FIFTH HIGH SCHOOL EDITION

The Norton Field Guide to Writing
with readings and handbook

FIFTH HIGH SCHOOL EDITION

The Norton
Field Guide
to Writing

with readings and handbook

Richard Bullock
WRIGHT STATE UNIVERSITY

Maureen Daly Goggin
ARIZONA STATE UNIVERSITY

Francine Weinberg

W. W. NORTON & COMPANY
Independent Publishers Since 1923

W. W. Norton & Company has been independent since its founding in 1923, when William Warder Norton and Mary D. Herter Norton first published lectures delivered at the People's Institute, the adult education division of New York City's Cooper Union. The firm soon expanded its program beyond the Institute, publishing books by celebrated academics from America and abroad. By mid-century, the two major pillars of Norton's publishing program—trade books and college texts—were firmly established. In the 1950s, the Norton family transferred control of the company to its employees, and today—with a staff of four hundred and a comparable number of trade, college, and professional titles published each year—W. W. Norton & Company stands as the largest and oldest publishing house owned wholly by its employees.

Editor: Sarah Touborg
Director of High School Publishing:
 Jenna Bookin Barry
Project Editor: Christine D'Antonio
Associate Editor: Claire Wallace
Assistant Editor: Madeline Rombes
Manuscript Editor: Jude Grant
Managing Editor, College: Marian Johnson
Managing Editor, College Digital Media: Kim Yi
Production Managers: Liz Marotta, Brad Abromaitis
Media Editors: Erica Wnek, Samantha Held
Media Project Editor: Cooper Wilhelm
Media Assistant Editor: Ava Bramson

Ebook Production Manager: Danielle Lehman
Marketing Manager, Composition: Lib Triplett
High School Marketing and Market Development
 Manager: Christina Magoulis
Design Director: Hope Miller Goodell
Book Designer: Anna Palchik
Photo Editor: Catherine Abelman
Photo Research: Dena Digilio Betz
Permissions Manager: Megan Schindel
Permissions Clearing: Bethany Salminen
Composition: Graphic World
Manufacturing: Transcontinental—
 Beauceville

Permission to use copyrighted material is included in the Acknowledgments section of this book, which begins on page A-1.

The Library of Congress has catalogued another edition as follows:

Library of Congress Cataloging-in-Publication Data
Names: Bullock, Richard H. (Richard Harvey) author. | Goggin, Maureen Daly,
 author. | Weinberg, Francine, author.
Title: The Norton Field Guide to writing with readings and handbook / Richard
 Bullock, Wright State University, Maureen Daly Goggin, Arizona State
 University, Francine Weinberg.
Description: Fifth edition. | New York ; London : W. W. Norton & Company,
 [2019] | Includes bibliographical references and index.
Identifiers: LCCN 2018007983 | **ISBN 9780393655803** (paperback)
Subjects: LCSH: English language—Rhetoric—Handbooks, manuals, etc. |
 English language—Grammar—Handbooks, manuals, etc. | Report
 writing—Handbooks, manuals, etc. | College readers.
Classification: LCC PE1408 .B883825 2019 | DDC 808/.042—dc23 LC record available at
 https://lccn.loc.gov/2018007983

ISBN 978-0-393-88567-5

W. W. Norton & Company, Inc., 500 Fifth Avenue, New York, NY 10110
wwnorton.com

W. W. Norton & Company Ltd., 15 Carlisle St., London W1D 3BS

1 2 3 4 5 6 7 8 9 10   23 22 21

Preface

The Norton Field Guide to Writing began as an attempt to offer the kind of writing guides found in the best rhetorics in a format as user-friendly as the best handbooks, and on top of that, to be as brief as could be. We wanted to create a handy guide to help students with all their written work. Just as there are field guides for bird watchers, for gardeners, and for accountants, this would be one for writers. In its first four editions, the book has obviously touched a chord with many writing instructors, and it remains a best-selling rhetoric—a success that leaves us humbled and grateful. Student success is now on everyone's mind. As teachers, we want our students to succeed, and writing courses offer one of the best opportunities to help them develop the skills and habits of mind they need to succeed, whatever their goals may be. Success, though, doesn't end with writing; students need to transfer their knowledge and skills to other courses and other writing tasks. To that end, we've added new chapters on reading and writing across fields of study and new guidance on writing literature reviews. We've also added "Taking Stock" questions to each Genre chapter to help students develop their metacognitive abilities by reflecting on their work.

The Norton Field Guide still aims to offer both the guidance new teachers and writers need and the flexibility many experienced teachers want. In our own teaching we've seen how well explicit guides to writing work for students and novice teachers. But too often, writing textbooks provide far more information than students need or instructors can assign and as a result are bigger and more expensive than they should be. So we've tried to provide enough structure without too much detail—to give the information writers need to know while resisting the temptation to tell them everything there is to know.

Most of all, we've tried to make the book easy to use, with menus, directories, a glossary/index, and color-coded links to help students find what they're looking for. The links are also the way we keep the book brief: chapters are short, but the links send students to pages elsewhere in the book if they need more detail.

What's in the Book

The Norton Field Guide covers 14 genres. Much of the book is in the form of guidelines, designed to help students consider the choices they have as writers. The book is organized into ten parts:

1. **ACADEMIC LITERACIES.** Chapters 1–4 focus on writing and reading in academic contexts, summarizing and responding, and developing academic habits of mind.

2. **RHETORICAL SITUATIONS.** Chapters 5–9 focus on purpose, audience, genre, stance, and media and design. In addition, almost every chapter includes tips to help students focus on their rhetorical situations.

3. **GENRES.** Chapters 10–23 cover 14 genres, 4 of them—literacy narrative, textual analysis, report, and argument—treated in greater detail.

4. **FIELDS.** Chapters 24–26 cover the key features of major fields of study and give guidance on reading and writing in each of those fields.

5. **PROCESSES.** Chapters 27–34 offer advice for generating ideas and text, drafting, revising and rewriting, editing, proofreading, compiling a portfolio, collaborating with others, and writing as inquiry.

6. **STRATEGIES.** Chapters 35–46 cover ways of developing and organizing text—writing effective beginnings and endings, titles and thesis statements, comparing, describing, taking essay exams, and so on.

7. **RESEARCH/DOCUMENTATION.** Chapters 47–55 offer advice on how to do academic research; work with sources; quote, paraphrase, and summarize source materials; and document sources using MLA and APA styles. Chapter 54 presents the "official MLA style" introduced in 2021.

8. **MEDIA/DESIGN.** Chapters 56–60 give guidance on choosing the appropriate print, digital, or spoken medium; designing text; using images and sound; giving spoken presentations; and writing online.

9. **READINGS.** Chapters 61–70 provide readings in 10 genres, plus one chapter of readings that mix genres. Discussion questions are color-coded to refer students to relevant details elsewhere in the book.

10. **HANDBOOK.** At the end of the book is a handbook to help students edit what they write, organized around the intuitive categories of sentences, language, and punctuation to make it easy to use.

What's Online for Students

Ebooks. All versions of *The Norton Field Guide* are available as ebooks and include all the readings and images found in the print books. Highlighted links are active in the ebook so students can quickly navigate to more detail as needed. The ebook is accessible from any computer, tablet, or mobile device and lets students highlight, annotate, or even listen to the text.

InQuizitive for Writers. With InQuizitive, students learn to edit sentences and practice working with sources to become better writers and researchers. InQuizitive is adaptive: students receive additional practice on the areas where they need more help. Links to *The Little Seagull Handbook* and explanatory feedback give students advice, right when they need it. And it's formative: by wagering points, students think about what they know and don't know. Visit inquizitive.wwnorton.com.

Norton/write. Just a click away with no passcode required, find a library of model student papers; more than 1,000 online exercises and quizzes; research and plagiarism tutorials; documentation guidelines for MLA, APA, *Chicago*, and CSE styles; MLA citation drills—and more. All MLA materials reflect 2021 style. Access the site at digital.wwnorton.com/write.

What's Available for Instructors

A Guide to Teaching with *The Norton Field Guides*. Written by Richard Bullock and several other teachers, this is a comprehensive guide to teaching writing, from developing a syllabus to facilitating group work, teaching multimodal writing to assessing student writing. Free of charge.

Coursepacks are available for free and in a variety of formats, including *Blackboard*, *D2L*, *Moodle*, *Canvas*, and *Angel*—and work within your existing learning management system, so there's no new system to learn, and access is free and easy. The *Field Guide* Coursepack includes model student papers; reading comprehension quizzes; reading strategy exercises; quizzes and exercises on grammar and research; documentation guidelines; and author biographies. Coursepacks are ready to use, right from the start—but are also easy to customize, using the system you already know and understand. Access the Coursepack at wwnorton.com/instructors.

PowerPoints. Ready-made PowerPoints feature genre organization flow-charts and documentation maps from the book to help you show examples during class. Download the PowerPoints at wwnorton.com/instructors.

Worksheets available in Word and PDF can be edited, downloaded, and printed with guidance on editing paragraphs, responding to a draft, and more. Download the worksheets at wwnorton.com/instructors.

Highlights

It's easy to use. Menus, directories, and a glossary/index make it easy for students to find what they're looking for. Color-coded templates and documentation maps even make MLA and APA documentation easy.

It has just enough detail, with short chapters that include color-coded links sending students to more detail if they need more.

It's uniquely flexible for teachers. Short chapters can be assigned in any order—and color-coded links help draw from other chapters as need be.

A user-friendly handbook, with an intuitive organization around sentences, language, and punctuation to make it easy for students to find what they need. And we go easy on the grammatical terminology, with links to the glossary for students who need detailed definitions.

What's New

A new part on fields of study with 3 new chapters on reading and writing in the disciplines (Part 4):

- **A new chapter on the fields of study** surveys the distinctions among the major discipline areas and includes an overview of why a general education matters. (Chapter 24)

- **A new chapter on reading across fields of study** includes short examples drawn from a variety of courses and genres, along with tips, techniques, and key terms specific to each. (Chapter 25)

- **A new chapter on writing in academic fields** includes summaries of the key features of writing in the major disciplines, along with descriptions and short examples of typical writing assignments in each. (Chapter 26)

New advice on detecting "false news" and unreliable sources, including how to read sources with a critical eye and how to use the elements of a rhetorical situation to determine whether or not a potential source is genuine and reputable. (Chapter 49)

A new section on reviews of scholarly literature with advice on how to develop, organize, and write a literature review. This section also includes an overview of the key features of the genre, as well as a new student example. (Chapter 15)

New "Taking Stock of Your Work" questions: each Genre chapter now ends with a series of questions to help students develop their metacognitive abilities by thinking about their writing processes and products.

New guidelines for peer review with detailed advice on how to read and respond to peers' drafts. (Chapter 32)

Expanded coverage of synthesizing ideas: a new sample essay that shows students how to synthesize multiple sources. (Chapter 50)

New advice on arguing with a hostile audience, including how to use Rogerian argument techniques to engage with audiences who may not share students' perspectives or values. (Chapter 38)

12 new readings in the rhetoric: new essays in nearly every genre, including a literacy narrative on working in an auto repair shop, a report on popcorn, a rhetorical analysis of a speech by former president Barack Obama, a profile of the modern-day plastic straw, and many more. In addition, there is a new APA research paper on the benefits of nurseries in women's prisons.

21 new readings in the anthology: at least one new essay in every genre, including an illustrated literacy narrative, a text analysis about Disney princesses, a profile of a plastic cooler, a proposal for a playground, and many more.

Ways of Teaching with *The Norton Field Guide to Writing*

The Norton Field Guide is designed to give you both support and flexibility. It has clear assignment sequences if you want them, or you can create your own. If, for example, you assign a position paper, there's a full chapter. If you want students to use sources, add the appropriate research chapters. If you want them to submit a topic proposal, add that chapter.

If you're a new teacher, the Genre chapters offer explicit assignment sequences—and the color-coded links will remind you of detail you may want to bring in. The instructor's manual offers advice on creating a syllabus, responding to writing, and more.

If you focus on genres, there are complete chapters on all the genres students are often assigned. Color-coded links will help you bring in details about research or other writing strategies as you wish.

If you organize your course thematically, a Thematic Guide will lead you to readings on 23 themes. Chapter 29 on generating ideas can help get students thinking about a theme. You can also assign them to do research on the theme, starting with Chapter 48 on finding sources, or perhaps with Chapter 27 on writing as inquiry. If they then write in a particular genre, there will be a chapter to guide them.

If you want students to do research, there are 9 chapters on the research process, including guidelines and sample papers for MLA and APA styles.

If you focus on modes, you'll find chapters on using narration, description, and so on as strategies for many writing purposes, and links that lead students through the process of writing an essay organized around a particular mode.

If you teach a stretch, ALP, IRW, or dual credit course, the academic literacies chapters offer explicit guidelines to help students write and read in academic contexts, summarize and respond to what they read, and develop academic habits of mind that will help them succeed.

If you teach online, the book is available as an ebook—and a companion Coursepack includes exercises, quizzes, video tutorials, and more.

Acknowledgments

As we've traveled around the country and met many of the students, teachers, and WPAs who are using *The Norton Field Guide*, we've been gratified to hear that so many find it helpful. As much as we like the positive response, though, we are especially grateful when we receive suggestions for ways the book might be improved. In this fifth edition, as we did in the fourth edition, we have tried to respond to the many good suggestions we've gotten from students, colleagues, reviewers, and editors. Thank you all, both for your kind words and for your good suggestions.

Some people need to be singled out for thanks, especially Marilyn Moller, the guiding editorial spirit of the *Field Guide* through all five editions. When we presented Marilyn with the idea for this book, she encouraged us and helped us conceptualize it—and then taught us how to write a text-book. The quality of the *Field Guide* is due in large part to her knowledge of the field of composition, her formidable editing and writing skills, her sometimes uncanny ability to see the future of the teaching of writing— and her equally formidable, if not uncanny, stamina.

Editor Sarah Touborg guided us through this new edition with good humor and better advice. Just as developmental editor John Elliott did with the third and fourth editions, Sarah shepherded this fifth edition through revisions and additions with a careful hand and a clear eye for appropriate content and language. Her painstaking editing shows throughout the book, and we're grateful for her ability to make us appear to be better writers than we are.

Many others have contributed, too. Thanks to project editor Christine D'Antonio for her energy, patience, and great skill in coordinating the tightly scheduled production process for the book. Claire Wallace brought her astute eye and keen judgment to all of the readings, while Maddy Rombes managed the extensive reviewing process and took great care of the man-uscript at every stage. *The Norton Field Guide* is more than just a print book, and we thank Erica Wnek, Samantha Held, Kim Yi, Ava Bramson, and Cooper Wilhelm for creating and producing the superb ebook and instruc-tors' site. Anna Palchik designed the award-winning, user-friendly, and attractive interior, Pete Garceau created the beautiful new cover design, and Debra Morton Hoyt and Tiani Kennedy further enhanced the design and coordinated it all, inside and out. Liz Marotta transformed a scribbled-over manuscript into a finished product with extraordinary speed and pre-cision, while Jude Grant copyedited. Megan Schindel and Bethany Salminen cleared text permissions, coping efficiently with ongoing changes, and Catherine Abelman cleared permission for the images found by Dena Digilio Betz. Steve Dunn, Lib Triplett, Elizabeth Pieslor, and Doug Day helped us all keep our eyes on the market. Thanks to all, and to Roby Harrington, Drake McFeely, and Julia Reidhead for supporting this project in the first place.

Rich has many, many people at Wright State University to thank for their support and assistance. Jane Blakelock taught Rich most of what he knows about electronic text and writing on and for the web and assembled an impressive list of useful links for the book's website. Adrienne Cassel (now at Sinclair Community College) and Catherine Crowley read and commented on many drafts. Peggy Lindsey (now at Georgia Southern University) shared her students' work and the idea of using charts to show how various genres might be organized. Brady Allen, Debbie Bertsch (now at Columbus State Community College), Vicki Burke, Melissa Carrion, Jimmy Chesire, Carol Cornett, Mary Doyle, Byron Crews, Deborah Crusan, Sally DeThomas, Stephanie Dickey, Scott Geisel, Karen Hayes, Chuck Holmes, Beth Klaisner (now at Colorado State University), Nancy Mack, Marty Maner, Cynthia Marshall, Sarah McGinley, Kristie McKiernan, Michelle Metzner, Kristie Rowe, Bobby Rubin, Cathy Sayer, David Seitz, Caroline Simmons, Tracy Smith, Rick Strader, Mary Van Loveren, and A. J. Williams responded to drafts, submitted good models of student writing, contributed to the instructor's manual, tested the *Field Guide* in their classes, provided support, and shared with Rich some of their best teaching ideas. Henry Limouze and then Carol Loranger, chairs of the English Department, gave him room to work on this project with patience and good humor. Sandy Trimboli, Becky Traxler, and Lynn Morgan, the secretaries to the writing programs, kept him anchored. And he thanks especially the more than 300 graduate teaching assistants and 10,000 first-year students who class-tested various editions of the *Field Guide* and whose experiences helped—and continue to help—to shape it.

At Arizona State, Maureen wants to acknowledge the unwavering support of Neal A. Lester, Vice President of Humanities and Arts and former chair of the English Department, and the assistance of Jason Diller, her former graduate research assistant, and Judy Holiday, her former graduate mentee, for their reading suggestions. She thanks her colleagues, all exemplary teachers and mentors, for creating a supportive intellectual environment, especially Patricia Boyd, Peter Goggin, Mark Hannah, Kathleen Lamp, Elenore Long, Paul Matsuda, Keith Miller, Ersula Ore, Alice Robison, Shirley Rose, and Doris Warriner. Thanks also go to ASU instructors and first-year students who have used the *Field Guide* and have offered good suggestions. Finally, Maureen wants to pay tribute to her students, who are themselves among her best teachers.

Thanks to the teachers across the country who reviewed the fourth edition of the *Field Guide* and helped shape this fifth edition: Elizabeth Acosta, El Paso Community College; Thomas Barber, City College of New York; Keri Behre, Marylhurst University; David Bell, University of North Georgia; Dean Blumberg, Horry–Georgetown Technical College; Abdallah Boumarate, Valencia College; Tabitha Bozeman, Gadsden State Community College; Laurie E. Buchanan, Clark State Community College; Ashley Buzzard, Midlands Technical College; Emma Carlton, University of New Orleans; Danielle Carr, City College of New York; Toni I. Carter, Ivy Tech Community College of Indiana; Carla Chwat, University of North Georgia; Marie Coffey, Northeast Lakeview College; Stephanie Conner, College of Coastal Georgia; Robert Derr, Danville Community College; Cheryl Divine, Columbia College; Amber Duncan, Northwest Vista College; Gloria Estrada, El Paso Community College; Kevin Ferns, Woodland Community College; Dianne Flickinger, Cowley County Community College; Michael Flood, Horry–Georgetown Technical College; Dan Fuller, Hinds Community College–Utica; Robert Galin, University of New Mexico–Gallup; Jennifer P. Gray, College of Coastal Georgia; Julie Groesch, San Jacinto College; Elizabeth Hair, Trident Technical College; Mark Hankerson, Albany State University; Pamela Hardman, Cuyahoga Community College; Michael Hedges, Horry–Georgetown Technical College; Michael Hill, Henry Ford College; Lorraine M. Howland, New Hampshire Technical Institute, Concord's Community College; Alyssa Johnson, Horry–Georgetown Technical College; Luke Johnson, Mesabi Range College; Elaine M. Jolayemi, Ivy Tech Community College of Indiana; George Kanieski, Cuyahoga Community College; Elizabeth Kuehne, Wayland Baptist University; Matt Laferty, Cuyahoga Community College; Robin Latham, Nash Community College; Adam Lee, Concordia University Irvine; Bronwen Llewellyn, Daytona State College; Chelsea Lonsdale, Henry Ford College; Jeffery D. Mack, Albany State University; Devona Mallory, Albany State University; Katheryn McCoskey, Butler Community College; Jenny McHenry, Tallahassee Community College; James McWard, Johnson County Community College; Eileen E. Medeiros, Johnson & Wales University; Kristina Meehan, Spartanburg Community College; Cathryn Meyer, Tallahassee Community College; Josephine Mills, Arapahoe Community College; James Minor, South Piedmont Community College; Erin O'Keefe, Allen Community College–Burlingame; Jeff Owens, Lassen Community College; Anthony Guy Patricia, Concord University; Brenda Reid, Tallahassee Community College; Emily Riser, Mississippi Delta Community College; Emily Rosenblatt, City College of New York; Kent Ross, Northeastern Junior College; Jessica Schreyer, University of Dubuque; Sunita Sharma, Mississippi Delta Community College; Taten Sheridan, Kodiak College; Ann Spurlock, Mississippi State University; Derrick Stewart, Midlands Technical College; Pamela Stovall, University of New Mexico–Gallup; James D. Suderman, Northwest Florida State College; Harun K. Thomas, Daytona State College; Alison Van Nyhuis, Fayetteville State University; Anna Voisard; City College of New York; Elisabeth von Uhl, City College of New York; Ellen Wayland-Smith, University of Southern California; James Williams, Soka University; Michael Williams, Horry–Georgetown Technical College; Mark W. Wilson, Southwestern Oregon Community College; and Michelle Zollars, Patrick Henry Community College.

Thanks also to those instructors who reviewed the *Field Guide* resources, helping us improve them for the fifth edition: Jessica Adams, Clark State Community College; Megan Anderson, Limestone College; Jamee Atkinson, Texas State Technical College; David Bach, Northwest Vista College; Ryan Baechle, University of Toledo; Aaron Barrell, Everett Community College; Soky Barrenechea, Penn State Abington; Lauren Baugus, Pensacola State College; Kristina Baumli, University of the Arts; Kay Berry, Dixie High School; Marie Bischoff, Sierra Community College; Matt Bloom, Hawkeye Community College; Allison Brady, Toccoa Falls College; Hannah Bingham Brunner, Oklahoma Christian University; Sybil Canon, Northwest MS Community College; Marie Coffey, Northeast Lakeview College; Susan Cowart, Texas State Technical College; Kennette Crockett, Harold Washington College; Anthony D'Ariea, Regis College; Mary Rutledge-Davis, North Lake College; Courtney Doi, Alamance Community College; Zona Douthit, Roger Williams University; Amber Duncan, Northwest Vista College; Michelle Ellwood, Keuka College; Michael Esquivel, Tarrant County College; Julie Felux, Northwest Vista College; Monika Fleming, Edgecombe Community College; Dianne Flickinger, Cowley County Community College; Barbara Z.

Flinn, Youngstown State University; P. Foster, Alabama State University; Darius Frasure, Mountain View College; Robert Galin, University of New Mexico; Chanda Gilmore, Immaculata University; William Godbey, Tarrant County College; Deborah Goodwyn, Virginia State University; Ben Graydon, Daytona State College; Lamarr Green, Northwest Vista College; Marie Green, Northern VA Community College; Ricardo Guzman, Northwest Vista College; Lori Hicks, Ivy Tech Community College; Lana Highfill, Ivy Tech Community College; Lorraine M. Howland, NHTI, Concord's Community College; N. Luanne J. Hurst, Pasco Hernando State College; Judith Isakson, Daytona State College; Jeanine Jewell, Southeast Community College; Lori Johnson, Rappahannock Community College; Randy Johnson, Capital Community College; Wesley Johnson, Pasco-Hernando State College; Kelsea Jones, Treasure Valley Community College; Lisa Jones, Pasco-Hernando State College; Erin Kalish, Bridgewater State University; Amber Kovach, Boise State University; Julie Kratt, Cowley College; Robin Latham, Nash Community College; Stephanie Legarreta, El Paso Community College; Amy Ludwig, College of the Canyons; Carol Luvert, Hawkeye Community College; Barbara Lyras, Youngstown State University; Crystal Manboard, Northwest Vista College; Margaret Marangione, Blue Ridge Community College; Kristen Marangoni, Tulsa Community College; Christina McCleanhan, Maysville Community and Technical College; Sara McDonald, Saint Cloud Technical and Community College and Saint Cloud State University; Kelly McDonough, Clarendon College; Shannon McGregor, Des Moines Area Community College; Lisa McHarry, West Hills College, Coalinga; Craig McLuckie, Okanagan College; James McWard, Johnson County Community College; Eileen Medeiros, Pasco-Hernando State College; Kristy Meehan, Spartanburg Community College; Jason Melton, Sacramento State University; John Miller, Ivy Tech Community College; Erik Moellering, Asheville Buncombe Technical Community College; Michael Murray, Columbus State Community College; Briana Murrell, Fayetteville State University; Anthony Nelson, El Paso Community College; Andrew Nye, Minnesota State University Mankato; Alison Van Nyhuis, Fayetteville State University; Oluwatosin Ogunnika, Virginia State University; Judith Oster, Valley Community College; Deb Paczynski, Central New Mexico Community College; Susan Passmore, Colquitt County High School; Diane Paul, Southeast Community College; Patricia Penn, Cowley

College; Mike Peterson, Dixie State University; Larissa L. Pierce, Eastfield College; David Pittard, Fossil Ridge High School; Robert Ramos, City College; Cynthia Fox Richardson, Clark State Community College; Alice Waits-Richardson, Southern State Community College; Maurisa Riley, Tarrant County College NW; Stephanie Roberts, Georgia Military College; Adrian Rosa, Jackson College; Erin Mahoney-Ross, Tarrant County College Northwest Campus; Jennifer Royal, Santa Rosa Junior College; Julia Ruengert, Pensacola State College; Shirley Rutter, Johnson & Wales University; Eli Ryder, Antelope Valley College; Jessica Schreyer, University of Dubuque; Jennifer Scowron, Youngstown State University; Claudia Skutar, University of Cincinnati Blue Ash College; Jennifer Smith, Pepperdine University; Michael Stewart, University of Alabama; Michelle Sufridge, Madison-Plains High School; Harun Karim Thomas, Daytona State College; Zainah Usman, Tarrant County College; Jennifer Vega, El Paso Community College; Ashley Waterman, Community College of Aurora; Ann Henson Webb, Moraine Valley Community College; Maggie M. Werner, Hobart and William Smith College; Kaci L. West, Abraham Baldwin Agricultural College; Cassandra Wettlaufer, Tarrant County College; Holly White, Cuyahoga County Community College; Casey Wiley, Penn State University; Karen Wilson, Hawkeye Community College; Sabine Winter, Eastfield College; Jonathan Wood, College of Western Idaho; and Marilyn S. Yamin, Pellissippi State Community College.

The Norton Field Guide has also benefited from the good advice and conversations we've had with writing teachers across the country, including (among many others) Maureen Mathison, Susan Miller, Tom Huckin, Gae Lyn Henderson, and Sundy Watanabe at the University of Utah; Christa Albrecht-Crane, Doug Downs, and Brian Whaley at Utah Valley State College; Anne Dvorak and Anya Morrissey at Longview Community University; Jeff Andelora at Mesa Community College; Robin Calitri at Merced College; Lori Gallinger, Rose Hawkins, Jennifer Nelson, Georgia Standish, and John Ziebell at the Community College of Southern Nevada; Stuart Blythe at Indiana University–Purdue University Fort Wayne; Janice Kelly at Arizona State University; Jeanne McDonald at Waubonsee Community College; Web Newbold, Mary Clark-Upchurch, Megan Auffart, Matt Balk, Edward James Chambers, Sarah Chavez, Desiree Dighton, Ashley Ellison, Theresa Evans, Keith Heller, Ellie Isenhart, Angela Jackson-Brown,

Naoko Kato, Yuanyuan Liao, Claire Lutkewitte, Yeno Matuki, Casey McArdle, Tibor Munkacsi, Dani Nier-Weber, Karen Neubauer, Craig O'Hara, Martha Payne, Sarah Sandman, and Kellie Weiss at Ball State University; Patrick Tompkins at Tyler Community College; George Kanieski and Pamela Hardman at Cuyahoga Community College; Daniela Regusa, Jeff Partridge, and Lydia Vine at Capital Community College; Elizabeth Woodworth, Auburn University–Montgomery; Stephanie Eason at Enterprise Community College; Kate Geiselman at Sinclair Community College; Ronda Leathers Dively at Southern Illinois University; Debra Knutson at Shawnee State University; Guy Shebat and Amy Flick at Youngstown State University; Martha Tolleson, Toni McMillen, and Patricia Gerecci at Collin College; Sylva Miller at Pikes Peak Community College; Dharma Hernandez at Los Angeles Unified School District; Ann Spurlock at Mississippi State University; Luke Niiler at the University of Alabama; and Jeff Tix at Wharton County Junior College.

We wouldn't have met most of these people without the help of the Norton travelers, the representatives who spend their days visiting faculty, showing and discussing the *Field Guide* and Norton's many other fine textbooks. Thanks to Kathy Carlsen, Scott Cook, Marilyn Rayner, Peter Wentz, Krista Azer, Sarah Wolf, Mary Helen Willett, Susyn Dietz, and all the other Norton travelers. Thanks also to regional sales managers Paul Ducham, Dennis Fernandes, Deirdre Hall, Dan Horton, Katie Incorvia, Jordan Mendez, Annie Stewart, Amber Watkins, and Natasha Zabohonski. And we'd especially like to thank Mike Wright and Doug Day for promoting this book so enthusiastically and professionally.

It's customary to conclude by expressing gratitude to one's spouse and family, and for good reason. Writing and revising *The Norton Field Guide* over the past several years, we have enjoyed the loving and unconditional support of our spouses, Barb, Peter, and Larry, who provide the foundation for all we do. Thank you. We couldn't have done it without you.

How to Use This Book

There's no one way to do anything, and writing is no exception. Some people need to do a lot of planning on paper; others write entire drafts in their heads. Some writers compose quickly and loosely, going back later to revise; others work on one sentence until they're satisfied with it, then move on to the next. And writers' needs vary from task to task, too: sometimes you know what you're going to write about and why, but need to figure out how to do it; other times your first job is to come up with a topic. *The Norton Field Guide* is designed to allow you to chart your own course as a writer, offering guidelines that suit your writing needs. It is organized in ten parts:

1. **ACADEMIC LITERACIES**: The chapters in this part will help you know what's expected in the reading and writing you do for academic purposes, and in summarizing and responding to what you read. One chapter even provides tips for developing habits of mind that will help you succeed, whatever your goals.

2. **RHETORICAL SITUATIONS**: No matter what you're writing, it will always have some purpose, audience, genre, stance, and medium and design. This part will help you consider each of these elements, as well as the particular kinds of rhetorical situations created by academic assignments.

3. **GENRES**: Use these chapters for help with specific kinds of writing, from abstracts to lab reports to memoirs and more. You'll find more detailed guidance for four especially common assignments: literacy narratives, textual analyses, reports, and arguments.

4. **FIELDS**: The chapters in this part will help you apply what you're learning in this book to your other courses.

5. **PROCESSES**: These chapters offer general advice for all writing situations—from generating ideas and text to drafting, revising and rewriting, compiling a portfolio—and more.

6. **STRATEGIES**: Use the advice in this part to develop and organize your writing—to write effective beginnings and endings, to guide readers through your text, and to use comparison, description, dialogue, and other strategies as appropriate.

7. **RESEARCH / DOCUMENTATION**: Use this section for advice on how to do research, work with sources, and compose and document research-based texts using MLA and APA styles.

8. **MEDIA / DESIGN**: This section offers guidance in designing your work and using visuals and sound, and in deciding whether and how to deliver what you write on paper, on screen, or in person.

9. **READINGS**: This section includes readings in 10 genres, and one chapter of texts that mix genres—42 readings in all that provide good examples of the kinds of writing you yourself may be assigned to do.

10. **HANDBOOK**: Look here for help with sentence-level editing.

Ways into the Book

The Norton Field Guide gives you the writing advice you need, along with the flexibility to write in the way that works best for you. Here are some of the ways you can find what you need in the book.

Brief menus. Inside the front cover you'll find a list of all the chapters; start here if you are looking for a chapter on a certain kind of writing or a general writing issue. Inside the back cover is a menu of all the topics covered in the **HANDBOOK**.

Complete contents. Pages xxiii–xlv contain a detailed table of contents. Look here if you need to find a reading or a specific section in a chapter.

Guides to writing. If you know the kind of writing you need to do, you'll find guides to writing 14 common genres in Part 3. These guides are designed to help you through all the decisions you have to make—from coming up with a topic to editing and proofreading your final draft.

Color-coding. The parts of this book are color-coded for easy reference: light blue for **ACADEMIC LITERACIES**, red for **RHETORICAL SITUATIONS**, green for **GENRES**, pink for **FIELDS**, lavender for **PROCESSES**, orange for **STRATEGIES**, blue for **RESEARCH / DOCUMENTATION**, gold for **MEDIA / DESIGN**, apple green for the **READINGS**, and yellow for the **HANDBOOK**. You'll find a key to the colors on the front cover flap and also at the foot of each left-hand page. When you see a word highlighted in a color, that tells you where you can find additional detail on the topic.

Glossary / index. At the back of the book is a combined glossary and index, where you'll find full definitions of key terms and topics, along with a list of the pages where everything is covered in detail.

Directories to MLA and APA documentation. A brief directory inside the back cover will lead you to guidelines on citing sources and composing a list of references or works cited. The documentation models are color-coded so you can easily see the key details.

Ways of Getting Started

If you know your genre, simply turn to the appropriate genre chapter. There you'll find model readings, a description of the genre's Key Features, and a Guide to Writing that will help you come up with a topic, generate text, organize and write a draft, get response, revise, edit, and proofread. The genre chapters also point out places where you might need to do research, use certain writing strategies, design your text a certain way—and direct you to the exact pages in the book where you can find help doing so.

If you know your topic, you might start with some of the activities in Chapter 29, Generating Ideas and Text. From there, you might turn to Chapter 48, for help Finding Sources on the topic. When it comes time to narrow your topic and come up with a thesis statement, Chapter 36 can help. If you get stuck at any point, you might turn to Chapter 27, Writing as Inquiry; it provides tips that can get you beyond what you already know about your topic. If your assignment or your thesis defines your genre, turn to that chapter; if not, consult Chapter 27 for help determining the appropriate genre, and then turn to that genre chapter.

Contents

xxiii

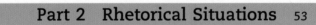

Part 2   Rhetorical Situations   53

Part 3   Genres   73

13 Arguing a Position   157

14 Abstracts   185

Part 4   Fields   289

Part 6   Strategies   371

Part 7 Doing Research 477

Part 9   Readings   685

Part 10   Handbook   HB-1

Sentences   HB-3

Language   HB-41

Punctuation / Mechanics   *HB-77*

Thematic Guide to the Readings

Class Issues

Creative Play and Gaming

Crime and Justice

Death and Dying

Digital and Social Media

Education and Schooling

Immigration

Language and Literacy

Nature and the Environment

Race and Ethnicity

Science and Technology

Work

World Cultures and Global Issues

part 1

Academic Literacies

Whenever we enter a new community—start a new job, move to a new town, join a new club—there are certain things we need to learn. The same is true upon entering the academic world. We need to be able to **READ** and **WRITE** in certain ways. We're routinely called on to **SUMMARIZE** something we've heard or read and to **RESPOND** in some way. And to succeed, we need to develop certain **HABITS OF MIND**—everyday things such as asking questions and being persistent. The following chapters provide guidelines to help you develop these fundamental academic literacies—and know what's expected of you in academic communities.

1

Academic Literacies

Writing in Academic Contexts   **1**

Write an essay arguing whether genes or environment do more to determine people's intelligence. Research and write a report on the environmental effects of electricity-generating windmills. Work with a team to write a proposal and create a multimedia presentation for a sales campaign. Whatever you're studying, you're surely going to be doing a lot of writing, in classes from various disciplines—the above assignments, for example, are from psychology, environmental science, and marketing. Academic writing can serve a number of different purposes—to **ARGUE** for what you think about a topic and why, to **REPORT** on what's known about an issue, to **PROPOSE A SOLUTION** for some problem, and so on. Whatever your topics or purposes, all academic writing follows certain conventions, ones you'll need to master in order to join the conversations going on across campus. This chapter describes what's expected of academic writing—and of academic writers.

▲ 157–84

131–56

246–55

What's Expected of Academic Writing

Evidence that you've considered the subject thoughtfully. Whether you're composing a report, an argument, or some other kind of writing, you need to demonstrate that you've thought seriously about the topic and done any necessary research. You can use various ways to show that you've considered the subject carefully, from citing authoritative sources to incorporating information you learned in class to pointing out connections among ideas.

academic literacies | rhetorical situations | genres | fields | processes | strategies | research MLA / APA | media / design | readings | handbook

An indication of why your topic matters. You need to help your readers understand why your topic is worth exploring and why your writing is worth reading. Even if you are writing in response to an assigned topic, you can better make your point and achieve your purpose by showing your readers why your topic is important and why they should care about it. For example, in the prologue to *Our Declaration*, political philosopher Danielle Allen explains why her topic, the Declaration of Independence, is worth writing about:

> The Declaration of Independence matters because it helps us see that we cannot have freedom *without* equality. It is out of an egalitarian commitment that a people grows—a people that is capable of protecting us all collectively, and each of us individually, from domination. If the Declaration can stake a claim to freedom, it is only because it is so clear-eyed about the fact that the people's strength resides in its equality.
>
> The Declaration also conveys another lesson of paramount importance. It is this: language is one of the most potent resources each of us has for achieving our own political empowerment. The men who wrote the Declaration of Independence grasped the power of words. This reveals itself in the laborious processes by which they brought the Declaration, and their revolution, into being. It shows itself forcefully, of course, in the text's own eloquence.

By explaining that the topic matters because freedom and equality matter—and language gives us the means for empowering ourselves—Allen gives readers reason to read her careful analysis.

A response to what others have said. Whatever your topic, it's unlikely that you'll be the first one to write about it. And if, as this chapter assumes, all academic writing is part of a larger conversation, you are in a way adding your own voice to that conversation. One good way of doing that is to present your ideas as a response to what others have said about your topic—to begin by quoting, paraphrasing, or summarizing what others have said and then to agree, disagree, or both.

For example, in an essay arguing that organ sales will save lives, MIT student Joanna MacKay says, "Some agree with Pope John Paul II that the selling of organs is morally wrong and violates 'the dignity of the human

person.'" But she then responds—and disagrees, arguing that "the morals we hold are not absolute truths" and that "peasants of third-world countries" might not agree with the pope.

A clear, appropriately qualified thesis. When you write in an academic context, you're expected to state your main point explicitly, often in a THESIS STATEMENT. Joanna MacKay states her thesis clearly in her essay "Organ Sales Will Save Lives": "Governments should not ban the sale of human organs; they should regulate it." Often you'll need to QUALIFY your thesis statement to acknowledge that the subject is complicated and there may be more than one way of seeing it or exceptions to the generalization you're making about it. Here, for example, is a qualified thesis, from an essay evaluating the movie *Juno* by Ali Heinekamp, a student at Wright State University: "Although the situations *Juno*'s characters find themselves in and their dialogue may be criticized as unrealistic, the film, written by Diablo Cody and directed by Jason Reitman, successfully portrays the emotions of a teen being shoved into maturity way too fast." Heinekamp makes a claim that *Juno* achieves its main goal, while acknowledging at the beginning of the sentence that the film may be flawed.

387–89

388–89

Good reasons supported by evidence. You need to provide good reasons for your thesis and evidence to support those reasons. For example, Joanna MacKay offers several reasons why sales of human kidneys should be legalized: there is a surplus of kidneys, the risk to the donor is not great, and legalization would allow the trade in kidneys to be regulated. Evidence to support your reasons sometimes comes from your own experience but more often from published research and scholarship, research you do yourself, or firsthand accounts by others.

Compared with other kinds of writing, academic writing is generally expected to be more objective and less emotional. You may find *Romeo and Juliet* deeply moving or cry when you watch *The Fault in Our Stars*—but when you write about the play or the film for a class, you must do so using evidence from the text to support your thesis. You may find someone's ideas deeply offensive, but you should respond to them with reason rather than with emotional appeals or personal attacks.

Acknowledgment of multiple perspectives. Debates and arguments in popular media are often framed in "pro/con" terms, as if there were only two sides to any given issue. Once you begin seriously studying a topic, though, you're likely to find that there are several sides and that each of them deserves serious consideration. In your academic writing, you need to represent fairly the range of perspectives on your topic—to explore three, four, or more positions on it as you research and write. In her report, "Does Texting Affect Writing?," Marywood University student Michaela Cullington, for example, examines texting from several points of view: teachers' impressions of the influence of texting on student writing, the results of several research studies, and her own survey research.

A confident, authoritative stance. If one goal of academic writing is to contribute to a larger conversation, your tone should convey confidence and establish your authority to write about your subject. Ways to achieve such a tone include using active verbs ("X claims" rather than "it seems"), avoiding such phrases as "in my opinion" and "I think," and writing in a straightforward, direct style. Your writing should send the message that you've done the research, analysis, and thinking and know what you're talking about. For example, here is the final paragraph of Michaela Cullington's essay on texting and writing:

> On the basis of my own research, expert research, and personal observations, I can confidently state that texting is not interfering with students' use of standard written English and has no effect on their writing abilities in general. It is interesting to look at the dynamics of the arguments over these issues. Teachers and parents who claim that they are seeing a decline in the writing abilities of their students and children mainly support the negative-impact argument. Other teachers and researchers suggest that texting provides a way for teens to practice writing in a casual setting and thus helps prepare them to write formally. Experts and students themselves, however, report that they see no effect, positive or negative. Anecdotal experiences should not overshadow the actual evidence.

Cullington's use of simple, declarative sentences ("Other teachers and researchers suggest . . ."; "Anecdotal experiences should not overshadow . . .")

and her straightforward summary of the arguments surrounding texting, along with her strong, unequivocal ending ("texting is not interfering with students' use of standard written English"), lend her writing a confident tone. Her stance sends the message that she's done the research and knows what she's talking about.

Carefully documented sources.   Clearly acknowledging sources and documenting them carefully and correctly is a basic requirement of academic writing. When you use the words or ideas of others—including visuals, video, or audio—those sources must be documented in the text and in a works-cited or references list at the end. (If you're writing something that will appear online, you may also refer readers to your sources by using hyperlinks in the text; ask your instructor if you need to include a list of references or works cited as well.)

Careful attention to correctness.   Whether you're writing something formal or informal, in an essay or an email, you should always write in complete sentences, use appropriate capitalization and punctuation, and check that your spelling is correct. In general, academic writing is no place for colloquial language, slang, or texting abbreviations. If you're quoting someone, you can reproduce that person's writing or speech exactly, but in your own writing you try hard to be correct—and always proofread carefully.

What's Expected of College Writers: The WPA Outcomes

Writing is not a multiple-choice test; it doesn't have right and wrong answers that are easily graded. Instead, your readers, whether they're teachers or anyone else, are likely to read your writing with various questions in mind: does it make sense, does it meet the demands of the assignment, is the grammar correct, to name just a few of the things readers may look for. Different readers may notice different things, so sometimes it may seem to you that their response—and your grade—is unpredictable. It should be good to know, then, that writing teachers across the nation have come to some agreement on certain "outcomes," what college students should know and be able to do by the time they finish a first-year writing course. These outcomes have been defined by the National Council of Writing Program Administrators (WPA). Here's a brief summary of these outcomes and how *The Norton Field Guide* can help you meet them:

Knowledge of Rhetoric

- *Understand the rhetorical situation of texts that you read and write.* See Chapters 5–9 and the many prompts for Considering the Rhetorical Situation throughout the book.
- *Read and write texts in a number of different genres, and understand how your purpose may influence your writing.* See Chapters 10–22 for guidelines on writing in thirteen genres and Chapter 23 on mixing genres.
- *Adjust your voice, tone, level of formality, design, and medium as is necessary and appropriate.* See Chapter 8 on stance and tone and Chapter 9 for help thinking about medium and design.
- *Choose the media that will best suit your audience, purpose, and the rest of your rhetorical situation.* See Chapters 9 and 56.

Critical Thinking, Reading, and Composing

- *Read and write to inquire, learn, think critically, and communicate.* See Chapters 1 and 2 on academic writing and reading, and Chapter 27 on writing as inquiry. Chapters 10–23 provide genre-specific prompts to help you think critically about a draft.
- *Read for content, argumentative strategies, and rhetorical effectiveness.* Chapter 7 provides guidance on reading texts with a critical eye, Chapter 11 teaches how to analyze a text, and Chapter 49 shows how to evaluate sources.
- *Find and evaluate popular and scholarly sources.* Chapter 48 teaches how to use databases and other methods to find sources, and Chapter 49 shows how to evaluate the sources you find.

- *Use sources in various ways to support your ideas.* Chapter 38 suggests strategies for supporting your ideas, and Chapter 51 shows how to incorporate ideas from sources into your writing to support your ideas.

Processes

- *Use writing processes to compose texts and explore ideas in various media.* Part 5 covers all stages of the processes writers use, from generating ideas and text to drafting, getting response and revising, and editing and proofreading. Each of the thirteen genre chapters (10–22) includes a guide that leads you through the process of writing in that genre.
- *Collaborate with others on your own writing and on group tasks.* Chapter 28 offers guidelines for working with others, Chapter 32 provides general prompts for getting and giving response, and Chapters 10–23 provide genre-specific prompts for reading a draft with a critical eye.
- *Reflect on your own writing processes.* Chapters 10–23 provide genre-specific questions to help you take stock of your work, and Chapter 31 offers guidance in thinking about your own writing process. Chapter 34 provides prompts to help you reflect on a writing portfolio.

Knowledge of Conventions

- *Use correct grammar, punctuation, and spelling.* Chapter 33 provides tips to help you edit and proofread for your writing. Chapters 10–23 offer genre-specific advice for editing and proofreading.
- *Understand and use genre conventions and formats in your writing.* Chapter 7 provides an overview of genres and how to think about them. Part 3 covers thirteen genres, describing the key features and conventions of each one.
- *Understand intellectual property and document sources appropriately.* Chapter 52 offers guidance on the ethical use of sources, Chapter 53 provides an overview of documentation styles, and Chapters 54 and 55 provide templates for documenting in MLA and APA styles.

2 Reading in Academic Contexts

We read newspapers to know about the events of the day. We read textbooks to learn about history, chemistry, and other academic topics—and other academic sources to do research and develop arguments. We read tweets and blogs to follow (and participate in) conversations about issues that interest us. And as writers, we read our own writing to make sure it says what we mean it to say and proofread our final drafts to make sure they say it correctly. In other words, we read many kinds of texts for many different purposes. This chapter offers a number of strategies for various kinds of reading you do in academic contexts.

TAKING STOCK OF YOUR READING

One way to become a better reader is to understand your reading process; if you know what you do when you read, you're in a position to decide what you need to change or improve. Consider the answers to the following questions:

- What do you read for pleasure? for work? for school? Consider all the sorts of reading you do: books, magazines, and newspapers, websites, *Facebook*, texts, blogs, product instructions.

- When you're facing a reading assignment, what do you do? Do you do certain things to get comfortable? Do you play music or seek quiet? Do you plan your reading time or set reading goals for yourself? Do you flip through or skim the text before settling down to read it, or do you start at the beginning and work through it?

- When you begin to read something for an assignment, do you make sure you understand the purpose of the assignment—why you must

read this text? Do you ever ask your instructor (or whoever else assigned the reading) what its purpose is?

- How do you motivate yourself to read material you don't have any interest in? How do you deal with boredom while reading?

- Does your mind wander? If you realize that you haven't been paying attention and don't know what you just read, what do you do?

- Do you ever highlight, underline, or annotate text as you read? Do you take notes? If so, what do you mark or write down? Why?

- When you read text you don't understand, what do you do?

- As you anticipate and read an assigned text, what attitudes or feelings do you typically have? If they differ from reading to reading, why do they?

- What do you do when you've finished reading an assigned text? Write out notes? Think about what you've just read? Move on to the next task? Something else?

- How well do your reading processes work for you, both in school and otherwise? What would you like to change? What can you do to change?

The rest of this chapter offers advice and strategies that you may find helpful as you work to improve your reading skills.

READING STRATEGICALLY

Academic reading is challenging because it makes several demands on you at once. Textbooks present new vocabulary and new concepts, and picking out the main ideas can be difficult. Scholarly articles present content and arguments you need to understand, but they often assume that readers already know key concepts and vocabulary and so don't generally provide background information. As you read more texts in an academic field and begin to participate in its conversations, the reading will become easier, but in the meantime you can develop strategies that will help you read effectively.

Thinking about What You Want to Learn

To learn anything, we need to place new information into the context of what we already know. For example, to understand photosynthesis, we need to already know something about plants, energy, and oxygen, among other things. To learn a new language, we draw on similarities and differences between it and any other languages we know. A method of bringing to conscious attention our current knowledge on a topic and of helping us articulate our purposes for reading is a list-making process called KWL+. To use it, create a table with three columns:

K: What I Know	W: What I Want to Know	L: What I Learned

Before you begin reading a text, list in the "K" column what you already know about the topic. Brainstorm ideas, and list terms or phrases that come to mind. Then group them into categories. Also before reading, or after reading the first few paragraphs, list in the "W" column questions you have that you expect, want, or hope to be answered as you read. Number or reorder the questions by their importance to you.

Then, as you read the text or afterward, list in the "L" column what you learned from the text. Compare your "L" list with your "W" list to see what you still want or need to know (the "+")—and what you learned that you didn't expect.

Previewing the Text

It's usually a good idea to start by skimming a text—read the title and subtitle, any headings, the first and last paragraphs, the first sentences

academic literacies · rhetorical situations · genres · fields · processes · strategies · research MLA / APA · media / design · readings · handbook

of all the other paragraphs. Study any illustrations and other visuals. Your goal is to get a sense of where the text is heading. At this point, don't stop to look up unfamiliar words; just mark them in some way to look up later.

Adjusting Your Reading Speed to Different Texts

Different texts require different kinds of effort. Some that are simple and straightforward can be skimmed fairly quickly. With academic texts, though, you usually need to read more slowly and carefully, matching the pace of your reading to the difficulty of the text. You'll likely need to skim the text for an overview of the basic ideas and then go back to read it closely. And then you may need to read it yet again. (But do try always to read quickly enough to focus on the meanings of sentences and paragraphs, not just individual words.) With visual texts, too, you'll often need to look at them several times, moving from gaining an overall impression to closely examining the structure, layout, and other visual features—and exploring how those features relate to any accompanying verbal text.

Looking for Organizational Cues

As you read, look for cues that signal the way the text's ideas are organized and how each part relates to the ones around it.

The introductory paragraph and thesis often offer a preview of the topics to be discussed and the order in which they will be addressed. Here, for example, is a typical thesis statement for a report: *Types of prisons in the United States include minimum and medium security, close security, maximum security, and supermax.* The report that follows should explain each type of prison in the order stated in the thesis.

391

Transitions help **GUIDE READERS** in following the direction of the writer's thinking from idea to idea. For example, "however" indicates an idea that contradicts or limits what has just been said, while "furthermore" indicates one that adds to or supports it.

Headings identify a text's major and minor sections, by means of both the headings' content and their design.

Thinking about Your Initial Response

Some readers find it helps to make brief notes about their first response to a text, noting their reaction and thinking a little about why they reacted as they did.

What are your initial reactions? Describe both your intellectual reaction and any emotional reaction, and identify places in the text that caused you to react as you did. An intellectual reaction might consist of an evaluation ("I disagree with this position because . . ."), a connection ("This idea reminds me of . . ."), or an elaboration ("Another example of this point is . . ."). An emotional reaction could include approval or disapproval ("YES! This is exactly right!" "NO! This is so wrong!"), an expression of feeling ("This passage makes me so sad"), or one of appreciation ("This is said so beautifully"). If you had no particular reaction, note that, too.

What accounts for your reactions? Are they rooted in personal experiences? aspects of your personality? positions you hold on an issue? As much as possible, you want to keep your opinions from interfering with your understanding of what you're reading, so it's important to try to identify those opinions up front.

Dealing with Difficult Texts

Let's face it: some texts are difficult. You may have no interest in the subject matter, or lack background knowledge or vocabulary necessary for understanding the text, or simply not have a clear sense of why you have to read the text at all. Whatever the reason, reading such texts can be a challenge. Here are some tips for dealing with them:

Look for something familiar.   Texts often seem difficult or boring because we don't know enough about the topic or about the larger conversation surrounding it to read them effectively. By skimming the headings, the abstract or introduction, and the conclusion, you may find something that relates to something you already know or are at least interested in—and being aware of that prior knowledge can help you see how this new material relates to it.

Look for "landmarks."   Reading a challenging academic text the first time through can be like driving to an unfamiliar destination on roads you've never traveled: you don't know where you're headed, you don't recognize anything along the way, and you're not sure how long getting there will take. As you drive the route again, though, you see landmarks along the way that help you know where you're going. The same goes for reading a difficult text: sometimes you need to get through it once just to get some idea of what it's about. On the second reading, now that you have "driven the route," look for the ways that the parts of the text relate to one another, to other texts or course information, or to other knowledge you have.

Monitor your understanding.   You may have had the experience of reading a text and suddenly realizing that you have no idea what you just read. Being able to monitor your reading—to sense when you aren't understanding the text and need to reread, focus your attention, look up unfamiliar terms, take some notes, or take a break—can make you a more efficient and better reader. Keep these questions in mind as you read: What is my purpose for reading this text? Am I understanding it? Does it make sense? Should I slow down, reread, annotate? skim ahead and then come back? pause to reflect?

Be persistent.   Research shows that many students respond to difficult texts by assuming they're "too dumb to get it"—and quit reading. Successful students, on the other hand, report that if they keep at a text, they will come to understand it. Some of them even see difficult texts as challenges: "I'm going to keep working on this until I make sense of it." Remember that reading is an active process, and the more you work at it the more successful you will be.

Annotating

Many readers find it helps to annotate as they read: highlighting keywords, phrases, sentences; connecting ideas with lines or symbols; writing comments or questions in the margin or on sticky notes; circling new words so you can look up the definitions later; noting anything that seems noteworthy or questionable. Annotating forces you to read for more than just the surface meaning. Especially when you are going to be writing about or responding to a text, annotating creates a record of things you may want to refer to.

Annotate as if you're having a conversation with the author, someone you take seriously but whose words you do not accept without question. Put your part of the conversation in the margin, asking questions, talking back: "What's this mean?" "So what?" "Says who?" "Where's evidence?" "Yes!" "Whoa!" or even ☺ or ☹ or texting shorthand like LOL or INTRSTN. If you're reading a text online, you may be able to copy it and annotate it electronically. If so, make your annotations a different color from the text itself.

What you annotate depends on your **PURPOSE**, or what you're most interested in. If you're analyzing a text that makes an explicit argument, you would probably underline the **THESIS STATEMENT** and then the **REASONS** and **EVIDENCE** that support that statement. It might help to restate those ideas in your own words in the margins—in order to understand them, you need to put them in your own words! If you are trying to **IDENTIFY PATTERNS**, you might highlight each pattern in a different color or mark it with a sticky note and write any questions or notes about it in that color. You might annotate a visual text by circling and identifying important parts of the image.

There are some texts that you cannot annotate, of course—library books, some materials you read on the web, and so on. Then you will need to use sticky notes or make notes elsewhere, and you might find it useful to keep a reading log for this purpose.

55–56

387–89
400–401
401–8

23–25

Coding

You may also find it useful to record your thoughts as you read by using a coding system—for example, using "X" to indicate passages that contradict your assumptions, or "?" for ones that puzzle you. You can make up your own coding system, of course, but you could start with this one*:

- ✔ Confirms what you thought
- X Contradicts what you thought
- ? Puzzles you
- ?? Confuses you
- ! Surprises you
- ☆ Strikes you as important
- ➜ Is new or interesting to you

You might also circle new words that you'll want to look up later and highlight or underline key phrases.

---

*Adapted from Harvey Daniels and Steven Zemelman, *Subjects Matter: Every Teacher's Guide to Content-Area Reading*.

A Sample Annotated Text

Here is an excerpt from Justice: What's the Right Thing to Do?, *a book by Harvard professor Michael J. Sandel, annotated by a writer who was doing research for a report on the awarding of military medals:*

What Wounds Deserve the Purple Heart?

✔

On some issues, questions of virtue and honor are too obvious to deny. Consider the recent debate over who should qualify for the Purple Heart. Since 1932, the U.S. military has awarded the medal to soldiers wounded or killed in battle by enemy action. In addition to the honor, the medal entitles recipients to special privileges in veterans' hospitals.

PTSD increasingly common among veterans.

Since the beginning of the current wars in Iraq and Afghanistan, growing numbers of veterans have been diagnosed with post-traumatic stress disorder and treated for the condition. Symptoms include recurring nightmares, severe depression, and suicide. At least three hundred thousand veterans reportedly suffer from traumatic stress or major depression. Advocates for these veterans have proposed that they, too, should qualify for the Purple Heart. Since psychological injuries can be at least as debilitating as physical ones, they argue, soldiers who suffer these wounds should receive the medal.

Argument: Vets with PTSD should be eligible for PH because psych. injuries are as serious as physical.

No PH for PTSD vets? Seems unfair!

After a Pentagon advisory group studied the question, the Pentagon announced, in 2009, that the Purple Heart would be reserved for soldiers with physical injuries. Veterans suffering from mental disorders and psychological trauma would not be eligible, even though they qualify for government-supported medical treatment and disability payments. The Pentagon offered two reasons for its decision: traumatic stress disorders are not intentionally caused by enemy action, and they are difficult to diagnose objectively.

Argument: PTSD is like punctured eardrums, which do get the PH.

Did the Pentagon make the right decision? Taken by themselves, its reasons are unconvincing. In the Iraq War, one of the most common injuries recognized with the Purple Heart has been a punctured eardrum, caused by explosions at close range. But unlike bullets and bombs, such explosions are not a deliberate enemy tactic intended to injure or kill; they are (like traumatic stress) a damaging side effect of battlefield action. And while traumatic disorders may be more difficult

academic literacies | rhetorical situations | genres | fields | processes | strategies | research MLA / APA | media / design | readings | handbook

to diagnose than a broken limb, the injury they inflict can be more severe and long-lasting.

As the wider debate about the Purple Heart revealed, the real issue is about the meaning of the medal and the virtues it honors. What, then, are the relevant virtues? Unlike other military medals, <u>the Purple Heart honors sacrifice, not bravery</u>. It requires no heroic act, only an injury inflicted by the enemy. The question is what kind of injury should count.

PH "honors sacrifice, not bravery." Injury enough. So what kind of injury?

A veteran's group called the Military Order of the Purple Heart opposed awarding the medal for psychological injuries, claiming that doing so would "debase" the honor. A spokesman for the group stated that "shedding blood" should be an essential qualification. He didn't explain why bloodless injuries shouldn't count. But Tyler E. Boudreau, a former Marine captain who favors including psychological injuries, offers a compelling analysis of the dispute. He attributes the opposition to a deep-seated attitude in the military that views post-traumatic stress as a kind of weakness. "The same culture that demands tough-mindedness also encourages skepticism toward the suggestion that the violence of war can hurt the healthiest of minds . . . Sadly, <u>as long as our military culture bears at least a quiet contempt for the psychological wounds of war, it is unlikely those veterans will ever see a Purple Heart</u>."

Wow: one vet's group insists that for PH, soldier must bleed!

☆

So the debate over the Purple Heart is more than a medical or clinical dispute about how to determine the veracity of injury. At the heart of the disagreement are rival conceptions of <u>moral character and military valor</u>. Those who insist that only bleeding wounds should count believe that post-traumatic stress reflects a weakness of character unworthy of honor. Those who believe that psychological wounds should qualify argue that veterans suffering long-term trauma and severe depression have sacrificed for their country as surely, and as honorably, as those who've lost a limb. The dispute over the Purple Heart illustrates the moral logic of Aristotle's theory of justice. We can't determine who deserves a military medal without asking what virtues the medal properly honors. And to answer that question, we have to assess competing conceptions of character and sacrifice.

Argument based on different ideas about what counts as a military virtue.

— Michael J. Sandel, *Justice: What's the Right Thing to Do?*

Summarizing

Writing a summary, boiling down a text to its main ideas, can help you understand it. To do so, you need to identify which ideas in the text are crucial to its meaning. Then you put those crucial ideas into your own words, creating a brief version that accurately sums up the text. Here, for example, is a summary of Sandel's analysis of the Purple Heart debate:

> In "What Wounds Deserve the Purple Heart?," Harvard professor Michael J. Sandel explores the debate over eligibility for the Purple Heart, the medal given to soldiers who die or are wounded in battle. Some argue that soldiers suffering from post-traumatic stress disorder should qualify for the medal because psychological injuries are as serious as physical ones. However, the military disagrees, since PTSD injuries are not "intentionally caused by enemy action" and are hard to diagnose. Sandel observes that the dispute centers on how "character" and "sacrifice" are defined. Those who insist that soldiers must have had physical wounds to be eligible for the Purple Heart see psychological wounds as reflecting "weakness of character," while others argue that veterans with PTSD and other psychological traumas have sacrificed honorably for their country.

READING CRITICALLY

When we read critically, we apply our analytical skills in order to engage with a text to determine not only what a text says but also what it means and how it works. The following strategies can help you read texts critically.

Believing and Doubting

One way to develop a response to a text is to play the believing and doubting game, sometimes called reading with and against the grain.
332–33 ⊙
331–32
Your goal is to **LIST** or **FREEWRITE** notes as you read, writing out as many

reasons as you can think of for believing what the writer says (reading with the grain) and then as many as you can for doubting it (reading against the grain).

First, try to look at the world through the writer's perspective. Try to understand their reasons for arguing as they do, even if you strongly disagree. Then reread the text, trying to doubt everything in it: try to find every flaw in the argument, every possible way it can be refuted—even if you totally agree with it. Developed by writing theorist Peter Elbow, the believing and doubting game helps you consider new ideas and question ideas you already have—and at the same time see where you stand in relation to the ideas in the text you're reading.

Thinking about How the Text Works: What It Says, What It Does

Sometimes you'll need to think about how a text works, how its parts fit together. You may be assigned to analyze a text, or you may just need to make sense of a difficult text, to think about how the ideas all relate to one another. Whatever your purpose, a good way to think about a text structure is by **OUTLINING** it, paragraph by paragraph. If you're interested in analyzing its ideas, look at what each paragraph *says*; if, on the other hand, you're concerned with how the ideas are presented, pay attention to what each paragraph *does*.

◯ 335–37

What it says.   Write a sentence that identifies what each paragraph says. Once you've done that for the whole text, look for patterns in the topics the writer addresses. Pay attention to the order in which the topics are presented. Also look for gaps, ideas the writer has left unsaid. Such paragraph-by-paragraph outlining of the content can help you see how the writer has arranged ideas and how that arrangement builds an argument or develops a topic. Here, for example, is an outline of Michael Granof's proposal,

"Course Requirement: Extortion"; the essay may be found on pages 246–49. The numbers in the left column refer to the essay's paragraphs.

1	College textbooks cost several times more than other books.
2	However, a proposed solution to the cost problem would only make things worse.
3	This proposal, to promote sales of used textbooks, would actually cause textbook costs to rise, because the sale of used books is a main reason new texts cost so much.
4	There is another way to lower costs.
5	Used textbooks are already being marketed and sold very efficiently.
6	Because of this, most new textbook sales take place in the first semester after they're published, forcing publishers to raise prices before used books take over the market.
7	In response, textbooks are revised every few years, whether or not the content is outdated, and the texts are "bundled" with other materials that can't be used again.
8–9	A better solution would be to consider textbooks to be like computer software and issue "site licenses" to universities. Once instructors choose textbooks, the university would pay publishers fees per student for their use.
10	Publishers would earn money for the use of the textbooks, and students' costs would be much lower.
11	Students could use an electronic text or buy a print copy for additional money. The print copies would cost less because the publisher would make most of its profits on the site license fees.
12	This arrangement would have no impact on teaching, unlike other proposals that focus on using electronic materials or using "no frills" textbooks and that might negatively affect students' learning.
13	This proposal would reduce the cost of attending college and help students and their families.

What it does. Identify the function of each paragraph. Starting with the first paragraph, ask, What does this paragraph do? Does it introduce a topic? provide background for a topic to come? describe something? define some-

thing? entice me to read further? something else? What does the second paragraph do? the third? As you go through the text, you may identify groups of paragraphs that have a single purpose. Here is a functional outline of Granof's essay (again, the numbers on the left refer to the paragraphs):

1	Introduces the topic by defining a problem
2	Introduces a flawed solution
3	Explains the flawed solution and the problem with it
4	Introduces a better solution
5–7	Describes the current situation and the dynamics of the problem
8	Outlines the author's proposed solution
9–10	Explains the proposed solution
11–12	Describes the benefits and effects of the proposed solution
13	Concludes

Identifying Patterns

Look for notable patterns in the text—recurring words and their synonyms, as well as repeated phrases, metaphors and other images, and types of sentences. Some readers find it helps to highlight patterns in various colors. Does the author repeatedly rely on any particular writing strategies: **NARRATION**? **COMPARISON**? Something else?

462–70
424–31

Another kind of pattern that might be important to consider is the kind of evidence the text provides. Is it more opinion than facts? nothing but statistics? If many sources are cited, is the information presented in any patterns—as **QUOTATIONS**? **PARAPHRASES**? **SUMMARIES**? Are there repeated references to certain experts or sources?

526–38

In visual texts, look for patterns of color, shape, and line. What's in the foreground, and what's in the background? What's completely visible, partly visible, or hidden? In both verbal and visual texts, look for omissions and anomalies: What isn't there that you would expect to find? Is there anything that doesn't really fit in?

If you discover patterns, then you need to consider what, if anything, they mean in terms of what the writer is saying. What do they reveal about the writer's underlying premises and beliefs? What do they tell you about the writer's strategies for persuading readers to accept the truth of what they are saying?

See how color-coding an essay by *New York Times* columnist William Safire on the meaning of the Gettysburg Address reveals several patterns in the language Safire uses. In this excerpt from the essay, which was published just before the first anniversary of the September 11, 2001, terrorist attacks, Safire develops his analysis through several patterns. Religious references are colored yellow; references to a "national spirit," green; references to life, death, and rebirth, blue; and places where Safire directly addresses the reader, gray.

But the selection of this poetic political sermon as the oratorical centerpiece of our observance need not be only an exercise. . . . Now, as then, a national spirit rose from the ashes of destruction.

Here is how to listen to Lincoln's all-too-familiar speech with new ears.

In those 266 words, you will hear the word *dedicate* five times. . . .

Those five pillars of dedication rested on a fundament of religious metaphor. From a president not known for his piety—indeed, often criticized for his supposed lack of faith—came a speech rooted in the theme of national resurrection. The speech is grounded in conception, birth, death, and rebirth.

Consider the barrage of images of birth in the opening sentence. . . .

Finally, the nation's spirit rises from this scene of death: "that this nation, under God, shall have a new birth of freedom." Conception, birth, death, rebirth. The nation, purified in this fiery trial of war, is resurrected. Through the sacrifice of its sons, the sundered nation would be reborn as one. . . .

Do not listen on Sept. 11 only to Lincoln's famous words and comforting cadences. Think about how Lincoln's message encompasses but goes beyond paying "fitting and proper" respect to the dead and the bereaved. His sermon at Gettysburg reminds "us the living" of our "unfinished work" and "the great task remaining before us"—to resolve that this generation's response to the deaths of thousands of our people leads to "a new birth of freedom."

The color coding helps us to see patterns in Safire's language, just as Safire reveals patterns in Lincoln's words. He offers an interpretation of

academic literacies rhetorical situations genres fields processes strategies research MLA / APA media / design readings handbook

Lincoln's address as a "poetic political sermon," and the words he uses throughout support that interpretation. At the end, he repeats the assertion that Lincoln's address is a sermon, inviting us to consider it differently. Safire's repeated commands ("Consider," "Do not listen," "Think about") offer additional insight into how he wishes to position himself in relation to his readers.

READING RHETORICALLY

To read academic texts effectively, you need to look beyond the words on the page or screen to the **RHETORICAL CONTEXT** of the text and the argument it makes. Academic texts—both the ones you read and the ones you write—are parts of ongoing scholarly conversations, in which writers respond to the ideas and assertions of others in order to advance knowledge. To enter those conversations, you must first read carefully and critically to understand the rhetorical situation, the larger context within which a writer wrote, and the argument the text makes.

▲ 116–17

Considering the Rhetorical Situation

As a reader, you need to think about the message that the writer wants to articulate, including the intended audience and the writer's attitude toward that audience and the topic, as well as about the genre, medium, and design of the text.

PURPOSE What is the writer's purpose? To entertain? inform? persuade readers to think something or take some action? What is *your* purpose for reading this text?

■ 55–56

AUDIENCE Who is the intended audience? Are you a member of that group? If not, should you expect that you'll need to look up unfamiliar terms or concepts or that you'll run into assumptions you don't necessarily share? How is the writer addressing the audience—as an expert addressing those less knowledgeable? an outsider addressing insiders?

■ 57–60

GENRE What is the genre? Is it a report? an argument? an analysis? something else? Knowing the genre can help you to anticipate certain key features.

STANCE Who is the writer, and what is their stance? Critical? Curious? Opinionated? Objective? Passionate? Indifferent? Something else? Knowing the stance affects the way you understand a text, whether you're inclined to agree or disagree with it, to take it seriously, and so on.

MEDIA / DESIGN What is the medium, and how does it affect the way you read? If it's a print text, what do you know about the publisher? If it's on the web, who sponsors the site, and when was it last updated? Are there any headings, summaries, or other elements that highlight key parts of the text?

Analyzing the Argument

All texts make some kind of argument, claiming something and then offering reasons and evidence as support for any claim. As a critical reader, you need to look closely at the argument a text makes—to recognize all the claims it makes, consider the support it offers for those claims, and decide how you want to respond. What do you think, and why? Here are some questions to consider when analyzing an argument:

- *What claim is the text making?* What is the writer's main point? Is it stated as a **THESIS** or only implied? Is it limited or **QUALIFIED** somehow? If not, should it have been?

- *How is the claim supported?* What **REASONS** does the writer provide for the claim, and what **EVIDENCE** is given for the reasons? What kind of evidence is it? Facts? Statistics? Examples? Expert opinions? Images? How convincing do you find the reasons and evidence? Is there enough evidence?

- *What appeals besides logical ones are used?* Does the writer appeal to readers' **EMOTIONS**? try to establish **COMMON GROUND**? demonstrate their **CREDIBILITY** as trustworthy and knowledgeable? How successful are these appeals?

◆ 401–13

- *Are any* **COUNTERARGUMENTS** *acknowledged?* If so, are they presented accurately and respectfully? Does the writer concede any value to them or try to refute them? How successfully does the writer deal with them?

◆ 411–12

- *What outside sources of information does the writer cite?* What kinds of sources are they, and how credible do they seem? Are they current and authoritative? How well do they support the argument?

- *Do you detect any* **FALLACIES**? Fallacies are arguments that involve faulty reasoning. Because they often seem plausible, they can be persuasive. It is important, therefore, that you question the legitimacy of such reasoning when you run across it.

◆ 414–16

Considering the Larger Context

All texts are part of ongoing conversations with other texts that have dealt with the topic of the text. An essay arguing for an assault-weapons ban is part of an ongoing conversation on gun legislation, which is itself part of a conversation on individual rights and responsibilities. Academic texts document their sources in part to show their relationship to the ongoing scholarly conversation on a particular topic. In fact, any time you're reading to learn, you're probably reading for some larger context. Whatever your reading goals, being aware of that larger context can help you better understand what you're reading. Here are some specific aspects of the text to pay attention to:

Who else cares about this topic?   Especially when you're reading in order to learn about a topic, the texts you read will often reveal which people or groups are part of the conversation—and might be sources of further reading. For example, an essay describing the formation of Mammoth Cave in Kentucky could be of interest to geologists, cave explorers, travel writers, or tourists. If you're reading such an essay while doing research on the cave, you should consider how the audience to whom the writer is writing determines the nature of the information provided—and its suitability as a source for your research.

What conversations is this text part of? Does the text refer to any concepts or ideas that give you some sense that it's part of a larger conversation? An argument on airport security measures, for example, is part of larger conversations about government response to terrorism, the limits of freedom in a democracy, and the possibilities of using technology to detect weapons and explosives, among others.

What terms does the writer use? Do any terms or specialized language reflect the writer's allegiance to a particular group or academic discipline? If you run across words like *false consciousness, ideology,* and *hegemony,* for example, you might guess that the text was written by a Marxist scholar.

What other writers or sources does the writer cite? Do the other writers have a particular academic specialty, belong to an identifiable intellectual school, share similar political leanings? If an article on politics cites Paul Krugman and Gail Collins in support of its argument, you might assume that the writer holds liberal opinions; if it cites Ross Douthat and Jennifer Rubin, the writer is likely a conservative.

READING VISUAL TEXTS

Photos, drawings, graphs, diagrams, and charts are frequently used to help convey important information and often make powerful arguments themselves. So learning to read and interpret visual texts is just as necessary as it is for written texts.

Taking visuals seriously. Remember that visuals are texts themselves, not just decoration. When they appear as part of a written text, they may introduce information not discussed elsewhere in the text. Or they might illustrate concepts hard to grasp from words alone. In either case, it's important to pay close attention to any visuals in a written text.

academic literacies · rhetorical situations · genres · fields · processes · strategies · research MLA / APA · media / design · readings · handbook

Looking at any title, caption, or other written text that's part of a visual will help you understand its main idea. It might also help to think about its purpose: Why did the writer include it? What information does it add or emphasize? What argument is it making? See, for example, how a psychology textbook uses visuals to help explain two ways that information can be represented:

Analogical and Symbolic Representations

When we think about information, we use two basic types of internal representations: analogical and symbolic.

Analogical representations usually correspond to images. They have some characteristics of actual objects. Therefore, they are analogous to actual objects. For example, maps correspond to geographical layouts. Family trees depict branching relationships between relatives. A clock corresponds directly to the passage of time. **Figure 2.1a** is a drawing of a violin from a particular perspective. This drawing is an analogical representation.

Figure 2.1 Analogical Versus Symbolic Representations

(a) (b)

Violin

(a) Analogical representations, such as this picture of a violin, have some characteristics of the objects they represent.
(b) Symbolic representations, such as the word *violin*, are abstract and do not have relationships to the physical qualities of objects.

By contrast, **symbolic representations** are abstract. These representations usually consist of words or ideas. They do not have relationships to physical qualities of objects in the world. The word *hamburger* is a symbolic representation that usually represents a cooked patty of beef served on a bun. The word *violin* stands for a musical instrument (**Figure 2.1b**). — Sarah Grison, Todd Heatherton, and Michael Gazzaniga, *Psychology in Your Life*

The headings tell you the topic: analogical and symbolic representations. The paragraphs define the two types of representation, and the illustrations present a visual example of each type. The visuals make the information in the written text easier to understand by illustrating the differences between the two.

Reading charts and graphs. To read the information in charts and graphs, you need to look for different things depending on what type of chart or graph you're considering. A line graph, for example, usually contains certain elements: title, legend, x axis, y axis, and source information. Figure 2.2 shows one such graph taken from a sociology textbook.

Other types of charts and graphs include some of these same elements. But the specific elements vary according to the different kinds of

Title: Indicates the topic.

Legend: Explains the symbols used. Here, colors show the different categories.

Source: The origin of the data.

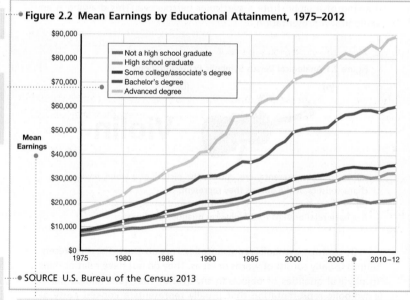

Figure 2.2 Mean Earnings by Educational Attainment, 1975–2012

Legend:
- Not a high school graduate
- High school graduate
- Some college/associate's degree
- Bachelor's degree
- Advanced degree

Mean Earnings (y axis): $0, $10,000, $20,000, $30,000, $40,000, $50,000, $60,000, $70,000, $80,000, $90,000

x axis: 1975, 1980, 1985, 1990, 1995, 2000, 2005, 2010–12

SOURCE U.S. Bureau of the Census 2013

y axis: Defines the independent variable (something that doesn't change depending on other factors).

x axis: Defines the dependent variable (something that changes, depending on other factors).

✳ academic literacies   ■ rhetorical situations   ▲ genres   ● fields   ○ processes   ◆ strategies   ● research MLA / APA   ▢ media / design   ▮ readings   ⬥ handbook

Figure 2.3 Women's Participation in the Labor Force in the United States, 1948–2012

*Women in the labor force as a percent of all civilian women age sixteen and over.
†Women in the labor force as a percent of the total labor force (both men and women) age sixteen and over.

SOURCE U.S. Bureau of Labor Statistics 2014

information being presented, and some charts and graphs can be challenging to read. For example, the chart in Figure 2.3, from the same textbook, includes elements of both bar and line graphs to depict two trends at once: the red line shows the percentage of women in the United States who were in the labor force over a sixty-five-year period, and the blue bars show the percentage of U.S. workers who were women during that same period. Both trends are shown in two-year increments. To make sense of this chart, you need to read the title, the y-axis labels, and the labels and their definitions carefully.

Reading Onscreen

Research shows that we tend to read differently onscreen than we do when we read print texts: we skim and sample, often reading a sentence or two and then jumping to another site, another text. If we need to scroll the page to continue, we often don't bother. In general, we don't read as carefully as we do when reading print texts, and we're less likely to reread or take other steps if we find that we don't understand something. Following are some strategies that might help you read effectively onscreen.

Adjust your reading speed and effort to your purpose. Many students use the web to get an overview of a topic and find potential sources. In that case, skimming and browsing are sensible and appropriate tactics. If you're reading to evaluate a source or find specific information on a topic, though, you probably need to read more slowly and carefully.

Keep your purpose in mind as you read. Clicking on hyperlinks and jumping from site to site can be tempting. Resist the temptation! Making a list of specific questions you're seeking to answer can help you stay focused and on task.

Print out longer texts. Some people find reading online to be harder on their eyes than reading pages of print, and many find that they comprehend and remember information in longer texts better if they read them in print. Reading a long text is similar to walking through an unfamiliar neighborhood: we form a mental map of the text as we read and then associate the information with its location in the text, making remembering easier. Since forming such a map is more difficult when reading an electronic text, printing out texts you need to read carefully may be a good strategy.

IF YOU NEED MORE HELP

511–18
331–39
343–47
348–55
356–60

See Chapter 49, **EVALUATING SOURCES**, for questions to help you analyze a text's rhetorical situation. See also Chapter 29 on **GENERATING IDEAS AND TEXT**; you can adapt those methods as ways of looking at texts, especially clustering and cubing. And see also Chapter 31 on **ASSESSING YOUR OWN WRITING**, Chapter 32 on **GETTING RESPONSE AND REVISING**, and Chapter 33 on **EDITING AND PROOF-READING** if you need advice for reading your own writing.

Summarizing and Responding: *Where Reading Meets Writing*

Summarizing a text helps us to see and understand its main points and to think about what it says. Responding to that text then prompts us to think about—*and say*—what we think. Together, summarizing and responding to texts is one way that we engage with the ideas of others. In a history course, you might summarize and respond to an essay arguing that Civil War photographers did not accurately capture the realities of the battlefield. In a philosophy course, you might summarize Plato's "Allegory of the Cave" and respond to its portrayal of knowledge as shadows on a wall.

And in much of the writing that you do, you'll need to cite the ideas of others, both as context for your own thinking and as evidence to support your arguments. In fact, unless you're Adam, there's probably no topic you'll write about that someone else hasn't already written about—and one way of introducing what you have to say is as a response to something others have said about your topic. A good way of doing that is by summarizing what they've said, using the summary as a launching pad for what you say. This chapter offers advice for summarizing and responding, writing tasks you'll have occasion to do in many of your college classes—and provides a short guide to writing a summary/response essay, a common assignment in composition classes.

SUMMARIZING

In many of your college courses, you'll likely be asked to summarize what someone else has said. Boiling down a text to its basic ideas helps you focus on the text, figure out what the writer has said, and understand (and remember) what you're reading. In fact, summarizing is an essential academic skill, a way to incorporate the ideas of others into your own writing. Following are some guidelines for summarizing effectively:

Read the text carefully.   To write a good summary, you need to read the original text carefully to capture the writer's intended meaning as clearly and evenhandedly as you can. Start by **SKIMMING** the text to get a general sense of what it's saying. If some parts don't make sense, don't worry; at this point, you're reading just to get the gist. Then reread the text more slowly, **ANNOTATING** it paragraph by paragraph. If there's an explicit **THESIS** stating the main point, highlight it in some way. Then try to capture the main idea of each paragraph in a single sentence.

12–13 ❋

16–17 ❋
387–89 ◆

State the main points concisely and accurately.   Summaries of a complete text are generally between 100 and 250 words in length, so you need to choose your words carefully and to focus only on the text's main ideas. Leave out supporting evidence, anecdotes, and counterarguments unless they're crucial to understanding the text. For instance, in summarizing "A Brief History of the Modern-Day Straw, the World's Most Wasteful Commodity" (see p. 233), Ernie Smith's essay explaining why drinking straws are wasteful, you would omit its description of the invention of the rye straw in the nineteenth century.

Describe the text accurately and fairly—and using neutral language. Present the author's ideas evenhandedly and fairly; a summary isn't the place to share your opinion of what the text says. Use neutral verbs such as *states*, *asserts*, or *concludes*, not verbs that imply praise or criticism like *proves* or *complains*.

535–38 ●

Use SIGNAL PHRASES to distinguish what the author says from what you say.   Introducing a statement with phrases such as "he says" or "the essay concludes" indicates explicitly that you're summarizing what the author said. When first introducing an author, you may need to say something about their credentials. For example:

> In "Our Declaration," political philosopher Danielle Allen analyzes the language of the Declaration of Independence.

❋
academic literacies

■
rhetorical situations

▲
genres

●
fields

○
processes

◆
strategies

●
research MLA / APA

▢
media / design

❚❚
readings

⌃
handbook

Daniel Felsenfeld, a music composer who also writes about music, describes how he developed a passion for twentieth-century classical music in "Rebel Music."

Later in the text, you may need to refer to the author again as you summarize specific parts of the text. These signal phrases are typically briefer: *In Felsenfeld's view . . . , Allen then argues . . .*

Use quotations sparingly, if at all. You may need to **QUOTE** keywords or memorable phrases, but most or all of a summary should be written in your own words, using your own sentence structures.

    DOCUMENT any text you summarize in a works-cited or references list. A summary of a lengthy work should include **IN-TEXT DOCUMENTATION** noting the pages summarized; they aren't needed with a brief text like the one summarized below (see p. 143).

528–31

544–47
MLA 551–57
APA 600–604

An Example Summary

In "The Reason College Costs More than You Think," Jon Marcus, a higher-education editor at the *Hechinger Report*, reports that a major reason why college educations are so expensive is the amount of time students stay in college. Although almost all first-year students and their families assume that earning a bachelor's degree will take four years, the reality is that more than half of all students take longer, with many taking six years or more. This delay happens for many reasons, including students changing majors, having to take developmental courses, taking fewer courses per term than they could have, and being unable to register for required courses. As a result, their expenses are much greater—financial aid seldom covers a fifth or sixth year, so students must borrow money to finish—and the additional time they spend in college is time they aren't working, leading to significant losses in wages.

This summary begins with a signal phrase stating the author's name and credentials and the title of the text being summarized. The summary includes only the main ideas, in the summary writer's own words.

RESPONDING

When you summarize a text, you show that you understand its main ideas; responding to a text pushes you to engage with those ideas—and gives you the opportunity to contribute your ideas to a larger conversation. You can respond in various ways, for instance, by taking a **POSITION** on the text's argument, by **ANALYZING THE TEXT** in some way, or by **REFLECTING** on what it says.

157–84
98–130
256–63

Deciding How to Respond

You may be assigned to write a specific kind of response—an argument or analysis, for instance—but more often than not, the nature of your response is left largely up to you. If so, you'll need to read closely and critically to understand what the text says, to get a sense of how—and how well—it does so, and to think about your own reaction to it. Only then can you decide how to respond. You can respond to what the text says (its ideas), to how it says it (the way it's written), or to where it leads your own thinking (your own personal reaction). Or you might write a response that mixes those ways of responding. You might, for example, combine a personal reaction with an examination of how the writing caused that reaction.

If you're responding to what a text says, you might agree or disagree with the author's argument, supporting your position with good reasons and evidence for your response. You might agree with parts of the argument and disagree with others. You might find that the author has ignored or downplayed some important aspect of the topic that needs to be discussed or at least acknowledged. Here are some questions to consider that can help you think about what a text says:

- What does the writer claim?

400–401
401–8

- What **REASONS** and **EVIDENCE** does the writer provide to support that claim?

- What parts of the text do you agree with? Is there anything you disagree with—and if so, why?
- Does the writer represent any views other than their own? If not, what other perspectives should be considered?
- Are there any aspects of the topic that the writer overlooks or ignores?
- If you're responding to a visual text, how do the design and any images contribute to your understanding of what the text "says"?

Here is a brief response to Jon Marcus's "The Reason College Costs More than You Think," one that responds to his argument:

> It's true that one reason college costs so much more is that students take longer than four years to finish their degrees, but Jon Marcus's argument in "The Reason College Costs More than You Think" is flawed in several ways. He ignores the fact that over the past years state governments have reduced their subsidies to state-supported colleges and universities, forcing higher tuition, and that federal scholarship aid has declined as well, forcing students to pay a greater share of the costs. He doesn't mention the increased number of administrators or the costs of fancy athletic facilities and dormitories. Ultimately, his argument places most of the blame for higher college costs on students, who, he asserts, make poor choices by changing majors and "taking fewer courses per term than they could." College is supposed to present opportunities to explore many possible career paths, so changing majors should be considered a form of growth and education. Furthermore, many of us are working full-time to pay the high costs of college, leaving us with little extra time to study for four or five courses at once and sometimes forcing us to take fewer classes per term because that's all we can afford. Marcus is partly right—but he gets much of the problem wrong.

If you're focusing on the way a text is written, you'll consider what elements the writer uses to convey their message—facts, stories, images, and so on. You'll likely pay attention to the writer's word choices and look for any patterns that lead you to understand the text in a particular way. To think about the way a text is written, you might find some of these questions helpful:

- What is the writer's message? Is there an explicit statement of that message?

- How well has the writer communicated the message?

- How does the writer support what they say: by citing facts or statistics? by quoting experts? by noting personal experiences? Are you persuaded?

- Are there any words, phrases, or sentences that you find notable and that contribute to the text's overall effect?

119–25 ▲

- How does the text's design affect your response to it? If it's a **VISUAL TEXT**—a photo or ad, for example—how do the various parts of the text contribute to its message?

Here is a brief response to Marcus's essay that analyzes the various ways it makes its argument:

> In "The Reason College Costs More than You Think," *Time* magazine writer Jon Marcus argues that although several factors contribute to high college costs, the main one is how long it takes students to graduate. Marcus introduces this topic by briefly profiling a student who is in his fifth year of school and has run out of financial aid because he "changed majors and took courses he ended up not needing." This profile gives a human face to the topic, which Marcus then develops with statistics about college costs and the numbers of students who take more than four years to finish. Marcus's purpose is twofold: to inform readers that the assumption that most students finish college in four years is wrong and to persuade them that poor choices like those this student made are the primary reason college takes so long and costs so much. He acknowledges that the extra costs are "hidden" and "not entirely the student's fault" and suggests that poor high school preparation and unavailable required courses play a role, as do limits on financial aid. However, his final paragraph quotes the student as saying of the extra years, "That's time you're wasting that you could be out making money." As the essay's final statement, this assertion that spending more time in school is time wasted and that the implicit goal of college is career preparation reinforces Marcus's argument that college *should* take only four years and that students who take longer are financially irresponsible.

academic literacies   rhetorical situations   genres   fields   processes   strategies   research MLA / APA   media / design   readings   handbook

If you're reflecting on your own reaction to a text, you might focus on how your personal experiences or beliefs influenced the way you understood the text or on how it reinforced or prompted you to reassess some of those beliefs. You could also focus on how it led you to see the topic in new ways—or note questions that it's led you to wonder about. Some questions that may help you reflect on your own reaction to a text include:

- How did the text affect you personally?
- Is there anything in the text that really got your attention? If so, what?
- Do any parts of the text provoke an emotional reaction—make you laugh or cry, make you uneasy? What prompted that response?
- Does the text bring to mind any memories or past experiences? Can you see anything related to you and your life in the text?
- Does the text remind you of any other texts?
- Does the text support (or challenge) any of your beliefs? How?
- Has reading this text given you any new ideas or insight?

Here is a brief response to Jon Marcus's essay that reflects on an important personal issue:

> Jon Marcus's "Why College Costs More than You Think" made me think hard about my own educational plans. Because I'm working to pay for as much of my education as I can, I'm taking a full load of courses so I can graduate in four years, but truth be told I'm starting to question the major I've chosen. That's one aspect of going to college that Marcus fails to discuss: how your major affects your future career choices and earnings—and whether or not some majors that don't lead immediately to a career are another way of "wasting" your time. After taking several courses in English and philosophy, I find myself fascinated by the study of literature and ideas. If I decide to major in one or both of those subjects, am I being impractical? Or am I "following my heart," as Steve Jobs said in his Stanford commencement speech? Jobs did as he told those graduates to do, and it worked out well for him, so maybe majoring in something "practical" is less practical than it seems. If I graduate in four years and am "out making money" but doing something I don't enjoy, I might be worse off than if I take longer in college but find a path that is satisfying and enriching.

WRITING A SUMMARY / RESPONSE ESSAY

You may be assigned to write a full essay that summarizes and responds to something you've read. Following is one such essay. It was written by Jacob MacLeod, a student at Wright State University, and responds to a *New York Times* column by Nicholas Kristof, "Our Blind Spot about Guns" (see p. 162).

JACOB MacLEOD

Guns and Cars Are Different

In "Our Blind Spot about Guns," *The New York Times* columnist Nicholas Kristof compares guns to cars in order to argue for sensible gun regulation. Kristof suggests that gun regulations would dramatically decrease the number of deaths caused by gun use. To demonstrate this point, he shows that the regulations governments have instituted for cars have greatly decreased the number of deaths per million miles driven. Kristof then argues that guns should be regulated in the same way that cars are, that car regulation provides a model for gun regulation. I agree with Kristof that there should be more sensible gun regulation, but I have difficulty accepting that all of the regulations imposed on cars have made them safer, and I also believe that not all of the safety regulations he proposes for guns would necessarily have positive effects.

Kristof is right that background checks for those who want to buy guns should be expanded. According to Daniel Webster, director of the Johns Hopkins Center for Gun Policy and Research, state laws prohibiting firearm ownership by members of high-risk groups, such as perpetrators of domestic violence and the mentally ill, have been shown to reduce violence. Therefore, Webster argues, universal background checks would significantly reduce the availability of guns to high-risk groups, as well as reducing the number of guns diverted to the illegal market by making it easier to prosecute gun traffickers.

Kristof also argues that lowering the speed limit made cars safer. However, in 1987, forty states raised their top speed limit from 55 to 65 miles per hour. An analysis of this change by the University of California Transportation Center shows that after the increase, traffic fatality rates on interstate highways in those forty states decreased between 3.4 percent and 5.1 percent. After the higher limits went into effect, the study suggested, some drivers may have switched to safer interstates from other, more dangerous roads, and highway patrols

may have focused less on enforcing interstate speed limits and more on activities yielding greater benefits in terms of safety (Lave and Elias 58–61). Although common sense might suggest that lowered speed limits would mean safer driving, research showed otherwise, and the same may be true for gun regulation.

Gun control advocates argue that more guns mean more deaths. However, an article by gun rights advocates Don B. Kates and Gary Mauser argues that murder rates in many developed nations have bear no relation to the rate of gun ownership (652). The authors cite data on firearms ownership in the United States and England that suggest that crime rates are lowest where the density of gun ownership is highest and highest where gun density is lowest (653) and that increased gun ownership has often coincided with significant reductions in violence. For example, in the United States in the 1990s, criminal violence decreased, even though gun ownership increased (656). However, the authors acknowledge that "the notion that more guns reduce crime is highly controversial" (659).

All in all, then, Kristof is correct to suggest that sensible gun regulation is a good idea in general, but the available data suggest that some of the particular measures he proposes should not be instituted. I agree that expanding background checks would be a good way to regulate guns and that failure to require them would lead to more guns in the hands of criminals. While background checks are a good form of regulation, however, lower speed limits and trigger locks are not. The problem with this solution is that although it is based on commonsense thinking, the empirical data show that it may not work.

Works Cited

Kates, Don B., and Gary Mauser. "Would Banning Firearms Reduce Murder and Suicide? A Review of International and Some Domestic Evidence." *Harvard Journal of Law and Public Policy*, vol. 30, no. 2, Jan. 2007, pp. 649–94.

Kristof, Nicholas. "Our Blind Spot about Guns." *The New York Times,* 31 July 2014, www.nytimes.com/2014/07/31/opinion/nicholas -kristof-our-blind-spot-about-guns.html.

Lave, Charles, and Patrick Elias. "Did the 65 mph Speed Limit Save Lives?" *Accident Analysis & Prevention*, vol. 26, no. 1, Feb. 1994, pp. 49–62, www.sciencedirect.com/science/article/ pii/000145759490068X.

Webster, Daniel. "Why Expanding Background Checks Would, in Fact, Reduce Gun Crime." Interview by Greg Sargent. *The Washington Post,* 3 Apr. 2013, www.washingtonpost.com/blogs/plum-line/wp/2013/04/03/why-expanding-background-checks-would-in-fact-reduce-gun-crime/.

In his response, MacLeod both agrees and disagrees with Kristof's argument, using several sources to support his argument that some of Kristof's proposals may not work. MacLeod states his thesis at the end of the first paragraph, after his summary, and ends with a balanced assessment of Kristof's proposals. He cites several sources, both in the text with signal phrases and in-text documentation and at the end in a works-cited section.

Key Features of Summary / Response Essays

A clearly identified author and title.   Usually the author and title of the text being summarized are identified in a signal phrase in the first sentence. The author (or sometimes the title) may then be referred to in an abbreviated form if necessary in the rest of the essay: for example, "Kristof argues . . ." or "according to 'Our Blind Spot about Guns' . . ."

A concise summary of the text.   The summary presents the main and supporting ideas in the text, usually in the order in which they appear. MacLeod, for example, reduces Kristof's argument to four sentences that capture Kristof's main points while leaving out his many examples.

An explicit response.   Your essay should usually provide a concise statement (one sentence if possible) of your overall response to the text.

- *If you're responding to the argument,* you'll likely agree or disagree (or both), and so your response itself will constitute an argument, with an explicit thesis statement. For example, MacLeod first agrees with Kristof that "there should be more sensible gun regulation," but then introduces a two-part thesis: that not all automobile regulations have made cars safer and that not all gun regulations would make guns safer.

- *If you're analyzing the text,* you'll likely need to explain what you think the author is saying and how the text goes about conveying that

message. An analysis of Kristof's text, for example, might focus on his comparison of automobile regulations with gun regulations.

- *If you're responding with a reflection,* you might explore the ideas, emotions, or memories that the text evokes, the effects of its ideas on your own beliefs, or how your own personal experiences support or contradict the author's position. One response to Kristof's essay might begin by expressing surprise at the comparison of guns to cars and then explore the reasons you find that comparison surprising, leading to a new understanding of the ways regulations can work to save lives.

Support for your response.   Whatever your response, you need to offer reasons and evidence to support what you say.

- *If you're responding to what the text says,* you may offer facts, statistics, anecdotal evidence, and textual evidence, as MacLeod does. You'll also need to consider—and acknowledge—any possible counterarguments, positions other than yours.

- *If you're responding to the way the text is written,* you may identify certain patterns in the text that you think mean something, and you'll need to cite evidence from the text itself. For example, Kristof twice invokes a popular slogan among gun rights advocates, "Guns don't kill people. People kill people," changing "guns" to "cars" to advance his argument that regulating guns may make them safer, just as has happened with cars.

- *If you're reflecting on your own reaction to the text,* you may connect its ideas with your own experiences or beliefs or explore how the text reinforced, challenged, or altered your beliefs. A staunch gun-rights advocate, for example, might find in Kristof's essay a reasonable middle ground too often lacking in polarized debates like the one on gun control.

Ways of Organizing a Summary and Response Essay

You can organize a summary and response essay in various ways. You may want to use a simple, straightforward structure that starts out by

387–89

summarizing the text and then gives the **THESIS** of your response followed by details that develop the thesis.

[Summary, followed by response]

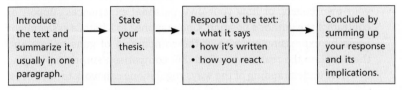

Or you may want to start out with the thesis and then, depending on whether your response focuses on the text's argument or its rhetorical choices, provide a paired summary of each main point or each aspect of the writing and a response to it.

[Introduction and thesis, followed by point-by-point summary and response]

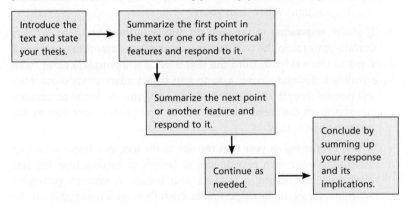

340–42
343–47
348–55
356–60
539–43

IF YOU NEED MORE HELP

See Chapter 30 for guidelines on **DRAFTING** and Chapter 36 for help writing a thesis and coming up with a title. See Chapter 31 on **ASSESSING YOUR OWN WRITING**, Chapter 32 on **GETTING RESPONSE AND REVISING**, and Chapter 33 on **EDITING AND PROOFREADING**. See Chapter 52 on **ACKNOWLEDGING SOURCES, AVOIDING PLAGIARISM**.

academic literacies · rhetorical situations · genres · fields · processes · strategies · research MLA / APA · media / design · readings · handbook

Developing Academic Habits of Mind   4

A little advice from Serena Williams: "Stick to it and work hard." She wasn't just talking about tennis, and her words resonate for all of us, for everything we set out to do. And here's Michael Jordan, who tells us "Never quit!" and then goes on to issue a warning: "If you quit once, it becomes a habit." Serena Williams and Michael Jordan may be two of the greatest athletes ever, but neither of them was born a champion. They became great by working hard, hanging in there, never giving up.

They succeeded, in other words, by developing certain habits of mind that can serve us all well—and that are especially valuable when it comes to succeeding in school. This chapter is about developing *academic habits of mind.* Just as Serena Williams wasn't born with her powerful serve, none of us was born knowing how to write academic papers or ace exams. But we too can learn and can develop the habits we need to succeed. This chapter offers advice for developing habits of mind that writing teachers nationwide have identified as essential for college success.

Engage

We all know people who see school as a series of hoops to jump through, who seem uninvolved—and even bored. We also know people who are passionate about something—a video game, a hobby, a profession—and who invest themselves, their time, and their emotions wholeheartedly in those activities. Successful students make that investment in school.

In other words, they engage with what they're studying, what they're doing, and what they're learning.

Think about your purpose for being in college.   What are your goals? To get a degree? To qualify for a particular job or profession? To find intellectual stimulation? To explore life? Try to define why you are in school, both in larger terms ("to get a degree in accounting") and in terms of the specific courses you are taking ("Learning to write better will help me be a better student in general and communicate effectively at work").

Fight off boredom.   Every job, including the job of being a student, involves some tasks that are dull but need to be done. When you encounter such a task, ask yourself how it helps you reach a larger goal. Shooting a hundred free throws for practice may not seem interesting, but it can help you win games. When you're listening to a lecture or reading a textbook, take notes, highlight, and annotate; doing that forces you to pay attention and increases what you remember and learn. Trying to identify the main ideas as you listen to a lecture will help you stay focused. When you're studying, try alternating between different tasks: reading, writing, doing problem sets, drawing, and so on.

If you get distracted, figure out ways to deal with it.   It's hard to engage with what you're reading or studying when you're thinking about something else—paying a tuition bill, the last episode of *The Walking Dead*, whatever. Try taking a few moments to write out what's on your mind, in a journal or somewhere else. Sometimes that simple act frees your mind to think about your work, even if it doesn't solve anything.

Raise your hand.   When you think you know the answer to a teacher's question (or when you yourself have a question), raise your hand. Most teachers appreciate students who take chances and who participate in class. At the same time, be polite: don't monopolize discussion or interrupt others when they're speaking.

Get involved. Get to know other students; study with them; join a campus organization. People who see themselves as part of something larger, even just a study group with three or four others, engage more in what they're doing than those who try to go it alone.

Be Curious

When we're young, we're curious about everything, and we learn by asking questions (why? why *not*?) and by exploring our surroundings (digging holes, cutting up magazines, investigating attics and basements). As we get older, though, we focus on things that interest us—and may as a result start to ignore other things or even to forget how to explore. In college, you'll be asked to research, study, and write about many topics you know nothing about. Seize the opportunity. Be curious! And take a tip from Dr. Seuss: "The more that you read, the more things you will know. / The more that you learn, the more places you'll go."

Ask questions. It's tempting to stay within our comfort zones, thinking about things we know and like, listening to those whose views we tend to agree with—to say what we already believe rather than to stop and think. Resist that temptation! Take every opportunity to ask questions, to learn more about things you're already interested in, and especially to learn about things you don't (yet) know anything about. As marine biologist Sylvia Earle says, "The best scientists and explorers have the attributes of kids! They ask questions and have a sense of wonder. They have curiosity. Who, what, where, why, when, and how! They never stop asking questions, and I never stop asking questions, just like a five year old."

Listen! Pay attention to what others say, including those who you don't necessarily agree with. The words and ideas of others can challenge the way we think, prompt us to rethink what we think—and spark our curiosity: Why does X think that? What do *I* think—*and why*? Why do my neighbors oppose the Common Core? What do educators think about it? Paying attention to all sides of an argument, doing research to find out what others have said about a topic, or searching social media to see the latest postings on a trending topic are all ways you can listen in on (and engage in) conversations on important issues of all kinds.

Be Open to New Ideas

No matter where you're in school, you're going to encounter ideas and concepts and even facts that challenge your own beliefs; you're also likely to meet people whose backgrounds and ways of looking at life are very different from your own. Be open-minded, open to new ideas and to what others think and say. Consider the perspectives and arguments of others. Learning involves accepting new ideas, acknowledging the value of different perspectives, and coming to understand our own beliefs in new ways. Listen to what others say, and think before you respond.

- *Treat the ideas of others with respect,* whether you agree with them or not, and encourage others to do the same. We don't open up if we don't feel safe.

- *Try to withhold judgment.* Be willing to listen to the thoughts of others and to consider ideas that may at first seem alien or weird (or wrong). Remember that your weird is likely someone else's normal—and the reverse.

- *Look for common ground between your perspectives and those of others*— places where you can agree, even in the midst of serious disagreement.

Be Flexible

Being flexible means being adaptable. In college, you'll likely face novel situations and need to find new ways to address problems, such as juggling school, work, and family; adjusting to roommates and making new friends; and figuring out how to do unfamiliar new assignments and how to take tests. You'll even have to do new kinds of writing: lab reports, reflections,

literacy narratives, and many, many more; if your school writing up until this point has usually (or always) called for a five-paragraph theme, that's not going to be the case anymore.

Look for new ways to do things. As the saying goes, "If all you have is a hammer, everything looks like a nail." Look for other tools to add to your toolbox: try solving math problems with words or by drawing, or starting a writing project by sketching out the parts.

Try not to see things as right or wrong, good or bad. Be willing to consider alternative points of view and to withhold judgment. Often ideas or actions can only be judged in context; they may be true in some cases or in part, and you often need to understand the larger situation or take into account various perspectives. For example, you may believe that lying is wrong, but is it excusable if telling the truth will cause someone pain? You find a required reading assignment boring and useless, but why, then, did your instructor assign it?

Approach academic assignments rhetorically. Analyze each assignment's purpose, intended audience, and the rest of its RHETORICAL SITUATION. Think about what's required in terms of content and format—and also about what's appropriate in terms of language and style. And what's expected in the discipline: informal language, sentence fragments, and photographs without captions might be appropriate for a sociology blog, for example, whereas a research project for a history course might have different requirements for how it's organized, formatted, and documented.

53

Be Creative

If you think that creativity is something artists have (and are born with), think again. From the young man selling homemade granola at a local farm market to the woman who puts together an eye-catching outfit from thrift-store bins, many of us are at work expressing ourselves in distinctive ways. Psychologists tell us that acting creatively opens us up to becoming more creative—and it is safe to say that doing so will make your work more productive and very likely more fun.

- *Play with ideas.* Freewrite. Make lists. Try looping, clustering, and the other ways of **GENERATING IDEAS** covered in this book. Take some time to think about the ideas you come up with.

331–39 ◯

- *Don't wait until the last minute.* Some students say they do better under the pressure of a deadline. Don't believe it! It's *always* better to give yourself time to think, to explore ideas, to "sleep on" assignments that first stump you.

- *Take risks!* Explore questions and topics that you haven't thought about before. Try out methods you haven't used previously. Challenge yourself to come up with ten ideas. Or twenty.

- *Ask questions.* And remember that there's no such thing as a dumb question.

Persist

Sometimes the key to success is simply sticking to the task at hand: ignoring distractions, hanging in there, forgetting frustration, getting the work done even in the face of setbacks and failures. Here's some advice from actress and singer Julie Andrews: "Perseverance is failing 19 times and succeeding the 20th."

- *Don't quit.* Assume that you can complete the task, and make up your mind to do it. If you're reading a book that seems hopelessly confusing or over your head, for example, keep at it until it starts to make sense. Reread, **OUTLINE CHAPTERS**, **SUMMARIZE**, **ANNOTATE**, and do whatever else you need to do to understand it.

335–37 ◯
20 ❄
16–17

- *Remember that sometimes you'll encounter setbacks*—and that the goal (a passing grade, a degree, a job) is still reachable if you keep trying. Those who play video games know that failing is an inherent part of playing them; the same is true of many other things as well.

academic literacies · rhetorical situations · genres · fields · processes · strategies · research MLA / APA · media / design · readings · handbook

- *Make a plan and establish a schedule,* and stick to them.
- *Break large projects into smaller goals.* Especially with assignments that call for a huge amount of work, approach it in stages: focus on getting through the next chapter, the next draft, the next whatever. It may be good to "keep your eyes on the prize," but it's usually best to take it one step at a time.
- *When you're working on several assignments, tackle the hardest ones first.* Work on them when you're fresh and your mind is clear.
- *If you don't understand something, ask for clarification.* Better to admit to confusion than to act as if you know something when you don't.
- *Ask for help when you need it.* Teachers are usually happy to help students during office hours or by appointment, before or after class, or over email. Get to know your teachers: they're there to help you.
- *Take advantage of whatever help is available* at your school's writing center or learning center and in class. An important part of being persistent is getting help when you need it.

Reflect

Pay attention to the ways you work and make decisions. Reflect on the ways you think and on how you think about the world. This kind of "meta-cognitive" thinking is one of the most important habits of mind, and it's one that will continue to serve you well throughout your life.

- *Figure out when you are most efficient* and do your best work—and try to schedule your work accordingly.
- *Pay attention to what you're reading and how you're doing it.* Think about why you're reading x, and use **READING STRATEGIES** appropriate to your purpose. If you lose the thread of an explanation or argument, figure out where you got lost and why.

  ✳ 10–32

- *After completing an assignment, reflect in writing* on what you did well, what problems you had, and how you solved them (or not). What would you do differently next time—or if you had more time? You'll find prompts for "Taking Stock of Your Work" at the end of Chapters 10–23 that can help.

- *Troubleshoot.* Pay attention to bumps in the road as you encounter them. Try to understand what caused the problem, what you did to solve it, how successful you were and why.

- *Try to focus on your achievements, what you can do*, rather than on what you may not be able to do or to do as well as you'd like.

Take Responsibility

In one way or another, all the habits of mind discussed above involve taking responsibility for your own actions. It may be tempting to blame others or society or bad luck for problems in your academic life, but the more you take ownership of your own learning, the more control you have over the results. Some ways you can enhance your sense of responsibility and demonstrate it include these:

- *Acknowledge that how much you learn and what grades you get depend mostly on you.* Teachers often say that they don't *give* grades, students *earn* grades—an important difference.

- *Treat school as you do a job,* one for which you must show up on time, perform tasks at a certain level of competence, and meet deadlines. In college, where your time is mostly unstructured, you have to become your own boss. So attend class regularly, follow instructions, and turn in assignments on time.

- *Get organized.* Maintain a calendar so you know what's due when. Create a schedule for your day that includes time for class, studying, working, and personal activities. Develop a system for organizing your written work and notes for each course you're taking. Learn where to find the materials you need to do your classwork.

526–38
544–47

- *Use research sources responsibly.* QUOTE , PARAPHRASE , and SUMMARIZE the work of others accurately, and DOCUMENT it correctly. Give appropriate credit to those whose ideas and words you are using.

academic literacies · rhetorical situations · genres · fields · processes · strategies · research MLA / APA · media / design · readings · handbook

part 2

Rhetorical Situations

Whenever we write, whether it's a text to a friend or a toast for a wedding, an English essay or a résumé, we face some kind of rhetorical situation. We have a PURPOSE, a certain AUDIENCE, a particular STANCE, a GENRE, and a MEDIUM to consider—and, as often as not, a DESIGN. All are important elements that we need to think about carefully. The following chapters offer brief discussions of those elements of the rhetorical situation, along with questions that can help you make the choices you need to as you write. See also the GENRE chapters for guidelines for considering your rhetorical situation in each of these specific kinds of writing.

Rhetorical Situations

Purpose   5

All writing has a purpose. We write to explore our thoughts and emotions, to express ourselves, to entertain; we write to record words and events, to communicate with others, to try to persuade others to believe as we do or to behave in certain ways. In fact, we often have several purposes at the same time. We may write an essay in which we try to explain something to an audience, but at the same time we may be trying to persuade that audience of something. Look, for example, at this passage from a 2012 *New York Times* op-ed essay by economist and editorial columnist Paul Krugman about social and economic trends among "the traditional working-class family"—declining rates of marriage and of male participation in the labor force and increasing numbers of out-of-wedlock births. Krugman asserts that the primary reason for those statistics is a "drastic reduction in the work opportunities available to less-educated men":

> Most of the numbers you see about income trends in America focus on households rather than individuals, which makes sense for some purposes. But when you see a modest rise in incomes for the lower tiers of the income distribution, you have to realize that all—yes, all—of this rise comes from the women, both because more women are in the paid labor force and because women's wages aren't as much below male wages as they used to be.
>
> For lower-education working men, however, it has been all negative. Adjusted for inflation, entry-level wages of male high school graduates have fallen 23 percent since 1973. Meanwhile, employment benefits have collapsed. In 1980, 65 percent of recent high-school graduates working in the private sector had health benefits, but, by 2009, that was down to 29 percent.
>
> So we have become a society in which less-educated men have great difficulty finding jobs with decent wages and good benefits.
>
> —Paul Krugman, "Money and Morals"

academic literacies · rhetorical situations · genres · fields · processes · strategies · research MLA / APA · media / design · readings · handbook

Krugman is reporting information here, outlining how the earnings and benefits of less-educated men have dropped over the last forty years. He is also making an argument, that these economic setbacks are a cause of the social ills among working-class Americans and not, as some would have it, the result of them. (Krugman, writing for a newspaper, is also using a style—including dashes, contractions, and other informal elements—that strives to be engaging while it informs and argues.)

Even though our purposes may be many, knowing our primary reason for writing can help us shape that writing and understand how to proceed with it. Our purpose can determine the genre we choose, our audience, even the way we design what we write.

Identify your purpose.   While a piece of writing often has many purposes, a writer usually focuses on one. When you get an assignment or see a need to write, ask yourself what the primary purpose of the writing task is: to entertain? to inform? to persuade? to demonstrate your knowledge or your writing ability? What are your own goals? What are your audience's expectations, and do they affect the way you define your purpose?

Thinking about Purpose

- *What do you want your audience to do, think, or feel?* How will your readers use what you tell them?

- *What does this writing task call on you to do?* Do you need to show that you have mastered certain content or skills? Do you have an assignment that specifies a particular **STRATEGY** or **GENRE**—to compare two things, perhaps, or to argue a position?

- *What are the best ways to achieve your purpose?* What **STANCE** should you take? Should you write in a particular genre? Do you have a choice of **MEDIUM**, and does your text require any special format or **DESIGN** elements?

371 ◆
73 ▲
66–68 ■
637 □

Audience 6

Who will read (or hear) what you are writing? A seemingly obvious but crucially important question. Your audience affects your writing in various ways. Consider a piece of writing as simple as a text from a mother to her son:

> *Pls. take chicken out to thaw and feed Annye. Remember Dr. Wong at 4.*

On the surface, this brief note is a straightforward reminder to do three things. But in fact it is a complex message filled with compressed information for a specific audience. The writer (the mother) counts on the reader (her son) to know a lot that can be left unsaid. She expects that he knows that the chicken is in the freezer and needs to thaw in time to be cooked for dinner; she knows that he knows who Annye is (a pet?), what they are fed, and how much; she assumes that he knows who (and where) Dr. Wong is. She doesn't need to spell out any of that because she knows what her son knows and what he needs to know—and in her text she can be brief. She understands her audience. Think how different such a reminder would be were it written to another audience—a babysitter, perhaps, or a friend helping out while Mom is out of town.

What you write, how much you write, how you phrase it, even your choice of **GENRE** (memo, essay, email, text, speech)—all are influenced by the audience you envision. And your audience will interpret your writing according to their own expectations and experiences, not yours.

When you are a student, your audience is most often your teachers, so you need to be aware of their expectations and know the conventions (rules, often unstated) for writing in specific academic fields. You may make statements that seem obvious to you, not realizing that your instructors may consider them assertions that must be proved with evidence

61–65

of one sort or another. Or you may write more or less formally than teachers expect. Understanding your audience's expectations—by asking outright, by reading materials in your field of study, by trial and error—is important to your success as a college writer.

This point is worth dwelling on. You are probably reading this textbook for a writing course. As a student, you will be expected to produce essays with few or no errors. If you correspond with family, friends, or coworkers using email and texts, you may question such standards; after all, many of the messages you get in these contexts are not grammatically perfect. But in a writing class, the instructor needs to see your best work. Whatever the rhetorical situation, your writing must meet the expectations of your audience.

Identify your audience.   Audiences may be defined as *known*, *multiple*, or *unknown*. *Known audiences* can include people with whom you're familiar as well as people you don't know personally but whose needs and expectations you do know. You yourself are a known, familiar audience, and you write to and for yourself often. Class notes, to-do lists, reminders, and journals are all written primarily for an audience of one: you. For that reason, they are often in shorthand, full of references and code that you alone understand.

Other known, familiar audiences include anyone you actually know—friends, relatives, teachers, classmates—and whose needs and expectations you understand. You can also know what certain readers want and need, even if you've never met them personally, if you write for them within a specific shared context. Such a known audience might include PC gamers who read cheat codes that you have posted on the internet for beating a game; you don't know those people, but you know roughly what they know about the game and what they need to know, and you know how to write about it in ways they will understand.

You often have to write for *multiple audiences*. Business memos or reports may be written initially for a supervisor, who may pass them along to others. Grant proposals may be reviewed by four to six levels of readers—each, of course, with its own expectations and perspectives.

academic literacies · rhetorical situations · genres · fields · processes · strategies · research MLA / APA · media / design · readings · handbook

Even writing for a class might involve multiple audiences: your instructor and your classmates.

Unknown audiences can be the most difficult to address since you can't be sure what they know, what they need to know, how they'll react. Such an audience could be your downstairs neighbor, with whom you've chatted occasionally in the laundry room. How will she respond to your letter asking her to sponsor you in an upcoming charity walk? Another unknown audience—perhaps surprisingly—might be many of your instructors, who want—and expect!—you to write in ways that are new to you. While you can benefit from analyzing any audience, you need to think most carefully about those you don't know.

Thinking about Audience

- *Whom do you want to reach?* To whom are you writing (or speaking)?

- *What is your audience's background—their education and life experiences?* It may be important for you to know, for example, whether your readers attended college, fought in a war, or have young children.

- *What are their interests?* What do they like? What motivates them? What do they care about?

- *Is there any demographic information that you should keep in mind?* Consider whether race, gender, sexual orientation, disabilities, occupation, religious beliefs, economic status, and so on should affect what or how you write. For example, writers for *Men's Health*, *InStyle*, and *Out* must consider the particular interests of each magazine's readers.

- *What political circumstances may affect their reading?* What attitudes—opinions, special interests, biases—may affect the way your audience reads your piece? Are your readers conservative, liberal, or middle of the road? Politics may take many other forms as well—retirees on a fixed income may object to increased school taxes, so a letter arguing for such an increase would need to appeal to them differently than would a similar letter sent to parents of young children.

- *What does your audience already know—or believe—about your topic? What do you need to tell them? What is the best way to do so?* Those retirees who oppose school taxes already know that taxes are a burden for them; they may need to know why schools are justified in asking for more money every few years. A good way to explain this may be with a bar graph showing how property values benefit from good schools with adequate funding. Consider which **STRATEGIES** will be effective—narrative, comparison, something else?

371 ◆

- *What's your relationship with your audience, and how should it affect your language and tone?* Do you know them, or not? Are they friends? colleagues? mentors? adversaries? strangers? Will they likely share your **STANCE**? In general, you need to write more formally when you're addressing readers you don't know, and you may address friends and colleagues more informally than you would a boss.

66–68 ◼

- *What does your audience need and expect from you?* Your history professor, for example, may need to know how well you can discuss the economy of the late Middle Ages in order to assess your learning; he may expect you to write a carefully reasoned argument, drawing conclusions from various sources, with a readily identifiable thesis in the first paragraph. Your boss, on the other hand, may need an informal email that briefly lists your sales contacts for the day; she may expect that you list the contacts in the order in which you saw them, that you clearly identify each one, and that you briefly say how well each contact went. What **GENRE** is most appropriate?

73 ▲

- *What kind of response do you want?* Do you want readers to believe or do something? to accept as valid your information on a topic? to understand why an experience you once had matters to you?

637 ◻

- *How can you best appeal to your audience?* Is there a particular **MEDIUM** that will best reach them? Are there any **DESIGN** requirements? (Elderly readers may need larger type, for instance.)

Genres are kinds of writing. Letters, profiles, reports, position papers, poems, blog posts, instructions, parodies—even jokes—are genres. For example, here is the beginning of a **PROFILE** of a mechanic who repairs a specific kind of automobile:

▲ 233–45

> Her business card reads Shirley Barnes, M.D., and she's a doctor, all right—a Metropolitan Doctor. Her passion is the Nash Metropolitan, the little car produced by Austin of England for American Motors between 1954 and 1962. Barnes is a legend among southern California Met lovers—an icon, a beacon, and a font of useful knowledge and freely offered opinions.

A profile offers a written portrait of someone or something that informs and sometimes entertains, often examining its subject from a particular angle—in this case, as a female mechanic who fixes Nash Metropolitans. While the language in this example is informal and lively ("she's a doctor, all right"), the focus is on the subject, Shirley Barnes, "M.D." If this same excerpt were presented as a poem, however, the new genre would change our reading:

> Her business card reads
> Shirley Barnes, M.D.,
> and she's a doctor, all right
> —a Metropolitan Doctor.
> Her passion is the Nash Metropolitan,
> the little car produced by Austin of England
> for American Motors between 1954 and 1962.
> Barnes is a legend
> among southern California Met lovers
> —an icon,

a beacon,
and a font of useful knowledge and
freely offered opinions.

The content hasn't changed, but the different presentation invites us to read not only to learn about Shirley Barnes but also to explore the significance of the words and phrases on each line, to read for deeper meaning and greater appreciation of language. The genre thus determines how we read and how we interpret what we read.

Genres help us write by establishing features for conveying certain kinds of content. They give readers clues about what sort of information they're likely to find and so help them figure out how to read ("This article begins with an abstract, so it's probably a scholarly source" or "Thank goodness! I found the instructions for editing videos on my phone"). At the same time, genres are flexible; writers often tweak the features or combine elements of different genres to achieve a particular purpose or connect with an audience in a particular way. Genres also change as writers' needs and available technologies change. For example, computers have enabled us to add audio and video content to texts that once could appear only on paper.

Choosing the Appropriate Genre

How do you know which genre you should choose? Often the words and phrases used in writing assignments can give you clues to the best choice. Here are typical terms used in assignments and the genres they usually call for.

75–97 ▲

LITERACY NARRATIVE If you're assigned to explore your development as a writer or reader or to describe how you came to be interested in a particular subject or career, you'll likely need to write a literacy narrative or a variation on one. Some terms that might signal a literacy narrative: *describe a learning experience, tell how you learned, trace your development, write a story.*

98–130 ▲
211–23

TEXTUAL ANALYSIS or **LITERARY ANALYSIS** If your assignment calls on you to look at a nonfiction text to see not only what it says but how it works,

you likely need to write a textual analysis. If the text is a short story, novel, poem, or play, you probably need to write a literary analysis. If you are analyzing a text or texts in multiple media, you might choose either genre or mix the two. Some terms that might signal that a textual or literary analysis is being asked for: *analyze, examine, explicate, read closely, interpret*.

REPORT　If your task is to research a topic and then tell your audience in a balanced, neutral way what you know about it, your goal is probably to write a report. Some terms that might signal that a report is being asked for: *define, describe, explain, inform, observe, record, report, show*.

▲ 131–56

POSITION PAPER or **ARGUMENT**　Some terms that might signal that your instructor wants you to take a position or argue for or against something: *agree or disagree, argue, claim, criticize, defend, justify, position paper, prove*.

▲ 157–84

SUMMARY　If your assignment is to reduce a text into a single paragraph or so, is called for. Some terms that might signal that a summary is expected: *abridge, boil down, compress, condense, recap, summarize*.

EVALUATION　If your instructor asks you to say whether or not you like something or whether it's a good or bad example of a category or better or worse than something else, an evaluation is likely being called for. Some terms that might signal that an evaluation is expected: *assess, critique, evaluate, judge, recommend, review*.

▲ 202–10

MEMOIR　If you're asked to explore an important moment or event in your life, you're probably being asked to write a memoir. Some terms that likely signal that a memoir is desired: *autobiography, chronicle, narrate, a significant personal memory, a story drawn from your experience*.

▲ 224–32

PROFILE　If your instructor assigns you the task of portraying a subject in a way that is both informative and entertaining, you're likely being asked to write a profile. Some terms that might indicate that a profile is being asked for: *angle, describe, dominant impression, interview, observe, report on*.

▲ 233–45

PROPOSAL　If you're asked to offer a solution to a problem, to suggest some action—or to make a case for pursuing a certain project, a proposal

▲ 246–55

is probably in order. Some terms that might indicate a proposal: *argue for [a solution or action], propose, put forward, recommend.*

256–63 ▲

REFLECTION If your assignment calls on you to think in writing about something or to play with ideas, you are likely being asked to write a reflection. Some terms that may mean that a reflection is called for: *consider, explore, ponder, probe, reflect, speculate.*

Dealing with Ambiguous Assignments

Sometimes even the key term in an assignment doesn't indicate clearly which genre is wanted, so you need to read such an assignment especially carefully. A first step might be to consider whether it's asking for a report or an argument. For example, here are two sample assignments:

> Discuss ways in which the invention of gas and incandescent lighting significantly changed people's daily lives in the nineteenth century.
>
> Discuss why Willy Loman in *Death of a Salesman* is, or is not, a tragic hero.

Both assignments use the word *discuss*, but in very different ways. The first may be simply be requesting an informative, researched report: the thesis—new forms of lighting significantly changed people's daily lives in various ways—is already given, and you may be simply expected to research and explain what some of these changes were. It's also possible, though, that this assignment is asking you to make an argument about which of these changes were the most significant ones.

In contrast, *discuss* in the second assignment is much more open-ended. It does not lead to a particular thesis but is more clearly asking you to present an argument: to choose a position (Willy Loman *is* a tragic hero; Willy Loman is *not* a tragic hero; even, possibly, Willy Loman both *is and is not* a tragic hero) and to marshal reasons and evidence from the play to support your position. A clue that an argument is being asked for lies in the way the assignment offers a choice of paths.

Other potentially ambiguous words in assignments are *show* and *explore*, both of which could lead in many directions. If after a careful reading of the entire assignment you still aren't sure what it's asking for, ask your instructor to clarify the appropriate genre or genres.

Thinking about Genre

- *How does your genre affect what content you can or should include?* Objective information? Researched source material? Your own opinions? Personal experience? A mix?

- *Does your genre call for any specific* **STRATEGIES?** Profiles, for example, usually include some narration; lab reports often explain a process. ◆ 371

- *Does your genre require a certain organization?* **PROPOSALS**, for instance, usually need to show a problem exists before offering a solution. Some genres leave room for choice. Business letters delivering good news might be organized differently than those making sales pitches. ▲ 246–55

- *Does your genre affect your tone?* An abstract of a scholarly paper calls for a different **TONE** than a memoir. Should your words sound serious and scholarly? brisk and to the point? objective? opinionated? Sometimes your genre affects the way you communicate your **STANCE**. ■ 67–68 ■ 66–68

- *Does the genre require formal (or informal) language?* A letter to the mother of a friend asking for a summer job in her bookstore calls for more formal language than does an email to the friend thanking him for the lead.

- *Do you have a choice of medium?* Some genres call for print; others for an electronic medium. Sometimes you have a choice: a résumé, for instance, can be printed to bring to an interview, or it may be downloaded or emailed. Some teachers want reports turned in on paper; others prefer that they be emailed or posted in the class course management system. If you're not sure what **MEDIUM** you can use, ask. ☐ 637

- *Does your genre have any design requirements?* Some genres call for paragraphs; others require lists. Some require certain kinds of fonts—you wouldn't use **impact** for a personal narrative, nor would you likely use chiller for an invitation to Grandma's sixty-fifth birthday party. Different genres call for different **DESIGN** elements. ☐ 637

8 Stance

Whenever you write, you have a certain stance, an attitude toward your topic. The way you express that stance affects the way you come across to your audience as a writer and a person. This email from a college student to his father, for example, shows a thoughtful, reasonable stance for a carefully researched argument:

> Hi Dad,
> I'll get right to the point: I'd like to buy a car. I saved over $4,500 from working this summer, and I've found three different cars that I can get for under $3,000. That'll leave me $1,400 to cover the insurance. I can park in Lot J, over behind Monte Hall, for $75 for both semesters. And I can earn gas and repair money by upping my hours at the cafeteria. It won't cost you any more, and if I have a car, you won't have to come and pick me up when I want to come home. May I buy it?
> Love,
> Michael

While such a stance can't guarantee that Dad will give permission, it's more likely to produce results than this version:

> Hi Dad,
> I'm buying a car. A guy in my Western Civ course has a cool Nissan he wants to get rid of. I've got $4,500 saved from working this summer, it's mine, and I'm going to use it to get some wheels. Mom said you'd freak if I did, but I want this car. OK?
> Michael

The writer of the first email respects his reader and offers reasoned arguments and evidence of research to convince him that buying a car is an action that will benefit them both. The writer of the second, by contrast, seems impulsive, ready to buy the first car that comes along, and defiant—

he's picking a fight. Each email reflects a certain stance that shows the writer as a certain kind of person dealing with a topic in a certain way and establishing a certain relationship with his audience.

Identify your stance.   What is your attitude toward your topic? Objective? Critical? Curious? Opinionated? Passionate? Indifferent? Your stance may be affected by your relationship to your **AUDIENCE**. How do you want them to see you? As a colleague sharing information? a good student showing what you can do? an advocate for a position? Often your stance is affected by your **GENRE**: for example, lab reports require an objective, unemotional stance that emphasizes the content and minimizes the writer's own attitudes. Memoir, by comparison, allows you to reveal your feelings about your topic. Your stance is also affected by your **PURPOSE**, as the two emails about cars show. Your stance in a piece written to entertain will likely differ from the stance you'd adopt to persuade.

■ 57–60

▲ 73

■ 55–56

You communicate (or downplay) your stance through your tone—through the words you use and other ways your text expresses an attitude toward your subject and audience. For example, in an academic essay you would state your position directly—"*The Bachelor* reflects the values of American society today"—using a confident, authoritative tone. In contrast, using qualifiers like "might" or "I think" can give your writing a wishy-washy, uncertain tone: "I think *The Bachelor* might reflect some of America's values." A sarcastic tone might be appropriate for a comment on a blog post but isn't right for an academic essay: "*The Bachelor*'s star has all the personality of a bowling ball."

Like every other element of writing, your tone must be appropriate for your rhetorical situation.

Just as you likely alter what you say depending on whether you're speaking to a boss, an instructor, a parent, or a good friend, so you need to make similar adjustments as a writer. It's a question of appropriateness: we behave in certain ways in various social situations, and writing is a social situation. You might sign an email to a friend with an XO, but in an email to your supervisor you'll likely sign off with a "Many thanks" or "Sincerely." To write well, you need to write with integrity, to say as much as possible what you wish to say; yet you also must understand that in writing, as in speaking, your stance and tone need to suit your purpose, your relationship to your audience, the way in which you wish your audience to perceive you, and your medium.

In writing as in other aspects of life, the Golden Rule applies: "Do unto audiences as you would have them do unto you." Address readers respectfully if you want them to respond to your words with respect.

Thinking about Stance

- *What is your stance, and how does it relate to your purpose for writing?* If you feel strongly about your topic and are writing an argument that tries to persuade your audience to feel the same way, your stance and your **PURPOSE** fit naturally together. But suppose you are writing about the same topic with a different purpose—to demonstrate the depth of your knowledge about the topic, for example, or your ability to consider it in a detached, objective way. You will need to adjust your stance to meet the demands of this different purpose.

- *How should your stance be reflected in your tone?* Can your tone grow directly out of your stance, or do you need to "tone down" your attitude toward the topic or take a different tone altogether? Do you want to be seen as reasonable? angry? thoughtful? gentle? funny? ironic? If you're writing about something you want to be seen as taking very seriously, be sure that your language and even your font reflect that seriousness. Check your writing for words that reflect the tone you want to convey—and for ones that do not (and revise as necessary).

- *How is your stance likely to be received by your audience?* Your tone and especially the attitude it projects toward your **AUDIENCE** will affect how they react to the content of what you say.

- *Should you openly discuss your stance?* Do you want or need to announce your own perspective on your topic? Will doing so help you reach your audience, or would it be better not to say directly where you're coming from?

academic literacies · rhetorical situations · genres · fields · processes · strategies · research MLA / APA · media / design · readings · handbook

Media/Design 9

In its broadest sense, a medium is a go-between: a way for information to be conveyed from one person to another. We communicate through many media, verbal and nonverbal: our bodies (we catch someone's eye, wave, nod); our voices (we whisper, talk, shout, groan); and various technologies, including handwriting, print, telephone, radio, video, and computer.

Each medium has unique characteristics that influence both what and how we communicate. As an example, consider this message: "I haven't told you this before, but I love you." Most of the time, we communicate such a message in person, using the medium of voice (with, presumably, help from eye contact and touch). A phone call will do, though most of us would think it a poor second choice, and a handwritten letter or note would be acceptable, if necessary. Few of us would break such news on a website, with a tweet, or during a radio call-in program.

By contrast, imagine whispering the following sentence in a darkened room: "By the last decades of the nineteenth century, the territorial expansion of the United States had left almost all Indians confined to reservations." That sentence starts a chapter in a history textbook, and it would be strange indeed to whisper it into someone's ear. It is appropriate, however, in the textbook, in print or in an e-book, or as a quotation in an oral presentation.

As you can see, we can often choose among various media depending on our purpose and audience. In addition, we can often combine media to create **MULTIMEDIA** texts. And different media allow us to use different ways or modes of expressing meaning, from words to images to sound to hyperlinks, that can be combined into **MULTIMODAL** formats.

641–42

No matter the medium or media, a text's design affects the way it is received and understood. A typed letter on official letterhead sends a different message than the same words handwritten on pastel stationery. Classic type

654–60 ☐

sends a different message than *flowery italics*. Some genres and media (and audiences) demand **PHOTOS**, **DIAGRAMS**, or color. Some information is easier to explain—and read—in the form of a **PIE CHART** or a **BAR GRAPH** than in the form of a paragraph. Some reports and documents are so long and complex that they need to be divided into sections, which are then best

650–52 ☐

labeled with **HEADINGS**. These are some of the elements to consider when you are thinking about how to design what you write.

Identify your media and design needs. Does your writing situation call for a certain medium and design? A printed essay? An oral report with visual aids? A blog? A podcast? Academic assignments often assume a particular medium and design, but if you're unsure about your options or the degree of flexibility you have, check with your instructor.

Thinking about Media

- *What medium are you using*—print? spoken? electronic? a combination?—and how does it affect the way you will create your text? A printed résumé is usually no more than one page long; an electronic résumé posted on an employer's website has no length limits. An oral presentation should contain detailed information; accompanying slides should provide only an outline.

371 ◆

- *How does your medium affect your organization and* **STRATEGIES**? Long paragraphs are fine on paper but don't work well on the web. On presentation slides, phrases or keywords work better than sentences. In print, you need to define unfamiliar terms; on the web, you can sometimes just add a link to a definition found elsewhere.

- *How does your medium affect your language?* Some print documents require a more formal voice than spoken media; email and texting often invite greater informality.

- *How does your medium affect what modes of expression you use?* Should your text include photos, graphics, audio or video files, or links? Do you need slides, handouts, or other visuals to accompany an oral presentation?

academic literacies rhetorical situations genres fields processes strategies research MLA / APA media / design readings handbook

Thinking about Design

- *What's the appropriate look for your* RHETORICAL SITUATION*?* Should your text look serious? whimsical? personal? something else? What design elements will suit your audience, purpose, stance, genre, and medium?

- *What elements need to be designed?* Is there any information you would like to highlight by putting it in a box? Are there any key terms that should be boldfaced? Do you need navigation buttons? How should you indicate links?

- *What font(s) are appropriate* to your audience, purpose, stance, genre, and medium?

- *Are you including any* VISUALS*?* Should you? Will your AUDIENCE expect or need any? Is there any information in your text that would be easier to understand as a chart or graph? If you need to include video or audio clips, how should the links be presented?

- *Should you include headings?* Would they help you organize your materials and help readers follow the text? Does your GENRE or MEDIUM require them?

- *Should you use a specific format?* MLA? APA?

53

653–63
57–60

61–65
69–71

MLA 548–96
APA 597–636

part 3

Genres

When we make a shopping list, we automatically write each item we need in a single column. When we email a friend, we begin with a salutation: "Hi, Jordan." Whether we are writing a letter, a résumé, or a proposal, we know generally what it should contain and what it should look like because we are familiar with each of those genres. Genres are kinds of writing, and texts in any given genre share goals and features—a proposal, for instance, generally starts out by identifying a problem and then suggests a certain solution. The chapters in this part provide guidelines for writing in thirteen common academic genres. First come detailed chapters on four genres often assigned in writing classes—LITERACY NARRATIVES, TEXTUAL ANALYSES, REPORTS, and ARGUMENTS— followed by brief chapters on NINE OTHER GENRES and one on MIXING GENRES.

Genres

Writing a Literacy Narrative **10**

Narratives are stories, and we read and tell them for many different purposes. Parents read their children bedtime stories as an evening ritual. College applicants write about significant moments in their lives. In *psychology* courses, you may write a personal narrative to illustrate how individuals' stories inform the study of behavior. In *education* courses, you may share stories of your teaching experiences. And in *computer science* courses, you may write programming narratives to develop programming skills.

This chapter provides detailed guidelines for writing a specific kind of narrative: a literacy narrative. Writers of literacy narratives traditionally explore their experiences with reading or writing, but we'll broaden the definition to include experiences with various literacies, which might include learning an academic skill, a sport, an artistic technique, or something else. For example, the third narrative in this chapter explores one writer's realization that she needs "automotive literacy" to work in her parents' car repair shop. Along with this essay, this chapter includes two additional good examples, the first annotated to point out the key features found in most literacy narratives.

EMILY VALLOWE

Write or Wrong Identity

Emily Vallowe wrote this literacy narrative for a writing class at the University of Mary Washington in Virginia. In it, she explores her lifelong identity as a writer—and her doubts about that identity.

I'm sitting in the woods with a bunch of Catholic people I just met yesterday. Suddenly, they ask me to name one of the talents God has given me. I panic for a split second and then breathe an internal sigh of relief. I tell them I'm a writer. As the group leaders move on to ques-

Attention-getting opening.

75

tion someone else, I sit trying to mentally catch my breath. It will take a moment before the terror leaves my forearms, chest, and stomach, but I tell myself that I have nothing to fear. I am a writer. Yes, I most definitely am a writer. *Now breathe*, I tell myself . . . *and suppress that horrifying suspicion that you are actually not a writer at all.*

The retreat that prepared me for my eighth-grade confirmation was not the first time I found myself pulling out the old "I'm a writer" card and wondering whether I was worthy enough to carry this sacred card in the wallet of my identity. Such things happen to people with identity crises.

Clearly described details.

In kindergarten I wrote about thirty books. They were each about five pages long, with one sentence and a picture on each page. They were held together with three staples on the left side or top and had construction paper covers with the book's title and the phrase "by Emily Vallowe" written out in neat kindergarten-teacher handwriting. My mom still has all of these books in a box at the bottom of her closet.

One day at the very end of the school year, my kindergarten teacher took me to meet my future first-grade teacher, Mrs. Meadows. I got to make a special trip to meet her because I had been absent on the day the rest of the kindergarteners had gone to meet their future teachers. Mrs. Meadows's classroom was big and blue and different from the kindergarten class, complete with bigger, different kids (I think Mrs. Meadows had been teaching third or fourth graders that year, so her students were much older than I was). During this visit, Mrs. Meadows showed me a special writing desk, complete with a small, old-fashioned desk lamp (with a lamp shade and everything). I'm not sure if I understood why she was showing me this writing area. She may have said that she'd heard good things about me.

Vallowe traces her identity as a writer through her life.

This handful of images is all I can remember about the most 5 significant event in my writing life. I'm not sure why I connect the memory of my kindergarten books with the image of me sitting in Mrs. Meadows's old classroom (for by the time I had her she was in a room on the opposite side of the school). I guess I don't even know exactly when this major event happened. Was it kindergarten? First grade? Somewhere in between? All I know is that some event occurred in early elementary school that made me want to be a writer. I don't

academic literacies · rhetorical situations · genres · fields · processes · strategies · research MLA / APA · media / design · readings · handbook

even clearly remember what this event was, but it is something that has actively affected me for the fourteen years since then.

I have wanted to be a writer my entire life—or at least that's what I tell people. Looking back, I don't know if I ever *wanted* to be a writer. The idea might never have even occurred to me. Yet somehow I was marked as a writer. My teachers must have seen something in my writing that impressed them and clued me in on it. Teachers like to recognize kids for their strengths, and at the age of five, I probably started to notice that different kids were good at different things: Bobby was good at t-ball; Sally was good at drawing; Jenny could run really fast. I was probably starting to panic at the thought that I might not be good at anything—and then a teacher came along and told me I was good at writing. Someone gave me a compliment, and I ran with it. I declared myself to be a writer and have clung to this writer identity ever since.

There are certain drawbacks to clinging to one unchanging identity since the age of five. Constant panic is one of these drawbacks. It is a strange feeling to grow up defining yourself as something when you don't know if that something is actually true. By the time I got to middle school, I could no longer remember having become a writer; I had just always been one—and had been one without any proof that I deserved to be called one. By the age of ten, I was facing a seasoned writer's terror of "am I any good?!" and this terror has followed me throughout my entire life since then. Every writing assignment I ever had was a test—a test to see if I was a real writer, to prove myself to teachers, to classmates, to myself. I approached every writing assignment thinking, "I am supposed to be good at this," not "I am going to try to make this good," and such an attitude is not a healthy way to approach anything.

Ongoing discussion of the central issue: is she a writer or not?

It doesn't help that if I am a writer, I am a very slow one. I can't sit down and instantly write something beautiful like some people I know can. I have been fortunate to go to school with some very smart classmates, some of whom can whip out a great piece of writing in minutes. I still find these people threatening. If they are faster than I am, does that make them better writers than I am? *I thought I was supposed to be "the writer"!*

My obsession with being "the" writer stems from my understanding of what it means to be "the" anything. My childhood was marked by a belief in many abstract absolutes that I am only now allowing to crumble. I was born in Chicago (and was thus the fourth generation of my family to live there), but I grew up in northern Virginia. I came to look down on my Virginia surroundings because I had been taught to view Chicago as this great Mecca—the world's most amazing city to which I must someday return, and to which all other places on earth pale in comparison. Throughout my childhood, I gathered that Chicago is a real city in which average people live and which has an economy historically based in shipping and manufacturing; Washington, D.C., on the other hand, where my dad works, has a population that includes a bizarre mix of impoverished people and the most influential leaders and diplomats in the world—and so manufactures nothing but political power. People in Chicago know how to deal with snow; Virginians panic at the *possibility* of snow. Chicago rests on soil that is so fertile it's *black*; Virginia does not even have soil—it has reddish clay suitable for growing nothing except tobacco. Even Chicago's tap water tastes amazing; D.C.'s tap water is poisoned with lead. I grew up thinking that every aspect of Chicago was perfect—so perfect that Chicago became glorious to the point of abstraction. No other city could compare, and after a while I forgot *why* no other city could compare. I just knew that Chicago was "the" city . . . and that if "the" city exists, there must also be an abstract "the" everything.

Vallowe examines the roots of her identity as a writer—and why she questions that identity.

I grew up with this and many other abstract ideals that I would defend against my friends' attacks . . . until I learned that they were just abstractions—and so was I. My writing identity was just another ideal, an absolute that I clung to without any basis in fact. I used to use writing as an easy way to define myself on those over-simplistic surveys teachers always asked us to fill out in elementary and middle school—the surveys that assumed that someone could know all about me simply by finding out my favorite color, my favorite TV show, or my hobbies. I used to casually throw out the "I'm a writer" card just to get these silly surveys over with. "I'm a writer" was just an easy answer to the complicated question, "Who are you?" I always thought the surveys avoided asking this question, but maybe I was the one avoiding it. For years, I had been defining myself as "the writer" without really pondering what this writer identity meant. Is a writer simply someone who writes all the time? Well, I often went through long stretches in which I did not write anything, so this definition did not seem to suit me. Is a writer someone who is good at writing? Well, I've

10

already mentioned that I've been having "am I any good?!" thoughts since elementary school, so this definition didn't seem to fit me, either. I was identifying myself as "the writer" as an abstraction, without any just cause to do so.

The funny thing is that I recognized my writing identity as an abstract ideal before I recognized any of the other ideals I was clinging to, but that didn't make the situation any better. It is one thing to learn that dead people have been voting in Chicago elections for decades, and so perhaps Chicago isn't the perfect city, but what happens when the absolute ideal is you? More important, what would happen if *this* absolute were to crumble? It was terrifying to think that I might discover that I was not a writer because to not be a writer was to suddenly be nothing. If a writer was the only thing that I had ever been, what would happen if writing was a lie? I would vanish. Looking back, the logical part of my brain tells me that, if I am not a writer, I am still plenty of other things: I am a Catholic; I am a Vallowe; people tell me that I have other good qualities. But when facing these horrifying spells of writer's doubt, my brain doesn't see these other things. I am driven only by the fear of nothingness and the thought that I have to be a writer because I'm not good at anything else.

Am I really not good at anything else? I used to blame this entire writer's complex on whoever it was that told me I was a writer. If that person hadn't channeled this burdensome identity into me, I might never have expected great literary things from myself, and life would have been easier. I had these thoughts until one day in high school I mentioned something to my mom about the fact that I'd been writing since I was five years old. My mom corrected me by saying that I'd been writing since I was three years old. At the age of three I couldn't even physically form letters, but apparently I would dictate stories to my mom on a regular basis. My mom explained to me how I would run to her and say, "Mommy, Mommy, write my story for me!"

This new information was both comforting and unsettling. On one hand, it was a great relief to know that I had been a writer all along—that I would have been a writer even if no one had told me that I was one. On the other hand, the knowledge that I had been a writer all along drove me into an entirely new realm of panic.

I've been a writer my entire life?

WHAT?!

She continues to explore her identity as a writer.

15

I've been a writer since I was three? Three? *Three* years old: How is that even possible? I didn't know it was possible to be anything at age three, let alone the thing that might define me for my entire life.

I have been taught that each person has a vocation—a calling that they must use to spread God's love to others. Yet I've also assumed that one must go on some sort of journey to figure out what this vocation is. If I found my vocation at the age of three, have I skipped this journey? And if I've skipped the journey, does that mean that the vocation isn't real? Or am I just really lucky for having found my vocation so early? Was I really born a writer? Was I born to do one thing, and will I do that one thing for my entire life? Can anything be that consistent? That simple? And if I am living out some divine vocation, is that any comfort at all? If I am channeling some divine being in my writing, and everything I write comes from some outside source, where does that leave me? Am I nothing even if I am a writer?

This questioning has not led me to any comforting conclusions. I still wonder if my writer identity has been thrust upon me, and what it means to have someone else determine who I am. If I am a writer, then I am someone who passionately seeks originality—someone who gets pleasure from inventing entire fictional worlds. Yet if someone—either a teacher or a divine being—is channeling an identity into me, then I am no more original than the characters that I create in my fiction. If my identity is not original, then this identity is not real, and if I am not real . . . I can't even finish this sentence.

I don't know if I really wrote thirty books in kindergarten. It might have been twenty—or fifteen—or ten—or five. I might have made up that part about the special writing desk in Mrs. Meadows's old classroom. I don't know if God predestined me to write masterpieces or if a teacher just casually mentioned that I wrote well and I completely overreacted to the compliment. Questioning my identity as "the writer" has led me to new levels of fear and uncertainty, but this questioning is not going to stop. Even if I one day sit, withered and gray, with a Nobel Prize for Literature proudly displayed on my desk as I try to crank out one last novel at the age of ninety-two, my thoughts will probably drift back to Mrs. Meadows and those books I wrote in kindergarten. In my old age, I still might not understand my writer identity,

Ending refers back to the opening anecdote.

Conclusion is tentative (since the end of the story is decades in the future).

but maybe by that point, I will have written a novel about a character with an identity crisis—and maybe the character will have come
through all right.

In this literacy narrative, Vallowe reflects on the origins of her identity as a
writer: her early teachers, her parents, God, herself. The significance of her story
lies in her inability to settle on any one of these possibilities.

DANIEL FELSENFELD

Rebel Music

Daniel Felsenfeld is a composer of classical music, a writer of several books on
music, and a contributor to NewMusicBox, a multimedia publication whose
mission "is to support and promote new music created in the United States." In
this essay, which originally appeared in 2010 in Opinionator, *a commentary*
blog of the New York Times, *he explores his journey of becoming literate in*
classical music.

Music may be the universal language, but those of us who spend our
lives with it are expected to know it in depth, from early on. Many
composers, whether traditional or experimental, have been steeped in
Western classical music from the cradle. That was not the case with me.

My primal time was the middle of the '80's in Orange County,
Calif. I was 17 years old. The O.C. was billed as the ideal suburban
community, but when you are raised in a palm-tree lined Shangri-La
as I was, it is hard to grasp what's missing without that crucial glimpse
beyond. Now I realize: even though we had enough water to keep the
manicured lawns just so, I was experiencing a personal drought, an arid
lack of culture of all kinds, especially music.

I was by no means unmusical, though any talent I have remains
a mystery, coming as I do from perhaps the least musical of families
(who would be the first to admit this). To her credit, my mother signed
me up for the de rigueur piano lessons. Each week I dazzled poor Ms.
Shimizu with either an astonishing performance of a Mozart sonata or
a heretofore unseen level of ill-preparedness. I slogged my way through

Chopin Preludes, culminating my high school piano study with a mid-dling performance of Beethoven's "Pathétique" sonata. Probably not unlike most kids' first encounter with formal music study: uninspiring.

Eventually I quit lessons, but had developed chops enough to work in both piano bars (an underage piano man, traveling with my own snifter) and community theater orchestra pits. The music was dull, or at least had a dulling effect on me—it didn't sparkle, or ask questions. I took a lot of gigs, but at 17 I was already pretty detached. I was attracted to music for some reason I lacked vocabulary to explain, and neither *Oklahoma!* nor *Annie* offered answers.

That might have been it—working my way through junior college playing in pits or at Nordstrom's, settling into some career or other—a piano studio, weddings, writing songs for mild amusement. Thankfully, it was not.   5

Some afternoons I would go to my friend Mike's house at the end of my cul-de-sac to listen to tapes of bands a lot of my friends were listening to: General Public, Howard Jones, the Thompson Twins (or David Bowie, Bauhaus and The Clash in our edgier moments). One day, bored with the music, Mike flipped his double-decked cassette case over to reveal rows of hidden tapes in a concealed compartment.

"Want to hear something really wild?" he said.

"But of course."

At 17, rebellion was of course a staple in my life. The smartest kids I knew took the route of dolling themselves up in anti-establishment finery—goth, punk, straight edge—forming bands, going to clubs in Los Angeles, spouting manifestos. I had auditioned this mode, joining a band (whose name escapes me) and, in one of my great (mercifully unphotographed) late high school moments, taking a long, throbbing solo at a school assembly on one of those bygone over-the-shoulder keyboards.

It seems implausible now, but the "something really wild" Mike held was not goth, metal, or punk. It was a neatly hand-labeled tape of Beethoven's Ninth Symphony. He put it on, and I listened. I think it was then I actually heard music for the first time.   10

Was this the same Beethoven to whose sonata I had done such violence? It unrolled from the small speakers, this big, gorgeous, unruly beast of a thing, contemporary, horrifying, a juggernaut that moved from the dark to unbearable brightness, soaring and spitting, malin-gering and dancing wildly, the Most Beautiful Thing I Ever Heard. This

"symphony" by this Beethoven had a drug-like effect on me. At my insistence we listened again. And again. I wished it would just keep going.

Mike, who was just a kid in the neighborhood with odd—evolved? sophisticated?—taste, had dozens more tapes: Brahms, Mozart, Bach, Prokofiev, Tchaikovsky, Sibelius, Rachmaninoff, Strauss. I may have known that this kind of music was called classical, but I certainly did not understand that it was considered "great" or that it was revered as the foundation of musical culture in the West. I just loved it more than anything I'd heard before, and I must have sensed it was also miles away from Orange County, exactly as far as my adolescent self longed to be. I dubbed Mike's tapes, and listened to them in secret. Driving to school with Beethoven blaring, I'd switch to KROQ as I entered the parking lot, swerving into my spot believing I'd put one over on people again.

My passion for this "other" kind of music felt like the height of rebellion: I was the lone Bolshevik in my army. I loved this new (to me) music, but loved my abstract role in it even more. Rebels sought to break the mold, to do something that was exclusively "theirs," to be weird by way of self-expression. And since I was the only one I knew listening to symphonies and concerti, operas and string quartets, I felt I was the weirdest of them all; it served my adolescent need to be misunderstood. And so I decided, with little prior experience or interest, to become a composer.

Little did I know, right?

All too soon, I came to understand what hard work this was. 15 I studied scores, read biographies, got a serious piano teacher and logged hours a day practicing, traded up Mike's cassettes for the then-novel compact discs, and boarded the spaceship bound for planet New York once or twice (always returning, at least then, to warmer climes). After signing up for theory classes at Fullerton Junior College, I met my first living composers: Brent Pierce taught me counterpoint and harmony (one summer I wrote a daily fugue), and Lloyd Rodgers was my private teacher (who encouraged me to copy out the entire "Well Tempered Clavier" by hand). In the meantime, I heard my first examples of what is called "New Music," that is, classical music written more recently than the 19th century.

Of course, some of my illusions vanished as soon as I realized there were composers I could actually meet. I was no longer a rebellion of one, but this halcyon innocence was traded for the ability to interact with artists who were always taking on the obscene challenge of creating music that was totally new, completely theirs.

Now I live far from the O.C., in New York, having long ago colonized this distant planet and gone native, an active member of a community I once admired from what seemed an impossible distance. And while there are moments I lament not having been raised in a musical family, or my late and clumsy start, I also strive to make my less-than-ideal origins an asset. I've learned I do my best work when I remove myself and try to return to that Age of Wonder when I first heard the gorgeous dissonances of pieces like Samuel Barber's *Hermit Songs* or *Prayers of Kierkegaard*, Elliott Carter's Second String Quartet, Michael Nyman's "The Kiss," George Crumb's *Black Angels*, Arnold Schoenberg's *Pierrot Lunaire*, Benjamin Britten's *Turn of the Screw*, John Corigliano's First Symphony, and Stephen Sondheim's *Sweeney Todd,* and took them to be the *same* dissonances, not contrasting sides of a sometimes-contentious or politicized art world. When I am composing, I try to return to that time and place of inexperience when I was knocked sideways by dangerous sounds. Why else write? Why else listen?

Felsenfeld portrays the significance of his narrative as a specific moment: when he first heard Beethoven's Ninth Symphony, which marked a turning point in his life. To capture the evolution of his musical tastes and talent, he provides detailed lists of the musicians and musical pieces that influenced him as a composer and music lover.

ANA-JAMILEH KASSFY

Automotive Literacy

In the following literacy narrative, Ana-Jamileh Kassfy describes an experience that taught her that literacy takes many forms, as well as the importance of knowing what goes on in the family business, auto repair. She wrote this essay in a college writing class at the University of Texas at El Paso and posted it on her class blog.

My father runs a well-known family-owned auto shop here in El Paso, Texas. I come from a family of five, which consists of me, two older brothers, and my parents. My father manages the place, while one of

my brothers works as a mechanic in charge of most of the heavy labor and the other spends all day standing by a state inspection machine making sure the cars can run safely on the streets of El Paso. My mother works as the shop's secretary, answering the phone and handling all paperwork. I, on the other hand, was not given the option of being a part of the family business; my job is to graduate from college. And I'll gladly accept going to school and learning in place of spending my days working on cars, even though I spent a lot of time at the shop throughout my childhood.

Since I come from a family whose life revolves around cars, and since I practically lived at the auto shop until I was able to drive, you'd think that I'd understand most of the jargon a mechanic would use, right? Wrong. During my first sixteen years of life, I did manage to learn the difference between a flathead and a Torx screwdriver. I also learned what brake pads do and that a car uses many different colorful fuses. However, rather than paying attention to what was happening and what was being said around me, most of the time I chose to focus on the social aspect of the business. While everyone was running around ordering different pads, filters, and starters or explaining in precise detail why a customer needed a new engine, I preferred to sit and speak with customers and learn their life stories. Being social worked for me—until it didn't.

One day my mother couldn't come to work and decided to have me fill in for her. That was fine with me. I thought to myself, "How hard could it be to answer a phone and say, 'Good afternoon, M & J Service, how may I help you?' or to greet customers and then turn them over to my dad?"

My morning went by pretty smoothly. I thought I had my duties down to a science. I figured aside from the permanent ringing in my ear from the annoyingly loud air compressors, a few minor paper cuts, and the almost perpetual stench of gasoline and burnt oil, my day was going to fly by.

Then, around lunchtime, my dad left to pick up a part at a car dealership and my brothers went out for lunch. A woman pulled up in a '01 Hyundai Elantra that was desperately in need of a new paint job and walked into the shop. The woman seemed to be in her late forties and was wearing professional clothing with green eye shadow and bright orange lipstick. Her copper-brown hair was feathered out and she wore extremely large gold earrings. And she was angry. She demanded I tell her why she was having a difficult time starting her car. As I began to dust off the file stored in my memory as "Automotive Terms I Will Never Use," I attempted to calm her down, and then I made the mistake of asking her what the problem was.

She said in a harsh tone, "My car doesn't start, your dad just replaced the spark plugs and the motor head, and now my 'blah blah blah' is making noise! I took it to my friend who's a mechanic and he told me your dad fixed the wrong part."

I took a few seconds and just stood there looking at her, trying to add up what I had learned in my life as a "mechanic" and recall what spark plugs were. But it was useless. After a few moments, I gave up. I told her that I couldn't help her, but that she was more than welcome to wait for a mechanic to return.

After giving me an unpleasant look, she proceeded to say, while waving her hands in front of me, "I want my money back! Here is my receipt. I'm taking my car elsewhere. Your dad screwed me over. I told him it was the 'blah blah blah.' Why did he take out the 'blah blah blah'? WHY CAN'T YOU HELP ME? WHY ARE YOU HERE? BLAH BLAH BLAH!"

I stood there, overwhelmed. I began to fidget and push my hair back nervously as I wished some knowledge would kick in. It seemed unbelievable, but despite growing up in a family that lived and breathed automobiles, there was nothing I could do to help her. And my sixteen years of socializing with customers hadn't even paid off because I couldn't calm her down. When I saw my dad walk in, I sighed with relief, explained the problem to him, and it was resolved. But standing in front of that woman like a deer caught in headlights was so embarrassing. Having somebody shout, "Why can't you help me?" and "Why are you here?" made me feel so ignorant.

Unfortunately, that was only the first of many occasions when 10
people have automatically expected that I know how to take apart and rebuild an engine, or perform some other auto-related task. In reality, I know as much about cars as the next person. After that incident, it became clear to me that I could be literate on very different levels. I'm an expert at running social networks like my *Twitter* feed, and I can zip through and analyze an entire novel written in Spanish, but in other subjects, like automobiles, I am completely illiterate. And when I'm expected to know them, I feel anything but competent.

academic literacies ✳ rhetorical situations ■ genres ▲ fields ⬡ processes ○ strategies ◆ research MLA / APA ● media / design ☐ readings ᚹ handbook ⌃

A confrontation with an irate costumer forces Kassfy to realize that she could be very literate in some situations but almost illiterate in others, and that her lack of knowledge in a workplace context put her at a real disadvantage.

Key Features / Literacy Narratives

A well-told story. As with most narratives, those about literacy often set up some sort of situation that needs to be resolved. That need for resolution makes readers want to keep on reading. We want to know how Kassfy will deal with an irate customer. Some literacy narratives simply explore the role that developing literacy of some kind played at some time in someone's life, as when Felsenfeld "was knocked sideways" by classical music. And some, like Vallowe's, speculate on the origins of the writer's literacy.

Vivid detail. Details can bring a narrative to life for readers by giving them vivid mental sensations of the sights, sounds, smells, tastes, and textures of the world in which your story takes place. The details you use when describing something can help readers picture places, people, and events; dialogue can help them hear what is being said. We grasp the depth of Felsenfeld's reaction to hearing Beethoven's Ninth Symphony from his description of it: "big, gorgeous, unruly beast of a thing, contemporary, horrifying, a juggernaut." Similarly, we can picture and hear Vallowe as a little girl running to her mother and saying, "Mommy, Mommy, write my story for me!"

Some indication of the narrative's significance. By definition, a literacy narrative tells something the writer remembers about learning to read, write, or gain competence in a specific area. In addition, the writer needs to make clear why the incident matters to them. You may reveal its significance in various ways. Now a composer, Felsenfeld tries to "return to that Age of Wonder when [he] first heard" what he calls "dangerous sounds." Kassfy comes to understand that to work in an auto repair shop, she needs to understand automotive repair terms. Vallowe's narrative would be less effective if, instead of questioning her identity as a writer from several perspectives, she had simply said, "I became a writer at the age of three."

A GUIDE TO WRITING LITERACY NARRATIVES

Choosing a Topic

In general, it's a good idea to focus on a single event that took place during a relatively brief period of time—though sometimes learning to do or understand something may take place over an extended period. In that case, several snapshots or important moments may be needed. Here are some suggestions for topics:

- any early memory about writing, reading, speaking, or another form of literacy that you recall vividly
- someone who taught you to read or write
- someone who helped you understand how to do something
- a book, video game, recording, or other text that has been significant for you in some way
- an event at school that was related to your literacy and that you found interesting, humorous, or embarrassing
- a literacy task that you found (or still find) especially difficult or challenging
- a memento that represents an important moment in your literacy development (perhaps the start of a **LITERACY PORTFOLIO**)
- the origins of your current attitudes about writing, reading, speaking, or doing something
- learning to text, learning to write email appropriately, creating and maintaining a *Facebook* page or blog

361–70 ◯

Make a list of possible topics, and then choose one that you think will be interesting to you and to others—and that you're willing to share with others. If several seem promising, try them out on a friend or classmate.

Or just choose one and see where it leads; you can switch to another if need be. If you have trouble coming up with a topic, try **FREEWRITING**, **LISTING**, **CLUSTERING**, or **LOOPING**.

331–34

Considering the Rhetorical Situation

<table>
<tr>
<td>

PURPOSE
</td>
<td>

Why do you want to tell this story? To share a memory with others? To fulfill an assignment? To teach a lesson? To explore your past learning? Think about the reasons for your choice and how they will shape what you write.
</td>
<td>

55–56
</td>
</tr>
<tr>
<td>

AUDIENCE
</td>
<td>

Are your readers likely to have had similar experiences? Would they tell similar stories? How much explaining will you have to do to help them understand your narrative? Can you assume that they will share your attitudes toward your story, or will you have to work at making them see your perspective? How much about your life are you willing to share with this audience?
</td>
<td>

57–60
</td>
</tr>
<tr>
<td>

STANCE
</td>
<td>

What attitude do you want to project? Affectionate? Neutral? Critical? Do you wish to be sincere? serious? humorously detached? self-critical? self-effacing? something else? How do you want your readers to see you?
</td>
<td>

66–68
</td>
</tr>
<tr>
<td>

MEDIA / DESIGN
</td>
<td>

Will your narrative be in print? presented orally? online? Should you use photos, tables, graphs, or video or audio clips? Is there a font that conveys the right tone? Do you need headings?
</td>
<td>

69–71
</td>
</tr>
</table>

Generating Ideas and Text

Good literacy narratives share certain elements that make them interesting and compelling for readers. Remember that your goals are to tell the story as clearly and vividly as you can and to convey the meaning the incident has for you today. Start by thinking about what you already know about writing a literacy narrative. Then write out what you remember about the setting of your narrative and those involved, perhaps trying out some of the methods in the chapter on **GENERATING IDEAS AND TEXT**. You may also want to **INTERVIEW** a teacher or parent or other person who figures in your narrative.

331–39
506–7

Explore what you already know about writing a literacy narrative. Think about recent occasions when you've had to narrate a story, either orally or in writing, in school or out. Take a few moments to think about a couple of those occasions, especially ones involving your reading, writing, speaking, or learning to do something. Why and to whom were you telling these stories? How successful do you think your narratives were? What aspects of telling the story did you feel most confident about or do especially well? What could you have done better? What do you still need to learn about writing a literacy narrative?

Describe the setting. Where does your narrative take place? List the places where your story unfolds. For each place, write informally for a few minutes, **DESCRIBING** what you remember:

443–51

- *What do you see?* If you're inside, what color are the walls? What's hanging on them? What can you see out any windows? What else do you see? Books? Lined paper? Red ink? Are there people? places to sit? a desk or a table?

- *What do you hear?* A radiator hissing? Leaves rustling? The wind howling? Rain? Someone reading aloud? Shouts? Cheers? Children playing? Music? The chime of a text arriving on your phone?

- *What do you smell?* Sweat? Perfume? Incense? Food cooking?

- *How and what do you feel?* Nervous? Happy? Cold? Hot? A scratchy wool sweater? Tight shoes? Rough wood on a bench?

- *What do you taste?* Gum? Mints? Graham crackers? Juice? Coffee?

Think about the key people. Narratives include people whose actions play an important role in the story. In your literacy narrative, you are

probably one of those people. A good way to develop your understanding of the people in your narrative is to write about them:

- *Describe each person in a paragraph or so.* What do the people look like? How do they dress? How do they speak? Quickly? Slowly? With an accent? Do they speak clearly, or do they mumble? Do they use any distinctive words or phrases? You might begin by describing their movements, their posture, their bearing, their facial expressions. Do they have a distinctive scent?

- *Recall (or imagine) some characteristic dialogue.* A good way to bring people to life and move a story along is with **DIALOGUE**, to let readers hear them rather than just hearing about them. Try writing six to ten lines of dialogue between two people in your narrative. If you can't remember an actual conversation, make up one that could have happened. (After all, you are telling the story, and you get to decide how it is to be told.) Try to remember (and write down) some of the characteristic words or phrases that the people in your narrative used.

452–56

Write about "what happened." At the heart of every good **NARRATIVE** is the answer to the question "What happened?" The action in a literacy narrative may be as dramatic as winning a spelling bee or as subtle as a conversation between two friends; both contain action, movement, or change that the narrative tries to capture for readers. A good story dramatizes the action. Try **SUMMARIZING** the action in your narrative in a paragraph—try to capture what happened. Use active and specific verbs (*pondered*, *shouted*, *laughed*) to describe the action as vividly as possible.

462–70

526–38

Consider the significance of the narrative. You need to make clear the ways in which any event you are writing about is significant for you now. Write a page or so about the meaning it has for you. How did it change or otherwise affect you? What aspects of your life now can you trace to that event? How might your life have been different if this event had not happened or had turned out differently? Why does this story matter to you?

Ways of Organizing a Literacy Narrative

335–37 ◯

Start by **OUTLINING** the main events in your narrative. Then think about how you want to tell the story. Don't assume that the only way to tell your story is just as it happened. That's one way—starting at the beginning of the action and continuing to the end. But you could also start in the middle—or even at the end. Daniel Felsenfeld, for example, could have begun his narrative by discussing his influences as a composer and then gone back to the origins of his interest in music at seventeen. Several ways of organizing a narrative follow.

[Chronologically, from beginning to end]

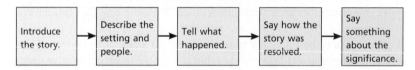

Introduce the story. → Describe the setting and people. → Tell what happened. → Say how the story was resolved. → Say something about the significance.

[Beginning in the middle]

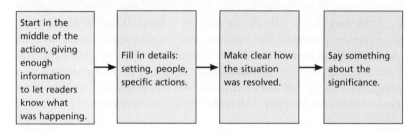

Start in the middle of the action, giving enough information to let readers know what was happening. → Fill in details: setting, people, specific actions. → Make clear how the situation was resolved. → Say something about the significance.

[Beginning at the end]

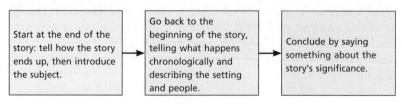

Start at the end of the story: tell how the story ends up, then introduce the subject. → Go back to the beginning of the story, telling what happens chronologically and describing the setting and people. → Conclude by saying something about the story's significance.

Writing Out a Draft

Once you have generated ideas and thought about how you want to organize your narrative, it's time to begin **DRAFTING**. Do this quickly—try to write a complete draft in one sitting, concentrating on getting the story on paper or screen and on putting in as much detail as you can. Some writers find it helpful to work on the beginning or ending first. Others write out the main event first and then draft the beginning and ending.

340–42

Draft a BEGINNING. A good narrative grabs readers' attention right from the start. Here are some ways of beginning:

373–80

- *Create a question to be answered.* Felsenfeld describes the typical composer's upbringing, but then states that his was not typical—so his narrative should describe his unique introduction to classical music.
- *Describe the context.* You may want to provide background information at the start of your narrative, as Vallowe does with an anecdote exposing her fears that she may not be who she thinks she is.
- *Describe the setting, especially if it's important to the narrative.* Kassfy begins by describing her family's roles working in her father's auto shop.

Draft an ENDING. Think about what you want readers to read last. An effective ending helps them understand the meaning of your narrative. Here are some possibilities:

380–85

- *End where your story ends.* It's up to you to decide where a narrative ends. Vallowe ends far in the future, in her imagined old age.
- *Say something about the significance of your narrative.* Vallowe explores the meaning of her experience over several paragraphs, and Kassfy discusses her ignorance and resulting embarrassment. The trick is to touch on the narrative's significance without stating it too directly.
- *Refer back to the beginning.* Vallowe refers back to her kindergarten writing, and Felsenfeld to his first encounter with classical music.

353–55 ○

Consider REWRITING. If you have time and want to explore alternatives, you might try rewriting your draft to see if a different plan or approach might work better.

386–87 ◆

Come up with a title. A good **TITLE** indicates something about the subject of your narrative—and makes readers want to take a look. Kassfy's title joins two terms—"automotive" and "literacy"—that aren't usually seen together. Vallowe uses word play—"Write or Wrong Identity", to question whether she is actually a writer. Felsenfeld captures the irony in calling his secret love of classical music an act of rebellion with his title "Rebel Music."

Considering Matters of Design

You'll probably write your narrative in paragraph form, but think about the information you're presenting and how you can design it to enhance your story and appeal to your audience.

648–49 ▢

- What would be an appropriate **FONT**? Something serious, like Times Roman? Something whimsical, like *Comic Sans*? Something else?

650–52 ▢

- Would it help your readers if you added **HEADINGS** in order to divide your narrative into shorter sections?

653–63 ▢

- Would photographs or other **VISUALS** show details better than you can describe them with words alone? If you're writing about learning to read, for example, you might scan in an image of one of the first books you read. Or if your topic is learning to write, you could include something you wrote. You could even include a video or audio recording. Would your narrative best be conveyed as a multimodal composition that combines written text, images, and video or audio?

Getting Response and Revising

The following questions can help you study your draft with a critical eye. **GETTING RESPONSE** from others is always good, and these questions can guide their reading, too. Make sure they know your purpose and audience.

348–50

- Do the title and first few sentences make readers want to read on? If not, how else might you begin?

- Is the sequence of events in the narrative clear? Does it flow, and are there effective transitions? Does the narrative get sidetracked at any point?

- Is anything confusing?

- Is there enough detail, and is it interesting? Will readers be able to imagine the setting? Can they picture the characters and sense what they're like? Would it help to add some dialogue so that readers can "hear" them?

- Are visuals used effectively and integrated smoothly with the written text? If there are no visuals, would using some strengthen the narrative?

- Have you made the narrative meaningful enough for readers so that they wonder and care about what will happen?

- Do you narrate any actions clearly? vividly? Does the action keep readers engaged?

- Is the significance of the narrative clear?

- Is the ending satisfying? What are readers left thinking?

The preceding questions should identify aspects of your narrative you need to work on. When it's time to **REVISE**, make sure your text appeals to your audience and achieves your purpose as successfully as possible.

350–53

Editing and Proofreading

Readers equate correctness with competence. Once you've revised your draft, follow these guidelines for **EDITING** a narrative:

356–59
462–70
391

- Make sure events are **NARRATED** in a clear order and include appropriate time markers, **TRANSITIONS**, and summary phrases to link the parts and show the passing of time.

HB-40

- Be careful that **VERB TENSES ARE CONSISTENT** throughout. If you start your narrative in the past tense ("he *taught* me how to use a computer"), be careful not to switch to the present ("So I *look* at him and *say* . . . ") along the way.

HB-12–14

- Check to see that **VERB TENSES** correctly indicate when an action took place. If one action took place before another action in the past, for example, you should use the past perfect tense: "I forgot to dot my i's, a mistake I *had made* many times before."

452–56

- Punctuate **DIALOGUE** correctly. Whenever someone speaks, surround the speech with quotation marks ("No way," I said). Periods and commas go inside quotation marks; exclamation points and question marks go inside if they're part of the quotation, outside if they're part of the whole sentence:

  INSIDE   Opening the door, Ms. Cordell announced, "Pop quiz!"

  OUTSIDE   It wasn't my intention to announce "I hate to read"!

359–60

- **PROOFREAD** your finished narrative carefully before turning it in.

Taking Stock of Your Work

- How well do you think you told the story?
- What did you do especially well?
- What could still be improved?
- How did you go about coming up with ideas and generating text?
- How did you go about drafting your narrative?

- Did you use photographs or any other visual or audio elements? What did they add? Can you think of such elements you might have used?
- How did others' responses influence your writing?
- What would you do differently next time?

IF YOU NEED MORE HELP

See also **MEMOIRS** (Chapter 18), a kind of narrative that focuses more generally on a significant event from your past, and **REFLECTIONS** (Chapter 21), a kind of essay for thinking about a topic in writing. See Chapter 34 if you are required to submit your literacy narrative as part of a writing **PORTFOLIO**.

▲ 224–32
256–63

◉ 361–70

---

11 Analyzing Texts

Both the *Huffington Post* and *National Review* cover the same events, but each one interprets them differently. All toothpaste ads claim to make teeth "the whitest." The Environmental Protection Agency is a guardian of America's air, water, and soil—or an unconstitutional impediment to economic growth, depending on which politician is speaking. Those are but three examples that demonstrate why we need to be careful, analytical readers of magazines, newspapers, blogs, websites, ads, political documents, even textbooks.

Text is commonly thought of as words, as a piece of writing. In the academic world, however, text can include not only writing but images—photographs, illustrations, videos, films—and even sculptures, buildings, and music and other sounds. And many texts combine words, images, and sounds. We are constantly bombarded with texts: on the web, in print, on signs and billboards, even on our clothing. Not only does text convey information, but it also influences how and what we think. We need to read, then, to understand not only what texts say but also how they say it and how they try to persuade or influence what we think.

Because understanding how texts say what they say and achieve their effects is so crucial, assignments in many disciplines ask you to analyze texts. You may be asked to analyze candidates' speeches in a *political science* course or to analyze the imagery in a poem for a *literature* class. In a *statistics* course, you might analyze a set of data—a numerical text—to find the standard deviation from the mean.

This chapter offers detailed guidelines for writing an essay that closely examines a text both for what it says and for how it does so, with the goal of demonstrating for readers how—and how well—the text achieves its effects. We'll begin with three good examples, the first annotated to point out the key features found in most textual analyses.

HANNAH BERRY

The Fashion Industry: Free to Be an Individual

Hannah Berry wrote this analysis of two visual texts, shoe ads, for a first-year writing course at Wright State University.

As young women, we have always been told through the medium of advertisement that we must use certain products to make ourselves beautiful. For decades, ads for things like soap, makeup, and mouthwash have established a sort of misplaced control over our lives, telling us what will make us attractive and what will not. Recently, however, a new generation of advertisement has emerged in the fashion industry, one that cleverly equates the products shown in the ads with the quest for confident individuality. Ads such as the two for Clarks and Sorel discussed below encourage us to break free from the standard beauty mold and be ourselves; using mostly imagery, they remind us that being unique is the true origin of beauty.

> *Attention to the context of the ads Berry will analyze.*

> *Clear thesis.*

The first ad promotes Clarks fashion as band geek chic, quite literally raising a unique personality onto a pedestal, with the subject poised on a decorative stone platform as shown in fig. 1. Photographed in standing profile, this quirky-looking young woman is doing what she loves—playing some kind of trumpet—and looks great doing it. She is wearing her hair in a French twist with a strand tucked behind her ear, as if she recently moved it out of her face to play the music she loves without distraction. The downturn of her nose points to the short gray-black dress that stops several inches above her knees but covers her chest and shoulders modestly, with a collar situated at the base of her neck and sleeves that reach for her elbows. The dress is plain,

> *Detailed description of the first text.*

Fig. 1. Clarks ad shows a band geek doing what she loves (Clarks).

> *Illustrations are labeled in MLA format.*

but it is a perfect fit for the personality implied in the photo. Set against the background of a light-tan wall, the model leans back slightly as if supporting the weight of her instrument. Her right knee is bent while her left knee remains straight. The positioning of her legs not only accentuates her unbalanced posture but also points out the pair of simple brown pumps that complete the look. She wears the shoes with a pair of socks in a much darker shade of brown pulled up around her shins. Around her ankles are sandy-colored rings of shaggy fabric that are most likely attached to the socks, giving the whole outfit a sense of nerdy flair. Her expression is a simple mix of calm and concentration. It's as if the photographer happened to take the picture while she was practicing for a school recital.

Clarks has taken what looks like your average high school student and dressed her in an outfit that speaks to her own distinctive character and talents. The image sparks the idea that her beauty comes from an internal base of secure self-confidence and moves outward to infuse her physical appearance and sense of style. This ad urges us to celebrate individuality with the right look. Using an image alone, Clarks advertises its products with the simple promise that they will support you in doing what you love and keep you original.

Taking a narrower perspective on originality, the ad for Sorel boots shown in fig. 2 dramatizes the idea that spontaneity is key to a distinctive personal identity. This abstract idea is depicted in a vividly concrete way, using the featured fur-topped boots as a base for encouraging a bold sense of self. The ad dares us to break free from the mold of society and do something "fearless" (Sorel). It shows us a dark-haired, red-lipped woman sitting in a formal French upholstered chair in a

Fig. 2. Sorel ad flaunts devil-red boots worn by a fearless woman with a shotgun (Sorel).

Analysis of the first text.

Description of the second text.

dark-blue, elaborately paneled parlor. An expression of triumph and mischief adorns her sultry visage. She's wearing a revealing short white dress that overlaps slightly around her chest and falls strategically over her hips so that large portions of her upper thighs are visible. Feathers in autumn colors cover her shoulders, and a gold belt accentuates her waist. Next to her is a polished wood table supporting a lighted candle, a small glass vase of pink and white flowers, and a black-and-white-patterned orb. There is a dormant, ornate fireplace to her left. But what makes this scene extraordinary is what seems to have taken place moments before the picture was taken. One of the young woman's feet, clad in the devil-red black-laced boots being advertised, rests defiantly on top of the shattered remains of a crystal chandelier. In her right hand, the woman holds an old-looking shotgun with her forefinger still resting on the trigger.

Speculation about the story behind the image.

In Sorel's explosive ad, it is apparent that the woman not only shot down the ceiling fixture but also has no regrets about doing so. Her white dress represents a sort of purity and innocence that is completely contradicted by the way she wears it—and by the boots. They gave her the power to shoot down the chandelier, the push she needed to give in to a long-held desire that perhaps she couldn't have indulged in without the extra help. They symbolize her liberty to decide to be herself and do what she wants. Along with the white dress, the formal decor represents the bounds that society tells her she must fit into—but that she decides to take a potshot at instead. Focusing on the beauty of inner power, not just the power of outer beauty, this Sorel ad punctuates its bold visual statement with a single verbal phrase: "Après anything" (Sorel). In the French language, the word *après* means "after." So, the ad suggests, no matter what outrageous or outlandish deed you do, the Sorel boots will be there for you, suitable for slipping into afterward like a negligee.

Analysis of the second text.

With these pioneering fashion ads that celebrate blowing your own horn or shooting up fancy French lighting fixtures for fun, young women are told to accessorize their inner beauty with articles of clothing geared toward their distinctive individual desires. "You don't have to just try to be beautiful in the ways other women do," they say; "you can strike out on your own, and our products will help you do it." The extent to which women will respond to these messages remains to be seen, but certainly the ads themselves achieve a strikingly different look. Whether celebrating individual talents or random acts of defiance in our everyday lives, they dare us to accessorize our personalities.

Conclusion ties together the strands of the analysis.

Works Cited

Advertisement for Clarks. *Lucky*, Sept. 2011, p. 55.

Advertisement for Sorel. *Lucky*, Sept. 2011, p. 65.

Berry summarizes each ad clearly and focuses her analysis on a theme run-ning through both ads: that clothing is an expression of one's individuality. She describes patterns of images in both ads as evidence.

DANIELLE ALLEN

Our Declaration

Danielle Allen is a political theorist, teaches at Harvard University, and directs Harvard's Edmond J. Safra Center for Ethics. This analysis is a chapter from her book Our Declaration: A Reading of the Declaration of Independence in Defense of Equality.

There's something quite startling about the phrase "We hold these truths to be self-evident." Perhaps it can be made visible most easily with a comparison.

The Catholic Church, too, is committed to a set of truths. At every mass priest and parishioners together recite a list of their beliefs called the *Credo*. One version, called the Apostles' Creed, starts like this: "I believe in God, the Father almighty, creator of heaven and earth. I believe in Jesus Christ, his only son and Lord." Each section begins with the words "I believe," and that's why this recitation is called the *Credo*. Latin, "credo" simply means "I believe."

The Declaration launches its list of truths altogether differently. Jefferson and his colleagues do not say, "I believe," or even "we believe," that all men are created equal. Instead, they say, "We hold these truths to be self-evident," and then they give us a set of either three or five truths, depending on how you count.

What's the difference between "We believe" and "We hold these truths to be self-evident"? In the Catholic *Credo*, when one says, "I believe," the basis for that belief is God's revealed word. In contrast, when Jefferson and his colleagues say, "We hold these truths to be self-evident," they are claiming to know the truths thanks to their own powers of perception and reasoning. These truths are self-evident, and so humans can grasp and hold them without any external or divine assistance.

In order to understand what "We hold these truths to be self-evident" 5 really means, then, it is important to know what "self-evident" means.

Sometimes people take it to mean that we can instantly understand an idea, but that's not really right. It's true that sometimes the idea of self-evidence is used for things that we simply perceive. For instance, when I look out my window I immediately perceive that the world includes things like trees and flowers. If outside my window there are many different kinds of tree—hickory and maple and oak, for instance—when I look at them, I nonetheless rapidly perceive that they are all the same kind of thing. That many different kinds of a particular sort of growing thing are all trees is self-evident. We can call this self-evidence from sense perception.

The immediacy of perception, though, is not the same as instantly understanding an idea. And, in fact, to call a proposition self-evident is not at all to say that you will instantly get it. It means instead that if you look into the proposition, if you entertain it, if you reflect upon it, you will inevitably come to affirm it. All the evidence that you need in order to believe the proposition exists within the proposition itself.

This second kind of self-evidence comes not from perception but from logic and how language works.

For instance, we define a chair as an object with a seat and some structure of legs to hold that seat up; and the artifact serves the purpose of having someone sit on it. Then, if I say that a chair is for sitting on, I am expressing a self-evident truth based only on the definition of a chair. Of course a chair is for sitting on! That is how I've defined the word, after all. That's a pretty trivial example of self-evidence. If that were all there were to the idea of self-evidence, it wouldn't be very interesting.

So here is where matters get more interesting: one can string 10 together more than one kind of self-evident proposition—let's call them "premises"—in order to lead to a new piece of knowledge, a conclusion, which will also count as self-evident, since it has been deduced from a few basic self-evident premises.

Aristotle called this method of stringing together valid premises to yield a self-evident conclusion, a syllogism. Above, I said that "syllogism" is a technical word. Here is a basic example:

FIRST PREMISE: *Bill Gates is a human being.*
SECOND PREMISE: *All human beings are mortal.*
CONCLUSION: *Bill Gates is mortal.*

This is a bit like math. We can use a Venn diagram to show how the syllogism works. Venn diagrams represent sets of things and how they overlap, and the argument of a syllogism can be thought of as expressing facts about sets and their members. Bill Gates is in the set of human beings. And the set of human beings is entirely contained within the set of mortals. It follows that Bill Gates is in the set of mortals. The validity of this syllogism becomes self-evident when those facts are represented as in this Venn diagram:

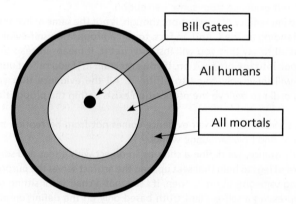

Now, in this syllogism, our two premises are both self-evident truths based on sense perception. We know Bill Gates is a human being by looking at and listening to him. As to the idea that human beings are mortal, we know that human beings die by seeing it happen all around us and never seeing a counterexample. Then we take these two premises, each self-evident through sense perception, and generate a third self-evident proposition, in this case a conclusion, through deduction. From the two premises, we can deduce the certain conclusion that Bill Gates will die.

The Declaration introduces a similar kind of argument when it says, "We hold these truths to be self-evident." At first glance, it looks as if we just have three separate self-evident truths. But if we look closer, we notice that our truths also represent an argument with two premises, which are true from sense perception, and a conclusion that is deduced from them.

Here's how it works.   15

After the Declaration says, "We hold these truths to be self-evident," the text proceeds to identify three truths: one about human beings, one about government, and one about revolution. The truth about human beings, though, is a three-part truth.

It is self-evidently true:

> that all men are created equal, that they are endowed by their Creator with certain unalienable Rights, that among these are Life, Liberty and the pursuit of Happiness.

How do these three claims make a single truth? Human beings are equal in all acquiring the same rights at the moment of their creation. From the moment of their emergence as living beings, human beings seek to survive, to be free from domination, and to be happy. This is something we simply observe about human beings. For that matter, we observe it about other animals, too. For instance, I've never seen a cat that didn't want to survive, to be free, and to be happy.

Then, with the next truth, we come to the difference between human beings and animals. The Declaration says, it is self-evidently true

> —That to secure these rights, Governments are instituted among Men, deriving their just powers from the consent of the governed.

This is a truly salient point. The signers are saying that, in contrast to the animal kingdom, the world of human beings is indeed full of kingdoms and other kinds of governments. The so-called animal kingdom is a kingdom only metaphorically. There are no governments among animals. Animals have social hierarchies, and they have their own methods for seeking their survival, freedom, and happiness, but human beings use politics. Human beings display self-conscious thought about social organization, and politics is the activity that flows from that self-consciousness about power. Again, this is simply a matter of observation. From the beginning of time to the present day, human beings have formed governments. Human beings have done this just as regularly as birds build nests.

Then the Declaration puts these first two truths together. Since human beings seek their own survival, freedom, and happiness, and since they have a special tool for doing so—namely, the ability to form governments—it makes sense for them to stick with any particular version of that tool, any particular government, only if it's doing the work it's been built to do. 20

Compare it to a bird with a nest. What's the point of a bird's staying in a nest if it turns out that the nest has been built out of material inimical or poisonous to the bird? What's the use, in other words, of having a government, if it doesn't serve the purposes of protecting life, liberty, and the pursuit of happiness for which governments are set up in the first place?

The Declaration puts it this way: It is self-evidently true

> *— That whenever any Form of Government becomes destructive of these ends, it is the Right of the People to alter or to abolish it, and to institute new Government, laying its foundation on such principles and organizing its powers in such form, as to them shall seem most likely to effect their Safety and Happiness.*

From the facts, first, that people are simply wired, as are all animals, to seek their survival, freedom, and happiness, and, second, that human beings use governments as their central instrument for protecting their life, liberty, and pursuit of happiness, we can deduce that people have a right to change governments that aren't working for them.

This makes an argument that goes like this:

PREMISE 1:　　All people have rights to life, liberty, and the pursuit of happiness.

PREMISE 2:　　Properly constituted government is necessary to their securing their rights

CONCLUSION:　All people have a right to a properly constituted government.

academic literacies　rhetorical situations　genres　fields　processes　strategies　research MLA / APA　media / design　readings　handbook

In fact, a philosopher would say that a premise is missing from that 25 argument and that the full formally valid syllogism would look like this:

PREMISE 1: All people have rights to life, liberty, and the pursuit of happiness.

PREMISE 2: Properly constituted government is necessary to their securing these rights.

PREMISE 3: [All people have a right to whatever is necessary to secure what they have a right to].

CONCLUSION: All people have a right to a properly constituted government.

Politicians often craft maxims simply by dropping out pieces of their argument. With the missing premise inserted, the Declaration's truths fit together almost like the pieces of a mathematical equation; we intuitively feel the puzzle pieces snap together. That is how self-evidence should feel.

Allen's analysis focuses on the Declaration's second sentence, unpacking its logic through a careful examination of its key term, "self-evident," and explaining how the rest of the sentence forms a syllogism that "snaps together." She looks carefully at every word, restricting her analysis here to a very brief part of the text—but provides insights that illuminate the whole document.

ROY PETER CLARK

Why It Worked: A Rhetorical Analysis of Obama's Speech on Race

Roy Peter Clark teaches writing at the Poynter Institute. This essay, which Clark describes as "an X-ray reading of the text," appeared online on the Poynter Institute's website, first in 2008 and again in 2017, with a new introduction.

The National Conference of Teachers of English (NCTE) has declared today [October 20, 2017] a National Day on Writing. I celebrate such a day. The introduction of my book *Writing Tools* imagines what America might look like and sound like if we declared ourselves a "nation of writers." After all, what good is freedom of expression if we lack the means to express ourselves?

To mark this day—and to honor language arts teachers every-where—Poynter is republishing an essay I wrote almost a decade ago. Remember? It was the spring of 2008 and Barack Obama was running for president. Many of us wondered if America was ready to elect an African-American president (a man with the middle name Hussein).

To dispel the fears of some white Americans and to advance his chances for election, Obama delivered a major address on race in America, a speech that was praised even by some of his adversaries. Obama had / has a gift for language. He is a skilled orator. To neutral-ize that advantage, his opponents—including Hillary Clinton at one point—would characterize Obama's words as empty "rhetoric"—an elaborate trick of language.

The spring of 2008 seems like such a long time ago. A time just before the Great Recession [that affected the U.S. from 2008 to 2009]. A time just before the ascendancy of social networks and the trolls who try to poison them. A time before black lives were said to matter in a more assertive way. A time before fake news was anything more dangerous than a piece of satire in the *Onion*. A time before Colin Kaepernick took a knee—except when he was tired. A time before torch-bearing white supremacists marched through the night in Charlottesville, Virginia.

It feels like the perfect time for a restart on a conversation about 5 race. To prepare us, let's take another look at the words of Barack Obama before he was president. Let's review what he said, and, more important, how and why he said it. My X-ray analysis of that speech is meant not as a final word on that historical moment, but as an invitation, a doorway to a room where we can all reflect on American history and the American language.

Have a great National Day on Writing.

More than a century ago, scholar and journalist W. E. B. Du Bois wrote a single paragraph about how race is experienced in America. I have learned more from those 112 words than from most book-length studies of the subject:

After the Egyptian and Indian, the Greek and Roman, the Teuton and Mongolian, the Negro is a sort of seventh son, born with a veil,

academic literacies · rhetorical situations · genres · fields · processes · strategies · research MLA / APA · media / design · readings · handbook

and gifted with second-sight in this American world, a world which yields him no true self-consciousness, but only lets him see himself through the revelation of the other world. It is a peculiar sensation, this double-consciousness, this sense of always looking at one's self through the eyes of others, of measuring one's soul by the tape of a world that looks on in amused contempt and pity. One ever feels his two-ness,—an American, a Negro; two souls, two thoughts, two unreconciled strivings; two warring ideals in one dark body, whose dogged strength alone keeps it from being torn asunder.

Much has been said about the power and brilliance of Barack Obama's March 18, 2008, speech on race, even by some of his detractors. The focus has been on the orator's willingness to say things in public about race that are rarely spoken at all, even in private, and his expressed desire to move the country to a new and better place. There has also been attention to the immediate purpose of the speech, which was to reassure white voters that they had nothing to fear from the congregant of a fiery African-American pastor, the Rev. Jeremiah Wright.

Amid all the commentary, I have yet to see an X-ray reading of the text that would make visible the rhetorical strategies that the orator and authors used so effectively. When received in the ear, these effects breeze through us like a harmonious song. When inspected with the eye, these moves become more apparent, like reading a piece of sheet music for a difficult song and finally recognizing the chord changes.

Such analysis, while interesting in itself, might be little more than a scholarly curiosity if we were not so concerned with the language issues of political discourse. The popular opinion is that our current president [George W. Bush], though plain spoken, is clumsy with language. Fair or not, this perception has produced a hope that our next president will be a more powerful communicator, a Kennedy or Reagan, perhaps, who can use language less as a way to signal ideology and more as a means to bring the disparate parts of the nation together. Journalists need to pay closer attention to political language than ever before.

Like most memorable pieces of oratory, Obama's speech sounds better than it reads. We have no way of knowing if that was true of Lincoln's Gettysburg Address, but it is certainly true of Dr. King's "I Have a Dream" speech. If you doubt this assertion, test it out. Read the speech[1] and then experience it in its original setting[2] recited by his soulful voice.

The effectiveness of Obama's speech rests upon four related rhetorical strategies:

1. The power of allusion and its patriotic associations.
2. The oratorical resonance of parallel constructions.
3. The "two-ness" of the texture, to use Du Bois's useful term.
4. His ability to include himself as a character in a narrative about race.

Allusion

Part of what made Dr. King's speech resonate, not just for black people, but for some whites, was its framing of racial equality in familiar patriotic terms: "This will be the day when all of God's children will be able to sing with new meaning, 'My country 'tis of thee, sweet land of liberty, of thee I sing. Land where my fathers died, land of the pilgrim's pride, from every mountainside, let freedom ring.'" What follows, of course, is King's great litany of iconic topography that carries listeners across the American landscape: "Let freedom ring from the snowcapped Rockies of Colorado! . . ."

In this tradition, Obama begins with "We the people, in order to form a more perfect union," a quote from the Constitution that becomes a recurring refrain linking the parts of the speech. What comes next is "Two hundred and twenty one years ago," an opening that places him in the tradition of Lincoln at Gettysburg and Dr. King at the Lincoln Memorial: "Five score years ago."

On the first page, Obama mentions the words democracy, Declaration of Independence, Philadelphia convention, 1787, the colonies, the founders, the Constitution, liberty, justice, citizenship under the law, parchment, equal, free, prosperous, and the presidency. It is not as well known as it should be that many black leaders, including Dr. King, use two different modes of discourse when addressing white vs. black audiences, an ignorance that has led to some of the hysteria over some of Rev. Wright's comments.

Obama's patriotic lexicon is meant to comfort white ears and soothe white fears. What keeps the speech from falling into a pan-

15

1. http://www.americanrhetoric.com/speeches/mlkihaveadream.htm
2. https://archive.org/details/MLKDream

academic literacies · rhetorical situations · genres · fields · processes · strategies · research MLA / APA · media / design · readings · handbook

dering sea of slogans is language that reveals, not the ideals, but the failures of the American experiment: "It was stained by this nation's original sin of slavery, a question that divided the colonies and brought the convention to a stalemate until the founders chose to allow the slave trade to continue for at least twenty more years, and to leave any final resolution to future generations." And "what would be needed were Americans in successive generations who were willing to do their part . . . to narrow that gap between the promise of our ideals and the reality of their time."

Lest a dark vision of America disillusion potential voters, Obama returns to familiar evocations of national history, ideals, and language:

- — "Out of many, we are truly one."
- — "survived a Depression."
- — "a man who served his country"
- — "on a path of a more perfect union"
- — "a full measure of justice"
- — "the immigrant trying to feed his family"
- — "where our union grows stronger"
- — "a band of patriots signed that document."

Parallelism

At the risk of calling to mind the worst memories of grammar class, I invoke the wisdom that parallel constructions help authors and orators make meaning memorable. To remember how parallelism works, think of equal terms to express equal ideas. So Dr. King dreamed that one day his four children "will not be judged by the color of their skin but by the content of their character." (*By the content of their character* is parallel to *by the color of their skin*.)

Back to Obama: "This was one of the tasks we set forth at the beginning of this campaign—to continue the long march of those who came before us, a march for a more just, more equal, more free, more caring and more prosperous America." If you are counting, that's five parallel phrases among 43 words.

And there are many more: 20

    ". . . we may not have come from the same place, but we all want to move in the same direction."

"So when they are told to bus their children to a school across town; when they hear that an African American is getting an advantage in landing a good job or a spot in a good college because of an injustice that they themselves never committed; when they're told that their fears about crime in urban neighborhoods are somehow prejudiced, resentment builds over time."

". . . embracing the burdens of our past without becoming victims of our past."

Two-ness

I could argue that Obama's speech is a meditation upon Du Bois's theory of a dual experience of race in America. There is no mention of Du Bois or two-ness, but it is all there in the texture. In fact, once you begin the search, it is remarkable how many examples of two-ness shine through:

— "through protests and struggles"
— "on the streets and in the courts"
— "through civil war and civil disobedience"
— "I am the son of a black man from Kenya and a white woman from Kansas."
— "white and black"
— "black and brown"
— "best schools . . . poorest nations"
— "too black or not black enough"
— "the doctor and the welfare mom"
— "the model student and the former gang-banger"
— "raucous laughter and sometimes bawdy humor"
— "political correctness or reverse racism"
— "your dreams do not have to come at the expense of my dreams"

Such language manages to create both tension and balance and, without being excessively messianic, permits Obama to present himself as the bridge builder, the reconciler of America's racial divide.

Autobiography

There is an obnoxious tendency among political candidates to frame their life story as a struggle against poverty or hard circumstances. As satirist Stephen Colbert once noted of presidential candidates, it is not

academic literacies rhetorical situations genres fields processes strategies research MLA / APA media / design readings handbook

enough to be an average millionaire. To appeal to populist instincts it becomes de rigueur to be descended from "goat turd farmers" in France.

Without dwelling on it, Obama reminds us that his father was black and his mother white, that he came from Kenya, but she came from Kansas: "I am married to a black American who carries within her the blood of slaves and slave owners—an inheritance we pass on to our two precious daughters. I have brothers, sisters, nieces, nephews, uncles, and cousins, of every race and every hue, scattered across three continents, and for as long as I live, I will never forget that in no other country on Earth is my story even possible."

The word "story" is a revealing one, for it is always the candidate's job (as both responsibility and ploy) to describe himself or herself as a character in a story of his or her own making. In speeches, as in homilies, stories almost always carry the weight of parable, with moral lessons to be drawn.

Most memorable, of course, is the story at the end of the speech— 25 which is why it appears at the end. It is the story of Ashley Baia, a young, white Obama volunteer from South Carolina, whose family was so poor she convinced her mother that her favorite meal was a mustard and relish sandwich.

"Anyway, Ashley finishes her story and then goes around the room and asks everyone else why they're supporting the campaign. They all have different stories and reasons. Many bring up a specific issue. And finally they come to this elderly black man who's been sitting there quietly the entire time. . . . He simply says to everyone in the room, 'I am here because of Ashley.'"

During most of the 20th century, demagogues, especially in the South, gained political traction by pitting working class whites and blacks against each other. How fitting, then, that Obama's story points in the opposite direction through an old black man who feels a young white woman's pain.

Clark traces four patterns of rhetorical strategies used by President Obama in his speech: allusion, parallelism, W. E. B. Du Bois's "two-ness," and autobiography. His analysis shows how these strategies combine to provide Obama with the opportunity to address and bring together a broad audience through memorable prose.

For four more textual analyses, see CHAPTER 62.

Key Features / Textual Analyses

A summary or description of the text. Your readers may not know the text you are analyzing, so you need to include it or tell them about it before you analyze it. Allen's text, the Declaration of Independence, is well known, so she assumes that her readers already know its first sentences. Texts that are not so well known require a more detailed summary or description. For example, Berry includes the ads she analyzes and also describes them in detail.

Attention to the context. Texts don't exist in isolation: they are influenced by and contribute to ongoing conversations, controversies, debates, and cultural trends. To fully engage a particular text, you need to understand its larger context. Clark begins by quoting a 1903 book on race in America, and Berry places shoe ads into the context of fashion advertising.

A clear interpretation or judgment. Your goal in analyzing a text is to lead readers through careful examination of the text to some kind of interpretation or reasoned judgment, sometimes announced clearly in a thesis statement. When you interpret something, you explain what you think it means, as Berry does when she argues that the two ads suggest that our clothing choices enhance our individuality. She might instead have chosen to judge the effectiveness of the ads, perhaps noting that they promise the impossible: uniqueness through mass-produced clothing. Clark argues that through Obama's use of four rhetorical strategies, he "present[s] himself as the bridge builder, the reconciler of America's racial divide."

Reasonable support for your conclusions. Written analysis of a text is generally supported by evidence from the text itself and sometimes from other sources as well. The writer might support their interpretation by quoting words or passages from a verbal text or referring to images in a visual text. Allen, for example, interprets the term "self-evident" by referring to formal logic, Venn diagrams, and the Catholic Credo. Berry examines patterns of both language and images in her analysis of two ads. Clark provides lists of phrases from Obama's speech to support his thesis. Note that the support you offer for your interpretation need only be "reasonable"—there is never only one way to interpret something.

A GUIDE TO WRITING TEXTUAL ANALYSES

Choosing a Text to Analyze

Most of the time, you will be assigned a text or a type of text to analyze: a poem in a literature class, the work of a political philosopher in a political science class, a speech in a history or communications course, a painting or sculpture in an art class, a piece of music in a music theory course. If you must choose a text to analyze, look for one that suits the demands of the assignment—one that is neither too large or complex to analyze thoroughly (a Dickens novel or a Beethoven symphony is probably too big) nor too brief or limited to generate sufficient material (a ten-second TV news brief or a paragraph from *Hillbilly Elegy* would probably be too small). You might also choose to analyze three or four texts by examining elements common to all. Be sure you understand what the assignment asks you to do, and ask your instructor for clarification if you're not sure.

Considering the Rhetorical Situation

PURPOSE	Why are you analyzing this text? To demonstrate that you understand it? To show how its argument works—or doesn't? Or are you using the text as a way to make some other point?	55–56
AUDIENCE	Are your readers likely to know your text? How much detail will you need to supply?	57–60
STANCE	What interests you (or not) about your text? Why? What do you know or believe about it, and how will your own beliefs affect your analysis?	66–68
MEDIA / DESIGN	Will your analysis appear in print? on the web? How will your medium affect your analysis? If you are analyzing a visual text, you will probably need to include an image of it.	69–71

Generating Ideas and Text

In analyzing a written text, your goal is to understand what it says, how it works, and what it means. To do so, you may find it helpful to follow a certain sequence: read, respond, summarize, analyze, and draw conclusions from your analysis.

12–13
16–17
14

Read to see what the text says. Start by reading carefully, to get a sense of what it says. This means first skimming to **PREVIEW THE TEXT**, rereading for the main ideas, then questioning and **ANNOTATING**.

Consider your **INITIAL RESPONSE**. Once you have a sense of what the text says, what do you think? What's your reaction to the argument, the tone, the language, the images? Do you find the text difficult? puzzling? Do you agree with what the writer says? disagree? agree *and* disagree? Your reaction to a text can color your analysis, so start by thinking about how you react—and why. Consider both your intellectual and any emotional reactions. Identify places in the text that trigger or account for those reactions. If you think that you have no particular reaction or response, try to articulate why. Whatever your response, think about what accounts for it.

534–35
335–37

Next, consolidate your understanding of the text by **SUMMARIZING** what it says in your own words. You may find it helpful to **OUTLINE** its main ideas. For instance, Allen carefully maps out the parts of the syllogism at the heart of her analysis.

Decide what you want to analyze. Having read the text carefully, think about what you find most interesting or intriguing and why. Does the argument interest you? its logic? its attempt to create an emotional response? its reliance on the writer's credibility or reputation? its use of design to achieve its aims? its context? Does the text's language, imagery, or structure intrigue you? something else? You might begin your analysis by exploring what attracted your notice.

Think about the larger context. All texts are part of larger conversations with other texts that have dealt with the same topic. An essay arguing for handgun trigger locks is part of an ongoing conversation about gun regulation, which is itself part of a conversation on individual rights and responsibilities. Academic texts include documentation in part to weave in voices from the conversation. And, in fact, anytime you're reading to learn, you're probably reading for some larger context. Whatever your reading goals, being aware of that larger context can help you better understand what you're reading. Here are some specific aspects of the text to pay attention to:

- *Who else cares about this topic?* Especially when you're reading in order to learn about a topic, the texts you read will often reveal which people or groups are part of the conversation—and might be sources of further reading. For example, an essay describing the formation of the Grand Canyon could be of interest to geologists, environmentalists, Native Americans, travel writers, or tourists. If you're reading such an essay while doing research on the canyon, you should consider how the audience addressed determines the nature of the information provided—and its suitability as a source for your research.

- *Ideas.* Does the text refer to any concepts or ideas that give you some sense that it's part of a larger conversation? An argument on airport security measures, for example, is part of larger conversations about government response to terrorism, the limits of freedom in a democracy, and the possibilities of using technology to detect weapons and explosives, among others.

- *Terms.* Is there any terminology or specialized language that reflects the writer's allegiance to a particular group or academic discipline? If you run across words like *false consciousness*, *ideology*, and *hegemony*, for example, you might guess the text was written by a Marxist scholar.

- *Citations.* Whom does the writer cite? Do the other writers have a particular academic specialty, belong to an identifiable intellectual school, share similar political leanings? If an article on politics cites Michael Moore and Maureen Dowd in support of its argument, you might assume the writer holds liberal opinions; if it cites Rush Limbaugh and Sean Hannity, the writer is likely a conservative.

Write a brief paragraph describing the larger context surrounding the text and how that context affects your understanding of the text.

Consider what you know about the writer. What you know about the person who created a text can influence your understanding of it. Their **CREDENTIALS**, other work, reputation, stance, and beliefs are all useful windows into understanding a text. You may need to conduct an online search to find information on the writer. Then write a sentence or two summarizing what you know about the writer and how that information affects your understanding of the text.

512 ●

Study how the text works. Written texts are made up of various components, including words, sentences, paragraphs, headings, lists, punctuation—and sometimes images as well. Look for patterns in the way these components are used and try to decide what those patterns reveal about the text. How do they affect its message? See the sections on **THINKING ABOUT HOW THE TEXT WORKS** and **IDENTIFYING PATTERNS** for specific guidelines on examining patterns this way. Then write a sentence or two describing the patterns you've discovered and how they contribute to what the text says.

21–23 ✳
23–25

Analyze the argument. Every text makes an argument and provides some kind of support for it. An important part of understanding any text is to recognize its argument—what the writer wants the audience to believe, feel, or do. Here are some questions you'll want to consider when you analyze an argument:

- *What is the claim?* What is the main point the writer is trying to make? Is there a clearly stated **THESIS**, or is the thesis merely implied? Is it appropriately qualified?

387–89 ◆

- *What support does the writer offer for the claim?* What **REASONS** are given to support the claim? What **EVIDENCE** backs up those reasons? Facts? Statistics? Examples? Testimonials by authorities? Anecdotes or stories? Are the reasons and evidence appropriate, plausible, and sufficient? Are you convinced by them? If not, why not?

400–401 ◆
401–8

- *How does the writer appeal to readers?* Do they appeal to your **EMOTIONS**? rely on **LOGIC**? try to establish **COMMON GROUND**? demonstrate **CREDIBILITY**?

413 ◆
398–408
410–11
410–13

- *How evenhandedly does the writer present the argument?* Is there any mention of **COUNTERARGUMENTS**? If so, how does the writer deal with them? By refuting them? By acknowledging them and responding to them reasonably? Does the writer treat other arguments respectfully? dismissively? 411–12

- *Does the writer use any logical* **FALLACIES**? Are the arguments or beliefs of others distorted or exaggerated? Is the logic faulty? 414–16

- *What authorities or other sources of outside information does the writer use?* How are they used? How credible are they? Are they in any way biased or otherwise unreliable? Are they current?

- *How does the writer address you as the reader?* Does the writer assume that readers know something about what is being discussed? Does their language include you or exclude you? (Hint: If you see the word *we*, do you feel included?) Do you sense that you and the writer share any beliefs or attitudes? If the writer is not writing to you, what audience is the target? How do you know?

Then write a brief paragraph summarizing the argument the text makes and the main way the writer argues it, along with your reactions to or questions about that argument.

In analyzing a visual text, your goal is to understand its intended effect on viewers as well as its actual effect, the ways it creates that effect, and its relationship to other texts. If the visual text accompanies a written one, you need to understand how the texts work together to convey a message or make an argument.

Describe the text. Your first job is to examine the image carefully. Focus on specific details; given the increasing use of *Photoshop* and other digital image manipulation tools, you can usually assume that every detail in the image is intentional. Ask yourself these questions:

- What kind of image is it? Does it stand alone, or is it part of a group? Are there typical features of this kind of image that it includes—or lacks?

- What does the image show? What stands out? What is in the background? Are some parts of the image grouped together or connected? Are any set apart from one another?

- As you look at the image, does the content seem far away, close up, or in between? Are you level with it, looking down from above, or looking up from below? What is the effect of your viewing position?

- Does the image tell or suggest a story about what has happened (as in Berry's ad for Sorel shoes) or is about to happen?

- Does the image allude to or refer to anything else? For example, the Starbucks logo features the image of a Siren, a mythical being who lured sailors to their doom.

Explore your response. Images, particularly those in advertisements, are often trying to persuade us to buy something or to feel, think, or behave a certain way. News photographs and online videos also try to evoke **EMOTIONAL** responses, from horror over murdered innocents to amusement at cute kittens. Think about your response:

413

- How does the image make you feel? What emotional response, if any, does the image make you feel? Sympathy? Concern? Anger? Happiness? Contentment? Something else?

- What does the image lead you to think about? What connections does it have to things in your life, in the news, in your knowledge of the world?

- Do the image and any words accompanying seem to be trying to persuade you to think or do something? Do they do so directly, such as by pointing out the virtues of a product (Buick Encore: "Sized to Fit Your Life")? Or indirectly, by setting a tone or establishing a mood (the Clarks shoe ad that Berry analyzes)?

73

- Does the **GENRE** affect your response? For example, do you expect to laugh at a comic? feel empathy with victims of a tragedy in a photo accompanying a news story? find a satirical editorial cartoon offensive?

Consider the context. Like written texts, visual texts are part of larger conversations with other texts that have dealt with the same topic or used similar imagery. This editorial cartoon on global warming, for example, is part of an ongoing conversation about climate change and the role our lifestyles play in it:

Consider what you know about the artist or sponsor. Editorial cartoons, like the one above, are usually signed, and information about the artist and their other work is usually readily available on the web. Many commercials and advertisements, however, are created by ad agencies, so the organization or company that sponsored or posted the image should be identified and researched. How does that information affect your understanding of the text?

Decide on a focus for your analysis. What do you find most interesting about the text, and why? Its details and the way they work together (or not)? The argument it makes? The way it uses images to appeal to its audience? The emotional response it evokes? The way any words and images work together to deliver a message? These are just some ways of thinking about a visual text, ones that can help you find a focus.

However you choose to focus your analysis, it should be limited in scope so that you can zero in on the details of the visual you're analyzing. Here, for example, is an excerpt from an essay from 2014 by an art historian responding to a statement made by former president Barack Obama that manufacturing skills may be worth more than a degree in art history:

> *"I promise you, folks can make a lot more potentially with skilled manufacturing or the trades than they might with an art history degree."* President Barack Obama

> Charged with interrogating this quote from the president, I Google "Obama art history." I click on the first result, a video from CNN, in which the quote is introduced by a gray-haired man in a dark and serious suit, standing in front of a bank of monitors in a digitally created nonspace. The camera cuts from this man to President Obama, who stands in shirtsleeves, his tie slightly loosened. His undershirt is visible through his buttondown under the intense light from what I assume is the work-day sun.

> Behind him is a crowd of men and women in more casual clothing, some wearing sweatshirts that have the name of a union printed across them. Their presence creates a spectrum of skin tones. Each person was clearly vetted for visual effect, as were the president's and the newscaster's costumes, the size of their flag lapel pins, the shape of the microphones they speak into, and the angle of the light on their faces. The president makes the comment in question, immediately declares his love for art history, and says that he doesn't want to get a bunch of angry emails from art historians. The crowd behind him laughs and the clip cuts off abruptly.

> A click away, I find a digitized copy of a handwritten note from President Obama, apologizing to an angry art history professor who emailed him to complain about his comments. The card on which the note is written is plain, undecorated save for two lines of text printed in a conservative, serif font in a shade of blue that is just on the vibrant

side of navy—THE WHITE HOUSE—and under it in smaller letters, WASHINGTON. Its tasteful, minimal aesthetic pulls double duty, meant to convey both populist efficiency (note the absence of gold gilding) and stern superiority (you know where Washington is, right?). It sets up a productive contrast with the friendliness of the president's own handwriting, particularly his looping signature, soft on the outside with a strong slash through the middle.

Like the video of the president's speech, it is a screen-scale tour de force of political imagecraft, certainly produced with the full knowledge that it would be digitized and go viral, at least among a particular demographic.

—Joel Parsons, "Richness in the Eye of the Beholder"

Parsons begins by describing the images—Obama's clothing, the people standing behind him, the letterhead on his note card, his "looping

Barack Obama speaking at a General Electric plant in Waukesha, Wisconsin, 2014.

THE WHITE HOUSE

WASHINGTON

Ann —

Let me apologize for my off-the-cuff remarks. I was making a point about the job market, not the value of art history. As it so happens, art history was one of my favorite subjects in high school, and it has helped me take in a great deal of joy in my life that

I might otherwise have missed.

So please pass on my apology for the glib remark to the entire department, and understand that I was trying to encourage young people who may not be predisposed to a four year college experience to be open to technical training that can lead them to an honorable career.

Sincerely,

Obama's apology note to Ann Johns, art history professor at the University of Texas at Austin.

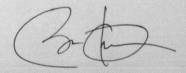

signature"—followed by an analysis of how every aspect of the video and the note card was "certainly produced with the full knowledge that it would be digitized and go viral." Notice as well that Parsons's analysis focuses more on the visual aspects of the video and note card than on what was said or written. And in a part of his essay not shown here, he notes that his analysis is grounded in "tools . . . he learned in a first-year art history course"—a not-so-subtle response to what President Obama said.

Coming Up with a Thesis

When you analyze a text, you are basically **ARGUING** that the text should be read or seen in a certain way. Once you've studied the text thoroughly, you need to identify your analytical goal: do you want to show that the text has a certain meaning? uses certain techniques to achieve its purposes? tries to influence its audience in particular ways? relates to some larger context in some significant manner? should be taken seriously—or not? something else? Come up with a tentative **THESIS** to guide your thinking and analyzing—but be aware that your thesis may change as you continue to work.

397–417

387–89

Ways of Organizing a Textual Analysis

Examine the information you have to see how it supports or complicates your thesis. Look for clusters of related information that you can use to structure an **OUTLINE**. Your analysis might be structured in at least two ways. You might, as Clark does, discuss patterns, elements, or themes that run through the text. Alternatively, you might analyze each text or section of text separately, as Berry does. Following are graphic representations of some ways of organizing a textual analysis:

335–37

[Thematically]

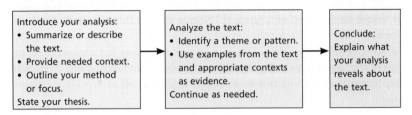

Introduce your analysis:
- Summarize or describe the text.
- Provide needed context.
- Outline your method or focus.

State your thesis.

→

Analyze the text:
- Identify a theme or pattern.
- Use examples from the text and appropriate contexts as evidence.

Continue as needed.

→

Conclude: Explain what your analysis reveals about the text.

[Part by part, or text by text]

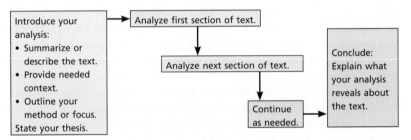

Introduce your analysis:
- Summarize or describe the text.
- Provide needed context.
- Outline your method or focus.

State your thesis.

→ Analyze first section of text.

↓

Analyze next section of text.

↓

Continue as needed.

→

Conclude: Explain what your analysis reveals about the text.

[Spatially, as the text is likely to be experienced by viewers]

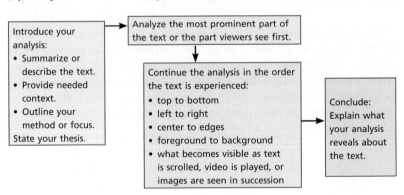

Introduce your analysis:
- Summarize or describe the text.
- Provide needed context.
- Outline your method or focus.

State your thesis.

→ Analyze the most prominent part of the text or the part viewers see first.

↓

Continue the analysis in the order the text is experienced:
- top to bottom
- left to right
- center to edges
- foreground to background
- what becomes visible as text is scrolled, video is played, or images are seen in succession

→

Conclude: Explain what your analysis reveals about the text.

Writing Out a Draft

In drafting your analysis, your goal should be to integrate the various parts into a smoothly flowing, logically organized essay. However, it's easy to get bogged down in the details. Consider writing one section of the analysis first, then another and another, until you've drafted the entire middle; then draft your beginning and ending. Alternatively, start by summarizing the text and moving from there to your analysis and then to your ending. However you do it, you need to support your analysis with evidence: from the text itself (as Berry's analysis of advertisements does), or from **RESEARCH** on the larger context of the text (as Allen does), or by comparing the text you are analyzing to another text (as Clark does).

477

Draft a **BEGINNING**. The beginning of an essay that analyzes a text generally has several tasks: to introduce or summarize the text for your readers, to offer any necessary information on the larger context, and to present your thesis.

373–80

- *Summarize or describe the text.* If the text is one your readers don't know, you need to **SUMMARIZE** or **DESCRIBE** it early on to show that you understand it fully. For example, Berry begins each analysis of a shoe advertisement with a description of its content.

534–35

- *Show the text.* If you're analyzing a visual text online, consider starting off with an image, a video, or a link to it or something similar, as Berry does by embedding the ads she analyzes in her text.

- *Provide a context for your analysis.* If there is a larger context that is significant for your analysis, you might mention it in your introduction. Allen does this by comparing the Declaration's statement about self-evident truths to the statements of belief in the Apostles' Creed of the Catholic Church.

- *State your* **THESIS**. Berry ends her first paragraph by stating her thesis explicitly: These ads "for Clarks and Sorel . . . encourage us to break free from the standard beauty mold and be ourselves; using mostly imagery, they remind us that being unique is the true origin of beauty." Clark promises to analyze "the rhetorical strategies that the orator and authors used so effectively."

387–89

380–85 **Draft an ENDING.** Think about what you want your readers to take away from your analysis, and end by getting them to focus on those thoughts.

- *Restate your thesis—and say why it matters.* Berry, for example, ends by asserting that the ads she examines invite women to "be ourselves" by "accessoriz[ing] our personalities."

- *Explain what your analysis reveals.* Your analysis should tell your readers something about the way the text works or about what it means or says. Allen, for example, concludes by noting that "the Declaration's truths fit together almost like the pieces of a mathematical equation; we intuitively feel the puzzle pieces snap together. That is how self-evidence should feel."

386–87 **Come up with a TITLE.** A good title indicates something about the subject of your analysis—and makes readers want to see what you have to say about it. Berry's title provides a preview of her thesis that the ads she is analyzing are selling a vision of clothing as a vehicle for being unique, while Clark's title straightforwardly announces his topic.

353–55 **Consider REWRITING.** If you have time and want to explore alternatives, you might try rewriting your draft to see if a different plan or approach might work better.

Considering Matters of Design

544–47 - If you cite written text as evidence, be sure to set long quotations and **DOCUMENTATION** according to the style you're using.

650–52 - If your essay is lengthy, consider whether **HEADINGS** would make your analysis easier for readers to follow.

- If you're analyzing a visual text, include a copy of the image and a caption identifying it.

- If you're submitting your essay electronically, provide links to whatever text you are analyzing.

- If you're analyzing an image or a screen shot, consider annotating elements of it right on the image.

academic literacies | rhetorical situations | genres | fields | processes | strategies | research MLA / APA | media / design | readings | handbook

Getting Response and Revising

The following questions can help you and others study your draft with a critical eye. Make sure that anyone you ask to read and **RESPOND** to your text knows your purpose and audience.

348–50

- Is the beginning effective? Does it make a reader want to continue?
- Does the introduction provide an overview of your analysis? Is your thesis clear?
- Is the text described or summarized clearly and sufficiently?
- Is the analysis well organized and easy to follow? Do the parts fit together coherently? Does it read like an essay rather than a collection of separate bits of analysis?
- Does each part of the analysis relate to and support the thesis?
- Is anything confusing or in need of more explanation?
- Are all quotations accurate and correctly documented?
- Is it clear how the analysis leads to the interpretation? Is there adequate evidence to support the interpretation?
- Does the ending make clear what your analysis shows?

Then it's time to **REVISE**. Make sure your text appeals to your audience and think hard about whether it will achieve your purpose.

350–53

Editing and Proofreading

Readers equate correctness with competence. Once you've revised your draft, edit carefully:

- Is your **THESIS** clearly stated?
- Check all **QUOTATIONS**, **PARAPHRASES**, and **SUMMARIES** for accuracy and form. Be sure that each has the required **DOCUMENTATION**.
- Make sure that your analysis flows clearly from one point to the next and that you use **TRANSITIONS** to help readers move through your text.
- **PROOFREAD** your finished analysis carefully before turning it in.

387–89
526–38
544–47

391

359–60

Taking Stock of Your Work

Take stock of what you've written and learned by writing out answers to these questions:

- How did you go about analyzing the text? What methods did you use—and which ones were most helpful?
- How did you go about drafting your essay?
- How well did you organize your written analysis? What, if anything, could you do to make it easier to read?
- Did you provide sufficient evidence to support your analysis?
- What did you do especially well?
- What could still be improved?
- Did you include any visuals, and if so, what did they add? Could you have shown the same thing with words?
- How did other readers' responses influence your writing?
- What would you do differently next time?
- Are you pleased with your analysis? What did it teach you about the text you analyzed? Did it make you want to study more works by the same writer or artist?

<table>
<tr><td>340–42</td><td rowspan="6">

IF YOU NEED MORE HELP

See Chapter 30 for guidelines on **DRAFTING**, Chapter 31 on **ASSESSING YOUR OWN WRITING**, Chapter 32 on **GETTING RESPONSE AND REVISING**, and Chapter 33 on **EDITING AND PROOFREADING**. See Chapter 34 if you are required to submit your analysis in a writing **PORTFOLIO**. See Chapter 58 for help **USING VISUALS**.

</td></tr>
</table>

340–42
343–47
348–55
356–60
361–70
653–63

academic literacies / rhetorical situations / genres / fields / processes / strategies / research MLA / APA / media / design / readings / handbook

Reporting Information 12

Many kinds of writing report information. Newspapers report on local and world events; textbooks give information about biology, history, writing; websites provide information about products (*jcrew.com*), people (*pharrellwilliams.com*), institutions (*smithsonian.org*). We write out a lot of information ourselves, from a note we post on our door saying we've gone to choir practice to a text we send to tell a friend where to meet us for dinner and how to get there.

College assignments often call for reporting information as well. In a *history* class, you may be assigned to report what you've learned about the state of U.S. relations with Japan just before the bombing of Pearl Harbor. A *biology* course may require you to report the effects of an experiment in which plants are deprived of sunlight for different periods of time. In a *nursing* class, you may have to report the changes in a patient's symptoms after the administration of a particular drug.

This chapter focuses on reports that are written to inform readers about a particular topic. Very often this kind of writing calls for some kind of research: you need to know your subject in order to report on it! When you write to report information, you are the expert. We'll begin with three good examples, the first annotated to show the key features found in most reports.

MICHAELA CULLINGTON

Does Texting Affect Writing?

This essay by a student at Marywood University was published in Young Scholars in Writing, *a journal of undergraduate writing published by the University of Missouri–Kansas City.*

It's taking over our lives. We can do it almost anywhere—walking to class, waiting in line at the grocery store, or hanging out at home. It's quick, easy, and convenient. It has become a concern of doctors, parents, and teachers alike. What is it? It's texting!

Text messaging—or *texting*, as it's more commonly called—is the process of sending and receiving typed messages via a cellular phone. It is a common means of communication among teenagers and is even becoming popular in the business world because it allows quick messages to be sent without people having to commit to a telephone conversation. A person is able to say what is needed, and the other person will receive the information and respond when it's convenient to do so.

Definitions of key terms.

In order to more quickly type what they are trying to say, many people use abbreviations instead of words. The language created by these abbreviations is called *textspeak*. Some people believe that using these abbreviations is hindering the writing abilities of students, and others argue that texting is actually having a positive effect on writing. In fact, it seems likely that texting has no significant effect on student writing.

Here's the thesis.

Concerns about Textspeak

A September 2008 article in *USA Today* entitled "Texting, Testing Destroys Kids' Writing Style" summarizes many of the most common complaints about the effect of texting. It states that according to the National Center for Education Statistics, only twenty-five percent of high school seniors are "proficient" writers. The article quotes Jacquie Ream, a former teacher and author of *K.I.S.S.—Keep It Short and Simple*, a guide for writing more effectively. Ream states, "[W]e have a whole generation being raised without communication skills." She blames the use of acronyms and shorthand in text messages for students' inability to spell and ultimately to write well. Ream also points out that students struggle to convey emotion in their writing because, as she states, in text messages "emotions are always sideways smiley faces."

Analysis of causes and effects.

This debate became prominent after some teachers began to believe they were seeing a decline in the writing abilities of their students. Many attributed this perceived decline to the increasing popularity of text messaging and its use of abbreviations. Naomi Baron, a linguistics professor at American University, blames texting for what she sees as the fact that "so much of American society has become sloppy and laissez faire about

5

the mechanics of writing" ("Should"). Teachers report finding "2" for "to," "gr8" for "great," "dat" for "that," and "wut" for "what," among other examples of textspeak, in their students' writing. A Minnesota teacher of the seventh and ninth grades says that she has to spend extra time in class editing papers and must "explicitly" remind her students that it is not acceptable to use text slang and abbreviations in writing (Walsh). Another English teacher believes that text language has become "second nature" to her students (Carey); they are so used to it that they do not even catch themselves doing it.

Many also complain that because texting does not stress the importance of punctuation, students are neglecting it in their formal writing. Teachers say that their students are forgetting commas, apostrophes, and even capital letters to begin sentences. Another complaint is that text messages lack emotion. Many argue that texts lack feeling because of their tendency to be short, brief, and to the point. Because students are not able to communicate emotion effectively through texts, some teachers worry, they may lose the ability to do so in writing.

To get a more personal perspective on the question of how teachers perceive texting to be influencing student writing, I interviewed two of my former high school teachers—my junior-year English teacher and my senior-year theology teacher. Both teachers stress the importance of writing in their courses. They maintain that they notice text abbreviations in their students' writing often. To correct this problem, they point it out when it occurs and take points off for its use. They also remind their students to use proper sentence structure and complete sentences. The English teacher says that she believes texting inhibits good writing—it reinforces simplistic writing that may be acceptable for conversation but is "not so good for critical thinking or analysis." She suggests that texting tends to generate topic sentences without emphasizing the following explanation. According to these teachers, then, texting is inhibiting good writing. However, their evidence is limited, based on just a few personal experiences rather than on a significant amount of research.

Responses to Concerns about Textspeak

In response to these complaints that texting is having a negative impact on student writing, others insist that texting should be viewed as beneficial because it provides students with motivation to write, practice in specific writing skills, and an opportunity to gain confidence in their writing. For example, Betty Sternberg and her coauthors argue that texting is a good way to motivate students: teens enjoy texting, and if they frequently write through texts, they will be more motivated to write formally. Texting also helps to spark students' creativity, these authors argue, because they are always coming up with new ways to express their ideas (417).

In addition, because they are engaging in written communication rather than oral speech, texting teens learn how to convey their message to a reader in as few words as possible. In his book *Txtng: The Gr8 Db8*, David Crystal discusses a study that concludes that texting actually helps foster "the ability to summarize and express oneself concisely" in writing (168). Furthermore, Crystal explains that texting actually helps people to "sharpen their diplomatic skills . . . [because] it allows more time to formulate their thoughts and express them carefully" (168). One language arts teacher from Minnesota believes that texting helps students develop their own "individual voice" (qtd. in Walsh). Perfecting such a voice allows the writer to offer personal insights and express feelings that will interest and engage readers.

Synthesis of various sources of information. Quotations are introduced with signal phrases.

Supporters of texting also argue that it not only teaches elements of writing but provides extra practice to those who struggle with the conventions of writing. As Crystal points out, children who struggle with literacy will not choose to use a technology that requires them to do something that is difficult for them. However, if they do choose to text, the experience will help them "overcome their awkwardness and develop their social and communication skills" (*Txtng* 171). Shirley Holm, a junior high school teacher, describes texting as a "comfortable form of communication" (qtd. in Walsh). Teenagers are used to texting, enjoy doing so, and as a result are always writing. Through this experience of writing in ways they enjoy, they can learn to take pleasure in writing formally. If students are continually writing in some form, they will eventually develop better skills.

Furthermore, those who favor texting explain that with practice comes the confidence and courage to try new things, which some observers believe they are seeing happen with writing as a result of texting. Teenagers have, for example, created an entirely new language—one that uses abbreviations and symbols instead of words, does not require punctuation, and uses short, incomplete phrases throughout the entire

10

conversation. It's a way of speaking that is a language in and of itself. Crystal, among others, sees this "language evolution" as a positive effect of texting; he seems, in fact, fascinated that teenagers are capable of creating such a phenomenon, which he describes as the "latest manifestation of the human ability" (*Txtng* 175). David Warlick, a teacher and author of books about technology in the classroom, would agree with Crystal. He believes students should be given credit for "inventing a new language ideal for communicating in a high-tech world" (qtd. in Carey).

Methods

I decided to conduct my own research into this controversy. I wanted to get different, more personal, perspectives on the issue. First, I surveyed seven students on their opinions about the impact of texting on writing. Second, I questioned two high school teachers, as noted above. Finally, in an effort to compare what students are actually doing to people's perceptions of what they are doing, I analyzed student writing samples for instances of textspeak.[1]

To let students speak for themselves, I created a list of questions for seven high school and college students, some of my closest and most reliable friends. Although the number of respondents was small, I could trust my knowledge of them to help me interpret their responses. In addition, these students are very different from one another, and I believed their differences would allow for a wide array of thoughts and opinions on the issue. I was thus confident in the reliability and diversity of their answers but was cautious not to make too many assumptions because of the small sample size.

Firsthand research: interviews and survey.

I asked the students how long they had been texting; how often they texted; what types of abbreviations they used most and how often they used them; and whether they noticed themselves using any type of textspeak in their formal writing. In analyzing their responses, I looked for commonalities to help me draw conclusions about the students' texting habits and if/how they believed their writing was affected.

I created a list of questions for teachers similar to the one for the students and asked two of my high school teachers to provide their input. I asked if they had noticed their students using textspeak in their writing assignments and, if so, how they dealt with it. I also asked if they believed texting had a positive or negative effect on writing. Next, I asked if they were texters themselves. And, finally, I solicited their

15

opinions on what they believed should be done to prevent teens from using text abbreviations and other textspeak in their writing.

I was surprised at how different the students' replies and opinions were from the teachers'. I decided to find out for myself whose impressions were more accurate by comparing some students' actual writing with students' and teachers' perceptions of that writing. To do this I looked at twenty samples of student writing—end-of-semester research arguments written in two first-year college writing courses with different instructors. The topics varied from increased airport security after September 11 to the weapons of the Vietnam War to autism, and lengths ranged from eight to ten pages. To analyze the papers for the presence of textspeak, I looked closely for use of abbreviations and other common slang terms, especially those usages that the students had stated in their surveys were most common. These included "hbu" ("How about you?"); "gtg" ("Got to go"); and "cuz" ("because"). I also looked for the numbers 2 and 4 used instead of the words "to" and "for."

Comparison and contrast.

Discussion of Findings

My research suggests that texting actually has a minimal effect on student writing. It showed that students do not believe textspeak is appropriate in formal writing assignments. They recognize the difference between texting friends and writing formally and know what is appropriate in each situation. This was proven true in the student samples, in which no examples of textspeak were used. Many experts would agree that there is no harm in textspeak, as long as students continue to be taught and reminded that occasions where formal language is expected are not the place for it. As Crystal explains, the purpose of the abbreviations used in text messages is not to replace language but rather to make quick communications shorter and easier, since in a standard text message, the texter is allowed only 160 characters for a communication ("Texting" 81).

Dennis Baron, an English and linguistics professor at the University of Illinois, has done much research on the effect of technology on writing, and his findings are aligned with those of my own study. In his book *A Better Pencil: Readers, Writers, and the Digital Revolution,* he concludes that students do not use textspeak in their writing. In fact, he suggests students do not even use abbreviations in their text messages very often. Baron says that college students have "put away such

Summary and quotations of sources.

academic literacies · rhetorical situations · genres · fields · processes · strategies · research MLA / APA · media / design · readings · handbook

childish things, and many of them had already abandoned such signs of middle-school immaturity in high school" (qtd. in Golden).

In surveying the high school and college students, I found that most have been texting for a few years, usually starting around ninth grade. The students said they generally text between thirty and a hundred messages every day but use abbreviations only occasionally, with the most common being "lol" ("Laugh out loud"), "gtg" ("Got to go"), "hbu" ("How about you?"), "cuz" ("because"), and "jk" ("Just kidding"). None of them believed texting abbreviations were acceptable in formal writing. In fact, research has found that most students report that they do not use textspeak in formal writing. As one Minnesota high school student says, "[T]here is a time and a place for everything," and formal writing is not the place for communicating the way she would if she were texting her friends (qtd. in Walsh). Another student admits that in writing for school she sometimes finds herself using these abbreviations. However, she notices and corrects them before handing in her final paper (Carey). One teacher reports that, despite texting, her students' "formal writing remains solid." She occasionally sees an abbreviation; however, it is in informal, "warm-up" writing. She believes that what students do in everyday writing is up to them as long as they use standard English in formal writing (qtd. in Walsh).

Summary of survey results with quotations.

Also supporting my own research findings are those from a study that took place at a midwestern research university. This study involved eighty-six students who were taking an Introduction to Education course at the university. The participants were asked to complete a questionnaire that included questions about their texting habits, the spelling instruction they had received, and their proficiency at spelling. They also took a standardized spelling test. Before starting the study, the researchers had hypothesized that texting and the use of abbreviations would have a negative impact on the spelling abilities of the students. However, they found that the results did not support their hypothesis. The researchers did note that text messaging is continuing to increase in popularity; therefore, this issue should continue to be examined (Shaw et al.).

20

Summary of research that supports her own.

I myself am a frequent texter. I chat with my friends from home every day through texting. I also use texting to communicate with my school friends, perhaps to discuss what time we are going to meet for dinner or to ask quick questions about homework. According to my cell phone bill, I send and receive around 6,400 texts a month. In the messages I send, I

Pertinent personal experience.

rarely notice myself using abbreviations. The only time I use them is if I do not have time to write out the complete phrase. However, sometimes I find it more time-consuming to try to figure out how to abbreviate something so that my message will still be comprehensible.

Since I rarely use abbreviations in my texting, I never use them in my formal writing. I know that they are unacceptable and that it would make me look unintelligent if I included acronyms and symbols instead of proper and formal language. I also have not noticed an effect on my spelling as a result of texting. I am confident in my spelling abilities, and even when I use an abbreviation, I know how to spell the word(s) it stands for.

Conclusion: summary of research and restatement of claim.

On the basis of my own research, expert research, and personal observations, I can confidently state that texting is not interfering with students' use of standard written English and has no effect on their writing abilities in general. It is interesting to look at the dynamics of the arguments over these issues. Teachers and parents who claim that they are seeing a decline in the writing abilities of their students and children mainly support the negative-impact argument. Other teachers and researchers suggest that texting provides a way for teens to practice writing in a casual setting and thus helps prepare them to write formally. Experts and students themselves, however, report that they see no effect, positive or negative. Anecdotal experiences should not overshadow the actual evidence.

Note

[1] All participants in the study have given permission for their responses to be published.

Works Cited

Baron, Dennis. *A Better Pencil: Readers, Writers, and the Digital Revolution.* Oxford UP, 2009.

Carey, Bridget. "The Rise of Text, Instant Messaging Vernacular Slips into Schoolwork." *The Miami Herald,* 6 Mar. 2007. *Academic OneFile,* search.ebscohost.com/login.aspx?.direct=true&db=edsgao&AN= edsgcl.160190230&site=eds-live.

Crystal, David. "Texting." *ELT Journal,* vol. 62, no. 1, Jan. 2008, pp. 77–83. *Academic OneFile,* search.ebscohost.com/login.aspx?direct=true&db =edsgao&AN=edsgcl.177163353&site=eds-live.

———. *Txtng: The Gr8 Db8.* Oxford UP, 2008.

Golden, Serena. Review of *A Better Pencil*, by Dennis Baron. *Inside Higher Ed*, 18 Sept. 2009, insidehighered.com/news/2009/09/18/barron.

Shaw, Donita M., et al. "An Exploratory Investigation into the Relationship between Text Messaging and Spelling." *New England Reading Association Journal*, vol. 43, no. 1, pp. 57–62. *EBSCO Discovery Service for Marywood University*, search.ebscohost.com/login.aspx?direct=true&db=edb&AN=25648081&site=eds-live.

"Should We Worry or LOL?" *NEA Today*, Mar. 2004, p. 12. *ProQuest*, search.proquest.com/docview/198894194?accountid=42654.

Sternberg, Betty, et al. "Enhancing Adolescent Literacy Achievement through Integration of Technology in the Classroom." *Reading Research Quarterly*, vol. 42, no. 3, July–Sept. 2007, pp. 416–20. *ProQuest*, search.proquest.com/docview/212128056?accountid=42654.

"Texting, Testing Destroys Kids' Writing Style." *USA Today Magazine*, vol. 137, no. 2760, Sept. 2008, p. 8. *ProQuest*, search.proquest.com/docview/214595644?accountid=42654.

Walsh, James. "Txt Msgs Creep in2 class; Some Say That's gr8." *McClatchy-Tribune News Service*, 23 Oct. 2007. *ProQuest*, search.proquest.com/docview/456879133?accountid=42654.

Cullington's essay examines whether or not texting affects students' writing. Her information is based on both published scholarship and a small survey of students and teachers.

FRANKIE SCHEMBRI

Edible Magic

In the following report, Massachusetts Institute of Technology student Frankie Schembri explains the science behind how popcorn pops. Her essay was originally published in Angles 2016: Selected Essays from Introductory Writing Subjects at MIT.

Life is studded with little pockets of magic. These are the moments with mysterious emergent qualities, when the whole is greater than the sum of the parts, when one plus one somehow equals three. Such magic is even better when it comes in edible form.

When an unassuming little kernel of corn meets hot oil, it is transformed. It is elevated with an unmistakable "pop!" into a fluffy cloud of goodness ready to be dressed with butter, caramel, or whatever your heart desires.

This magic is called popcorn.

Popcorn exploded in popularity in the early 20th century but surprisingly only made it into movie theaters with the advent of sound films, or "talkies," in 1927. Silent films catered to a smaller, more exclusive clientele and owners worried that the sound of the snack being munched would detract from the experience (Geiling, 2013).

By the 1940s, popcorn had become an inextricable part of going   5
to the movies, and from then on, over half of the popcorn consumed yearly in America was eaten at movie theaters (Geiling, 2013). Fast-forward some 70 years and the relationship remains unbreakable.

Step into any movie theater lobby across America and your senses are bombarded with the unmistakable scent of salt and butter.

Popcorn snuck into the American household in the 1960s with Jiffy Pop, a self-contained stovetop popper including kernels, oil, and even the pan, and it flourished with the popularity of microwave ovens in the 1970s (Smith, 1999, p. 124). Popcorn cultivated an important relationship with microwaves in the latter half of the 20th century, important enough that popcorn was eventually given the rare honor of its own designated microwave button (Smith, 1999, p. 127).

"But how?" you might ask. How do these ordinary kernels magically spring to life with a little heat and oil, enchanting kids and grown-ups alike?

Like most acts of magic, popcorn's "pop" can be understood with a little science.

Botanically speaking, popcorn is a type of maize, the only domesticated subgroup in the genus *Zea*, a group of plants in the grass family. The different types of maize are classified based on their kernel's size, shape, and composition (Smith, 1999, p. 6).

Corn kernels have three main structural components. First, there is the germ (from the Latin *germen*, meaning seed or sprout), a small pocket of genetic material that is essentially a baby corn plant waiting to grow. The germ is surrounded by the endosperm (the Greek *endon*, within, and *sperma,* seed), a larger parcel of water mixed with soft and hard starch granules that make up most of the kernel's weight and would provide food for the corn plant if it were to sprout. Finally, the germ-endosperm complex is surrounded by the pericarp (from the Greek *peri,* around, and *karpos,* fruit), the hard shell that winds up stuck between your molars after you enjoy a bag of popcorn (Ghose, 2015).

Popcorn kernels are unique in that they are relatively small, they have endosperms containing a larger number of hard starch granules, and their pericarps are hard and impermeable, essentially sealing off the contents of the kernel from the outside environment. These characteristics have endowed popcorn kernels with the ability to pop (Ghose, 2015).

In an attempt to better understand the physics of popcorn, aeronautical engineer Emmanuel Virot and physicist Alexandre Ponomarenko, who seem to have also fallen under popcorn's spell (judging by the language of their published report), experimented with the temperature at which a kernel pops. As Virot and Ponomarenko (2015) explained, when heat is applied to the kernels via hot oil on a stovetop or in a microwave, the temperature of the kernels begins to rise accordingly. Most affected by this increase in heat is the water stored between the starch granules in the endosperm. Much like a bubbling pot of water brought to a boil, the water in the kernel begins to change from liquid into gas.

While liquid water is content to stay put, gaseous water in the form of steam craves space to move, but the hard shell of the pericarp effectively keeps the water trapped inside the kernel. As a result, the kernel acts like a tiny steamer and the starch granules inside are cooked into a gooey mass. As the mass gets hotter and hotter, the steam presses harder and harder on the inside surface of the kernel's shell like the hands of a million tiny creatures trapped inside a bubble (Virot & Ponomarenko, 2015).

The tension is palpable. The kernel begins to shake with anticipation. It rocks back and forth, back and forth, faster and faster, and faster still. Then finally . . . pop! The bubble bursts, the lid flies off the pot, and fireworks explode as the hard shell of the pericarp cracks and the steam breaks free from its kernel prison. The starchy goop also bubbles out into the world, where it meets cold, fresh air and rapidly hardens into spongy cloudlike shapes. Just like that, in just one-fifteenth of a second, a new piece of popcorn is born (Virot & Ponomarenko, 2015).

Virot and Ponomarenko (2015) determined that the temperature at which kernels typically pop is 180 degrees Celsius. The pair also determined that the resulting popped kernel can be up to 40 times its unpopped volume, although usually the kernel's radius merely doubles. 15

But what propels the kernel, with what Virot and Ponomarenko (2015) called "all the grace of a seasoned gymnast," into the air as it pops? When the pericarp fractures, it does so in only one place first, giving some of the steam and starchy goop a head start on escaping. The starch released first extends to create a leg of sorts, off of which the rest of the kernel springboards, launching it somersaulting into the air like an Olympic gymnast. Popcorn jumps typically only reach a height of a few centimeters, but still manage to create endless entertainment for the hungry viewer.

Where does the "pop" sound come from? Arguably the most important part of the whole experience, popcorn's characteristic noise is not, contrary to popular belief, the sound of the kernel's shell breaking open. The popping sound is created by the release of trapped water vapor resonating in the kernel, similar to how, when removed, a champagne cork makes a popping sound that resonates in the glass bottle (Virot & Ponomarenko, 2015).

Making popcorn hardly seems like an opportunity to learn about physics, but the kernels' unique transformation illustrates some principles of thermodynamics, biomechanics, and acoustics, as the properties of different materials dictate how they respond to pressure and heat.

Life is studded with little pockets of magic. From the enticing smell during a night at the movies to the rising staccato sound of a bag coming to life in your microwave, popcorn is magic-meets-science in its most delicious form. And it always leaves you hungry for more.

References

Geiling, N. (2013, October 3). Why do we eat popcorn at the movies? *Smithsonianmag.com*. https://www.smithsonianmag.com/arts-culture/why-do-we-eat-popcorn-at-the-movies-475063/

Ghose, T. (2015, February 10). *The secret acrobatics of popcorn revealed*. Live Science. https://www.livescience.com/49768-mechanics-of-popcorn.html

Smith, A. (1999). *Popped culture: A social history of popcorn in America*. University of South Carolina Press.

Virot, E., & Ponomarenko, A. (2015). Popcorn: Critical temperature, jump and sound. *Journal of the Royal Society Interface*, *12*(104). https://doi.org/10.1098/rsif.2014.1247

Schembri introduces her subject by placing it in a cultural context of the movies, Jiffy Pop, and microwave popcorn. She then distinguishes popcorn from other varieties of corn or maize and goes on to describe what happens when popcorn kernels are heated, pop, and fly into the air. To explore her subject from these various perspectives, she draws on scientific, historical, and popular sources.

JON MARCUS

The Reason College Costs More than You Think

Writing online for Time *in 2014, Hechinger Report editor Jon Marcus examines the length of time students take to graduate and how that affects the cost of getting a degree.*

When Alex Nichols started as a freshman at the University of Mississippi, he felt sure he'd earn his bachelor's degree in four years. Five years later, and Nichols is back on the Oxford, Mississippi, campus for what he hopes is truly his final semester.

"There are a lot more students staying another semester or another year than I thought there would be when I got here," Nichols says. "I meet people once a week who say, 'Yes, I'm a second-year senior,' or, 'I've been here for five years.'"

The Lyceum, the oldest building at the University of Mississippi.

They're likely as surprised as Nichols still to be toiling away in school.

Nearly nine out of 10 freshmen think they'll earn their bachelor's degrees within the traditional four years, according to a nationwide survey conducted by the Higher Education Research Institute at UCLA. But the U.S. Department of Education reports that fewer than half that many actually will. And about 45 percent won't have finished even after six years.

That means the annual cost of college, a source of so much anxiety for families and students, often overlooks the enormous additional expense of the extra time it will actually take to graduate.

"It's a huge inconvenience," says Nichols, whose college career has been prolonged for the common reason that he changed majors and took courses he ended up not needing. His athletic scholarship—Nichols was a middle-distance runner on the cross-country team—ran out after four years. "I had to get some financial help from my parents."

The average added cost of just one extra year at a four-year public university is $63,718 in tuition, fees, books, and living expenses, plus lost wages each of those many students could have been earning had

5

 academic literacies
 rhetorical situations
 genres
 fields
processes
 strategies
 research MLA / APA
media / design
readings
handbook

they finished on time, according to the advocacy group Complete College America.

A separate report by the Los Angeles–based Campaign for College Opportunity finds that the average student at a California State University campus who takes six years instead of four to earn a bachelor's degree will spend an additional $58,000 and earn $52,900 less over their lifetimes than a student who graduates on time, for a total loss of $110,900.

"The cost of college isn't just what students and their families pay in tuition or fees," says Michele Siqueiros, the organization's executive director. "It's also about time. That's the hidden cost of a college education."

So hidden that most families still unknowingly plan on four years for a bachelor's degree, says Sylvia Hurtado, director of the Higher Education Research Institute at UCLA. 10

Although the institute does not poll parents in its annual survey, "that high percentage of freshmen [who are confident they'll finish in four years] is probably reflecting their parents' expectation—'This is costing me a lot, so you're going to be out in four years.' So the students think, 'Sure, why not?' I don't think the parents even initially entertain or plan for six years or some possible outcome like that."

Yet many students almost immediately doom themselves to taking longer, since they register for fewer courses than they need to stay on track. Surveys of incoming freshmen in California and Indiana who said they expected to graduate in four years found that half signed up for fewer courses than they'd needed to meet that goal, according to a new report by the higher-education consulting firm HCM Strategists.

It's not entirely the students' fault.

More than half of community-college students are slowed down by having to retake subjects such as math and reading that they should have learned in high school, says Complete College America. And at some schools, budget cuts have made it difficult to register for the courses students do need to take. Two-thirds of students at one California State University campus weren't able to get into their required courses, according to a 2010 study by the University of California's Civil Rights Project.

Most state financial-aid programs, meanwhile, cover only four years. "They do not fund a fifth or sixth year," says Stan Jones, president of 15

Complete College America and a former Indiana commissioner of higher education. "And by that time the parents' resources and the students' resources have run out. So that fifth year is where you borrow."

Students at the most elite colleges and universities tend not to have this problem, which means that schools with some of the highest annual tuition can turn out to be relative bargains. These schools "would have a revolt if their students had to go a fifth year," Jones says. "But that recognition has really not hit the public sector yet, about the hidden cost of that extra year."

Policymakers urge speeding students through remedial classes more quickly, adding more sections of required courses so students can get in when they need them, and encouraging students to take 15 credits per semester instead of the typical 12.

Change won't come soon enough for Nichols, who is determined that it won't take more than one extra semester to finish his degree in integrated marketing communications.

"That's time you're wasting," he says, "that you could be out making money."

■■ For four more reports, see CHAPTER 63.

Marcus combines information from various research institutes, advocacy groups, surveys, and academic sources to support his argument. His statistics are given a human face by quotations from a student who is taking longer to graduate than he expected.

Key Features / Reports

A tightly focused topic. The goal of this kind of writing is to inform readers about something without digressing—and without, in general, bringing in the writer's own opinions. All three examples focus on a particular topic—texting, popping popcorn, and the cost of college—and present information about the topics evenhandedly.

Accurate, well-researched information. Reports usually require research. The kind of research depends on the topic. Sometimes internet research will suffice, though reports done for college courses may require library research to locate scholarly sources—Cullington, for example, uses various

sources available through her university library's databases. Other topics may require or benefit from field research—interviews, observations, surveys, and so on. In addition to doing library and online research, for example, Marcus interviewed a student, and Cullington conducted a survey of students and analyzed twenty samples of student writing.

A synthesis of ideas. Reports seldom rely on a single source of information. Rather, they draw on several sources, making connections among the facts and ideas found in them. For example, Schembri combines information from a magazine article and a book to provide a brief history of the growth of popcorn's popularity in the United States. Marcus compares undergraduate students' expectations of finishing college in four years with statistics showing that more than half will take longer, using information from a university study and a government report as well as an interview with a student.

Various writing strategies. Presenting information usually requires various organizing patterns—defining, comparing, classifying, explaining processes, analyzing causes and effects, and so on. Schembri explains the process governing popcorn popping and classifies different kinds of maize. Marcus analyzes the financial effects of delaying graduation, and Cullington analyzes the effects (or lack of effects) of texting on students' writing ability.

Clear definitions. Reports need to provide clear definitions of any key terms that their audience may not know. Cullington defines both *texting* and *textspeak*. Schembri defines several components of corn kernels, including the germ, endosperm, and pericarp.

Appropriate design. Reports often combine paragraphs with information presented in lists, tables, diagrams, and other illustrations. When you're presenting information, you need to think carefully about how to design it—numerical data, for instance, can be easier to understand and remember in a table than in a paragraph. Often a photograph can bring a subject to life, as does the photo on page 140, which accompanies "Edible Magic." Online reports offer the possibility of video and audio clips as well as links to source materials and more detailed information.

A GUIDE TO WRITING REPORTS

Choosing a Topic

Whether you get to choose your topic or are working with an assigned one, see if you can approach the topic from an angle that interests you.

If you get to choose. What interests you? What do you wish you knew more about? The possible topics for informational reports are limitless, but the topics that you're most likely to write well on are those that engage you. They may be academic in nature or reflect your personal interests or both. If you're not sure where to begin, here are some places to start:

- an intriguing technology: driverless cars, touchscreens, tooth whiteners
- sports: soccer, snowboarding, ultimate Frisbee, basketball
- an important world event: the Arab Spring, the fall of Rome, the Black Death
- a historical period: the African diaspora, the Middle Ages, the Ming dynasty, the Great Depression
- a common object: hoodies, gel pens, mascara, Post-it notes
- a significant environmental issue: melting Arctic ice, deer overpopulation, mercury and the fish supply
- the arts: rap, outsider art, the Crystal Bridges Museum of American Art, Savion Glover, Mary Cassatt

332–33 ○ **LIST** a few possibilities, and then choose one that you'd like to know more about—and that your audience might find interesting, too. You might start out by phrasing your topic as a question that your research will attempt to answer. For example:

How is *Google* different from *Yahoo!*?

How was the Great Pyramid constructed?

What kind of training do football referees receive?

academic literacies · rhetorical situations · genres · fields · processes · strategies · research MLA / APA · media / design · readings · handbook

If your topic is assigned. If your assignment is broad—"Explain some aspect of the U.S. government"—try focusing on a more limited topic within the larger topic: federalism, majority rule, political parties, states' rights. Even if an assignment seems to offer little flexibility—"Explain the physics of roller coasters"—your task is to decide how to research the topic, and sometimes even narrow topics can be shaped to fit your own interests and those of your audience.

Considering the Rhetorical Situation

PURPOSE	Why are you presenting this information? To teach readers about the subject? To demonstrate your research and writing skills? For some other reason?	55–56
AUDIENCE	Who will read this report? What do they already know about the topic? What background information do they need in order to understand it? Will you need to define any terms? What do they want or need to know about the topic? Why should they care about it? How can you attract their interest?	57–60
STANCE	What is your own attitude toward your subject? What interests you most about it? What about it seems important?	66–68
MEDIA / DESIGN	What medium are you using? What is the best way to present the information? Will it all be in paragraph form, or is there information that is best presented as a chart, table, or infographic? Do you need headings? Would diagrams, photographs, or other illustrations help you explain the information?	69–71

Generating Ideas and Text

Good reports share certain features that make them useful and interesting to readers. Remember that your goal is to present information clearly and accurately. Start by exploring your topic.

331–34 ◯

Explore what you already know about your topic. Write out whatever you know or want to know about your topic, perhaps by **FREEWRITING**, **LISTING**, or **CLUSTERING**. Why are you interested in this topic? What questions do you have about it? Such questions can help you decide what you'd like to focus on and how you need to direct your research efforts.

Narrow your topic. To write a good report, you need to narrow your focus—and to narrow your focus, you need to know a fair amount about your subject. If you are assigned to write on a subject like biodiversity, for example, you need to know what it is, what the key issues are, and so on. If you do, you can simply list or brainstorm possibilities, choose one, and start your research. If you don't know much about the subject, though, you need to do some research to discover focused, workable topics. This research may shape your thinking and change your focus. Start with **SOURCES** that can give you a general sense of the subject, such as a *Wikipedia* entry, a magazine article, a website, perhaps an interview with an expert. Your goal at this point is simply to find out what issues your topic might include and then to focus your efforts on an aspect of the topic you will be able to cover.

489–510 ●

Come up with a tentative thesis. Once you narrow your topic, write out a statement that explains what you plan to report or explain. A good **THESIS** is potentially interesting (to you and your readers) and limits your topic enough to make it manageable. Schembri phrases her thesis as a question: "How do these ordinary kernels magically spring to life with a little heat and oil?" Cullington frames her thesis in relation to the context surrounding her topic: "Some people believe that using these abbreviations is hindering the writing abilities of students, and others argue that texting is actually having a positive effect on writing. In fact, it seems likely that texting has no significant effect on student writing." At this point, however, you need only a tentative thesis that will help focus any research you do.

387–89 ◆

Do any necessary research, and revise your thesis. To focus your research efforts, **OUTLINE** the aspects of your topic that you expect to discuss. Identify any aspects that require additional research and develop a research plan.

335–37 ◯

academic literacies   rhetorical situations   genres   fields   processes   strategies   research MLA / APA   media / design   readings   handbook

Expect to revise your outline as you do your research, since more information will be available for some aspects of your topic than others, some may prove irrelevant to your topic, and some may turn out to be more than you need. You'll need to revisit your tentative thesis once you've done any research, to finalize your statement.

Ways of Organizing a Report

Reports can be organized in various ways. Here are three common organizational structures:

[Reports on topics that are unfamiliar to readers]

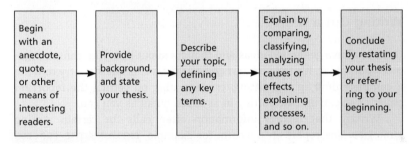

[Reports on events]

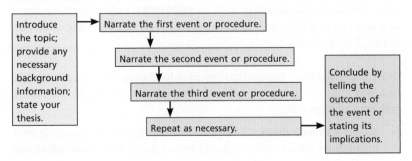

[Reports that compare and contrast]

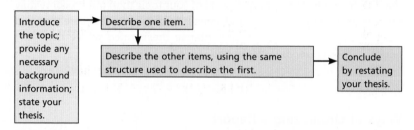

Many reports use a combination of organizational structures; don't be afraid to use whatever method of organization best suits your material and your purpose.

Writing Out a Draft

340–42 Once you have generated ideas and thought about how you want to organize your report, it's time to start **DRAFTING**. Do this quickly—try to write a complete draft in one sitting, concentrating on getting the report on paper or screen and on putting in as much detail as you can.

457–61
392–96 Writing that reports information often calls for certain writing strategies. The report on popcorn, for example, **EXPLAINS THE PROCESS** of popping, whereas the report on college costs **ANALYZES THE EFFECTS** of delaying college graduation. When you're reporting on a topic your readers 424–31 aren't familiar with, you may wish to **COMPARE** it with something more familiar; you can find useful advice on these and other writing strategies in Part 6 of this book.

373–80 Draft a **BEGINNING**.   Essays that report information often need to begin in a way that will get your audience interested in the topic. Here are a few ways of beginning:

- *Simply state your thesis.* Cullington states her thesis about texting after only a brief introduction. Opening with a thesis works well when you

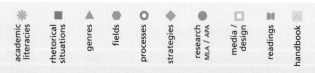

can assume your readers have enough familiarity with your topic that you don't need to give much detailed background information.

- *Start with something that will provoke readers' interest.* Marcus's report begins with an anecdote about a college student.

- *Begin with an illustrative example.* Schembri evokes the childhood wonder of popping corn before exploring its history and physics.

Draft an ENDING.   Think about what you want your readers to read last. An effective ending leaves them thinking about your topic.

380–85

- *Summarize your main points.* This is a good way to end when you've presented several key points you want readers to remember. Cullington ends this way, summarizing the debate about texting's effects and the results of her research.

- *Point out the implications of your report.* Cullington ends by affirming the importance of researched evidence when drawing conclusions not only about texting but in general.

- *Frame your report by referring to its introduction.* Marcus begins and ends his report by quoting the same student, and Schembri returns to her introductory evocation of popcorn as "little pockets of magic."

- *Tell what happened.* If you are reporting on an event, you could conclude by telling how it turns out.

Come up with a title.   You'll want a title that tells readers something about your subject—and makes them want to know more. Cullington's title, "Does Texting Affect Writing?," is a straightforward description of what's to come. Marcus suggests that his essay will disclose the reason college costs more than you think—but doesn't tell us in the title. See the chapter on **GUIDING YOUR READER** for tips on coming up with titles that are informative and enticing enough to make readers wish to read on.

386–91

Considering Matters of Design

You'll probably write the main text of your report in paragraph form, but think about what kind of information you're presenting and how you can design and format it to make it as easy as possible for your readers to understand. You might ask yourself these questions:

648–49
- What is an appropriate **FONT**? A font like Times New Roman that is easy to read in print? A font like Ariel or **Verdana** that looks good onscreen? Something else?

650–52
- Would it help your readers if you divided your report into shorter sections and added **HEADINGS**?

649–50
- Is there any information that would be easier to follow in a **LIST**?

656
- Could any of your information be summarized in a **TABLE** or **FIGURE**?

656
- Do you have any data that readers would more easily understand in the form of a bar **GRAPH**, line graph, or pie chart?

653–63
- Would **ILLUSTRATIONS** (diagrams, photos, drawings, and so on), video or audio clips, or links help you explain anything in your report?

Getting Response and Revising

The following questions can help you study your draft with a critical eye. **GETTING RESPONSE** from others is always good, and these questions can guide their reading, too. Make sure they know your purpose and audience.

348–50
- Do the title and opening sentences get readers' interest? If not, how might they do so?

- What information does this text provide, and for what purpose?

- Does the introduction explain why this information is being presented? Does it place the topic in a larger context?

- Are all key terms defined that need to be?

- Do you have any questions? Where might more explanation or an example help you understand something better?

academic literacies · rhetorical situations · genres · fields · processes · strategies · research MLA / APA · media / design · readings · handbook

- Is any information presented visually, with a chart, graph, table, drawing, or photograph? If so, is it clear how the illustration relates to the written text? Is there any text that would be more easily understood if it were presented visually?

- Is any information presented through digital media, such as hyperlinks, video clips, or audio files? If so, is the relation of these elements to the written text made clear? Would any aspect of the report be clearer if presented using such elements?

- Does the organization help make sense of the information? Does the text include description, comparison, or any other writing strategies? Does the topic or rhetorical situation call for any particular strategies that should be added?

- If the report cites any sources, are they quoted, paraphrased, or summarized effectively (and with appropriate documentation)? Is information from sources introduced with **SIGNAL PHRASES**?

  535–38

- Does the report end in a satisfying way? What are readers left thinking?

These questions should identify aspects of your report you need to work on. When it's time to **REVISE**, make sure your report appeals to your audience and achieves your purpose as successfully as possible. If you have time and want to explore alternatives, you might try **REWRITING** your draft to see if a different plan or approach might work better.

350–53

353–55

Editing and Proofreading

Readers equate correctness with the writer's competence. Once you've revised your draft, follow these guidelines for **EDITING** a report:

356–59

- Check your use of key terms. Repeating key words is acceptable in reports; using synonyms for unfamiliar words may confuse readers, while the repetition of key words or the use of clearly identified **PRONOUNS** for them can be genuinely helpful.

  HB-29–34

- Check to be sure you have **TRANSITIONS** where you need them.

  391

650–52 ☐
- If you have included **HEADINGS**, make sure they're parallel in structure and consistent in design.

653–63 ☐
- Make sure that any photos or other **ILLUSTRATIONS** have captions, that charts and graphs have headings—and that all are referred to in the main text. Use white space as necessary to separate sections of your report and to highlight graphic elements.

544–47 ●
- Check any **DOCUMENTATION** to see that it follows the appropriate style.

359–60 ○
- **PROOFREAD** and spell-check your report carefully.

Taking Stock of Your Work

- How well did you convey the information? Is it complete enough for your audience's needs?
- What strategies did you rely on, and how did they help you achieve your purpose?
- How well did you organize the report?
- How did you go about researching the information for this piece?
- How did you go about drafting this piece?
- Did you use any tables, graphs, diagrams, photographs, illustrations, or other graphics effectively?
- How did others' responses influence your writing?
- What did you do especially well?
- What could still be improved?
- What would you do differently next time?

IF YOU NEED MORE HELP

361–70 ○
185–89 ▲
233–45
See Chapter 34 if you are required to submit your report in a writing **PORTFOLIO**. See also Chapter 14 on **ABSTRACTS** if your report requires one; and Chapter 19 on **PROFILES**, a report based on firsthand research.

Arguing a Position **13**

Everything we say or do presents some kind of argument, takes some kind of position. Often we take overt positions: "Everyone in the United States is entitled to affordable health care." "The university needs to offer more language courses." "Photoshopped images should carry disclosure notices." But arguments can be less direct and specific as well, from yellow ribbons that honor U.S. troops to a yellow smiley face, which might be said to argue for a good day.

In college course work, you are constantly called on to argue positions: in an *English* class, you may argue for a certain interpretation of a poem; in a *business* course, you may argue for the merits of a flat tax; in a *linguistics* class, you may argue that English is now a global language. All of those positions are arguable—people of goodwill can agree or disagree with them and present reasons and evidence to support their positions.

This chapter provides guidelines for writing an essay that argues a position. We'll begin with three good examples, the first one annotated to point out key features of this kind of writing.

JOANNA MACKAY

Organ Sales Will Save Lives

In this essay, written for a class on ethics and politics in science, MIT student Joanna MacKay argues that the sale of human organs should be legal.

> There are thousands of people dying to buy a kidney and thousands of people dying to sell a kidney. It seems a match made in heaven. So why are we standing in the way? Governments should not ban the sale of human organs; they should regulate it. Lives should not be wasted; they should be saved.

Clear and arguable position.

157

About 350,000 Americans suffer from end-stage renal disease, a state of kidney disorder so advanced that the organ stops functioning altogether. There are no miracle drugs that can revive a failed kidney, leaving dialysis and kidney transplantation as the only possible treatments (McDonnell and Mallon, pars. 2 and 3).

Dialysis is harsh, expensive, and, worst of all, only temporary. Acting as an artificial kidney, dialysis mechanically filters the blood of a patient. It works, but not well. With treatment sessions lasting three hours, several times a week, those dependent on dialysis are, in a sense, shackled to a machine for the rest of their lives. Adding excessive stress to the body, dialysis causes patients to feel increasingly faint and tired, usually keeping them from work and other normal activities.

Kidney transplantation, on the other hand, is the closest thing to a cure that anyone could hope for. Today the procedure is both safe and reliable, causing few complications. With better technology for confirming tissue matches and new anti-rejection drugs, the surgery is relatively simple.

But those hoping for a new kidney have high hopes indeed. In the year 2000 alone, 2,583 Americans died while waiting for a kidney transplant; worldwide the number of deaths is around 50,000 (Finkel 27). With the sale of organs outlawed in almost every country, the number of living donors willing to part with a kidney for free is small. When no family member is a suitable candidate for donation, the patient is placed on a deceased donors list, relying on the organs from people dying of old age or accidents. The list is long. With over 60,000 people in line in the United States alone, the average wait for a cadaverous kidney is ten long years.

Daunted by the low odds, some have turned to an alternative solution: purchasing kidneys on the black market. For about $150,000, they can buy a fresh kidney from a healthy, living donor. There are no lines, no waits. Arranged through a broker, the entire procedure is carefully planned out. The buyer, seller, surgeons, and nurses are flown to a predetermined hospital in a foreign country. The operations are performed, and then all are flown back to their respective homes. There is no follow-up, no paperwork to sign (Finkel 27).

The illegal kidney trade is attractive not only because of the promptness but also because of the chance at a living donor. An organ from a cadaver will most likely be old or damaged, estimated

5

Necessary background information.

to function for about ten years at most. A kidney from a living donor can last over twice as long. Once a person's transplanted cadaverous kidney stops functioning, he or she must get back on the donor list, this time probably at the end of the line. A transplanted living kidney, however, could last a person a lifetime.

While there may seem to be a shortage of kidneys, in reality there is a surplus. In third-world countries, there are people willing to do anything for money. In such extreme poverty these people barely have enough to eat, living in shacks and sleeping on dirt floors. Eager to pay off debts, they line up at hospitals, willing to sell a kidney for about $1,000. The money will go toward food and clothing, or perhaps to pay for a family member's medical operation (Goyal et al. 1590–91). Whatever the case, these people need the money.

Reason (donors need the money) supported by evidence.

There is certainly a risk in donating a kidney, but this risk is not great enough to be outlawed. Millions of people take risks to their health every day for money, or simply for enjoyment. As explained in *The Lancet*, "If the rich are free to engage in dangerous sports for pleasure, or dangerous jobs for high pay, it is difficult to see why the poor who take the lesser risk of kidney selling for greater rewards . . . should be thought so misguided as to need saving from themselves" (Radcliffe-Richards et al. 1951). Studies have shown that a person can live a healthy life with only one kidney. While these studies might not apply to the poor living under strenuous conditions in unsanitary environments, the risk is still theirs to take. These people have decided that their best hope for money is to sell a kidney. How can we deny them the best opportunity they have?

Counterargument (donating a kidney is risky) acknowledged.

Some agree with Pope John Paul II that the selling of organs is morally wrong and violates "the dignity of the human person" (qtd. in Finkel 26), but this is a belief professed by healthy and affluent individuals. Are we sure that the peasants of third-world countries agree? The morals we hold are not absolute truths. We have the responsibility to protect and help those less fortunate, but we cannot let our own ideals cloud the issues at hand.

Counterargument (selling organs is wrong) acknowledged.

In a legal kidney transplant, everybody gains except the donor. The doctors and nurses are paid for the operation, the patient receives a new kidney, but the donor receives nothing. Sure, the donor will have the warm, uplifting feeling associated with helping a fellow human being, but this is not enough reward for most people to part with a

Reason (altruism is not enough) supported by evidence.

piece of themselves. In an ideal world, the average person would be altruistic enough to donate a kidney with nothing expected in return. The real world, however, is run by money. We pay men for donating sperm, and we pay women for donating ova, yet we expect others to give away an entire organ for no compensation. If the sale of organs were allowed, people would have a greater incentive to help save the life of a stranger.

While many argue that legalizing the sale of organs will exploit the poorer people of third-world countries, the truth of the matter is that this is already the case. Even with the threat of a $50,000 fine and five years in prison (Finkel 26), the current ban has not been successful in preventing illegal kidney transplants. The kidneys of the poor are still benefiting only the rich. While the sellers do receive most of the money promised, the sum is too small to have any real impact on their financial situation. A study in India discovered that in the long run, organ sellers suffer. In the illegal kidney trade, nobody has the interests of the seller at heart. After selling a kidney, their state of living actually worsens. While the $1,000 pays off one debt, it is not enough to relieve the donor of the extreme poverty that placed them in debt in the first place (Goyal et al. 1591).

Counterargument (poor people are exploited) acknowledged.

These impoverished people do not need stricter and harsher penalties against organ selling to protect them, but quite the opposite. If the sale of organs were made legal, it could be regulated and closely monitored by the government and other responsible organizations. Under a regulated system, education would be incorporated into the application process. Before deciding to donate a kidney, the seller should know the details of the operation and any hazards involved. Only with an understanding of the long-term physical health risks can a person make an informed decision (Radcliffe-Richards et al. 1951).

Reason (regulating organ sales would lead to better decisions).

Regulation would ensure that the seller is fairly compensated. In the illegal kidney trade, surgeons collect most of the buyer's money in return for putting their careers on the line. The brokers arranging the procedure also receive a modest cut, typically around ten percent. If the entire practice were legalized, more of the money could be directed toward the person who needs it most, the seller. By eliminating the middleman and allowing the doctors to settle for lower prices, a regulated system would benefit all those in need of a kidney, both rich

Reason (fairness to sellers) followed by evidence.

academic literacies | rhetorical situations | genres | fields | processes | strategies | research MLA / APA | media / design | readings | handbook

and poor. According to Finkel, the money that would otherwise be spent on dialysis treatment could not only cover the charge of a kidney transplant at no cost to the recipient, but also reward the donor with as much as $25,000 (32). This money could go a long way for people living in the poverty of third-world countries.

Critics fear that controlling the lawful sale of organs would be too 15 difficult, but could it be any more difficult than controlling the unlaw- ful sale of organs? Governments have tried to eradicate the kidney market for decades to no avail. Maybe it is time to try something else. When "desperately wanted goods" are made illegal, history has shown that there is more opportunity for corruption and exploitation than if those goods were allowed (Radcliffe-Richards et al. 1951). (Just look at the effects of the prohibition of alcohol, for example.) Legalization of organ sales would give governments the authority and the opportunity to closely monitor these live kidney operations.

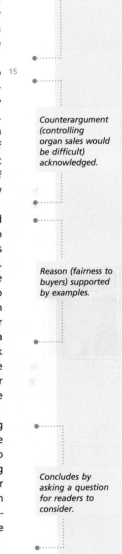

Counterargument (controlling organ sales would be difficult) acknowledged.

Regulation would also protect the buyers. Because of the need for secrecy, the current illegal method of obtaining a kidney has no contracts and, therefore, no guarantees. Since what they are doing is illegal, the buyers have nobody to turn to if something goes wrong. There is nobody to point the finger at, nobody to sue. While those participating in the kidney market are breaking the law, they have no other choice. Without a new kidney, end-stage renal disease will soon kill them. Desperate to survive, they are forced to take the only offer available. It seems immoral to first deny them the opportunity of a new kidney and then to leave them stranded at the mercy of the black market. Without laws regulating live kidney transplants, these people are subject to possibly hazardous procedures. Instead of turning our backs, we have the power to ensure that these operations are done safely and efficiently for both the recipient and the donor.

Reason (fairness to buyers) supported by examples.

Those suffering from end-stage renal disease would do anything for the chance at a new kidney, take any risk or pay any price. There are other people so poor that the sale of a kidney is worth the profit. Try to tell someone that they have to die from kidney failure because selling a kidney is morally wrong. Then turn around and try to tell another person that they have to remain in poverty for that same reason. In matters of life and death, our stances on moral issues must be reevalu- ated. If legalized and regulated, the sale of human organs would save lives. Is it moral to sentence thousands to unnecessary deaths?

Concludes by asking a question for readers to consider.

Works Cited

Finkel, Michael. "This Little Kidney Went to Market." *The New York Times Magazine,* 27 May 2001, pp. 26+.

Goyal, Madhav, et al. "Economic and Health Consequences of Selling a Kidney in India." *Journal of the American Medical Association,* vol. 288, 2002, pp. 1589–92.

McDonnell, Michael B., and William K. Mallon. "Kidney Transplant." *eMedicine Health,* 18 Aug. 2008, www.emedicinehealth.com/articles/24500-1.asp.

Radcliffe-Richards, J., et al. "The Case for Allowing Kidney Sales." *The Lancet,* vol. 351, no. 9120, 27 June 1998, pp. 1950–52.

MacKay clearly states her position at the beginning of her text: "Governments should not ban the sale of human organs; they should regulate it." Her argument appeals to her readers' sense of fairness; when kidney sales are legalized and regulated, both sellers and buyers will benefit from the transaction. She uses MLA style to document her sources.

NICHOLAS KRISTOF

Our Blind Spot about Guns

In this essay, which first appeared in the New York Times *in 2014, columnist Nicholas Kristof argues that if guns and their owners were regulated in the same way that cars and their drivers are, thousands of lives could be saved each year.*

If we had the same auto fatality rate today that we had in 1921, by my calculations we would have 715,000 Americans dying annually in vehicle accidents.

Instead, we've reduced the fatality rate by more than 95 percent— not by confiscating cars, but by regulating them and their drivers sensibly.

We could have said, "Cars don't kill people. People kill people," and there would have been an element of truth to that. Many accidents are a result of alcohol consumption, speeding, road rage or driver distraction. Or we could have said, "It's pointless because even if you regulate cars, then people will just run each other down with bicycles," and that, too, would have been partly true.

Yet, instead, we built a system that protects us from ourselves. This saves hundreds of thousands of lives a year and is a model of what we should do with guns in America.

Whenever I write about the need for sensible regulation of guns, some readers jeer: *Cars kill people, too, so why not ban cars? Why are you so hypocritical as to try to take away guns from law-abiding people when you don't seize cars?*

That question is a reflection of our national blind spot about guns. The truth is that we regulate cars quite intelligently, instituting evidence-based measures to reduce fatalities. Yet the gun lobby is too strong, or our politicians too craven, to do the same for guns. So guns and cars now each kill more than 30,000 in America every year.

One constraint, the argument goes, is the Second Amendment. Yet the paradox is that a bit more than a century ago, there was no universally recognized individual right to bear arms in the United States, but there was widely believed to be a "right to travel" that allowed people to drive cars without regulation.

A court struck down an early attempt to require driver's licenses, and initial attempts to set speed limits or register vehicles were met with resistance and ridicule. When authorities in New York City sought in 1899 to ban horseless carriages in the parks, the idea was lambasted in the *New York Times* as "devoid of merit" and "impossible to maintain."

Yet, over time, it became increasingly obvious that cars were killing and maiming people, as well as scaring horses and causing accidents. As a distinguished former congressman, Robert Cousins, put it in 1910: "Pedestrians are menaced every minute of the days and nights by a wanton recklessness of speed, crippling and killing people at a rate that is appalling."

Courts and editorial writers alike saw the carnage and agreed that something must be done. By the 1920s, courts routinely accepted driver's license requirements, car registration and other safety measures.

That continued in recent decades with requirements of seatbelts and air bags, padded dashboards and better bumpers. We cracked down on drunken drivers and instituted graduated licensing for young people, while also improving road engineering to reduce accidents. The upshot is that there is now just over 1 car fatality per 100 million miles driven.

Yet as we've learned to treat cars intelligently, we've gone in the opposite direction with guns. In his terrific new book, *The Second Amendment: A Biography,* Michael Waldman, the president of the Brennan Center for Justice at the New York University School of Law, notes that "gun control laws were ubiquitous" in the nineteenth century. Visitors to Wichita, Kansas, for example, were required to check their revolvers at police headquarters.

And Dodge City, symbol of the Wild West? A photo shows a sign on the main street in 1879 warning: "The Carrying of Fire Arms Strictly Prohibited."

Dodge City, Kansas, 1879. The sign reads, "The Carrying of Fire Arms strictly prohibited."

academic literacies · rhetorical situations · genres · fields · processes · strategies · research MLA / APA · media / design · readings · handbook

The National Rifle Association supported reasonable gun control for most of its history and didn't even oppose the landmark Gun Control Act of 1968. But, since then, most attempts at safety regulation have stalled or gone backward, and that makes the example of cars instructive.

"We didn't ban cars, or send black helicopters to confiscate them," notes Waldman. "We made cars safer: air bags, seatbelts, increasing the drinking age, lowering the speed limit. There are similar technological and behavioral fixes that can ease the toll of gun violence, from expanded background checks to trigger locks to smart guns that recognize a thumbprint, just like my iPhone does." 15

Some of these should be doable. A Quinnipiac poll this month found 92 percent support for background checks for all gun buyers.

These steps won't eliminate gun deaths any more than seatbelts eliminate auto deaths. But if a combination of measures could reduce the toll by one-third, that would be 10,000 lives saved every year.

A century ago, we reacted to deaths and injuries from unregulated vehicles by imposing sensible safety measures that have saved hundreds of thousands of lives a year. Why can't we ask politicians to be just as rational about guns?

Kristof argues that because regulating cars has made them much safer, guns should be regulated similarly. He supports his argument with data on fatality rates and the history of automobile and gun regulation in the United States.

MOLLY WORTHEN

U Can't Talk to Ur Professor Like This

Molly Worthen is an assistant professor of history at the University of North Carolina–Chapel Hill and a frequent contributor to the New York Times, *where this essay arguing that manners and etiquette matter in the college classroom originally appeared.*

At the start of my teaching career, when I was fresh out of graduate school, I briefly considered trying to pass myself off as a cool professor. Luckily, I soon came to my senses and embraced my true identity as a young fogey. After one too many students called me by my first name and sent me email that resembled a drunken late-night *Facebook* post, I took a very fogeyish step. I began attaching a page on etiquette to every syllabus: basic rules for how to address teachers and write polite, grammatically correct emails.

Over the past decade or two, college students have become far more casual in their interactions with faculty members. My colleagues around the country grumble about students' sloppy emails and blithe informality.

Mark Tomforde, a math professor at the University of Houston who has been teaching for almost two decades, added etiquette guidelines to his website. "When students started calling me by my first name, I felt that was too far, and I've got to say something," he told me. "There were also the emails written like text messages. Worse than the text abbreviations was the level of informality, with no address or signoff."

His webpage covers matters ranging from appropriate email addresses (if you're still using "cutie_pie_98@hotmail.com," then "it's time to retire that address") to how to be gracious when making a request ("do not make demands").

Sociologists who surveyed undergraduate syllabuses from 2004 and 2010 found that in 2004, 14 percent addressed issues related to classroom etiquette; six years later, that number had more than doubled, to 33 percent. This phenomenon crosses socio-economic lines. My colleagues at Stanford gripe as much as the ones who teach at state schools, and students from more privileged backgrounds are often the worst offenders.

Why are so many teachers bent out of shape because a student fails to call them "Professor" or neglects to proofread an email? Are academics really that insecure? Is this just another case of scapegoating millennials for changes in the broader culture?

Don't dismiss these calls for old-fashioned courtesy as a case of fragile ivory tower egos or misplaced nostalgia. There is a strong liberal case for using formal manners and titles to ensure respect for all university professionals, regardless of age, race or gender. More important, doing so helps defend the university's dearest values at a time when they are under continual assault.

It's true that the conventions that have, until recently, ruled higher education did not rule from time immemorial. Two centuries ago, students often rejected expectations of deference. In 1834, Harvard

students rebelled when some of their classmates were punished for refusing to memorize their Latin textbook. They broke the windows of a teacher's apartment and destroyed his furniture. When the president of the college cracked down and suspended the entire sophomore class, the juniors retaliated by hanging and burning him in effigy and setting off a rudimentary explosive in the campus chapel.

Later in the 19th century, etiquette manuals proliferated in bookstores, and Americans began to emphasize elaborate social protocols. As colleges expanded and academic disciplines professionalized, they mimicked the hierarchical cultures of the German research universities, where students cowered before "Herr Professor Doktor."

The historian John Kasson has noted that back then, formal etiquette was not aimed at ensuring respect for all. It was, in part, a system to enforce boundaries of race, class and gender at a time when the growth of cities and mass transit forced Americans into close quarters with strangers. Codes of behavior served "as checks against a fully democratic order and in support of special interests, institutions of privilege and structures of domination," he writes in his book *Rudeness and Civility*.

But today, on the other side of the civil rights revolution, formal titles and etiquette can be tools to protect disempowered minorities and ensure that the modern university belongs to all of us. Students seem more inclined to use casual forms of address with professors who are young, nonwhite and female—some of whom have responded by becoming vocal defenders of old-fashioned propriety.

Angela Jackson-Brown, a professor of English at Ball State University in Muncie, Ind., told me that "most of my students will acknowledge that I'm the first and only black teacher they've ever had." Insisting on her formal title is important, she said: "I feel the extra burden of having to go in from Day 1 and establish that I belong here."

When Professor Jackson-Brown began teaching in the 1990s, most students respected her authority. But in recent years, that deference has waned (she blames the informality of social media). "I go out of my way now to not give them access to my first name," she said. "On every syllabus, it states clearly: 'Please address me as Professor Jackson-Brown.'"

She linked this policy to the atmosphere of mutual respect that she cultivates in her classes. These days, simply being considerate can feel like a political act. "After this recent election, I've had several female students come to me and say, 'I'm noticing differences in how

10

men are treating me.' It's heartbreaking," she said. "We're trying to set standards for them that they may not see outside the classroom, places where you'd think there would be decorum."

This logic resonates with some students. "Having these titles forces everyone to give that respect," Lyndah Lovell, a graduating senior at the College of William & Mary in Williamsburg, Va., said. "They know they have to use these manners with everyone. Even if the underlying thoughts of prejudice will still be there to some extent, you give these thoughts less power." 15

Insisting on traditional etiquette is also simply good pedagogy. It's a teacher's job to correct sloppy prose, whether in an essay or an email. And I suspect that most of the time, students who call faculty members by their first names and send slangy messages are not seeking a more casual rapport. They just don't know they should do otherwise—no one has bothered to explain it to them. Explaining the rules of professional interaction is not an act of condescension; it's the first step in treating students like adults.

That said, the teacher-student relationship depends on a special kind of inequality. "Once I refer to them as I would my best friend, I eliminate that boundary of clarity," Ms. Lovell told me. She recalled how awkward she felt when the head of the research lab where she worked asked undergraduates to call him Willy. "All my friends were saying: 'Oh, man, do we do this? He has a Ph.D. He's a professor. Is it O.K. to do this?' Sometimes I do, but he's a great mentor, and it's confusing. A lot of us like to preserve that distance."

Alexis Delgado, a sophomore at the University of Rochester, is skeptical of professors who make a point of insisting on their title. "I always think it's a power move," she told me. "Just because someone gave you a piece of paper that says you're smart doesn't mean you can communicate those ideas to me. I reserve the right to judge if you're a good professor."

But she ruefully recalled one young professor who made the mistake of telling the class that he didn't care if they used his first name. "He didn't realize how far it would go, and we all thought, this is awkward," she said. "I had no desire to be friends. I only wanted to ask questions."

During office hours, we have frank conversations about career choices, mental health crises and family tribulations. But the last thing most students want from a mentor is the pretense of chumminess. 20

academic literacies   rhetorical situations   genres   fields   processes   strategies   research MLA / APA   media / design   readings   handbook

Ms. Lovell said the very act of communicating more formally helps her get some distance on a personal problem. "When I explain my difficulties and struggles, I try to explain in a mature way," she said. "I want to know: How would someone older than me think through this?"

The facile egalitarianism of the first-name basis can impede good teaching and mentoring, but it also presents a more insidious threat. It undermines the message that academic titles are meant to convey: esteem for learning. The central endeavor of higher education is not the pursuit of money or fame but knowledge. "There needs to be some understanding that degrees mean something," Professor Jackson-Brown said. "Otherwise, why are we encouraging them to get an education?"

The values of higher education are not the values of the commercial, capitalist paradigm. At a time when corporate executives populate university boards and politicians demand proof of a diploma's immediate cash value, this distinction needs vigilant defense.

The erosion of etiquette encourages students to view faculty members as a bunch of overeducated customer service agents. "More and more, students view the process of going to college as a business transaction," Dr. Tomforde, the math professor, told me. "They see themselves as a customer, and they view knowledge as a physical thing where they pay money and I hand them the knowledge—so if they don't do well on a test, they think I haven't kept up my side of the business agreement." He added, "They view professors in a way similar to the person behind the counter getting their coffee."

But if American culture in general—including many work- 25 places—has become less formal, are professors doing students a disservice by insisting on old-fashioned manners?

When Anna Lewis left a Ph.D. program in English to work at a technology firm, she had to learn to operate in a different culture. Yet she has noticed that the informality of the tech industry can mislead new millennial employees.

"They see they can call everyone from the C.E.O. down by their first name, and that can be confusing—because what they often don't realize is that there's still a high standard of professionalism," she told me. "At the intern level, these things are basic, but they require reminders: show up to meetings on time; be aware that you, yourself, are fully responsible for your work schedule. No one is going to tell you to attend a meeting." In other words, young graduates mistake informality for license to act unprofessionally.

"There is some value in being schooled in more formal etiquette, developing personal and professional accountability, a work ethic and a level of empathy, which is very much valued in the tech industry," Ms. Lewis said.

Here's an analogy: We should teach students traditional etiquette for the same reason most great abstract painters first mastered figurative painting. In order to abandon or riff on a form, you have to get the hang of its underlying principles.

That means that professors should take the time to explain these   30 principles, making it clear that learning how to write a professional email and relate to authority figures is not just preparation for a job after graduation. The real point is to stand up for the values that have made our universities the guardians of civilization.

And if you're going to write an angry email telling me how wrong I am, I beg you: Please proofread it before you hit "send."

For four more arguments, see CHAPTER 64.

Worthen argues that using "formal manners and titles" shows respect for both academic professionals and the ideals for which they stand, protects minorities and women, and is part of a complete education. Much of the support for her position is in the form of testimony from college teachers and students.

Key Features / Arguments

A clear and arguable position. At the heart of every argument is a claim with which people may reasonably disagree. Some claims are not arguable because they're completely subjective, matters of taste or opinion ("I hate sauerkraut"), because they are a matter of fact ("The first *Star Wars* movie came out in 1977"), or because they are based on belief or faith ("There is life after death"). To be arguable, a position must reflect one of at least two points of view, making reasoned argument necessary: Guns should (or should not) be regulated; selling human organs should be legal (or illegal). In college writing, you

will often argue not that a position is correct but that it is plausible—that it is reasonable, supportable, and worthy of being taken seriously.

Necessary background information. Sometimes we need to provide some background on a topic we are arguing so that readers can understand what is being argued. MacKay establishes the need for kidney donors before launching her argument for legalizing the selling of organs; Kristof describes the history of automobile regulation.

Good reasons. By itself, a position does not make an argument; the argument comes when a writer offers reasons to back up the position. There are many kinds of good reasons. Kristof makes his argument by comparing cars to guns. MacKay bases her argument in favor of legalizing the sale of human organs on the grounds that doing so would save more lives, that impoverished people should be able to make risky choices, and that regulation would protect such people who currently sell their organs on the black market as well as desperate buyers.

Convincing evidence. Once you've given reasons for your position, you then need to offer evidence for your reasons: facts, statistics, expert testimony, anecdotal evidence, case studies, textual evidence. All three arguments use a mix of these types of evidence. MacKay cites statistics about Americans who die from renal failure to support her argument for legalizing organ sales. Kristof shows how regulating cars led to dramatic decreases in driving deaths and injuries. Worthen offers testimony from several college faculty and students who assert the value of etiquette and manners in the classroom.

Appeals to readers' values. Effective arguers try to appeal to readers' values and emotions. MacKay appeals to basic values of compassion and fairness. These are deeply held values that we may not think about very much and as a result may see as common ground we share with the writers. And some of MacKay's evidence appeals to emotion—her descriptions of people dying from kidney disease and of poor people selling their organs are likely to evoke an emotional response in many readers.

A trustworthy tone. Arguments can stand or fall on the way readers perceive the writer. Very simply, readers need to trust the person who's making the argument. One way of winning this trust is by demonstrating that you know what you're talking about. Kristof offers plenty of facts to show his knowledge of the history of automotive regulation—and he does so in a self-assured tone. There are many other ways of establishing yourself (and your argument) as trustworthy—by showing that you have some experience with your subject, that you're fair, and of course that you're honest.

Careful consideration of other positions. No matter how reasonable and careful we are in arguing our positions, others may disagree or offer counterarguments. We need to consider those other views and to acknowledge and, if possible, refute them in our written arguments. MacKay, for example, acknowledges that some believe that selling organs is unethical, but she counters that it's usually healthy, affluent people who say this—not people who need either an organ or the money they could get by selling one.

A GUIDE TO WRITING ARGUMENTS

Choosing a Topic

A fully developed argument requires significant work and time, so choosing a topic in which you're interested is very important. Students often find that widely debated topics such as "animal rights" or "abortion" can be difficult to write on because they don't feel any personal connection to them. Better topics include those that

- interest you right now
- are focused but not too narrowly
- have some personal connection to your life

331–39 ○ One good way to **GENERATE IDEAS** for a topic that meets those three criteria is to explore your own roles in life.

academic literacies · rhetorical situations · genres · fields · processes · strategies · research MLA / APA · media / design · readings · handbook

Start with your roles in life. Make four columns with the headings "Personal," "Family," "Public," and "School." Then **LIST** the roles you play that relate to it. Here is a list one student wrote:

332–33

Personal	Family	Public	School
gamer	son	voter	college student
dog owner	younger	homeless-shelter volunteer	work-study employee
old-car owner	brother	American	dorm resident
male	grandson	resident of Texas	primary-education major
white			
middle class			

Identify issues that interest you. Think, then, about issues or controversies that may concern you as a member of one or more of those groups. For instance, as a primary-education major, this student cares about the controversy over whether teachers' jobs should be focused on preparing kids for high-stakes standardized tests. As a college student, he cares about the costs of a college education. Issues that stem from these subjects could include the following: Should student progress be measured by standardized tests? Should college cost less than it does?

Pick four or five of the roles you list. In 5 or 10 minutes, identify issues that concern or affect you as a member of each of those roles. It might help to word each issue as a question starting with *Should*.

Frame your topic as a problem. Most position papers address issues that are subjects of ongoing debate—their solutions aren't easy, and people disagree on which ones are best. Posing your topic as a problem can help you think about the topic, find an issue that's suitable to write about, and find a clear focus for your essay.

For example, if you wanted to write an argument on the lack of student parking at your school, you could frame your topic as one of several problems: What causes the parking shortage? Why are the university's parking garages and lots limited in their capacity? What might alleviate the shortage?

Choose one issue to write about. Remember that the issue should be interesting to you and have some connection to your life. It is a tentative choice; if you find later that you have trouble writing about it, simply go back to your list of roles or issues and choose another.

Considering the Rhetorical Situation

55–56 **PURPOSE**
Do you want to persuade your audience to do something? Change their minds? Consider alternative views? Accept your position as plausible—see that you have thought carefully about an issue and researched it appropriately?

57–60 **AUDIENCE**
Who is your intended audience? What do they likely know and believe about this issue? How personal is it for them? To what extent are they likely to agree or disagree with you—and with one another? Why? What common ground can you find with them?

66–68 **STANCE**
What's your attitude toward your topic, and why? How do you want your audience to perceive your attitude? How do you want your audience to perceive you? As an authority on your topic? As someone much like them? As calm? reasonable? impassioned or angry? something else?

69–71 **MEDIA/DESIGN**
What media will you use, and how do your media affect your argument? Does your print or online argument call for photos or charts? If you're giving an oral presentation, should you put your reasons and support on slides? If you're writing electronically, should you include audio or video evidence or links to counterarguments or your sources?

Generating Ideas and Text

Most essays that successfully argue a position share certain features that make them interesting and persuasive. Remember that your goal is to stake out a position and convince your readers that it is plausible.

Explore what you already know about the issue. Write out whatever you know about the issue by **FREEWRITING** or as a **LIST** or **OUTLINE**. Why are you interested in this topic? What is your position on it at this point, and why? What aspect do you think you'd like to focus on? Where do you need to focus your research efforts? This activity can help you discover what more you need to learn. Chances are you'll need to learn a lot more about the issue before you even decide what position to take.

331–32
335–37

Do some research. At this point, try to get an overview. Start with one **GENERAL SOURCE** of information that will give you a sense of the ins and outs of your issue, one that isn't overtly biased. *The Atlantic, Time, Slate*, and other online newspapers and magazines can be good starting points on current issues. For some issues, you may need to **INTERVIEW** an expert. For example, one student who wanted to write about chemical abuse of animals at 4-H competitions interviewed an experienced show competitor. Use your overview source to find out the main questions raised about your issue and to get some idea about the various ways in which you might argue it.

498–99

506–7

Explore the issue strategically. Most issues may be argued from many different perspectives. You'll probably have some sense of the different views that exist on your issue, but you should explore multiple perspectives before deciding on your position. The following methods are good ways of exploring issues:

- As a matter of **DEFINITION**. What is it? How should it be defined? How can *organic* or *genetically modified food* be defined? How do proponents of *organic food* define it—and how do they define *genetically modified food*? How do advocates of *genetically modified food* define it—and how do they define *organic food*? Considering such definitions is one way to identify different perspectives on the topic.

432–42

- As a matter of **CLASSIFICATION**. Can the issue be divided into categories? Are there different kinds of, or different ways of, producing organic foods and genetically modified foods? Do different categories suggest particular positions or perhaps a way of supporting a certain position? Are there other ways of categorizing foods?

418–23

424–31

- As a matter of **COMPARISON**. Is one subject being considered better than another? Is organic food healthier or safer than genetically modified food? Is genetically modified food healthier or safer than organic? Is the answer somewhere in the middle?

457–61

- As a matter of **PROCESS**. Should somebody do something? What? Should people buy and eat more organic food? More genetically modified food? Should they buy and eat some of each?

Reconsider whether the issue can be argued. Is this issue worth discussing? Why is it important to you and to others? What difference will it make if one position or another prevails? Is it **ARGUABLE**? At this point, you want to be sure that your topic is worth arguing about.

397–417

Draft a thesis. Having explored the possibilities, decide your position, and write it out as a complete sentence. For example:

> Parents should be required to have their children vaccinated.
>
> Pod-based coffeemakers should be banned.
>
> Genetically modified foods should not be permitted in the United States.

Qualify your thesis. Rather than taking a strict pro or con position, in most cases you'll want to **QUALIFY YOUR POSITION**—in certain circumstances, with certain conditions, with these limitations, and so on. This is not to say that we should settle, give in, sell out; rather, it is to say that our position may not be the only "correct" one and that other positions may be valid as well. **QUALIFYING YOUR THESIS** also makes your topic manageable by limiting it. For example:

399

388–89

> Parents should be required to have their children vaccinated, with only medical exemptions allowed.
>
> Pod-based coffeemakers should be banned unless the pods are recyclable.
>
> Genetically modified foods should not be permitted in the United States if a link between GMOs and resistance to antibiotics is proven.

academic literacies · rhetorical situations · genres · fields · processes · strategies · research MLA / APA · media / design · readings · handbook

Come up with good reasons. Once you have a thesis, you need to come up with good **REASONS** to convince your readers that it's plausible. Write out your position, and then list several reasons. For instance, if your thesis is that pod-based coffeemakers should be banned, two of your reasons might be:

400–401

> The pods cannot be recycled.
>
> Other methods of making coffee are more environmentally sound.

Think about which reasons are best for your purposes. Which seem the most persuasive? Which are most likely to be accepted by your audience? Which seem to matter the most now? If your list of reasons is short or you think you'll have trouble developing them enough to write an appropriate essay, this is a good time to rethink your topic—before you've invested too much time in it.

Develop support for your reasons. Next you have to come up with **EVIDENCE** to support your reasons: facts, statistics, examples, testimony by authorities and experts, anecdotal evidence, scenarios, case studies and observation, and textual evidence. For some topics, you may want or need to use evidence in visual form like photos, graphs, and charts; online, you could also use video or audio evidence and links to evidence in other websites.

401–8

What counts as evidence varies across audiences. Statistical evidence may be required in certain disciplines but not in others; anecdotes may be accepted as evidence in some courses but not in engineering. Some audiences will be persuaded by emotional appeals while others will not. For example, if you argue that foods produced from genetically modified organisms (GMOs) should be allowed to be sold because they're safe, you could support that reason with *facts*: GMOs are tested thoroughly by three separate U.S. government agencies. Or you could support it with *statistics*: A study of 29 years of data on livestock fed GMO feed found that GMO-fed cattle had no adverse health effects on people who ate them. *Expert testimony* might include R. E. Goodman of the Department of Food Science and Technology at the University of Nebraska–Lincoln, who writes that "there is an absence of proof of harm to consumers from commercially available GMOs."

Identify other positions.   Now think about positions other than yours and the reasons people are likely to give for those positions. Be careful to represent their points of view as accurately and fairly as you can. Then decide whether you need to acknowledge or to refute each position.

Acknowledging other positions.   Some positions can't be refuted but are too important to ignore, so you need to **ACKNOWLEDGE** concerns and objections they raise to show that you've considered other perspectives. For example, in an essay arguing that vacations are necessary to maintain good health, medical writer Alina Tugend acknowledges that "in some cases, these trips—particularly with entire families in tow—can be stressful in their own way. The joys of a holiday can also include lugging around a ridiculous amount of paraphernalia, jet-lagged children sobbing on airplanes, hotels that looked wonderful on the Web but are in reality next to a construction site." Tugend's acknowledgment moderates her position and makes her argument appear more reasonable.

411 ◆

Refuting other positions.   State the position as clearly and as fairly as you can, and then **REFUTE** it by showing why you believe it is wrong. Perhaps the reasoning is faulty or the supporting evidence inadequate. Acknowledge the merits of the position, if any, but emphasize its shortcomings. Avoid the **FALLACY** of attacking the person holding the position or bringing up a competing position that no one seriously entertains.

413–14 ◆

414–16 ◆

Ways of Organizing an Argument

Readers need to be able to follow the reasoning of your argument from beginning to end; your task is to lead them from point to point as you build your case. Sometimes you'll want to give all the reasons for your argument first, followed by discussion of any other positions. Alternatively, you might discuss each reason and any opposing arguments together.

academic literacies   rhetorical situations   genres   fields   processes   strategies   research MLA / APA   media / design   readings   handbook

[Reasons to support your argument, followed by opposing arguments]

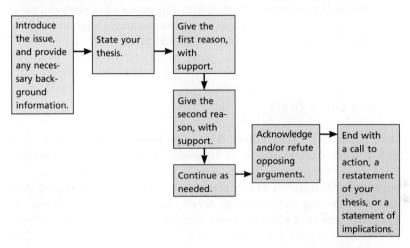

[Reason/opposing argument, reason/opposing argument]

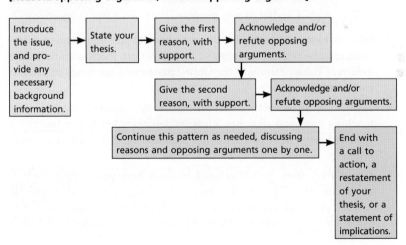

Consider carefully the order in which you discuss your reasons. Usually what comes last makes the strongest impression on readers and what comes in the middle the least impression, so you might want to put your most important or strongest reasons first and last.

Writing Out a Draft

340–42 ◉
Once you have generated ideas, done some research, and thought about how you want to organize your argument, it's time to start **DRAFTING**. Your goal in the initial draft is to develop your argument—you can fill in support and transitions as you revise. You may want to write your first draft in one sitting, so that you can develop your reasoning from beginning to end. Or you may write the main argument first and the introduction and conclusion after you've drafted the body of the essay; many writers find that beginning and ending an essay are the hardest tasks they face.
373–85 ◆
Here is some advice on how you might **BEGIN AND END** your argument:

Draft a beginning.   There are various ways to begin an argument essay, depending on your audience and purpose. Here are a few suggestions:

- *Offer background information.* You may need to give your readers information to help them understand your position. MacKay outlines the extent of kidney failure in the United States and the limits of dialysis as treatment.

- *Begin with an anecdote.* Worthen starts by summarizing her early teaching days and how her students' behavior led her to become a "young fogey" who instructed her students on classroom and email etiquette.

- *Define a key term.* You may need to show how you're using certain keywords. MacKay, for example, defines *end-stage renal disease* as "a state of kidney disorder so advanced that the organ stops function-432–42 ◆ing altogether," a **DEFINITION** that is central to her argument.

- *Begin with something that will get readers' attention.* MacKay begins emphatically: "There are thousands of people dying to buy a kidney and thousands of people dying to sell a kidney . . . So why are we standing in the way?"
- *Explain the context for your position.* All arguments are part of a larger, ongoing conversation, so you might begin by showing how your position fits into the arguments others have made. Kristof places his argument about guns in the **CONTEXT** of government regulation of other dangerous technologies.

▲ 114

Draft an ending.   Your conclusion is the chance to wrap up your argument in such a way that readers will remember what you've said. Here are a few ways of concluding an argument essay:

- *Summarize your main points.* Especially when you've presented a complex argument, it can help readers to **SUMMARIZE** your main point. MacKay sums up her argument with the sentence "If legalized and regulated, the sale of human organs would save lives."

● 534–35

- *Call for action.* Kristof does this by asking politicians to consider "sensible safety measures." Worthen asks professors to teach the principles underlying etiquette.
- *Frame your argument by referring to the introduction.* MacKay does this when she ends by reiterating that selling organs benefits both seller and buyer. Worthen mentions the need for correct emails in both her first and last few paragraphs.

Come up with a title.   Most often you'll want your title to tell readers something about your topic—and to make them want to read on. MacKay's "Organ Sales Will Save Lives" tells us both her topic and position. Kristof's title, "Our Blind Spot about Guns," entices us to find out what that blind spot is. Worthen's "U Can't Talk to Ur Professor Like This" leads us to ask, "Like what?" See the chapter on **GUIDING YOUR READER** for more advice on composing a good title.

◆ 386–87

Considering Matters of Design

You'll probably write the main text of your argument in paragraph form, but think about what kind of information you're presenting and how you can design it to make your argument as easy as possible for your readers to understand. Think also about whether any visual or audio elements would be more persuasive than written words.

648–49
- What would be an appropriate **FONT**? Something serious like Times Roman? Something traditional like Courier? Something else?

650–52
- Would it help your readers if you divided your argument into shorter sections and added **HEADINGS**?

649–50
- If you're making several points, would they be easier to follow if you set them off in a **LIST**?

656
- Do you have any supporting evidence that would be easier to understand in the form of a bar **GRAPH**, line graph, or pie chart?

653–63
- Would **ILLUSTRATIONS**—photos, diagrams, or drawings—add support for your argument? Online, would video, audio, or links help?

Getting Response and Revising

At this point you need to look at your draft closely, and if possible **GET RESPONSE** from others as well. Following are some questions for looking at an argument with a critical eye.

348–50

- Is there sufficient background or context?
- Have you defined terms to avoid misunderstandings?
- Is the thesis clear and appropriately qualified?
- Are the reasons plausible?
- Is there enough evidence to support these reasons? Will readers accept the evidence as valid and sufficient?
- Can readers follow the steps in your reasoning?

academic literacies | rhetorical situations | genres | fields | processes | strategies | research MLA / APA | media / design | readings | handbook

- Have you considered potential objections or other positions? Are there any others that should be addressed?
- Have you cited enough sources, and are these sources credible?
- Are source materials documented carefully and completely, with in-text citations and a works-cited or references section?
- Are any visuals or links that are included used effectively and integrated smoothly with the rest of the text? If there are no visuals or links, would using some strengthen the argument?

Next it's time to **REVISE**, to make sure your argument offers convincing evidence, appeals to readers' values, and achieves your purpose. If you have time and want to explore alternatives, you might try **REWRITING** your draft to see if a different plan or approach might work better.

○ 348–50

○ 353–55

Editing and Proofreading

Readers equate correctness with competence. Once you've revised your draft, follow these guidelines for **EDITING** an argument:

○ 356–59

- Check to see that your tone is appropriate and consistent throughout, reflects your **STANCE** accurately, and enhances the argument you're making.

■ 66–68

- Be sure readers will be able to follow the argument; check to see you've provided **TRANSITIONS** and summary statements where necessary.

◆ 391

- Make sure you've smoothly integrated **QUOTATIONS**, **PARAPHRASES**, and **SUMMARIES** from source material into your writing and **DOCUMENTED** them accurately.

● 526–38
544–47

- Look for phrases such as "I think" or "I feel" and delete them; your essay itself expresses your opinion.
- Make sure that **ILLUSTRATIONS** have captions and that charts and graphs have headings—and that all are referred to in the main text.

□ 653–63

- If you're writing online, make sure all your links work.
- **PROOFREAD** and spell-check your essay carefully.

○ 359–60

Taking Stock of Your Work

Take stock of what you've written by writing out answers to these questions:

- What did you do well in this piece?
- What could still be improved?
- How did you go about researching your topic?
- How did others' responses influence your writing?
- How did you go about drafting this piece?
- Did you use visual elements (tables, graphs, diagrams, photographs), audio elements, or links effectively? If not, would they have helped?
- What would you do differently next time?
- What have you learned about your writing ability from writing this piece? What do you need to work on in the future?

361–70 ○
98–130 ▲
202–10
246–55

> **IF YOU NEED MORE HELP**
>
> See Chapter 34 if you are required to submit your argument as part of a writing PORTFOLIO. See also Chapter 11 on **ANALYZING A TEXT**, Chapter 16 on **EVALUATIONS**, and Chapter 20 on **PROPOSALS** for advice on writing those specific types of arguments.

Abstracts 14

Abstracts are summaries written to give readers the gist of a **REPORT** or presentation. Sometimes they are published in conference proceedings or databases. In courses in the *sciences, social sciences,* and *engineering,* you may be asked to create abstracts of your proposed projects and completed reports and essays. Abstracts are brief, typically 100–200 words, sometimes even shorter. Two common kinds are *informative abstracts* and *proposal abstracts.*

▲ 131–56

INFORMATIVE ABSTRACTS

Informative abstracts state in one paragraph the essence of a whole paper about a study or a research project. That one paragraph must mention all the main points or parts of the paper: a description of the study or project, its methods, the results, and the conclusions. Here is an example of the abstract accompanying a seven-page article that appeared in the *Journal of Clinical Psychology:*

> The relationship between boredom proneness and health-symptom reporting was examined. Undergraduate students ($N = 200$) completed the Boredom Proneness Scale and the Hopkins Symptom Checklist. A multiple analysis of covariance indicated that individuals with high boredom-proneness total scores reported significantly higher ratings on all five subscales of the Hopkins Symptom Checklist (Obsessive–Compulsive, Somatization, Anxiety, Interpersonal Sensitivity, and Depression). The results suggest that boredom proneness may be an

important element to consider when assessing symptom reporting. Implications for determining the effects of boredom proneness on psychological- and physical-health symptoms, as well as the application in clinical settings, are discussed.

—Jennifer Sommers and Stephen J. Vodanovich,
"Boredom Proneness"

The first sentence states the nature of the study being reported. The next summarizes the method used to investigate the problem, and the following one gives the results: students who, according to specific tests, are more likely to be bored are also more likely to have certain medical or psychological symptoms. The last two sentences indicate that the paper discusses those results and examines the conclusion and its implications.

PROPOSAL ABSTRACTS

Proposal abstracts contain the same basic information as informative abstracts, but their purpose is very different. You prepare proposal abstracts to persuade someone to let you write on a topic, pursue a project, conduct an experiment, or present a paper at a scholarly conference. This kind of abstract is not written to introduce a longer piece but rather to stand alone, and often the abstract is written before the paper itself. Titles and other aspects of the proposal deliberately reflect the theme of the proposed work, and you may use the future tense, rather than the past, to describe work not yet completed. Here is a possible proposal for doing research on boredom:

Undergraduate students will complete the Boredom Proneness Scale and the Hopkins Symptom Checklist. A multiple analysis of covariance will be performed to determine the relationship between boredom-proneness total scores and ratings on the five subscales of the Hopkins Symptom Checklist (Obsessive–Compulsive, Somatization, Anxiety, Interpersonal Sensitivity, and Depression).

Key Features / Abstracts

A summary of basic information. An informative abstract includes enough information to substitute for the report itself, and a proposal abstract gives an overview of the planned work.

Objective description. Abstracts present information on the contents of a report or a proposed study; they do not present arguments about or personal perspectives on those contents. The informative abstract on boredom proneness, for example, offers only a tentative conclusion: "The results *suggest* that boredom proneness *may* be an important element to consider."

Brevity. Although the length of abstracts may vary, journals and organizations often restrict them to 120–200 words — meaning you must carefully select and edit your words.

A BRIEF GUIDE TO WRITING ABSTRACTS

Considering the Rhetorical Situation

PURPOSE	Are you giving a brief but thorough overview of a completed study? only enough information to create interest? a proposal for a planned study or presentation?	55–56
AUDIENCE	For whom are you writing this abstract? What information about your project will your readers need?	57–60
STANCE	Whatever your stance in the longer work, your abstract must be objective.	66–68
MEDIA / DESIGN	How will you set off your abstract from the rest of the text? If you are publishing it online, should it be on a separate page? What format do your readers expect?	69–71

Generating Ideas and Text

Write the paper first, the abstract last. You can then use the finished work as the guide for the abstract, which should follow the same basic structure. *Exception:* You may need to write a proposal abstract months before the work it describes will be complete.

387–89 **Copy and paste key statements.** If you've already written the work, highlight your **THESIS**, objective, or purpose; basic information on your methods; your results; and your conclusion. Copy and paste those sentences into a new document to create a rough version of your abstract.

534–35 **Pare down the rough abstract.** **SUMMARIZE** the key ideas in the document, editing out any nonessential words and details. In your first sentence, introduce the overall scope of your study. Also include any other information that seems crucial to understanding your paper. Avoid phrases that add unnecessary words, such as "It is concluded that." In general, you probably won't want to use "I"; an abstract should cover ideas, not say what you think or will do.

Conform to any requirements. In general, an informative abstract should be at most 10 percent of the length of the entire work and no longer than the maximum length allowed. Proposal abstracts should conform to the requirements of the organization calling for the proposal.

Ways of Organizing an Abstract

Organizing abstracts is straightforward: in a single paragraph, briefly state the nature of the report or presentation, followed by an overview of the paper or the proposal.

academic literacies · rhetorical situations · genres · fields · processes · strategies · research MLA / APA · media / design · readings · handbook

[An informative abstract]

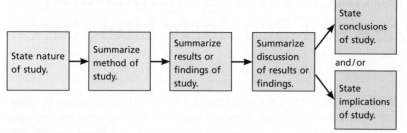

[A proposal abstract]

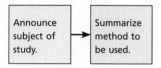

Taking Stock of Your Work

Take stock of what you've written by writing out answers to these questions:

- How did you decide on the type of abstract—informative or proposal— to write?

- How did you identify key statements in your finished work?

- What did you do well in this piece? What could still be improved? What would you do differently next time?

IF YOU NEED MORE HELP

See Chapter 30 for guidelines on **DRAFTING**, Chapter 31 on **ASSESSING YOUR OWN WRITING**, Chapter 32 on **GETTING RESPONSE AND REVISING**, and Chapter 33 on **EDITING AND PROOFREADING**.

340–42
343–47
348–55
356–60

15 Annotated Bibliographies and Reviews of Scholarly Literature

When we do research, we may consult annotated bibliographies to evaluate potential sources and literature reviews when we need an overview of the important research ("literature") on a topic. In some courses, you may be asked to create annotated bibliographies or literature reviews to demonstrate that you have researched your topic thoroughly. This chapter offers advice on writing both.

ANNOTATED BIBLIOGRAPHIES

Annotated bibliographies describe, give publication information for, and sometimes evaluate each work on a list of sources. There are two kinds of annotations, *descriptive* and *evaluative*; both may be brief, consisting only of phrases, or more formal, consisting of sentences and paragraphs. Sometimes an annotated bibliography is introduced by a short statement explaining its scope.

Descriptive annotations simply summarize the contents of each work, without comment or evaluation. They may be very short, just long enough to capture the flavor of the work, like the examples in the following excerpt from a bibliography of books and articles on teen films, published in the *Journal of Popular Film and Television*.

MICHAEL BENTON, MARK DOLAN, AND REBECCA ZISCH

Teen Film$

In the introduction to his book *The Road to Romance and Ruin*, Jon Lewis points out that over half of the world's population is currently under the age of twenty. This rather startling fact should be enough to make most Hollywood producers drool when they think of the potential profits from a target movie audience. Attracting the largest

academic literacies | rhetorical situations | genres | fields | processes | strategies | research MLA / APA | media / design | readings | handbook

demographic group is, after all, the quickest way to box-office success. In fact, almost from its beginning, the film industry has recognized the importance of the teenaged audience, with characters such as Andy Hardy and locales such as Ridgemont High and the 'hood.

Beyond the assumption that teen films are geared exclusively toward teenagers, however, film researchers should keep in mind that people of all ages have attended and still attend teen films. Popular films about adolescents are also expressions of larger cultural currents. Studying the films is important for understanding an era's common beliefs about its teenaged population within a broader pattern of general cultural preoccupations.

This selected bibliography is intended both to serve and to stimulate interest in the teen film genre. It provides a research tool for those who are studying teen films and their cultural implications. Unfortunately, however, in the process of compiling this list we quickly realized that it was impossible to be genuinely comprehensive or to satisfy every interest.

Doherty, Thomas. *Teenagers and Teenpics: The Juvenilization of American Movies in the 1950s.* Unwin Hyman, 1988. Historical discussion of the identification of teenagers as a targeted film market.

Foster, Harold M. "Film in the Classroom: Coping with 'Teenpics.'" *English Journal*, vol. 76, no. 3, Mar. 1987, pp. 86–88. Evaluation of the potential of using teen films such as *Sixteen Candles*, *The Karate Kid*, *Risky Business*, *The Flamingo Kid*, and *The Breakfast Club* to instruct adolescents on the difference between film as communication and film as exploitation.

Washington, Michael, and Marvin J. Berlowitz. "Blaxploitation Films and High School Youth: Swat Superfly." *Jump Cut*, vol. 9, Oct.–Dec. 1975, pp. 23–24. Marxist reaction to the trend of youth-oriented black action films. Article seeks to illuminate the negative influences the films have on high school students by pointing out the false ideas about education, morality, and the black family espoused by the heroes in the films.

These annotations are purely descriptive; the authors express none of their own opinions. They describe works as "historical" or "Marxist" but do not indicate whether they're "good." The bibliography entries are documented in MLA style.

Evaluative annotations offer opinions on a source as well as describe it. They are often helpful in assessing how useful a source will be for your own writing. The following evaluative annotations are from a bibliography by Kelly Green, a student at Arizona State University. Following her instructor's directions, she labeled each required part of her annotation—summary, degree of advocacy, credibility, and reliability.

KELLY GREEN

Researching Hunger and Poverty

Abramsky, Sasha. "The Other America, 2012: Confronting the Poverty Epidemic." *The Nation,* vol. 294, no. 20, 25 Apr. 2012, www.thenation .com/article/other-america-2012-confronting-poverty-epidemic/.

> The author presents the image of American poverty in 2012 with examples from various families living in poverty. The author explores the conditions that make up the new recession and suggests that people in America notice the scale of the issue and take action to solve it [Summary]. The author advocates poverty reform and shows bias toward the interests of low-income families. He acknowledges other perspectives on the issue respectfully [Degree of Advocacy]. Abramsky is a freelance journalist with experience in several magazines and newspapers. He has written several books on the topic of poverty [Credibility]. *The Nation* is one of the oldest-running magazines in the United States and contains opinions on politics and culture [Reliability].

Ambler, Marjane. "Sustaining Our Home, Determining Our Destiny." *Tribal College Journal,* vol. 13, no. 3, Spring 2002, www .tribalcollegejournal.org/sustaining-home-determining-destiny/.

> The author examines the causes of poverty on Native American reservations, the factors that lead to solutions to Native American poverty, and the ways in which tribal colleges have

helped improve life on reservations [Summary]. The author is strongly biased toward Native American interests and advocates that effective solutions to poverty originate within the reservations, especially in tribal colleges and universities [Degree of Advocacy]. Marjane Ambler was an editor for the *Tribal College Journal* for nine years and worked in national park service for nearly a decade [Credibility]. This article was published in 2002 in the *Tribal College Journal,* a national magazine published by the American Indian Higher Education Consortium [Reliability].

These annotations not only summarize the sources in detail but also evaluate their bias, or "degree of advocacy"; credibility; and reliability.

Key Features / Annotated Bibliographies

A statement of scope. Sometimes you need or are asked to provide a brief introductory statement to explain what you're covering. The authors of the bibliography on teen films introduce their bibliography with three paragraphs establishing a context for the bibliography and announcing their purpose for compiling it.

Complete bibliographic information. Provide all the information about each source using one documentation system (MLA, APA, or another one) so that you, your readers, or other researchers will be able to find the source easily. It's a good idea to include sources' URLs or **PERMALINKS** to make accessing online sources easier.

487

A concise description of the work. A good annotation describes each item as carefully and objectively as possible, giving accurate information and showing that you understand the source. These qualities will help to build authority—for you as a writer and for your annotations.

Relevant commentary. If you write an evaluative bibliography, your comments should be relevant to your purpose and audience. The best way to achieve relevance is to consider what questions a potential reader might have about each source: What are the main points of the source? What is its argument? How even-handed or biased is it? How current and reliable is it? Will the source be helpful for your project?

Consistent presentation. All annotations should follow a consistent pattern: if one is written in complete sentences, they should all be. Each annotation in the teen films bibliography, for example, begins with a phrase (not a complete sentence) characterizing the work.

A BRIEF GUIDE TO WRITING ANNOTATED BIBLIOGRAPHIES

Considering the Rhetorical Situation

55–56 ▪ **PURPOSE** Will your bibliography need to demonstrate the depth or breadth of your research? Will your readers actually track down and use your sources? Do you need or want to convince readers that your sources are good?

57–60 ▪ **AUDIENCE** For whom are you compiling this bibliography? What does your audience need to know about each source?

66–68 ▪ **STANCE** Are you presenting yourself as an objective describer or evaluator? Or are you expressing a particular point of view toward the sources you evaluate?

69–71 ▪ **MEDIA / DESIGN** If you are publishing the bibliography electronically, will you provide links from each annotation to the source itself? Online or offline, should you distinguish the bibliographic information from the annotation by using a different font?

Generating Ideas and Text

Decide what sources to include. You may be tempted to include in a bibliography every source you find or look at. A better strategy is to include only those sources that you or your readers may find potentially useful in researching your topic. For an academic bibliography, you need to consider the qualities in the list below. Some of these qualities should not rule a source in or out; they simply raise issues you need to think about.

- *Appropriateness.* Is this source relevant to your topic? Is it a primary source or a secondary source? Is it aimed at an appropriate audience? General or specialized? Elementary, advanced, or somewhere in between?

- *Credibility.* Is the author reputable? Is the publication, publishing company, or sponsor of the site reputable? Do the ideas more or less agree with those in other sources you've read?

- *Balance.* Does the source present enough evidence for its assertions? Does it show any particular bias? Does it present countering arguments fairly?

- *Timeliness.* Is the source recent enough? Does it reflect current thinking or research about the subject?

If you need help **FINDING SOURCES**, see Chapter 48.

489–510

Compile a list of works to annotate. Give the sources themselves in whatever documentation style is required; see the guidelines for **MLA** and **APA** styles in Chapters 54 and 55.

MLA 548–96
APA 597–636

Determine what kind of bibliography you need to write. Will your bibliography be descriptive or evaluative? Will your annotations be in the form of phrases? complete sentences? paragraphs? The form will shape your reading and note taking. If you're writing a descriptive bibliography, your reading goal will be just to understand and capture the writer's message as clearly as possible. If you're writing an evaluative bibliography, you will also need to assess the source as you read in order to include your own opinions of it.

Read carefully. To write an annotation, you must understand the source's argument, but when you are writing an annotated bibliography as part of a **PROPOSAL**, you may have neither the time nor the need to read the whole text. Here's a way of quickly determining whether a source is likely to serve your needs:

246–55 ▲

- Check the publisher or sponsor (university press? scholarly journal? popular magazine? website sponsored by a reputable organization?).

- Read the preface (of a book), abstract (of a scholarly article), introduction (of an article in a nonscholarly magazine or a website).

- Skim the table of contents or the headings.

- Read the parts that relate specifically to your topic.

Research the writer, if necessary. If you are required to indicate the writer's credentials, you may need to do additional research. You may find information by typing the writer's name into a search engine or looking up the writer in *Contemporary Authors*. In any case, information about the writer should take up no more than one sentence in your annotation.

443–51 ◆

Summarize the work in a sentence or two. **DESCRIBE** it as objectively as possible: even if you are writing an evaluative annotation, you can evaluate the central point of a work better by stating it clearly first. *If you're writing a descriptive annotation, you're done.*

511–18 ●

66–68 ▪

Establish criteria for evaluating sources. If you're **EVALUATING** sources for a project, you'll need to evaluate them in terms of their usefulness for your project, their **STANCE**, and their overall credibility.

Write a brief evaluation of the source. If you can generalize about the worth of the entire work, fine. You may find, however, that some parts are useful while others are not, and what you write should reflect that mix.

Be consistent—in content, sentence structure, and format.

- *Content.* Try to provide about the same amount of information for each entry. If you're evaluating, don't evaluate some sources and just describe others.

- *Sentence structure.* Use the same style throughout—**COMPLETE SEN-TENCES**, brief phrases, or a mix.

HB-4–7

- *Format.* Use one documentation style throughout; use a consistent **FONT** for each element in each entry—for example, italicize or underline all book titles.

648–49

Ways of Organizing an Annotated Bibliography

Depending on their purpose, annotated bibliographies may or may not include an introduction. Most annotated bibliographies cover a single topic and so are organized alphabetically by author's or editor's last name. When a work lacks a named author, alphabetize it by the first important word in its title. Consult the documentation system you're using for additional details about alphabetizing works appropriately.

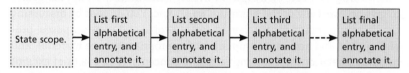

Sometimes an annotated bibliography needs to be organized into several subject areas (or genres, periods, or some other category); if so, the entries are listed alphabetically within each category. For example, a bibliography about terrorism breaks down into subjects such as "Global Terrorism" and "Weapons of Mass Destruction."

[Multicategory bibliography]

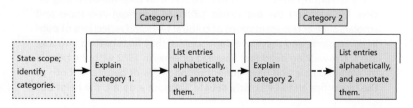

Taking Stock of Your Work

Take stock of what you've written by writing out answers to these questions:

- How did you go about researching the entries in this bibliography?
- How did you decide which sources to include and which to leave out?
- How did you go about drafting your bibliography?
- Did you cite your sources accurately?
- What did you do well? What could still be improved? What would you do differently next time?

REVIEWS OF SCHOLARLY LITERATURE

Reviews of scholarly literature describe and evaluate important research ("literature") available on a topic. In writing a literature review, your goal is to give an overview of the literature on a topic. You do that by discussing the literature that is most relevant to your topic and your purposes, providing clear and accurate summaries of appropriate source material, and describing relationships among facts and concepts. Here is a brief excerpt from a literature review that describes scholarship in zombie movies by a student at the University of Mary Washington.

CAMERON CARROLL

Zombie Film Scholarship: A Review of the Literature

Zombies are the shambling undead creatures that attack in hordes and strike terror into the hearts of moviegoers with their mindless aggression. Monsters on the big screen fascinate American audiences and scholars alike as representations of cultural fears and reflections of public perceptions, and they have done so since they first shuffled into theaters. The walking dead first haunted cinemas in 1932 with the release of *White Zombie* and have gone through cycles of popularity both at the box office and in scholarly debate. Without a doubt, the height of

zombie scholarship began in the mid-2000s with only shallow mentions made in horror analyses before then. Only the English discipline gave the zombie credit as a subject worthy of study. As author and English professor Kyle Bishop wrote in 2010, "The zombie phenomenon has yet to be plumbed to its depths by the academic and literary markets."[1] Although significant zombie research has only surfaced in the 2000s, a valiant effort is currently being made to explore zombie symbolism and its historical and cultural context across non-traditional scholarly fields, such as anthropology, psychology, sociology, and philosophy.

. . .

Zombies, as creatures that waver between living and dead, necessarily bring forth questions on the nature of being and thus also fall into the realm of philosophy as seen in *Zombies, Vampires, and Philosophy: New Life for the Undead* published in 2010 and edited by Richard Greene and K. Silem Mohammed, professors of philosophy and English, respectively. Philosophers in the study of zombies seek to answer such questions as, is it better to be undead or dead? Richard Greene argues that since death is a state of non-existence and Undeath is at least a primal existence, the question comes down to the classic "to be, or not to be?" For him, Undeath is the only option for a state of being, since death is non-existence. Existence in any form is inherently better than utterly ceasing to be.[16] Greene's philosophy colleague, William Larkin, counters that zombies are driven to actions seen as evil and mindless, both states that humans do not usually choose. He cites how zombie films repeatedly depict survivors who ask their friends and family to kill them should it appear that they will turn into zombies, so desperate are they to avoid Undeath.[17] Simon Clark, a writer with a master's degree in Fine Arts, discusses morality in relation to zombies: if zombies are non-moral and whether or not they are the freest creatures because of their lack of morality. Clark writes that they become ultimately free in their modern incarnations from turn of the millennium cinema.[18] Zombies break through barriers that survivors put up to keep them confined and are so primal that they cannot be held accountable for their actions, making them truly liberated. A fictional creature encourages real discussions in philosophical debate, demonstrating yet another area that inspires scholars to reexamine their own field because of zombies.

. . .

The message to take away from zombie scholarship is that what it represents is evolutionary and infinitely debatable, but the victory for zombie studies is that zombies are being studied at all. After decades of being underrepresented in horror scholarship, zombies are finally getting their due as a cultural icon, complete with varying opinions and interpretations. Scholarly debate proves that the zombie is a valid resource for understanding American culture and worthy of the enthusiastic pursuit of interdepartmental scholarship. As shown within the scholarly works above, the debate over the meaning of the living dead is quite lively, indeed.

Notes

1. Kyle William Bishop, *American Zombie Gothic: The Rise and Fall (and Rise) of the Walking Dead in Popular Culture* (Jefferson, NC: McFarland, 2010), 7.

. . .

16. Richard Greene and K. Silem Mohammed, eds., *Zombies, Vampires, and Philosophy: New Life for the Undead* (Chicago: Open Court, 2010), 13.

17. Greene and Mohammed, 20.

18. Greene and Mohammed, 208.

Carroll begins by establishing a context for her discussion and then focuses on her topic, the scholarship of zombies in film. In her review, she discusses the history of zombie scholarship in general and then in psychology, social trends, fiction, and, in this excerpt, philosophy. A history major, she follows Chicago style; in addition to the notes, she included a bibliography listing all her sources, including the two noted here.

Key Features / Reviews of Scholarly Literature

Careful, thorough research. A review of scholarly literature demands that you research all the major literature on the topic—or at least the major literature available to you, given the time you have.

Accurate, objective summaries of the relevant literature. Readers expect a literature review to objectively summarize the main ideas or conclusions of the texts reviewed.

academic literacies · rhetorical situations · genres · fields · processes · strategies · research MLA / APA · media / design · readings · handbook

Critical evaluation for the literature. A literature review offers considered selection of the most important, relevant, and useful sources of information on its topic, so you must evaluate each source to decide whether it should be included and then to determine how it advances understanding of the topic.

SYNTHESIS of the scholarship. A literature review differs from an annotated bibliography in that the review identifies key concepts, similarities, and differences within the body of literature, showing how the sources relate to one another by method, study findings, themes, main ideas, or something else.

519–25

A clear focus. Because a literature review provides an overview of your topic's main issues and explains the main concepts underlying your research, it must be carefully organized and clearly focused on your specific topic.

Taking Stock of Your Work

Take stock of what you've written by writing out answers to these questions:

- How did you go about researching the sources you used?
- How did you decide which sources to include and which to leave out?
- What led you to group related sources together as you did?
- How did you go about synthesizing similar sources?
- What did you do well? What could still be improved? What would you do differently next time?

IF YOU NEED MORE HELP

See Chapter 30 for guidelines on **DRAFTING**, Chapter 31 on **ASSESSING YOUR OWN WRITING**, Chapter 32 on **GETTING RESPONSE AND REVISING**, and Chapter 33 on **EDITING AND PROOFREADING**. See Chapter 34 if you are required to submit your bibliography in a writing **PORTFOLIO**.

340–42
343–47
348–55
356–60
361–70

16 Evaluations

TestFreaks evaluates audio equipment and appliances. The *Princeton Review* and *U.S. News & World Report* evaluate colleges and universities. You probably consult such sources to make decisions, and you probably evaluate things all the time—when you recommend a film (or not) or a teacher (ditto). An evaluation is at bottom a judgment; you judge something according to certain criteria, supporting your judgment with reasons and evidence. You need to give your reasons for evaluating it as you do because often your evaluation will affect your audience's actions: they must see this movie, needn't bother with this book, should be sure to have the Caesar salad at this restaurant, and so on.

In college courses, students in *literature, film, drama,* and *art* classes may be assigned to evaluate poems, fiction, movies, plays, and artwork,

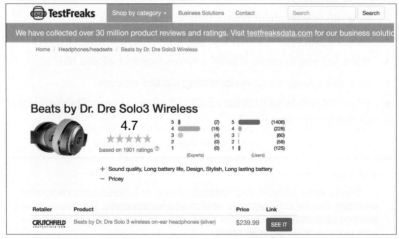

TestFreaks crawls the web for expert reviews and user opinions.

and those in *business* and *political science* classes may be asked to evaluate advertising or political campaigns or plans for business or public-policy initiatives. In a review that follows, written for *The Daily Bruin*, UCLA's student newspaper, William Thorne offers his evaluation of the film *The Circle*.

WILLIAM THORNE

Movie Review: The Circle

The Circle imagines a world in which internet stardom is just a daily vlog away, and giant tech companies battle governments over privacy issues. Sound familiar?

The latest offering from up-and-coming indie director James Ponsoldt aims to be both a reflection on documenting one's life online and a warning against millennials' unchecked faith in tech giants. But the film falls short of being a well-rounded piece.

If anyone can get millennials to put down their iPhones and listen, it's the film's main star, Emma Watson. Fresh off her all-singing all-dancing performance in the Disney behemoth *Beauty and the Beast*, Watson plays Mae Holland, a frustrated young woman trapped in a dull office job in the modern-day Bay Area. Mae's problems stretch beyond her career concerns, though, as her father, played by the late, great Bill Paxton in his final film role, has multiple sclerosis. And Mae's relationship with her ex-boyfriend Mercer (Ellar Coltrane), a local lad who makes antler chandeliers, doesn't seem to be going anywhere.

The solution to all of Mae's problems? Joining The Circle, a powerful internet company co-founded by Eamon Bailey (Tom Hanks), a bearded, ambitious genius who is a turtleneck and a pair of glasses away from Steve Jobs. Bailey's motto is "Knowing is good. Knowing everything is better," yet somehow hardly anyone at the company can see the creepy, maniacal implications of these two sentences, and so Bailey and his co-founder Tom Stenton (Patton Oswalt) act on their crazy ideas unchallenged.

The Circle starts out as a promising and intriguing sci-fi thriller, 5 exploring the pros and cons of having minute, camouflaged cameras on every street corner. Hanks does a Jobsian job of selling Big Brother surveillance to the audience, channeling a mixture of his trademark

American Dream optimism and "Go get 'em, Woody" attitude. But, as with most Hanks performances, there's more to the character than meets the eye, and Bailey's enthusiasm masks his stalkerish desire to see what everyone is doing.

Some of the best moments in the movie occur when Mae volunteers to wear a tiny camera on her chest and document her every move for the world to see as part of The Circle's latest venture. Although Mae is reluctant at first to expose her life to the online world, she soon becomes addicted to the millions of faceless followers and begins to sacrifice real relationships with her family and friends for superficial interactions with often offensive users. The character adopts a fake smile and exudes nauseating enthusiasm, echoing many of today's *YouTube* vloggers and providing a clever commentary on how online fame can come with a price.

Tonally, however, the film can't quite decide what it wants to be. At one point, Ty Lafitte (John Boyega), who seems to be the only person even slightly worried by The Circle's practices, leads Mae into the sewers underneath The Circle's colossal offices, referred to as "the campus," to warn her about the dangers of the company's omniscience. The

scene suggests that the two will team up to take down the company and escape together in a heart-racing thriller. Yet Ty is subsequently sidelined, and the uneasy sexual tension between him and Mae is left unresolved.

The film's tonal issues begin even earlier, during a scene that critiques millennials' obsession with social media and their trademark fear of missing out on socializing. Two "Circlers," acting under the pretense of getting her settled in at the company, approach Mae and inform her that The Circle's company barbecues and impromptu Beck concerts are not mandatory, but that if she doesn't show up, she'll drop in the company participation rankings. The moment is laugh-out-loud funny, but it makes the seriousness of subsequent scenes dealing with Mae's father's disease and Mercer's detachment feel empty and tasteless.

The Circle lurches from tense thriller to weepy family drama to savvy, knowing comedy from scene to scene, leaving the audience wondering why it couldn't just settle for one of the above. The film only avoids rotten-apple status because of the elements of clever commentary on modern-day surveillance and the power of information in the hands of tech companies, and because of the solid acting. Watson and Hanks both shine, and it's definitely worth getting off *Instagram* for a few hours to see the final film performance from the legendary Paxton.

Thorne quickly summarizes The Circle's *plot and then evaluates the film using clear criteria: the performances of Tom Hanks and Emma Watson, the complexity of their characters, the film's coherence, and its message.*

For four more evaluations, see CHAPTER 65.

Key Features / Evaluations

A concise description of the subject.   You should include just enough information to let readers who may not be familiar with your subject understand what it is; the goal is to evaluate, not summarize. Depending on your topic and medium, some of this information may be in visual or audio form. Thorne briefly describes *The Circle*'s main plot points, only providing what readers need to understand the context of his evaluation.

Clearly defined criteria. You need to determine clear criteria as the basis for your judgment. In reviews or other evaluations written for a broad audience, you can integrate the criteria into the discussion as reasons for your assessment, as Thorne does in his evaluation of *The Circle*. In more formal evaluations, you may need to announce your criteria explicitly. Thorne evaluates the film based on the stars' performances, the complexity of their characters, and the film's coherence.

A knowledgeable discussion of the subject. To evaluate something credibly, you need to show that you know it yourself and that you understand its context. Thorne cites many examples from *The Circle*, showing his knowledge of the film, and he draws parallels to other topics, such as Steve Jobs's iconic look, Tom Hanks's tendency to play complicated characters, and modern society's obsession with social media. Some evaluations require that you research what other authoritative sources have said about your subject. Thorne might have referred to other reviews of the film to show that he'd researched others' views.

A balanced and fair assessment. An evaluation is centered on a judgment. Thorne concedes that *The Circle* doesn't quite know what kind of movie it is, so it "lurches from tense thriller to weepy family drama to savvy, knowing comedy." Nevertheless, he thinks the film is worth seeing due to its "clever commentary on modern-day surveillance" and some of the actors' performances. It is important that any judgment be balanced and fair. Seldom is something all good or all bad. A fair evaluation need not be all positive or all negative; it may acknowledge both strengths and weaknesses. For example, a movie's soundtrack may be wonderful while the plot is not.

Well-supported reasons. You need to argue for your judgment, providing reasons and evidence that might include visual and audio as well as verbal material. Thorne gives several reasons for his assessment of *The Circle*—the strong performances by Hanks and Watson, the ways in which "the film can't quite decide what it wants to be"—and he supports these reasons with several examples from the film.

academic literacies | rhetorical situations | genres | fields | processes | strategies | research MLA / APA | media / design | readings | handbook

A BRIEF GUIDE TO WRITING EVALUATIONS

Choosing Something to Evaluate

You can more effectively evaluate a limited subject than a broad one: review certain dishes at a local restaurant rather than the entire menu; review one film or episode rather than all the films by Alfred Hitchcock or all seventy-three *Game of Thrones* episodes. The more specific and focused your subject, the better you can write about it.

Considering the Rhetorical Situation

PURPOSE	Are you writing to affect your audience's opinion of a subject? to help others decide what to see, do, or buy? to demonstrate your expertise in a field?	55–56
AUDIENCE	To whom are you writing? What will your audience already know about the subject? What will they expect to learn from your evaluation of it? Are they likely to agree with you or not?	57–60
STANCE	What is your attitude toward the subject, and how will you show that you have evaluated it fairly and appropriately? Think about the tone you want to use: should it be reasonable? passionate? critical?	66–68
MEDIA/DESIGN	How will you deliver your evaluation? In print? Electronically? As a speech? Can you show images or audio or video clips? If you're submitting your text for publication, are there any format requirements?	69–71

Generating Ideas and Text

Explore what you already know. **FREEWRITE** to answer the following questions: What do you know about this subject or subjects like it? What are your initial or gut feelings, and why do you feel as you do? How does

331–32

this subject reflect or affect your basic values or beliefs? How have others evaluated subjects like this?

Identify criteria. Make a list of criteria you think should be used to evaluate your subject. Think about which criteria will likely be important to your **AUDIENCE**. You might find **CUBING** and **QUESTIONING** to be useful processes for thinking about your criteria.

57–60

334–35

Evaluate your subject. Study your subject closely to determine to what extent it meets each of your criteria. You may want to list your criteria and take notes related to each one, or you may develop a rating scale for each criterion to help stay focused on it. Come up with a tentative judgment.

Compare your subject with others. Often, evaluating something involves **COMPARING AND CONTRASTING** it with similar things. We judge movies in comparison with the other movies we've seen and french fries with the other fries we've tasted. Sometimes those comparisons can be made informally. For other evaluations, you may have to do research—to try on several pairs of jeans before buying any, for example—to see how your subject compares.

424–31

State your judgment as a tentative thesis statement. Your **THESIS STATEMENT** should be one that addresses both pros and cons. "*Hawaii Five-O* is fun to watch despite its stilted dialogue." "Of the five sport-utility vehicles tested, the Toyota 4Runner emerged as the best in comfort, power, and durability, though not in styling or cargo capacity." Both of these examples offer a judgment but qualify it according to the writer's criteria.

387–89

Anticipate other opinions. I think Will Ferrell is a comic genius whose movies are first-rate. You think Will Ferrell is a terrible actor who makes awful movies. How can I write a review of his latest film that you will at least consider? One way is by **ACKNOWLEDGING** other opinions—and **REFUTING** those opinions as best I can. I may not persuade you to see Ferrell's next film, but I can at least demonstrate that by certain criteria he should be appreciated. You may need to **RESEARCH** how others have evaluated your subject.

411

412–13

477

Identify and support your reasons.   Write out all the REASONS you can think of that will convince your audience to accept your judgment. Review your list to identify the most convincing or important reasons. Then review how well your subject meets your criteria and decide how best to SUPPORT your reasons: through examples, authoritative opinions, statistics, visual or audio evidence, or something else.

◆ 400–401

◆ 401–8

Ways of Organizing an Evaluation

Evaluations are usually organized in one of two ways. One way is to introduce what's being evaluated, followed by your judgment, discussing your criteria along the way. This is a useful strategy if your audience may not be familiar with your subject.

[Start with your subject]

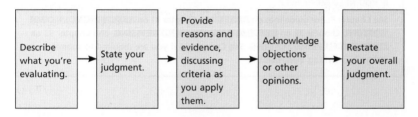

Describe what you're evaluating. → State your judgment. → Provide reasons and evidence, discussing criteria as you apply them. → Acknowledge objections or other opinions. → Restate your overall judgment.

You might also start by identifying your criteria and then follow with a discussion of how well your subject meets those criteria. This strategy foregrounds the process by which you reached your conclusions.

[Start with your criteria]

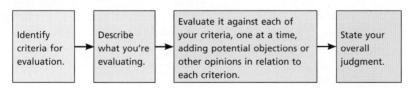

Identify criteria for evaluation. → Describe what you're evaluating. → Evaluate it against each of your criteria, one at a time, adding potential objections or other opinions in relation to each criterion. → State your overall judgment.

Taking Stock of Your Work

Take stock of what you've written by writing out answers to these questions:

- What did you do well in this piece?

- What could still be improved?

- How did you develop criteria for your evaluation?

- How did others' responses influence your writing?

- What would you do differently next time?

- What have you learned about your writing ability or writing processes from writing this piece? What do you need to work on in the future?

340–42
343–47
348–55
356–60
361–70

> **IF YOU NEED MORE HELP**
>
> See Chapter 30 for guidelines on **DRAFTING**, Chapter 31 on **ASSESSING YOUR OWN WRITING**, Chapter 32 on **GETTING RESPONSE AND REVISING**, and Chapter 33 on **EDITING AND PROOFREADING**. See Chapter 34 if you are required to submit your report in a writing **PORTFOLIO**.

Literary Analyses 17

Literary analyses are essays that examine literary texts closely to understand their messages, interpret their meanings, appreciate their techniques, or understand their historical or social contexts. Such texts traditionally include novels, short stories, poems, and plays but may also include films, TV shows, videogames, music, and comics. You might read *Macbeth* and notice that Shakespeare's play contains a pattern of images of blood. You could explore the distinctive point of view in Ambrose Bierce's story "An Occurrence at Owl Creek Bridge." Or you could point out the differences between Stephen King's *The Shining* and Stanley Kubrick's screenplay based on that novel. In all these cases, you use specific analytical techniques to go below the surface of the work to deepen your understanding of how it works and what it means.

You may be assigned to analyze works of literature in courses in *English, film, drama,* and many other subjects. Here is a poem by the twentieth-century American poet Robert Frost, followed by a student's analysis of it written for a literature course at the University of South Dakota and chosen as a winner of the 2017 Norton Writer's Prize.

ROBERT FROST

The Road Not Taken

Two roads diverged in a yellow wood,
And sorry I could not travel both
And be one traveler, long I stood
And looked down one as far as I could
To where it bent in the undergrowth;   5

211

Then took the other, as just as fair,
And having perhaps the better claim,
Because it was grassy and wanted wear;
Though as for that the passing there
Had worn them really about the same,   10

And both that morning equally lay
In leaves no step had trodden black.
Oh, I kept the first for another day!
Yet knowing how way leads on to way,
I doubted if I should ever come back.   15

I shall be telling this with a sigh
Somewhere ages and ages hence:
Two roads diverged in a wood, and I—
I took the one less traveled by,
And that has made all the difference.   20

MATTHEW MILLER
Frost's Broken Roads

"The Road Not Taken" by Robert Frost is arguably one of the most popular poems ever written. Read at graduations, eulogies, even in movies and car commercials, it is often interpreted as an ode to individualism. Frost's image of the road "less traveled" has become synonymous with daring life choices that make "all the difference" in living a fulfilling life (lines 19–20). Some may latch on to this as the poem's deeper meaning. However, this convenient conclusion ignores several conflicting, yet beautiful, details that lead the poem down a path of broken metaphor and temporal inconsistency. To truly recognize what Frost is building in this poem, a few nagging inconsistencies must be considered.

academic literacies   rhetorical situations   genres   fields   processes   strategies   research MLA / APA   media / design   readings   handbook

In the first line of the poem, the traveler is depicted hiking in a "yellow wood" wherein he finds a fork in his path (1). This setting is the foundation of a common metaphor, but transposing familiar notions of a figurative fork in the road onto Frost's poem requires acceptance of the traveler's metaphoric natural world and its "temporal scheme," or some form of unified movement through time, as the critic Cleanth Brooks describes it in his classic book on poetic structure, *The Well Wrought Urn* (203). If the path that is covered "[i]n leaves no step had trodden black" (12) makes "all the difference" (20) in a life, common sense indicates the decision to choose that path has to occur early enough during a lifetime to properly affect its outcome. The speaker/traveler affirms this, telling the reader that he "shall be telling" them the story of his decision "with a sigh / Somewhere ages and ages hence" (16–17). In other words, the traveler must be fairly young, otherwise he wouldn't have "ages and ages" (17) left to tell his story. It may not be apparent at a surface level, but this complicates our understanding of the poem's implicit story.

It is common knowledge that morning, the beginning of the day, is often paralleled figuratively with the beginning of other things (e.g. "the dawn of civilization"). In this sense, the setting helps to solidify the poem's established temporal sense; the earliness of the day—"morning" (16)—parallels the early point in life when the traveler makes his life-altering decision. However, the description of the scene, the "yellow wood" (1) where the ground "lay / In leaves" (11–12), indicates that late autumn has set in around the forest. Parallels between seasonal progression and the human life cycle saturate literature and art with such metaphors as the "springtime of youth" and the "hoary winter of old age" (Kammen 23). With that in mind, the end of autumn represents the bitter end of productive years and the first step into the cold and death of winter. So, embedded in the poem is a temporal inconsistency; the traveler is young, with "ages and ages" (17) yet to live, but the autumn setting implies his world is quickly coming to an end.

Another question that complicates a traditional understanding of the poem is that of identity. The narrator claims he is "sorry" he "could not travel both" paths "and be one traveler" (2–3). For him to stray off his path would equal becoming a different person; he "could not travel both / *And be one traveler*" (2–3, emphasis added). However, one person can easily be two different travelers in a lifetime (i.e., one person can take both a cruise vacation and a backpacking trip: two very different traveling styles). The traveler/speaker even admits this is possible by saying he *could* keep "the first for another day" (13). His excuse for not traveling both paths was not that it was impossible but rather that "knowing how way leads on to way, / I doubted if I should ever come back" (14–15). Although he believes one of the paths has "the better claim, / Because it was grassy and wanted wear" (7–8), in practically the same breath he casts doubt on the claim that it is "less traveled" (19), admitting other travelers have worn down the two trails "really about the same" (10). The speaker in this poem is not Emerson's self-reliant transcendentalist, who can "speak what [he] think[s] to-day in words as hard as cannon balls, and to-morrow speak what to-morrow thinks in hard words again, though it contradict every thing [he] said to-day" (214).

Frost's syntax and punctuation add even more nuance. The poem consists of one sentence that takes up the first two stanzas and part of the third, in which our traveler deliberates and, eventually, makes his decision; and the three sentences of the third and fourth stanzas, in which our traveler lives with his choice. As the poem progresses to the point where our traveler makes his decision, we see punctuation that is irregular when compared with the rest of the poem: an exclamation point when the traveler finally makes a decision (possibly showing excess emotion); an em dash (—) followed by a repeated word when re-telling his story that functions almost like a stutter, possibly showing regret/lack of confidence in his choice. With this in mind, it seems as though our traveler had a tough time making his decision, and afterward, there is no obvious approval or happiness with it, only that it "made all the difference" (20), which could be positive or negative.

Placing the poem in its historical context further complicates these questions. According to an article written for the Poetry Foundation by the poet Katherine Robinson, "The Road Not Taken" was actually written "as a joke for a friend, the poet Edward Thomas."

Indeed, when Frost and Thomas went walking together, Thomas would often choose one fork in the road because he was convinced it would lead them to something, perhaps a patch of rare wild flowers or a particular bird's nest. . . . In a letter, Frost goaded Thomas, saying, "No matter which road you take, *you'll always sigh*, and wish you'd taken another" (Robinson, emphasis added).

Introducing the poet's biography might be considered by many a sin against the work, especially for those espousing Cleanth Brooks's celebration of poetic unity and universal meaning. However, knowing this information fills in several gaps about the poem; instead of confusing inconsistencies and paradoxical meanings, the poem can now be viewed—at least partly—as teasing from a friend. It is easy to imagine an indecisive Thomas, standing and staring down the fork in the path, afraid of what he'll miss if he picks the wrong trail, and then on the way home "telling" Frost, "with a sigh" (16), about all he swore he missed on *the road he didn't take* (16). This being said, Frost published this work knowing full well of its depth and epistemological possibilities, saying in a letter, "My poems . . . are all set to trip the reader head foremost into the boundless" (qtd. in Robinson).

Frost's timeless poem is an elegant narrative, filled with serene imagery and laced with layers of mystery. Readers of this canonical work can easily find themselves slipping into the easy, traditional reading of an ode to individualism. Upon closer inspection, there is only one thing clear about "The Road Not Taken," which is said best in words Frost loved to tell his readers regarding his classic poem: "[Y]ou have to be careful of that one; it's a tricky poem—very tricky" (qtd. in Robinson).

Works Cited

Brooks, Cleanth. *The Well Wrought Urn: Studies in the Structure of Poetry*. Harcourt, 1975.

Emerson, Ralph Waldo. "Self-Reliance." *The Norton Anthology of American Literature*, edited by Robert S. Levine et al., 9th ed., vol. B, W. W. Norton, 2017, pp. 236–53.

Frost, Robert. "The Road Not Taken." *Poetry Foundation,* www.poetryfoundation.org/poems/44272/the-road-not-taken.

Kammen, Michael G. *A Time to Every Purpose: The Four Seasons in American Culture*. U of North Carolina P, 2004.

Robinson, Katherine. "Robert Frost: 'The Road Not Taken.'" *Poetry Foundation,* 27 May 2016, www.poetryfoundation.org/articles/89511/robert-frost-the-road-not-taken.

For two more literary analyses, see CHAPTER 66.

Miller focuses his analysis on "tricky" aspects of Frost's poem. In addition, he uses aspects of Frost's biography and letters to resolve some of the seeming contradictions and tensions in the poem.

Key Features / Literary Analyses

An arguable thesis. A literary analysis is a form of argument; you are arguing that your analysis of a literary work is valid. Your thesis, then, should be arguable, as Miller's is: "To truly recognize what Frost is building in this poem, a few nagging inconsistencies must be considered." A mere summary—"Frost writes about someone trying to decide which road to take"—would not be arguable and therefore is not a good thesis.

Careful attention to the language of the text. The key to analyzing a text is looking carefully at the language, which is the foundation of its meaning. Specific words, images, metaphors—these are where analysis begins. You may also bring in contextual information, such as cultural, historical, or biographical facts, or you may refer to similar texts. But the words, phrases, and sentences that make up the text you are analyzing are your primary source when dealing with texts. That's what literature teachers mean by "close reading": reading with the assumption that every word of a text is meaningful.

Attention to patterns or themes. Literary analyses are usually built on evidence of meaningful patterns or themes within a text or among several texts. These patterns and themes reveal meaning. In Frost's poem, images of diverging roads and yellow leaves create patterns of meaning, while the regular rhyme scheme (*wood/stood/could, both/undergrowth*) creates patterns of sound and structure that may contribute to the overall meaning.

A clear interpretation. A literary analysis demonstrates the plausibility of its thesis by using evidence from the text and, sometimes, relevant

contextual evidence to explain how the language and patterns found there support a particular interpretation. When you write a literary analysis, you show readers one way the text may be read and understood; that is your interpretation.

MLA style.   Literary analyses usually follow MLA style. Miller's essay includes a works-cited list and refers to line numbers using MLA style.

A BRIEF GUIDE TO WRITING LITERARY ANALYSES

Considering the Rhetorical Situation

PURPOSE	What do you need to do? Show that you have examined the text carefully? Offer your own interpretation? Demonstrate a particular analytical technique? Or some combination? If you're responding to an assignment, does it specify what you need to do?	55–56
AUDIENCE	What do you need to do to convince your readers that your interpretation is plausible and based on sound analysis? Can you assume that readers are already familiar with the text you are analyzing, or do you need to tell them about it?	57–60
STANCE	How can you see your subject through interested, curious eyes—and then step back in order to see what your observations might *mean*?	66–68
MEDIA/DESIGN	Will your analysis focus on an essentially verbal text or one that has significant visual content, such as a graphic novel? Will you need to show visual elements in your analysis? Will it be delivered in a print, spoken, or electronic medium? Are you required to follow MLA or some other style?	69–71

Generating Ideas and Text

Look at your assignment. Does it specify a particular kind of analysis? Does it ask you to consider a particular theme? To use any specific critical approaches? Look for any terms that tell you what to do, words like *analyze, compare, interpret,* and so on.

Study the text with a critical eye. When we read a literary work, we often come away with a reaction to it: we like it, we hate it, it made us cry or laugh, it perplexed us. That may be a good starting point for a literary analysis, but to write about literature you need to go beyond initial reactions, to think about **HOW THE TEXT WORKS**: What does it *say*, and what does it *do*? What elements make up this text? How do those elements work together or fail to work together? Does this text lead you to think or feel a certain way? How does it fit into a particular context (of history, culture, technology, genre, and so on)?

21–23

Choose a method for analyzing the text. There are various ways to analyze your subject. Three common focuses are on the text itself, on your own experience reading it, and on other cultural, historical, or literary contexts.

- *The text itself*. Trace the development and expression of themes, characters, and language through the work. How do they help to create the overall meaning, tone, or effect for which you're arguing? To do this, you might look at the text as a whole, something you can understand from all angles at once. You could also pick out parts from the beginning, middle, and end as needed to make your case, **DEFINING** key terms, **DESCRIBING** characters and settings, and **NARRATING** key scenes. Miller's essay about "The Road Not Taken" offers a text-based analysis that looks at Frost's treatment of time in the poem. You might also examine the same theme in several different works.

  432–42
  443–51
  462–70

- *Your own response as a reader*. Explore the way the text affects you or develops meanings as you read through it from beginning to end. By doing such a close reading, you're slowing down the process to notice

how one element of the text leads you to expect something, confirming earlier suspicions or surprises. You build your analysis on your experience of reading the text—as if you were pretending to drive somewhere for the first time, though in reality you know the way intimately. By closely examining the language of the text as you experience it, you explore how it leads you to a set of responses, both intellectual and emotional. If you were responding in this way to the Frost poem, you might discuss how the narrator keeps trying to assert that one road is preferable to another but admits that both are the same, so that his willful assertion that one is "less traveled by" and that his choice "made all the difference" is no difference at all.

- *Context.* Analyze the text as part of some **LARGER CONTEXT**—as part of a certain time or place in history or as an expression of a certain culture (how does this text relate to the time and place of its creation?), as one of many other texts like it, a representative of a genre (how is this text like or unlike others of its kind? how does it use, play with, or flout the conventions of the genre?). A context-based approach to the Frost poem might look at Frost's friendship with another poet, Edward Thomas, for whom Frost wrote the poem, and its influence on Thomas's decision to enlist in the army at the start of World War I.

◆ 427

Read the work more than once. Reading literature, watching films, or listening to speeches is like driving to a new destination: the first time you go, you need to concentrate on getting there; on subsequent trips, you can see other aspects—the scenery, the curve of the road, other possible routes—that you couldn't pay attention to earlier. When you experience a piece of literature for the first time, you usually focus on the story, the plot, the overall meaning. By experiencing it repeatedly, you can see how its effects are achieved, what the pieces are and how they fit together, where different patterns emerge, how the author crafted the work.

To analyze a literary work, then, plan to read it more than once, with the assumption that every part of the text is there for a reason. Focus on details, even on a single detail that shows up more than once: Why is it there? What can it mean? How does it affect our experience of reading or studying the text? Also, look for anomalies, details that *don't* fit the patterns: Why are they part of the text? What can they mean? How do they affect the experience of the text? See the **READING IN ACADEMIC CONTEXTS** chapter for several different methods for reading a text.

10–32

387–89

Compose a strong thesis. The **THESIS** of a literary analysis should be specific, limited, and open to potential disagreement. In addition, it should be analytical, not evaluative: avoid thesis statements that make overall judgments, such as a reviewer might do: "Virginia Woolf's *The Waves* is a failed experiment in narrative" or "No one has equaled the achievement of *The Lego Movie*." Rather, offer a way of seeing the text: "The choice presented in Robert Frost's 'The Road Not Taken' ultimately makes no difference"; "The plot of *The Lego Movie* reflects contemporary American media culture."

Read the text carefully. When you analyze a text, you need to find specific, brief passages that support your interpretation. Then you should interpret those passages in terms of their language, their context, or your reaction to them as a reader. To find such passages, you must read the text closely, questioning it as you go, asking, for example:

- What language provides evidence to support your thesis?
- What does each word (phrase, passage) mean exactly?
- Why does the writer choose *this* language, *these* words? What are the implications or connotations of the language? If the language is dense or difficult, why might the writer have written it that way?
- What images or metaphors are used? What is their effect on the meaning?
- What patterns of language, imagery, or plot do you see? If something is repeated, what significance does the repetition have?
- How does each word, phrase, or passage relate to what precedes and follows it?
- How does the experience of reading the text affect its meaning?

- What words, phrases, or passages connect to a larger **CONTEXT**? What language demonstrates that this work reflects or is affected by that context?

10–32

- How do these various elements of language, image, and pattern support your interpretation?

Your analysis should focus on analyzing and interpreting your subject, not simply summarizing or paraphrasing it. Many literary analyses also use the strategy of **COMPARING** two or more works.

424–31

Find evidence to support your interpretation.   The parts of the text you examine in your close reading become the evidence you use to support your interpretation. Some think that we're all entitled to our own opinions about literature. And indeed we are. But when writing a literary analysis, we're entitled only to our own *well-supported* and *well-argued* opinions. When you analyze a text, you must treat it like any other **ARGUMENT**: you need to discuss how the text creates an effect or expresses a theme, and then you have to show **EVIDENCE** from the text—significant plot or structural elements; important characters; patterns of language, imagery, or action—to back up your argument.

397–417

401–8

Pay attention to matters of style.   Literary analyses have certain conventions for using pronouns and verbs.

- In informal papers, it's okay to use the first person: "I believe Frost's narrator has little basis for claiming that one road is 'less traveled.'" In more formal essays, make assertions directly; claim authority to make statements about the text: "Frost's narrator has no basis for claiming that one road is 'less traveled.'"

- Discuss textual features in the **PRESENT TENSE** even if quotations from the text are in another tense: "When Nick finds Gatsby's body floating in the pool, he says very little about it: 'the laden mattress moved irregularly down the pool.'" Describe the historical context of the setting in the **PAST TENSE**: "In the 1920s, such estates as Gatsby's were rare."

HB-12–14

HB-12–14

MLA 548–96
528–31
535–38

650–52
391

Cite and document sources appropriately. Use **MLA** citation and documentation style unless told otherwise. Format **QUOTATIONS** properly, and use **SIGNAL PHRASES** to introduce quoted material.

Think about format and design. Brief essays do not require **HEADINGS**; text divisions are usually marked by **TRANSITIONS** between paragraphs. In longer papers, though, headings can be helpful.

Organizing a Literary Analysis

[Of a single text]

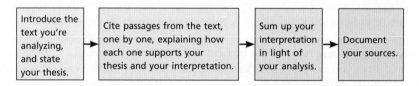

[Comparing two texts]

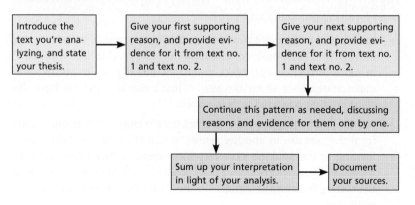

academic literacies · rhetorical situations · genres · fields · processes · strategies · research MLA / APA · media / design · readings · handbook

Taking Stock of Your Work

Take stock of what you've written by writing out answers to these questions:

- How did you go about analyzing the text? Which method did you use? Why?
- Was your thesis specific and limited? Did it offer a way to see the text?
- Did you provide sufficient evidence from the text or its context to support your analysis?
- What did you do especially well? What could still be improved?
- How did other readers' responses influence your writing?
- What would you do differently next time?
- Are you pleased with your analysis? What did it teach you about the text you analyzed? Did it make you want to study more works by the same author?

IF YOU NEED MORE HELP

See Chapter 30 for guidelines on **DRAFTING**, Chapter 31 on **ASSESSING YOUR OWN WRITING**, Chapter 32 on **GETTING RESPONSE AND REVISING**, and Chapter 33 on **EDITING AND PROOFREADING**. See Chapter 34 if you are required to submit your analysis in a writing **PORTFOLIO**.

340–42
343–47
348–55
356–60
361–70

18 Memoirs

We write memoirs to explore our past—about shopping for a party dress with Grandma, or driving a car for the first time, or breaking up with our first love. Memoirs focus on events and people and places that are important to us. We usually have two goals when we write a memoir: to capture an important moment and to convey something about its significance for us. You may be asked to write memoirs or personal reflections that include memoirs in *psychology*, *education*, and *English* courses. The following example is from Pulitzer Prize–winning journalist Rick Bragg's autobiography, *All Over but the Shoutin'*. Bragg grew up in Alabama, and in this memoir he recalls when, as a teenager, he paid a final visit to his dying father.

RICK BRAGG

All Over but the Shoutin'

He was living in a little house in Jacksonville, Alabama, a college and mill town that was the closest urban center—with its stoplights and a high school and two supermarkets—to the country roads we roamed in our raggedy cars. He lived in the mill village, in one of those houses the mills subsidized for their workers, back when companies still did things like that. It was not much of a place, but better than anything we had ever lived in as a family. I knocked and a voice like an old woman's, punctuated with a cough that sounded like it came from deep in the guts, told me to come on in, it ain't locked.

It was dark inside, but light enough to see what looked like a bundle of quilts on the corner of a sofa. Deep inside them was a ghost of a man, his hair and beard long and going dirty gray, his face pale and cut with deep grooves. I knew I was in the right house because my daddy's only

academic literacies · rhetorical situations · genres · fields · processes · strategies · research MLA / APA · media / design · readings · handbook

real possessions, a velvet-covered board pinned with medals, sat inside a glass cabinet on a table. But this couldn't be him.

He coughed again, spit into a can and struggled to his feet, but stopped somewhere short of standing straight up, as if a stoop was all he could manage. "Hey, Cotton Top," he said, and then I knew. My daddy, who was supposed to be a still-young man, looked like the walking dead, not just old but damaged, poisoned, used up, crumpled up and thrown in a corner to die. I thought that the man I would see would be the trim, swaggering, high-toned little rooster of a man who stared back at me from the pages of my mother's photo album, the young soldier clowning around in Korea, the arrow-straight, good-looking boy who posed beside my mother back before the fields and mop handle and the rest of it took her looks. The man I remembered had always dressed nice even when there was no cornmeal left, whose black hair always shone with oil, whose chin, even when it wobbled from the beer, was always angled up, high.

I thought he would greet me with that strong voice that sounded so fine when he laughed and so evil when, slurred by a quart of corn likker, he whirled through the house and cried and shrieked, tormented by things we could not see or even imagine. I thought he would be the man and monster of my childhood. But that man was as dead as a man could be, and this was what remained, like when a snake sheds its skin and leaves a dry and brittle husk of itself hanging in the Johnson grass.

"It's all over but the shoutin' now, ain't it, boy," he said, and when he let the quilt slide from his shoulders I saw how he had wasted away, how the bones seemed to poke out of his clothes, and I could see how it killed his pride to look this way, unclean, and he looked away from me for a moment, ashamed.

He made a halfhearted try to shake my hand but had a coughing fit again that lasted a minute, coughing up his life, his lungs, and after that I did not want to touch him. I stared at the tops of my sneakers, ashamed to look at his face. He had a dark streak in his beard below his lip, and I wondered why, because he had never liked snuff. Now I know it was blood.

I remember much of what he had to say that day. When you don't see someone for eight, nine years, when you see that person's life red on their lips and know that you will never see them beyond this day, you listen close, even if what you want most of all is to run away.

"Your momma, she alright?" he said.

I said I reckon so.

"The other boys? They alright?"   10

I said I reckon so.

Then he was quiet for a minute, as if trying to find the words to a question to which he did not really want an answer.

"They ain't never come to see me. How come?"

I remember thinking, fool, why do you think? But I just choked down my words, and in doing so I gave up the only real chance I would ever have to accuse him, to attack him with the facts of his own sorry nature and the price it had cost us all. The opportunity hung perfectly still in the air in front of my face and fists, and I held my temper and let it float on by. I could have no more challenged him, berated him, hurt him, than I could have kicked some three-legged dog. Life had kicked his ass pretty good.

"How come?"   15

I just shrugged.

For the next few hours—unless I was mistaken, having never had one before—he tried to be my father. Between coughing and long pauses when he fought for air to generate his words, he asked me if I liked school, if I had ever gotten any better at math, the one thing that just flat evaded me. He asked me if I ever got even with the boy who blacked my eye ten years ago, and nodded his head, approvingly, as I described how I followed him into the boys' bathroom and knocked his dick string up to his watch pocket, and would have dunked his head in the urinal if the aging principal, Mr. Hand, had not had to pee and caught me dragging him across the concrete floor.

He asked me about basketball and baseball, said he had heard I had a good game against Cedar Springs, and I said pretty good, but it was two years ago, anyway. He asked if I had a girlfriend and I said, "One," and he said, "Just one?" For the slimmest of seconds he almost grinned and the young, swaggering man peeked through, but disappeared again in the disease that cloaked him. He talked and talked and never said a word, at least not the words I wanted.

He never said he was sorry.

He never said he wished things had turned out different.   20

He never acted like he did anything wrong.

Part of it, I know, was culture. Men did not talk about their feelings in his hard world. I did not expect, even for a second, that he would bare his soul. All I wanted was a simple acknowledgment that he was wrong, or at least too drunk to notice that he left his pretty wife and sons alone again and again, with no food, no money, no way to get any, short of begging, because when she tried to find work he yelled, screamed, refused. No, I didn't expect much.

After a while he motioned for me to follow him into a back room where he had my present, and I planned to take it and run. He handed me a long, thin box, and inside was a brand-new, well-oiled Remington .22 rifle. He said he had bought it some time back, just kept forgetting to give it to me. It was a fine gun, and for a moment we were just like anybody else in the culture of that place, where a father's gift of a gun to his son is a rite. He said, with absolute seriousness, not to shoot my brothers.

I thanked him and made to leave, but he stopped me with a hand on my arm and said wait, that ain't all, that he had some other things for me. He motioned to three big cardboard egg cartons stacked against one wall.

Inside was the only treasure I truly have ever known.   25

I had grown up in a house in which there were only two books, the King James Bible and the spring seed catalog. But here, in these boxes, were dozens of hardback copies of everything from Mark Twain to Sir Arthur Conan Doyle. There was a water-damaged Faulkner, and the nearly complete set of Edgar Rice Burroughs's *Tarzan*. There was poetry and trash, Zane Grey's *Riders of the Purple Sage,* and a paperback with two naked women on the cover. There was a tiny, old copy of *Arabian Nights,* threadbare Hardy Boys, and one Hemingway. He had bought most of them at a yard sale, by the box or pound, and some at a flea market. He did not even know what he was giving me, did not recognize most of the writers. "Your momma said you still liked to read," he said.

There was Shakespeare. My father did not know who he was, exactly, but he had heard the name. He wanted them because they were pretty, because they were wrapped in fake leather, because they looked like rich folks' books. I do not love Shakespeare, but I still have those books. I would not trade them for a gold monkey.

"They's maybe some dirty books in there, by mistake, but I know you ain't interested in them, so just throw 'em away," he said. "Or at least, throw 'em away before your momma sees 'em." And then I swear to God he winked.

I guess my heart should have broken then, and maybe it did, a little. I guess I should have done something, anything, besides mumble "Thank you, Daddy." I guess that would have been fine, would not have betrayed in some way my mother, my brothers, myself. But I just stood there, trapped somewhere between my long-standing, comfortable hatred, and what might have been forgiveness. I am trapped there still.

Bragg's memoir illustrates all the features that make a memoir good: how the son and father react to each other creates the kind of suspense that keeps us reading; vivid details and rich dialogue bring the scene to life. His later reflections make the significance of that final meeting very clear.

For four more memoirs, see CHAPTER 67.

Key Features / Memoirs

A good story.   Your memoir should be interesting, to yourself and others. It need not be about a world-shaking event, but your topic—and how you write about it—should interest your readers. At the center of most good stories stands a conflict or question to be resolved. The most compelling memoirs feature some sort of situation or problem that needs resolution. That need for resolution is another name for suspense. It's what makes us want to keep reading.

Vivid details.   Details bring a memoir to life by giving readers mental images of the sights, sounds, smells, tastes, and textures of the world in which your story takes place. The goal is to show as well as tell, to take readers there. When Bragg describes a "voice like an old woman's, punctuated with a cough that sounded like it came from deep in the guts," we can hear his dying father ourselves. A memoir is more than simply a report of what happened; it uses vivid details and dialogue to bring the events of the past to life, much as good fiction brings to life events that the writer makes up or embellishes. Depending on your topic and medium, you may want to provide some of the details in audio or visual form.

Clear significance. Memories of the past are filtered through our view from the present: we pick out some moments in our lives as significant, some as more important or vivid than others. Over time, our interpretations change, and our memories themselves change.

A good memoir conveys something about the significance of its subject. As a writer, you need to reveal something about what the incident means to you. You don't, however, want to simply announce the significance as if you're tacking on the moral of the story. Bragg tells us that he's "trapped between [his] long-standing, comfortable hatred, and what might have been forgiveness," but he doesn't come right out and say that's why the incident is so important to him.

A BRIEF GUIDE TO WRITING MEMOIRS

Choosing an Event to Write About

LIST several events or incidents from your past that you consider significant in some way. They do not have to be earthshaking; indeed, they may involve a quiet moment that only you see as important—a brief encounter with a remarkable person, a visit to a special place, a memorable achievement (or failure), something that makes you laugh whenever you think about it. Writing about events that happened at least a few years ago is often easier than writing about recent events because you can more easily step back and see those events with a clear perspective. To choose the event that you will write about, consider how well you can recall what happened, how interesting it will be to readers, and whether you want to share it with an audience.

332–33

Considering the Rhetorical Situation

PURPOSE   What is the importance of the memory you are trying to convey? How will this story help you understand yourself and your readers understand you, as you were then and as you are now?

55–56

57–60 ■ **AUDIENCE** Who are your readers? Why will they care about your memoir? What do you want them to think of you after reading it? How can you help them understand your experience?

66–68 ■ **STANCE** What impression do you want to give, and how can your words contribute to that impression? What tone do you want to project? Sincere? Serious? Humorous? Detached? Self-critical?

69–71 ■ **MEDIA / DESIGN** Will your memoir be a print document? A speech? Will it be posted on a website? Can you include photographs, audio or video clips, or other visual texts?

Generating Ideas and Text

334–35 ○ **Think about what happened.** Take a few minutes to write out an account of the incident: **WHAT** happened, **WHERE** it took place, **WHO** else was involved, what was said, how you feel about it, and so on. Can you identify any tension or conflict that will make for a compelling story? If not, you might want to rethink your topic.

Consider its significance. Why do you still remember this event? What effect has it had on your life? What makes you want to tell someone else about it? Does it say anything about you? What about it might interest someone else? If you have trouble answering these questions, you should probably find another topic. But in general, once you have defined the significance of the incident, you can be sure you have a story to tell—and a reason for telling it.

Think about the details. The best memoirs connect with readers by giving them a sense of what it was like to be there, leading them to experience in words and images what the writer experienced in life. Spend some time 443–51 ◆ **DESCRIBING** the incident, writing what you see, hear, smell, touch, and taste when you envision it. Do you have any photos or memorabilia or other **VISUAL** materials you might include in your memoir? Try writing out **DIALOGUE**, things that were said (or, if you can't recall exactly, things that might have been said). Look at what you come up with—is there detail enough to bring the scene to life? Anything that might be called vivid? If you don't have enough detail, you might reconsider whether you recall enough about the incident to write about it. If you have trouble coming up with plenty of detail, try **FREEWRITING**, **LISTING**, or **LOOPING**.

653–63
452–56

331–33

Ways of Organizing Memoirs

[Tell about the event from beginning to end]

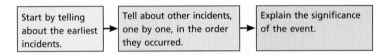

[Start at the end and tell how the event came about]

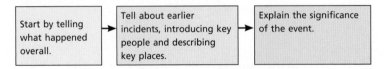

Taking Stock of Your Work

Take stock of what you've written by writing out answers to these questions:

- How well do you think you told the story?

- How did you go about coming up with ideas and generating text?

- How did you go about drafting your narrative?

- Did you use photographs or any other visual or audio elements? What did they add? Can you think of such elements you might have used?

- How did others' responses influence your writing?

- What did you do especially well? What could be improved? What would you do differently next time?

340–42
343–47
348–55
356–60
361–70

IF YOU NEED MORE HELP

See Chapter 30 for guidelines on **DRAFTING**, Chapter 31 on **ASSESSING YOUR OWN WRITING**, Chapter 32 on **GETTING RESPONSE AND REVISING**, and Chapter 33 on **EDITING AND PROOFREADING**. See Chapter 34 if you are required to submit your memoir in a writing **PORTFOLIO**.

Profiles

Profiles are written portraits—of people, places, events, or other things. We find profiles of celebrities, travel destinations, and offbeat festivals in magazines and newspapers, on radio and TV. A profile presents a subject in an entertaining way that conveys its significance, showing us something or someone that we may not have known existed or that we see every day but don't know much about. In college *journalism* classes, students learn to create profiles using words and, in many cases, photos and video as well. Here is a profile of a common, everyday object: the drinking straw. The writer, Ernie Smith, is a social media journalist, blogger, and founder of the *Tedium* newsletter, where a version of this essay originally appeared. It was revised and reposted on *Atlas Obscura*, an online news site.

ERNIE SMITH

A Brief History of the Modern-Day Straw, the World's Most Wasteful Commodity

The plastic straw is a simple invention with relatively modest value: For a few moments, the device helps make beverages easier to drink. And then, due to reasons of sanitation and ease of use, the straws are thrown away, never to be seen again.

Except, of course, the straw you use in your iced coffee doesn't biodegrade, and stays around basically forever, often as ocean junk. That, understandably, is leading to chatter around banning plastic straws—notably in Berkeley, California, often the first place to ban anything potentially damaging to the environment.

And while the rest of the world won't be banning straws anytime soon, maybe they should start thinking about it, because the problem

with straws is one of scale. According to *National Geographic*, Americans use *500 million* straws every single day — more than one per person daily.

The resulting waste is difficult to recycle and often shows up in landfills, at sea, and on the beach; the plastic is particularly dangerous for marine wildlife.

But it wasn't always this way. The modern day-straw was an attempt to solve the failings of a device that was very much biodegradable. And that replacement was itself biodegradable. The problem, really, is what came after.

Marvin Stone, perhaps more than any other person, deserves credit for making artificial straws useful and popular. But he doesn't deserve the blame for what straws have become.

Stone was a serial inventor who was known for manufacturing a variety of products with a cylinder shape, such as cigarette holders. Born in Ohio in 1842, but based in Washington, D.C., for much of his life, he launched his career as a journalist, but eventually followed his father's inventive spirit into the realm of manufacturing. Being a D.C. resident, he was a big fan of mint juleps, a drink popularized in the

city during the 19th century by famed Kentucky Senator Henry Clay. Stone would order the drinks at Aman's, a well-known restaurant in D.C. during the era—though he was disappointed by the rye straws, which had a negative effect on his drink.

Yes, that's right, before plastic straws, we used straws made of rye grass—produced naturally, from the ground. The manufacturing process, according to a *The Small Grains*, a book by Mark Alfred Carleton, was closer to wheat than plastic.

"After bleaching, the straws are assorted by hand, each individual stalk being examined, and the imperfect ones removed," Carleton explained. "They are then cut, the five lower joints only being utilized for drinking purposes. The sheaths are then removed, and the straw washed and bound into bundles ready for the market."

The rye straw, while the first widely used variety of drinking straw, 10 had some significant problems—including that the straws affected the taste of the drink and that they had a tendency to disintegrate into the beverage, leaving sediment at the bottom of the drink.

Stone was just the guy to fix the problem. He was already making cigarette holders at his nearby factory, and had recently patented a fountain pen holder, so he knew a thing or two about building cylinder-shaped objects. So he wrapped a sheet of paper around a pencil, added some glue, and suddenly he had invented the paper straw. He gave his initial supply to Aman's for his own personal use, but found

that people he ran into at the bar were impressed enough with his invention that they wanted their own. That led Stone to patent the device, and within a few years, he had cornered the market on paper straws, which became popular with the rise of soda fountains at pharmacies.

According to a 1889 article from *The Lafayette Advertiser*, Stone's factory was producing 2 million straws per day not long after he filed for that patent. And when he died in 1899, Stone was well-regarded in obituaries.

"Although few pharmacists have had the pleasure of personally meeting Mr. Stone, his name is, nevertheless, known wherever there is a soda fountain," the pharmacy trade publication *The Spatula* wrote at the time.

But the straws had a problem—simply, they weren't as durable as plastic, and while they didn't negatively affect the taste of the soda like rye straws did, they did eventually disintegrate in the beverages. By the 1960s, plastic straws, which initially carried a sense of novelty for the public because they could be made clear, had usurped the paper version entirely.

Good for plastic. Bad for the environment.

In 2017, we're perhaps more aware than ever of the weaknesses of the plastic straw, bendable or not. And more than one entrepreneur has tried to create new alternatives that solve the problems of both paper and plastic.

Many of these straw varieties rely on permanence over disposability and biodegradability, which means you'll be carrying a straw around with you—no matter how weird that seems.

Perhaps the most intriguing natural option for straw drinking is the bamboo straw. The company Brush With Bamboo, which makes a bamboo-based toothbrush (and sports support from Ed Begley Jr. on its website), also sells a set of bamboo drinking straws, which are handmade in India and designed to be reused for many years. As a result, the company sells a 12-pack of bamboo straws for $20—or more than a dollar a straw.

Other materials, like metal, have also become common straw vectors. And more than one small-scale manufacturer, like the Michigan company Strawesome, has tried selling straws made from glass. (That said, neither of these straws sound good for your teeth.)

On the disposable front, the primary alternative that's revealed itself is corn, which has perhaps gotten the closest in terms of disposability and flexibility. Eco-Products, a Certified B Corporation, sells plastic materials to stores and other retailers made from Ingeo, a biopolymer often produced from corn that's compostable and renewable.

While not horribly cheap compared to standard plastic straws—they sell for about a quarter a pop in small quantities—Eco-Products' compostable straws are a lot better for the environment.

And hey, if you can't beat 'em, eat 'em—the straws that is. Starbucks earned a whole lot of buzz a couple years ago after it started

selling cookie straws to go with its Frappuccinos, and it's not a phenomenon that's completely unheard of—candy straws and beef straws are things that exist. But perhaps the most natural approach to edible straw-making might be ice straws. Just make sure you don't want a refill.

All these alternative materials are great—but the concerns about plastic have brought long-dormant paper straws back from the brink.

And you can thank an eccentric billionaire for that.

A couple years ago, I called Ted Turner "the Steve Jobs of television," as well as a "genius," and emphasized I was not being hyperbolic by making this claim—because what he did for television in the '70s was genuinely groundbreaking. 25

Now, while Turner no longer has the level of influence and power he once did—he no longer owns Turner Broadcasting (which he regrets), and he literally gave a billion dollars to the United Nations in 1997, which probably did a number on his checkbook—he does own a lot of land, and that land contains a lot of bison. And that means that he's well suited for being a restaurant entrepreneur.

Ted's Montana Grill, a chain he started in 2002, is quietly an environmental maverick—the entire chain was built around the idea of ensuring the bison would stick around for generations to come by building business value around the animal. Despite the fact you're eating bison, it's actually hugely beneficial for the species' long-term survival because there's a business case for investing in ranching bison. But beyond that, Turner and his business partner George McKerrow Jr. saw an opportunity to build an eco-friendly legacy even greater than that of *Captain Planet*.

And the straw is kind of the key element of the whole thing. In a 2011 interview with the podcast and news site *Southeast Green*, McKerrow (who is also known for starting the LongHorn Steakhouse and Capital Grille chains) explained how he helped bring the paper straw back to life as a tool of environmentalism—and how it was one of the biggest challenges he faced in his efforts to minimize the amount of plastic used by the chain.

"I remember growing up with a paper straw," McKerrow explained in an interview with the podcast's Beth Bond. "It collapsed a lot, but heck, it was better for the environment than a plastic straw, which might be in a landfill for a hundred-plus years, or for eternity."

McKerrow looked online for info and soon found himself on 30
the phone with the owner of Precision Products Group—the parent
company of Paramount Tube, the direct descendant of Stone's manufacturing company. McKerrow noted that paper straws hadn't been
manufactured anywhere since 1970, but that the firm was willing to pay
top-dollar to get those straws. Precision had the equipment around, but
it had fallen into disuse. But inspired by the phone call, the company
pledged to check to see what was possible.

"About two weeks later, he got back to me, and he said, 'We
found that machine,' and I could hear it in his voice that he was really
excited," McKerrow continued. "He said, 'The engineers think that they
can make it work.'"

And they did. Ted's Montana Grill became the first company to
use paper straws in more than 30 years, but the quality issues with the
straws—made from paper and coated in beeswax—were still apparent, leading to customer complaints. Initially, McKerrow relented for a
time, letting plastic into the cups at the restaurant, but eventually, he
got a hold of Precision again, only to find that the phone call a couple
years prior had led the firm to shift its entire corporate direction.

Precision, seeing a market need for eco-friendly straws, launched
a brand-new subsidiary, Aardvark, to bring their paper straws back to
the market.

"The story goes, we recreated a whole industry, something that
was old became new again, something that was better for the environment by at least 50 percent," McKerrow added.

They aren't cheap—at 1.5 cents each, the cost is far above the 35
commodity price of standard plastic straws. But in some ways, the extra
cost on the front end means it's a whole lot cheaper for the environment.

Like most people, I drink a lot of beverages on an average day,
often out of cups, sometimes with straws. There's something strangely
appealing about the basic disposability of cups that you don't have
to carry around everywhere. We live in a disposable culture and we
probably throw away more disposable cups than anything else.

But there are consequences to that disposability. In 2015, a sea
turtle became the face of a budding anti-straw movement after a gruesome video of that turtle getting a straw removed from its nose drew
millions of views online. (Aardvark launched a new bendy straw, with
sea turtle art, directly inspired by the story.)

academic literacies · rhetorical situations · genres · fields · processes · strategies · research MLA / APA · media / design · readings · handbook

That video is one of a few reasons why we're starting to see campaigns to cut back on straw usage pick up in a big way. It's easy fodder for corporate responsibility campaigns—Bacardi, a company that has probably benefited more than most from the existence of straws, started one last year—and multiple nonprofit campaigns have coalesced around the issue, including The Last Plastic Straw and One Less Straw.

Which doesn't mean we have to ban straws to stop them from polluting the environment, but there is a reason to discuss changing habits. How much harder is it to drink your coffee out of a cup that you bring with you? If you end up using a straw, is there a way to get just a little bit more mileage out of that piece of plastic? And if the issue matters to you, does that affect the places you go to buy things? (And no, this isn't a commercial for Ted Turner's restaurant chain.)

The problem with straws are that they're so insignificant that we take them for granted. Perhaps we shouldn't.   40

Smith's profile examines the environmental impacts of a common household and restaurant object, the plastic drinking straw. The writer engages our interest first with the title, which claims that straws, seemingly inconsequential, are "the world's most wasteful commodity." He then provides a history of the drinking straw, alternatives to plastic straws, and a tale of the reemergence of the paper straw.

📖 For four more profiles, see CHAPTER 68.

Key Features / Profiles

An interesting subject.   The subject may be something unusual, or it may be something ordinary shown in an intriguing way. You might profile an interesting person (like billionaire Ted Turner), a place (like the company that makes paper straws), an event (like the rescue of the sea turtle), or an object (like the drinking straw).

Any necessary background.   A profile usually includes just enough information to let readers know something about the subject's larger context. Smith quickly explains the problems with plastic straws: there are billions of them, they don't degrade, and they're hard to recycle, making them dangerous to wildlife, but leaves out other details about straws that don't matter for this profile.

An interesting angle.   A good profile captures its subject from a particular angle. Sometimes finding an angle will be fairly easy because your topic—like the history of the drinking straw—is offbeat enough to be interesting in and of itself. Other topics, though, may require you to find a particular aspect that you can focus on. For example, a profile of a person might focus on the important work the person does or a challenging hobby they pursue; it would likely ignore aspects of the person's life that don't relate to that angle.

A firsthand account.   Whether you are writing about a person, place, object, or event, you need to spend time observing and interacting with your subject. With a person, interacting means watching and conversing. Journalists tell us that "following the guy around," getting your subject to do something and talk about it at the same time, yields excellent material for a profile. When one writer met Theodor Geisel (Dr. Seuss) before profiling him, she asked him not only to talk about his characters but also to draw one—resulting in an illustration for her profile. With a place, object, or event, interacting may mean visiting and participating, although sometimes you may gather even more information by playing the role of the silent observer.

Engaging details.   You need to include details that bring your subject to life. These may include *specific information* ("Americans use *500 million* straws every single day—more than one per person daily"); *sensory images* ("[Rye] straws affected the taste of the drink and . . . had a tendency to disintegrate into the beverage, leaving sediment at the bottom of the drink"); *figurative language* (Giving a billion dollars to the UN "did a number on [Ted Turner's] checkbook"); *dialogue* ("He said, 'The engineers think that they can make it work'"); and *anecdotes* ("He wrapped a sheet of paper around a pencil, added some glue, and suddenly he had invented the paper

straw"). Choose details that show rather than tell—that let your audience see and hear your subject rather than merely read an abstract description of it. Sometimes you may let them see and hear it literally, by including *photographs* or *video and audio clips*. And be sure all the details create some *dominant impression* of your subject: the impression that we get out of this profile, for example, is of a simple device that is more complicated and destructive than it seems.

A BRIEF GUIDE TO WRITING PROFILES

Choosing a Suitable Subject

A person, a place, an object, an event—whatever you choose, make sure it's something that arouses your curiosity and that you're not too familiar with. Knowing your subject too well can blind you to interesting details. **LIST** five to ten interesting subjects that you can experience firsthand. Obviously, you can't profile a person who won't be interviewed or a place or activity that can't be observed. So before you commit to a topic, make sure you'll be able to carry out firsthand research.

331–32

Considering the Rhetorical Situation

PURPOSE   Why are you writing the profile? What angle will best achieve your purpose? How can you inform *and engage* your audience?

55–56

AUDIENCE   Who is your audience? How familiar are they with your subject? What expectations of your profile might they have? What background information or definitions do you need to provide? How interested will they be—and how can you get their interest?

57–60

66–68 ■
STANCE What view of your subject do you expect to present? Sympathetic? Critical? Sarcastic? Will you strive for a carefully balanced perspective?

69–71 ■
MEDIA/DESIGN Will your profile be a print document? electronic? an oral presentation? Can (and should) you include images or any other visuals? Will it be recorded as an audio file or multimodal text?

Generating Ideas and Text

Explore what you already know about your subject. Why do you find this subject interesting? What do you know about it now? What do you expect to find out about it from your research? What preconceived ideas about or emotional reactions to this subject do you have? Why do you have them? It may be helpful to try some of the activities in the chapter on 331–39 ○ **GENERATING IDEAS AND TEXT**.

Visit your subject. If you're writing about an amusement park, go there; if you're profiling the man who runs the carousel, make an appointment to meet and interview him. Get to know your subject—if you profile Ben and Jerry, sample the ice cream! Take photos or videos if there's anything you might want to show visually in your profile. Find helpful hints for 506–8 ● **OBSERVING** and **INTERVIEWING** in the chapter on finding sources.

If you're planning to interview someone, prepare questions. If Smith had interviewed manufacturers of alternatives to plastic straws, he might have asked questions like "How do you manufacture them?" and "If we're supposed to use them over and over again, how can we clean them?"

Do additional research. You may be able to write a profile based entirely on your field research. You may, though, need to do some library or web 477 ● **RESEARCH** as well, to deepen your understanding, get a different perspective, or fill in gaps. Often the people you interview can help you find sources of additional information; so can the sponsors of events and those in charge of places. To learn more about a city park, for instance, contact the government office that maintains it. Download any good photos of your subject that you find online (such as the photos of straws and the soda fountain), both to refer to as you write and to illustrate your profile.

Analyze your findings. Look for patterns, images, recurring ideas or phrases, and engaging details. Look for contrasts or discrepancies: between a subject's words and actions, between the appearance of a place and what goes on there, between your expectations and your research findings. Smith probably expected plastic straws to be an environmental problem, but he may not have expected that problem to be as big as it is. You may find the advice in the **READING IN ACADEMIC CONTEXTS** chapter helpful here.

10–32

Come up with an angle. What's most memorable about your subject? What most interests you? What will interest your audience? Smith focuses on the environmental impact and usability of straws and alternatives to plastic straws. Sometimes you'll know your angle from the start; other times you'll need to look further into your topic. You might try **CLUSTERING**, **CUBING**, **FREEWRITING**, and **LOOPING**, to help you look at your topic from many different angles.

331–34

Note details that support your angle. Use your angle to focus your research and generate text. Try **DESCRIBING** your subject as clearly as you can, **COMPARING** your subject with other subjects of its sort, writing **DIALOGUE** that captures your subject. Smith, for instance, tells us how rye straws were manufactured and provides an intriguing look at how Ted Turner's desire for an eco-friendly restaurant chain led to the resurgence of the paper straw. Engaging details will bring your subject to life for your audience. Together, these details should create a dominant impression of your subject.

443–51
424–31
452–56

Ways of Organizing a Profile

462–70

One common way to organize a profile is by **NARRATING**. For example, if you are profiling a chess championship, you may write about it chronologically, creating suspense as you move from start to finish.

[As a narrative]

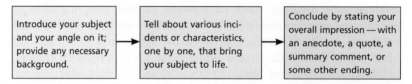

Introduce your subject and your angle on it; provide any necessary background. → Tell about various incidents or characteristics, one by one, that bring your subject to life. → Conclude by stating your overall impression — with an anecdote, a quote, a summary comment, or some other ending.

443–51

Sometimes you may organize a profile by **DESCRIBING**—a person or a place, for instance.

[As a description]

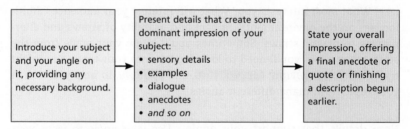

Introduce your subject and your angle on it, providing any necessary background. → Present details that create some dominant impression of your subject:
• sensory details
• examples
• dialogue
• anecdotes
• *and so on* → State your overall impression, offering a final anecdote or quote or finishing a description begun earlier.

Taking Stock of Your Work

Take stock of what you've written by writing out answers to these questions:

* How did you go about choosing a subject—and an angle on that subject?

* How did you go about doing the necessary research? Did you encounter any difficulties?

academic literacies · rhetorical situations · genres · fields · processes · strategies · research MLA / APA · media / design · readings · handbook

- How did you go about drafting your profile?
- Did you use photographs or any other visual or audio elements? What did they add? Can you think of such elements you might have used?
- How did others' responses influence your writing?
- What did you do especially well? What could still be improved? What would you do differently next time?

IF YOU NEED MORE HELP

See Chapter 30 for guidelines on **DRAFTING**, Chapter 31 on **ASSESSING YOUR OWN WRITING**, Chapter 32 on **GETTING RESPONSE AND REVISING**, and Chapter 33 on **EDITING AND PROOFREADING**. See Chapter 34 if you are required to submit your analysis in a writing **PORTFOLIO**.

340–42
343–47
348–55
356–60
361–70

20 Proposals

Proposals are part of our personal lives: lovers propose marriage, friends propose sharing dinner and a movie, you offer to pay half the cost of a car and insurance if your parents will pay the other half. They are also part of our academic and professional lives: student leaders lobby for lights on bike paths. Musicians, artists, writers, and educators apply for grants. Researchers in all fields of the humanities, social sciences, sciences, and technology seek funding for their projects. In business, contractors bid on building projects, and companies and freelancers solicit work from potential clients. These are all examples of proposals, ideas put forward for consideration that say, "Here is a solution to a problem" or "This is what ought to be done." For example, here is a proposal for reducing the costs of college textbooks, written by an accounting professor at the University of Texas who is chairman of the university's Co-op Bookstore and himself a textbook author.

MICHAEL GRANOF

Course Requirement: Extortion

By now, entering college students and their parents have been warned: textbooks are outrageously expensive. Few textbooks for semester-long courses retail for less than $120, and those for science and math courses typically approach $180. Contrast this with the $20 to $30 cost of most hardcover best sellers and other trade books.

Perhaps these students and their parents can take comfort in knowing that the federal government empathizes with them, and in an attempt to ease their pain Congress asked its Advisory Committee on Student Financial Assistance to suggest a cure for the problem.

Unfortunately, though, the committee has proposed a remedy that would only worsen the problem.

The committee's report, released in May, mainly proposes strengthening the market for used textbooks—by encouraging college bookstores to guarantee that they will buy back textbooks, establishing online book swaps among students, and urging faculty to avoid switching textbooks from one semester to the next. The fatal flaw in that proposal (and similar ones made by many state legislatures) is that used books are the cause of, not the cure for, high textbook prices.

Yet there is a way to lighten the load for students in their budgets, if not their backpacks. With small modifications to the institutional arrangements between universities, publishers, and students, textbook costs could be reduced—and these changes could be made without government intervention.

Today the used-book market is exceedingly well organized and efficient. Campus bookstores buy back not only the books that will be used at their university the next semester but also those that will not. Those that are no longer on their lists of required books they resell to national wholesalers, which in turn sell them to college bookstores on campuses where they will be required. This means that even if a text is being adopted for the first time at a particular college, there is almost certain to be an ample supply of used copies.

As a result, publishers have the chance to sell a book to only one of the multiple students who eventually use it. Hence, publishers must cover their costs and make their profit in the first semester their books are sold—before used copies swamp the market. That's why the prices are so high.

As might be expected, publishers do what they can to undermine the used-book market, principally by coming out with new editions every three or four years. To be sure, in rapidly changing fields like biology and physics, the new editions may be academically defensible. But in areas like algebra and calculus, they are nothing more than a transparent attempt to ensure premature textbook obsolescence. Publishers also try to discourage students from buying used books by bundling the text with extra materials like workbooks and CDs that are not reusable and therefore cannot be passed from one student to another.

The system could be much improved if, first of all, colleges and publishers would acknowledge that textbooks are more akin to computer software than to trade books. A textbook's value, like that of a software program, is not in its physical form, but rather in its intellectual content. Therefore, just as software companies typically "site license" to colleges, so should textbook publishers.

Here's how it would work: A teacher would pick a textbook, and the college would pay a negotiated fee to the publisher based on the number of students enrolled in the class. If there were 50 students in the class, for example, the fee might be $15 per student, or $750 for the semester. If the text were used for ten semesters, the publisher would ultimately receive a total of $150 ($15 × 10) for each student enrolled in the course, or as much as $7,500.

In other words, the publisher would have a stream of revenue for as long as the text was in use. Presumably, the university would pass on this fee to the students, just as it does the cost of laboratory supplies and computer software. But the students would pay much less than the $900 a semester they now typically pay for textbooks.

Once the university had paid the license fee, each student would have the option of using the text in electronic format or paying more to purchase a hard copy through the usual channels. The publisher could set the price of hard copies low enough to cover only its production and distribution costs plus a small profit, because it would be covering most of its costs and making most of its profit by way of the license fees. The hard copies could then be resold to other students or back to the bookstore, but that would be of little concern to the publisher.

A further benefit of this approach is that it would not affect the way courses are taught. The same cannot be said for other recommendations from the Congressional committee and from state legislatures, like placing teaching materials on electronic reserve, urging faculty to adopt cheaper "no frills" textbooks, and assigning mainly electronic textbooks. While each of these suggestions may have merit, they force faculty to weigh students' academic interests against their fiscal concerns and encourage them to rely less on new textbooks.

Neither colleges nor publishers are known for their cutting-edge innovations. But if they could slightly change the way they do business, they would make a substantial dent in the cost of higher education and provide a real benefit to students and their parents.

academic literacies · rhetorical situations · genres · fields · processes · strategies · research MLA / APA · media / design · readings · handbook

This proposal clearly defines the problem—some textbooks cost a lot—and explains why. It proposes a solution to the problem of high textbook prices and offers reasons why this solution will work better than others. Its tone is reasonable and measured, yet decisive.

For four more proposals, see CHAPTER 69.

Key Features / Proposals

A well-defined problem. Some problems are self-evident and relatively simple, and you would not need much persuasive power to make people act—as with the problem "This university discards too much paper." While some people might see nothing wrong with throwing paper away, most are likely to agree that recycling is a good thing. Other issues are controversial: some people see them as problems while others do not, such as this one: "Motorcycle riders who do not wear helmets risk serious injury and raise health-care costs for everyone." Some motorcyclists believe that wearing or not wearing a helmet should be a personal choice; you would have to present arguments to convince your readers that not wearing a helmet is indeed a problem needing a solution. Any written proposal must establish at the outset that there is a problem—and that it's serious enough to require a solution. For some topics, visual or audio evidence of the problem may be helpful.

A recommended solution. Once you have defined the problem, you need to describe the solution you are suggesting and to explain it in enough detail for readers to understand what you are proposing. Again, photographs, diagrams, or other visuals may help. Sometimes you might suggest several solutions, weigh their merits, and choose the best one.

A convincing argument for your proposed solution. You need to convince readers that your solution is feasible—and that it is the best way to solve the problem. Sometimes you'll want to explain in detail how your proposed solution would work. See, for example, how the textbook proposal details the way a licensing system would operate. Visuals may strengthen this part of your argument as well.

Granof's proposal for reducing textbook prices via licensing fees might benefit from a photograph like this one, which provides a comparison of other approaches to the problem, such as buying used books or renting them.

A response to anticipated questions.   You may need to consider any questions readers may have about your proposal—and to show how its advantages outweigh any disadvantages. Had the textbook proposal been written for college budget officers, it would have needed to anticipate and answer questions about the costs of implementing the proposed solution.

A call to action.   The goal of a proposal is to persuade readers to accept your proposed solution. This solution may include asking readers to take action.

An appropriate tone.   Since you're trying to persuade readers to act, your tone is important—readers will always react better to a reasonable, respectful presentation than to anger or self-righteousness.

A BRIEF GUIDE TO WRITING PROPOSALS

Deciding on a Topic

Choose a problem that can be solved. Complex, large problems, such as poverty, hunger, or terrorism, usually require complex, large solutions. Most of the time, focusing on a smaller problem or a limited aspect of a large problem will yield a more manageable proposal. Rather than tackling the problem of world poverty, for example, think about the problem faced by people in your community who have lost jobs and need help until they find employment.

Considering the Rhetorical Situation

PURPOSE	Do you have a stake in a particular solution, or do you simply want to eliminate the problem by whatever solution might be adopted?	▮ 55–56
AUDIENCE	Do your readers share your view of the problem as a serious one needing a solution? Are they likely to be open to possible solutions or resistant? Do they have the authority to carry out a proposed solution?	▮ 57–60
STANCE	How can you show your audience that your proposal is reasonable and should be taken seriously? How can you demonstrate your own authority and credibility?	▮ 66–68
MEDIA / DESIGN	How will you deliver your proposal? In print? Electronically? As a speech? Would visuals, or video or audio clips help support your proposal?	▮ 69–71

Generating Ideas and Text

Explore potential solutions to the problem. Many problems can be solved in more than one way, and you need to show your readers that you've examined several potential solutions. You may develop solutions

477

424–31

on your own; more often, though, you'll need to do **RESEARCH** to see how others have solved—or tried to solve—similar problems. Don't settle on a single solution too quickly—you'll need to **COMPARE** the advantages and disadvantages of several solutions in order to argue convincingly for one.

Decide on the most desirable solution(s). One solution may be head and shoulders above others—but be open to rejecting all the possible solutions on your list and starting over if you need to, or to combining two or more potential solutions in order to come up with an acceptable fix.

Think about why your solution is the best one. Why did you choose your solution? Why will it work better than others? What has to be done to enact it? What will it cost? What makes you think it can be done? Writing out answers to these questions will help you argue for your solution: to show that you have carefully and objectively outlined a problem, analyzed the potential solutions, weighed their merits, and determined the reasons the solution you propose is the best.

Ways of Organizing a Proposal

You can organize a proposal in various ways, but always you will begin by establishing that there is a problem. You may then identify several possible solutions before recommending one of them or a combination of several. Sometimes, however, you might discuss only a single solution.

[Several possible solutions]

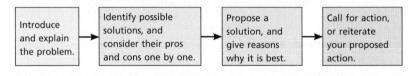

Introduce and explain the problem. → Identify possible solutions, and consider their pros and cons one by one. → Propose a solution, and give reasons why it is best. → Call for action, or reiterate your proposed action.

academic literacies · rhetorical situations · genres · fields · processes · strategies · research MLA / APA · media / design · readings · handbook

[A single solution]

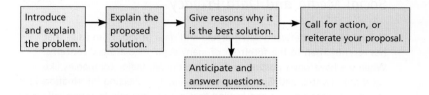

Taking Stock of Your Work

Take stock of what you've written by writing out answers to these questions:

- How did you decide on and limit your topic?
- How did you go about researching your topic?
- How did you determine the best solution to the problem you defined?
- Did you use visual elements (tables, graphs, diagrams, photographs), audio elements, or links effectively? If not, would they have helped?
- What did you do well in this piece? What could still be improved? What would you do differently next time?
- What have you learned about the processes of writing from writing this piece? What do you need to work on in the future?

TOPIC PROPOSALS

Instructors often ask students to write topic proposals to ensure that their topics are appropriate or manageable. Some instructors may also ask for an ANNOTATED BIBLIOGRAPHY showing that appropriate sources of information are available—more evidence that the project can be carried out. Here a student proposes a topic for an assignment in a writing course in which she has been asked to take a position on a global issue.

▲ 190–98

CATHERINE THOMS

Social Media and Data Privacy

The relationship between social media and data privacy is an issue that has recently risen to the forefront of many social media users' concerns. While we have been posting and sharing online, major companies like Facebook, Twitter, and Google have been silently collecting information about our personal lives and leaving that data vulnerable to potentially harmful exposure. As someone who has had their private information compromised multiple times by large-scale data breaches, I feel compelled to share my research on the dangers of such security breaches and how they can happen.

In this paper, I will argue that it is crucial for consumers to be aware of the ways in which social media platforms can gain access to consumers' private data and what those platforms can do with that data. In March 2018, it was revealed that 87 million Facebook profiles were exposed to manipulation by the political consulting firm Cambridge Analytica during the 2016 presidential election. I will use this scandal as an example of how the unlawful exposure of personal data can have far-reaching effects on external world events, and I plan to analyze how this scandal has functioned as a global catalyst for further scrutiny into the privacy mechanisms of social media.

I will concentrate on the specific ways personal data may be misused. Although sharing thoughts and pictures on social media may not seem like anything to think twice about, many people don't realize just how much is at stake should enough of that personal data fall into the wrong hands. Much of my research will be done on specific social media applications such as Facebook and Google Analytics, as that is where the heart of the issue resides and where consumers can learn the most about their personal data exposure and protection.

Thoms defines and narrows her topic (from data breaches to the specific ways consumers' data may be misused), discusses her interest, outlines her argument, and discusses her research strategy. Her goal is to convince her instructor that she has a realistic writing project and a clear plan.

Key Features / Topic Proposals

You'll need to explain what you want to write about, why you want to explore it, and what you'll do with your topic. Unless your instructor has additional requirements, here are the features to include:

A concise discussion of the subject. Topic proposals generally open with a brief discussion of the subject, outlining any important areas of controversy or debate associated with it and clarifying the extent of the writer's current knowledge of it. In its first two paragraphs, Thoms's proposal includes a concise statement of the topic she wishes to address.

A clear statement of your intended focus. State what aspect of the topic you intend to write on as clearly as you can, narrowing your focus appropriately. Thoms does so by stating her intended topic—data breaches—and then showing how she will focus on the specific ways consumers' data may be misused.

A rationale for choosing the topic. Tell your instructor why this topic interests you and why you want to write about it. Thoms both states what made her interested in her topic and hints at a practical reason for choosing it: plenty of information is available.

Mention of resources. To show your instructor that you can achieve your goal, you need to identify the available research materials.

IF YOU NEED MORE HELP

See Chapter 30 for guidelines on **DRAFTING**, Chapter 31 on **ASSESSING YOUR OWN WRITING**, Chapter 32 on **GETTING RESPONSE AND REVISING**, and Chapter 33 on **EDITING AND PROOFREADING**. See Chapter 34 if you are required to submit your proposal in a writing **PORTFOLIO**.

340–42
343–47
348–55
356–60
361–70

21 Reflections

Sometimes we write essays just to think about something—to speculate, ponder, probe; to play with an idea, develop a thought; or simply to share something. Reflective essays are our attempt to think something through by writing about it and to share our thinking with others. If such essays make an argument, it is about things we care or think about more than about what we believe to be "true." In college, you might be asked in courses across the curriculum to write formal or informal reflections in the form of essays, journals, design reports, or learning logs. Have a look at one example of a reflection by Edan Lepucki, a novelist and non-fiction writer. This essay originally appeared on the Op-Ed page of the *New York Times*.

EDAN LEPUCKI

Our Mothers as We Never Saw Them

In one of my favorite photographs of my mother, she's about 18 and very tan, with long, blond hair. It's the 1970s and she's wearing a white midriff and cutoffs. My dad is there, too, hugging her from behind, and from the looks of it, they're somewhere rural—maybe some pastoral patch of small-town New Jersey where they met.

I haven't seen this photo for years, I have no idea where it is now, but I still think of it—and, specifically, my mom in it. She looks really sexy; wars have been waged over less impressive waist-to-hip ratios. And she is so young and innocent. She hasn't yet dropped out of college, or gotten married. The young woman in this photo has no idea that life will bring her five children and five grandchildren, a conversion to Judaism, one divorce, two marriages, a move across the country.

For me, as for many daughters, the time before my mother became a mother is a string of stories, told and retold: the time she got hit by a car and had amnesia; the time she sold her childhood Barbie to buy a ticket to Woodstock; the time she worked as a waitress at Howard Johnson's, struggling to pay her way through her first year at Rutgers. The old photos of her are even more compelling than the stories because they're a historical record, carrying the weight of fact, even if the truth there is slippery: the trick of an image, and so much left outside the frame. These photos serve as a visual accompaniment to the myths. Because any story about your mother is part myth, isn't it?

After finishing my most recent novel, in part about mother-daughter relationships, I put out a call on social media for photos from women of their mothers before they were mothers. A character in the book, a young artist, does something similar, so I'd thought a lot about what the process might be like. I wasn't prepared, however, for how powerful the images I received would be.

The young women in these pictures are beautiful, fierce, sassy, goofy, cool, sweet—sometimes all at once. I asked contributors to tell me about their moms or the photo submitted, and they often wrote that something specific and special about their present-day mother—her smile, say, or her posture—was present in this earlier version.

What solace to know that time, aging and motherhood cannot take away a woman's essential identity. For daughters who closely resemble their moms, it must be an even bigger comfort; these mothers and daughters are twins, separated by a generation, and an old photo serves as a kind of mirror: How do I look? Even if there isn't a resemblance, we can't help but compare ourselves to our young mothers before they were mothers.

"I locate something of myself in the slope of her shoulders," said one contributor, Molly. "This makes me feel adjacent to her coolness."

Sometimes, too, a photo deepens the mystery of a mother. Emma, whose mom died when she was 8, says that she "cobbles together" an image of her mother from other people's memories. "Those

Adalena can see her own expression in this image of her mother, Hua Sou, which she contributed to the author's project.

points only give an outline," she writes, "let alone a shadow or full likeness of a person." She's heard plenty of stories about her mother's childhood, and about her early years as a mother, but very little about the years after her mother graduated college and before she got married. Emma calls this period her mother's "lost years." She notes that she, at age 29, is in that same phase of life now.

Many of us find a breezy toughness in the bygone versions of our mothers, and we envy it. Before a kid or two tied her down, Mom was hitchhiking, or she was playing softball with guys, or like Julia's mom, she was "transcribing tapes from her time as a war reporter like it's the most casual thing in the world." Paria, whose mother fled Iran during the Revolution, notes her mother's resilience; then, as now, her mom maintains a "joie de vivre."

The photos women sent me offer a key to how we, as daughters, want to perceive young womanhood. Pluck, sex appeal, power, kindness,

Julia's mother, Anne, during her time as a war reporter.

persistence: We admire and celebrate these characteristics, and we long for the past versions of our moms to embody them. But if these characteristics are a prerequisite for a properly executed womanhood, does becoming a mother divest a woman of such qualities? In studying these photos, and each daughter's interpretation of them, I've come to wonder what traits we allow our mothers to have, and which ones we view as temporary, expiring with age and the beginning of motherhood. Can a woman be both sexual and maternal, daring and responsible, innocent and wise? Mothers are either held up as paragons of selflessness, or they're discounted and parodied. We often don't see them in all their complexity.

For daughters, these old photos of our mothers feel like both a 10 chasm and a bridge. The woman in the picture is someone other than the woman we know. She is also exactly the person in the photo—still, right now. Finally, we see that the woman we've come

academic literacies | rhetorical situations | genres | fields | processes | strategies | research MLA / APA | media / design | readings | handbook

Zan submitted this photo of her mother, Darcy, to the project.

to think of as Mom — whether she's nurturing, or disapproving, or thoughtful, or delusional, or pestering, or supportive, or sentimental — is also a mysterious, fun, brave babe.

She's been here all this time.

Photographs of people's mothers when they were young sparks Lepucki's reflection on the lenses through which we see our mothers. She considers the stories our mothers tell and the way photos complement the stories, then examines several photos contributed by others, noting how we compare ourselves to our parents. Finally, her reflections lead her to explore how "we, as daughters, want to perceive young womanhood" — and how the women in the photos combine distance, familiarity, and youthful allure.

For four more reflections, see CHAPTER 70.

Key Features / Reflections

A topic that intrigues you. A reflective essay has a dual purpose: to ponder something you find interesting or puzzling and to share your thoughts with an audience. Your topic may be anything that interests you. You might write about someone you have never met and are curious about, an object or occurrence that makes you think, a place where you feel comfortable or safe. Your goal is to explore the meaning that the person, object, event, or place has for you in a way that will interest others. One way to do that is by making connections between your personal experience and more general ones that readers may share. Lepucki writes about her own and other women's photos of their mothers, and in doing so she raises questions and offers insights about the way people relate to their mothers.

Some kind of structure. A reflective essay can be structured in many ways, but it needs to *be* structured. It may seem to wander, but all its paths and ideas should relate, one way or another. The challenge is to keep your readers' interest as you explore your topic and to leave readers satisfied that the journey was pleasurable, interesting, and profitable. Lepucki begins by describing a remembered photo of her mother and relating it to her mother's stories. She then explores the significance of several photos of other women's mothers and examines the ways daughters interpret photos of their mothers as young women—and how those interpretations may change when those young women become mothers.

Specific details.   You'll need to provide specific details to help readers understand and connect with your subject, especially if it's an abstract or unfamiliar one. Lepucki offers a wealth of details about a favorite photo: "She's about 18 and very tan, with long, blond hair. It's the 1970s and she's wearing a white midriff and cutoffs. My dad is there, too, hugging her from behind." Anecdotes can bring your subject to life. Writing of that photo, Lepucki continues: "And she is so young and innocent. She hasn't yet dropped out of college, or gotten married. The young woman in this photo has no idea that life will bring her five children and five grandchildren, a conversion to Judaism, one divorce, two marriages, a move across the country." Reflections may be about causes, such as how our parents affect our self-images; comparisons, such as when Lepucki compares the photos sent to her; and examples, as the photos included in Lepucki's essay exemplify the "beautiful, fierce, sassy, goofy, cool, sweet" young women she sees in all the photos sent to her.

A questioning, speculative tone.   In a reflective essay, you are working toward answers, not providing them neatly organized and ready for consumption. So your tone is usually tentative and open, demonstrating a willingness to entertain, accept, and reject various ideas as your essay progresses from beginning to end. Lepucki achieves this tone by questioning her own insights: "Any story about your mother is part myth, isn't it?"; and by admitting that she doesn't have all the answers: "In studying these photos, and each daughter's interpretation of them,

academic literacies · rhetorical situations · genres · fields · processes · strategies · research MLA / APA · media / design · readings · handbook

I've come to wonder what traits we allow our mothers to have, and which ones we view as temporary, expiring with age and the beginning of motherhood."

A BRIEF GUIDE TO WRITING REFLECTIONS

Deciding on a Topic

Choose a subject you want to explore. Write a list of things that you think about, wonder about, find puzzling or annoying. They may be big things—life, relationships—or little things—quirks of certain people's behavior, curious objects, everyday events. Try **CLUSTERING** one or more of those things, or begin by **FREEWRITING** to see what comes to mind as you write.

○ 333–34
331–32

Considering the Rhetorical Situation

PURPOSE   What's your goal in writing this essay? To introduce a topic that interests you? Entertain? Provoke readers to think about something? What aspects of your subject do you want to ponder and reflect on?

■ 55–56

AUDIENCE   Who is the audience? How familiar are they with your subject? How will you introduce it in a way that will interest them?

■ 57–60

STANCE   What is your attitude toward the topic you plan to explore? Questioning? Playful? Critical? Curious? Something else?

■ 66–68

MEDIA / DESIGN   Will your essay be a print document? an oral presentation? Will it be posted on a website or blog? Would it help to include any visuals or video or audio files?

■ 69–71

Generating Ideas and Text

Explore your subject in detail. Reflections often include descriptive details. Lepucki, for example, describes the aspects of the women in the photos that help her see how daughters want to see young women: as having "pluck, sex appeal, power, kindness, persistence." She also provides details in the form of several photographs. You may also make your point by **DEFINING**, **COMPARING**, even **CLASSIFYING**. Virtually any organizing pattern will help you explore your subject.

432–42
424–31
418–23

Back away. Ask yourself why your subject matters: why is it important or intriguing or significant? You may try **LISTING** or **OUTLINING** possibilities, or you may want to start **DRAFTING** to see where the writing takes your thinking. Your goal is to think on screen (or paper) about your subject, to play with its possibilities.

332–33
335–37
340–42

Think about how to keep readers with you. Reflections may seem loose or unstructured, but they must be carefully crafted so that readers can follow your train of thought. It's a good idea to sketch out a rough **THESIS** to help focus your thoughts. You may not include the thesis in the essay itself, but every part of the essay should in some way relate to it.

387–89

Ways of Organizing a Reflective Essay

Reflective essays may be organized in many ways because they mimic the way we think, associating one idea with another in ways that make sense but do not necessarily form a "logical" progression. In general, you might consider organizing a reflection using this overall strategy:

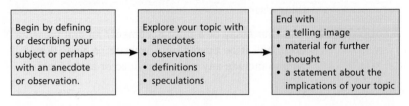

Begin by defining or describing your subject or perhaps with an anecdote or observation. → Explore your topic with
• anecdotes
• observations
• definitions
• speculations → End with
• a telling image
• material for further thought
• a statement about the implications of your topic

academic literacies · rhetorical situations · genres · fields · processes · strategies · research MLA / APA · media / design · readings · handbook

Another way to organize this type of essay is as a series of brief reflections that together create an overall impression:

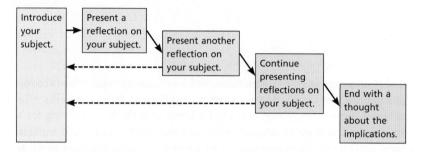

Taking Stock of Your Work

Take stock of what you've written by writing out answers to these questions:

- How did you decide on your topic?
- Why did you organize it as you did?
- Did you use visual elements (photographs, diagrams, drawings), audio elements, or links? If so, what did they add? If not, what might you have used?
- What did you do well in this piece? What could still be improved? What would you do differently next time?
- What have you learned about your writing ability from writing this piece? What do you need to work on in the future?

IF YOU NEED MORE HELP

See Chapter 30 for guidelines on **DRAFTING**, Chapter 31 on **ASSESSING YOUR OWN WRITING**, Chapter 32 on **GETTING RESPONSE AND REVISING**, and Chapter 33 on **EDITING AND PROOFREADING**. See Chapter 34 if you are required to submit your reflection in a writing **PORTFOLIO**.

340–42
343–47
348–55
356–60
361–70

22

Résumés and Job Letters

Résumés summarize our education, work experience, and other accomplishments for prospective employers. Application letters introduce us to those employers. When you send a letter and résumé applying for a job, you are making an argument for why that employer should want to meet you and perhaps hire you. In a way, the two texts together serve as an advertisement selling your talents and abilities to someone who likely has to sift through many applications to decide whom to invite for an interview. That's why résumés and application letters require a level of care that few other documents do. In the same way, sending a thank-you letter following an interview completes your presentation of yourself to potential employers. Résumés, application letters, and thank-you letters are obviously very different genres—yet they share one common purpose: to help you find a job. Thus, they are presented together in this chapter.

Understanding Your Audiences

When you apply for a job, you will likely post your application materials online. They may then be read by a recruiter or a hiring manager. Before that happens, though, your résumé may be searched by an ATS, or applicant tracking system. These systems are designed to ease recruiters' and managers' workloads by ranking applicants, usually on the basis of keywords that appear in their résumés. These keywords usually match the words used in the job posting, so to increase your chances of success, you should describe your skills and experience using the same keywords. One way to do this is to paste the job posting into an online word cloud generator, such as *Wordle*, *WordItOut*, or *Jobscan*. For example, here is a posting for an internship and a word cloud; the larger the word, the more often it is used in the posting:

academic literacies | rhetorical situations | genres | fields | processes | strategies | research MLA / APA | media / design | readings | handbook

Interns will receive full-on training in their respective departments and be responsible for generating sales, conducting presentations, scheduling promotions, and working within our team.

You will assist Account Executives in their events or retail demonstration and sales and marketing campaigns.

Our company generates over $1 million in revenue through direct marketing campaigns. Interns must be prepared to interact with clients and customers and deliver sales presentations.

This is a hands-on opportunity and interns will gain experience and skills in promotional sales, direct marketing, and working in a team atmosphere and with clients.

Requirements: student mentality; goal-oriented; confidence; self-motivation; punctuality; reliability; strong work ethic; desire to make a difference; passionate about helping people

The word cloud suggests that these words should appear in an applicant's résumé: *Sales, marketing, clients, business, interns, team,* and *customers*. (While it's tempting to use "soft skill" terms as listed under the requirements, you're better off describing actions that demonstrate those skills.

For example, "self-motivation" and "passionate about helping people" might be shown by volunteer work at a homeless shelter.)

Social Media and Job Hunting

Social media have become important aspects of finding a job, for both good and ill. In fact, over half of all employers always search for job applicants' online profiles—and in many cases, those profiles reduce the applicants' chances of being hired. So it's important to create or revise your profiles on *Facebook, LinkedIn,* and *Twitter,* the three most-searched social media sites, as well as other sites. Emphasize any volunteer or charity work you do, and highlight potential qualifications for and interest in the kind of work you want. Make sure your profiles contain no profanity or references to your sexual activity, or use of alcohol, guns, or illegal drugs—and proofread your posts for grammar and spelling. Your photos of yourself should project a professional image, too. Also, Google yourself to see what a search reveals about you.

You can also use social media to improve your job search. Read the descriptions of positions you would like to have, looking for keywords that describe what employers want in such employees; then use those keywords in your profiles. Also, join *LinkedIn* groups related to your desired job or industry to stay current with the conversations in those fields; then follow the companies where you'd like to work, as new job opportunities are sometimes posted there before they appear in other places.

RÉSUMÉS

A résumé is one of a job seeker's most important tools. If done well, a résumé not only tells potential employers about your education and work history, it says a lot about your attention to detail, writing skills, and professionalism. Taking the time to craft an excellent résumé, then, is time well spent. Here's an example, a résumé written by a college student applying for an internship before her senior year.

Emily W. Williams •·················· *Name in boldface.*
28 Murphy Lane
Springfield, Ohio 45399
Phone: 937-555-2640
Email: ewilliams22@gmail.com
LinkedIn: www.linkedin.com/EmilyWWilliams

SKILLS
- Communicating in writing and verbally, face-to-face and in various media
- Organizing and analyzing data
- Collaborating with other people on a team to achieve goals within deadlines
- Fluent in French
- Software: Microsoft Word, Microsoft Excel, SPSS, ATLAS.ti, Avid Pro Tools

EDUCATION
Wittenberg University, Springfield, Ohio
- BA in Marketing expected in May 2020
- Minor in Psychology
- Current GPA: 3.67
- Recipient, Community Service Scholarship

Clark State Community College, Springfield, Ohio
- AA in Business Administration, 2018
- GPA: 3.88
- Honors: Alpha Lambda Delta National Honor Society

EXPERIENCE
Aug. 2018–Present: Department of Psychology, Wittenberg •······· *Work experience*
University, Springfield, Ohio *in reverse*
Research Assistant *chronological*
- Collect and analyze data *order.*
- Interview research study participants

Summer 2018: Landis and Landis Public Relations, Springfield, OH
Events Coordinator
- Organized local charity campaigns
- Coordinated database of potential donors
- Produced two radio spots for event promotion

Summers 2016–17: Springfield Aquatic Club, Springfield, OH
Assistant Swim Coach
- Instructed children ages 5–18 in competitive swimming

•············ *Format to fill*
entire page.

Emily Williams's résumé is arranged to highlight her social media presence and skills; her education and experience are arranged chronologically. Because she is in college, readers can assume that she graduated from high school, so that information isn't needed here. She describes her skills and work responsibilities using action verbs to highlight what she actually did—"communicating," "collaborating," "produced," "instructed"—and so on.

Key Features / Résumés

A structure that suits your goals and experience. There are conventional ways of organizing a résumé but no one right way. You can organize a résumé chronologically or functionally, and it can be targeted (customized for a particular job application) or not. A *chronological résumé* is the most general, listing pretty much all your academic and work experience from the most recent to the earliest. A *targeted résumé* will generally announce the specific goal up top, just beneath your name, and will offer information selectively, showing only the experience and skills relevant to your goal. A *functional résumé* is organized around various kinds of experience and is not chronological. You might write a functional résumé if you wish to demonstrate a lot of experience in more than one area and perhaps if you wish to downplay dates. *Combination résumés*, like Emily Williams's, allow you to combine features from various types of résumés to present yourself in the best light; Emily's initial emphasis on skills is functional, while her education and experience are listed chronologically.

Succinct. A résumé should almost always be short—one page if at all possible. Entries should be parallel but do not need to be written in complete sentences—"Produced two radio spots," for instance, rather than "I produced two radio spots." Use action verbs ("instructed," "produced") to emphasize what you accomplished.

A design that highlights key information. It's important for a résumé to look good and to be easy to skim; typography, white space, and alignment matter. Your name should be bold at the top, and the information you

academic literacies · rhetorical situations · genres · fields · processes · strategies · research MLA / APA · media / design · readings · handbook

want your readers to see first should be near the top of the page. Major sections should be labeled with headings, all of which should be in one slightly larger or bolder font. And you need to surround each section and the text as a whole with adequate white space to make the parts easy to read—and to make the entire document look professional.

A BRIEF GUIDE TO WRITING RÉSUMÉS

Considering the Rhetorical Situation

PURPOSE   Are you seeking a job? an internship? some other position? How will the position for which you're applying affect what you include on your résumé?   ▮ 55–56

AUDIENCE   What sort of employee is the company or organization seeking? What experience and qualities will the person doing the hiring be looking for?   ▮ 57–60

STANCE   What personal and professional qualities do you want to convey? Think about how you want to come across— as eager? polite? serious? ambitious?—and choose your words accordingly.   ▮ 66–68

MEDIA/DESIGN   Are you planning to send your résumé and letter as PDFs? on paper? as an email attachment? Whatever your medium, be sure both documents are formatted appropriately and proofread carefully.   ▮ 69–71

Generating Ideas and Text for a Résumé

Define your objective.   Are you looking for a particular job for which you should create a targeted résumé? Are you preparing a generic chronological résumé to use in a search for work of any kind? Defining your objective as specifically as possible helps you decide on the form the résumé will take and the information it will include.

Consider how you want to present yourself. Begin by gathering the information you will need to include. As you work through the steps of putting your résumé together, think about the method of organization that works best for your purpose—chronological, targeted, functional, or combination.

- *Contact information.* At the top of your résumé, list your full name, a permanent address (rather than your school address), and a permanent telephone number with area code.

- *Your email address.* Your email address should sound professional; addresses like hotbabe334@gmail.com do not make a good first impression on potential employers. If possible, get an address that uses your name and a common provider, such as Gmail, iCloud mail, or Outlook.

- *Your social media presence.* Many employers routinely check applicants' social media presence to evaluate their personality and character, so yours should reflect your professional self and highlight your skills. Anything from an inappropriate photo or reference to drinking to poor writing can hurt your chances, while evidence of communication skills and a professional image can help them, so you should shape your social media presence to highlight or demonstrate your qualifications and skills. Don't scrub your sites and post nothing, though—use your online presence to enhance your employability. That includes checking for jobs on company *Facebook* pages and *Twitter* feeds and in *LinkedIn* groups.

- *Your skills.* What have you learned to do, both in school and in jobs or volunteer work that you've done? Make a list, and phrase each one in terms of what you can *do*, as Williams does. Avoid such phrases as "hard worker," "detail-oriented," and "self-starter." As you revise your résumé to fit different job postings, choose skills from your list that match the job's requirements. As you list your education, experience, and other activities, think in terms of the skills you acquired and add them to your list.

academic literacies | rhetorical situations | genres | fields | processes | strategies | research MLA / APA | media / design | readings | handbook

- *Your education.* Start with the most recent: degree, major, college attended, and minor (if any). You may want to list your GPA (if it's over 3.0) and any academic honors you've received. If you don't have much work experience, list education first.

- *Your work experience.* As with education, list your most recent job first and work backward. Include job title, organization name, city and state, start and end dates, and responsibilities. Describe them in terms of your duties and accomplishments. If you have extensive work experience in the area in which you're applying, list that first.

- *Community service, volunteer, and charitable activities.* Many high school students are required to perform community service, and many students participate in various volunteer activities that benefit others. List the skills and aptitudes that participation helped you develop or demonstrate.

- *Other activities, interests, and abilities.* What do you do for fun? What skills do your leisure activities require? (For example, if you play a sport, you probably have a good grasp of the value of teamwork and the drive to practice something until you've mastered it. You should describe your skills in a way that an employer might find attractive.)

Choose references. It's assumed that if you get to the interview stage, employers will ask you to provide references, so you don't need to list them on your résumé or say "References on request." Before you start applying for jobs, ask people to serve as references, so they will be ready. It's a good idea to provide each reference with a one-page summary of relevant information about you (for example, give professors a list of courses you took with them, including the grades you earned and the titles of papers you wrote).

Choose your words carefully. Remember, your résumé is a sales document—you're trying to present yourself as someone worth a second look. Focus on your achievements, using action verbs that say what you've done. Be honest—employers expect truthfulness, and embellishing the truth can cause you to lose a job later.

Consider key design elements.   Make sure your résumé is centered on the page and that it looks clean and clear. It's usually best to use a single, simple **FONT** (Times New Roman, Calibri, Arial, and Cambria are good ones) throughout and to print on white paper. Use bold type and bullets to make the résumé easy to read, and limit it to no more—and no less—than one full page.

648–49 ☐

Edit and proofread carefully.   Your résumé must be perfect. Show it to others, and proofread again. You don't want even one typo or other error.

Send the résumé as a PDF.   PDFs look the same on all devices, whereas *Word* or other formats may not. Make sure potential employers see your résumé as you intended.

Ways of Organizing a Résumé

If you don't have much work experience or if you've just gone back to school to train for a new career, put education before work experience; if you have extensive work experience in the area in which you're applying, list work before education.

[Chronological]

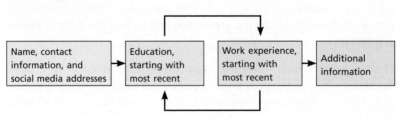

If you have limited work experience, gaps in your employment or education, or wish to focus on your skills, rather than your work history, use a functional résumé.

[Functional]

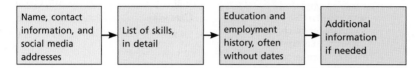

| Name, contact information, and social media addresses | → | List of skills, in detail | → | Education and employment history, often without dates | → | Additional information if needed |

A combination résumé is flexible: it lets you focus on both your skills and your experience by listing skills and also your education and employment history, and it can be tailored to specific job prospects.

[Combination]

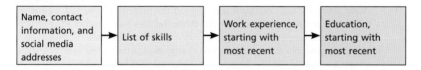

| Name, contact information, and social media addresses | → | List of skills | → | Work experience, starting with most recent | → | Education, starting with most recent |

APPLICATION AND THANK-YOU LETTERS

The application letter argues that the writer should be taken seriously as a candidate for a job or some other opportunity. Generally, it is sent together with a résumé, so it doesn't need to give that much information. It does, however, have to make a favorable impression: the way it's written and presented can get you in for an interview—or not. On the following page is an application letter that Emily Williams wrote seeking a position at the end of her junior year. Williams tailored her letter to one specific reader at a specific organization. The letter cites details, showing that it is not a generic application letter being sent to many possible employers. Rather, it identifies a particular position—the public relations internship—and

Application Letter

Equal space at top and bottom of page, all text aligning at left margin.

Street address, city, state, ZIP, date.

28 Murphy Lane
Springfield, OH 45399
May 19, 2019

Line space.

Recipient's name and title, organization, address.

Barbara Jeremiah, President
Jeremiah Enterprises
44322 Commerce Way
Worthington, OH 45322

Line space.

Re: Public Relations Internship Opening (Ref. ID: 27C)

Subject line with position information.

Salutation, with a colon.

Dear Ms. Jeremiah:

Line space.

Position identified.

I am writing to apply for the public relations internship advertised in the Sunday, May 15, *Columbus Dispatch*. The success of your company makes me eager to work with you and learn from you.

Line space between paragraphs.

Match between experience and job description.

My grasp of public relations goes beyond the theories I have learned in the classroom. I applied those theories last summer at Landis and Landis, the Springfield public relations firm, where I was responsible for organizing two charity events that drew over two hundred potential donors each. I also learned to use sound productions software to produce promotional radio spots. Since

Show knowledge of company.

Jeremiah Enterprises focuses on nonprofit public relations, my experience, training, and initiative will allow me to contribute to your company's public relations team..

Availability.

I will be available to begin any time after May 23, when the spring term at Wittenberg ends. I have attached my résumé, which provides detailed information about my background. I will phone this week to see if I might arrange an interview.

Line space.

Closing.

Sincerely,

Emily W. Williams (signature)

4 lines space for signature if mailed. Electronic letters need only typed name.

Emily W. Williams

Sender's name, typed.

stresses the fit between Williams's credentials and the position. Williams also states her availability. Send a thank-you email to each person who interviewed you within twenty-four hours of the interview; follow up by mailing a printed note that follows the same format as the application letter. Doing so is a way of showing appreciation for the interview and restating your interest in the position. It also shows that you have good manners and understand proper business etiquette. Below is an email that Emily Williams sent to the person who interviewed her. Williams thanks the interviewer for her time and the opportunity to meet, and she reiterates her interest in the position and her qualifications for it.

Thank-You Email

Line space.

Dear Ms. Jeremiah: •·· *Salutation, with a colon.*

Thank you for the opportunity to meet with you yesterday. I enjoyed talking with you and meeting the people who work with you, and I continue to be very interested in becoming an intern with Jeremiah Enterprises. *Thanks and confirmation of interest.*

Line space between paragraphs.

As we discussed, I worked with a public relations firm last summer, and since then I have completed three courses in marketing and public relations that relate directly to the work I would be doing as an intern. *Brief review of qualifications.*

Invitation for further contact.

I have attached a list of references, as you requested. If you need any more information, please do not hesitate to contact me by email at ewilliams22@gmail.com or by phone at 937-555-2640. Thanks again; I hope to hear from you soon. *Attachments.*

Repeat thanks.

Line space.

Sincerely, •·· *Closing.*

Emily W. Williams

Key Features / Application and Thank-You Letters

A succinct indication of your qualifications. In an application letter, you need to make clear why you're interested in the position or the organization—and at the same time give some sense of why the person you're writing to should at least want to meet you. In a thank-you letter, you should remind the interviewer of your qualifications.

A reasonable and pleasing tone. When writing application and thank-you letters, you need to go beyond simply stating your accomplishments or saying thank you. Through your words, you need to demonstrate that you will be the kind of employee the organization wants. Presentation is also important—your letter should be neat and error-free.

A conventional, businesslike format. Application and thank-you letters typically follow a prescribed format. The most common is the block format shown in the examples. It includes the writer's address, the date, the recipient's name and address, a salutation, the message, a closing, and a signature.

A BRIEF GUIDE TO WRITING JOB LETTERS

Generating Ideas and Text for Application and Thank-You Letters

Focus. Application and thank-you letters are not personal and should not be chatty. Keep them focused: when you're applying for a position, include only information relevant to the position. Don't make your audience wade through irrelevant side issues. Stay on topic.

State the reason for the letter. Unlike essays, which develop a thesis over several paragraphs, or emails, which announce their topic in a subject line, letters need to explicitly introduce their reason for being written, usually in the first paragraph. When you're applying for something or thanking someone, say so in the first sentence: "I am writing to apply

academic literacies · rhetorical situations · genres · fields · processes · strategies · research MLA / APA · media / design · readings · handbook

for the Margaret Branscomb Peabody Scholarship for students majoring in veterinary science." "Thank you for meeting with me."

Think of your letter as an argument.   When you're asking for a job, you're making an **ARGUMENT**. You're making a claim—that you're qualified for a certain position—and you need to support your claim with reasons and evidence. Therefore, it's important to read the position's requirements carefully and tailor the letter to show that you meet them. In her letter, for example, Williams shows how her combined education and work experience make her successful in her summer job, and she connects that experience to the specific internship she's applying for.

◆ 397–417

Choose an appropriate salutation.   If you know the person's name and title, use it: "Dear Professor Turnigan." If you don't know the person's title, one good solution is to address them by first and last name: "Dear Julia Turnigan." If, as sometimes happens, you must write to an unknown reader, your options include "To Whom It May Concern" and the more old-fashioned "Dear Sir or Madam." Another option in such situations might be to omit the salutation completely and instead use a subject line, for example: "Subject: Public Relations Internship Application." Whenever possible, though, write to a specific person; research or contact the organization and find out whom to write to. Once you've had an interview, write to your interviewer.

Consider the medium.   If you're applying for a job with a printed letter and résumé, follow standard business-letter format, as Williams does. If you're applying via email, paste your entire letter into the body of the email, but move your contact information below your signature. Also, list the job for which you are applying in your subject line—and if the employer asks for specific information in the subject line, be sure to include it exactly.

Proofread.   Few writing situations demand greater perfection than professional letters—especially job letters. Employers receive dozens, sometimes hundreds, of applications, and often can't look at them all. Typos, grammar errors, and other forms of sloppiness prejudice readers against applicants: an employer is likely to think that if this applicant can't take the time and care to **PROOFREAD**, how badly do they want this position? To compete, strive for perfection.

359–60

Ways of Organizing an Application or Thank-You Letter

Application and thank-you letters should both follow a conventional organization, though you might vary the details somewhat. Here are two standard organizations:

[Application letter]

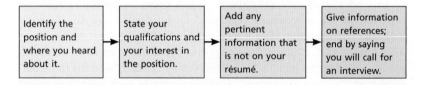

| Identify the position and where you heard about it. | State your qualifications and your interest in the position. | Add any pertinent information that is not on your résumé. | Give information on references; end by saying you will call for an interview. |

[Thank-you letter]

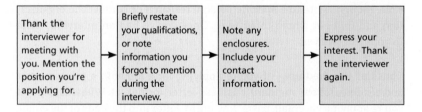

| Thank the interviewer for meeting with you. Mention the position you're applying for. | Briefly restate your qualifications, or note information you forgot to mention during the interview. | Note any enclosures. Include your contact information. | Express your interest. Thank the interviewer again. |

Taking Stock of Your Work

Take stock of what you've written by writing out answers to these questions:

- How did you go about identifying your strengths and qualifications?
- Why did you choose the résumé structure you did?

academic literacies · rhetorical situations · genres · fields · processes · strategies · research MLA / APA · media / design · readings · handbook

- Did you maintain an appropriate tone throughout your job letters?
- What did you do well in your résumé and letters? What could still be improved?
- What have you learned about your writing ability and your job qualifications from writing these pieces? What do you need to work on in the future?

IF YOU NEED MORE HELP

See Chapter 30 for guidelines on **DRAFTING**, Chapter 31 on **ASSESSING YOUR OWN WRITING**, Chapter 32 on **GETTING RESPONSE AND REVISING**, and Chapter 33 on **EDITING AND PROOFREADING**.

340–42
343–47
348–55
356–60

23 Mixing Genres

202–10
233–45
246–55
131–56

Musicians regularly mix genres, blending, for instance, reggae, hip-hop, and jazz to create a unique sound. Like musicians, writers often combine different genres in a single text. An **EVALUATION** of mining practices might include a **PROFILE** of a coal company CEO. A **PROPOSAL** to start a neighborhood watch might begin with a **REPORT** on crime in the area. Here's a column that mixes genres, written by Anna Quindlen for *Newsweek* magazine in 2007.

ANNA QUINDLEN

Write for Your Life

The new movie *Freedom Writers* isn't entirely about the themes the trailers suggest. It isn't only about gang warfare and racial tensions and tolerance. It isn't only about the difference one good teacher can make in the life of one messed-up kid. *Freedom Writers* is about the power of writing in the lives of ordinary people. That's a lesson everyone needs. The movie, and the book from which it was taken, track the education of a young teacher named Erin Gruwell, who shows up shiny-new to face a class of what are called, in pedagogical jargon, "at risk" students. It's a mixed bag of Latino, Asian, and black teenagers with one feckless white kid thrown in. They ignore, belittle, and dismiss her as she proffers lesson plans and reading materials seriously out of step with the homelessness, drug use, and violence that are the stuff of their precarious existences.

Textual analysis.

And then one day, she gives them all marbled composition books and the assignment to write their lives, ungraded, unjudged, and the world breaks open.

"My probation officer thinks he's slick; he swears he's an expert on gangs."

"Sorry, diary, I was going to try not to do it tonight, but the little baggy of white powder is calling my name."

"If you pull up my shirtsleeves and look at my arms, you will see 5 black and blue marks."

"The words 'Eviction Notice' stopped me dead in my tracks."

"When I was younger, they would lock me up in the closet because they wanted to get high and beat up on each other."

Ms. G, as the kids called her, embraced a concept that has been lost in modern life: writing can make pain tolerable, confusion clearer and the self stronger.

How is it, at a time when clarity and strength go begging, that we have moved so far from everyday prose? Social critics might trace this back to the demise of letter writing. The details of housekeeping and child rearing, the rigors of war and work, advice to friends and family: none was slated for publication. They were communications that gave shape to life by describing it for others.

But as the letter fell out of favor and education became pro- 10 fessionalized, with its goal less the expansion of the mind than the acquisition of a job, writing began to be seen largely as the purview of writers. Writing at work also became so stylistically removed from the story of our lives that the two seemed to have nothing in common. Corporate prose conformed to an equation: information × polysyllabic words + tortured syntax = aren't you impressed?

Report.

And in the age of the telephone most communication became evanescent, gone into thin air no matter how important or heartfelt. Think of all those people inside the World Trade Center saying goodbye by phone. If only, in the blizzard of paper that followed the collapse of the buildings, a letter had fallen from the sky for every family member and friend, something to hold on to, something to read and reread. Something real. Words on paper confer a kind of immortality. Wouldn't all of us love to have a journal, a memoir, a letter, from those we have loved and lost? Shouldn't all of us leave a bit of that behind?

Reflection.

The age of technology has both revived the use of writing and pro- vided ever more reasons for its spiritual solace. Emails are letters, after all, more lasting than phone calls, even if many of them r 2 cursory 4 u.

And the physical isolation they and other arms-length cyber-advances create makes talking to yourself more important than ever. That's also what writing is: not just a legacy, but therapy. As the novelist Don DeLillo once said, "Writing is a form of personal freedom. It frees us from the mass identity we see in the making all around us. In the end, writers will write not to be outlaw heroes of some underculture but mainly to save themselves, to survive as individuals."

Argument.

That's exactly what Gruwell was after when she got the kids in her class writing, in a program that's since been duplicated at other schools. Salvation and survival for teenagers whose chances of either seemed negligible. "Growing up, I always assumed I would either drop out of school or get pregnant," one student wrote. "So when Ms. G started talking about college, it was like a foreign language to me." Maybe that's the moment when that Latina girl began to speak that foreign language, when she wrote those words down. Today she has a college degree.

One of the texts Erin Gruwell assigned was *The Diary of a Young Girl* by Anne Frank. A student who balked at reading a book about someone so different, so remote, went on to write: "At the end of the book, I was so mad that Anne died, because as she was dying, a part of me was dying with her." Of course Anne never dreamed her diary would be published, much less read by millions of people after her death at the hands of the Nazis. She wrote it for the same reason the kids who called themselves Freedom Writers wrote in those composition books: to make sense of themselves. That's not just for writers. That's for people.

Quindlen argues that writing helps us understand ourselves and our world. She uses several genres to help advance her argument—textual analysis of the film Freedom Writers, *a brief report on the decline of letter writing, and a reflection on the technologies we use to write. Together, these genres help her develop her argument that writing helps us "make sense of [our]selves."*

For four more multigenre texts, see CHAPTER 71.

Key Features / Texts That Mix Genres

One primary genre. Your writing situation will often call for a certain genre that is appropriate for your purpose—an argument, a proposal, a

report, a textual analysis, and so forth. Additional genres then play supporting roles. Quindlen's essay, for example, primarily argues a position and mixes in other genres, including report and reflection, to elaborate her argument and bring it to life.

A clear focus. A text that mixes genres approaches the topic several different ways, but each genre must contribute to your main point. One genre may serve as the introduction, and others may be woven throughout the text in other ways, but all must address some aspect of the topic and support the central claim. Quindlen's analysis of the film *Freedom Writers*, for example, supports her claim that writing is one way we learn about ourselves.

Careful organization. A text that combines several genres requires careful organization—the various genres must fit together neatly and clearly. Quindlen opens by analyzing the theme of *Freedom Writers*, noting that it's about "the power of writing in the lives of ordinary people." She then switches genres, reporting on how "we have moved so far from everyday prose" and then reflecting on the consequences of that move.

Clear transitions. When a text includes several genres, those genres need to be connected in some way. Transitions do that, and in so doing, they help readers make their way through the text. Transitions may include words such as *in addition* and *however*, and they may also consist of phrases that sum up an idea and move it forward. See, for example, how Quindlen ends one paragraph by quoting Don DeLillo as saying that writers write "to save themselves, to survive as individuals" and then begins the next paragraph by referring to DeLillo's words, saying "That's exactly what Gruwell was after."

Some Typical Ways of Mixing Genres

It's possible to mix almost any genres together. Following are some of the most commonly mixed genres and how they combine with other genres.

157–84
131–56

Memoirs.   Sometimes a personal anecdote can help support an **ARGUMENT** or enhance a **REPORT**. Stories from your personal experience can help readers understand your motivations for arguing a certain position and can enhance your credibility as a writer.

131–56

Profiles.   One way to bring a **REPORT** on an abstract topic to life is to include a profile of a person, place, or event. For example, if you were writing a report for your boss on the need to hire more sales representatives, including a profile of one salesperson's typical day might drive home the point that your sales force is stretched too thin.

157–84

Textual analyses.   You might need to analyze a speech or other document as part of an **ARGUMENT**, especially on a historical or political topic. For instance, you might analyze speeches by Abraham Lincoln and Jefferson Davis if you're writing about the causes of the Civil War, or an advertisement for e-cigarettes if you're making an argument about teen smoking.

246–55

Evaluations.   You might include an evaluation of something when you write a **PROPOSAL** about it. For example, if you were writing a proposal for additional student parking on your campus, you would need to evaluate the current parking facilities to discuss their inadequacy.

A BRIEF GUIDE TO WRITING TEXTS THAT MIX GENRES

Considering the Rhetorical Situation

55–56

PURPOSE   Why are you writing this text? To inform? persuade? entertain? explore an idea? something else? What genres will help you achieve your purpose?

57–60

AUDIENCE   Who are your readers? Which genres will help these readers understand your point? Will starting with a memoir or profile draw them in? Will some analysis help them

academic literacies · rhetorical situations · genres · fields · processes · strategies · research MLA / APA · media / design · readings · handbook

understand the topic? Will a profile make the topic less abstract or make them more sympathetic to your claim?

GENRE   What is your primary genre? What other genres might support that primary genre?

■ 61–65

STANCE   What is your stance on your topic—objective? opinionated? something else? Will including a textual analysis or report help you establish an objective or analytical tone? Will some reflection or a brief memoir show your personal connection to your topic?

■ 66–68

MEDIA / DESIGN   Will your text be an electronic or a print document? an oral presentation? Will it be published on a blog or other website? Should you include illustrations? audio or video clips? Do you need to present any information that would be best shown in a chart or graph?

■ 69–71

Generating Ideas and Text

Identify your primary genre.   If you're writing in response to an assignment, does it specify a particular genre? Look for key verbs that name specific genres—for example, *analyze*, *argue*, *evaluate*, and so on. Be aware that other verbs imply certain genres: *explain*, *summarize*, *review*, and *describe* ask for a report; *argue*, *prove*, and *justify* signal that you need to argue a position; and *evaluate* and *propose* specify evaluations and proposals.

If the choice of genre is up to you, consider your **PURPOSE** and **AUDIENCE** carefully to determine what genre is most appropriate. Consult the appropriate genre chapter to identify the key features of your primary genre and to generate ideas and text.

■ 55–56
■ 57–60

Determine if other genres would be helpful.   As you write a draft, you may identify a need—for a beginning that grabs readers' attention, for a satisfying ending, for ways to make an abstract concept more concrete or to help in analyzing something. At this point, you may want to try mixing one or more genres within your draft. Determine what genre will help you achieve your purpose and consult the appropriate genre chapter for advice on writing in that genre. Remember, however, that you're mixing genres into your draft to support and enhance it—so your supporting genres may not be as developed as complete texts in that genre would be and may not include all the key features. For example, if you include a brief memoir as part of an argument, it should include a good story and vivid details—but its significance may well be stated as part of the argument rather than revealed through the storytelling itself.

Integrate the genres. Your goal is to create a focused, unified, coherent text. So you need to make sure that your genres work together to achieve that goal. Make sure that each genre fulfills a purpose within the text. For example, writing that **TAKES A POSITION** rarely jumps into the argument immediately. Instead, it may include several paragraphs in which the context for the disputed position is explained or information crucial to the audience's understanding is reported. Sometimes that **REPORT** will be introduced by a brief **MEMOIR** that makes the topic personal to the writer and so less abstract. And the argument itself may well do much more than simply take a position—it may **EVALUATE** alternatives and end with a **PROPOSAL**, and even include genres in other media, such as a video clip **PROFILING** the subject of the argument. Also, use **TRANSITIONS** to help readers move from section to section in your text.

Multigenre Projects

Sometimes a collection of texts can together represent an experience or advance an argument. For example, you might document a trip to the Grand Canyon in an album that contains journal entries written during the trip, photographs, a map of northern Arizona showing the canyon, postcards, an essay on the geology of the canyon, and a souvenir coin stamped with an image of the canyon. Each represents a different way of experiencing the Grand Canyon, and together they offer a multifaceted way to understand your trip.

157–84
131–56
224–32
202–10
246–55
233–55
391

You might also write in several different genres on the same topic. If you begin by **ARGUING** that the government should provide universal health care, for example, writing a **MEMOIR** about a time you were ill could help you explore a personal connection to the topic. Composing a **PROFILE** of a doctor might give you new insights into the issue, and writing a **PROPOSAL** for how universal health care could work might direct you to potential solutions. You could assemble all these texts in a folder, with a title page and table of contents so that readers can see how it all fits together—or you could create an online multimodal text, combining text, images, video, sound, and links to other sites.

◆ 397–417
▲ 224–32
233–45
246–55

Taking Stock of Your Work

Take stock of what you've written by writing out answers to these questions:

- What led you to choose a mix of genres? How did your mix meet your purpose and your audience's needs?
- How well did you organize your piece?
- What strategies helped you achieve your purpose?
- Did you use visual elements (tables, graphs, diagrams, photographs), audio elements, or links effectively? If not, would they have helped?
- What did you do well in this piece? What could still be improved? What would you do differently next time?
- What have you learned about the processes of writing from writing this piece? What do you need to work on in the future?

IF YOU NEED MORE HELP

See Chapter 31 for guidelines on **DRAFTING**, Chapter 32 on **ASSESSING YOUR OWN WRITING**, Chapter 35 on **BEGINNING AND ENDING**, and Chapter 36 on **GUIDING YOUR READER**.

 340–42
343–47
◆ 373–85
389–91

part 4

Fields

When we study at a college or university, we take courses in many academic fields of study, or disciplines, in the humanities, social sciences, the sciences, and various career-oriented fields. Each field of study has its own methods of doing research and communicating, requiring us to learn how to READ and WRITE in the ways appropriate to that field. The chapters that follow offer advice on how to adapt your reading and writing to the demands of various fields of study.

Fields

Fields of Study **24**

Most colleges and universities are organized around fields of study, often referred to as *disciplines*, that share ways of seeing the universe, doing research, and presenting information—each through a different lens. Historians examine the way people behave differently than do economists; biologists look for different aspects of the natural world than do physicists. The various majors that colleges and universities offer invite you to learn to see the world in their distinctive ways and join professions that use distinctive skills. Marketing majors, for example, learn ways of influencing human behavior, while education majors learn ways of teaching students and music majors learn the intricacies of playing an instrument or singing. As you immerse yourself in a major, you come to see the world with a particular perspective.

Academic Fields and General Education

Your general education courses have a different goal: to prepare you for the demands of living in a complex and changing world—a world in which you'll need to use your ability to understand a wide range of facts, theories, and concepts to interact with a wide variety of people, work in various jobs, and make important decisions. In other words, these courses are designed to teach you how to learn and think. They are also helpful if you're not sure what you'd like to major in, because you can sample courses in various disciplines to help you decide. In your first couple of years, you will likely take general education courses in the following subject areas:

- the humanities, which include the arts, communications, history, literature, music, philosophy, and religion

academic literacies   rhetorical situations   genres   fields   processes   strategies   research MLA / APA   media / design   readings   handbook

- the social sciences, which may include anthropology, economics, political science, geography, psychology, and sociology
- the sciences, which usually include such disciplines as astronomy, biology, chemistry, geology, mathematics, and physics

It's important to note that these lists are far from comprehensive; schools differ in the courses and majors they offer, so some schools may offer courses in fields that are not on any of these lists—and some of these courses won't be available at your school. You may also take courses in career-oriented fields such as education, business, engineering, and nursing.

Studying, Reading, and Writing in Academic Fields

Each field focuses on the study of particular subjects and issues. In *psychology*, you study the human mind—what it is and why we behave as we do. In *sociology*, you study the way society shapes our actions. In *biology*, you study life itself, from bacteria and fungi to organisms interacting with their environment. In *history*, you study the past to understand the present. In *nursing*, you study best ways of providing patient care within the health-care system. In *engineering*, you learn how to solve technical problems and design engineering systems.

Each field also examines the world through a distinctive lens, using its own methods to study and analyze those subjects. For example, scientists test hypotheses with experiments designed to prove or disprove their accuracy; sociologists study groups by using statistical evidence; and historians examine diaries, speeches, or photographs from the past. In addition, disciplines develop technical terms and ways of using language that allow scholars to understand one another—but that can be hard to understand. For example, consider the word *significant*. When people say that something is *significant* in day-to-day conversation, they usually mean that it's important, a big deal; in statistics, though, a *significant* result is one that is probably true—but it may or may not be important.

academic literacies · rhetorical situations · genres · fields · processes · strategies · research MLA / APA · media / design · readings · handbook

Disciplines also present information using methods standard in that discipline. In *business* courses, you're likely to read case studies of specific companies and write business cases and other communications. In *education* courses, you'll read and write lesson plans; in *science* courses, you'll read and write laboratory reports; in *English* courses, you'll read fiction, poetry, and plays and write literary analyses. In each, you'll present information in ways used in conversations among scholars in the discipline. And that means that you may need to adapt your reading and writing to the genres, concepts, and methods of the various academic fields you encounter.

THINKING ABOUT READING AND WRITING IN THE FIELDS

- What reading assignments do you have in your other courses?

- What makes them easy or hard to read? What helps you read them?

- Do you enjoy reading some genres or subjects more than others? Why?

- What writing assignments do you have in your other courses?

- Do you alter or adjust your writing processes in different courses? Why or why not?

- What makes writing in some courses hard or easy?

- Do you enjoy writing in certain genres or on certain topics? Why?

25   Reading across Fields of Study

We read shopping lists differently from graphic novels and operating instructions differently from poems. For that matter, we read novels and poems differently—and go about reading textbooks differently still. Just as we write using various processes—generating ideas and text, drafting, getting responses and revising, editing, and proofreading—we vary our reading processes from task to task. We will likely read a mathematics textbook differently from a case study in nursing, and read a speech by Abraham Lincoln in a history course differently from the way we'd read it in a rhetoric course. This chapter offers advice on how to engage with texts in a variety of fields.

Considering the Rhetorical Situation

A good way to approach reading in academic fields is to treat reading as a process that you adapt to the demands of each new situation. Instead of diving in and focusing your reading on the details of the content, it's often useful to take some time to consider the text's purpose, your purpose, the audience, the author, the author's stance, the genre, and the medium. This information can help you decide how to get the most out of the text.

55–56 ■

- *The text's* **PURPOSE**. When was the text written, and why? Is it a textbook? a classic work that lays out concepts that have become fundamental to the field? a work proposing a new way of looking at an issue?

- *Your purpose as a reader.* Why are you reading this text? To study for a test? To find sources for a research project? To learn about something on your own?

- *The* **AUDIENCE**. For whom was the text written? Students like you? Scholars in the field? Interested nonspecialists? Readers who lived at some point in the past or in a particular location? What facts and concepts does the text assume its readers already know and understand?
57–60

- *The author.* Who wrote what you are reading? Does knowing the author's identity matter? Is the author reliable and credible? For example, is the author a respected scholar? Is the author known for a particular point of view?

- *The author's* **STANCE**. What is the author's stance toward the subject? toward the reader? Approving? Hostile? Critical? Passionate? What elements of the text reveal the author's stance?
66–68

- *The* **GENRE**. What is the text's genre? How was it meant to be read? Is that how you're reading it? What are the genre's key features? Knowing the key features of the genre can help you understand the text's content as you read and predict the text's organization.
61–65

- *The* **MEDIUM** *and* **DESIGN**. The medium and design of a text affect how you must read it. You may need to read a textbook differently from an article found on the internet, for example. An online textbook may require different commenting and note-taking strategies from a print text. Understanding the limitations and the advantages of a particular genre, medium, and design will help you get the most out of your reading.
69–71

Advice for Reading across Fields of Study

Becoming knowledgeable in a field of study requires learning its specialized ways of thinking, writing, and reading, including the terminology specific to the field and the kinds of texts the field is likely to produce and study. However, there is some general advice that can help you as you begin to read the kinds of texts you are likely to encounter in college.

Pay attention to vocabulary.   All disciplines require that you learn their vocabulary, which includes not only concepts and facts but also the names of important figures in the field and what they represent. Scholars typically write for other scholars in the same field, so they may assume that readers understand these terms and references and refer to them without explanation—and even "popular" writing often makes the same assumption. You'll find that much of the work in all your courses consists of learning terms and concepts. So it's important to take good notes in lectures, writing down terms your instructor emphasizes as they are defined, or, if they aren't, writing them down to look up later. Your textbooks introduce and define key terms and often include a glossary in the back that provides definitions.

In addition, be aware that disciplinary vocabularies use different kinds of words. In the sciences, the language is likely very technical, with many terms based on Greek and Latin roots (for example, the Greek prefix *gastr-* forms *gastropod* [snail], *gastric* [stomach], and *gastroscopy* [examination of the abdomen and stomach]). In the humanities, the vocabulary often alludes to complex concepts. Consider, for example, these sentences from *The Swerve*, a book by literary historian Stephen Greenblatt:

> The household, the kinship network, the guild, the corporation—these were the building blocks of personhood. Independence and self-reliance had no cultural purchase.

Almost every term, from "household" to "guild" to "personhood" to "cultural purchase," carries a wealth of information that must be understood. While understanding the scientific terms requires a good dictionary, these particular terms require an encyclopedia—or the knowledge gained by much reading.

Consider the author—or not.   In some disciplines, it's important to know who wrote a text, while in others the identity or **STANCE** of the author is seen as irrelevant. Historians, for example, need to know who the author of a text is, and the perspective that author brings to the text is central to reading history. Literary scholars may try not to consider the author at all, focusing solely on a close reading of the text itself. Scientists may consider the author's identity or the school or lab where the author works

66–68

academic literacies · rhetorical situations · genres · fields · processes · strategies · research MLA / APA · media / design · readings · handbook

to decide whether or not to read a text. Mathematicians resolutely ignore the author, focusing solely on the information in the text itself. So to make sense of a text in a discipline, you need to find out how that discipline sees the role of the author.

Identify key ideas and make comparisons. Whatever the discipline, look for the main ideas its texts present. Rather than highlight or underline them, write out the key ideas in your own words. As you read texts on the same subject, you may want to develop a matrix to help you **COMPARE AND CONTRAST** as well as **SYNTHESIZE** the main ideas. The following chart, adapted from one developed by two librarians, presents the main ideas in two sources, and then synthesizes the two versions. This example synthesizes a key idea found in two articles on how social media affects political participation among youths:

◆ 424–31

● 519–25

Source #1: Skorik, M. M. "Youth Engagement in Singapore"	Source #2: Ahmad, K. "Social Media and Youth Participatory Politics"	Synthesis: Main Ideas
Singapore's government has consistently applied controls on traditional media outlets but has left social media outlets untouched and unregulated.	Online participation in political campaigns and issues was almost five times greater than traditional participation. Researches concluded that this "could provide the participant with anonymity, in turn less vulnerability to political vengeance."	**Main idea #1:** Government control and censorship of mainstream media has caused protesters to look for alternative communication tools.
Key idea in source #1	Key idea in source #2	Synthesis of ideas
Key idea in source #1	Key idea in source #2	Synthesis of ideas

Michelle Chiles and Emily Brown, "Literature Review." Bristol Community College, Fall River, MA, 2015. Unpublished *PowerPoint*.

You might also get into the habit of skimming the works-cited or references list at the end of articles and books. As you do so, you'll begin to see who the most important people are in the discipline and what counts as evidence.

Build a map of the discipline. To make sense of a new idea, we need to have some way of fitting it into what we already know. Reading in an unfamiliar discipline can be hard because we don't have a sense of where the information in the text fits into the conversations of the discipline, its history, or our own goals—what we'd like to know or do in this field. It's useful to visualize the discipline so that we can place readings into the appropriate context. Possible ways of organizing a discipline follow.

Draw a word map. Using your textbook and perhaps some online sources as guides, draw an overview of the field. Here's one for psychology:

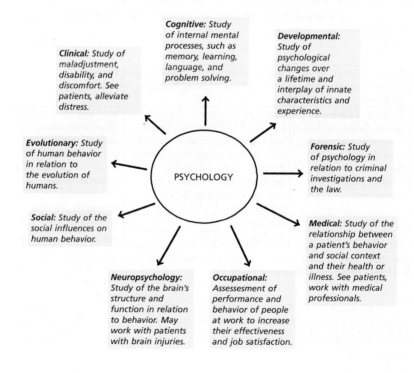

Cognitive: Study of internal mental processes, such as memory, learning, language, and problem solving.

Developmental: Study of psychological changes over a lifetime and interplay of innate characteristics and experience.

Clinical: Study of maladjustment, disability, and discomfort. See patients, alleviate distress.

Evolutionary: Study of human behavior in relation to the evolution of humans.

Forensic: Study of psychology in relation to criminal investigations and the law.

PSYCHOLOGY

Social: Study of the social influences on human behavior.

Medical: Study of the relationship between a patient's behavior and social context and their health or illness. See patients, work with medical professionals.

Neuropsychology: Study of the brain's structure and function in relation to behavior. May work with patients with brain injuries.

Occupational: Assessement of performance and behavior of people at work to increase their effectiveness and job satisfaction.

academic literacies / rhetorical situations / genres / fields / processes / strategies / research MLA / APA / media / design / readings / handbook

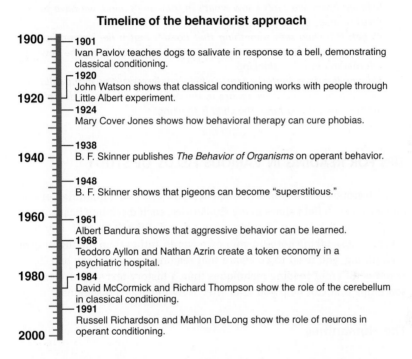

Create a timeline.   Sometimes it's helpful to understand how a discipline developed over time, how its research methods or emphases came to be, so you can place its texts and key developments within that history. Here, for example, is a timeline of the behaviorist approach in psychology:

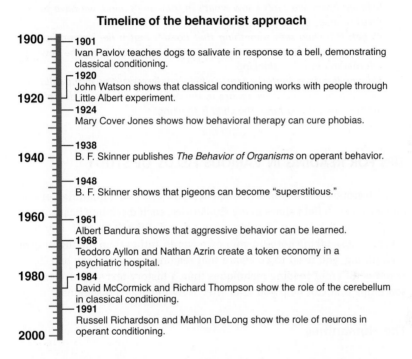

Timeline of the behaviorist approach

1900
1901
Ivan Pavlov teaches dogs to salivate in response to a bell, demonstrating classical conditioning.
1920
John Watson shows that classical conditioning works with people through **1920** Little Albert experiment.
1924
Mary Cover Jones shows how behavioral therapy can cure phobias.

1938
1940 B. F. Skinner publishes *The Behavior of Organisms* on operant behavior.

1948
B. F. Skinner shows that pigeons can become "superstitious."

1960
1961
Albert Bandura shows that aggressive behavior can be learned.
1968
Teodoro Ayllon and Nathan Azrin create a token economy in a psychiatric hospital.
1980
1984
David McCormick and Richard Thompson show the role of the cerebellum in classical conditioning.
1991
Russell Richardson and Mahlon DeLong show the role of neurons in **2000** operant conditioning.

Write a conversation among researchers.   To better understand the similarities and differences among various schools of thought within a discipline, choose some of the most prominent proponents of each school and write a fictional conversation among them, outlining where they agree and disagree and where they published or disseminated their theories and findings. Here, for instance, is a snippet of a dialogue that might have taken place between developmental psychologist Jean Piaget and behavioral psychologist B. F. Skinner:

> **Piaget:** *Children learn by adapting to conflicts between what they already know and challenges to that knowledge.*
> **Skinner:** *Bosh! We can't know what's in someone's mind; we have to focus on their behavior.*
> **Piaget:** *If a child sees something that doesn't match her preconceptions, she learns from it and through her behavior assimilates the new information into her thinking.*
> **Skinner:** *But if we reinforce a certain behavior by rewarding it, the child will do it more, and if we ignore it, the behavior will stop. It doesn't matter what, if anything, the child is thinking.*

TIPS FOR READING IN VARIOUS FIELDS OF STUDY

Though groups of disciplines (the sciences, the arts and humanities, and so on) within each field share many similarities, each discipline has features unique to it. While you should expect to read difficult texts in any field several times, taking notes in your own words, rather than highlighting or underlining, you need to be aware that reading, say, a biology text likely requires different reading techniques than a history text would. Here are some tips that can help you read effectively in various disciplines.

The Humanities

- Much of the scholarship in the humanities is based on texts of one sort or another—the Constitution, the Bible, Toni Morrison's novels, Mozart's piano concertos, Georgia O'Keeffe's paintings. When reading in the humanities, then, be aware of the differences between reading **PRIMARY SOURCES** like those and **SECONDARY SOURCES** (commentaries; analyses; evaluations; and interpretations of primary).

489–90

- When reading a primary source, you may need to ask questions like these: What kind of document is this? Who created it? When and where was the source produced? Who was it intended for? What is

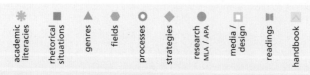

academic literacies · rhetorical situations · genres · fields · processes · strategies · research MLA / APA · media / design · readings · handbook

its historical context? Why did the creator of the source create it? How was it received at the time of its creation? Has that reception changed?

- Read primary sources carefully and expect to reread them, perhaps several times. The way a text is organized, its sentence structure, its wording, and its imagery can all contribute to its overall message, and that's true of documents like the Declaration of Independence, the Torah, and Descartes's *Principles of Philosophy*.

- Reading secondary sources requires that you examine them with a critical eye. The questions on pages 513–14 can help you understand the source and evaluate its accuracy, perspective or angle, and usefulness for your own work.

- Similarly, plan to reread secondary sources. The argument of interpretations, analyses, or critical works requires close attention to their logic and use of evidence.

- Remember that in the humanities, "criticism" doesn't necessarily mean looking for flaws and errors. Rather, it's another term for analyzing or evaluating.

- Some key terms you need to know in order to read texts in the humanities include: *analogy, allusion, argument, deductive reasoning, inductive reasoning, irony, metaphor, natural law, natural rights, political rights, premise*. If you don't understand the meaning of any of these terms, be sure to look up their definitions.

The Social Sciences

- As you read writing in the social sciences, you need to pay attention to the hypotheses, claims, reasons, and evidence presented in the texts. Are they persuasive? How do they compare or contrast with other arguments?

- Be sure you understand what a theory in the social sciences is: a way of organizing information to help enhance our understanding of behavior, events, phenomena, or issues. For example, in sociology, social exchange theory assumes that we behave according to our sense of whether we'll be rewarded or punished by those with whom we interact. Remember that a theory is not an unsupported opinion but rather a coherent, logical frame for understanding and describing.

198–201 ▲

- Many articles include a **LITERATURE REVIEW** that summarizes and critiques previous work on the topic. Since scholarly work always grows out of the work of others, authors need to connect their work to articles and books previously published on the topic. Many literature reviews discuss imitations and problems in previous studies, ultimately identifying missing elements or gaps in them (often identified with words like *but*, *however*, and *although*), leading to a rationale for why this new work is needed.

- The "Discussion" and "Conclusion" sections (which are sometimes combined into a single section) explain and interpret the results of a study in the context of the previous literature, note any limitations in the current study, and recommend future research to address those limitations. In other words, these sections discuss what the author thinks the study means. As you read, consider possible flaws or omissions in the author's thinking as well as in the research design; for example, the study is too broad, the research question is poorly defined, or the study doesn't address its significance—the "so what?" question. Your insights could lead you to a better understanding of the topic—or to a research project of your own.

- Some key terms you need to know in order to read texts in the social sciences include *adaptation*, *aggregate*, *alienation*, *capital*, *class system*, *deviance*, *interest*, *markets*, *motivation*, *norm*, *power*, *schema*, *supply and demand*, and *value*. If you don't understand the meaning of any of these terms, be sure to look up their definitions.

The Sciences

- Remember that scientific texts are not collections of settled facts. They make claims and argue for them, using reasons and evidence to support those arguments. Scientific texts report the results of studies

and experiments and are written by scientists for an audience of other scientists in the same field. These texts are different from science writing, which is often a form of nonfiction sometimes written by scientists, journalists, or other writers and aimed at general audiences to inform about scientific topics.

- If you're examining potential sources for a research project, read selectively: use articles' **ABSTRACTS** to decide whether an article is likely to be useful for your project, and skim the text to find the information relating to your needs. Many scientific articles follow a structure nicknamed IMRaD (Introduction, Methods, Results, and Discussion), so you may need to read only the sections of the article that discuss what you're looking for.

▲ 185–89

- Pay attention to the sample size—the number of units of whatever is being studied that are included in the study (a larger sample size is generally better than a smaller one)—and error bars in graphs, which show the uncertainty in the findings of the study being described.

- Scientists often make their arguments through visuals as much as words, so read images, graphs, and charts as carefully as you would the words in the text.

- For math problems or exercises, read the entire problem. Draw a picture or diagram to help you visualize the problem. Read it again, identifying the most important information; be sure you understand what the problem is asking for. Then decide on a method for solving it and come up with an answer. If you get stuck, think about how you'd deal with this information if it weren't a math problem. How would you go about solving it? Finally, reread the problem and ask yourself if you've answered the question that was asked.

- Some key terms you need to know in order to read texts in the sciences include *skepticism, data, evidence/observation, hypothesis, variables, biodiversity, falsifiability, theory, evolution, experimentation, population, qualitative, quantitative, repeatability, empirical, paradigm, rational/agnostic, cosmos.* If you don't understand the meaning of any of these terms, be sure to look up their definitions.

A Note on Career-Focused Fields

In general, the advice here for reading texts in general-education courses holds for reading in every major, including career-oriented disciplines, such as business administration, nursing, teaching, and education. At the same time, it's worth paying attention to the ways of thinking and the priorities of every field as you read in them. Here are a few examples:

Both business administration and education focus on processes. In business, much reading discusses how businesspeople do things, manage workers, set up systems, follow best accounting practices, and the like; in education, your reading will likely focus on how to write lesson plans, how to present information appropriately, and so on. Drawing flowcharts and diagrams of processes can help you understand the steps involved and help you remember them.

Engineers solve problems. So when reading engineering texts, look for relationships among concepts and ideas, and think about ways those concepts can be used to solve complex problems. Pay close attention to charts, graphs, diagrams, and visuals, as they often pack considerable information into a single image. When reading a graph, for example, consider not only the data as presented but also relationships in the data, and look for inferences and predictions you can make from the data presented.

Engineering and nursing texts contain a lot of information, much of which you won't need right away, so don't try to master every fact or procedure. Instead, read the chapter introductions, summaries, and questions, and skim, looking for the answers to the questions. You might also review a study guide for the NCLEX nursing licensing exam or the NCEES PE exam in engineering and focus your reading on the subject areas the exam focuses on. In general, work to understand the concepts you need rather than trying to memorize an avalanche of information; look for patterns in the information and how concepts are interrelated.

Writing in Academic **26** Fields of Study

In a *literature* course, you're asked to write an analysis of a short story. In a *biology* course, you must complete several lab reports. In a *management* course, you may create a detailed business plan. In fact, just about every course you take in college will require writing, so to write successfully, you must understand the rhetorical situation of your writing in every course and discipline—to write as if you're an insider, a member of the discipline, even if you're just learning the ropes. This chapter offers help in determining the general expectations of writing done in various academic fields of study.

Considering the Rhetorical Situation

To write in academic fields, you need to use the same processes and strategies you're asked to use in your writing classes, including analyzing the RHETORICAL SITUATION in which you're writing. These questions can help:

53

55–56

PURPOSE Why do people in this discipline write? To share scholarship and research findings? persuade? teach or provide guidance? show learning or mastery? track progress? propose solutions or plans of action? explore ideas or the self? earn grants or other rewards? something else?

57–60 **AUDIENCE**

To whom do people in this discipline write? To colleagues and other scholars? students? managers? employees? customers? clients? granting agencies? the public? others? What do they already know about the discipline and the topic? What specialized terms or concepts do they understand, and which need to be defined or explained? How much evidence or support is required, and what kinds (empirical data, research findings, logical analysis, personal testimony, something else) will they accept?

61–65 **GENRE**

What genres—reports, analyses, arguments, instructions, case studies, résumés, to name only a few—are typically used in this discipline? Are they organized in a certain way, and do they contain specific kinds of information? How much flexibility or room for innovation and creativity is allowed? What counts as evidence or support for assertions, and how is it cited (in citations in the text, in footnotes, in a works-cited page, informally in the text, or in some other way)?

66–68 **STANCE**

What attitude is considered appropriate in this discipline? Objective? Unemotional? Critical? Passionate? Should you write as a good student showing what you can do? an instructor of others? an advocate for a position? someone exploring an idea? something else? Does the discipline require a certain tone? formal or informal language? Can you include your personal perspective and write using "I"? Should you write only in the third person and use passive voice?

69–71 **MEDIA/DESIGN**

What media are typically used in this discipline? Print? Spoken? Electronic? A combination? Are certain design elements expected? to be avoided? Are visuals commonly used? What kinds—charts, graphs, photos, drawings, video or audio clips, or something else? In which genres? How much design freedom do you have?

WRITING IN ACADEMIC FIELDS OF STUDY

Generalizing about the requirements of writing in academic disciplines is tricky; what constitutes a discipline is sometimes unclear, and universities group academic fields together in various ways. For example, in some universities psychology is considered a science, while in others it's a social science. Economics is sometimes part of a college of business administration, sometimes in a college of arts and sciences. In addition, the writing required in, say, history, differs from that required in English literature, though both are considered parts of the humanities.

Furthermore, certain genres of writing, like *case studies* and *research reports*, can share the same name but have very different organizational structures and content, depending on the discipline in which they are used. For example, research reports in psychology and the natural sciences include a review of relevant scholarly literature in the introduction; in reports in sociology and other social sciences, the literature review is a separate section. A case study in business identifies a problem or issue in an organization; provides background information; includes a section, "Alternatives," that discusses possible solutions to the problem and why they were rejected; outlines and argues for a proposed solution; and proposes specific strategies for achieving the proposed solution. A case study in nursing, on the other hand, includes three sections: patient status, an overview of the patient's condition and treatment; the nurse's assessment of the patient's symptoms and their possible causes; and a plan for helping the patient improve. The guide below offers general advice on how to write in broad academic disciplines, but as the differences between two disciplines' expectations for case studies show, it's always a good idea to ask each of your professors for guidance on writing for their particular fields.

WRITING IN THE ARTS AND HUMANITIES

The arts and humanities focus on human culture and the expressions of the human mind, and the purpose of writing in these fields is to explore and analyze aspects of the human experience across time and sometimes to create original works of literature, music, and art. The methods used in these disciplines include careful reading, critical analysis, historical research, interpretation, questioning, synthesis, and imitation. Courses in the arts and humanities typically include fine arts, architecture, music, dance, theater, film, photography, literature, history, classical and modern languages, linguistics, and philosophy.

Writing in the arts and humanities is generally done for a broad audience that includes professors and scholars, other students, the general public, and oneself. Genres may include ANNOTATED BIBLIOGRAPHIES, ANALYSES, ARGUMENTS, essays, EVALUATIONS, JOURNALS, personal narratives, REPORTS, PRESENTATIONS, PROPOSALS, REFLECTIONS, and LITERATURE REVIEWS, as well as fiction and poetry. Support is often based on textual and observational evidence and personal insight, though in some fields empirical evidence and data are also valued. Writers in the arts and humanities tend to use modifiers to acknowledge that their insights and conclusions are interpretive, not definitive. Documentation is usually done in MLA or *Chicago* style. Elements of style favored in writing in the arts and humanities may include the use of "I"; the active voice; an informal vocabulary, if appropriate; and vivid language.

190–201 ▲
98–130
157–84
202–10
337–38 ○
131–56 ▲
673–84 □
246–55 ▲
256–63
198–201

MLA 548–96 ●

A Sample of Writing in History: A Researched Essay

Identifies a problem in current understanding of a historical event.

Offers a narrative of a past event.

Demonstrates familiarity with relevant sources.

The Pueblo Revolt of 1680 was one of the most significant yet misrepresented events in the history of American Indians. After three generations of being oppressed by Spanish rule, the Pueblo Indians throughout the southwest region of North America banded together, organizing a widespread rebellion in the blistering summer heat of 1680 and successfully liberating themselves from their oppressors by springtime. When examining the causes of the revolt, the lack of authentic Pueblo voices within the written records challenges the validity of the available sources and makes one wonder if we will ever know what went on through the eyes of the Pueblo. Although in

academic literacies ✳
rhetorical situations ■
genres ▲
fields ●
processes ○
strategies ◆
research MLA / APA ●
media / design □
readings ▮▮
handbook ⌃

the traditional narrative, the Spaniards are regarded as missionaries sent by God to "save" the "barbaric" Pueblos, the event, if seen from the Pueblo perspective, can be understood as a violent retaliation by the Pueblo against the Spanish oppression. The Pueblo uprisings, from burning down churches to the violent deaths of Catholic friars, reveal spiritual abuse as the major cause of the revolt. Moreover, without texts written by the Pueblo, their architecture and spatial organization provide valuable insight into the causes of the revolt era and help to overcome the veneer of Spanish colonialism.

Offers a strong thesis.

Clear, engaging writing style.

Adapted from "Letting the Unspoken Speak: A Reexamination of the Pueblo Revolt of 1680," by E. McHugh, April 2015, Armstrong Undergraduate Journal of History 5, no. 1, https://www.armstrong.edu/history-journal/history-journal-letting-the-unspoken-speak-a-reexamination-of-the-pueblo-re.

Sources in essay cited in Chicago format.

Typical Organization of Arts and Humanities Essays

Typical essays in the arts and humanities include these elements:

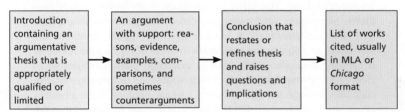

| Introduction containing an argumentative thesis that is appropriately qualified or limited | → | An argument with support: reasons, evidence, examples, comparisons, and sometimes counterarguments | → | Conclusion that restates or refines thesis and raises questions and implications | → | List of works cited, usually in MLA or *Chicago* format |

WRITING IN SCIENCE AND MATHEMATICS

The sciences include biology, chemistry, geology, earth sciences, and physics. Mathematics may include statistics and logic as well. All these fields aim to increase our knowledge of the physical and natural world and its phenomena through observation, experiment, logic, and computation.

185–89 ▲
198–201
131–56
157–84
246–55

APA 597–636 ●

Scientists and mathematicians typically write **ABSTRACTS**, **LITERATURE REVIEWS**, **REPORTS**, **ARGUMENTS**, poster presentations, **PROPOSALS**, and lab reports for audiences that may include other researchers, granting agencies, teachers, students, and the general public. Support in the sciences most often consists of repeatable empirical evidence; in mathematics, careful reasoning and the posing and solving of problems; in both, careful attention to the work of previous researchers. The writing in these fields focuses on the subject of the study, not the researcher, so most often the passive voice is used. Source material is paraphrased and summarized and cited in CSE or **APA** style.

A Sample of Scientific Writing: A Scientific Proposal in Biology

Careful reference to previous sentence.

Specialized disciplinary vocabulary.

Sources paraphrased and summarized.

Planarians, flatworms widely known for their incredible regenerative capabilities, are able to restore an entire organism from even a small fragment of tissue. This ability to regenerate is attributed solely to neoblasts, pluripotent adult stem cells located throughout the parenchyma of the animal (Newmark & Sanchez Alvarado, 2002). Neoblasts are stimulated to migrate and proliferate in times of injury (Guedelhoefer & Sanchez Alvarado, 2012). Lethally irradiated planarians (devoid of stem cells and therefore unable to regenerate) can restore regenerative capability through transplantation of a single neoblast from a healthy planarian (Wagner et al., 2011). Many studies have concluded that the population of neoblasts is not homogenous (Scimone et al., 2014), and there are different responses to different injury types. Wenemoser and Reddien (2012) observed a body-wide increase in mitotic activity, such as cell division and migration, with any injury.

Third person, passive voice.

Adapted from *"Identifying Genes Involved in Suppression of Tumor Formation in the Planarian Schmidtea mediterranea,"* by E. Dorsten, 2015, Best Integrated Writing, 2, *https://corescholar.libraries.wright.edu/biw/vol2/iss1/6/*

academic literacies   rhetorical situations   genres   fields   processes   strategies   research MLA / APA   media / design   readings   handbook

Typical Organization of Research Reports in the Sciences

Typical reports in the sciences include elements that follow the IMRaD structure: Introduction, Methods, Results, and Discussion. They also include an abstract and list of references.

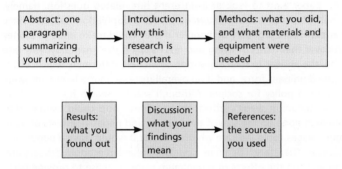

WRITING IN THE SOCIAL SCIENCES

Anthropology, archaeology, criminal justice, cultural studies, gender studies, geography, psychology, political science, and sociology are considered social sciences because they all explore human behavior and society using observation, experimentation, questionnaires, and interviews.

 Social scientists typically write for fellow scholars, teachers, students, and the general public. They may write in several genres: **ABSTRACTS**, **ANNOTATED BIBLIOGRAPHIES**, **ANALYSES**, **ARGUMENTS**, case studies, ethnographies, **LITERATURE OR RESEARCH REVIEWS**, **REPORTS**, **SUMMARIES**, and **PRESENTATIONS**. Claims are typically supported by empirical evidence, fieldwork done in natural settings, observation, and interviews. Writers in these fields strive for an objective tone, often using the passive voice. Sources may be cited in **APA** or *Chicago* style.

185–89
190–98
98–130
157–84
198–201
131–56
33–34
673–84

APA 597–636

A Sample of Writing in the Social Sciences:
A Research Report

Traditional economic theory states that a minimum wage above the marginal product of labor will lead to increased unemployment. . . . This paper aims to look at a different but related question, namely, *Objective tone.* whether or not a minimum wage makes a population happier. Since people would arguably be happier if they could make enough money to cover their costs of living and less happy if the unemployment rate rose, the answer to such a question could help determine which effect *Research question.* is the dominant force and if an overall increase in the minimum wage is a good policy for society. Although scant research has been done *Specialized language.* on a minimum wage's effect on happiness, one could assume that research done on the size of the positive and negative effects of minimum wages could indicate whether or not it would leave a population *Literature review.* happier. Therefore, I begin by reviewing relevant economic theory and research on the effects of a minimum wage increase to provide background information and describe what related questions have been *Empirical method.* approached and answered. I then describe the data and method used to answer this question, followed by the interpretation of such results *Analysis and evaluation of results.* as well as the implications.

Adapted from "The Effect of Minimum Wages on Happiness," by J. Nizamoff, Beyond Politics 2014, pp. 85–94, https://beyondpolitics.nd.edu/wp-content/uploads/2015/03/2013-14-Full-Journal.pdf

Typical Organization of a Research Report in the Social Sciences

Typical research reports in social science courses might include the following elements, though the order and names of the elements may differ from discipline to discipline. For example, in psychology, the literature review is part of the introduction, not a separate section as shown here.

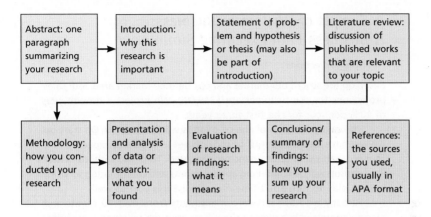

WRITING IN BUSINESS

The focus of the academic discipline of business is business-management principles and their application, and the purpose of writing in business is often to cause readers to make a decision and then act on it. The primary methods used include problem solving, planning, and experiential learning, or learning by doing. Courses typically taught include finance, economics, human resources, marketing, operations management, and accounting.

The audiences for writing in business typically include colleagues, employees in other departments, supervisors, managers, clients, customers, and other stakeholders—often several at the same time as a text moves through an organization. Genres may include memos, emails, letters, case studies, executive summaries, **RÉSUMÉS**, business plans, **REPORTS**, and **ANALYSES**. Support usually takes the form of facts and figures, examples, narratives, and expert testimony, and documentation is usually done in **APA** or *Chicago* style. Elements of style favored in business writing include these features: the main point is presented early; the language used is simple, direct, and positive; and the active voice is used in most cases.

264–79
131–56
98–130

APA 597–636

A Sample of Writing in Business: A Business Plan Executive Summary:

Financial Projections

Precise numbers, confidently stated.

Based on the size of our market and our defined market area, our sales projections for the first year are $340,000. We project a growth rate of 10% per year for the first three years.

Clear, direct writing, free of jargon and hedging.

The salary for each of the co-owners will be $40,000. On start up we will have six trained staff to provide pet services and expect to hire four more this year once financing is secured. To begin with, co-owner Pat Simpson will be scheduling appointments and coordinating services, but we plan to hire a full-time receptionist this year as well.

Positive tone.

Already we have service commitments from over 40 clients and plan to aggressively build our client base through newspaper, website, social media, and direct mail advertising. The loving on-site professional care that Pet Grandma will provide is sure to appeal to cat and dog owners throughout the West Vancouver area.

Adapted from "Business Plan Executive Summary Sample," by S. Ward, March 29, 2017, The Balance, *https://thebalance.com/business-plan-executive -summary-example-2948007*

Typical Organization of Business Plans

A common assignment in business courses is a business plan. Business plans typically include these sections:

Executive summary: outlines your proposal and what makes it likely to succeed

Company overview: includes a mission statement and describes the company's ownership, structure, and location

Products and services: defines the problem your company will try to solve and how it will do so; the competition and how you can do better; what, specifically, you are selling

Target market: includes a list of who your customers are

Marketing plan: specifies how you will reach your customers

Implementation plan: provides a schedule, a management team, and a financial plan

academic literacies · rhetorical situations · genres · fields · processes · strategies · research MLA / APA · media / design · readings · handbook

WRITING IN EDUCATION

The focus of study in education is how people learn and how to teach effectively. Its primary methods include observation, problem solving, and practice teaching. Courses typically center on teaching methods, the philosophy of education, educational measurement and assessment, educational psychology, and instructional technology, among others.

Educators typically write for audiences that include their students, parents, other teachers, administrators, and the public. Genres may include lesson plans, **SUMMARIES**, **REPORTS**, **ANNOTATED BIBLIOGRAPHIES**, **PORTFOLIOS**, and **REFLECTIONS**. Support for claims may include facts, statistics, test scores, personal narratives, observations, and case studies. Sources are documented in **APA** style. Clarity and correctness are important in writing in education; "I" may be used in reflective writing and informal communication, while in formal writing the third person is preferred.

33–34

131–56

190–98

361–70

256–63

APA 600–604

A Sample of Writing in Education: A Teaching Philosophy Statement

My Image of the Child: •⋯⋯⋯⋯⋯⋯⋯⋯⋯⋯⋯⋯⋯⋯

Sections labeled with headings.

I believe that the student should be at the center of the instructional •⋯⋯ process. I have an image of children as strong and capable beings. The classroom is a place where the teacher serves as a facilitator and guide as the students construct their own understanding of the world around them. Although it is the teacher's role to plan lessons and evaluate students' progress, it is of the utmost importance to always take the children and their own unique needs into consideration. For my second field experience, I was placed at Margaret Manson Elementary. Their school motto is that "the children come first." When children are the priority in teaching, an amazing amount of learning can take place. I believe in creating opportunities for students to develop to their fullest potential while developing and expanding their horizons and world-views. In order to accomplish this, there must be a welcoming, positive environment that is open and honest. When students feel comfortable

Argument is constructed to show teaching priorities.

Writing carefully crafted and proofread.

As a reflective piece, "I" is appropriate.

Discusses both teaching and personal qualities.

at school they will surely be more engaged and responsive to class activities. I also consider it essential to be passionate and enthusiastic about learning so that the students can have a most relevant and meaningful experience.

Adapted from "Statement of Teaching Philosophy," by K. Tams (n.d.), Kelly Tams' Teaching Portfolio, http://tams.yolasite.com/my-philosophy-of-education.php

Typical Organization of Lesson Plans in Education

Frequent assignments in education courses are lesson plans, which typically include these elements:

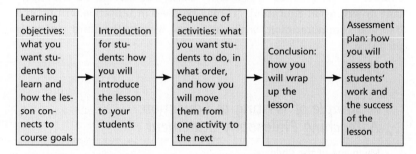

Learning objectives: what you want students to learn and how the lesson connects to course goals → Introduction for students: how you will introduce the lesson to your students → Sequence of activities: what you want students to do, in what order, and how you will move them from one activity to the next → Conclusion: how you will wrap up the lesson → Assessment plan: how you will assess both students' work and the success of the lesson

WRITING IN ENGINEERING AND TECHNOLOGY

In the fields of engineering and technology, the focus is how to create and maintain useful structures, systems, processes, and machines. Engineers and technicians define problems as well as solve them, weigh various alternatives, and test possible solutions before presenting them to clients. This is a broad set of disciplines that may include civil, computer, electrical, mechanical, and structural engineering; computer science; and various technology specialties such as HVAC and automotive technology.

Engineers and technicians typically write for their peers and team members, their clients, and the public. Writing tasks may include **ABSTRACTS**, **EVALUATIONS**, instructions, **LITERATURE REVIEWS**, memos, **PROPOSALS**, **REPORTS**, and **SUMMARIES**. Support usually includes data, examples, mathematical and logical reasoning, and experimental results, and sources are usually cited in **APA** format. Engineers and technicians value writing that includes logical ordering of ideas and precise language. Tables, charts, figures, illustrations, and headings and subheadings within the writing—all ways of quickly and efficiently getting information—are also valued.

▲ 185–89
202–10
198–201
246–55
131–56
✳ 33–34
● APA 597–636

A Sample of Writing in Engineering: A Research Report

2. MATERIALS AND METHODS •⋯⋯⋯⋯⋯⋯⋯⋯⋯⋯⋯⋯⋯⋯ *Headings used.*

To begin testing, an ATV test bed was designed (fig. 1). To secure the machine, a loose rope was attached to the front of the machine and then to the testing platform. An additional rope was then attached at a 90° angle to the front of the machine to act as the lifting force. The test bed platform could be raised to a maximum of 60°, which simulated hills or steep terrain. Each test was started at 0° and then increased by increments of 10 (angles were determined by a digital level attached to platform). Once the machine was at the appropriate angle, a lift force was applied to observe turnover weight. Once the machine's tires lifted off of the platform, the scale was read to determine the amount of weight. Each machine was tested from to rear and side to side.

Charts, graphs, and photos included.

Precise description of procedure.

Technical language used for precision.

Adapted from "Analysis of All Terrain Vehicle Crash Mechanisms," by S. Tanner, M. Aitken, and J. N. Warnock, 2008–10, Journal of Undergraduate Research in Bioengineering, *https://www.uweb.engr.washington.edu/education/pdf/ tanner.pdf*

Typical Organization of Lab Reports in Engineering

Lab reports, a typical assignment in engineering classes, usually include the IMRaD elements, along with an abstract and a list of references. This format may vary depending on the engineering field and the requirements of the experiment or task.

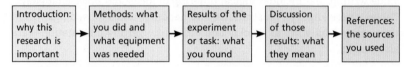

Introduction: why this research is important → Methods: what you did and what equipment was needed → Results of the experiment or task: what you found → Discussion of those results: what they mean → References: the sources you used

WRITING IN HEALTH SCIENCES AND NURSING

Health sciences and nursing is a broad set of fields that may include nursing, anatomy, physiology, nutrition, and pharmacology as well as athletic training, exercise science, physical or occupational therapy, and speech pathology. Consequently, the methods used are also broad and varied, and they may include study of theories and techniques, observation, role-playing, and experiential learning.

185–89 ▲
190–98
157–84
131–56
256–63
198–201
33–34 ✳
443–51 ◆

APA 597–636 ●

Writing in these fields may include **ABSTRACTS**, **ANNOTATED BIBLI-OGRAPHIES**, **ARGUMENTS**, case studies, instructions, personal narratives, **REPORTS**, **REFLECTIONS**, **REVIEWS**, **SUMMARIES**, and charts **DESCRIBING** patients' conditions and care. The audiences for this writing may include other patient care providers, clinic and hospital administrators and staff, insurance companies, and patients or clients. Support for assertions typically includes scholarly research, observation, and description, and high value is placed on accurate information and detail. Other aspects of this writing include a preference for writing in the third person, paraphrased source information, and the use of headings and subheadings. Sources are usually cited in **APA** format.

academic literacies · rhetorical situations · genres · fields · processes · strategies · research MLA / APA · media / design · readings · handbook

A Sample of Writing in Nursing:
A Case Study

Patient Status. • Ms. D is a morbidly obese 67 year old female, 240 lbs, 5'2" with type II diabetes mellitus. She was transferred from a nursing home to the hospital for pneumonia, but also suffers from congestive heart disease, sleep apnea, psoriasis, and osteoarthritis. She has a weak but productive cough with tonsil suction, and she was on breathing treatments with albuterol. Her skin is very dry and thin with several lesions and yeast infections, and the deep folds of her lower abdomen bled during the bed bath. She did not want to wear her breathing mask at night and refused to get out of bed. She cried when encouraged to use the bathroom or to move her legs. She expressed great fear of returning to the nursing home.

Careful description of patient's condition.

Detailed observation using precise terms.

Behavior as well as medical conditions taken into account.

From the outset, we realized that Ms. D needed care beyond physical therapy and treatment for pneumonia; we realized that her obesity and refusal to participate in her health care expressed important patterns of her life. Morbid obesity does not happen overnight; it is a progressive pattern associated with activity levels, diet, and self-care practices, as well as other possible physiological and psychosocial dimensions. Johnson's (1980) Behavioral System Model, which outlines seven behavioral subsystems, was helpful in providing a perspective of the complexity of Ms. D's health needs. We also assessed that Ms. D lacked confidence in taking care of herself (reflecting the *achievement subsystem*) and lacked a sense of family support from her two sons (*affiliative subsystem*). Her fear of returning to the nursing home coupled with her need for ongoing care challenged her sense of interdependency as addressed in Johnson's *dependency subsystem*.

Patient Assessment.

Use of paraphrased scholarly source to aid assessment.

Adapted from "Esthetic Knowing with a Hospitalized Morbidly Obese Patient," by R. Brinkley, K. Ricker, and K. Tuomey, Fall 2007, Journal of Undergraduate Nursing Scholarship, 9, no. 1, http://www.juns.nursing.arizona.edu/articles/Fall%202007/Esthetic%20knowing.htm

Typical Organization of Case Studies in Health Sciences and Nursing

Case studies, typical assignments in these fields, usually include the following elements:

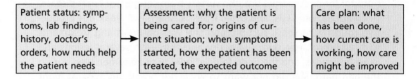

Patient status: symptoms, lab findings, history, doctor's orders, how much help the patient needs	→	Assessment: why the patient is being cared for; origins of current situation; when symptoms started, how the patient has been treated, the expected outcome	→	Care plan: what has been done, how current care is working, how care might be improved

academic literacies · rhetorical situations · genres · fields · processes · strategies · research MLA / APA · media / design · readings · handbook

part 5

Processes

To create anything, we generally break the work down into a series of steps. We follow a recipe (or the directions on a box) to bake a cake; we break a song down into different parts and the music into various chords to arrange a piece of music. So it is when we write. We rely on various processes to get from a blank screen or page to a finished product. The chapters that follow offer advice on some of these processes—from WRITING AS INQUIRY and GENERATING IDEAS to DRAFTING to GETTING RESPONSE to EDITING to COMPILING A PORTFOLIO, and more.

Processes

Writing as Inquiry **27**

Sometimes we write to say what we think. Other times, however, we write in order to figure out what we think. Much of the writing you do in college will be the latter. Even as you learn to write, you will be writing to learn. This chapter is about writing with a spirit of inquiry—approaching writing projects with curiosity, moving beyond the familiar, keeping your eyes open, tackling issues that don't have easy answers. It's about starting with questions and going from there—and taking risks. As Mark Twain once said, "Sail away from the safe harbor. . . . Explore. Dream. Discover." This chapter offers strategies for doing just that with your writing.

Starting with Questions

The most important thing is to start with questions—with what you don't know rather than with what you do know. Your goal is to learn about your subject and then to learn more. If you're writing about a topic you know well, you want to expand on what you already know. In academic writing, good topics arise from important questions, issues, and problems that are already being discussed. As a writer, you need to find out what's being said about your topic and then see your writing as a way of entering that larger conversation.

So start with questions, and don't expect to find easy answers. If there were easy answers, there would be no reason for discussion—or for you to write. For purposes of inquiry, the best questions can't be answered by looking in a reference book. Instead, they are ones that help you explore what you think—and why. As it happens, many of the strategies in this book can help you ask questions of this kind. Following are some questions to get you started:

432–42

How can it be DEFINED? What is it, and what does it do? Look it up in a dictionary; check *Wikipedia*. Remember, though, that these are only starting points. How *else* can it be defined? What more is there to know about it? If your topic is being debated, chances are that its very definition is subject to debate. If, for instance, you're writing about gay marriage, how you define marriage will affect how you approach the topic.

443–51

How can it be DESCRIBED? What details should you include? From what vantage point should you describe your topic? If, for example, your topic is the physiological effects of running a marathon, what are those effects—on the lungs, heart muscles, nerves, brain, and so on? How will you describe the physical experience of running over twenty-six miles from the runner's point of view?

457–61

How can it be EXPLAINED? What does it do? How does it work? If you're investigating the use of performance-enhancing drugs by athletes, for example, what exactly are the effects of these drugs? What makes them dangerous—and are they always dangerous or only in certain conditions? Why are they illegal—and should they be illegal?

424–31

What can it be COMPARED with? Again using performance-enhancing drugs by athletes as an example, how does taking such supplements compare with wearing high-tech footwear or uniforms? Does such a comparison make you see taking steroids or other performance-enhancing drugs in a new light?

392–96

What may have CAUSED it? What might be its EFFECTS? Who or what does it affect? What causes cerebral palsy in children, for example? What are its symptoms? If children with cerebral palsy are not treated, what might be the consequences?

418–23

How can it be CLASSIFIED? Is it a topic or issue that can be placed into categories of similar topics or issues? What categories can it be placed into? Are there legal and illegal performance-enhancing supplements (human growth hormone and steroids, for instance), and what's the difference? Are some safe and others less safe? Classifying your topic in this way can help you consider its complexities.

How can it be ANALYZED?   What parts can the topic be divided into?   ▲ 98–130
For example, if you are exploring the health effects of cell phone use, you
might ask these questions: What evidence suggests that cell phone radiation
causes cancer? What cancers are associated with cell phone use? What do
medical experts and phone manufacturers say? How can cell phone users
reduce their risk?

How can it be interpreted?   What does it really mean? How do you
interpret it, and how does your interpretation differ from others? What
evidence supports your interpretation, and what argues against it? Imagine you're exploring the topic of sports injuries among young women. Do
these injuries reflect a larger cultural preoccupation with competition? a
desire to win college scholarships? something else?

What expectations does it raise?   What will happen next? What makes
you think so? If this happens, how will it affect those involved? For
instance, will the governing bodies of professional sports require more
testing of athletes' blood, urine, and hair than they do now? Will such tests
be unfair to athletes taking drugs for legitimate medical needs?

What are the different POSITIONS on it?   What controversies or disagree-   ▲ 157–84
ments exist, and what evidence is offered for the various positions? What
else might be said? Are there any groups or individuals who seem especially authoritative? If so, you might want to explore what they have said.

What are your own feelings about it?   What interests you about the
topic? How much do you already know about it? For example, if you're
an athlete, how do you feel about competing against others who may
have taken supplements? If a friend has problems with drugs, do those
problems affect your thinking about drugs in sports? How do you react
to what others say about the topic? What else do you want to find out?

Are there other ways to think about it?   Is what seems true in this case
also true in others? How can you apply this subject in another situation?
Will what works in another situation also work here? What do you have to
do to adapt it? Imagine you are writing about traffic fatalities. If replacing
stop signs with roundabouts or traffic circles reduced traffic fatalities in
England, could doing so also reduce accidents in the United States?

334–35 ◉
You can also start with the journalist's **QUESTIONS**: *Who? What? When? Where? Why? How?* Asking questions from these various perspectives can help you deepen your understanding of your topic by leading you to see it from many angles.

Keeping a Journal

337–38 ◉
One way to get into the habit of using writing as a tool for inquiry is to keep a **JOURNAL**. You can use a journal to record your observations, reactions, whatever you wish. Some writers find journals especially useful places to articulate questions or speculations. You may be assigned by teachers to do certain work in a journal, but in general, you can use a journal to write for yourself. Note your ideas, speculate, digress—go wherever your thoughts lead you.

Keeping a Blog

667 ▢
You may also wish to explore issues or other ideas online in the form of a **BLOG**. Most blogs have a comments section that allows others to read and respond to what you write, leading to potentially fruitful discussions. You can also include links to other websites, helping you connect various strands of thought and research. The blogs of others, along with online discussion forums and groups, may also be useful sources of opinion on your topic, but keep in mind that they probably aren't authoritative research sources. There are a number of search engines that can help you find blog posts related to specific topics, including *Google Blog Search, Ask*, and *IceRocket*. You can create your own blog on sites such as *Blogger, Tumblr, Svbtle*, or *WordPress*.

Collaborating 28

Whether you're working in a face-to-face group, posting on an online discussion board, or exchanging drafts with a classmate, you likely spend a lot of time working with others on writing tasks. Even if you do much of your writing sitting alone at a computer, you probably get help from others at various stages in the writing process—and provide help as well. Two heads can be better than one—and learning to work well with a team is as important as anything else you'll learn in college. This chapter offers some guidelines for collaborating successfully with other writers.

Some Ground Rules for Face-to-Face Group Work

- Make sure everyone is facing everyone else and is physically part of the group. Doing that makes a real difference in the quality of the interactions—think how much better conversation works when you're sitting around a table than it does when you're sitting in a row.

- Thoughtfulness, respect, and tact are key, since most writers (as you know) are sensitive and need to be able to trust those commenting on their work. Respond to the contributions of others as you would like others to respond to yours.

- Each meeting needs an agenda—and careful attention paid to time. Appoint one person as timekeeper to make sure all necessary work gets done in the available time.

- Appoint another person to be group leader or facilitator. That person needs to make sure everyone gets a chance to speak, no one dominates the discussion, and the group stays on task.

- Appoint a member of the group to record the group's discussion, jotting down the major points as they come up and then writing a **SUMMARY** of the discussion that the group members then approve.

534–35

Online Collaboration

Sometimes you'll work with one or more people online. Working together online offers many advantages, including the ability to collaborate without being in the same place at the same time. Nonetheless, it also presents some challenges that differ from those of face-to-face group work. When sharing writing or collaborating with others online in other ways, consider the following suggestions:

- As with all online communication, remember that you need to choose your words carefully to avoid inadvertently hurting someone's feelings. Without facial expressions, gestures, and other forms of body language and without tone of voice, your words carry all the weight.

57–60

- Remember that the **AUDIENCE** for what you write may well extend beyond your group—your work might be forwarded to others, so there is no telling who else might read it.

- Decide as a group how best to deal with the logistics of exchanging drafts and comments. You can cut and paste text directly into email, send it as an attachment to a message, or post it to your class course management system site or a file-sharing site like *Dropbox* or *Google Docs*. You may need to use a combination of methods, depending on each group member's access to equipment and software. In any case, name your files carefully so that everyone knows which version to use.

Writing Conferences

Conferences with instructors or writing tutors can be an especially helpful kind of collaboration. These one-on-one sessions often offer the most strongly focused assistance you can get—and truly valuable instruction. Here are some tips for making the most of conference time:

- *Come prepared.* Bring all necessary materials, including the draft you'll be discussing, your notes, any outlines—and, of course, any questions.
- *Be prompt.* Your instructor or tutor has set aside a block of time for you, and once that time is up, there's likely to be another student writer waiting.
- *Listen carefully, discuss your work seriously, and try not to be defensive.* Your instructor or tutor is only trying to help you produce the best piece possible. If you sense that your work is being misunderstood, explain what you're trying to say. Don't get angry! If a sympathetic reader who's trying to help can't understand what you mean, maybe you haven't conveyed your meaning well enough.
- *Take notes.* During the conference, jot down keywords and suggestions. Immediately afterward, flesh out your notes so you'll have a complete record of what was said.
- *Reflect on the conference.* Afterward, think about what you learned. What do you have to do now? Create a plan for revising or doing further work, and write out questions you will ask at your next conference.

Group Writing Projects

Creating a document with a team is common in business and professional work and in some academic fields as well. Here are some tips for making collaboration of this kind work well:

- *Define the task as clearly as possible.* Make sure everyone understands and agrees with the stated goals.
- *Divide the task into parts.* Decide which parts can be done by individuals, which can be done by a subgroup, and which need to be done by everyone together.
- *Assign each group member certain tasks.* Try to match tasks to each person's skills and interests and to divide the work equally.

- *Establish a deadline for each task.* Allow time for unforeseen problems before the project deadline.
- *Try to accommodate everyone's style of working.* Some people value discussion; others want to get right down to the writing. There's no best way to get work done; everyone needs to be conscious that their way is not the only way.
- *Work for consensus—not necessarily total agreement.* Everyone needs to agree that the plan to get the task done is doable and appropriate—if not exactly the way you would do it if you were working alone.
- *Make sure everyone performs.* Sometimes your instructor may help, but the group itself may have to develop a way to ensure that the work gets done well and fairly. During the course of the project, it's sometimes helpful for each group member to write an assessment both of the group's work and of individual members' contributions.

academic literacies · rhetorical situations · genres · fields · processes · strategies · research MLA / APA · media / design · readings · handbook

Generating Ideas and Text

All good writing revolves around ideas. Whether you're writing a job-application letter, a sonnet, or an essay, you'll always spend time and effort generating ideas. Some writers can come up with a topic, put their thoughts in order, and flesh out their arguments in their heads; but most of us need to write out our ideas, play with them, tease them out, and examine them from some distance and from multiple perspectives. This chapter offers activities that can help you do just that. *Freewriting*, *looping*, *listing*, and *clustering* can help you explore what you know about a subject; *cubing* and *questioning* nudge you to consider a subject in new ways; and *outlining*, *letter writing*, *journal keeping*, and *discovery drafting* offer ways to generate a text.

Freewriting

An informal method of exploring a subject by writing about it, freewriting ("writing freely") can help you generate ideas and come up with materials for your draft. Here's how to do it:

1. Write as quickly as you can without stopping for 5 to 10 minutes (or until you fill a screen or page).

2. If you have a subject to explore, write it at the top and then start writing about it, but if you stray, don't worry—just keep writing. If you don't have a subject yet, just start writing and don't stop until the time is up. If you can't think of anything to say, write that ("I can't think of anything to say") again and again until you do—and you will!

3. Once the time is up, read over what you've written, and underline or highlight passages that interest you.

4. Write some more, starting with one of those underlined or highlighted passages as your new topic. Repeat the process until you've come up with a usable topic.

Looping

Looping is a more focused version of freewriting; it can help you explore what you know about a subject. You stop, reflect on what you've written, and then write again, developing your understanding in the process. It's good for clarifying your knowledge and understanding of a subject and finding a focus. Here's what you do:

1. Write for 5 to 10 minutes on whatever you know about your subject. This is your first loop.

2. Read over what you wrote, and then write a single sentence summarizing the most important or interesting idea. You might try completing one of these sentences: "I guess what I was trying to say was . . . " or "What surprises me most in reading what I wrote is . . ." This will be the start of another loop.

3. Write again for 5 to 10 minutes, using your summary sentence as your beginning and your focus. Again, read what you've written, and then write a sentence capturing the most important idea—in a third loop.

Keep going until you have enough understanding of your topic to be able to decide on a tentative focus—something you can write about.

Listing

Some writers find it useful to keep lists of ideas that occur to them while they are thinking about a topic. Follow these steps:

1. Write a list of potential ideas about a topic. Don't try to limit your list—include anything that interests you.

2. Look for relationships among the items on your list: what patterns do you see? If other ideas occur to you, add them to the list.

3. Arrange the items in an order that makes sense for your purpose and can serve as the beginning of an outline for your writing.

Clustering or Mapping Ideas

Clustering (also called idea mapping) is a way of generating and connecting ideas visually. It's useful for seeing how various ideas relate to one another and for developing subtopics. The technique is simple:

1. Write your topic in the middle of a sheet of paper and circle it.

2. Write ideas relating to that topic around it, circle them, and connect them to the central circle.

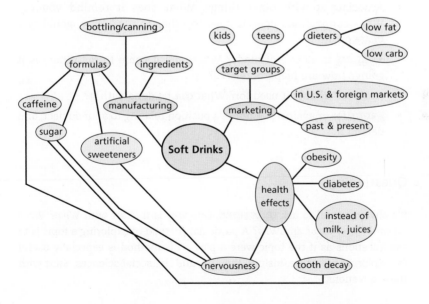

3. Write down examples, facts, or other details relating to each idea, and join them to the appropriate circles.

4. Keep going until you can't think of anything else relating to your topic.

You should end up with various ideas about your topic, and the clusters will allow you to see how they relate to one another. In the example cluster on the topic of "soft drinks" on the previous page, note how some ideas link not only to the main topic or related topics but also to other ideas.

Cubing

A cube has six sides. You can examine a topic as you might a cube, looking at it in these six ways:

443–51
- **DESCRIBE** it. What's its color? shape? age? size? What's it made of?

424–31
- **COMPARE** it to something else. What is it similar to or different from?

- Associate it with other things. What does it remind you of? What connections does it have to other things? How would you

418–23
  CLASSIFY it?

98–130
- **ANALYZE** it. How is it made? Where did it come from? Where is it going? How are its parts related?

- Apply it. What is it used for? What can be done with it?

157–84
- **ARGUE** for or against it. Choose a position relating to your subject, and defend it.

Questioning

334–35
It's always useful to ask **QUESTIONS**. One way is to start with *What? Who? When? Where? How?* and *Why?* A particular method of exploring a topic is to ask questions as if the topic were a play. This method is especially useful for exploring literature, history, the arts, and the social sciences. Start with these questions:

- *What?* What happens? How is it similar to or different from other actions?
- *Who?* Who are the actors? Who are the participants, and who are the spectators? How do the actors affect the action, and how are they affected by it?
- *When?* When does the action take place? How often does it happen? What happens before, after, or at the same time? Would it be different at another time? Does the time have historical significance?
- *Where?* What is the setting? What is the situation, and what makes it significant?
- *How?* How does the action occur? What are the steps in the process? What techniques are required? What equipment is needed?
- *Why?* Why did this happen? What are the actors' motives? What end does the action serve?

Using Genre Features

Genres typically include particular kinds of information and organize it in particular ways. One way to generate ideas and text, then, is to identify the key features of the genre in which you're writing and use them to guide you as you write. Of course, you may alter the genre's features or combine two or more genres in order to achieve your purpose, but the overall shape and content of the genre can give you a way to develop and organize your ideas and research.

Outlining

You may create an *informal outline* by simply listing your ideas and numbering them in the order in which you want to write about them. You might prefer to make a *working outline*, to show the hierarchy of relationships among your ideas. While still informal, a working outline distinguishes your main ideas and your support, often through simple indentation:

First main idea
  Supporting evidence or detail
  Supporting evidence or detail
Second main idea
  Supporting evidence or detail
  Supporting evidence or detail

A *formal outline* shows the hierarchy of your ideas through a system of indenting, numbering, and lettering. Remember that when you divide a point into more specific subpoints, you should have at least two of them—you can't divide something into only one part. Also, try to keep items at each level parallel in structure. Formal outlines work this way:

Thesis statement

I. First reason
   A. Supporting evidence
      1. Detail of evidence
      2. Detail of evidence
   B. Supporting evidence
II. Another reason

Here is a formal outline of the first part of the research report by Dylan Borchers on pages 588–96, "Against the Odds: Harry S. Truman and the Election of 1948," that shows how he organized it:

I. Introduction: Outcome of 1948 election
II. Bad predictions by pollsters
   A. Pollsters stopped polling.
   B. Dewey supporters became overconfident.
   C. Truman supporters were either energized or stayed home.
III. Dewey's campaign overly cautious
   A. He was overconfident.
   B. His message was vague—he avoided taking stands.

    IV. Dewey's public appearances poor
       A. He was seen as aloof, uncomfortable with crowds.
       B. He made blunders.
       C. His speeches were dull.

Writing out a formal outline can be helpful when you're dealing with a complex subject; as you revise your drafts, though, be flexible and ready to change your outline as your understanding of your topic develops.

Letter Writing

Sometimes the prospect of writing a report or essay can be intimidating. You may find that simply explaining your topic to someone will help you get started. In that case, write a letter or email to someone you know—your best friend, a parent or grandparent, a sibling—in which you discuss your subject. Explain it in terms that your reader can understand. Use the unsent letter to rehearse your topic; make it a kind of rough draft that you can then revise and develop to suit your actual audience.

Keeping a Journal

Some writers find that writing in a journal helps them generate ideas. Making note of your ideas, thoughts, feelings, or the events of your day can provide a wealth of topics, and a journal can also be a good place to explore what you think and why you think as you do.

Journals are private—you are the only audience—so you can feel free to write whatever comes to mind. And you can do more than write. If you choose a paper journal, doodle or draw in it, and keep clippings or scraps of paper between the pages; if you keep your journal on a computer, copy and paste interesting images or text you find online. Whatever form your journal takes, feel free to play with its contents, and don't worry about errors or grammar. The goal is to generate ideas; let yourself wander without censoring yourself or fretting that your writing is incorrect or incomplete or incoherent. That's okay.

331–32
332–33
334

One measure of the success of journaling and other personal writing is length: journal entries, **FREEWRITING**, **LISTING**, **CUBING**, and other types of informal writing are like warm-up exercises to limber you up and get you thinking. If you don't give them enough time and space, they may not do what you want them to. Often, students' best insights appear at the end of their journal entries. Had they stopped before that point, they would never have had those good ideas.

After you've written several journal entries, one way to study the ideas in them is to highlight useful patterns in different colors. For example, journal entries usually include some questioning and speculating, as well as summarizing and paraphrasing. Try color-coding each of these, sentence by sentence, phrase by phrase: yellow for summaries or paraphrases, green for questions, blue for speculations. Do any colors dominate? If, for example, your entries are mostly yellow, you may be restating the course content or quoting from the textbook too much and perhaps need to ask more questions. If you're generating ideas for an essay, you might assign colors to ideas or themes to see which ones are the most promising.

Discovery Drafting

Some writers do best by jumping in and writing. Here are the steps to take if you're ready to write a preliminary **DRAFT**:

340–42

1. Write your draft quickly, in one sitting if possible.

2. Assume that you are writing to discover what you want to say and how you need to say it—and that you will make substantial revisions in a later part of the process.

3. Don't worry about grammatical or factual correctness—if you can't think of a word, leave a blank space to fill in later. If you're unsure of a date or spelling, put a question mark in parentheses as a reminder to check it later. Just write.

IF YOU NEED MORE HELP

See each of the **GENRE** chapters for specific strategies for generating text in each genre.

▲ 73

30 Drafting

At some point, you need to write out a draft. By the time you begin drafting, you've probably written quite a bit—in the form of notes, lists, outlines, and other kinds of informal writing. This chapter offers some hints on how to write a draft—and reminds you that as you draft, you may well need to get more information, rethink some aspect of your work, or follow new ideas that occur to you as you write.

Establishing a Schedule with Deadlines

479–80

Don't wait until the last minute to write. Computers crash, printers jam. Life intervenes in unpredictable ways. You increase your chances of success immensely by setting and meeting **DEADLINES**: Research done by ____; rough draft done by ____; revisions done by ____; final draft edited, proofread, and submitted by ____. How much time you need varies with each writing task—but trying to compress everything into twenty-four or forty-eight hours before the deadline is asking for trouble.

Getting Comfortable

When are you at your best? When do you have your best ideas? For major writing projects, consider establishing a schedule that lets you write when you stand the best chance of doing good work. Schedule breaks for exercise and snacks. Find a good place to write, a place where you've got a good surface on which to spread out your materials, good lighting, a comfortable chair, and the right tools (computer, pen, paper) for the job. Often, however, we must make do: you may have to do your drafting in a busy computer lab or classroom. The trick is to make yourself as comfortable as you can manage. Sort out what you *need* from what you *prefer*.

340

Starting to Write

All of the above advice notwithstanding, don't worry so much about the trappings of your writing situation that you don't get around to writing. Write. Start by **FREEWRITING**, start with a first sentence, start with awful writing that you know you'll discard later—but write. That's what gets you warmed up and going.

331–32

Write quickly in spurts.   Write quickly with the goal of writing a complete draft, or a complete section of a longer draft, in one sitting. If you need to stop in the middle, make some notes about where you were headed when you stopped so that you can easily pick up your train of thought when you begin again.

Break down your writing task into small segments.   Big projects can be intimidating. But you can always write one section or, if need be, one paragraph or even a single sentence—and then another and another. It's a little like dieting. If I think I need to lose twenty pounds, I get discouraged and head for the doughnuts; but if I decide that I'll lose one pound and I lose it, well, I'll lose another—*that* I can do.

Expect surprises.   Writing is a form of thinking; the words you write lead you down certain roads and away from others. You may end up somewhere you didn't anticipate. Sometimes that can be a good thing—but sometimes you can write yourself into a dead end or out onto a tangent. Just know that this is natural, part of every writer's experience, and it's okay to double back or follow a new path that opens up before you.

Expect to write more than one draft.   A first sentence, first page, or first draft represents your attempt to organize into words your thoughts, ideas, feelings, research findings, and more. It's likely that some of that first try will not achieve your goals. That's okay—having writing on screen or on paper that you can change, add to, and cut means you're part of the way there. As you revise, you can fill in gaps and improve your writing and thinking.

Dealing with Writer's Block

You may sit down to write but find that you can't—nothing occurs to you; your mind is blank. Don't panic; here are some ways to get started writing again:

- Think of the assignment as a problem to be solved. Try to capture that problem in a single sentence: "How do I explain the context for my topic?" "What is the best way to organize my argument?" "What am I trying to do in the conclusion?"

- Start early and break the writing task into small segments drafted over several days. Waiting until the night before an assignment is due can create panic—and writer's block.

- Stop trying: take a walk, take a shower, do something else. Come back in a half hour, refreshed.

331–33 ◉ - Open a new document on your computer or get a fresh piece of paper and **FREEWRITE**, or try **LOOPING** or **LISTING**. What are you trying to say? Just let whatever comes come—you may write yourself out of your box.

- If you usually write on your computer, turn it off, get out paper and pencil, and write by hand.

333–34 ◉ - Try a graphic approach: try **CLUSTERING**, or draw a chart of what you want to say; draw a picture; doodle.

477 ● - Do some **RESEARCH** on your topic to see what others have said about it.

348–50 ◉ - Talk to someone about what you are trying to do. If there's a writing center at your school, talk to a tutor: **GET RESPONSE**. If there's no one to talk to, talk to yourself. It's the act of talking—using your mouth instead of your hands—that can free you up.

IF YOU NEED MORE HELP

331–39 ◉
343–47
348–55
See Chapter 29 on **GENERATING IDEAS AND TEXT** if you find you need more material. And once you have a draft, see Chapter 31 on **ASSESSING YOUR OWN WRITING** and Chapter 32 **GETTING RESPONSE AND REVISING** for help evaluating your draft.

Assessing Your Own Writing **31**

In school and out, our work is continually assessed by others. Teachers determine whether our writing is strong or weak; supervisors decide whether we merit raises or promotions; even friends and relatives size up in various ways the things we do. As writers, we need to assess our own work—to step back and see it with a critical eye. By developing standards of our own and being conscious of the standards others use, we can assess—and shape—our writing, making sure it does what we want it to do. This chapter will help you assess your own written work.

What we write for others must stand on its own because we usually aren't present when it is read—we rarely get to explain to readers why we did what we did and what it means. So we need to make our writing as clear as we can before we submit, post, display, or publish it. It's a good idea to assess your writing in two stages, first considering how well it meets the needs of your particular rhetorical situation, then studying the text itself to check its focus, argument, organization, and clarity. Sometimes some simple questions can get you started:

What works?
What still needs work?
Where do I need to say more (or less)?

Considering the Rhetorical Situation

PURPOSE What is your purpose for writing? If you have multiple purposes, list them, and then note which ones are the most important. How well does your draft achieve your purpose(s)? If you're writing for an assignment, what are

55–56

343

the requirements of the assignment, and does your draft meet those requirements?

57–60 **AUDIENCE**   To whom are you writing? What do those readers need and expect, as far as you can tell? Does your draft answer their needs? Do you define any terms and explain any concepts they won't know?

61–65 **GENRE**   What is the genre, and what are the key features of that genre? Does your draft include each of those features? If not, is there a good reason?

66–68 **STANCE**   Is your attitude toward your topic and your audience clear? Does your language project the personality and tone that you want?

69–71 **MEDIA / DESIGN**   What medium (print? spoken? electronic?) or combination of media is your text intended for, and how well does your writing suit it? How well does the design of the text suit your purpose and audience? Does it meet any requirements of the genre or of the assignment, if you're writing for one?

Examining the Text Itself

Look carefully at your text to see how well it says what you want it to say. Start with its focus, and then examine its reasons and evidence, organization, and clarity, in that order. If your writing lacks focus, the revising you'll do to sharpen the focus is likely to change everything else; if it needs more reasons and evidence, the organization may well change.

Consider your focus.   Your writing should have a clear point, and every part of the writing should support that point. Here are some questions that can help you see if your draft is adequately focused:

387–89

- What is your **THESIS**? Even if it is not stated directly, you should be able to summarize it for yourself in a single sentence.

academic literacies · rhetorical situations · genres · fields · processes · strategies · research MLA / APA · media / design · readings · handbook

- Is your thesis narrow or broad enough to suit the needs and expectations of your audience?
- How does the **BEGINNING** focus attention on your thesis or main point?   373–80
- Does each paragraph support or develop that point? Do any paragraphs or sentences stray from your focus?
- Does the **ENDING** leave readers thinking about your main point? Is there another way of concluding the essay that would sharpen your focus?   380–85

Consider the support you provide for your argument.   Your writing needs to give readers enough information to understand your points, follow your argument, and see the logic of your thinking. How much information is enough will vary according to your audience. If they already know a lot about your subject or are likely to agree with your point of view, you may need to give less detail. If, however, they are unfamiliar with your topic or are skeptical about your views, you will probably need to provide much more.

- What **REASONS** and **EVIDENCE** do you give to support your thesis? Where might more information be helpful? If you're writing online, could you provide links to it?   400–401
- What key terms and concepts do you **DEFINE**? Are there any other terms your readers might need to have explained? Could you do so by providing links?   432–42
- Where might you include more **DESCRIPTION** or other detail?   443–51
- Do you make any **COMPARISONS**? Especially if your readers will not be familiar with your topic, it can help to compare it with something more familiar.   424–31
- If you include **NARRATIVE**, how is it relevant to your point?   462–70
- See Part 6 for other useful **STRATEGIES**.   371

Consider the organization.   As a writer, you need to lead readers through your text, carefully structuring your material so that they will be able to follow your argument.

335–37
- Analyze the structure by **OUTLINING** it. An informal outline will do since you mainly need to see the parts, not the details.

626
MLA 558–87
- Is your text complete? Does your genre require an **ABSTRACT**, a **WORKS-CITED LIST**, or any other elements?

391
- What **TRANSITIONS** help readers move from idea to idea and paragraph to paragraph? Do you need more?

650–52
- If there are no **HEADINGS**, would adding them help orient readers?

Check for clarity.   Nothing else matters if readers can't understand what you write. Following are some questions that can help you see whether your meaning is clear and your text is easy to read:

386–87
- Does your **TITLE** announce the subject of your text and give some sense of what you have to say? If not, would a more direct title strengthen your argument?

387–89
- Do you state your **THESIS** directly? If not, will readers easily understand what your main point is? Try stating your thesis outright, and see if it makes your argument easier to follow.

373–80
380–85
- Does your **BEGINNING** tell readers what they need to understand your text, and does your **ENDING** help them make sense of what they've just read?

391
- How does each paragraph relate to the ones before and after? Are those relationships clear—or do you need to add **TRANSITIONS**?

- Do you vary your sentences? If all the sentences are roughly the same length or follow the same subject-verb-object pattern, your text probably lacks any clear emphasis and might even be difficult to read.

653–63
- Are **VISUALS** clearly labeled, positioned near the text they relate to, and referred to clearly in the text?

526–38
- If you introduce materials from other sources, have you clearly distinguished **QUOTED**, **PARAPHRASED**, or **SUMMARIZED** ideas from your own?

432–42
- Do you **DEFINE** all the words that your readers may not know?

- Does your punctuation make your writing more clear or less? Incorrect punctuation can make writing difficult to follow or, worse, change the meaning from what you intended. As a best-selling punctuation manual reminds us, there's a considerable difference between "eats, shoots, and leaves" and "eats shoots and leaves."

Thinking about Your Process

Your growth as a writer depends on how well you understand what you do when you write so that you can build on good habits. After you finish a writing project, consider the following questions to help you see the process that led to its creation—and find ways to improve the process next time:

- How would you tell the story of your thinking? Try writing these sentences: "When I first began with my topic, I thought _____. But as I did some thinking, writing, and research about the topic, my ideas changed and I thought _____."
- At some point in your writing, did you have to choose between two or more alternatives? What were they, and how did you choose?
- What was the most difficult problem you faced while writing? How did you go about trying to solve it?
- Whose advice did you seek while researching, organizing, drafting, revising, and editing? What advice did you take, and what did you ignore? Why?

Assessing a Body of Your Work

If you are required to submit a portfolio of your writing as part of a class, you will likely need to write a letter or essay that introduces the portfolio's contents and describes the processes that you used to create them and that **ASSESSES THE WRITING IN YOUR PORTFOLIO**. See Chapter 34 for detailed advice and a good example of a portfolio self-assessment.

⊙ 361–70

32 Getting Response and Revising

If we want to learn to play a song on the guitar, we play it over and over again until we get it right. If we play basketball or baseball, we likely spend hours shooting foul shots or practicing a swing. Writing works the same way. Making meaning clear can be tricky, and you should plan on revising and, if need be, rewriting in order to get it right. When we speak with someone face-to-face or on the phone or text a friend, we can get immediate response and restate or adjust our message if we've been misunderstood. In most other situations when we write, that immediate response is missing, so we need to seek out responses from readers to help us revise. This chapter includes a list of guidelines for those readers to consider, along with various strategies for subsequent revising and rewriting.

Giving and Getting Peer Response

When you meet with other students in pairs or small groups to respond to one another's work, in class or online, you have the opportunity to get feedback on your work from several readers who can help you plan revisions. At the same time, you learn from reading others' work how they approached the writing task—you're not writing in a vacuum. Some students wonder why class time is being taken up by peer response, assuming that their instructor's opinion is the only one that counts, but seeing the work of others and learning how others see your work can help you improve the clarity and depth of your writing. The key to responding effectively is to be as specific in your response as possible and avoid being either too harsh or too complimentary. These guidelines can help:

- Read your peer review partner's draft first from beginning to end as an interested reader, trying to understand the information and ideas.

academic literacies rhetorical situations genres fields processes strategies research MLA / APA media / design readings handbook

Don't look for problems. In fact, a good rule of thumb is this: read your partner's drafts in the same spirit that you want yours to be read.

- Before starting a second reading, ask your partner what questions they have about the draft or if you should focus on a particular aspect or part of the draft.

- As you read the draft again, take notes on a separate sheet of paper. Your notes might include positive comments ("I like the way you. . . . "), negative comments ("This sentence seems out of place"; "Is _____ the best word to use?"), and questions ("I'm not sure what you mean by _____"; "Would this paragraph work better on p. 2?").

- When you can, do more than identify issues. Offer suggestions or possible alternatives.

- When it's your draft's turn to be discussed, listen carefully to your partner's responses, take notes, and ask for clarification if necessary. Do not take issue with your partner's responses or argue over them; even if you're sure that what you wrote is perfectly clear, it's worth taking a second look if your partner has trouble understanding it.

Getting Effective Response

Ask your readers to consider some of the specific elements in the list below, but don't restrict them to those elements. Caution: if a reader says nothing about any of these elements, don't be too quick to assume that you needn't think about them yourself.

- What did you think when you first saw the **TITLE**? Is it interesting? informative? appropriate? Will it attract other readers' attention? ◆ 386–87

- Does the **BEGINNING** grab your attention? If so, how does it do so? Does it give enough information about the topic? offer necessary background information? How else might the piece begin? ◆ 373–80

- Is there a clear **THESIS**? What is it? ◆ 387–89

- Is there sufficient **SUPPORT** for the thesis? Is there anywhere you'd like to have more detail? Is the supporting material sufficiently **DOCUMENTED**?

- Does the text have a clear pattern of **ORGANIZATION**? Does each part relate to the thesis? Does each part follow from the one preceding it? Was the text easy to follow? How might the organization be improved?

- Is the **ENDING** satisfying? What did it leave you thinking? How else might the piece end?

- Can you tell the writer's **STANCE** or attitude toward the subject and audience? What words convey that attitude? Is it consistent throughout?

- How well does the text meet the needs and expectations of its **AUDIENCE**? Where might readers need more information, guidance, or clarification? How well does it achieve its **PURPOSE**? Does every part of the text help achieve the purpose? Could anything be cut? Should anything be added? Does the text meet the requirements of its **GENRE**? Should anything be added, deleted, or changed to meet those requirements?

- Do terms need **DEFINING**? Would examples, additional detail, explanations, **DIALOGUE**, or some other strategies help you understand the draft?

- Are **CHARTS**, **GRAPHS**, or **TABLES** clear and readable? If there are no **VISUALS**, should there be?

- Are sentences complete and grammatical? Are **TRANSITIONS** helpful or needed? Is the punctuation correct?

- Can any words or phrases be sharpened? Are verbs mostly active? Is **LANGUAGE THAT REFERS TO OTHERS** appropriate? Are all words spelled correctly?

Revising

Once you have studied your draft with a critical eye and, if possible, gotten responses from other readers, it's time to revise. Major changes may be necessary, and you may need to generate new material or do some rewriting. But assume that your draft is good raw material that you can revise to achieve your purposes. Revision should take place on several levels, from global (whole-text issues) to particular (the details). Work on your draft in that order, starting with the elements that are global in nature and gradually moving to smaller, more particular aspects. This allows you to use your time most efficiently and take care of bigger issues first. In fact, as you deal with the larger aspects of your writing, many of the smaller ones will be taken care of along the way.

Give yourself time to revise. When you have a due date, set deadlines for yourself that will give you time—preferably several days but as much as your schedule permits—to work on the text before it has to be delivered. Also, get some distance. Often when you're immersed in a project, you can't see the big picture because you're so busy creating it. If you can, get away from your writing for a while and think about something else. When you return to it, you're more likely to see it freshly. If there's not time to put a draft away for several days or more, even letting it sit overnight or for a few hours can help.

As you revise, assume that nothing is sacred. Bring a critical eye to all parts of a draft, not only to those parts pointed out by your reviewers. Content, organization, sentence patterns, individual words—all are subject to improvement. Be aware that a change in one part of the text may require changes in other parts.

At the same time, don't waste energy struggling with writing that simply doesn't work; you can always discard it. Look for the parts of your draft that do work—the parts that match your purpose and say what you want to say. Focus your efforts on those bright spots, expanding and developing them.

Revise to sharpen your FOCUS. Examine your **THESIS** to make sure it matches your **PURPOSE** as you now understand it. Read each paragraph to ensure that it contributes to your main point; you may find it helpful to **OUTLINE** your draft to help you see all the parts. One way to do this is to highlight one sentence in each paragraph that expresses the paragraph's main idea. Then copy and paste the highlighted sentences into a new document. Does one state the thesis of the entire essay? Do the rest relate to the thesis? Are they in the best order? If not, you need to either

🔘 344–45

◆ 387–89

▪ 55–56

🔘 335–37

modify the parts of the draft that don't advance your thesis or revise your thesis to reflect your draft's focus and to rearrange your points so they advance your discussion more effectively.

373–85 ◆   Read your **BEGINNING AND ENDING** carefully; make sure that the first paragraphs introduce your topic and provide any needed contextual information and that the final paragraphs provide a satisfying conclusion.

Revise to strengthen the argument. If readers find some of your claims 345 ◉ unconvincing, you need to provide more information or more **SUPPORT**. You may need to define terms you've assumed they will understand, offer additional examples, or provide more detail by describing, explaining 371 ◆ processes, adding dialogue, or using some other **STRATEGIES**. Make sure you show as well as tell—and don't forget that you might need to do so literally, with visuals like photos, graphs, or charts. You might try freewrit- 331–39 ◉ ing, clustering, or other ways of **GENERATING IDEAS AND TEXT**. If you need 477 ● to provide additional evidence, you might need to do additional **RESEARCH**.

345–46 ◉ **Revise to improve the ORGANIZATION.** If you've outlined your draft, number each paragraph, and make sure each one follows from the one before. If anything seems out of place, move it, or if necessary, cut it 391 ◆ completely. Check to see if you've included appropriate **TRANSITIONS** or 650–52 ☐ **HEADINGS** to help readers move through the text, and add them as needed. 61–65 ■ Check to make sure your text meets readers' expectations of the **GENRE** you're writing in.

346–47 ◉ **Revise for CLARITY.** Be sure readers will be able to understand what you're 386–87 ◆ saying. Look closely at your **TITLE** to be sure it gives a sense of what the 387–89 text is about and at your **THESIS**: will readers recognize your main point? If you don't state a thesis directly, consider whether you should. Provide 432–42 ◆ any necessary background information and **DEFINE** any key terms. Make 526–38 ● sure you've integrated any **QUOTATIONS**, **PARAPHRASES**, or **SUMMARIES** into your text smoothly. Are all paragraphs focused around one main point? Do the sentences in each paragraph contribute to that point? Finally, consider whether there are any data that would be more clearly presented in a **CHART**, **TABLE**, or **GRAPH**.

656

One way to test whether your text is clear is to switch audiences: write what you're trying to express as if you were talking to an eight-year-old. Your final draft probably won't be written that way, but the act of explaining your ideas to a young audience or readers who know nothing about your topic can help you discover any points that may be unclear.

Revise VISUALS.   Make sure images are as close as possible to the discussion to which they relate and that the information in the visual is explained in your text. Each image should be numbered and have a title or caption that identifies it and explains its significance. Each part of a **CHART**, **GRAPH**, or **TABLE** should be clearly labeled to show what it represents. If you didn't create the image yourself, make sure to cite its source, and if you're posting your work online, obtain permission from the copyright owner.

653–63

656

Read and reread — and reread.   Take some advice from writing theorist Donald Murray:

> Nonwriters confront a writing problem and look away from the text to rules and principles and textbooks and handbooks and models. Writers look at the text, knowing that the text itself will reveal what needs to be done and what should not yet be done or may never be done. The writer reads and rereads and rereads, standing far back and reading quickly from a distance, moving in close and reading slowly line by line, reading again and again, knowing that the answers to all writing problems lie within the evolving text.
>
> —Donald Murray, *A Writer Teaches Writing*

Rewriting

Some writers find it useful to try rewriting a draft in various ways or from various perspectives just to explore possibilities. Try it! If you find that your original plan works best for your purpose, fine. But you may find that another way will work better. Especially if you're not completely satisfied with your draft, consider the following ways of rewriting. Experiment with your rhetorical situation:

- Rewrite your draft from different points of view, through the eyes of different people perhaps or through the eyes of an animal or even from the perspective of an object. See how the text changes (in the information it presents, its perspective, its voice).

57–60
- Rewrite for a different **AUDIENCE**. How might an email detailing a recent car accident be written to a friend, an insurance agent, a parent?

66–68
- Rewrite in a different **TONE**. If the first draft was temperate and judicious, be extreme; if it was polite, be more direct. If the first draft was in standard English, rewrite it more informally.

61–65
70
- Rewrite the draft in a different **GENRE** or **MEDIUM**. Rewrite an essay as a letter, story, poem, speech, comic strip, *PowerPoint* presentation. Which genre and medium work best to reach your intended audience and achieve your purpose?

Ways of rewriting a narrative

452–56
- Rewrite one scene completely in **DIALOGUE**.
- Start at the end of the story and work back to the beginning, or start in the middle and fill in the beginning as you work toward the end.

Ways of rewriting a textual analysis

424–31
- **COMPARE** the text you're analyzing with another text (which may be in a completely different genre—film, TV, song lyrics, computer games, poetry, fiction, whatever).
- Write a parody of the text you're analyzing. Be as silly and as funny as you can while maintaining the structure of the original text. Alternatively, write a parody of your analysis, using evidence from the text to support an outrageous analysis.

academic literacies / rhetorical situations / genres / fields / processes / strategies / research MLA / APA / media / design / readings / handbook

Ways of rewriting a report

- Rewrite for a different **AUDIENCE**. For example, explain a concept to your grandparents; describe the subject of a profile to a visitor from another planet.

  57–60

- Be silly. Rewrite the draft as if for *The Daily Show* or the *Onion*, or rewrite it as if it were written by Bart Simpson.

Ways of rewriting an argument

- Rewrite taking another **POSITION**. Argue as forcefully for that position as you did for your actual one, acknowledging and refuting your original position. Alternatively, write a rebuttal to your first draft from the perspective of someone with different beliefs.

  157–84

- Rewrite your draft as a **STORY** —make it real in the lives of specific individuals. (For example, if you were writing about abortion rights, you could write a story about a young pregnant woman trying to decide what she believes and what to do.) Or rewrite the argument as a fable or parable.

  462–70

- Rewrite the draft as a letter responding to a hostile reader, trying at least to make them understand what you have to say.

- Rewrite the draft as an angry letter to someone or as a table-thumping dinner-with-the-relatives discussion. Write from the most extreme position possible.

- Write an **ANALYSIS** of the topic of your argument in which you identify, as carefully and as neutrally as you can, the various positions people hold on the issue.

  118–19

Once you've rewritten a draft in any of these ways, see whether there's anything you can use. Read each draft, considering how it might help you achieve your purpose, reach your audience, and convey your stance. Revise your actual draft to incorporate anything you think will make your text more effective, whether it's other genres or a different perspective.

33 Editing and Proofreading

Your ability to produce clear, error-free writing shows something about your ability as a writer and also leads readers to make assumptions about your intellect, your work habits, even your character. Readers of job-application letters and résumés, for example, may reject applications if they contain a single error, for no other reason than it's an easy way to narrow the field of potential candidates. In addition, they may well assume that applicants who present themselves sloppily in an application will do sloppy work on the job. This is all to say that you should edit and proofread your work carefully.

Editing

Editing is the stage where you work on the details of your paragraphs, sentences, words, and punctuation to make your writing as clear, precise, correct—and effective—as possible. Your goal is not to achieve "perfection" (whatever that may be) so much as to make your writing as effective as possible for your particular purpose and audience. Consult a good writing handbook for detailed advice, but use the following guidelines to help you check your drafts systematically for some common errors with paragraphs, sentences, and words:

Editing paragraphs

389–90 ◆
- Does each paragraph focus on one point? Does it have a **TOPIC SENTENCE** that announces that point, and if so, where is it located? If it's not the first sentence, should it be? If there's no clear topic sentence, should there be one?

356

- Does every sentence relate to the main point of the paragraph? If any sentences do not, should they be deleted, moved, or revised?

- Is there enough detail to develop the paragraph's main point? How is the point developed—with narrative? definition? some other **STRATEGY**? 371

- Where have you placed the most important information—at the beginning? the end? in the middle? The most emphatic spot is at the end, so in general that's where to put information you want readers to remember. The second most emphatic spot is at the beginning.

- Are any paragraphs especially long or short? Consider breaking long paragraphs if there's a logical place to do so—maybe an extended example should be in its own paragraph, for instance. If you have paragraphs of only a sentence or two, see if you can add to them or combine them with another paragraph, unless you're using a brief paragraph to provide emphasis.

- Check the way your paragraphs fit together. Does each one follow smoothly from the one before? Do you need to add any **TRANSITIONS**? 391

- Do the **BEGINNING** paragraphs catch readers' attention? In what other ways might you begin your text? 373–80

- Do the final paragraphs provide a satisfactory **ENDING**? How else might you conclude your text? 380–85

Editing sentences

- Is each sentence **COMPLETE**? Does it have someone or something (the subject) performing some sort of action or expressing a state of being (the verb)? Does each sentence begin with a capital letter and **END** with a period, question mark, or exclamation point? HB-4 / HB-85–86

- Check your use of the **PASSIVE VOICE**. Although there are some rhetorical situations in which the passive voice ("The prince was killed by a rival") is more appropriate than the active voice ("A rival killed the prince") because you want to emphasize an action rather than who performed it, you'll do well to edit it out unless you have a good reason for using it. HB-19–20

HB-35–37

- Check for **PARALLELISM**. Items in a list or series should be parallel in form—all nouns (lions, tigers, bears), all verbs (hopped, skipped, jumped), all clauses (he came, he saw, he conquered), and so on.

HB-58

- Do many of your sentences begin with **IT** or **THERE**? Too often these words make your writing wordy and vague or even conceal needed information. Why write "There are reasons we voted for him" when you can say "We had reasons to vote for him"?

391

- Are your sentences varied? If they all start with the subject or are the same length, your writing might be dull and maybe even hard to read. Try varying your sentence openings by adding **TRANSITIONS**, introductory phrases or clauses. Vary sentence lengths by adding detail to some or combining some sentences.

HB-78–84

- Make sure you've used **COMMAS** correctly. Is there a comma after each introductory element? ("After the lead singer quit, the group nearly disbanded. However, they then produced a string of hits.") Do commas set off nonrestrictive elements—parts that aren't needed to understand the sentence? ("The books I read in middle school, like the Harry Potter series, became longer and more challenging.") Are compound sentences connected with a comma? ("I'll eat broccoli steamed, but I prefer it roasted.")

Editing words

- Are you sure of the meaning of every word? Use a dictionary; be sure to look up words whose meanings you're not sure about. And remember your audience—do you use any terms they'll need to have defined?

HB-45

- Is any of your language too **GENERAL** or vague? Why write that you competed in a race, for example, if you could say you ran the 4 × 200 relay?

66–68

- What about the **TONE**? If your stance is serious (or humorous or critical or something else), make sure that your words all convey that attitude.

HB-31–32

- Do any pronouns have vague or unclear **ANTECEDENTS**? If you use "he" or "they" or "it" or "these," will readers know whom or what the words refer to?

HB-44

- Have you used any **CLICHÉS**—expressions that are used so frequently that they are no longer fresh? "Live and let live," avoiding something

"like the plague," and similar expressions are so predictable that your writing will almost always be better off without them.

- Be careful with **LANGUAGE THAT REFERS TO OTHERS**. Make sure that your words do not stereotype any individual or group. Mention age, gender, race, religion, sexual orientation, and so on only if they are relevant to your subject. When referring to an ethnic group, make every effort to use the terms members of the group prefer.

HB-66–68

- Edit out language that might be considered sexist. Have you used words like *manpower* or *policemen* to refer to people who may be female? If so, substitute less gendered words such as *personnel* or *police officers*. Do your words reflect any gender stereotypes—for example, that all engineers are male, or all nurses female? If you mention someone's gender, is it even necessary? If not, eliminate the unneeded words.

- How many of your verbs are forms of **BE** and **DO**? If you rely too much on these words, try replacing them with more specific verbs. Why write "She did a proposal for" when you could say "She proposed"?

HB-44–45

- Do you ever confuse **ITS** and **IT'S**? Use *it's* when you mean *it is* or *it has*. Use *its* when you mean *belonging to it*.

HB-53

Proofreading

Proofreading is the final stage of the writing process, the point where you clean up your work to present it to your readers. Proofreading is like checking your appearance in a mirror before going into a job interview: being neat and well groomed looms large in creating a good first impression, and the same principle applies to writing. Misspelled words, missing pages, mixed-up fonts, and other lapses send a negative message about your work—and about you. Most readers excuse an occasional error, but by and large readers are an intolerant bunch: too many errors will lead them to declare your writing—and maybe your thinking—flawed. There goes your credibility. So proofread your final draft with care to ensure that your message is taken as seriously as you want it to be.

Up to this point, you've been told *not* to read individual words on the page and instead to read for meaning. Proofreading demands the opposite: you must slow down your reading so that you can see every word, every punctuation mark.

- Use your computer's grammar checker and spelling checker, but only as a first step, and know that they're not very reliable. Computer programs don't read writing; instead, they rely on formulas and banks of words, so what they flag (or don't flag) as mistakes may or may not be accurate. If you were to write, "My brother was diagnosed with a leaning disorder," *leaning* would not be flagged as misspelled because it is a word (and might even be a disorder), even though it's the wrong word in that sentence.

- To keep your eyes from jumping ahead, place a ruler or piece of paper under each line as you read. Use your finger or a pencil as a pointer.

- Some writers find it helpful to read the text one sentence at a time, beginning with the last sentence and working backward.

- Read your text out loud to yourself—or better, to others, who may *hear* problems you can't see. Alternatively, have someone else read your text aloud to you while you follow along on the screen or page.

- Ask someone else to read your text. The more important the writing is, the more important this step is.

- If you find a mistake after you've printed out your text and are unable to print out a corrected version, make the change as neatly as possible in pencil or pen.

academic literacies | rhetorical situations | genres | fields | processes | strategies | research MLA / APA | media / design | readings | handbook

Compiling a Portfolio **34**

Artists maintain portfolios of their work to show gallery owners, collectors, and other potential buyers. Money managers work with investment portfolios of stocks, bonds, and various mutual funds. And often as part of a writing class, student writers compile portfolios of their work. As with a portfolio of paintings or drawings, a portfolio of writing includes a writer's best work and, sometimes, preliminary and revised drafts of that work, along with a statement by the writer articulating why they consider it good. The *why* is as important as the work, for it provides you with an occasion for assessing your overall strengths and weaknesses as a writer. This chapter offers guidelines to help you compile both a *writing portfolio* and a *literacy portfolio*, a project that writing students are sometimes asked to complete as part of a literacy narrative.

Considering the Rhetorical Situation

As with the writing you put in a portfolio, the portfolio itself is generally intended for a particular audience but could serve a number of different purposes. It's a good idea, then, to consider these and the other elements of your rhetorical situation when you begin to compile a portfolio.

PURPOSE	Why are you creating this portfolio? To show your learning? To create a record of your writing? As the basis for a grade in a course? To organize your research? To explore your literacy? For something else?	55–56
AUDIENCE	Who will read your portfolio? What will your readers expect it to contain? How can you help them understand the context or occasion for each piece of writing you include?	57–60

61–65 **GENRE**

What genres of writing should the portfolio contain? Do you want to demonstrate your ability to write one particular type of writing or in a variety of genres? Will your introduction to or assessment of the portfolio be in the form of a letter or an essay?

66–68 **STANCE**

How do you want to portray yourself in this portfolio? What items should you include to create this impression? What stance do you want to take in your written assessment of its contents? Thoughtful? Enthusiastic? Something else?

69–71 **MEDIA / DESIGN**

Will your portfolio be in print? Or will it be electronic? Will it include multiple media? Whichever medium you use, how can you help readers navigate its contents? What design elements will be most appropriate to your purpose and medium?

A WRITING PORTFOLIO

What to Include

A portfolio developed for a writing course typically contains examples of your best work in that course, including any notes, outlines, preliminary drafts, and so on, along with your own assessment of your performance in the course. You might include any of the following items:

- freewriting, outlines, and other work you did to generate ideas
- drafts, rough and revised
- in-class writing assignments
- source material—copies of articles and online sources, observation notes, interview transcripts, and other evidence of your research
- tests and quizzes

academic literacies · rhetorical situations · genres · fields · processes · strategies · research MLA / APA · media / design · readings · handbook

- responses to your drafts
- conference notes, error logs, lecture notes, and other course materials
- electronic material, including visuals, blogs, and multimedia texts
- reflections on your work

What you include will vary depending on what your instructor asks for. You may be asked to include three or four of your best papers or everything you've written. You may also be asked to show work in several different genres. In any case, you will usually need to choose, and to do that you will need to have criteria for making your choices. Don't base your decision solely on grades (unless grades are one criterion); your portfolio should reflect *your* assessment of your work, not your instructor's. What do you think is your best work? your most interesting work? your most ambitious work? Whatever criteria you use, you are the judge.

Organizing a Portfolio

If you set up a way to organize your writing at the start of the course, you'll be able to keep track of it throughout the course, making your job at term's end much easier. Remember that your portfolio presents you as a writer, presumably at your best. It should be neat, well organized, and easy to navigate. Your instructor may provide explicit guidelines for organizing your portfolio. If not, here are some guidelines:

Paper portfolios.   Choose something in which to gather your work. You might use a two-pocket folder, a three-ring binder, or a file folder, or you may need a box, basket, or some other container to accommodate bulky or odd-shaped items.

Label everything. Label each piece at the top of the first page, specifying the assignment, the draft, and the date: "Proposal, Draft 1, 9/12/18"; "Text Analysis, Final Draft, 10/10/18"; "Portfolio Self-Assessment, Final Draft, 11/11/18"; and so on. Write this information neatly on the page,

or put it on a Post-it note. For each assignment, arrange your materials chronologically, with your earliest material (freewriting, for example) on the bottom, and each successive item (source materials, say, then your outline, then your first draft, and so on) on top of the last, ending with your final draft on top. That way readers can see how your writing changed from draft to draft.

Electronic portfolios. You might also create an electronic portfolio, or e-portfolio. E-portfolios typically consist of a network of **LINKED** documents that might include not only your writing and reflections on that writing, but also sources, writing, and art you did for other courses or for your own enjoyment, audio and video clips, and other resources. Tools that can help you create an e-portfolio include:

661–62

- *Online tools.* Several websites, including *Weebly* and *Wix*, offer free tools to help you create a preformatted e-portfolio. For example, *GoogleSites* provides templates you can use to build an e-portfolio, uploading documents, images, and videos from your computer.

- *Blogging tools.* You can create an e-portfolio using a blogging platform, like *Tumblr* or *WordPress*, which allows you to upload files and create a network of linked pages. Readers can then comment on your e-portfolio, just as they might on your blog entries.

- *Wikis.* Wiki-based e-portfolios differ from blog-based ones in the level of interactivity they allow. In addition to commenting, readers may— if you allow them—make changes and add information. *PBworks* is one free provider, as is *WikiSpaces*.

- *Courseware.* Your school may use a learning platform, such as *Blackboard, Brightspace,* or *Moodle,* that allows you to create an e-portfolio of your work.

It's also possible to create an electronic portfolio using word processing, spreadsheet, or presentation software. The programs available for your use and the requirements for publishing your portfolio vary from school to school and instructor to instructor; ask your instructor or your school's help desk for assistance (and see Chapter 59 on **WRITING ONLINE** for general guidance).

664–72

Assessing Your Portfolio

An important part of your portfolio is your written self-assessment of your work. This is an opportunity to assess your work with a critical eye and to think about what you're most proud of, what you most enjoyed doing, what you want to improve. It's your chance to think about and say what you've learned during the class. Some instructors may ask you to write out your assessment in essay form, as an additional sample of your writing; others will want you to put it in letter form, which usually allows for a more relaxed and personal tone. Whatever form it takes, your statement should cover the following ground:

- *An evaluation of each piece of writing in the portfolio.* Consider both strengths and weaknesses, and give examples from your writing to support what you say. What would you change if you had more time? Which is your favorite piece, and why? your least favorite?

- *An assessment of your overall writing performance.* What do you do well? What still needs improvement? What do you *want* your work to say about you? What *does* your work say about you?

- *A discussion of how the writing you did in this course has affected your development as a writer.* How does the writing in your portfolio compare with writing you did in the past? What do you know now that you didn't know before? What can you do that you couldn't do before?

- *A description of your writing habits and process.* What do you usually do? How well does it work? What techniques seem to help you most, and why? Which seem less helpful? Cite passages from your drafts that support your conclusions.

- *An analysis of your performance in the course.* How did you spend your time? Did you collaborate with others? participate in peer review? have any conferences with your instructor? visit the writing center? Consider how these or any other activities contributed to your success.

A Sample Self-Assessment

Here is a self-assessment written by Nathaniel Cooney as part of his portfolio for his first-year writing class at Wright State University.

2 June 2018

Dear Reader,

It is my hope that in reading this letter you will gain an understanding of the projects contained in this portfolio. I enclose three works that I have submitted for an introductory writing class at Wright State University, English 102, Writing in Academic Discourse: an informative report, an argument paper, and a genre project based largely on the content of the argument paper. I selected the topics of these works for two reasons: First, they address issues that I believe to be relevant in terms of both the intended audience (peers and instructors of the course) and the times when they were published. Second, they speak to issues that are important to me personally. Below I present general descriptions of the works, along with my review of their strengths and weaknesses.

My purpose in writing the informative report "Higher Standards in Education Are Taking Their Toll on Students" was to present a subject in a factual manner and to support it with well-documented research. My intent was not to argue a point. However, because I chose a narrowly focused topic and chose information to support a thesis, the report tends to favor one side of the issue over the other. Because as a student I have a personal stake in the changing standards in the formal education system, I chose to research recent changes in higher education and their effects on students. Specifically, I examine students' struggles to reach a standard that seems to be moving further and further beyond their grasp.

I believe that this paper could be improved in two areas. The first is a bias that I think exists because I am a student presenting information from the point of view of a student. It is my hope, however, that my inclusion of unbiased sources lessens this problem somewhat and, furthermore, that it presents the

academic literacies · rhetorical situations · genres · fields · processes · strategies · research MLA / APA · media / design · readings · handbook

reader with a fair and accurate collection of facts and examples that supports the thesis. My second area of concern is the over-all balance in the paper between outside sources supporting my own thoughts and outside sources supporting opposing points of view. Rereading the paper, I notice many places where I may have worked too hard to include sources that support my ideas.

The second paper, "Protecting Animals That Serve," is an argument intended not only to take a clear position on an issue but also to argue for that position and convince the reader that it is a valid one. That issue is the need for legislation guaranteeing that certain rights of service animals be protected. I am blind and use a guide dog. Thus, this issue is especially important to me. During the few months that I have had him, my guide dog has already encoun-tered a number of situations where intentional or negligent treat-ment by others has put him in danger. At the time I was writing the paper, a bill was being written in the Ohio House of Represen-tatives that, if passed, would protect service animals and establish consequences for those who violated the law. The purpose of the paper, therefore, was to present the reader with information about service animals, establish the need for the legislation in Ohio and nationwide, and argue for passage of such legislation.

I think that the best parts of my argument are the introduction and the conclusion. In particular, I think that the conclusion does a good job of not only bringing together the various points but also convey-ing the significance of the issue for me and for others. In contrast, I think that the area most in need of further attention is the body of the paper. While I think the content is strong, I believe the overall organization could be improved. The connections between ideas are unclear in places, particularly in the section that acknowledges oppos-ing viewpoints. This may be due in part to the fact that I had diffi-culty understanding the reasoning behind the opposing argument.

The argument paper served as a starting point for the genre project, for which the assignment was to revise one paper writ-ten for this class in a different genre. My genre project consists of a poster and a brochure. As it was for the argument paper, my primary goal was to convince my audience of the importance of a particular issue and viewpoint—specifically, to convince my audience to support House Bill 369, the bill being introduced in the Ohio legislature that would create laws to protect the rights of service animals in the state.

Perhaps both the greatest strength and the greatest weakness of the genre project is my use of graphics. Because of my blindness, I was limited in my use of some graphics. Nevertheless, the pictures were carefully selected to capture the attention of readers and, in part, to appeal to their emotions as they viewed and reflected on the material.

I put a great deal of time, effort, and personal reflection into each project. While I am hesitant to say that they are finished and while I am dissatisfied with some of the finer points, I am satisfied with the overall outcome of this collection of works. Viewing it as a collection, I am also reminded that writing is an evolving process and that even if these works never become exactly what I envisioned them to be, they stand as reflections of my thoughts at a particular time in my life. In that respect, they need not be anything but what they already are, because what they are is a product of who I was when I wrote them. I hope that you find the papers interesting and informative and that as you read them, you, too, may realize their significance.

Respectfully,

Nathaniel J. Cooney

Nathaniel J. Cooney

Enclosures (3)

Cooney describes each of the works he includes and considers their strengths and weaknesses, citing examples from his texts to support his assessment.

A LITERACY PORTFOLIO

As a writing student, you may be asked to think back to the time when you first learned to read and write or to remember significant books or other texts you've read, and perhaps to put together a portfolio that chronicles your development as a reader and writer. You may also be asked to put together a literacy portfolio to accompany a **LITERACY NARRATIVE**.

▲ 75–97

What you include in such a portfolio will vary depending on what you've kept over the years and what your family has kept. You may have all of your favorite books, stories you dictated to a preschool teacher, notebooks in which you practiced writing the alphabet. Or you may have almost nothing. What you have or don't have is unimportant in the end: what's important is that you gather what you can and arrange it in a way that shows how you think about your development and growth as a literate person. What have been your experiences with reading and writing? What's your earliest memory of learning to write? If you love to read, what led you to love it? Who was most responsible for shaping your writing ability? Those are some of the questions you'll ask if you write a literacy narrative. You might also compile a literacy portfolio as a good way to generate ideas and text for that assignment.

What to Include in a Literacy Portfolio

- school papers
- drawings and doodles from preschool
- favorite books
- photographs you've taken
- drawings
- poems
- letters
- journals and diaries
- lists
- reading records or logs

- electronic texts you've created
- marriage vows
- speeches you've given
- awards you've received

Organizing a Literacy Portfolio

You may wish to organize your material chronologically, but there are other methods of organization to consider as well. For example, you might group items according to where they were written (at home, at school, at work), by genre (stories, poems, essays, letters, notes), or even by purpose (pleasure, school, work, church, and so on). Arrange your portfolio in the way that best conveys who you are as a literate person. Label each item you include, perhaps with a Post-it note, to identify what it is, when it was written or read, and why you've included it in your portfolio. Or you might create an e-portfolio, scanning print items to include in it with electronic items.

Reflecting on Your Literacy Portfolio

- Why did you choose each item?
- Is anything missing? Are there any other important materials that should be here?
- Why is the portfolio organized as it is?
- What does the portfolio show about your development as a reader and writer?
- What patterns do you see? Are there any common themes you've read or written about? Any techniques you rely on? Any notable changes over time?
- What are the most significant items, and why?

part 6

Strategies

Whenever we write, we draw on many different strategies to articulate what we have to say. We may DEFINE key terms, DESCRIBE people or places, and EXPLAIN how something is done. We may COMPARE one thing to another. Sometimes we may choose a pertinent story to NARRATE, and we may even want to include some DIALOGUE. The chapters that follow offer advice on how to use these and OTHER BASIC STRATEGIES for developing and organizing the texts you write.

Strategies

Beginning and Ending **35**

Whenever we pick up something to read, we generally start by looking at the first few words or sentences to see if they grab our attention, and based on them we decide whether to keep reading. Beginnings, then, are important, both attracting readers and giving them some information about what's to come. When we get to the end of a text, we expect to be left with a sense of closure, of satisfaction—that the story is complete, our questions have been answered, the argument has been made. So endings are important, too. This chapter offers advice on how to write beginnings and endings.

Beginning

How you begin depends on your **RHETORICAL SITUATION**, especially your purpose and audience. Academic audiences generally expect your introduction to establish context, explaining how the text fits into some larger conversation, addresses certain questions, or explores an aspect of the subject. Most introductions also offer a brief description of the text's content, often in the form of a thesis statement. The following opening of an essay on the effect of texting on student writing does all of this:

> It's taking over our lives. We can do it almost anywhere—walking to class, waiting in line at the grocery store, or hanging out at home. It's quick, easy, and convenient. It has become a concern of doctors, parents, and teachers alike. What is it? It's texting!
>
> Text messaging—or texting, as it's more commonly called—is the process of sending and receiving typed messages via a cellular phone. It is a common means of communication among teenagers and is even becoming popular in the business world because it allows quick messages

53

to be sent without people having to commit to a telephone conversation. A person is able to say what is needed, and the other person will receive the information and respond when it's convenient to do so.

In order to more quickly type what they are trying to say, many people use abbreviations instead of words. The language created by these abbreviations is called textspeak. Some people believe that using these abbreviations is hindering the writing abilities of students, and others argue that texting is actually having a positive effect on writing. In fact, it seems likely that texting has no significant effect on student writing.   —Michaela Cullington, "Does Texting Affect Writing?"

If you're writing for a nonacademic audience or genre—for a newspaper or a website, for example—your introduction may need to entice your readers to read on by connecting your text to their interests through shared experiences, anecdotes, or some other attention-getting device. Cynthia Bass, writing a newspaper article about the Gettysburg Address on its 135th anniversary, connects that date—the day her audience would read it—to Lincoln's address. She then develops the rationale for thinking about the speech and introduces her specific topic: debates about the writing and delivery of the Gettysburg Address:

November 19 is the 135th anniversary of the Gettysburg Address. On that day in 1863, with the Civil War only half over and the worst yet to come, Abraham Lincoln delivered a speech now universally regarded as both the most important oration in U.S. history and the best explanation—"government of the people, by the people, for the people"—of why this nation exists.

We would expect the history of an event so monumental as the Gettysburg Address to be well established. The truth is just the opposite. The only thing scholars agree on is that the speech is short—only ten sentences—and that it took Lincoln under five minutes to stand up, deliver it, and sit back down.

Everything else—when Lincoln wrote it, where he wrote it, how quickly he wrote it, how he was invited, how the audience reacted—has been open to debate since the moment the words left his mouth.

—Cynthia Bass, "Gettysburg Address: Two Versions"

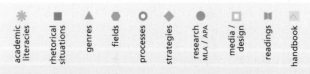

academic literacies · rhetorical situations · genres · fields · processes · strategies · research MLA / APA · media / design · readings · handbook

Ways of Beginning

Explain the larger context of your topic.   Most essays are part of an ongoing conversation, so you might begin by outlining the context of the subject to which your writing responds. An essay exploring the "emotional climate" of the United States after Barack Obama became president in 2008 begins by describing the national moods during some of his predecessors' administrations:

> Every president plays a symbolic, almost mythological role that's hard to talk about, much less quantify—it's like trying to grab a ball of mercury. I'm not referring to using the bully pulpit to shape the national agenda but to the way that the president, as America's most inescapably powerful figure, colors the emotional climate of the country. John Kennedy and Ronald Reagan did this affirmatively, expressing ideals that shaped the whole culture. Setting a buoyant tone, they didn't just change movies, music, and television; they changed attitudes. Other presidents did the same, only unpleasantly. Richard Nixon created a mood of angry paranoia, Jimmy Carter one of dreary defeatism, and George W. Bush, especially in that seemingly endless second term, managed to do both at once.
>
> —John Powers, "Dreams from My President"

State your thesis.   Sometimes the best beginning is a clear **THESIS** stating your position, like the following statement in an essay arguing that fairy tales and nursery rhymes introduce us to "the rudiments and the humanness of engineering":

387–89

> We are all engineers of sorts, for we all have the principles of machines and structures in our bones. We have learned to hold our bodies against the forces of nature as surely as we have learned to walk. We calculate the paths of our arms and legs with the computer of our brain, and we catch baseballs and footballs with more dependability than the most advanced weapons systems intercept missiles. We may wonder if human evolution may not have been the greatest engineering feat of all time. And though many of us forget how much we once knew about the principles and practices of engineering, the nursery rhymes and fairy tales of our youth preserve the evidence that we did know quite a bit.
>
> —Henry Petroski, "Falling Down Is Part of Growing Up"

Forecast your organization.   You might begin by briefly outlining the way in which you will organize your text. The following example from a scholarly paper on the role of immigrants in the U.S. labor market offers background on the subject and describes the points that the writer's analysis will discuss:

> Debates about illegal immigration, border security, skill levels of workers, unemployment, job growth and competition, and entrepreneurship all rely, to some extent, on perceptions of immigrants' role in the U.S. labor market. These views are often shaped as much by politics and emotion as by facts.
>
> To better frame these debates, this short analysis provides data on immigrants in the labor force at the current time of slowed immigration, high unemployment, and low job growth and highlights eight industries where immigrants are especially vital. How large a share of the labor force are they and how does that vary by particular industry? How do immigrants compare to native-born workers in their educational attainment and occupational profiles?
>
> The answers matter because our economy is dependent on immigrant labor now and for the future. The U.S. population is aging rapidly as the baby boom cohort enters old age and retirement. As a result, the labor force will increasingly depend upon immigrants and their children to replace current workers and fill new jobs. This analysis puts a spotlight on immigrant workers to examine their basic trends in the labor force and how these workers fit into specific industries and occupations of interest.
>
> —Audrey Singer, "Immigrant Workers in the U.S. Labor Force"

Offer background information.   If your readers may not know as much as you do about your topic, giving them information to help them understand your position can be important, as David Guterson does in an essay on the Mall of America:

> Last April, on a visit to the new Mall of America near Minneapolis, I carried with me the public-relations press kit provided for the benefit of reporters. It included an assortment of "fun facts" about the mall: 140,000 hot dogs sold each week, 10,000 permanent jobs, 44 escalators and 17 elevators, 12,750 parking places, 13,300 short tons of steel, $1 million in cash disbursed weekly from 8 automatic-teller machines.

academic literacies   rhetorical situations   genres   fields   processes   strategies   research MLA / APA   media / design   readings   handbook

The rotunda of the Mall of America.

Opened in the summer of 1992, the mall was built on the 78-acre site of the former Metropolitan Stadium, a five-minute drive from the Minneapolis–St. Paul International Airport. With 4.2 million square feet of floor space—including twenty-two times the retail footage of the average American shopping center—the Mall of America was "the largest fully enclosed combination retail and family entertainment complex in the United States."

—David Guterson, "Enclosed. Encyclopedic. Endured. One Week at the Mall of America"

653–63 □

VISUALS can also help provide context. For example, this essay on the Mall of America might have included a photo like the one on the preceding page to convey the size of the structure.

Define key terms or concepts.   The success of an argument often hinges on how key terms are **DEFINED**. You may wish to provide definitions up front, as an advocacy website, *Health Care Without Harm*, does in a report on the hazards of fragrances in health-care facilities:

432–42 ◆

To many people, the word "fragrance" means something that smells nice, such as perfume. We don't often stop to think that scents are chemicals. Fragrance chemicals are organic compounds that volatilize, or vaporize into the air—that's why we can smell them. They are added to products to give them a scent or to mask the odor of other ingredients. The volatile organic chemicals (VOCs) emitted by fragrance products can contribute to poor indoor air quality (IAQ) and are associated with a variety of adverse health effects.

—"Fragrances," *Health Care Without Harm*

Connect your subject to your readers' interests or values.   You'll always want to establish common ground with your readers, and sometimes you may wish to do so immediately, in your introduction, as in this example:

We all want to feel safe. Most Americans lock their doors at night, lock their cars in parking lots, try to park near buildings or under lights, and wear seat belts. Many invest in expensive security systems, carry pepper spray or a stun gun, keep guns in their homes, or take self-defense classes. Obviously, safety and security are important issues in American life.

—Andy McDonie, "Airport Security: What Price Safety?"

Start with something that will provoke readers' interest. Anna Quindlen opens an essay on feminism with the following eye-opening assertion:

> Let's use the F word here. People say it's inappropriate, offensive, that it puts people off. But it seems to me it's the best way to begin, when it's simultaneously devalued and invaluable.
> Feminist. Feminist, feminist, feminist.
>
> —Anna Quindlen, "Still Needing the F Word"

Start with an anecdote. Sometimes a brief **NARRATIVE** helps bring a topic to life for readers. See, for example, how an essay on the dozens, a type of verbal contest played by some African Americans, begins:

462–70

> Alfred Wright, a nineteen-year-old whose manhood was at stake on Longwood Avenue in the South Bronx, looked fairly calm as another teenager called him Chicken Head and compared his mother to Shamu the whale.
> He fingered the gold chain around his thin neck while listening to a detailed complaint about his sister's sexual abilities. Then he slowly took the toothpick out of his mouth; the jeering crowd of young men quieted as he pointed at his accuser.
> "He was so ugly when he was born," Wright said, "the doctor smacked his mom instead of him."
>
> —John Tierney, "Playing the Dozens"

Ask a question. Instead of a thesis statement, you might open with a question about the topic your text will explore, as this study of the status of women in science does:

> Are women's minds different from men's minds? In spite of the women's movement, the age-old debate centering around this question continues. We are surrounded by evidence of de facto differences between men's and women's intellects—in the problems that interest them, in the ways they try to solve those problems, and in the professions they choose. Even though it has become fashionable to view such differences as environmental in origin, the temptation to seek an explanation in terms of innate differences remains a powerful one.
>
> —Evelyn Fox Keller, "Women in Science: A Social Analysis"

Jump right in. Occasionally you may wish to start as close to the key action as possible. See how one writer jumps right into his profile of a blues concert:

> Long Tongue, the Blues Merchant, strolls onstage. His guitar rides side-saddle against his hip. The drummer slides onto the tripod seat behind the drums, adjusts the high-hat cymbal, and runs a quick, off-beat tattoo on the tom-tom, then relaxes. The bass player plugs into the amplifier, checks the settings on the control panel, and nods his okay. Three horn players stand off to one side, clustered, lurking like brilliant sorcerer-wizards waiting to do magic with their musical instruments.
>
> —Jerome Washington, "The Blues Merchant"

Ending

Endings are important because they're the last words readers read. How you end a text will depend in part on your **RHETORICAL SITUATION**. You may end by wrapping up loose ends, or you may wish to give readers something to think about. Some endings do both, as Cynthia Bass does in a report on the debate over the Gettysburg Address. In her two final paragraphs, she first summarizes the debate and then shows its implications:

> What's most interesting about the Lincoln-as-loser and Lincoln-as-winner versions is how they marshal the same facts to prove different points. The invitation asks Lincoln to deliver "a few appropriate remarks." Whether this is a putdown or a reflection of the protocol of the time depends on the "spin"—an expression the highly politicized Lincoln would have readily understood—which the scholar places on it.
>
> These diverse histories should not in any way diminish the power or beauty of Lincoln's words. However, they should remind us that history, even the history of something as deeply respected as the Gettysburg Address, is seldom simple or clear. This reminder is especially useful today as we watch expert witnesses, in an effort to divine what the founders meant by "high crimes and misdemeanors," club one another with conflicting interpretations of the same events, the same words, the same precedents, and the same laws.
>
> —Cynthia Bass, "Gettysburg Address: Two Versions"

Bass summarizes the dispute about Lincoln's address and then moves on to discuss the role of scholars in interpreting historical events. Writing in 1999 during President Bill Clinton's impeachment hearings, she concludes by pointing out the way in which expert government witnesses often offer conflicting interpretations of events to suit their own needs. The ending combines several strategies to bring various strands of her essay together, leaving readers to interpret her final words themselves.

Ways of Ending

Restate your main point.   Sometimes you'll simply **SUMMARIZE** your central idea, as in this example from an essay arguing that we have no "inner" self and that we should be judged by our actions alone:

534–35

> The inner man is a fantasy. If it helps you to identify with one, by all means, do so; preserve it, cherish it, embrace it, but do not present it to others for evaluation or consideration, for excuse or exculpation, or, for that matter, for punishment or disapproval.
>
>   Like any fantasy, it serves your purposes alone. It has no standing in the real world which we share with each other. Those character traits, those attitudes, that behavior—that strange and alien stuff sticking out all over you—*that's the real you!*
>
> —Willard Gaylin, "What You See Is the Real You"

Discuss the implications of your argument.   The following conclusion of an essay on the development of Post-it notes leads readers to consider how failure sometimes leads to innovation:

> Post-it notes provide but one example of a technological artifact that has evolved from a perceived failure of existing artifacts to function without frustrating. Again, it is not that form follows function but, rather, that the form of one thing follows from the failure of another thing to function as we would like. Whether it be bookmarks that fail to stay in place or taped-on notes that fail to leave a once-nice surface clean and intact, their failure and perceived failure is what leads to the true evolution of artifacts. That the perception of failure may take

centuries to develop, as in the case of loose bookmarks, does not reduce the importance of the principle in shaping our world.

—Henry Petroski, "Little Things Can Mean a Lot"

462–70 ◆

End with an anecdote, maybe finishing a **NARRATIVE** that was begun earlier in your text or adding one that illustrates the point you are making. See how Sarah Vowell uses a story to end an essay on students' need to examine news reporting critically:

> I looked at Joanne McGlynn's syllabus for her media studies course, the one she handed out at the beginning of the year, stating the goals of the class. By the end of the year, she hoped her students would be better able to challenge everything from novels to newscasts, that they would come to identify just who is telling a story and how that person's point of view affects the story being told. I'm going to go out on a limb here and say that this lesson has been learned. In fact, just recently, a student came up to McGlynn and told her something all teachers dream of hearing. The girl told the teacher that she was listening to the radio, singing along with her favorite song, and halfway through the sing-along she stopped and asked herself, "What am I singing? What do these words mean? What are they trying to tell me?" And then, this young citizen of the republic jokingly complained, "I can't even turn on the radio without thinking anymore."

—Sarah Vowell, "Democracy and Things Like That"

Refer to the beginning. One way to bring closure to a text is to bring up something discussed in the beginning; often the reference adds to or even changes the original meaning. For example, Amy Tan opens an essay on her Chinese mother's English by establishing herself as a writer and lover of language who uses many versions of English in her writing:

> I am not a scholar of English or literature. I cannot give you much more than personal opinions on the English language and its variations in this country or others.
>
> I am a writer. And by that definition, I am someone who has always loved language. I am fascinated by language in daily life. I spend a

great deal of my time thinking about the power of language — the way it can evoke an emotion, a visual image, a complex idea, or a simple truth. Language is the tool of my trade. And I use them all — all the Englishes I grew up with.

At the end of her essay, Tan repeats this phrase, but now she describes language not in terms of its power to evoke emotions, images, and ideas but in its power to evoke "the essence" of her mother. When she began to write fiction, she says,

> [I] decided I should envision a reader for the stories I would write. And the reader I decided upon was my mother, because these were stories about mothers. So with this reader in mind — and in fact she did read my early drafts — I began to write stories using all the Englishes I grew up with: the English I spoke to my mother, which for lack of a better term might be described as "simple"; the English she used with me, which for lack of a better term might be described as "broken"; my translation of her Chinese, which could certainly be described as "watered down"; and what I imagined to be her translation of her Chinese if she could speak in perfect English, her internal language, and for that I sought to preserve the essence, but neither an English nor a Chinese structure. I wanted to capture what language ability tests can never reveal: her intent, her passion, her imagery, the rhythms of her speech and the nature of her thoughts.
>
> —Amy Tan, "Mother Tongue"

Note how Tan not only repeats "all the Englishes I grew up with" but also provides parallel lists of what those Englishes can do for her: "evoke an emotion, a visual image, a complex idea, or a simple truth," on the one hand, and, on the other, capture her mother's "intent, her passion, her imagery, the rhythms of her speech and the nature of her thoughts."

Propose some action, as in the following conclusion of a report on the consequences of binge drinking among college students:

> The scope of the problem makes immediate results of any interventions highly unlikely. Colleges need to be committed to large-scale and long-term behavior-change strategies, including referral of alcohol abusers

to appropriate treatment. Frequent binge drinkers on college campuses are similar to other alcohol abusers elsewhere in their tendency to deny that they have a problem. Indeed, their youth, the visibility of others who drink the same way, and the shelter of the college community may make them less likely to recognize the problem. In addition to addressing the health problems of alcohol abusers, a major effort should address the large group of students who are not binge drinkers on campus who are adversely affected by the alcohol-related behavior of binge drinkers.

—Henry Wechsler et al., "Health and Behavioral Consequences of Binge Drinking in College: A National Survey of Students at 140 Campuses"

Considering the Rhetorical Situation

As a writer or speaker, think about the message that you want to articulate, the audience you want to reach, and the larger context you are writing in.

55–56 ■ **PURPOSE**
Your purpose will affect the way you begin and end. If you're trying to persuade readers to do something, you may want to open by clearly stating your thesis and end by calling for a specific action.

57–60 ■ **AUDIENCE**
Who do you want to reach, and how does that affect the way you begin and end? You may want to open with an intriguing fact or anecdote to entice your audience to read a profile, for instance, whereas readers of a report may expect it to conclude with a summary of your findings.

61–65 ■ **GENRE**
Does your genre require a certain type of beginning or ending? Arguments, for example, often provide a statement of the thesis near the beginning; proposals typically end with a call for some solution.

66–68 ■ **STANCE**
What is your stance, and can your beginning and ending help you convey that stance? For example, beginning an argument on the distribution of AIDS medications to underdeveloped countries with an anecdote may

demonstrate concern for the human costs of the disease, whereas starting with a statistical analysis may suggest the stance of a careful researcher. Ending a proposal by weighing the advantages and disadvantages of the solution you propose may make you seem reasonable.

MEDIA / DESIGN Your medium may affect the way you begin and end. A web text, for instance, may open with a homepage listing a menu of the site—and giving readers a choice of where they will begin. With a print text, you get to decide how it will begin and end.

69–71

IF YOU NEED MORE HELP

See also the guides to writing in Chapters 10–13 for ways of beginning and ending a **LITERACY NARRATIVE**, an essay **ANALYZING TEXT**, a **REPORT**, or an **ARGUMENT**.

75–97
98–130
131–56
157–84

36 Guiding Your Reader

Traffic lights, street signs, and lines on the road help drivers find their way. Readers need similar guidance—to know, for example, whether they're reading a report or an argument, an evaluation or a proposal. They also need to know what to expect: What will the report be about? What perspective will it offer? What will this paragraph cover? What about the next one? How do the two paragraphs relate to each other?

When you write, then, you need to provide cues to help your readers navigate your text and understand the points you're trying to make. This chapter offers advice on guiding your reader and, specifically, on using *titles*, *thesis statements*, *topic sentences*, and *transitions*.

Titles

A title serves various purposes, naming a text and providing clues to the content. It also helps readers decide whether they want to read further, so it's worth your while to come up with a title that attracts interest. Some titles include subtitles. You generally have considerable freedom in choosing a title, but always you'll want to consider the **RHETORICAL SITUATION** to be sure your title serves your purpose and appeals to the audience you want to reach.

Some titles simply announce the subject of the text:

"Black Men and Public Space"
The Pencil
"Why Colleges Shower Their Students with A's"
"Does Texting Affect Writing?"

53

Some titles provoke readers or otherwise entice them to read:

> "Kill 'Em! Crush 'Em! Eat 'Em Raw!"
> "Thank God for the Atom Bomb"
> "What Are Homosexuals For?"

Sometimes writers add a subtitle to explain or illuminate the title:

> *Aria: Memoir of a Bilingual Childhood*
> "It's in Our Genes: The Biological Basis of Human Mating Behavior"
> "From Realism to Virtual Reality: Images of America's Wars"

Sometimes when you're starting to write, you'll think of a title that helps you generate ideas and write. More often, though, a title is one of the last things you'll write, when you know what you've written and can craft a suitable name for your text.

Thesis Statements

A thesis identifies the topic of your text along with the claim you are making about it. A good thesis also helps readers understand an essay by forecasting its overall shape. In fact, some instructors call thesis statements *forecasting statements*. Working to create a sharp thesis can help you focus both your thinking and your writing. Here are three steps for moving from a topic to a thesis statement:

1. State your topic as a question. You may have an idea for a topic, such as "gasoline prices," "analysis of 'real women' ad campaigns," or "famine." Those may be good topics, but they're not thesis statements, primarily because none of them actually makes a statement. A good way to begin moving from topic to thesis statement is to turn your topic into a question:

> What causes fluctuations in gasoline prices?
>
> Are ads picturing "real women" who aren't models effective?
>
> What can be done to prevent famine in East Africa?

2. Turn your question into a position. A thesis statement is an assertion—it takes a stand or makes a claim. Whether you're writing a report or an argument, you are saying, "This is the way I see . . . ," "My research shows . . . ," or "This is what I believe about . . ." Your thesis statement announces your position on the question you are raising about your topic, so a relatively easy way of establishing a thesis is to answer your own question:

> Gasoline prices fluctuate for several reasons.
>
> Ads picturing "real women" instead of models are effective because women can easily identify with them.
>
> The most recent famine in Somalia could have been avoided if certain measures had been taken.

3. Narrow your thesis. A good thesis is specific, guiding you as you write and showing your audience exactly what your essay will cover, often in the same order you will cover it. The preceding thesis statements need to be qualified and focused—they need to be made more specific. For example:

> Gasoline prices fluctuate because of production procedures, consumer demand, international politics, and oil companies' policies.
>
> Dove's "Campaign for Self-Esteem" and Cover Girl's ads featuring Queen Latifah work because consumers can identify with the women's bodies and admire the women's confidence in displaying them.
>
> The 2017 famine in Somalia could have been avoided if farmers had received training in more effective methods and had planted drought-resistant crops and if other nations had provided more aid more quickly.

334–35 ○ A good way to narrow a thesis is to ask **QUESTIONS** about it: *Why* do gasoline prices fluctuate? *How* could the Somalia famine have been avoided? The answers will help you craft a narrow, focused thesis.

4. Qualify your thesis. Sometimes you want to make a strong argument and to state your thesis bluntly. Often, however, you need to acknowledge that your assertions may be challenged or may not be unconditionally true. In those cases, consider limiting the scope of your thesis by adding to it such terms as *may, probably, apparently, very likely, sometimes,* and *often.*

> Gasoline prices *very likely* fluctuate because of production procedures, consumer demand, international politics, and oil companies' policies.
>
> Dove's and Cover Girl's ad campaigns featuring "real women" *may* work because consumers can identify with the women's bodies and admire the women's confidence in displaying them.
>
> The 2017 famine in Somalia could *probably* have been avoided if farmers had received training in more effective methods and had planted drought-resistant crops and if other nations had provided more aid more quickly.

Thesis statements are typically positioned at or near the end of a text's introduction, to let readers know at the outset what is being claimed and what the text will be aiming to prove. While a thesis often forecasts your organization, it doesn't necessarily do so; the organization may be more complex than the thesis itself. For example, Notre Dame University student Sarah Dzubay's essay, "An Outbreak of the Irrational," contains this thesis statement:

> The movement to opt out of vaccinations is irrational and dangerous because individuals advocating for their right to exercise their personal freedom are looking in the wrong places for justification and ignoring the threat they present to society as a whole.

The essay that follows includes discussions of herd immunity; a socioeconomic profile of parents who choose not to vaccinate their children; outlines of the rationales those parents use to justify their choice, which include fear of autism, fear of causing other health problems, and political and ethical values; and a conclusion that parents who refuse to vaccinate their children are unreasonable and selfish. The paper delivers what the thesis promises but includes important information not mentioned in the thesis itself.

Topic Sentences

Just as a thesis statement announces the topic and position of an essay, a topic sentence states the subject and focus of a paragraph. Good paragraphs focus on a single point, which is summarized in a topic sentence. Usually, but not always, the topic sentence begins the paragraph:

Graduating from high school or college is an exciting, occasionally even traumatic event. Your identity changes as you move from being a high school teenager to a university student or a worker; your connection to home loosens as you attend school elsewhere, move to a place of your own, or simply exercise your right to stay out later. You suddenly find yourself doing different things, thinking different thoughts, fretting about different matters. As recent high school graduate T. J. Devoe puts it, "I wasn't really scared, but having this vast range of opportunity made me uneasy. I didn't know *what* was gonna happen." Jenny Petrow, in describing her first year out of college, observes, "It's a tough year. It was for all my friends."

—Sydney Lewis, *Help Wanted: Tales from the First Job Front*

Sometimes the topic sentence may come at the end of the paragraph or even at the end of the preceding paragraph, depending on the way the paragraphs relate to one another. Other times a topic sentence will summarize or restate a point made in the previous paragraph, helping readers understand what they've just read as they move on to the next point. See how the linguist Deborah Tannen does this in the first paragraphs of an article on differences in men's and women's conversational styles:

I was addressing a small gathering in a suburban Virginia living room—a women's group that had invited men to join them. Throughout the evening, one man had been particularly talkative, frequently offering ideas and anecdotes, while his wife sat silently beside him on the couch. Toward the end of the evening, I commented that women frequently complain that their husbands don't talk to them. This man quickly concurred. He gestured toward his wife and said, "She's the talker in our family." The room burst into laughter; the man looked puzzled and hurt. "It's true," he explained. "When I come home from work I have nothing to say. If she didn't keep the conversation going, we'd spend the whole evening in silence."

This episode crystallizes the irony that although American men tend to talk more than women in public situations, they often talk less at home. And this pattern is wreaking havoc with marriage.

—Deborah Tannen, "Sex, Lies, and Conversation:
Why Is It So Hard for Men and Women to Talk to Each Other?"

academic literacies | rhetorical situations | genres | fields | processes | strategies | research MLA / APA | media / design | readings | handbook

Transitions

Transitions help readers move from thought to thought—from sentence to sentence, paragraph to paragraph. You are likely to use a number of transitions as you draft; when you're **EDITING**, you should make a point of checking transitions. Here are some common ones:

356–59

- *To signal causes and effects:* accordingly, as a result, because, consequently, hence, so, then, therefore, thus
- *To signal comparisons:* also, in the same way, like, likewise, similarly
- *To signal changes in direction or expectations:* although, but, even though, however, in contrast, instead, nevertheless, nonetheless, on the contrary, on the one hand . . . on the other hand, still, yet
- *To signal examples:* for example, for instance, indeed, in fact, such as
- *To signal sequences or similarities:* again; also; and; and then; besides; finally; furthermore; last; moreover; next; too; first, second, third, etc.
- *To signal time relations:* after, as soon as, at first, at the same time, before, eventually, finally, immediately, later, meanwhile, next, simultaneously, so far, soon, then, thereafter
- *To signal a summary or conclusion:* as a result, as we have seen, finally, in a word, in any event, in brief, in conclusion, in other words, in short, in the end, in the final analysis, on the whole, therefore, thus, to summarize

---

IF YOU NEED MORE HELP

See also Chapter 58 on **USING VISUALS, INCORPORATING SOUND** for ways of creating visual signals for your readers.

653–63

37 Analyzing Causes and Effects

Analyzing causes helps us think about why something happened, whereas thinking about effects helps us consider what might happen. When we hear a noise in the night, we want to know what caused it. Children poke sticks into holes to see what will happen. Researchers try to understand the causes of diseases. Writers often have occasion to consider causes or effects as part of a larger topic or sometimes as a main focus: in a , we might consider the effects of reducing tuition or the causes of recent tuition increases; in a **MEMOIR**, we might explore why the person we had a date with failed to show up.

246–55
224–32

Usually we can only speculate about *probable* causes or *likely* effects. In writing about causes and effects, then, we are generally **ARGUING** for those we consider plausible, not proven. This chapter will help you analyze causes and effects in writing—and to do so in a way that suits your rhetorical situation.

397–417

Determining Plausible Causes and Effects

What causes ozone depletion? Sleeplessness? Obesity? And what are their effects? Those are of course large, complex topics, but whenever you have reason to ask why something happened or what could happen, there will likely be several possible causes and just as many predictable effects. There may be obvious causes, though often they will be less important than others that are harder to recognize. (Eating too much may be an obvious cause of being overweight, but *why* people eat too much has several less obvious causes: portion size, advertising, lifestyle, and psychological disorders are only a few possibilities.) Similarly, short-term effects are often less important than long-term ones. (A stomachache may be an

academic literacies · rhetorical situations · genres · fields · processes · strategies · research MLA / APA · media / design · readings · handbook

effect of eating too much candy, but the chemical imbalance that can result from consuming too much sugar is a much more serious effect.)

LISTING, **CLUSTERING**, and **OUTLINING** are useful processes for analyzing causes. And at times you might need to do some **RESEARCH** to identify possible causes or effects and to find evidence to support your analysis. When you've identified potential causes and effects, you need to analyze them. Which causes and effects are primary? Which seem to be secondary? Which are most relevant to your **PURPOSE** and are likely to convince your **AUDIENCE**? You will probably have to choose from several possible causes and effects for your analysis because you won't want or need to include all of them.

332–34
477

55–56
57–60

Arguing for Causes or Effects

Once you've identified several possible causes or predictable effects, you need to **ARGUE** that some are more plausible than others. You must provide convincing support for your argument because you usually cannot *prove* that x causes y or that y will be caused by z; you can only show, with good reasons and appropriate evidence, that x is *likely* to cause y or that y will *likely* follow from z. See, for example, how an essay on the psychological basis for risk taking speculates about two potential causes for the popularity of extreme sports:

397–417

> Studies now indicate that the inclination to take high risks may be hardwired into the brain, intimately linked to arousal and pleasure mechanisms, and may offer such a thrill that it functions like an addiction. The tendency probably affects one in five people, mostly young males, and declines with age. It may ensure our survival, even spur our evolution as individuals and as a species. Risk taking probably bestowed a crucial evolutionary advantage, inciting the fighting and foraging of the hunter-gatherer. . . .
>
> As psychologist Salvadore Maddi, PhD, of the University of California at Davis warns, "High-risk takers may have a hard time deriving meaning and purpose from everyday life." Indeed, this peculiar form of dissatisfaction could help explain the explosion of high-risk sports in America and other postindustrial Western nations. In unstable cultures, such as those at war or suffering poverty, people rarely seek

out additional thrills. But in a rich and safety-obsessed country like America, land of guardrails, seat belts, and personal-injury lawsuits, everyday life may have become too safe, predictable, and boring for those programmed for risk taking.   —Paul Roberts, "Risk"

Roberts suggests that genetics is one likely cause of extreme sports and that an American obsession with safety is perhaps a cause of their growing popularity. Notice, however, that he presents these as likely or possible, not certain, by choosing his words carefully: "studies now *indicate*"; "the inclination to take high risks *may* be hardwired"; "[r]isk taking *probably* bestowed a crucial evolutionary advantage"; "this . . . dissatisfaction *could help* explain." Like Roberts, you will almost always need to qualify what you say about causes and effects—to say that something *could explain* (rather than saying it "explains") or that it *suggests* (rather than "shows"). Causes and effects can seldom be proved definitively, so you need to acknowledge that your argument is not the last word on the subject.

Ways of Organizing an Analysis of Causes and Effects

Your analysis of causes and effects may be part of a proposal or some other genre of writing, or you may write a text whose central purpose is to analyze causes or speculate about effects. While there are many ways to organize an analysis of causes and effects, three common ways are to state a cause and then discuss its effects, to state an effect and then discuss its causes, and to identify a chain of causes and effects.

Identify a cause and then discuss its effects.   If you were writing about climate change, you might first show that many scientists fear it will have several effects, including more violent storms, the extinction of various kinds of plants, and elevated sea levels.

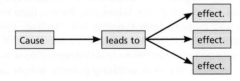

Identify an effect and then trace its causes. If you were writing about school violence, for example, you might argue that it is a result of sloppy dress, informal teacher-student relationships, low academic standards, and disregard for rules.

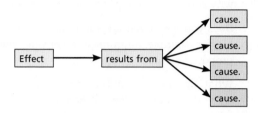

Identify a chain of causes and effects. You may sometimes discuss a chain of causes and effects. If you were writing about the right to privacy, for example, you might consider the case of Megan's law. A convicted child molester raped and murdered a girl named Megan; the crime caused New Jersey legislators to pass the so-called Megan's law (an effect), which requires that convicted sex offenders be publicly identified. As more states enacted versions of Megan's law, concern for the rights of those who are identified developed—the effect became a cause of further effects.

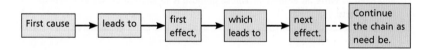

Considering the Rhetorical Situation

As a writer or speaker, you need to think about the message that you want to articulate, the audience you want to reach, and the larger context you are writing in.

PURPOSE   Your main purpose may be to analyze the causes and effects of something. But sometimes you'll have another goal that calls for such analysis — a business report, for

55–56

example, might need to explain what caused a decline in sales.

57–60   **AUDIENCE**   Who is your intended audience, and how will analyzing causes help you reach them? Do you need to tell them why some event happened or what effects resulted?

61–65   **GENRE**   Does your genre require you to analyze causes? Proposals, for example, often need to consider the effects of a proposed solution.

66–68   **STANCE**   What is your stance, and could analyzing causes or effects show that stance? Could it help demonstrate your seriousness or show that your conclusions are reasonable?

69–71   **MEDIA / DESIGN**   You can rely on words to analyze causes, but sometimes a drawing will help readers *see* how causes lead to effects.

IF YOU NEED MORE HELP

321 ○   See also the PROCESSES chapters for help generating ideas, drafting, and so on if you need to write an entire text whose purpose is to analyze causes or speculate about effects.

Arguing 38

Basketball fans argue about who's better, LeBron James or Steph Curry. Political candidates argue that they have the most experience or best judgment. A toilet paper ad argues that "you deserve a little luxury in your life, and so does your bottom." As you likely realize, we are surrounded by arguments, and much of the work you do as a college student requires you to read and write arguments. When you write a **LITERARY ANALYSIS**, for instance, you argue for a particular interpretation. In a **PROPOSAL**, you argue for a particular solution to a problem. Even a **PROFILE** argues that a subject should be seen in a certain way. This chapter offers advice on some of the key elements of making an argument, from developing an arguable thesis and identifying good reasons and evidence that supports those reasons to building common ground and dealing with viewpoints other than your own.

211–23
246–55
233–45

Reasons for Arguing

We argue for many reasons, and they often overlap: to convince others that our position on a subject is reasonable, to influence the way they think about a subject, to persuade them to change their point of view or to take some sort of action. In fact, many composition scholars and teachers believe that all writing makes an argument.

As a student, you'll be called on to make arguments continually: when you participate in class discussions, when you take an essay exam, when you post a comment to an online discussion or a blog. In all these instances, you are adding your opinions to some larger conversation, arguing for what you believe—and why.

Arguing Logically: Claims, Reasons, and Evidence

398–408 ◆

The basic building blocks of argument are **CLAIMS**, **REASONS**, and **EVIDENCE** that supports those reasons. Using these building blocks, we can construct a strong logical argument, also known as *logos*.

Claims.   Good arguments are based on arguable claims—statements that reasonable people may disagree about. Certain kinds of statements cannot be argued:

- *Verifiable statements of fact.* Most of the time, there's no point in arguing about facts like "the earth is round" or "George H. W. Bush was America's forty-first president." Such statements contain no controversy, no potential opposition—and so no interest for an audience. However, you might argue about the basis of a fact. For example, until recently it was a fact that our solar system had nine planets, but when further discoveries led to a change in the definition of *planet*, Pluto no longer qualified.

- *Issues of faith or belief.* By definition, matters of faith cannot be proven or refuted. If you believe in reincarnation or don't believe there is an afterlife, there's no way I can convince you otherwise. However, in a philosophy or religion course you may be asked to argue, for example, whether or not the universe must have a cause.

- *Matters of simple opinion or personal taste.* If you think cargo pants are ugly, no amount of arguing will convince you to think otherwise. If you've downloaded every Taylor Swift album and think she's the greatest singer ever, you won't convince your Nirvana-loving parents to like her, too. If matters of taste are based on identifiable criteria, though, they may be argued in an **EVALUATION**, where "Tom Cruise is a terrible actor" is more than just your opinion—it's an assertion you can support with evidence.

202–10 ▲

You may begin with an opinion: "I think wearing a helmet makes riding a bike more dangerous, not less." As it stands, that statement can't be considered a claim—it needs to be made more reasonable and informed. To do that, you might reframe it as a question—"Do bike riders who wear helmets get injured more often than those who don't?"—that may be answered as you do research and start to write. Your opinion or question should lead

you to an arguable claim, however, one that could be challenged by another thoughtful person. In this case, for example, your research might lead you to a focused, qualified claim: *Contrary to common sense, wearing a helmet while riding a bicycle increases the chances of injury, at least to adult riders.*

Qualifying a claim. According to an old saying, there are two sides to every story. Much of the time, though, arguments don't sort themselves neatly into two sides, pro and con. No matter what your topic, your argument will rarely be a simple matter of being for or against; in most cases, you'll want to qualify your claim—that it is true in certain circumstances, with certain conditions, with these limitations, and so on. Qualifying your claim shows that you're reasonable and also makes your topic more manageable by limiting it. The following questions can help you qualify your claim.

- *Can it be true in some circumstances or at some times but not others?* For example, freedom of speech should generally be unrestricted, but individuals can sue for slander or libel.

- *Can it be true only with certain conditions?* For instance, cell phones and computer monitors should be recycled, but only by licensed, domestic recyclers.

- *Can it be true for some groups or individuals but not others?* For example, nearly everyone should follow a low-carb diet, but some people, such as diabetics, should avoid it.

SOME WORDS FOR QUALIFYING A CLAIM

sometimes	nearly	it seems/seemingly
rarely	usually	some
in some cases	more or less	perhaps
often	for the most part	possibly
routinely	in many cases	in most cases

Drafting a thesis statement. Once your claim is focused and appropriately qualified, it can form the core of your essay's **THESIS STATEMENT**, which announces your position and forecasts the path your argument will follow. For example, here is the opening paragraph of an essay by the

387–89

executive director of the National Congress of American Indians arguing that the remains of Native Americans should be treated with the same respect given to others. The author outlines the context of her argument and then presents her thesis (here, in italics):

> What if museums, universities and government agencies could put your dead relatives on display or keep them in boxes to be cut up and otherwise studied? What if you believed that the spirits of the dead could not rest until their human remains were placed in a sacred area? The ordinary American would say there ought to be a law—and there is, for ordinary Americans. *The problem for American Indians is that there are too many laws of the kind that make us the archeological property of the United States and too few of the kind that protect us from such insults.* —Susan Shown Harjo, "Last Rites for Indian Dead: Treating Remains Like Artifacts Is Intolerable"

Reasons. Your claim must be supported by reasons that your audience will accept. A reason can usually be linked to a claim with the word *because*:

CLAIM	+	*BECAUSE*	+	REASON
College students should strive to graduate		*because*		they will earn far more over their lifetimes than those who do not.

Keep in mind that you likely have a further reason, a rule or principle that underlies the reason you link directly to your claim. In this argument, the underlying reason is that the economy values college graduates and pays them more. If your audience doesn't accept that principle, you may have to back it up with further reasons or evidence.

To come up with good reasons, start by stating your position and then answering the question *why?*

CLAIM: College students should strive to graduate. *Why?*

REASON: (Because) They will earn far more over their lifetimes than those who do not. *Why?*

UNDERLYING REASON: The economy values college graduates and pays them more.

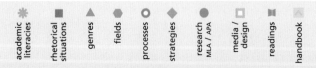

As you can see, this exercise can continue indefinitely as the underlying reasons grow more and more general and abstract. You can do the same with other positions:

CLAIM: Smoking should be banned. *Why?*

REASON: (Because) It is harmful to smokers and also to nonsmokers.

UNDERLYING REASON: People should be protected from harmful substances.

Evidence. Evidence to support your reasons can come from various sources. In fact, you may need to use several kinds of evidence to persuade your audience that your claim is true. Some of the most common types of evidence include facts, statistics, examples, authorities, anecdotes, scenarios, case studies, textual evidence, and visuals.

Facts are ideas that are proven to be true. Facts can include observations or scholarly research (your own or someone else's), but they need to be accepted as true. If your audience accepts the facts you present, they can be powerful means of persuasion. For example, an essay on junk email offers these facts to demonstrate the seasonal nature of spam:

> The flow of spam is often seasonal. It slows in the spring, and then, in the month that technology specialists call "black September"—when hundreds of thousands of students return to college, many armed with new computers and access to fast Internet connections—the levels rise sharply.
>
> —Michael Specter, "Damn Spam"

Specter offers this fact with only a general reference to its origin ("technology specialists"), but given what most people know—or think they know—about college students, it rings true. A citation from a study published by a "technology specialist" would offer even greater credibility.

Statistics are numerical data, usually produced through research, surveys, or polls. Statistics should be relevant to your argument, as current as possible, accurate, and from a reliable source. An argument advocating that Americans should eat less meat presents these data to support the writer's contention that we eat far too much of it:

Americans are downing close to 200 pounds of meat, poultry, and fish per capita per year (dairy and eggs are separate, and hardly insignificant), an increase of 50 pounds per person from 50 years ago. We each consume something like 110 grams of protein a day, about twice the federal government's recommended allowance; of that, about 75 grams come from animal protein. (The recommended level is itself considered by many dietary experts to be higher than it needs to be.) It's likely that most of us would do just fine on around 30 grams of protein a day, virtually all of it from plant sources.

—Mark Bittman, "Rethinking the Meat-Guzzler"

Bittman's statistics demonstrate the extent to which Americans have increased their meat consumption over the last half century, the proportion of our diets that comes from meat, and, by comparison, how much protein our bodies require—and summarize the heart of his argument in stark numeric terms.

Examples are specific instances that illustrate general statements. In a book on life after dark in Europe, a historian offers several examples to demonstrate his point that three hundred years ago, night—without artificial lighting—was treacherous:

Even sure-footed natives on a dark night could misjudge the lay of the land, stumbling into a ditch or off a precipice. In Aberdeenshire, a fifteen-year-old girl died in 1739 after straying from her customary path through a churchyard and tumbling into a newly dug grave. The Yorkshireman Arthur Jessop, returning from a neighbor's home on a cold December evening, fell into a stone pit after losing his bearings.

—A. Roger Ekirch, *At Day's Close: Night in Times Past*

Ekirch illustrates his point and makes it come alive for readers by citing two specific individuals' fates.

Authorities are experts on your subject. To be useful, authorities must be reputable, trustworthy, and qualified to address the subject. You should **EVALUATE** any authorities you consult carefully to be sure they have the credentials necessary for readers to take them seriously. When you cite

511–18

experts, you should clearly identify them and the origins of their authority in a **SIGNAL PHRASE**, as does the author of an argument that deforested land can be reclaimed:

535–38

> Reed Funk, professor of plant biology at Rutgers University, believes that the vast areas of deforested land can be used to grow millions of genetically improved trees for food, mostly nuts, and for fuel. Funk sees nuts used to supplement meat as a source of high-quality protein in developing-country diets.
>
> —Lester R. Brown, *Plan B 2.0: Rescuing a Planet under Stress and a Civilization in Trouble*

Brown cites Funk, an expert on plant biology, to support his argument that humans need to rethink the global economy in order to create a sustainable world. Without the information on Funk's credentials, though, readers would have no reason to take his proposal seriously.

Anecdotes are brief **NARRATIVES** that your audience will find believable and that contribute directly to your argument. Anecdotes may come from your personal experience or the experiences of others. In an essay arguing that it's understandable when athletes give in to the temptation to use performance-enhancing drugs, sports blogger William Moller uses an anecdote to show that the need to perform can outweigh the potential negative consequences of using drugs:

462–70

> I spent my high school years at a boarding school hidden among the apple orchards of Massachusetts. Known for a spartan philosophy regarding the adolescent need for sleep, the school worked us to the bone, regularly slamming us with six hours of homework. I pulled a lot more all-nighters (of the scholastic sort) in my years there than I ever did in college. When we weren't in class, the library, study hall, or formal sit-down meals, we were likely found on a sports field. We also had school on Saturday, beginning at 8 a.m. just like every other non-Sunday morning.
>
> Adding kindling to the fire, the students were not your laid-back types; everyone wanted that spot at the top of the class, and social life was rife with competition. The type A's that fill the investment banking,

legal, and political worlds—those are the kids I spent my high school years with.

And so it was that midway through my sophomore year, I found myself on my third all-nighter in a row, attempting to memorize historically significant pieces of art out of E. H. Gombrich's *The Story of Art*. I had finished a calculus exam the day before, and the day before that had been devoted to world history. And on that one cold night in February, I had had enough. I had hit that point where you've had so little sleep over such a long time that you start seeing spots, as if you'd been staring at a bright light for too long. The grade I would compete for the next day suddenly slipped in importance, and I began daydreaming about how easy the real world would be compared to the hell I was going through.

But there was hope. A friend who I was taking occasional study breaks with read the story in the bags beneath my eyes, in the slump of my shoulders, the nervous drumming of my fingers on the chair as we sipped flat, warm Coke in the common room. My personal *deus ex machina*,* he handed me a small white pill.

I was very innocent. I matured way after most of my peers, and was probably best known for being the kid who took all the soprano solos away from the girls in the choir as a first-year student. I don't think I had ever been buzzed, much less drunk. I'd certainly never smoked a cigarette. And knowing full well that what I was doing could be nothing better than against the rules (and less importantly, illegal) I did what I felt I needed to do, to accomplish what was demanded of me. And it worked. I woke up and regained focus like nothing I'd ever experienced. Unfortunately, it also came with serious side effects: I was a hypersensitized, stuffed-up, sweaty, wide-eyed mess, but I studied until the birds started chirping. And I aced my test.

Later I found out the pill was Ritalin, and it was classified as a class 3 drug.† I did it again, too—only a handful of times, as the side effects were so awful. But every time it was still illegal, still against

---

Deus ex machina: In ancient Greek and Roman drama, a god introduced into the plot to resolve complications.

†*Class 3 drug*: Drug that is illegal to possess without a prescription.

academic literacies   rhetorical situations   genres   fields   processes   strategies   research MLA / APA   media / design   readings   handbook

the rules. And as emphasized above, I was much more worried about the scholastic consequences if I were discovered abusing a prescription drug than the fact that I was breaking the law. Though I was using it in a far different manner than the baseball players who would later get caught with it in their systems, it was still very clearly a "performance-enhancing drug."

Just like every other person on this planet, I was giving in to the incentive scheme that was presented to me. The negative of doing poorly on the test was far greater than the negative of getting caught, discounted by the anesthetic of low probability.

—William Moller, "We, the Public,
Place the Best Athletes on Pedestals"

Moller uses this anecdote to demonstrate the truth of his argument, that given the choice between "breaking the rules and breaking my grades" or "getting an edge" in professional sports, just about everyone will choose to break the rules.

Scenarios are hypothetical situations. Like anecdotes, "what if" scenarios can help you describe the possible effects of particular actions or offer new ways of looking at a particular state of affairs. For example, a mathematician presents this lighthearted scenario about Santa Claus in a tongue-in-cheek argument that Christmas is (almost) pure magic:

Let's assume that Santa only visits those who are children in the eyes of the law, that is, those under the age of 18. There are roughly 2 billion such individuals in the world. However, Santa started his annual activities long before diversity and equal opportunity became issues, and as a result he doesn't handle Muslim, Hindu, Jewish and Buddhist children. That reduces his workload significantly to a mere 15% of the total, namely 378 million. However, the crucial figure is not the number of children but the number of homes Santa has to visit. According to the most recent census data, the average size of a family in the world is 3.5 children per household. Thus, Santa has to visit 108,000,000 individual homes. (Of course, as everyone knows, Santa only visits good children, but we can surely assume that, on an average, at least one child of the 3.5 in each home meets that criterion.)

> —Keith Devlin, "The Mathematics of Christmas"

Devlin uses this scenario, as part of his mathematical analysis of Santa's yearly task, to help demonstrate that Christmas is indeed magical—because if you do the math, it's clear that Santa's task is physically impossible.

Case studies and observations feature detailed reporting about a subject. Case studies are in-depth, systematic examinations of an occasion, a person, or a group. For example, in arguing that class differences exist in the United States, sociologist Gregory Mantsios presents studies of three "typical" Americans to show "enormous class differences" in their lifestyles.

Observations offer detailed descriptions of a subject. Here's an observation of the emergence of a desert stream that flows only at night:

> At about 5:30 water came out of the ground. It did not spew up, but slowly escaped into the surrounding sand and small rocks. The wet circle grew until water became visible. Then it bubbled out like a small fountain and the creek began.
>
> —Craig Childs, *The Secret Knowledge of Water*

Childs presents this and other observations in a book that argues (among other things) that even in harsh, arid deserts, water exists, and knowing where to find it can mean the difference between life and death.

526–38

Textual evidence includes QUOTATIONS, PARAPHRASES, and SUMMARIES. Usually, the relevance of textual evidence must be stated directly, as excerpts from a text may carry several potential meanings. For example, here is an excerpt from a student essay analyzing the function of the raft in *Huckleberry Finn* as "a platform on which the resolution of conflicts is made possible":

> [T]he scenes where Jim and Huck are in consensus on the raft contain the moments in which they are most relaxed. For instance, in chapter twelve of the novel, Huck, after escaping capture from Jackson's Island, calls the rafting life "solemn" and articulates their experience

as living "pretty high" (Twain 75–76). Likewise, subsequent to escaping the unresolved feud between the Grangerfords and Shepherdsons in chapter eighteen, Huck is unquestionably at ease on the raft: "I was powerful glad to get away from the feuds. . . . We said there warn't no home like a raft, after all. Other places do seem so cramped up and smothery, but a raft don't. You feel mighty free and easy and comfortable on a raft" (Twain 134).

—Dave Nichols, "'Less All Be Friends': Rafts as
Negotiating Platforms in Twain's *Huckleberry Finn*"

Huck's own words support Nichols's claim that he can relax on a raft. Nichols strengthens his claim by quoting evidence from two separate pages, suggesting that Huck's opinion of rafts pervades the novel.

Visuals can be a useful way of presenting evidence. Remember, though, that charts, graphs, photos, drawings, and other **VISUAL TEXTS** seldom speak for themselves and thus must be explained in your text. Below, for example, is a photograph of a poster carried by demonstrators at the 2008 Beijing Summer Olympics, protesting China's treatment of Tibetans.

653–63

If you were to use this photo in an essay, you would need to explain that the poster combines the image of a protester standing before a tank during the 1989 Tiananmen Square uprising with the Olympic logo, making clear to your readers that the protesters are likening China's treatment of Tibetans to its brutal actions in the past. Similarly, you could use this image of an American flag made from license plates in an argument about America's dependence on the auto industry.

Choosing appropriate evidence. The kinds of evidence you provide to support your argument depends on your **RHETORICAL SITUATION**. If your purpose is, for example, to convince readers to accept the need for a proposed solution, you'd be likely to include facts, statistics, and anecdotes. If you're writing for an academic audience, you'd be less likely to rely on anecdotes, preferring authorities, textual evidence, statistics, and case studies instead. And even within academic communities different disciplines and genres may focus primarily on different kinds of evidence. If you're not sure what counts as appropriate evidence, ask your instructor for guidance.

53

Arguing with a Hostile Audience

Academic arguments are often presented to an audience that is presumed to be open-minded and fair, and the goal of such arguments is to demonstrate that your position is plausible and reasonable. Sometimes, though, your goal is to change people's minds, to try to get them to see some issue differently. That can be more of a challenge, because your audience likely has good reasons for thinking as they do, or their views reflect their basic values, and they may well feel defensive, angry, or threatened when you challenge them. These situations call for different argumentative strategies, such as Rogerian argument.

Rogerian argument. This method of presenting an argument is based on the work of psychologist Carl Rogers. This method assumes that common ground—areas of shared values or beliefs—exist between people who disagree. If they can find that common ground, they're more likely to come to some agreement or compromise position.

Since the goal of a Rogerian argument is to find compromise, it is organized differently than a traditional argument. First you must show that you understand the position of your opponents, and then you offer your position. Here's how a typical Rogerian argument is organized; be aware that each section may require several paragraphs:

Introduction. Here, you introduce the issue, acknowledging the various sides of the controversy, being as fair as you can.

Describe the opposing view. In this section, you try to capture the opposing view as accurately and as neutrally as you can. There may be circumstances when that view might be valid, and you should include them, too. Your goal here is to show that you understand the opposing view and why your readers hold that view convincingly enough that they will agree that it's accurate. By doing so, you establish your credibility and honest desire to understand those whose views differ from yours.

387–89

66–68

State your THESIS and support it. Now it's time to outline your position and defend it with reasons and evidence. As with a traditional argument, your goal here is to show that you have thought carefully about your position and researched it thoroughly. As with all arguing, your TONE should show your openness to ideas and avoid sounding as if you and you alone know the truth about the issue or that you are intellectually or morally superior to your opponent.

Conclude. In your concluding section, you bring the two perspectives you've just outlined together to show how, while your opponent's views have merit, your position deals with the issue or solves the problem better—or how a compromise position, somewhere in the middle, allows both sides to benefit.

You may find value in using Rogerian techniques in traditional arguments, including seeking common ground, describing issues and positions in neutral terms, and addressing those with opposing views respectfully and with goodwill.

Convincing Readers You're Trustworthy

For your argument to be convincing, you need to establish your own credibility with readers (also known as *ethos*)—to demonstrate your knowledge about your topic, to show that you and your readers share some common ground, and to show yourself to be evenhanded in the way you present your argument.

Building common ground. One important element of gaining readers' trust is to identify some common ground, some values you and your audience share. For example, to introduce a book arguing for the compatibility of science and religion, author Chet Raymo offers some common memories:

> Like most children, I was raised on miracles. Cows that jump over the moon; a jolly fat man that visits every house in the world in a single night; mice and ducks that talk; little engines that huff and puff and

say, "I think I can"; geese that lay golden eggs. This lively exercise of credulity on the part of children is good practice for what follows—for believing in the miracle stories of traditional religion, yes, but also for the practice of poetry or science.

—Chet Raymo, *Skeptics and True Believers: The Exhilarating Connection between Science and Religion*

Raymo presents childhood stories and myths that are part of many people's shared experiences to help readers find a connection between two realms that are often seen as opposed.

Incorporating other viewpoints. To show that you have carefully considered the viewpoints of others, including those who may agree or disagree with you, you should incorporate those viewpoints into your argument by acknowledging, accommodating, or refuting them.

Acknowledging other viewpoints. One essential part of establishing your credibility is to acknowledge that there are viewpoints different from yours and to represent them fairly and accurately. Rather than weakening your argument, acknowledging possible objections to your position shows that you've thought about and researched your topic thoroughly. For example, in an essay about his experience growing up homosexual, writer Andrew Sullivan admits that not every young gay man or woman has the same experience:

I should add that many young lesbians and homosexuals seem to have had a much easier time of it. For many, the question of sexual identity was not a critical factor in their life choices or vocation, or even a factor at all. —Andrew Sullivan, "What Is a Homosexual?"

In response to a reasonable objection, Sullivan qualifies his assertions, making his own stance appear to be reasonable.

Accommodating other viewpoints. You may be tempted to ignore views you don't agree with, but in fact it's important to demonstrate that you are aware of them and have considered them carefully. You may find yourself conceding that opposing views have some merit and qualifying your claim or even making them part of your own argument. See, for example, how a philosopher arguing that torture is sometimes "not merely permissible but morally mandatory" addresses a major objection to his position:

> The most powerful argument against using torture as a punishment or to secure confessions is that such practices disregard the rights of the individual. Well, if the individual is all that important—and he is—it is correspondingly important to protect the rights of individuals threatened by terrorists. If life is so valuable that it must never be taken, the lives of the innocents must be saved even at the price of hurting the one who endangers them.
>
> —Michael Levin, "The Case for Torture"

Levin acknowledges his critics' argument that the individual is indeed important but then asserts that if the life of one person is important, the lives of many people must be even more important. In effect, he uses an opposing argument to advance his own.

Refuting other viewpoints. Often you may need to refute other arguments and make a case for why you believe they are wrong. Are the values underlying the argument questionable? Is the reasoning flawed? Is the evidence inadequate or faulty? For example, an essay arguing for the elimination of college athletics scholarships includes this refutation:

> Some argue that eliminating athletics scholarships would deny opportunity and limit access for many students, most notably black athletes. The question is, access to what? The fields of competition or an opportunity to earn a meaningful degree? With the six-year graduation rates of black basketball players hovering in the high 30-percent range, and black football players in the high 40-percent range, despite years of "academic reform," earning an athletics

scholarship under the current system is little more than a chance to
play sports.   —John R. Gerdy, "For True Reform,
                                       Athletics Scholarships Must Go"

Gerdy bases his refutation on statistics showing that for more than half
of African American college athletes, the opportunity to earn a degree by
playing a sport is an illusion.

When you incorporate differing viewpoints, be careful to avoid the
FALLACIES of attacking the person making the argument or refuting a
competing position that no one seriously entertains. It is also important
that you not distort or exaggerate opposing viewpoints. If *your* argument
is to be persuasive, other arguments should be represented fairly.

◆ 414–16

Appealing to Readers' Emotions

Logic and facts, even when presented by someone who seems reasonable
and trustworthy, may not be enough to persuade readers. Many successful arguments include an emotional component that appeals to readers'
hearts as well as to their minds. Advertising often works by appealing to
its audience's emotions, as in this paragraph from a Volvo ad:

> Choosing a car is about the comfort and safety of your passengers, most
> especially your children. That's why we ensure Volvo's safety research
> examines how we can make our cars safer for everyone who travels in
> them—from adults to teenagers, children to babies. Even those who
> aren't even born yet.   —*Volvo.com*

This ad plays on the fear that children—or a pregnant mother—may be
injured or killed in an automobile accident.

Keep in mind that emotional appeals, also known as *pathos*, can make
readers feel as though they are being manipulated and, consequently, less
likely to accept an argument. For most kinds of academic writing, use
emotional appeals sparingly.

Checking for Fallacies

Fallacies are arguments that involve faulty reasoning. It's important to avoid fallacies in your writing because they often seem plausible but are usually unfair or inaccurate and make reasonable discussion difficult. Here are some of the most common fallacies:

- *Ad hominem* arguments attack someone's character rather than address the issues. (*Ad hominem* is Latin for "to the man.") It is an especially common fallacy in political discourse and elsewhere: "Jack Turner has no business talking about the way we run things in this city. He's just another flaky liberal." Whether or not Turner is a "flaky liberal" has no bearing on the worth of his argument about "the way we run things in this city"; insulting one's opponents isn't an argument against their positions.

- *Bandwagon appeals* argue that because others think or do something, we should, too. For example, an advertisement for a breakfast cereal claims that it is "America's favorite cereal." It assumes that readers want to be part of the group and implies that an opinion that is popular must be correct.

- *Begging the question* is a circular argument. It assumes as a given what is trying to be proved, essentially asserting that A is true because A is true. Consider this statement: "Affirmative action can never be fair or just because you cannot remedy one injustice by committing another." This statement begs the question because to prove that affirmative action is unjust, it assumes that it is an injustice.

- *Either-or* arguments, also called *false dilemmas*, are oversimplifications that assert there can be only two possible positions on a complex issue. For example, "Those who oppose our actions in this war are enemies of freedom" inaccurately assumes that if someone opposes the war in question, they oppose freedom. In fact, people might have many other reasons for opposing the war.

- *False analogies* compare things that resemble each other in some ways but not in the most important respects—for example, "Trees pollute

the air just as much as cars and trucks do." Although it's true that plants emit hydrocarbons, and hydrocarbons are a component of smog, they also produce oxygen, whereas motor vehicles emit gases that combine with hydrocarbons to form smog. Vehicles pollute the air; trees provide the air that vehicles' emissions pollute.

- *Faulty causality,* also known as *post hoc, ergo propter hoc* (Latin for "after this, therefore because of this"), assumes that because one event followed another, the first event caused the second—for example, "Legalizing same-sex marriage in Sweden led to a decline in the marriage rate of opposite-sex couples." The statement contains no evidence to show that the first event caused the second.

- *Straw man* arguments misrepresent an opposing position to make it ridiculous or extreme and thus easy to refute, rather than dealing with the actual position. For example, if someone argues that funding for supplemental nutrition assistance should be cut, a straw man response would be, "You want the poor to starve," transforming a proposal to cut a specific program into an exaggerated argument that the proposer hasn't made.

- *Hasty generalizations* are conclusions based on insufficient or inappropriately qualified evidence. This summary of a research study is a good example: "Twenty randomly chosen residents of Brooklyn, New York, were asked whether they found graffiti tags offensive; fourteen said yes, five said no, and one had no opinion. Therefore, 70 percent of Brooklyn residents find tagging offensive." In Brooklyn, a part of New York City with a population of over two million, twenty residents is far too small a group from which to draw meaningful conclusions. To be able to generalize, the researcher would have had to survey a much greater percentage of Brooklyn's population.

- *Slippery slope* arguments assert that one event will inevitably lead to another, often cataclysmic event without presenting evidence that such a chain of causes and effects will in fact take place. Here's an example: "If the state legislature passes this 2 percent tax increase, it won't be long before all the corporations in the state move to other states and leave thousands unemployed." According to this argument, if taxes are raised, the state's economy will be ruined—not a likely scenario, given the size of the proposed increase.

Considering the Rhetorical Situation

To argue effectively, you need to think about the message that you want to articulate, the audience you want to persuade, the effect of your stance, and the larger context you are writing in.

<table>
<tr>
<td>55–56</td>
<td>**PURPOSE**</td>
<td>What do you want your audience to do? To think a certain way? To take a certain action? To change their minds? To consider alternative views to their current ones? To accept your position as plausible? To see that you have thought carefully about an issue and researched it appropriately?</td>
</tr>
<tr>
<td>57–60</td>
<td>**AUDIENCE**</td>
<td>Who is your intended audience? What do they likely know and believe about your topic? How personal is it for them? To what extent are they likely to agree or disagree with you? Why? What common ground can you find with them? How should you incorporate other viewpoints they have? What kind of evidence are they likely to accept?</td>
</tr>
<tr>
<td>61–65</td>
<td>**GENRE**</td>
<td>What genre will help you achieve your purpose? A position paper? An evaluation? A review? A proposal? An analysis?</td>
</tr>
<tr>
<td>66–68</td>
<td>**STANCE**</td>
<td>What's your attitude toward your topic, and why? What strategies will help you to convey that stance? How do you want your audience to perceive you? As an authority on your topic? As someone much like them? As calm? reasonable? impassioned or angry? something else?</td>
</tr>
</table>

MEDIA / DESIGN   What media will you use, and how do your media affect your argument? If you're writing on paper, does your argument call for photos or charts? If you're giving an oral presentation, should you put your reasons and support on slides? If you're writing online, should you add links to sites representing other positions or containing evidence that supports your position?

69–71

39 Classifying and Dividing

Classification and division are ways of organizing information: various items may be classified according to their similarities, or a single topic may be divided into parts. We might classify different kinds of flowers as annuals or perennials, for example, and classify the perennials further as dahlias, daisies, roses, and peonies. We might also divide a flower garden into distinct areas: for herbs, flowers, and vegetables.

Writers often use classification and division as ways of developing and organizing material. This book, for instance, classifies comparison, definition, description, and several other common ways of thinking and writing as strategies. It divides the information it provides about writing into seven parts: "Rhetorical Situations," "Genres," and so on. Each part further divides its material into various chapters. Even if you never write a book, you will have occasion to classify and divide material in 190–98 **ANNOTATED BIBLIOGRAPHIES**, essays **ANALYZING TEXTS**, and other kinds 98–130 of writing. This chapter offers advice for classifying and dividing information for various purposes—and in a way that suits your own rhetorical situation.

Classifying

When we classify something, we group it with similar things. A linguist would classify French, Spanish, and Italian as Romance languages, for example—and Russian, Polish, and Bulgarian as Slavic languages. In a phony news story from the *Onion* about a church bake sale, the writer classifies the activities observed there as examples of the seven deadly sins:

academic literacies · rhetorical situations · genres · fields · processes · strategies · research MLA / APA · media / design · readings · handbook

GADSDEN, AL—The seven deadly sins—avarice, sloth, envy, lust, gluttony, pride, and wrath—were all committed Sunday during the twice-annual bake sale at St. Mary's of the Immaculate Conception Church.

—"All Seven Deadly Sins Committed at Church Bake Sale," *Onion*

The article goes on to categorize the participants' behavior in terms of the sins, describing one parishioner who commits the sin of pride by bragging about her cookies and others who commit the sin of envy by envying the popularity of the prideful parishioner's baked goods (the consumption of which leads to the sin of gluttony). In all, the article notes, "347 individual acts of sin were committed at the bake sale," and every one of them can be classified as one of the seven deadly sins.

Dividing

As a writing strategy, division is a way of breaking something into parts — and a way of making the information easy for readers to follow and understand. See how this example about children's ways of nagging divides their tactics into seven categories:

James U. McNeal, a professor of marketing at Texas A&M University, is considered America's leading authority on marketing to children. In his book *Kids as Customers* (1992), McNeal provides marketers with a thorough analysis of "children's requesting styles and appeals." He [divides] juvenile nagging tactics into seven major categories. A *pleading* nag is one accompanied by repetitions of words like "please" or "mom, mom, mom." A *persistent* nag involves constant requests for the coveted product and may include the phrase "I'm gonna ask just one more time." *Forceful* nags are extremely pushy and may include subtle threats, like "Well, then, I'll go and ask Dad." *Demonstrative* nags are the most high risk, often characterized by full-blown tantrums in public places, breath holding, tears, a refusal to leave the store. *Sugar-coated* nags promise affection in return for a purchase and may rely on seemingly heartfelt declarations, like "You're the best dad in the world." *Threatening* nags are youthful forms of blackmail, vows of eternal hatred and of running away if something isn't bought. *Pity* nags claim the child will be heartbroken, teased, or socially stunted if the parent refuses to buy a certain item. "All of these appeals and styles may be used in combination," McNeal's research has discovered, "but kids tend to stick to one or two of each that prove most effective . . . for their own parents."

—Eric Schlosser, *Fast Food Nation: The Dark Side of the All-American Meal*

Here the writer announces the division scheme of "seven major categories." Then he names each tactic and describes how it works. Notice the italics: each tactic is italicized, making it easy to recognize and follow. Take away the italics, and the divisions would be less visible.

Creating Clear and Distinct Categories

When you classify or divide, you need to create clear and distinct categories. If you're writing about music, you might divide it on the basis of the genre (rap, rock, classical, gospel), artist (male or female, group or solo), or instruments (violins, trumpets, bongos, guitars). These categories must be distinct so that no information overlaps or fits into more than one category, and they must include every member of the group you're discussing. The simpler the criteria for selecting the categories, the better. The nagging categories in the example from *Fast Food Nation* are based on only one criterion: a child's verbal behavior.

Sometimes you may want to highlight your categories visually to make them easier to follow. Eric Schlosser does that by italicizing each category: the *pleading* nag, the *persistent* nag, the *forceful* nag, and so on. Other **DESIGN** elements—bulleted lists, pie charts, tables, images—might also prove useful.

644–52

Sometimes you might show categories visually, as in the following chart. The differences among the six varieties pictured are visible at a glance, and the chart next to the photos shows the best uses for each variety—and its level of tartness.

The photographs allow us to see the differences among the varieties at a glance. Although the varieties shown here are arranged according to the tartness of their flavor, they could have been arranged in other ways too—alphabetically or by shape or size.

	EATING	BAKING	COOKING	LESS TART
Red Delicious	✔	✔		
Honeycrisp	✔	✔	✔	
Red Rome		✔	✔	
Braeburn	✔		✔	
McIntosh	✔	✔	✔	MORE TART

All photos © New York Apple Association

For another example, see how *The World of Caffeine* authors Bennett Alan Weinberg and Bonnie K. Bealer use a two-column list to show what they say are the differing cultural connotations of coffee and tea:

Coffee Aspect	Tea Aspect
Male	Female
Boisterous	Decorous
Indulgence	Temperance
Hardheaded	Romantic
Topology	Geometry
Heidegger	Carnap
Beethoven	Mozart
Libertarian	Statist
Promiscuous	Pure

—Bennett Alan Weinberg and Bonnie K. Bealer,
The World of Caffeine

Considering the Rhetorical Situation

As a writer or speaker, you need to think about the message that you want to articulate, the audience you want to reach, and the larger context you are writing in.

55–56

PURPOSE   Your purpose for writing will affect how you classify or divide information. Weinberg and Bealer classify coffee as "boisterous" and tea as "decorous" to help readers understand the cultural styles the two beverages represent, whereas J. Crew might divide sweaters into cashmere, wool, and cotton to help shoppers find and buy clothing from their website.

57–60

AUDIENCE   Who do you want to reach, and will classifying or dividing your material help them follow your discussion?

academic literacies   rhetorical situations   genres   fields   processes   strategies   research MLA / APA   media / design   readings   handbook

GENRE   Does your genre call for you to categorize or divide information? A long report might need to be divided into sections, for instance.

61–65

STANCE   Your stance may affect the way you classify information. Weinberg and Bealer's classification of coffee as "Beethoven" and tea as "Mozart" reflects a stance that focuses on cultural analysis (and assumes an audience familiar with the difference between the two composers). If the authors were botanists, they might categorize the two beverages in terms of their biological origins ("seed based" and "leaf based").

66–68

MEDIA / DESIGN   You can classify or divide in paragraph form, but sometimes a pie chart or list will show the categories better.

69–71

IF YOU NEED MORE HELP

See also **CLUSTERING**, **CUBING**, and **LOOPING**, three methods of generating ideas discussed in Chapter 29 that can be especially helpful for classifying material. And see all the **PROCESSES** chapters for guidelines on drafting, revising, and so on if you need to write a classification essay.

332–34
321

40 Comparing and Contrasting

Comparing things looks at their similarities; contrasting them focuses on their differences. It's a kind of thinking that comes naturally and that we do constantly—for example, comparing Houston with Dallas, iPhones with Androids, or three paintings by Renoir. And once we start comparing, we generally find ourselves contrasting—Houston and Dallas have differences as well as similarities.

As a student, you'll often be asked to compare and contrast paintings or poems or other things. As a writer, you'll have cause to compare and contrast in most kinds of writing. In a **PROPOSAL**, for instance, you will need to compare your solution with other possible solutions; or in an **EVALUATION**, such as a movie review, you might contrast the film you're reviewing with some other film. This chapter offers advice on ways of comparing and contrasting things for various writing purposes and for your own rhetorical situations.

246–55
202–10

Most of the time, we compare obviously similar things: laptops we might purchase, three competing political candidates, two versions of a film. Occasionally, however, we might compare things that are less obviously similar. See how John McMurtry, an ex–football player, compares football with war in an essay arguing that the attraction football holds for spectators is based in part on its potential for violence and injury:

> The family resemblance between football and war is, indeed, striking. Their languages are similar: "field general," "long bomb," "blitz," "take a shot," "front line," "pursuit," "good hit," "the draft," and so on. Their principles and practices are alike: mass hysteria, the art of intimidation, absolute command and total obedience, territorial aggression, censorship, inflated insignia and propaganda, blackboard maneuvers and strategies, drills, uniforms, marching bands, and training

academic literacies · rhetorical situations · genres · fields · processes · strategies · research MLA / APA · media / design · readings · handbook

camps. And the virtues they celebrate are almost identical: hyper-aggressiveness, coolness under fire, and suicidal bravery.

—John McMurtry, "Kill 'Em! Crush 'Em! Eat 'Em Raw!"

McMurtry's comparison helps focus readers' attention on what he's arguing about football in part because it's somewhat unexpected. But the more unlikely the comparison, the more you might be accused of comparing apples and oranges. It's important, therefore, that the things we compare be legitimately compared—as is the case in the following comparison of the health of the world's richest and poorest people:

> World Health Organization (WHO) data indicate that roughly 1.2 billion people are undernourished, underweight, and often hungry. At the same time, roughly 1.2 billion people are overnourished and overweight, most of them suffering from excessive caloric intake and exercise deprivation. So while 1 billion people worry whether they will eat, another billion should worry about eating too much.
>
> Disease patterns also reflect the widening gap. The billion poorest suffer mostly from infectious diseases—malaria, tuberculosis, dysentery, and AIDS. Malnutrition leaves infants and small children even more vulnerable to such infectious diseases. Unsafe drinking water takes a heavier toll on those with hunger-weakened immune systems, resulting in millions of fatalities each year. In contrast, among the billion at the top of the global economic scale, it is diseases related to aging and lifestyle excesses, including obesity, smoking, diets rich in fat and sugar, and exercise deprivation, that cause most deaths.
>
> —Lester R. Brown, *Plan B 2.0: Rescuing a Planet under Stress and a Civilization in Trouble*

While the two groups of roughly a billion people each undoubtedly have similarities, this selection from a book arguing for global action on the environment focuses on the stark contrasts.

Two Ways of Comparing and Contrasting

Comparisons and contrasts may be organized in two basic ways: block and point by point.

The block method. One way is to discuss separately each item you're comparing, giving all the information about one item and then all the information about the next item. A report on Seattle and Vancouver, for example, compares the firearm regulations in each city using a paragraph about Seattle and then a paragraph about Vancouver:

> Although similar in many ways, Seattle and Vancouver differ markedly in their approaches to the regulation of firearms. In Seattle, handguns may be purchased legally for self-defense in the street or at home. After a thirty-day waiting period, a permit can be obtained to carry a handgun as a concealed weapon. The recreational use of handguns is minimally restricted.
>
> In Vancouver, self-defense is not considered a valid or legal reason to purchase a handgun. Concealed weapons are not permitted. Recreational uses of handguns (such as target shooting and collecting) are regulated by the province, and the purchase of a handgun requires a restricted-weapons permit. A permit to carry a weapon must also be obtained in order to transport a handgun, and these weapons can be discharged only at a licensed shooting club. Handguns can be transported by car, but only if they are stored in the trunk in a locked box.
>
> —John Henry Sloan et al., "Handgun Regulations, Crime, Assaults, and Homicide: A Tale of Two Cities"

The point-by-point method. The other way to compare things is to focus on specific points of comparison. In this paragraph, humorist David Sedaris compares his childhood with his partner's, discussing corresponding aspects of the childhoods one at a time:

> Certain events are parallel, but compared with Hugh's, my childhood was unspeakably dull. When I was seven years old, my family moved to North Carolina. When he was seven years old, Hugh's family moved to the Congo. We had a collie and a house cat. They had a monkey and two horses named Charlie Brown and Satan. I threw stones at stop signs. Hugh threw stones at crocodiles. The verbs are the same, but he definitely wins the prize when it comes to nouns and objects. An eventful day for my mother might have involved a trip to the dry

academic literacies · rhetorical situations · genres · fields · processes · strategies · research MLA / APA · media / design · readings · handbook

cleaner or a conversation with the potato-chip deliveryman. Asked one ordinary Congo afternoon what she'd done with her day, Hugh's mother answered that she and a fellow member of the Ladies' Club had visited a leper colony on the outskirts of Kinshasa.

—David Sedaris, "Remembering My Childhood on the Continent of Africa"

Using Graphs and Images to Present Comparisons

Some comparisons can be easier to understand if they're presented visually, as a **CHART**, **GRAPH**, or **ILLUSTRATION**. For example, this excerpt from a chart from the Gallup polling company's website shows the percentage of Americans who identified themselves as Republicans, Independents, or Democrats in 2012, broken down by race and ethnicity:

653–63

Racial and Ethnic Composition of U.S., by Party ID

	Republican	Independent	Democrat
Non-Hispanic white	89%	70%	60%
Non-Hispanic black	2%	8%	22%
Hispanic	6%	16%	13%
Asian	1%	3%	2%
Other	1%	1%	1%
Undesignated	1%	2%	2%

Gallup Daily tracking, January-December 2012

—*GALLUP*

The following bar graph, from an economics textbook, compares the incomes of various professions in the United States, both with one another and with the average U.S. income (defined as 100 percent). Again, it would be possible to write out this information in a paragraph—but it is much easier to understand it this way:

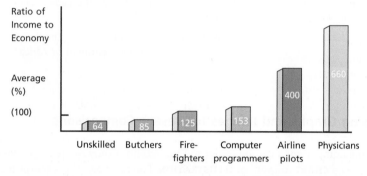

—Joseph E. Stiglitz, *Economics*

Sometimes photographs can make a comparison. The two photos below show a street in Houston before and after Hurricane Harvey in 2017.

Roadway in Houston before the 2017 hurricane (left) and after (right).

Using Figurative Language to Make Comparisons

Another way we make comparisons is with figurative language: words and phrases used in a nonliteral way to help readers see a point. Three kinds of figurative language that make comparisons are similes, metaphors, and analogies. When Robert Burns wrote that his love was "like a red, red rose," he was comparing his love with a rose and evoking an image—in this case, a simile—that helps us understand his feelings for her. A simile makes a comparison using *like* or *as*. In the following example, from an article in the food section of the *New York Times*, a restaurant critic uses several similes (underlined) to help us visualize an unusual food dish:

> Once upon a time, possibly at a lodge in Wyoming, possibly at a butcher shop in Maurice, Louisiana, or maybe even at a plantation in South Carolina, an enterprising cook decided to take a boned chicken, a boned duck, and a boned turkey, stuff them one inside the other <u>like Russian dolls</u>, and roast them. He called his masterpiece turducken. . . .
>
> A well-prepared turducken is a marvelous treat, a free-form poultry terrine layered with flavorful stuffing and moistened with duck fat. When it's assembled, it looks <u>like a turkey</u> and it roasts <u>like a turkey</u>, but when you go to carve it, you can slice through it <u>like a loaf of bread</u>. In each slice you get a little bit of everything: white meat from the breast; dark meat from the legs, duck, carrots, bits of sausage, bread, herbs, juices, and chicken, too.
>
> —Amanda Hesser, "Turkey Finds Its Inner Duck (and Chicken)"

Metaphors make comparisons without such connecting words as *like* or *as*. See how desert ecologist Craig Childs uses a metaphor to help us understand the nature of water during a flood in the Grand Canyon:

> Water splashed off the desert and ran all over the surface, looking for the quickest way down. It was too swift for the ground to absorb. When water flows like this, it will not be clean tap water. It will be <u>a gravy of debris</u>, snatching everything it finds.
>
> —Craig Childs, *The Secret Knowledge of Water*

Calling the water "a gravy of debris" allows us to see the murky liquid as it streams through the canyon.

Analogies are extended similes or metaphors that compare something unfamiliar with something more familiar. Arguing that corporations should not patent parts of DNA whose function isn't yet clear, a genetics professor uses the familiar image of a library to explain an unfamiliar concept:

> It's like having a library of books and randomly tearing pages out. You may know which books the pages came from but that doesn't tell you much about them. —Peter Goodfellow, quoted in John Vidal and John Carvel, "Lambs to the Gene Market"

Sometimes analogies are used for humorous effect as well as to make a point, as in this passage from a critique of history textbooks:

> Another history text—this one for fifth grade—begins with the story of how Henry B. Gonzalez, who is a member of Congress from Texas, learned about his own nationality. When he was ten years old, his teacher told him he was an American because he was born in the United States. His grandmother, however, said, "The cat was born in the oven. Does that make him bread?"
>
> —Frances FitzGerald, *America Revised: History Schoolbooks in the Twentieth Century*

The grandmother's question shows how an intentionally ridiculous analogy can be a source of humor—and can make a point memorably.

Considering the Rhetorical Situation

As a writer or speaker, you need to think about the message that you want to articulate, the audience you want to reach, and the larger context you are writing in.

55–56

PURPOSE Sometimes your main purpose for writing will be to compare two or more things. Other times, you may want to compare several things for some other purpose—to compare your views with those of others in an argument essay or to compare one text with another as you analyze them.

AUDIENCE   Who is your audience, and will comparing your topic with a more familiar one help them to follow your discussion?

57–60

GENRE   Does your genre require you to compare something? Evaluations often include comparisons—one book to another in a review, or ten different cell phones in *Consumer Reports*.

61–65

STANCE   Your stance may affect any comparisons you make. How you compare two things—evenhandedly, or clearly favoring one over the other, for example—will reflect your stance.

66–68

MEDIA / DESIGN   Some things you will want to compare with words alone (lines from two poems, for instance), but sometimes you may wish to make comparisons visually (two images juxtaposed on a page, or several numbers plotted on a line graph).

69–71

IF YOU NEED MORE HELP

See **LOOPING** and **CUBING**, two methods of generating ideas discussed in Chapter 29 that can be especially helpful for comparing and contrasting. If you're writing an essay whose purpose is to compare two or more things, see also the **PROCESSES** chapters for help drafting, revising, and so on.

332
334
321

41 Defining

Defining something says what it is—and what it is not. A terrier, for example, is a kind of dog. A fox terrier is a small dog now generally kept as a pet but once used by hunters to dig for foxes. Happiness is a jelly doughnut, at least according to Homer Simpson. All of those are definitions. As writers, we need to define any terms our readers may not know. And sometimes you'll want to stipulate your own definition of a word in order to set the terms of an **ARGUMENT**—as Homer Simpson does with a definition that's not found in any dictionary. This chapter details strategies for using definitions in your writing to suit your own rhetorical situations.

397–417

Formal Definitions

Sometimes to make sure readers understand you, you will need to provide a formal definition. If you are using a technical term that readers are unlikely to know or if you are using a term in a specific way, you need to say then and there what the word means. The word *mutual*, for example, has several dictionary meanings:

Definition of MUTUAL

1a: directed by each toward the other or the others • *mutual* affection
b: having the same feelings one for the other • they had long been *mutual* enemies
c: shared in common • enjoying their *mutual* hobby
d: joint • to their *mutual* advantage
2: characterized by intimacy • *mutual* contacts
3: of or relating to a plan whereby the members of an organization share in the profits and expenses; specifically: of, relating to, or taking

academic literacies | rhetorical situations | genres | fields | processes | strategies | research MLA / APA | media / design | readings | handbook

the form of an insurance method in which the policyholders constitute the members of the insuring company

—*Merriam-Webster.com*

The first two meanings are commonly understood and probably require no definition. But if you were to use *mutual* in the third sense, it might—depending on your audience. A general audience would probably need the definition; an audience from the insurance industry would not. A website that gives basic financial advice to an audience of non-specialists, for instance, offers a specific definition of the term *mutual fund*:

> *Mutual funds* are financial intermediaries. They are companies set up to receive your money and then, having received it, to make investments with the money.
>
> —Bill Barker, "A Grand, Comprehensive
> Overview to Mutual Funds Investing"

But even writers in specialized fields routinely provide formal definitions to make sure their readers understand the way they are using certain words. See how two writers define the word *stock* as it pertains to their respective (and very different) fields:

> Stocks are the basis for sauces and soups and important flavoring agents for braises. Admittedly, stock making is time consuming, but the extra effort yields great dividends.
>
> —Tom Colicchio, *Think Like a Chef*

> Want to own part of a business without having to show up at its office every day? Or ever? Stock is the vehicle of choice for those who do. Dating back to the Dutch mutual stock corporations of the sixteenth century, the modern stock market exists as a way for entrepreneurs to finance businesses using money collected from investors. In return for ponying up the dough to finance the company, the investor becomes a part owner of the company. That ownership is represented by stock—specialized financial "securities," or financial instruments, that are "secured" by a claim on the assets and profits of a company.
>
> —"Investing Basics: Stocks," *Motley Fool*

To write a formal definition

- Use words that readers are likely to be familiar with.
- Don't use the word being defined in the definition.
- Begin with the word being defined; include the general category to which the term belongs and the attributes that make it different from the others in that category.

For example:

Term	General Category	Distinguishing Attributes
Stock is	a specialized financial "security"	that is "secured" by a claim.
Photosynthesis is	a process	by which plants use sunlight to create energy.
Astronomers are	scientists	who study celestial objects and phenomena.
Zach Galifianakis,	an actor,	has been featured in several films, including *The Hangover* and *Birdman.*

Note that the category and distinguishing attributes cannot be stated too broadly; if they were, the definition would be too vague to be useful. It wouldn't be helpful in most circumstances, for example, to say, "Zach Galifianakis is a man who has acted" or "Photosynthesis is something having to do with plants."

Extended Definitions

Sometimes you need to provide a more detailed definition. Extended definitions may be several sentences long or several paragraphs long and may include pictures or diagrams. Sometimes an entire essay is devoted

to defining a difficult or important concept. Here is one writer's extended definition of *meme*:

> Richard Dawkins first came up with the idea of a meme in his 1976 book *The Selfish Gene*. Essentially, memes are ideas that evolve according to the same principles that govern biological evolution. Think about all the ideas that you have in your head right now. They are all memes, and they all came from somewhere. Some of them will have come from friends and some will have come from the internet or television. Examples of memes are musical tunes, jokes, trends, fashions, catch phrases, and car designs. Now, the memes that inhabit your mind are in competition with all the other memes in the *memepool* (the collection of all existing memes). This means that they are all competing to get themselves copied into other people's minds. Some of these memes do quite well. Every time you whistle your favorite tune or utter a useful catch phrase, you are facilitating the spread of those memes. Every time you wear something that is "in fashion" you are helping the idea of that fashion enter other people's minds. Consider the first four notes of Beethoven's 5th symphony, or the "Happy Birthday" song. These are ideas that inhabit our minds and have been very successful at replicating. Not only have these memes found their way into literally millions of minds, they have also managed to leave copies of themselves on paper, in books, on audiotape, on compact disks, and in computer hard-drives.
>
> There is a limited amount of memetic storage space on this planet, so only the best memes manage to implant themselves. Memes that are good at replicating tend to leave more copies of themselves in minds and in other mediums such as books. Memes that are not so good at replicating tend to die out. We can imagine what sorts of memes have become extinct. Ancient songs that were once sung and never written down are one example. Another example is the many stories that were once told but have since slipped into oblivion.
>
> —Brent Silby, "What Is a Meme?"

That definition includes a description of the basic features and behavior of memes, examples of them, and the origin of the term. We can assume that it's written for a general audience, one that doesn't know anything about memes.

Abstract concepts often require extended definitions because by nature they are more complicated to define. There are many ways of writing an extended definition, depending in part on the term being defined and on your audience and purpose. The following examples show some of the methods that can be used for composing extended definitions of *democracy*.

Explore the word's origins.   Where did the word come from? When did it first come into use? In the following example, from an essay considering what democracy means in the twenty-first century, the writer started by looking at the word's first known use in English. Though it's from an essay written for a first-year writing course and thus for a fairly general audience, it's a definition that might pique any audience's interest:

> According to the *Oxford English Dictionary*, the term *democracy* first appeared in English in a thirteenth-century translation of Aristotle's works—specifically, in his *Politics*, where he stated that the "underlying principle of democracy is freedom" and that "it is customary to say that only in democracies do men have a share in freedom, for that is what every democracy makes its aim." By the sixteenth century, the word was used much as it is now. One writer in 1586, for instance, defined it in this way: "where free and poore men being the greater number, are lords of the estate."
>
> —Susanna Mejía, "What Does Democracy Mean Now?"

Here's another example, this one written for a scholarly audience, from an essay about women, participation, democracy, and the information age:

> The very word *citizenship* carries with it a connotation of place, a "citizen" being, literally, the inhabitant of a city. Over the years the word has, of course, accumulated a number of associated meanings . . . and the word has come to stand in for such concepts as participation, equality, and democracy. The fact that the concept of locality is deeply embedded in the word *citizen* suggests that it is also fundamental to our current understanding of these other, more apparently abstract words.
>
> In Western thought, the concepts of citizenship, equality, and democracy are closely interlinked and can be traced back to a common source, in Athens in the fifth century B.C. Perhaps it is no accident that it was the same culture which also gave us, in its theater, the

academic literacies | rhetorical situations | genres | fields | processes | strategies | research MLA / APA | media / design | readings | handbook

Norman Rockwell's 1943 painting Freedom of Speech *presents a visual defini-*
tion of democracy: a citizen stands to speak at a public meeting while his fellow
citizens listen attentively.

concept of the unity of time and space. The Greek city-state has been represented for centuries as the ideal model of democracy, with free and equal access for all citizens to decision making. Leaving aside, for the moment, the question of who was included, and who excluded from this notion of citizenship, we can see that the sense of place is fundamental to this model. Entitlement to participate in the democratic process is circumscribed by geography; it is the inhabitants of the geographical entity of the city-state, precisely defined and bounded, who have the rights to citizenship. Those who are not defined as inhabitants of that specific city-state are explicitly excluded, although, of course, they may have the right to citizenship elsewhere.

—Ursula Huws, "Women, Participation, and Democracy in the Information Society"

Provide details. What are its characteristics? What is it made of? See how a historian explores the basic characteristics of democracy in a book written for an audience of historians:

As a historian I am naturally disposed to be satisfied with the meaning which, in the history of politics, men have commonly attributed to the word—a meaning, needless to say, which derives partly from the experience and partly from the aspirations of mankind. So regarded, the term *democracy* refers primarily to a form of government, and it has always meant government by the many as opposed to government by the one—government by the people as opposed to government by a tyrant, a dictator, or an absolute monarch. . . . Since the Greeks first used the term, the essential test of democratic government has always been this: the source of political authority must be and remain in the people and not in the ruler. A democratic government has always meant one in which the citizens, or a sufficient number of them to represent more or less effectively the common will, freely act from time to time, and according to established forms, to appoint or recall the magistrates and to enact or revoke the laws by which the community is governed. —Carl Becker, *Modern Democracy*

Compare it with other words. How is this concept like other similar things? How does it differ? What is it *not* like? **COMPARE AND CONTRAST**

424–31

it. See how a political science textbook defines a *majoritarian democracy* by comparing its characteristics with those of a *consensual democracy*:

> A majoritarian democracy is one
>
> 1. having only two major political parties, not many
>
> 2. having an electoral system that requires a bare majority to elect one clear winner in an election, as opposed to a proportional electoral system that distributes seats to political parties according to the rough share of votes received in the election
>
> 3. a strong executive (president or prime minister) and cabinet that together are largely independent of the legislature when it comes to exercising the executive's constitutional duties, in contrast to an executive and cabinet that are politically controlled by the parties in the legislature and therefore unable to exercise much influence when proposing policy initiatives.
>
> —Benjamin Ginsberg, Theodore J. Lowi, and Margaret Weir,
> *We the People: An Introduction to American Politics*

And here's an example in which democracy is contrasted with various other forms of governments of the past:

> Caesar's power derived from a popular mandate, conveyed through established republican forms, but that did not make his government any the less a dictatorship. Napoleon called his government a democratic republic, but no one, least of all Napoleon himself, doubted that he had destroyed the last vestiges of the democratic republic.
>
> —Carl Becker, *Modern Democracy*

Give examples. See how the essayist E. B. White defines democracy by giving some everyday examples of considerate behavior, humility, and civic participation—all things he suggests constitute democracy:

> It is the line that forms on the right. It is the don't in "don't shove." It is the hole in the stuffed shirt through which the sawdust slowly trickles; it is the dent in the high hat. Democracy is the recurrent suspicion that more than half of the people are right more than half of the time. . . . Democracy is a letter to the editor.   —E. B. White, "Democracy"

White's definition is elegant because he uses examples that his readers will know. His characteristics—metaphors, really—define democracy not as a conceptual way of governing but as an everyday part of American life.

418–23 ◆

Classify it.   Often it is useful to divide or **CLASSIFY** a term. The ways in which democracy unfolds are complex enough to warrant entire textbooks, of course, but the following definition, from a political science textbook, divides democracy into two kinds, representative and direct:

> A system of government that gives citizens a regular opportunity to elect the top government officials is usually called a representative democracy or republic. A system that permits citizens to vote directly on laws and policies is often called a direct democracy. At the national level, America is a representative democracy in which citizens select government officials but do not vote on legislation. Some states, however, have provisions for direct legislation through popular referendum. For example, California voters in 1995 decided to bar undocumented immigrants from receiving some state services.
>
> —Benjamin Ginsberg, Theodore J. Lowi, and Margaret Weir,
> *We the People: An Introduction to American Politics*

Stipulative Definitions

Sometimes a writer will stipulate a certain definition, essentially saying, "This is how I'm defining x." Such definitions are not usually found in a dictionary—and at the same time are central to the argument the writer is making. Here is one example, from an essay by Toni Morrison. Describing a scene from a film in which a newly arrived Greek immigrant, working as a shoe shiner in Grand Central Terminal, chases away an African American competitor, Morrison calls the scene an example of "race talk," a concept she then goes on to define:

This is race talk, the explicit insertion into everyday life of racial signs and symbols that have no meaning other than pressing African Americans to the lowest level of the racial hierarchy. Popular culture, shaped by film, theater, advertising, the press, television, and literature, is heavily engaged in race talk. It participates freely in this most enduring and efficient rite of passage into American culture: negative appraisals of the native-born black population. Only when the lesson of racial estrangement is learned is assimilation complete. Whatever the lived experience of immigrants with African Americans—pleasant, beneficial, or bruising—the rhetorical experience renders blacks as noncitizens, already discredited outlaws.

All immigrants fight for jobs and space, and who is there to fight but those who have both? As in the fishing ground struggle between Texas and Vietnamese shrimpers, they displace what and whom they can. Although U.S. history is awash in labor battles, political fights and property wars among all religious and ethnic groups, their struggles are persistently framed as struggles between recent arrivals and blacks. In race talk the move into mainstream America always means buying into the notion of American blacks as the real aliens. Whatever the ethnicity or nationality of the immigrant, his nemesis is understood to be African American.　—Toni Morrison, "On the Backs of Blacks"

The following example is from a book review of Nancy L. Rosenblum's *Membership and Morals: The Personal Uses of Pluralism in America*, published in the *American Prospect*, a magazine for readers interested in political analysis. In it a Stanford law professor outlines a definition of "the democracy of everyday life":

Democracy, in this understanding of it, means simply treating people as equals, disregarding social standing, avoiding attitudes of either deference or superiority, making allowances for others' weaknesses, and resisting the temptation to respond to perceived slights. It also means protesting everyday instances of arbitrariness and unfairness—from the rudeness of the bakery clerk to the sexism of the car dealer or the racism of those who vandalize the home of the first black neighbors on the block.　—Kathleen M. Sullivan, "Defining Democracy Down"

Considering the Rhetorical Situation

As a writer or speaker, you need to think about the message that you want to articulate, the audience you want to reach, and the larger context you are writing in.

55–56 **PURPOSE** Your purpose for writing will affect any definitions you include. Would writing an extended definition help you explain something? Would stipulating definitions of key terms help you shape an argument? Could an offbeat definition help you entertain your readers?

57–60 **AUDIENCE** What audience do you want to reach, and are there any terms your readers are unlikely to know (and therefore need to be defined)? Are there terms they might understand differently from the way you're defining them?

61–65 **GENRE** Does your genre require you to define terms? Chances are that if you're reporting information you'll need to define some terms, and some arguments rest on the way you define key terms.

66–68 **STANCE** What is your stance, and do you need to define key terms to show that stance clearly? How you define *fetus*, for example, is likely to reveal your stance on abortion.

69–71 **MEDIA / DESIGN** Your medium will affect the form your definitions take. In a print text, you will need to define terms in your text; if you're giving a speech or presentation, you might also provide images of important terms and their definitions. In an electronic text, you may be able to define terms by linking to an online dictionary definition.

IF YOU NEED MORE HELP

321 See also the **PROCESSES** chapters for help generating ideas, drafting, revising, and so on if you are writing a whole essay dedicated to defining a term or concept.

---

academic literacies · rhetorical situations · genres · fields · processes · strategies · research MLA / APA · media / design · readings · handbook

Describing 42

When we describe something, we indicate what it looks like—and some-times how it sounds, feels, smells, and tastes. Descriptive details are a way of showing rather than telling, of helping readers see (or hear, smell, and so on) what we're writing about—that the sky is blue, that Miss Havisham is wearing an old yellowed wedding gown, that the chemicals in the beaker have reacted and smell like rotten eggs. You'll have occasion to describe things in most of the writing you do—from describing a favorite hat in a **MEMOIR** to detailing a chemical reaction in a lab report. This chapter will help you work with description—and, in particular, help you think about the use of *detail*, about *objectivity and subjectivity*, about *vantage point*, about creating a clear *dominant impression*, and about using description to fit your rhetorical situation.

▲ 224–32

Detail

The goal of using details is to be as specific as possible, providing infor-mation that will help your audience imagine the subject or make sense of it. See, for example, how Nancy Mairs, an author with multiple sclerosis, describes the disease in clear, specific terms:

> During its course, which is unpredictable and uncontrollable, one may lose vision, hearing, speech, the ability to walk, control of bladder and/or bowels, strength in any or all extremities, sensitivity to touch, vibra-tion, and/or pain, potency, coordination of movements—the list of pos-sibilities is lengthy and, yes, horrifying. One may also lose one's sense of humor. That's the easiest to lose and the hardest to survive without.
>
> In the past ten years, I have sustained some of these losses. Char-acteristic of MS are sudden attacks, called exacerbations, followed by

remissions, and these I have not had. Instead, my disease has been slowly progressive. My left leg is now so weak that I walk with the aid of a brace and a cane, and for distances I use an Amigo, a variation on the electric wheelchair that looks rather like an electrified kiddie car. I no longer have much use of my left hand. Now my right side is weakening as well. I still have the blurred spot in my right eye. Overall, though, I've been lucky so far.   —Nancy Mairs, "On Being a Cripple"

Mairs's gruesome list demonstrates, through *specific details*, how the disease affects sufferers generally and her in particular. We know far more after reading this text than we do from the following more general description, from a National Multiple Sclerosis Society brochure:

Multiple sclerosis is a chronic, unpredictable disease of the central nervous system (the brain, optic nerves, and spinal cord). It is thought to be an autoimmune disorder. This means the immune system incorrectly attacks the person's healthy tissue.

MS can cause blurred vision, loss of balance, poor coordination, slurred speech, tremors, numbness, extreme fatigue, problems with memory and concentration, paralysis, and blindness. These problems may be permanent, or they may come and go.

—National Multiple Sclerosis Society, *Just the Facts*

Specific details are also more effective than labels, which give little meaningful information. Instead of saying that someone is a "moron" or "really smart," it's better to give details so that readers can understand the reasons behind the label: what does this person *do* or *say* that makes them deserve this label? See, for example, how the writer of a news story about shopping on the day after Thanksgiving opens with a description of a happy shopper:

Last Friday afternoon, the day ritualized consumerism is traditionally at its most frenetic, Alexx Balcuns twirled in front of a full-length mirror at the Ritz Thrift Shop on West Fifty-seventh Street as if inhabited by the soul of Eva Gabor in *Green Acres*. Ms. Balcuns was languishing in a $795 dyed-mink parka her grandmother had just bought her. Ms. Balcuns is six.

—Ginia Bellafante, "Staying Warm and Fuzzy during Uncertain Times"

academic literacies   rhetorical situations   genres   fields   processes   strategies   research MLA / APA   media / design   readings   handbook

The writer might simply have said, "A spoiled child admired herself in the mirror." Instead, she shows her subject twirling and "languishing" in a "$795 dyed-mink parka" and seemingly possessed by the soul of a glamorous actress—all details that create a far more vivid description.

Sensory details help readers imagine sounds, odors, tastes, and physical sensations in addition to sights. In the following example, writer Scott Russell Sanders recalls sawing wood as a child. Note how visual details, odors, and even the physical sense of being picked up by his father mingle to form a vivid scene:

> As the saw teeth bit down, the wood released its smell, each kind with its own fragrance, oak or walnut or cherry or pine—usually pine because it was the softest, easiest for a child to work. No matter how weathered and gray the board, no matter how warped and cracked, inside there was this smell waiting, as of something freshly baked. I gathered every smidgen of sawdust and stored it away in coffee cans, which I kept in a drawer of the workbench. When I did not feel like hammering nails I would dump my sawdust on the concrete floor of the garage and landscape it into highways and farms and towns, running miniature cars and trucks along miniature roads. Looming as huge as a colossus, my father worked over and around me, now and again bending down to inspect my work, careful not to trample my creations. It was a landscape that smelled dizzyingly of wood. Even after a bath my skin would carry the smell, and so would my father's hair, when he lifted me for a bedtime hug.
>
> —Scott Russell Sanders, *The Paradise of Bombs*

Whenever you describe something, you'll select from many possible details you might use. Simply put, to exhaust all the details available to describe something is impossible—and would exhaust your readers as well. To focus your description, you'll need to determine the kinds of details appropriate for your subject. They will vary, depending on your **PURPOSE**. See, for example, how the details might differ in three different genres:

■ 55–56

- *For a* **MEMOIR** *about an event,* you might choose details that are significant for you, that evoke the sights, sounds, and other sensations that give meaning to your event.

▲ 224–32

233–45

- *For a* **PROFILE**, you're likely to select details that will reinforce the dominant impression you want to give, that portray the event from the perspective you want readers to see.

- *For a lab report*, you need to give certain specifics—what equipment was used, what procedures were followed, what exactly were the results.

Deciding on a focus for your description can help you see it better, as you'll look for details that contribute to that focus.

Objectivity and Subjectivity

Descriptions can be written with objectivity, with subjectivity, or with a mixture of both. Objective descriptions attempt to be uncolored by personal opinion or emotion. Police reports and much news writing aim to describe events objectively; scientific writing strives for objectivity in describing laboratory procedures and results. See, for example, the following objective account of what happened at the World Trade Center on September 11, 2001:

> ### World Trade Center Disaster—Tuesday, September 11, 2001
>
> On Tuesday, September 11, 2001, at 8:45 a.m. New York local time, One World Trade Center, the north tower, was hit by a hijacked 767 commercial jet airplane loaded with fuel for a transcontinental flight. Two World Trade Center, the south tower, was hit by a similar hijacked jet eighteen minutes later, at 9:03 a.m. (In separate but related attacks, the Pentagon building near Washington, D.C., was hit by a hijacked 757 at 9:43 a.m., and at 10:10 a.m. a fourth hijacked jetliner crashed in Pennsylvania.) The south tower, WTC 2, which had been hit second, was the first to suffer a complete structural collapse, at 10:05 a.m., 62 minutes after being hit itself, 80 minutes after the first impact. The north tower, WTC 1, then also collapsed, at 10:29 a.m., 104 minutes after being hit. WTC 7, a substantial forty-seven-story office building in its own right, built in 1987, was damaged by the collapsing towers, caught fire, and later in the afternoon also totally collapsed.
>
> —"World Trade Center," *GreatBuildings.com*

Subjective descriptions, on the other hand, allow the writer's opinions and emotions to come through. A house can be described as comfortable, with a lived-in look, or as rundown and in need of a paint job and a new roof. Here's a subjective description of the planes striking the World Trade Center, as told by a woman watching from a nearby building:

> Incredulously, while looking out [the] window at the damage and carnage the first plane had inflicted, I saw the second plane abruptly come into my right field of vision and deliberately, with shimmering intention, thunder full-force into the south tower. It was so close, so low, so huge and fast, so intent on its target that I swear to you, I swear to you, I felt the vengeance and rage emanating from the plane.
>
> —Debra Fontaine, "Witnessing"

Vantage Point

Sometimes you'll want or need to describe something from a certain vantage point. Where you locate yourself in relation to what you're describing will determine what you can perceive (and so describe) and what you can't. You may describe your subject from a *stationary vantage point*, from which you (and your readers) see your subject from one angle only, as if you were a camera. This description of one of three photographs that captured a woman's death records only what the camera saw from one angle at one particular moment:

> The first showed some people on a fire escape—a fireman, a woman and a child. The fireman had a nice strong jaw and looked very brave. The woman was holding the child. Smoke was pouring from the build-ing behind them. A rescue ladder was approaching, just a few feet away, and the fireman had one arm around the woman and one arm reaching out toward the ladder.
>
> —Nora Ephron, "The Boston Photographs"

By contrast, this description of a drive to an Italian villa uses a *moving vantage point*; the writer recounts what he saw as he passed through a gate in a city wall, moving from city to country:

> La Pietra—"the stone"—is situated one mile from the Porta San Gallo, an entry to the Old City of Florence. You drive there along the Via Bolognese, twisting past modern apartment blocks, until you come to a gate, which swings open—and there you are, at the upper end of a long lane of cypresses facing a great ocher palazzo; with olive groves spreading out on both sides over an expanse of fifty-seven acres. There's something almost comically wonderful about the effect: here, the city, with its winding avenue; there, on the other side of a wall, the country, fertile and gray green.   —James Traub, "Italian Hours"

The description of quarries in the following section uses *multiple vantage points* to capture the quarries from many perspectives.

Dominant Impression

With any description, your aim is to create some dominant impression—the overall feeling that the individual details add up to. The dominant impression may be implied, growing out of the details themselves. For example, Scott Russell Sanders's memory of the smell of sawdust creates a dominant impression of warmth and comfort: the "fragrance . . . as of something freshly baked," sawdust "stored . . . away in coffee cans," a young boy "lifted . . . for a bedtime hug." Sometimes, though, a writer will state the dominant impression directly, in addition to creating it with details. In an essay about Indiana limestone quarries, Sanders makes the dominant impression clear from the start: "They are battlefields."

> The quarries will not be domesticated. They are not backyard pools; they are battlefields. Each quarry is an arena where violent struggles have taken place between machines and planet, between human ingenuity and brute resisting stone, between mind and matter. Waste rock litters the floor and brim like rubble in a bombed city. The ragged pits might have been the basements of vanished skyscrapers. Stones weighing tens of tons lean against one another at precarious angles, as if they have been thrown there by some gigantic strength and have

academic literacies · rhetorical situations · genres · fields · processes · strategies · research MLA / APA · media / design · readings · handbook

not yet finished falling. Wrecked machinery hulks in the weeds, grimly rusting, the cogs and wheels, twisted rails, battered engine housings, trackless bulldozers and burst boilers like junk from an armored regiment. Everywhere the ledges are scarred from drills, as if from an artillery barrage or machine-gun strafing. Stumbling onto one of these abandoned quarries and gazing at the ruins, you might be left wondering who had won the battle, men or stone.

— Scott Russell Sanders, *The Paradise of Bombs*

The rest of his description, full of more figurative language ("like rubble in a bombed city," "like junk from an armored regiment," "as if from an artillery barrage or machine-gun strafing") reinforces the direct "they are battlefields" statement.

Catch the late show.

11,000 inland lakes • Over 19 million acres of forest • 1,300 miles of scenic trails • More freshwater coastline than any other state   PURE *M*ICHIGAN
Your trip begins at michigan.org

The orange sunset and expanse of sky and water in this Michigan tourism ad create a dominant impression of spaciousness and warmth, while the text invites readers to visit a Michigan beach and enjoy watching the sun set, rather than watching television.

Organizing Descriptions

You can organize descriptions in many ways. When your description is primarily visual, you will probably organize it spatially: from left to right, top to bottom, outside to inside. One variation on this approach is to begin with the most significant or noteworthy feature and move outward from that center, as Ephron does in describing a photo. Or you may create a chronological description of objects as you move past or through them in space, as Traub does in his description of his drive. You might even pile up details to create a dominant impression, as Sanders and Mairs do, especially if your description draws on senses besides vision.

Considering the Rhetorical Situation

As a writer or speaker, you need to think about the message that you want to articulate, the audience you want to reach, and the larger context you are writing in.

<table>
<tr>
<td>55–56 ▮</td>
<td>**PURPOSE**</td>
<td>Your purpose may affect the way you use description. If you're arguing that a government should intervene in another country's civil war, for example, describing the anguish of refugees from that war could make your argument more persuasive. If you're analyzing a painting, you will likely need to describe it.</td>
</tr>
<tr>
<td>57–60 ▮</td>
<td>**AUDIENCE**</td>
<td>Who is your audience, and will they need detailed description to understand the points you wish to make?</td>
</tr>
<tr>
<td>61–65 ▮</td>
<td>**GENRE**</td>
<td>Does your genre require description? A lab report generally calls for you to describe materials and results; a memoir about Grandma should probably describe her—her smile, her dress, her apple pie.</td>
</tr>
<tr>
<td>66–68 ▮</td>
<td>**STANCE**</td>
<td>The way you describe things can help you convey your stance. For example, the details you choose can show you to be objective (or not), careful or casual.</td>
</tr>
</table>

academic literacies · rhetorical situations · genres · fields · processes · strategies · research MLA / APA · media / design · readings · handbook

MEDIA / DESIGN Your medium will affect the form your description can take. In a print or spoken text, you will likely rely on words, though you may also include visuals. In an electronic text, you can easily provide links to visuals as well as audio clips and so may need fewer words of your own.

69–71

IF YOU NEED MORE HELP

See also **FREEWRITING**, **CUBING**, and **LISTING**, three methods of generating ideas that can be especially helpful for developing detailed descriptions. Sometimes you may be assigned to write a whole essay describing something: see the **PROCESSES** chapters for help drafting, revising, and so on.

331–34
321

43 Dialogue

Dialogue is a way of including people's own words in a text, letting readers hear those people's voices—not just what you say about them. **MEMOIRS** and **PROFILES** often include dialogue, and many other genres do as well: **LITERARY ANALYSES** often quote dialogue from the texts they analyze, and essays **ARGUING A POSITION** might quote an authoritative source as support for a claim. This chapter provides brief guidelines for the conventions of paragraphing and punctuating dialogue and offers some good examples of how you can use dialogue most effectively to suit your own rhetorical situations.

Why Add Dialogue?

Dialogue is a way of bringing in voices other than your own, of showing people and scenes rather than just telling about them. It can add color and texture to your writing, making it memorable. Most important, however, dialogue should be more than just colorful or interesting. It needs to contribute to your rhetorical purpose, to support the point you're making. See how dialogue is used in the following excerpt from a magazine profile of the Mall of America, how it gives us a sense of the place that the journalist's own words could not provide:

> Two pubescent girls in retainers and braces sat beside me sipping coffees topped with whipped cream and chocolate sprinkles, their shopping bags gathered tightly around their legs, their eyes fixed on the passing crowds. They came, they said, from Shakopee—"It's nowhere," one of them explained. The megamall, she added, was "a buzz at first, but now it seems pretty normal. 'Cept my parents are like Twenty Questions every time I want to come here. 'Specially since the shooting."

academic literacies · rhetorical situations · genres · fields · processes · strategies · research MLA / APA · media / design · readings · handbook

On a Sunday night, she elaborated, three people had been wounded when shots were fired in a dispute over a San Jose Sharks jacket. "In the *mall*," her friend reminded me. "Right here at megamall. A shooting." "It's like nowhere's safe," the first added.

> —David Guterson, "Enclosed. Encyclopedic. Endured.
> One Week at the Mall of America"

Of course it was the writer who decided whom and what to quote, and Guterson deliberately chose words that capture the young shoppers' speech patterns, quoting fragments ("In the *mall*. . . . Right here at megamall. A shooting"), slang ("a buzz at first," "my parents are like Twenty Questions"), even contractions ("'Cept," "'Specially").

Integrating Dialogue into Your Writing

There are certain conventions for punctuating and paragraphing dialogue:

- **Punctuating.** Enclose each speaker's words in quotation marks, and put any end punctuation—periods, question marks, and exclamation marks—inside the closing quotation mark. Whether you're transcribing words you heard or making them up, you will sometimes need to add punctuation to reflect the rhythm and sound of the speech. In the last sentence of the example below, see how Chang-Rae Lee adds a comma after "Well" and italicizes "*practice*" to show intonation—and attitude.

- **Paragraphing.** When you're writing dialogue that includes more than one speaker, start a new paragraph each time the speaker changes.

- **Signal phrases.** Sometimes you'll need to introduce dialogue with SIGNAL PHRASES—"I said," "she asked," and so on—to make clear who is speaking. At times, however, the speaker will be clear enough, and you won't need any signal phrases.

535–38

Here is a conversation between a mother and her son that illustrates each of the conventions for punctuating and paragraphing dialogue:

> "Whom do I talk to?" she said. She would mostly speak to me in Korean, and I would answer back in English.

"The bank manager, who else?"

"What do I say?"

"Whatever you want to say."

"Don't speak to me like that!" she cried.

"It's just that you should be able to do it yourself," I said.

"You know how I feel about this!"

"Well, maybe then you should consider it *practice*," I answered lightly, using the Korean word to make sure she understood.

—Chang-Rae Lee, "Coming Home Again"

Interviews

Interviews are a kind of dialogue, with different conventions for punctuation. When you're transcribing an interview, give each speaker's name each time they speak, starting a new line but not indenting, and do not use quotation marks. Here is an excerpt from a National Public Radio interview that radio journalist Audie Cornish conducted with writer Susan Cain:

Audie Cornish: In the 1940s and '50s, the message to most Americans was, don't be shy. And in the era of reality television, Twitter and relentless self-promotion, it seems that cultural mandate is in overdrive.

A new book tells the story of how things came to be this way, and it's called *Quiet: The Power of Introverts in a World that Can't Stop Talking*. The author is Susan Cain, and she joins us from the NPR studios in New York to talk more about it. Welcome, Susan.

Susan Cain: Thank you. It's such a pleasure to be here, Audie.

Cornish: Well, we're happy to have you. And to start out—I think we should get this on the record—do you consider yourself an introvert or an extrovert?

Cain: Oh, I definitely consider myself an introvert, and that was part of the fuel for me to write the book.

Cornish: And what's the difference between being an introvert versus being shy? I mean, what's your definition?

Cain: So introversion is really about having a preference for lower-stimulation environments—so just a preference for quiet, for less noise, for less action—whereas extroverts really crave more stimulation in order to feel at their best. And what's important to understand

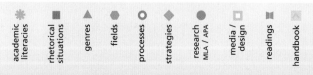

about this is that many people believe that introversion is about being antisocial. And that's really a misperception because actually, it's just that introverts are differently social. So they would prefer to have, you know, a glass of wine with a close friend as opposed to going to a loud party full of strangers.

Now shyness, on the other hand, is about a fear of negative social judgment. So you can be introverted without having that particular fear at all, and you can be shy but also be an extrovert.

Cornish: And in the book, you say that there's a spectrum. So if some people are listening and they think, well, I, too, like a glass of wine and a party. It's like we all have these tendencies.

Cain: Yeah, yeah. That's an important thing. And, in fact, Carl Jung, the psychologist who first popularized these terms all the way back in the 1920s—even he said there's no such thing as a pure introvert or a pure extrovert, and he said such a man would be in a lunatic asylum.

Cornish: That makes me worry because I took your test in the book and I'm like, 90 percent extroverted, basically.

[*soundbite of laughter*].

> —"Quiet, Please: Unleashing 'The Power of Introverts'"

In preparing the interview transcript for publication, NPR had to add punctuation, which of course was not part of the oral conversation, and probably deleted pauses and verbal expressions such as *um* and *uh*. At the same time, the editor kept informal constructions, such as incomplete sentences, which are typical answers to questions ("Yeah") to maintain the oral flavor of the interview and to reflect Cain's voice.

Considering the Rhetorical Situation

As a writer or speaker, you need to think about the message that you want to articulate, the audience you want to reach, and the larger context of your writing.

PURPOSE   Your purpose will affect any use of dialogue. Dialogue   ■ 55–56
can help bring a profile to life and make it memorable.
Interviews with experts or firsthand witnesses can add
credibility to a report or argument.

57–60 **AUDIENCE**
Whom do you want to reach, and will dialogue help? Sometimes actual dialogue can help readers hear human voices behind facts or reason.

61–65 **GENRE**
Does your genre require dialogue? If you're evaluating or analyzing a literary work, for instance, you may wish to include dialogue from that work. If you're writing a profile of a person or event, dialogue can help you bring your subject to life. Similarly, an interview with an expert can add credibility to a report or argument.

66–68 **STANCE**
What is your stance, and can dialogue help you communicate that stance? For example, excerpts of an interview may allow you to challenge someone's views and make your own views clear.

69–71 **MEDIA / DESIGN**
Your medium will affect the way you present dialogue. In a print text, you will present dialogue through written words. In an oral or electronic text, you might include actual recorded dialogue.

IF YOU NEED MORE HELP

506–7
526–38
See also the guidelines on **INTERVIEWING EXPERTS** for advice on setting up and recording interviews and those on **QUOTING**, **PARAPHRASING**, and **SUMMARIZING** for help deciding how to integrate dialogue into your text.

Explaining Processes 44

When you explain a process, you tell how something is (or was) done—how a bill becomes a law, how an embryo develops—or you tell someone how to do something—how to throw a curve ball, how to write a memoir. This chapter focuses on those two kinds of explanations, offering examples and guidelines for explaining a process in a way that works for your rhetorical situation.

Explaining a Process Clearly

Whether the process is simple or complex, you'll need to identify its key stages or steps and explain them one by one, in order. The sequence matters because it allows readers to follow your explanation; it is especially important when you're explaining a process that others are going to follow. Most often you'll explain a process chronologically, from start to finish. **TRANSITIONS**—words like *first*, *next*, *then*, and so on—are often necessary, therefore, to show readers how the stages of a process relate to one another and to indicate time sequences. Finally, you'll find that verbs matter; they indicate the actions that take place at each stage of the process.

391

Explaining How Something Is Done

All processes consist of steps, and when you explain how something is done, you describe each step, generally in order, from first to last. Here, for example, is an explanation of how french fries are made, from an essay published in the *New Yorker*:

> Fast-food French fries are made from a baking potato like an Idaho russet, or any other variety that is mealy, or starchy, rather than waxy. The potatoes are harvested, cured, washed, peeled, sliced, and then blanched—cooked enough so that the insides have a fluffy texture but not so much that the fry gets soft and breaks. Blanching is followed by drying, and drying by a thirty-second deep fry, to give the potatoes a crisp shell. Then the fries are frozen until the moment of service, when they are deep-fried again, this time for somewhere around three minutes. Depending on the fast-food chain involved, there are other steps interspersed in this process. McDonald's fries, for example, are briefly dipped in a sugar solution, which gives them their golden-brown color; Burger King fries are dipped in a starch batter, which is what gives those fries their distinctive hard shell and audible crunch. But the result is similar. The potato that is first harvested in the field is roughly 80 percent water. The process of creating a French fry consists, essentially, of removing as much of that water as possible—through blanching, drying, and deep-frying—and replacing it with fat.
>
> —Malcolm Gladwell, "The Trouble with Fries"

Gladwell clearly explains the process of making french fries, showing us the specific steps—how the potatoes "are harvested, cured, washed, peeled, sliced," and so on—and using clear transitions—"followed by," "then," "until," "when"—and action verbs to show the sequence. His last sentence makes his stance clear, pointing out that the process of creating a french fry consists of removing as much of a potato's water as possible "and replacing it with fat."

Explaining How to Do Something

In explaining how to do something, you are giving instruction so that others can follow the process themselves. See how Martha Stewart explains

the process of making french fries. She starts by listing the ingredients and then describes the steps:

4 medium baking potatoes
2 tablespoons olive oil
$1\frac{1}{2}$ teaspoons salt
$\frac{1}{4}$ teaspoon freshly ground pepper
malt vinegar (optional)

1. Heat oven to 400 degrees. Place a heavy baking sheet in the oven. Scrub and rinse the potatoes well, and then cut them lengthwise into $\frac{1}{2}$-inch-wide batons. Place the potato batons in a medium bowl, and toss them with the olive oil, salt, and pepper.

2. When baking sheet is hot, about 15 minutes, remove from the oven. Place prepared potatoes on the baking sheet in a single layer. Return to oven, and bake until potatoes are golden on the bottom, about 30 minutes. Turn potatoes over, and continue cooking until golden all over, about 15 minutes more. Serve immediately.

— Martha Stewart, *Favorite Comfort Food*

Stewart's explanation leaves out no details, giving a clear sequence of steps and descriptive verbs that tell us exactly what to do: "Heat," "Place," "Scrub and rinse," and so on. After she gives the recipe, she even goes on to explain the process of *serving* the fries—"Serve these French fries with a bowl of malt vinegar"—and reminds us that "they are also delicious dipped in spicy mustard, mayonnaise, and, of course, ketchup."

Explaining a Process Visually

Some processes are best explained **VISUALLY**, with diagrams or photographs. See, for example, how a blogger explains one process of shaping dough into a bagel—giving the details in words and then showing us in photos how to do it:

653–63

Gently press dough to deflate it a bit and divide into 6 equal portions.

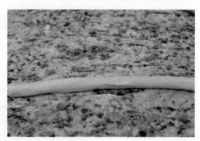

Roll each portion into a rope about 1/2-inch in diameter.

Wrap the dough around your hand like this.

Seal the ends together by rolling back and forth on the counter a few times.

Place bagels on a lined sheet pan. Allow to rise, uncovered.

—Patricia Reitz, *ButterYum*

Photos by Patricia Reitz (butteryum.org).

academic literacies　rhetorical situations　genres　fields　processes　strategies　research MLA / APA　media / design　readings　handbook

Considering the Rhetorical Situation

As always, you need to think about the message that you want to articulate, the audience you want to reach, and the larger context you are writing in.

PURPOSE Your purpose for writing will affect the way you explain a process. If you're arguing that we should avoid eating fast food, you might explain the process by which chicken nuggets are made. But to give information about how to fry chicken, you would explain the process quite differently.

 55–56

AUDIENCE Whom are you trying to reach, and will you need to provide any special background information or to interest them in the process before you explain it?

 57–60

GENRE Does your genre require you to explain a process? In a lab report, for example, you'll need to explain processes used in the experiment. You might want to explain a process in a profile of an activity or a proposal for a solution.

 61–65

STANCE If you're giving practical directions for doing something, you'll want to take a straightforward "do this, and then do that" perspective. If you're writing to entertain, you'll need to take a clever or amusing stance.

 66–68

MEDIA / DESIGN Your medium will affect the way you explain a process. In a print text, you can use both words and images. On the web, you may have the option of showing an animation of the process as well.

69–71

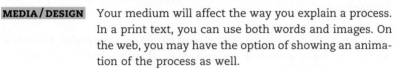

> **IF YOU NEED MORE HELP**
>
> See also **PROFILES** if you are writing about an activity that needs to be explained. See **NARRATING** for more advice on organizing an explanation chronologically. Sometimes you may be assigned to write a whole essay or report that explains a process; see **PROCESSES** for help drafting, revising, and so on.

▲ 233–45
◆ 462–70
○ 321

45 Narrating

157–84 ▲

233–45 ▲

Narratives are stories. As a writing strategy, a good narrative can lend support to most kinds of writing—in a **POSITION PAPER** arguing for Title IX compliance, for example, you might include a brief narrative about an Olympic sprinter who might never have had an opportunity to compete on a track-and-field team without Title IX. Or you can bring a **PROFILE** of a favorite coach to life with an anecdote about a pep talk they once gave before a championship track meet. Whatever your larger writing purpose, you need to make sure that any narratives you add support that purpose—they should not be inserted simply to tell an interesting story. You'll also need to compose them carefully—to put them in a clear *sequence*, include *pertinent detail*, and make sure they are appropriate to your particular rhetorical situation.

Sequencing

When we write a narrative, we arrange events in a particular sequence. Writers typically sequence narratives in chronological order, reverse chronological order, or as a flashback.

Use chronological order. Often you may tell the story chronologically, starting at the beginning of an event and working through to the end, as Maya Angelou does in this brief narrative from an essay about her high school graduation:

> The school band struck up a march and all classes filed in as had been rehearsed. We stood in front of our seats, as assigned, and on a signal from the choir director, we sat. No sooner had this been accomplished

than the band started to play the national anthem. We rose again and sang the song, after which we recited the pledge of allegiance. We remained standing for a brief minute before the choir director and the principal signaled to us, rather desperately I thought, to take our seats.   —Maya Angelou, "Graduation"

Use reverse chronological order.   You may also begin with the final action and work back to the first, as Aldo Leopold does in this narrative about cutting down a tree:

Now our saw bites into the 1890s, called gay by those whose eyes turn cityward rather than landward. We cut 1899, when the last passenger pigeon collided with a charge of shot near Babcock, two counties to the north; we cut 1898, when a dry fall, followed by a snowless winter, froze the soil seven feet deep and killed the apple trees; 1897, another drouth year, when another forestry commission came into being; 1896, when 25,000 prairie chickens were shipped to market from the village of Spooner alone; 1895, another year of fires; 1894, another drouth year; and 1893, the year of "the Bluebird Storm," when a March blizzard reduced the migrating bluebirds to near zero.

—Aldo Leopold, *A Sand County Almanac*

RÉSUMÉS are one genre where we generally use reverse chronological order, listing the most recent jobs or degrees first and then working backward. Notice, too, that we usually write these as narratives—telling what we have done rather than just naming positions we have held:

▲ 264–79

Sept. 2018–present	*Student worker*, Department of Information Management, Central State University, Wilberforce, OH. Compile data and format reports using Excel, Word, and university database.
June–Sept. 2018	*Intern*, QuestPro Corporation, West Louisville, KY. Assisted in development of software.
Sept. 2017–June 2018	*Bagger*, Ace Groceries, Elba, KY. Bagged customers' purchases.

Use a flashback. You can sometimes put a flashback in the middle of a narrative, to tell about an incident that illuminates the larger narrative. Terry Tempest Williams does this in an essay about the startling incidence of breast cancer in her family: she recalls a dinnertime conversation with her father right after her mother's death from cancer, when she learned for the first time what caused all of the cancer in her family:

> Over dessert, I shared a recurring dream of mine. I told my father that for years, as long as I could remember, I saw this flash of light in the night in the desert. That this image had so permeated my being, I could not venture south without seeing it again, on the horizon, illuminating buttes and mesas.
>
> "You did see it," he said.
>
> "Saw what?" I asked, a bit tentative.
>
> "The bomb. The cloud. We were driving home from Riverside, California. You were sitting on your mother's lap. She was pregnant. In fact, I remember the date, September 7, 1957. We had just gotten out of the Service. We were driving north, past Las Vegas. It was an hour or so before dawn, when this explosion went off. We not only heard it, but felt it. I thought the oil tanker in front of us had blown up. We pulled over and suddenly, rising from the desert floor, we saw it, clearly, this golden-stemmed cloud, the mushroom. The sky seemed to vibrate with an eerie pink glow. Within a few minutes, a light ash was raining on the car."
>
> I stared at my father. This was new information to me.
>
> —Terry Tempest Williams, "The Clan of the One-Breasted Women"

Williams could have simply announced this information as a fact—but see how much more powerful it is when told in narrative form.

Use time markers. Time markers help readers follow a sequence of events. The most obvious time markers are those that simply label the time, as the narrative entries in a diary, journal, or log might. For example, here is the final part of the narrative kept in a diary by a doomed Antarctic explorer:

WEDNESDAY, MARCH 21: Got within eleven miles of depot. Monday night; had to lay up all yesterday in severe blizzard. Today forlorn hope, Wilson and Bowers going to depot for fuel.

MARCH 22 and 23: Blizzard bad as ever—Wilson and Bowers unable to start—tomorrow last chance—no fuel and only one or two [days] of food left—must be near the end. Have decided it shall be natural— we shall march for the depot with or without our effects and die in our tracks.

THURSDAY, MARCH 29: Since the 21st we have had a continuous gale from W.S.W. and S.W. We had fuel to make two cups of tea apiece and bare food for two days on the 20th. Every day we have been ready to start for our depot eleven miles away, but outside the door of the tent it remains a scene of whirling drift. I do not think we can hope for any better things now. We shall stick it out to the end, but we are getting weaker, of course, and the end cannot be far. It seems a pity, but I do not think I can write more. . . .

Last Entry: For God's sake look after our people.

—Robert F. Scott, *Scott's Last Expedition: The Journals*

More often you will integrate time markers into the prose itself, as is done in this narrative about a woman preparing and delivering meals to workers at a cotton gin:

She made her plans meticulously and in secret. <u>One early evening</u> to see if she was ready, she placed stones in two five-gallon pails and carried them three miles to the cotton gin. She rested a little, and then, discarding some rocks, she walked in the darkness to the sawmill five miles farther along the dirt road. <u>On her way back</u> to her little house and her babies, she dumped the remaining rocks along the path.

<u>That same night</u> she worked into the early hours boiling chicken and frying ham. She made dough and filled the rolled-out pastry with meat. <u>At last</u> she went to sleep.

<u>The next morning</u> she left her house carrying the meat pies, lard, an iron brazier, and coals for a fire. <u>Just before lunch</u> she appeared in an empty lot behind the cotton gin. <u>As the dinner noon bell rang</u>, she

dropped the savors into boiling fat, and the aroma rose and floated over to the workers who spilled out of the gin, covered with white lint, looking like specters.

—Maya Angelou, *Wouldn't Take Nothing for My Journey Now*

391 ◆ **Use transitions.**   Another way to help readers follow a narrative is with TRANSITIONS, words like *first, then, meanwhile, at last,* and so on. See how the following paragraphs from Langston Hughes's classic essay about meeting Jesus use transitions (and time markers) to advance the action:

<u>Suddenly</u> the whole room broke into a sea of shouting, <u>as</u> they saw me rise. Waves of rejoicing swept the place. Women leaped in the air. My aunt threw her arms around me. The minister took me by the hand and led me to the platform.

    <u>When</u> things quieted down, in a hushed silence, punctuated by a few ecstatic "Amens," all the new young lambs were blessed in the name of God. <u>Then</u> joyous singing filled the room. <u>That night</u>, for the last time in my life but one—for I was a big boy twelve years old—I cried.   —Langston Hughes, "Salvation"

Including Pertinent Detail

When you include a narrative in your writing, you must decide which details you need—and which ones you don't need. For example, you don't want to include so much detail that the narrative distracts the reader from the larger text. You must also decide whether you need to include any background, to set the stage for the narrative. The amount of detail you include depends on your audience and purpose: How much detail does your audience need? How much detail do you need to make your meaning clear? In an essay on the suspicion African American men often face when walking at night, a journalist deliberately presents a story without setting the stage at all:

My first victim was a woman—white, well dressed, probably in her late twenties. I came upon her late one evening on a deserted street

in Hyde Park, a relatively affluent neighborhood in an otherwise mean, impoverished section of Chicago. As I swung onto the avenue behind her, there seemed to be a discreet, uninflammatory distance between us. Not so. She cast back a worried glance. To her, the youngish black man—a broad six feet two inches with a beard and billowing hair, both hands shoved into the pockets of a bulky military jacket—seemed menacingly close. After a few more quick glimpses, she picked up her pace and was soon running in earnest. Within seconds she disappeared into a cross street.   —Brent Staples, "Black Men and Public Space"

Words like "victim" and phrases like "came upon her" lead us to assume the narrator is scary and perhaps dangerous. We don't know why he is walking on the deserted street because he hasn't told us: he simply begins with the moment he and the woman encounter each other. For his purposes, that's all the audience needs to know at first, and details of his physical appearance that explain the woman's response come later, after he tells us about the encounter. Had he given us those details at the outset, the narrative would not have been nearly so effective. In a way, Staples lets the story sneak up on us, as the woman apparently felt he had on her.

Other times you'll need to provide more background information, as an MIT professor does when she uses an anecdote to introduce an essay about young children's experiences with electronic toys. First the writer tells us a little about Merlin, the computer tic-tac-toe game that the children in her anecdote play with. As you'll see, the anecdote would be hard to follow without the introduction:

Among the first generation of computational objects was Merlin, which challenged children to games of tic-tac-toe. For children who had only played games with human opponents, reaction to this object was intense. For example, while Merlin followed an optimal strategy for winning tic-tac-toe most of the time, it was programmed to make a slip every once in a while. So when children discovered strategies that allowed them to win and then tried these strategies a second time, they usually would not work. The machine gave the impression of not being "dumb enough" to let down its defenses twice. Robert, seven, playing with his friends on the beach, watched his friend Craig perform the "winning trick," but when he tried it, Merlin did not slip up and the game ended in a draw. Robert, confused and frustrated, threw Merlin into the sand and said, "Cheater. I hope your brains break." He was overheard by Craig and Greg, aged six and eight, who salvaged the by-now very sandy toy and took it upon themselves to set Robert straight. "Merlin doesn't know if it cheats," says Craig. "It doesn't know if you break it, Robert. It's not alive." Greg adds, "It's smart enough to make the right kinds of noises. But it doesn't really know if it loses. And when it cheats, it don't even know it's cheating." Jenny, six, interrupts with disdain: "Greg, to cheat you have to know you are cheating. Knowing is part of cheating."

—Sherry Turkle, "Cuddling Up to Cyborg Babies"

Opening and Closing with Narratives

373–80

Narratives are often useful as **BEGINNINGS** to essays and other kinds of writing. Everyone likes a good story, so an interesting or pithy narrative can be a good way to get your audience's attention. In the following introductory paragraph, a historian tells a gruesome but gripping story to attract our attention to a subject that might not otherwise merit our interest, bubonic plague:

In October 1347, two months after the fall of Calais, Genoese trading ships put into the harbor of Messina in Sicily with dead and dying men at the oars. The ships had come from the Black Sea port of Caffa (now Feodosiya) in the Crimea, where the Genoese maintained a trading post. The diseased sailors showed strange black swellings about the size of an egg or an apple in the armpits and groin. The swellings oozed blood and pus and were followed by spreading boils and black blotches on the skin from internal bleeding. The sick suffered severe pain and died quickly, within five days of the first symptoms. As the disease spread, other symptoms of continuous fever and spitting of blood appeared instead of the swellings or buboes. These victims coughed and sweated heavily and died even more quickly, within three days or less, sometimes in twenty-four hours. In both types everything that issued from the body—breath, sweat, blood from the buboes and lungs, bloody urine, and blood-blackened excrement—smelled foul. Depression and despair accompanied the physical symptoms, and before the end "death is seen seated on the face."

—Barbara Tuchman, "This Is the End of the World: The Black Death"

Imagine how different the preceding paragraph would be if it weren't in the form of a narrative. Imagine, for example, that Tuchman began by defining bubonic plague. Would that have gotten your interest? The piece was written for a general audience; how might it have been different if it had been written for scientists? Would they need (or appreciate) the story told here?

Narrative can be a good way of **ENDING** a text, too, by winding up a discussion with an illustration of the main point. Here, for instance, is a concluding paragraph from an essay on American values and Las Vegas weddings.

◆ 380–85

I sat next to one . . . wedding party in a Strip restaurant the last time I was in Las Vegas. The marriage had just taken place; the bride still wore her dress, the mother her corsage. A bored waiter poured out a few swallows of pink champagne ("on the house") for everyone but the bride, who was too young to be served. "You'll need something with more kick than that," the bride's father said with heavy jocularity to his new son-in-law; the ritual jokes about the wedding night had a certain Panglossian character, since the bride was clearly several months pregnant. Another round of pink champagne, this time not on the house, and the bride began to cry. "It was just as nice," she sobbed, "as I hoped and dreamed it would be."

—Joan Didion, "Marrying Absurd"

No doubt Didion makes her points about American values clearly and cogently in the essay. But concluding with this story lets us *see* (and hear) what she is saying about Las Vegas wedding chapels, which sell "'niceness,' the facsimile of proper ritual, to children who do not know how else to find it, how to make the arrangements, how to do it 'right.'"

Considering the Rhetorical Situation

As a writer or speaker, you need to think about the message that you want to articulate, the audience you want to reach, and the larger context you are writing in.

55–56   **PURPOSE**   Your purpose will affect the way you use narrative. For example, in an essay about seat belt laws, you might tell about the painful rehabilitation of a teenager who was not wearing a seat belt and was injured in an accident in order to persuade readers that seat belt use should be mandatory.

57–60   **AUDIENCE**   Whom do you want to reach, and do you have an anecdote or other narrative that will help them understand your topic or persuade them that your argument has merit?

61–65   **GENRE**   Does your genre require you to include narrative? A memoir about an important event might be primarily narrative, whereas a reflection about an event might focus more on the significance of the event than on what happened.

66–68   **STANCE**   What is your stance, and do you have any stories that would help you convey that stance? A funny story, for example, can help create a humorous stance.

69–71   **MEDIA / DESIGN**   In a print or spoken text, you will likely be limited to brief narratives, perhaps illustrated with photos or other images. In an electronic text, you might have the option of linking to full-length narratives or visuals available on the web.

IF YOU NEED MORE HELP

321

Glossary
264–79

See also the **PROCESSES** chapters if you are assigned to write a narrative essay and need help drafting, revising, and so on. Two special kinds of narratives are **LAB REPORTS** (which use narrative to describe the steps in an experiment from beginning to end) and **RÉSUMÉS** (which essentially tell the story of the work we've done, at school and on the job).

academic literacies · rhetorical situations · genres · fields · processes · strategies · research MLA / APA · media / design · readings · handbook

Taking Essay Exams 46

Essay exams present writers with special challenges. You must write quickly, on a topic presented to you on the spot, to show your instructor what you know about a specific body of information. This chapter offers advice on how to take essay exams.

Considering the Rhetorical Situation

PURPOSE   In an essay exam, your purpose is to show that you have mastered certain material and that you can analyze and apply it in an essay. You may need to make an argument or simply to convey information on a topic.   55–56

AUDIENCE   Will your course instructor be reading your exam, or a teaching assistant? Sometimes standardized tests are read by groups of trained readers. What specific criteria will your audience use to evaluate your writing?   57–60

GENRE   Does the essay question specify or suggest a certain genre? In a literature course, you may need to write a compelling literary analysis of a passage. In a history course, you may need to write an argument for the significance of a key historical event. In an economics course, you may need to contrast the economies of the North and South before the Civil War. If the essay question doesn't specify a genre, look for keywords such as *argue*, *evaluate*, or *explain*, which point to a certain genre.   61–65

STANCE   In an essay exam, your stance is usually unemotional, thoughtful, and critical.   66–68

69–71 ■

MEDIA / DESIGN Since essay exams are usually handwritten on lined paper or in an exam booklet, legible handwriting is a must. If you are taking an online test, write your essays in a word-processing program, edit there, and then paste them into the exam.

Analyzing Essay Questions

Essay questions usually include key verbs that specify the kind of writing you'll need to do—argue a position, compare two texts, and so on. Here are some of the most common kinds of writing you'll be asked to do on an essay exam:

98–130 ▲

- *Analyze.* Break an idea, theory, text, or event into its parts and examine them. For example, a world history exam might ask you to **ANALYZE** European imperialism's effect on Africa in the late nineteenth century and discuss how Africans responded.

- *Apply*. Consider how an idea or concept might work out in practice. For instance, a film studies exam might ask you to apply the concept of auteurism—a theory of film that sees the director as the primary creator, whose body of work reflects a distinct personal style—to two films by Clint Eastwood. An economics exam might ask you to apply the concept of opportunity costs to a certain supplied scenario.

397–417 ◆

- *Argue/prove/justify*. Offer reasons and evidence to support a position. A philosophy exam, for example, might ask you to **ARGUE** whether or not all stereotypes contain a "kernel of truth" and whether believing a stereotype is ever justified.

418–23 ◆

- *Classify.* Group something into categories. For example, a marketing exam might ask you to **CLASSIFY** shoppers in categories based on their purchasing behavior, motives, attitudes, or lifestyle patterns.

- *Compare/contrast.* Explore the similarities and/or differences between two or more things. An economics exam, for example, might ask you to **COMPARE** the effectiveness of patents and tax incentives in encouraging technological advances.

  424–31

- *Critique.* **ANALYZE** and **EVALUATE** a text or argument, considering its strengths and weaknesses. For instance, an evolutionary biology exam might ask you to critique John Maynard Smith's assertion that "scientific theories say nothing about what is right but only about what is possible" in the context of the theory of evolution.

  98–130
  202–10

- *Define.* Explain what a word or phrase means. An art history exam, for example, might ask you to **DEFINE** negative space and discuss the way various artists use it in their work.

  432–42

- *Describe.* Tell about the important characteristics or features of something. For example, a sociology exam might ask you to **DESCRIBE** Erving Goffman's theory of the presentation of self in ordinary life, focusing on roles, props, and setting.

  443–51

- *Evaluate.* Determine something's significance or value. A drama exam, for example, might ask you to **EVALUATE** the setting, lighting, and costumes in a filmed production of *Macbeth*.

  202–10

- *Explain.* Provide reasons and examples to clarify an idea, argument, or event. For instance, a rhetoric exam might ask you to explain the structure of the African American sermon and discuss its use in writings of Frederick Douglass and Martin Luther King Jr.

- *Summarize/review.* Give the major points of a text or idea. A political science exam, for example, might ask you to **SUMMARIZE** John Stuart Mill's concept of utilitarianism and its relation to freedom of speech.

  534–35

- *Trace.* Explain a sequence of ideas or order of events. For instance, a geography exam might ask you to trace the patterns of international migration since 1970 and discuss how these patterns differ from those of the period between 1870 and World War I.

Some Guidelines for Taking Essay Exams

Before the exam

16–17 ✳
- *Read* over your class notes and course texts strategically, **ANNOTATING** them to keep track of details you'll want to remember.

327–28 ◉
- *Collaborate* by forming a **STUDY GROUP** to help one another master the course content.

519–23 ●
- *Review* key ideas, events, terms, and themes. Look for common themes and **CONNECTIONS** in lecture notes, class discussions, and any read-ings—they'll lead you to important ideas.

- *Ask* your instructor about the form the exam will take: how long it will be, what kind of questions will be on it, how it will be evaluated, and so on. Working with a study group, write questions you think your instructor might ask, and then answer the questions together.

331–32 ◉
- *Warm up* just before the exam by **FREEWRITING** for 10 minutes or so to gather your thoughts.

During the exam

- *Scan the questions* to determine how much each part of the test counts and how much time you should spend on it. For example, if one essay is worth 50 points and two others are worth 25 points each, you'll want to spend half your time on the 50-point question.

- *Read over* the entire test before answering any questions. Start with the question you feel most confident answering, which may or may not be the first question on the test.

- *Don't panic.* Sometimes when students first read an essay question, their minds go blank, but after a few moments they start to recall the information they need.

- *Plan.* Although you won't have much time for revising or editing, you still need to plan and allow yourself time to make some last-minute

changes before you turn in the exam. So apportion your time. For a three-question essay test in a two-hour test period, you might divide your time like this:

Total Exam Time—120 minutes
Generating ideas—20 minutes (6–7 minutes per question)
Drafting—85 minutes (45 for the 50-point question,
                          20 for each 25-point question)
Revising, editing, proofreading—15 minutes

Knowing that you have built in time at the end of the exam period can help you remain calm as you write, as you can use that time to fill in gaps or reconsider answers you feel unsure about.

- *Jot down the main ideas* you need to cover in answering the question on scratch paper or on the cover of your exam book, number those ideas in the order you think makes sense—and you have an outline for your essay. If you're worried about time, plan to write the most important parts of your answers early on. If you don't complete your answer, refer your instructor to your outline to show where you were headed.

- *Turn the essay question into your introduction,* like this:

    Question: How did the outcomes of World War II differ from those of World War I?

    Introduction: The outcomes of World War II differed from those of World War I in three major ways: World War II affected more of the world and its people than World War I did, distinctions between citizens and soldiers were eroded, and the war's brutality made it impossible for Europe to continue to claim cultural superiority over other cultures.

- *State your thesis explicitly,* provide **REASONS** and **EVIDENCE** to support your thesis, and use transitions to move logically from one idea to the next. Restate your main point in your conclusion. You don't want to give what one professor calls a "garbage truck answer," dumping everything you know into a blue book and expecting the instructor to sort it all out.

◆ 400–408

- **Write on *every other line*** and only on one side of each page so that you'll have room to make additions or corrections. If you're typing on a computer, double space.
- ***If you have time left, go over your exam,*** looking for ideas that need elaboration as well as for grammatical and punctuation errors.

After the exam.   If your instructor doesn't return your exam, consider asking for a conference to go over your work so you can learn what you did well and where you need to improve—important knowledge to take with you into your next exam.

part 7

Doing Research

We do research all the time, for many different reasons. We search the web for information about a new computer, ask friends about the best place to get coffee, try on several pairs of jeans before deciding which ones to buy. You have no doubt done your share of library research before now, and you probably have visited a number of schools' websites before deciding which college you wanted to attend. Research, in other words, is something you do every day. The following chapters offer advice on the kind of research you'll need to do for your academic work and, in particular, for research projects.

Doing Research

Getting a Start on Research **47**

When you need to do research, it's sometimes tempting to jump in and start looking for information right away. However, doing research is complex and time-consuming. Research-based writing projects usually require you to follow several steps. You need to come up with a topic (or to analyze the requirements of an assigned topic) and come up with a research question to guide your research efforts. Once you do some serious, focused research to find the information you need, you'll be ready to turn your research question into a tentative thesis and sketch out a rough outline. After doing whatever additional research you need to fill in your outline, you'll write a draft—and get some response to that draft. You may then need to do additional research before revising. Once you revise, you'll need to edit and proofread. In other words, there's a lot to do. You need a schedule.

Establishing a Schedule and Getting Started

A good place to start a research project is by creating a time line for getting all this work done, perhaps using the form on the next page. Once you have a schedule, you can get started. The sections that follow offer advice on considering your rhetorical situation, coming up with a topic, and doing preliminary research; developing a research question, a tentative thesis, and a rough outline; and creating a working bibliography and keeping track of your sources. The chapters that follow offer guidelines for **FINDING SOURCES**, **EVALUATING SOURCES**, and **SYNTHESIZING IDEAS**.

459–510
511–18
519–25

academic literacies

rhetorical situations

genres

fields

processes

strategies

research MLA / APA

media / design

readings

handbook

Scheduling a Research Project

Complete by:

Analyze your rhetorical situation. _____

Choose a possible topic or analyze the assignment. _____

Plan a research strategy and do
    preliminary research. _____

Come up with a research question. _____

Schedule interviews and other field research. _____

Find sources. _____

Read sources and take notes. _____

Do any field research. _____

Come up with a tentative thesis and outline. _____

Write a draft. _____

Get response. _____

Do any additional research. _____

Revise. _____

Prepare a list of works cited. _____

Edit. _____

Proofread the final draft. _____

Submit the final draft. _____

Considering the Rhetorical Situation

As with any writing task, you need to start by considering your purpose,
your audience, and the rest of your rhetorical situation:

55–56 ■ **PURPOSE**   Is this project part of an assignment—and if so, does
it specify any one purpose? If not, what is your broad
purpose? To inform? argue? analyze? A combination?

57–60 ■ **AUDIENCE**   To whom are you writing? What does your audience
likely know about your topic, and is there any back-

academic literacies · rhetorical situations · genres · fields · processes · strategies · research MLA / APA · media / design · readings · handbook

ground information you'll need to provide? What opinions or attitudes do your readers likely hold? What kinds of evidence will they find persuasive? How do you want them to respond to your writing?

GENRE   Are you writing to report on something? to compose a profile? to make a proposal? an argument? What are the requirements of your genre in terms of the number and kind of sources you must use?

61–65

STANCE   What is your attitude toward your topic? What accounts for your attitude? How do you want to come across? Curious? Critical? Positive? Something else?

66–68

MEDIA / DESIGN   What medium or media will you use? Print? Spoken? Electronic? Will you need to create any charts, photographs, video, presentation software slides, or other visuals?

69–71

Coming Up with a Topic

If you need to choose a topic, consider your interests as they relate to the course for which you're writing. What do you want to learn about? What do you have questions about? What topics from the course have you found intriguing? What community, national, or global issues do you care about? Once you've thought of a potential topic, use the questions in Chapter 27, **WRITING AS INQUIRY**, to explore it and find an angle on it that you can write about—and want to.

323–26

If your topic is assigned, you need to make sure you understand exactly what it asks you to do. Read the assignment carefully, looking for keywords: does it ask you to **ANALYZE**, **COMPARE**, **EVALUATE**, **SUMMARIZE**, or **ARGUE**? If the assignment offers broad guidelines but allows you to choose within them, identify the requirements and the range of possible topics and define your topic within those constraints.

98–130
424–31
202–10
534–35
397–417

For example, in an American history course, your instructor might ask you to "discuss social effects of the Civil War." Potential but broad topics might include poverty among Confederate soldiers or former slaveholders, the migration of members of those groups to Mexico or Northern cities, the establishment of independent African American churches, or the spread of the Ku Klux Klan—to name only a few of the possibilities.

Think about what you know about your topic. Chances are you already know something about your topic, and articulating that knowledge can help you see possible ways to focus your topic or come up with potential sources of information. FREEWRITING, LISTING, CLUSTERING, and LOOPING are all good ways of tapping your knowledge of your topic. Consider where you might find information about it: Have you read about it in a textbook? heard stories about it on the news? visited websites focused on it? Do you know anyone who knows about this topic?

331–34 ○

Narrow the topic. As you consider possible topics, look for ways to narrow your topic's focus to make it specific enough to discuss in depth. For example:

> **Too general:** fracking
>
> **Still too general:** fracking and the environment
>
> **Better:** the potential environmental effects of extracting natural gas through the process of hydraulic fracturing, or fracking

If you limit your topic, you can address it with specific information that you'll be more easily able to find and manage. In addition, a limited topic will be more likely to interest your audience than a broad topic that forces you to use abstract, general statements. For example, it's much harder to write well about "the environment" than it is to address a topic that explores a single environmental issue.

Consulting with Librarians and Doing Preliminary Research

Consulting with a reference librarian at your school and doing some preliminary research in the library can save you time in the long run. Reference librarians can direct you to the best scholarly sources for your topic and help you focus your topic by determining appropriate search terms and KEYWORDS—significant words that appear in the title, abstract, or text of

495–98 ●

potential sources and that you can use to search for information on your topic in library catalogs, in databases, and on the web. These librarians can also help you choose the most appropriate reference works, sources that provide general overviews of the scholarship in a field. General internet searches can be time-consuming, as they often result in thousands of possible sites—too many to weed out efficiently, either by revising your search terms or by going through the sites themselves, many of which are unreliable. Library databases, on the other hand, include only sources that already have been selected by experts, and searches in them usually present manageable numbers of results.

Wikipedia can often serve as a jumping-off point for preliminary research, but since its entries are written and edited by people who may not have expertise in the subject, it is not considered a reliable academic source. Specialized encyclopedias, however, usually present subjects in much greater depth and provide more scholarly references that might suggest starting points for your research. Even if you know a lot about a subject, doing preliminary research can open you to new ways of seeing and approaching it, increasing your options for developing and narrowing your topic.

Coming Up with a Research Question

Once you've surveyed the territory of your topic, you'll likely find that your understanding of the topic has become broader and deeper. You may find that your interests have changed and your research has led to surprises and additional research. That's okay: as a result of exploring avenues you hadn't anticipated, you may well come up with a better topic than the one you'd started with. At some point, though, you need to develop a research question—a specific question that you will then work to answer through your research.

To write a research question, review your analysis of the **RHETORICAL SITUATION**, to remind yourself of any time constraints or length consider-ations. Generate a list of questions beginning with *What? When? Where? Who? How? Why? Would? Could?* and *Should?* Here, for example, are some questions

53

about the tentative topic "the potential environmental effects of extracting natural gas through the process of hydraulic fracturing, or fracking":

What are the environmental effects of fracking?

When was fracking introduced as a way to produce natural gas?

Where is fracking done, and how does this affect the surrounding people and environment?

Who will benefit from increased fracking?

How much energy does fracking use?

Why do some environmental groups oppose fracking?

Would other methods of extracting natural gas be safer?

Could fracking cause earthquakes?

Should fracking be expanded, regulated, or banned?

Select one question from your list that you find interesting and that suits your rhetorical situation. Use the question to guide your research.

Drafting a Tentative Thesis

387–89

Once your research has led you to a possible answer to your research question, try formulating that answer as a tentative **THESIS**. You need not be committed to the thesis; in fact, you should not be. The object of your research should be to learn about your topic, not to find information that simply supports what you already think you believe. Your tentative thesis may (and probably will) change as you learn more about your subject, consider the many points of view on it, and reconsider your topic and, perhaps, your goal: what you originally planned to be an argument for considering other points of view may become a call to action. However tentative, a thesis allows you to move forward by clarifying your purpose for doing research. Here are some tentative thesis statements on the topic of fracking:

Fracking is a likely cause of earthquakes in otherwise seismically stable regions of the country.

The federal government should strictly regulate the production of natural gas by fracking.

Fracking can greatly increase our supplies of natural gas, but other methods of producing energy should still be pursued.

As with a research question, a tentative thesis should guide your research efforts—but be ready to revise it as you learn still more about your topic. Research should be a process of **INQUIRY** in which you approach your topic with an open mind, ready to learn and possibly change. If you hold too tightly to a tentative thesis, you risk focusing only on evidence that supports your view, making your writing biased and unconvincing.

323–26

Creating a Rough Outline

After you've created a tentative thesis, write out a rough **OUTLINE** for your research project. Your outline can be a simple list of topics you want to explore, something that will help you structure your research efforts and organize your notes and other materials. As you read your sources, you can use your outline to keep track of what you need to find and where the information you do find fits into your argument. Then you'll be able to see if you've covered all the ideas you intended to explore—or whether you need to rethink the categories on your outline.

335–37

Keeping a Working Bibliography

A working bibliography is a record of all the sources you consult. You should keep such a record so that you can find sources easily when you need them and then cite any that you use. Your library likely offers tools to store source information you find in its databases and catalog, and software such as *Zotero* or *EasyBib* can also help you save, manage, and cite your sources. You may find it helpful to print out bibliographical data you find useful or to keep your working bibliography on index cards or in a notebook. However you decide to compile your working bibliography, include all the information you'll need later to document any sources you use; follow the **DOCUMENTATION** style you'll use when you write so that

544–47

Information for a Working Bibliography

FOR A BOOK

Library call number
Author(s) or editor(s)
Title and subtitle
Publication information: city, publisher, year of publication
Other information: edition, volume number, translator, and so on
If your source is an essay in a collection, include its author, title, and page numbers.

FOR A SOURCE FROM A DATABASE

Publication information for the source, as listed above
Name of database
DOI (digital object identifier) or URL of original source, such as the periodical in which an article was published.
Stable URL or permalink for database
Date you accessed source

FOR AN ARTICLE IN A PRINT PERIODICAL

Author(s)
Title and subtitle
Name of periodical
Volume number, issue number, date
Page numbers

FOR A WEB SOURCE

URL
Author(s) or editor(s) if available
Name of site
Sponsor of site
Date site was first posted or last updated
Date you accessed site
If the source is an article or book reprinted on the web, include its title, the title and publication information of the periodical or book, where it was first published, and any page numbers.

academic literacies · rhetorical situations · genres · fields · processes · strategies · research MLA / APA · media / design · readings · handbook

you won't need to go back to your sources to find the information. Some databases make this step easy by preparing rough-draft citations in several styles that you can copy, paste, and edit.

On the previous page is most of the basic information you'll want to include for each source in your working bibliography. Go to digital.wwnorton.com/fieldguide5rh for a worksheet you can use to keep track of this information.

Keeping Track of Your Sources

- *Staple together photocopies and printouts.* It's easy for individual pages to get shuffled or lost on a desk or in a backpack. Keep a stapler handy, and fasten pages together as soon as you copy them or print them out.

- *Bookmark web sources* or save them using a free bookmark management tool available through several library databases. For database sources, use the *DOI* or *stable URL*, *permalink*, or *document URL* (the terms used by databases vary)—not the URL in the "Address" or "Location" box in your browser, which will expire after you end your online session.

- *Label everything.* Label your copies with the source's author and title.

- *Highlight sections you plan to use.* When you sit down to draft, your goal will be to find what you need quickly, so as soon as you decide you might use a source, highlight the paragraphs or sentences that you think you'll use. If your instructor wants copies of your sources to see how you used them, you've got them ready. If you're using PDF copies, you can highlight or add notes using *Adobe Reader*.

- *Use your rough outline to keep track of what you've got.* In the margin of each highlighted section, write the number or letter of the outline division to which the section corresponds. (It's a good idea to write it in the same place consistently so you can flip through a stack of copies and easily see what you've got.) Alternatively, attach sticky notes to each copy, using a different color for each main heading in your outline.

- *Keep everything in an online folder, file folder, or box.* Keep everything related to your research in one place. If you create online subfolders or create folders that correspond to your rough outline, you'll be able to organize your material, at least tentatively. And if you highlight, label, and use sticky notes, your material will be even better organized, making writing a draft easier. The folder or box will also serve you well if you are required to create a portfolio that includes your research notes, copies of sources, and drafts.

- *Use a reference manager.* Web-based reference or citation management software allows you to create and organize a personal database of resources. You can import references from databases to a personal account, organize them, and draft citations in various formats. *RefWorks, EndNote, Mendeley,* and *Zotero* are four such systems; check with your librarian to see what system your library supports, or search online, as several of them are available for free. Be aware, though, that the citations generated are often inaccurate and need to be checked carefully for content and format. So treat them as rough drafts and plan to edit them.

489–510

511–18

> **IF YOU NEED MORE HELP**
>
> See the guidelines on **FINDING SOURCES** once you're ready to move on to in-depth research and those on **EVALUATING SOURCES** for help thinking critically about the sources you find.

academic literacies | rhetorical situations | genres | fields | processes | strategies | research MLA / APA | media / design | readings | handbook

Finding Sources **48**

To analyze media coverage of the 2016 Democratic National Convention, you examine news stories and blogs published at the time. To write an essay interpreting a poem by Maya Angelou, you study the poem and read several critical interpretations in literary journals. To write a report on career opportunities in psychology, you interview a graduate of your university who is working in a psychology clinic. In each of these cases, you go beyond your own knowledge to consult additional sources of information.

This chapter offers guidelines for locating a range of sources—print and online, general and specialized, published and firsthand. Keep in mind that as you do research, finding and **EVALUATING SOURCES** are two activities that usually take place simultaneously. So this chapter and the next one go hand in hand.

511–18

Kinds of Sources

Primary and secondary sources.   Your research will likely lead you to both primary and secondary sources. *Primary sources* include historical documents, literary works, eyewitness accounts, field reports, diaries, letters, and lab studies, as well as any original research you do through interviews, observation, experiments, or surveys. *Secondary sources* include scholarly books and articles, reviews, biographies, textbooks, and other works that interpret or discuss primary sources. Novels and films are primary sources; articles interpreting them are secondary sources. The Declaration of Independence is a primary historical document; a historian's description of the events surrounding the Declaration's writing is secondary. A published report of scientific findings is primary; a critique of that report is secondary.

Whether a work is considered primary or secondary sometimes depends on your topic and purpose. If you're analyzing a poem, a critic's article interpreting the poem is a secondary source—but if you're investigating that critic's work, the article would be a primary source for your own study and interpretation.

Secondary sources are often useful because they can help you understand and evaluate primary source material. Whenever possible, however, you should find and use primary sources, because secondary sources can distort or misrepresent the information in primary sources. For example, a seemingly reputable secondary source describing the 1948 presidential election asserted that the *New York Times* ran a headline reading, "Thomas E. Dewey's Election as President Is a Foregone Conclusion." But the actual article was titled "Talk Is Now Turning to the Dewey Cabinet," and it began by noting "[the] *popular view that* Gov. Thomas E. Dewey's election as President is a foregone conclusion." Here the secondary source got not only the headline wrong but also distorted the source's intended meaning by leaving out an important phrase. Your research should be as accurate and reliable as it can be; using primary sources whenever you can helps ensure that it is.

Scholarly and popular sources. Scholarly sources are written by academic experts or scholars in a particular discipline and are *peer-reviewed*— evaluated by other experts in the same discipline for their factual accuracy and lack of bias. They are also written largely *for* experts in a discipline, as a means of sharing research, insights, and in-depth analysis with one another; that's why they must meet high standards of accuracy and objectivity and adhere to the discipline's accepted research methods, including its style for documenting sources. Scholarly articles are usually published in academic journals; scholarly books may be published by university presses or by other academically focused publishers.

Popular sources include just about all other online and print publications, from websites to magazines to books written for nonspecialists. These sources generally explain or provide opinion on current events or topics of general interest; when they discuss scholarly research, they tend to simplify the concepts and facts, providing definitions, narratives, and examples to make them understandable to nonspecialist audiences. They are often written by journalists or other professional writers who may spe-

academic literacies · rhetorical situations · genres · fields · processes · strategies · research MLA / APA · media / design · readings · handbook

cialize in a particular area but who report or comment on the scholarship of others rather than doing any themselves. Their most important difference from scholarly sources is that popular sources are not reviewed by other experts in the field being discussed, although editors or fact-checkers review the writing before it's published.

In most of your college courses, you'll be expected to rely primarily on scholarly sources rather than popular ones. However, if you're writing about a very current topic or need to provide background information on a topic, a mix of scholarly and popular sources may be appropriate. To see how scholarly and popular sources differ in appearance, look at the Documentation Map for scholarly journals (p. 564) and at the illustrations on pages 492–93. Here's a guide to determining whether or not a potential source is scholarly:

IDENTIFYING SCHOLARLY SOURCES: WHAT TO LOOK FOR

- *Author.* Look for the author's scholarly credentials, including affiliations with academic or other research-oriented institutions.

- *Peer review.* Look for a list of reviewers at the front of the journal or on the journal's or publisher's website. If you don't find one, the source is probably not peer-reviewed.

- *Source citations.* Look for a detailed list of works cited or references at the end of the source and citations either parenthetically within the text or in footnotes or endnotes. (Popular sources may include a reference list but seldom cite sources within the text, except in signal phrases.)

- *Publisher.* Look for publishers that are professional scholarly organizations, such as the Modern Language Association or the Organization of American Historians, that are affiliated with universities or colleges, or that have a stated academic mission.

- *Language and content.* Look for abstracts (one-paragraph summaries of the contents) at the beginning of articles and for technical or specialized language and concepts that readers are assumed to be familiar with.

- *Other clues.* Look for little or no advertising on websites or within the journal; for a plain design with few or no illustrations, especially in print sources; and for listing in academic databases when you limit your search to *academic, peer-reviewed,* or *scholarly sources.*

Scholarly Source

Published in an academic journal.

Includes an abstract.

Cites academic research with consistent documentation style.

Describes research methods, includes numerical data.

Multiple authors who are academics.

Includes complete references list.

academic literacies

rhetorical situations

genres

fields

processes

strategies

research MLA / APA

media / design

readings

handbook

Popular Source

Published in general-interest periodical or website.

Catchy, provocative title; no abstract.

Author not an academic or other subject matter expert.

Academic experts cited but not documented.

Print and online sources.   Some sources are available only in print; some are available only online. But many print sources are also available on the web. You'll find print sources in your school's library, but chances are that many reference books and academic journal articles in your library will also be available online. In general, for academic writing it's best to try to find most of your online sources through the library's website rather than commercial search sites, which may lead you to unreliable sources and cause you to spend much more time sorting and narrowing search results.

Searching in Academic Libraries

College and university libraries typically offer several ways to search their holdings. Take a look at this search box, from the homepage of the Houston Community College libraries:

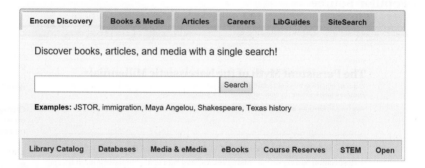

This box allows you to search through all the library's holdings at once an option that may be a good way to get started. You may already know, though, that you need to focus your search on one type of source, such as scholarly articles, leading you to choose the Articles search tab.

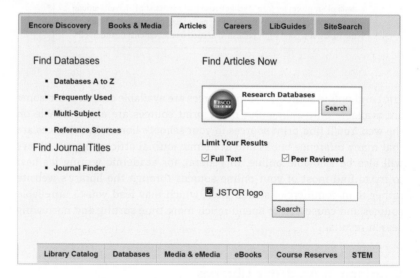

This box lets you shape and limit your search in several ways: by selecting a specific database, by choosing to search only for full-text articles

and only peer-reviewed articles, and by searching within a specific journal. "Ask a Librarian" options can be very useful; many libraries offer email, texting, chat, and phone conversations with reference librarians when you need help but aren't working in the library.

Searching Effectively Using Keywords

Whether you're searching for books, articles in periodicals, or other material available on the web, chances are you'll conduct most of your search online. Most materials produced since the 1980s and most library catalogs are online, and most periodical articles can be found by searching electronic indexes and databases. In each case, you can search for authors, titles, or subjects.

To search online, you'll need to come up with keywords. Keywords are significant words that stand for an idea or concept. The key to searching efficiently is to use keywords and combinations of them that will focus your searches on the information you need—but not too much of it. Often you'll start out with one general keyword that will yield far too many results; then you'll need to switch to more specific terms or combinations (*homeopathy* instead of *medicine* or *secondary education Japan* instead of *education Japan*).

Other times your keyword search won't yield enough sources; then you'll need to use broader terms or combinations (*education Japan* instead of *secondary education Japan*) or substitute synonyms (*home remedy* instead of *folk medicine*). Sometimes you'll need to learn terms used in academic disciplines or earlier in history for things you know by other names, such as *myocardial infarction* rather than *heart attack* or *the Great War* instead of *World War I*. Or look through the sources that turn up in response to other terms to see what keywords you might use in subsequent searches. Searching requires flexibility, in the words you use and the methods you try.

Finding keywords using word clouds.   One way to find keywords to help you narrow and focus your topic is to create a word cloud, a visual representation of words used in a text; the more often a word is used, the larger it looks in the word cloud. Several websites, including *Tagxedo*, *Wordle*, and *TagCrowd*, let you create word clouds. Examining a word cloud created from an article in a reference work may help you see what terms are used to discuss your topic—and may help you see new possible ways to narrow it. Above, for example, is a word cloud derived from an article in *Scientific American* discussing fracking. Many of the terms—*fracking, water, gas, wells, drilling*—are just what you'd expect. However, some terms—*USGS, DiGiulio, coalfired*—may be unfamiliar and lead to additional possibilities for research. For instance, *DiGiulio* is the last name of an expert on fracking whose publications might be worth examining, while *USGS* is an acronym for the United States Geological Survey, a scientific government agency.

Finding keywords using databases.   Once you've begun searching for and finding possible sources, you can expand your list of possible keywords by skimming the "detailed record" or "metadata" page for any scholarly articles you find, where full bibliographic information on the source may be found. A search for *fracking* resulted in this source:

Note the list of author-supplied keywords, which offers options for narrowing and focusing your topic. Each keyword is a link, so simply clicking on it will produce a new list of sources.

Advanced keyword searching.   Most search sites have "advanced search" options that will help you focus your research. Some allow you to ask

questions in conversational language: *What did Thomas Jefferson write about slavery?* Others allow you to focus your search by using specific words or symbols. Here are some of the most common ones:

- Type quotation marks around words to search for an exact phrase— "Thomas Jefferson."

- Type AND to specify that more than one keyword must appear in sources: Jefferson AND Adams. Some search engines require a plus sign instead: +Jefferson +Adams.

- Type OR if you're looking for sources that include any of several terms: Jefferson OR Adams OR Madison.

- Type NOT to find sources *without* a certain word: Jefferson NOT Adams. Some search engines call for a minus sign (actually, a hyphen) instead: +Jefferson –Adams.

- Type an asterisk to search for words in different form. For example, teach* will yield sources containing *teacher* and *teaching*.

Reference Works

The reference section of your school's library is the place to find encyclopedias, dictionaries, atlases, almanacs, bibliographies, and other reference works in print. Many of these sources are also online and can be accessed from any computer that is connected to the internet. Others are available only in the library. Remember, though, that whether in print or online, reference works are only a starting point, a place where you can get an overview of your topic.

General reference works. Consult encyclopedias for general background information on a subject, dictionaries for definitions of words, atlases for maps and geographic data, and almanacs for statistics and other data on current events. These are some works you might consult:

The New Encyclopaedia Britannica

The Columbia Encyclopedia

Webster's Third New International Dictionary

Oxford English Dictionary

National Geographic Atlas of the World

Statistical Abstract of the United States

The World Almanac and Book of Facts

Caution: *Wikipedia* is a popular online research tool, but since anyone can edit its entries, you can't be certain of its accuracy. Use it for general overviews, but look elsewhere—including *Wikipedia*'s own references and citations—for authoritative sources.

Specialized reference works. You can also go to specialized reference works, which provide in-depth information on a single field or topic. These may also include authoritative bibliographies, leading you to more specific works. A reference librarian can refer you to specialized encyclopedias in particular fields, but good places to start are online collections of many topic-specific reference works that offer overviews of a topic, place it in a larger context, and sometimes provide links to potential academic sources. Collections that are available through libraries include the following:

CQ Researcher offers in-depth reports on topics in education, health, the environment, criminal justice, international affairs, technology, the economy, and social trends. Each report gives an overview of a particular topic, outlines of the differing positions on it, and a bibliography of resources on it.

Gale Virtual Reference Library (*GVRL*) offers thousands of full-text specialized encyclopedias, almanacs, articles, and ebooks.

Oxford Reference contains hundreds of dictionaries, encyclopedias, and other reference works on a wide variety of subjects, as well as timelines with links to each item mentioned on each timeline.

SAGE Knowledge includes many encyclopedias and handbooks on topics in the social sciences.

Bibliographies.　Bibliographies provide an overview of what has been published on a topic, listing published works along with the information you'll need to find each work. Some are annotated with brief summaries of each work's contents. You'll find bibliographies at the end of scholarly articles and books, and you can also find book-length bibliographies, both in the reference section of your library and online. Check with a reference librarian for bibliographies on your research topic.

Books / Searching the Library Catalog

The library catalog is your primary source for finding books. Almost all library catalogs are computerized and can be accessed through the library's website. You can search by author, title, subject, or keyword. The image below shows the result of a keyword search for material on looted art in Nazi Germany. This search of the library's catalog revealed six items—print books and ebooks—on the topic; to access information on each one, the researcher must simply click on the title or thumbnail image. The image on the next page shows detailed information for one source: bibliographic data about author, title, and publication;

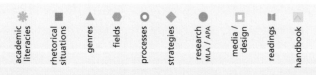

related subject headings (which may lead to other useful materials in the library)—and more. Library catalogs also supply a call number, which identifies the book's location on the library's shelves.

Ebooks / Finding Books Online

Many books in the library catalog are available online. Some may be downloaded to a tablet or mobile device. In addition, thousands of classic works that are in the public domain—no longer protected by copyright—may be read online. *Bartleby*, *Google Books*, *Open Library*, and *Project Gutenberg* are four collections of public-domain works. Here are some other sources of ebooks:

> *Hathi Trust Digital Library* offers access to millions of ebooks, about a third of them in the public domain, contributed by university libraries.

> *Internet Archive* includes millions of ebooks as well as audio, video, music, software, images, and the Way Back Machine, which archives historical webpages.

> The *Gale Virtual Reference Library (GVRL)*, *Oxford Reference*, and *SAGE Knowledge* all contain large ebook collections.

Periodicals / Searching Indexes and Databases

To find journal, magazine, and newspaper articles, you will need to search periodical indexes and databases. Indexes provide listings of articles organized by topics; many databases provide the full texts. Some indexes are in print and can be found in the reference section of the library; most are online. Some databases are available for free; most of the more authoritative ones, however, are available only by subscription and so must be accessed through a library.

Many databases now include not only scholarly articles but also dissertations, theses, book chapters, book reviews, and conference proceedings. Dissertations and theses are formal works of scholarship done as requirements for graduate degrees; book reviews offer critical evaluations of scholarly and popular books; and conference proceedings are papers presented, usually orally, at scholarly meetings.

When you access a source through a database, the URL or link address is different each time you log in, so if you want to return to a source, look for a *stable URL*, *permalink*, or *document URL* option and choose it to copy and paste into your list of sources.

General indexes and databases.   A reference librarian can help you determine which databases will be most helpful to you, but here are some useful ones:

Academic Search Complete and *Academic Search Premier* are multidisciplinary indexes and databases containing the full text of articles in thousands of journals and indexing of even more, with abstracts of their articles.

FirstSearch offers access to millions of full-text, full-image articles in dozens of databases covering many disciplines.

InfoTrac offers millions of full-text articles in a broad spectrum of disciplines and on a wide variety of topics from thousands of scholarly and popular periodicals, including the *New York Times*.

JSTOR archives scanned copies of entire publication runs of scholarly journals in many disciplines, but it may not include current issues of the journals.

academic literacies · rhetorical situations · genres · fields · processes · strategies · research MLA / APA · media / design · readings · handbook

LexisNexis contains full-text publications and articles from a large number of newspapers and business and legal resources.

ProQuest Central provides access to full-text articles from thousands of books, scholarly journals, conference papers, magazines, newspapers, blogs, podcasts, and websites and a large collection of dissertations and theses.

Single-subject indexes and databases.   The following are just a sample of what's available; check with a reference librarian for indexes and databases in the subject you're researching.

America: History and Life indexes scholarly literature on the history and culture of the United States and Canada.

BIOSIS Previews provides abstracts and indexes for thousands of sources on a wide variety of biological and medical topics.

ERIC is the U.S. Department of Education's Educational Resource Information Center database. It includes hundreds of journal titles as well as conference papers, technical reports, and other resources on education.

Historical Abstracts includes abstracts of articles on the history of the world, excluding the United States and Canada, since 1450.

Humanities International Index contains bibliographic references to more than 2,200 journals dealing with the humanities.

MLA International Bibliography indexes scholarly articles on modern languages, literature, folklore, and linguistics.

PsycINFO indexes scholarly literature in a number of disciplines relating to the behavioral and social sciences.

PubMed includes millions of citations for biomedical literature, many with links to full-text content.

Print indexes.   You may need to consult print indexes to find articles published before the 1980s. Here are six useful ones:

The Readers' Guide to Periodical Literature (print, 1900–; online, 1983–)

InfoTrac Magazine Index (print, 1988–; online, 1973–)

The New York Times Index (print and online, 1851–)

Humanities Index (print, 1974–; online, 1984–)

Social Sciences Index (print, 1974–; online, 1983–)

General Science Index (print, 1978–; online, 1984–)

Images, Sound, and More

Your library likely subscribes to various databases that allow you to find and download video, audio, and image files. Here is a sampling:

AP Images provides access to photographs taken for the Associated Press, the cooperative agency of thousands of newspapers and radio and television stations worldwide.

ArtStor provides images in the arts, architecture, humanities, and sciences.

Dance in Video offers hundreds of videos of dance productions and documentaries on dance.

Education in Video includes thousands of videos of teaching demonstrations, lectures, documentaries, and footage of students and teachers in their classrooms.

Naxos Music Library contains more than 130,000 classical, jazz, and world music recordings, as well as libretti and synopses of hundreds of operas and other background information.

Theatre in Video provides videos of hundreds of performances of plays and film documentaries.

The following indexes and databases are freely available on the internet:

The WWW Virtual Library is a catalog of websites on a wide range of subjects, compiled by volunteers with expertise in particular subject areas.

CSA Discovery Guides provide comprehensive information on current issues in the arts and humanities, natural sciences, social sciences, and technology, with an overview of each subject, key citations with abstracts, and links to websites.

Voice of the Shuttle, or *VoS,* offers information on subjects in the humanities, arranged to mirror "the way the humanities are organized for research and teaching as well as the way they are adapting to social, cultural, and technological changes."

The Library of Congress offers online access to information on a wide range of subjects, including academic subjects, as well as prints, photographs, and government documents.

JURIST is a university-based online gateway to authoritative legal instruction, information, scholarship, and news.

academic literacies   rhetorical situations   genres   fields   processes   strategies   research MLA / APA   media / design   readings   handbook

Searching the Web

The web provides access to countless sites containing information posted by governments, educational institutions, organizations, businesses, and individuals. Such websites are different from other sources—including the kinds of online sources you access through indexes and databases—in two key ways: (1) their content varies greatly in its reliability and (2) they are not stable, which means that what you see on a site today may be different (or gone) tomorrow. Anyone who wants to can post material on the web, so you need to evaluate carefully what you find there to eliminate sources that are not current, lack credibility, or are primarily advertisements or promotional in nature.

Because it is so vast and dynamic, finding what you need on the web for academic writing can be a challenge. The primary way of finding information on the web is with a search site. You may find the most suitable results for academic writing by using *Google Scholar*, a search site that finds scholarly literature, including peer-reviewed papers, technical reports, and abstracts. Here are other ways of searching the web:

- *Keyword searches. Google, Yahoo!, Bing,* and most other search sites all scan the web looking for keywords that you specify.
- *Subject directories. Google, Yahoo!,* and some other search sites offer directories that arrange information by topics, much like a library cataloging system. Such directories allow you to broaden or narrow your search if you need to—for example, a search for "birds" can be broadened to "animals" or narrowed to "blue-footed booby."
- *Metasearches. Yippy, Dogpile,* and *ZapMeta* are metasearch sites that allow you to use several search engines simultaneously. They are best for searching broadly; use a single search site for the most precise results.
- **Twitter** *searches.* In addition to *Twitter* Search, you can find *Twitter* content through search sites such as *Social Mention* and *Keyhole.*

Each search site and metasearch site has its own protocols for searching; most have an "advanced search" option that will help you search more productively. Remember, though, that you need to be careful about **EVALUATING SOURCES** that you find on the web because the web is unregulated and no one independently verifies the information posted on its sites.

● 511–18

Doing Field Research

Sometimes you'll need to do your own research, to go beyond the information you find in published sources and gather data by doing field research. Three kinds of field research you might want to consider are interviews, observations, and questionnaires.

Interviewing experts. Some kinds of writing—a profile of a living person, for instance—almost require that you conduct an interview. And sometimes you may just need to find information that you haven't been able to find in published sources. To get firsthand information on the experience of serving as a soldier in Afghanistan, you might interview your cousin who served a tour of duty there; to find current research on pesticide residues in food, you might need to interview a toxicologist. Whatever your goal, you can conduct interviews in person, using video-calling software such as *Skype* or *FaceTime*, by telephone, through email, or by mail. In general, you will want to use interviews to find information you can't find elsewhere. Below is some advice on planning and conducting an interview.

Before the interview

1. Once you identify someone you want to interview, email or phone to ask the person, stating your **PURPOSE** for the interview and what you hope to learn.

55–56

2. Once you've set up an appointment, send a note or email confirming the time and place. If you wish to record the interview, be sure to ask for permission to do so. If you plan to conduct the interview by mail or email, state when you will send your questions.

3. Write out questions. Plan questions that invite extended response and supporting details: "What accounts for the recent spike in gasoline prices?" forces an explanation, whereas "Is the recent spike in gas prices a direct result of global politics?" is likely to elicit only a yes or a no.

At the interview

4. Record the full name of the person you interview, along with the date, time, and place of the interview; you'll need this information to cite and document the interview accurately.

5. Take notes, even if you are recording the interview.
6. Keep track of time: don't take more than you agreed to beforehand unless both of you agree to keep talking. End by thanking your subject and offering to provide a copy of your final product.

After the interview

7. Flesh out your notes with details as soon as possible after the interview, while you still remember them. What did you learn? What surprised you? Summarize both the interviewee's words and your impressions.
8. Make sure you've reproduced quotations from the interview accurately and fairly. Avoid editing quotations in ways that distort the speaker's intended meaning.
9. Be sure to send a thank-you note or email.

Observation.   Some writing projects are based on information you get by observing something. For a sociology report, you may observe how students behave in large lectures. For an education course, you may observe one child's progress as a writer over a period of time. The following advice can help you conduct observations.

Before observing

1. Think about your research **PURPOSE**: What are you looking for? What do you expect to find? How will your presence as an observer affect what you observe? What do you plan to do with what you find?

55–56

2. If necessary, set up an appointment. You may need to ask permission of the people you wish to observe and of your school as well. (Check with your instructor about your school's policy in this area.) Be honest and open about your goals and intentions; college students doing research assignments are often welcomed where others may not be.

While observing

3. If you're taking notes on paper, you may want to divide each page down the middle vertically and write only on the left side of the page, reserving the right side for information you will fill in later. If you're using a laptop, you can set up two columns or a split screen.

4. Note descriptive details about the setting. What do you see? What do you hear? Do you smell anything? Get down details about color, shape, size, sound, and so on. Consider photographing or making a sketch of what you see.

443–51
5. Who is there, and what are they doing? **DESCRIBE** what they look like, and make notes about what they say. Note any significant demographic details—about gender, race, occupation, age, dress, and so on.

6. What is happening? Who's doing what? What's being said? Make note
462–70
of these kinds of **NARRATIVE** details.

After observing

7. As soon as possible after you complete your observations, use the right side of your notes to fill in gaps and include additional details.

98–130
8. **ANALYZE** your notes, looking for patterns. Did some things appear or happen more than once? Did anything stand out? surprise or puzzle you? What did you learn?

Questionnaires and surveys.   Various kinds of questionnaires and surveys can provide information or opinions from a large number of people. For a political science course, you might conduct a survey to ask students who they plan to vote for. Or, for a marketing course, you might distribute a questionnaire asking what they think about an advertising campaign. The advice in this section will help you create useful questionnaires and surveys.

Define your goal.   The goal of a questionnaire or survey should be limited and focused, so that every question will contribute to your research question. Also, people are more likely to respond to a brief, focused survey.

Define your sample.   A survey gets responses from a representative sample of the whole group. The answers to these questions will help you define that sample:

1. Who should answer the questions? The people you contact should represent the whole population. For example, if you want to survey undergraduate students at your school, your sample should reflect your school's enrollment in terms of gender, year, major, age, ethnicity, and so forth as closely as possible.

2. How many people make up a representative sample? In general, the larger your sample, the more the answers will reflect those of the whole group. But if your population is small—200 students in a history course, for example—your sample must include a large percentage of that group.

Decide on a medium.   Will you ask the questions face-to-face? over the phone? on a website such as *SurveyMonkey*? by mail? by email? Face-to-face questions work best for simple surveys or for gathering impersonal information. You're more likely to get responses to more personal questions with printed or online questionnaires, which should be neat and easy to read. Phone interviews may require well-thought-out scripts that anticipate possible answers and make it easy to record these answers.

Design good questions.   The way you ask questions will determine the usefulness of the answers you get, so take care to write questions that are clear and unambiguous. Here are some typical question types:

- *Multiple-choice*

  What is your current age?

  _____ 15–20   _____ 21–25   _____ 26–30   _____ 31–35   _____ Other

- *Rating scale*

  How would you rate the service at the campus bookstore?

  _____ Excellent   _____ Good   _____ Fair   _____ Poor

- *Agreement scale*

  How much do you agree with the following statements?

	Strongly Agree	Agree	Disagree	Strongly Disagree
The bookstore has sufficient numbers of textbooks available.	❒	❒	❒	❒

	Strongly Agree	Agree	Disagree	Strongly Disagree
Staff at the bookstore are knowledgeable.	❒	❒	❒	❒
Staff at the bookstore are courteous.	❒	❒	❒	❒

- *Open-ended*

  How often do you visit the campus bookstore?

  How can the campus bookstore improve its service?

Include all potential alternatives when phrasing questions to avoid biasing the answers. And make sure each question addresses only one issue—for example, "Bookstore staff are knowledgeable and courteous" could lead to the response "knowledgeable, agree; courteous, disagree."

When arranging questions, place easier ones at the beginning and harder ones near the end (but if the questions seem to fall into a different natural order, follow it). Make sure each question asks for information you will need—if a question isn't absolutely necessary, omit it.

Include an introduction.   Start by stating your survey's purpose and how the results will be used. It's also a good idea to offer an estimate of the time needed to complete the questions. Remind participants of your deadline.

Test the survey or questionnaire.   Make sure your questions elicit the kinds of answers you need by asking three or four people who are part of your target population to answer them. They can help you find unclear instructions, questions that aren't clear or that lack sufficient alternatives, or other problems that you should correct to make sure your results are useful. But if you change the questionnaire as a result of their responses, don't include their answers in your total.

511–18
526–28

> **IF YOU NEED MORE HELP**
>
> See **EVALUATING SOURCES** for help determining their usefulness. See also Chapter 49 for help **TAKING NOTES** on your sources.

academic literacies   rhetorical situations   genres   fields   processes   strategies   research MLA / APA   media / design   readings   handbook

Evaluating Sources **49**

Searching the *Health Source* database for information on the incidence of meningitis among college students, you find seventeen articles. A *Google* search on the same topic produces over 600,000 hits. How do you decide which sources to read? This chapter presents advice on evaluating sources—first to determine whether a source might be useful for your purposes and is worth looking at more closely and then to read with a critical eye the ones you choose.

Considering Whether a Source Might Be Useful

Think about your **PURPOSE**. Are you trying to persuade readers to believe or do something? to inform them about something? If the former, it will be especially important to find sources representing various positions; if the latter, you may need sources that are more factual or informative. Reconsider your **AUDIENCE**. What kinds of sources will they find persuasive? If you're writing for readers in a particular field, what counts as evidence in that field? Following are some questions that can help you judge whether a possible source you've found deserves your time and attention:

55–56

57–60

490–93

- *Is it reliable?* Is it **SCHOLARLY**? peer-reviewed? published in a reputable journal or magazine, or by a reputable publisher? Did you find it in a library database? on the web? Evaluating web-based texts may require more work than using results from library databases. But whatever kind of search you do, skim the results quickly to evaluate their reliability.

- *Is it relevant?* How does the source relate to your purpose? What will it add to your work? Look at the title and at any introductory material— a preface, abstract, or introduction—to see what the source covers.

- *What are the author's credentials?* How is the author qualified to write on the subject? Are they associated with a particular position on the issue? See whether the source mentions other works this author has written. In any case, you might do a web search to see what else you can learn about the author.

66–68

- *What is the* **STANCE**? Consider whether a source covers various perspectives or advocates one particular point of view. Does its title suggest a certain slant? If it's online, you might check to see whether it includes links to other sites and, if so, what their perspectives are. You'll want to consult sources with a variety of viewpoints.

- *Who is the publisher or sponsor?* If it's a book, what kind of company published it; if an article, what kind of periodical did it appear in? Books published by university presses and articles in scholarly journals are reviewed by experts before they are published. Books and articles written for the general public typically do not undergo rigorous review—and they may lack the kind of in-depth discussion that is useful for research.

    If the source is online, is the site maintained by an organization? an interest group? a government agency? an individual? Look for clues in the URL: *.edu* is used mostly by colleges and universities, *.gov* by government agencies, *.org* by nonprofit organizations, *.mil* by the military, and *.com* by commercial organizations. Evaluate the publisher's or sponsor's motives: to present information even-handedly? to promote a certain point of view, belief, or position? to sell something?

- *What is the level?* Can you understand the material? Texts written for a general audience might be easier to understand but not authoritative enough for academic work. Texts written for scholars will be more authoritative but may be hard to comprehend.

- *When was it published?* See when books and articles were published. Check to see when online sources were created and last updated. (If the site lists no date, see if links to other sites still work.) Recent does not necessarily mean better—some topics may require very current information whereas others may call for older sources.

academic literacies | rhetorical situations | genres | fields | processes | strategies | research MLA / APA | media / design | readings | handbook

- *Does it include other useful information?* Is there a bibliography that might lead you to other sources? How current are the sources it cites?
- *Is it available?* Is it a source you can get hold of? If it's a book and your school's library doesn't have it, can you get it through interlibrary loan?

Once you've decided that a source should be examined more closely, use the following questions to give it critical scrutiny.

Reading Sources with a Critical Eye

- *What* ARGUMENTS *does the author make?* Does the author present a number of different positions, or do they argue for a particular position? Do you need to ANALYZE THE ARGUMENT?

  ▲ 157–84

  ✳ 26–27

- *How persuasive do you find the argument?* What reasons and evidence does the author provide in support of any position(s)? Are there citations or links—and if so, are they credible? Is any evidence presented without citations? Do you find any of the author's assumptions questionable? How thoroughly does the author consider opposing arguments?

- *What is the author's* STANCE? Does the author strive for objectivity, or does the content or language reveal a particular bias? Does the author consider opposing views and treat them fairly?

  ■ 66–68

- *Do you recognize ideas you've run across in other sources?* Does the source leave out any information or perspective that other sources include—or include any that other sources leave out?

- *Does this source support or challenge your own position—or does it do both?* Does it support your thesis? offer a different argument altogether? Does it represent a position you may need to ACKNOWLEDGE or REFUTE? Don't reject a source just because it challenges your views; your sources should reflect a variety of views on your topic, showing that you've considered the subject thoroughly.

  ▲ 178
  178

- *What can you tell about the intended* AUDIENCE *and* PURPOSE? Is the author writing to a general audience, to a subset of that audience, to specialists in a particular field? Are you a member of that audience? If

  ■ 57–60
  55–56

not, does that affect the way you interpret what you read? Is the main purpose to inform readers about a topic or to argue a certain point?

Comparing Sources

You may find that two or more of your sources present similar information or arguments. How do you decide which one to use? Compare them, using these questions as a guide:

- *Which source is most current?* Generally, a more recent source is better than an older one, because the newer source includes information or data that is more up to date—and may include (or refute) the information in the earlier source. Be aware, though, that in some fields, such as literary criticism, decades-old sources may still be important.

398–408
- *Which argument is more persuasive?* Examine the **CLAIMS**, **REASONS**, and **EVIDENCE** presented in each source. Which source's argument is most logical? Which one has the best supporting reasons and evidence? Which one best **ACKNOWLEDGES**, **ACCOMMODATES**, or **REFUTES** opposing arguments?
411–13

- *Which author or authors are most authoritative?* An expert in the subject is more authoritative than, say, a journalist writing on the subject. An article published in a scholarly journal is more authoritative than one published in a general-circulation magazine or website. The journalist's article may be easier to read and more interesting, but you're best off looking for the best information—not the best read.

66–68
- *Which source has the most appropriate* **STANCE**? In general, look for sources that strive for objectivity, rather than a particular bias. Also, be aware that we all tend to favor information that agrees with our views—and that may lead us to choose sources we agree with rather than sources that present all sides of an issue.

- *Which source best fits your needs?* All other things being equal, the best source to choose is the one that will give you the information you need, support the argument you're making, and perhaps provide useful quotations to add to your writing. The best source will show that you've done appropriate research and will enhance your own credibility as a thinker, reader, researcher, and writer.

academic literacies • rhetorical situations • genres • fields • processes • strategies • research MLA / APA • media / design • readings • handbook

A Note of Caution: False News

As you read to find sources or simply to find out what's happening in the world, you need to be on guard against false or "fake" news. False news—propaganda, hoaxes, misinformation, and lies—includes satires and counterfeit news stories. Satires, which range from Jonathan Swift's "A Modest Proposal" to *Onion* stories like "NFL to Curb Excessive Celebrations by Removing Areas of Players' Brains Responsible for Emotions" and episodes of *The Daily Show*, offer humorous exaggerations to expose and criticize people and governments. Counterfeit news stories, though, are malicious fabrications created usually for political ends. World War II Nazi propaganda and recent fraudulent stories such as "Pope Francis Endorses Donald Trump," a story that went viral on Facebook, are intended to mislead readers. Further complicating things, some politicians and other public figures have taken to calling news reports with which they disagree and even entire newspapers and networks "fake news"—even though the stories reported are verifiably true and the news outlets are considered trustworthy.

Although false news has been around at least since the invention of the printing press, the internet and social media have led to a huge increase in false news stories, especially during the 2016 presidential election, seriously challenging and muddying "real" news. Each false story can rapidly multiply over sites such as *Facebook* and *Twitter* and through email. As a reader and researcher, you need to be able to see whether or not a story is false. As a writer, you risk harming your credibility if you cite a false news story as evidence.

All news outlets have a bias, but some are more trustworthy than others. Here is some advice on how to determine whether a potential news source is unfairly biased or can be safely used as a source in your own research.

Investigate the source. Some news media outlets' political bias is well known, but to determine the bias of other sources, you may have to do some research: Read the "About" pages of online sources to see how the source characterizes itself, who owns or runs it, and how the site may be contacted. A site without such information (or with only a link to a personal email account) is probably not a good source. If a site includes a disclaimer to the effect of, "We are not responsible for the reliability or accuracy of this information," assume that it's a site to avoid.

- See what websites that evaluate news sources say about the bias of the source. These sites rate the bias of sources using a combination of research into the content of a news source and votes on the site's judgment by the website's readers. While these sites acknowledge that such judgments are by nature subjective, they present a rough consensus on the direction and extent of bias.

- See whether the site appears in lists of websites that post fake or satirical stories. FactCheck.org and Wikipedia are two sites that publish such lists.

- Check the URL of online sources. Counterfeit websites mimic real news sources but either alter the URL (Breaking-CNN.com imitates CNN.com) or add a .co or .ma to a legitimate URL (usatoday.com.co or Bloomberg.com.ma). While reputable sites usually end in .org, .net, or .com, these endings don't necessarily mean the site is trustworthy—so exercise caution, especially with .com addresses.

- Check to see if other news media are reporting the same story. If the story appears in only one source, it's likely false.

- Check the date of the story and dates within the story. Sometimes old stories resurface as "news." They aren't any truer now than they were then.

- Do a search for the story's author. Does the author appear to be an expert on your topic? Does the author write for or belong to other organizations or sites that are biased or suspect? What other articles has the author written? If there's no author listed, the site is probably not trustworthy.

Use Your Own Judgment.   Sometimes you need to judge the trustworthiness of your sources yourself. Begin by assessing the story's plausibility: how likely is it to be true, given what you already know about the world? For example, the likelihood of a U.S. senator's father being involved in the

assassination of President John F. Kennedy or that vast, secret conspiracies are running the world is pretty slim—though such stories are common on the internet and believed by some people.

A story that seems designed to generate a strong emotional response in readers, especially anger or fear, rather than appealing to logic or sound evidence, may be false. For example, stories circulating on the internet asserting that childhood immunizations cause autism—and even that the president enacted a temporary ban on vaccinations—prey on parents' fears for their children's safety. But they are completely false.

You should also consider the source in light of the rhetorical situation:

PURPOSE
Consider the headline: Is it inflammatory or outrageous? Read beyond the headline. Does the story match the headline? Is the piece meant to inform? persuade? entertain? confirm readers' current beliefs? Is the story written to manipulate your emotions by making you angry? sad? Something else?

55–56

AUDIENCE
For whom is the piece written? Would this piece be considered reliable by the extreme political partisans on one side or another? To what extent does the piece confirm or challenge the expectations of its readers? Does the story appear only on social media, or is it also on other publication sites?

57–60

GENRE
Is the genre of the piece appropriate for its purpose and audience? If it's an argument, does it offer multiple perspectives on the topic? What evidence is offered—and can it be confirmed through links, references, or other sources? Do links or references actually exist and support the claims in the story? Does the information in the piece appear in other, reputable publications?

61–65

STANCE
What is the author's attitude toward the subject: objective? serious? angry? outraged? astonished? amused? snide? disrespectful? Is the author's tone appropriate for the content of the story?

66–68

69–71 ▮

MEDIA/DESIGN Does the website appear to be well designed or the work of an amateur? Does the headline or the story use ALL CAPS? Are photographs, charts, or tables included in the story? Do they seem real—again, do they appear in other, reputable sources—or doctored? Could a photograph, for example, have been Photoshopped?

Consider, too, the effect of your own biases. Does the story confirm what you already believe? Confirmation bias (our tendency to believe things that match what we already believe) makes us more likely to accept stories that confirm our beliefs and to discount information that doesn't. Be wary of assuming a story or article is trustworthy just because you agree with the author—you need to step back and make sure your own beliefs aren't clouding your judgment.

As a final check, you can go to sites whose purpose is investigating news for its veracity. Some to visit:

- FactCheck.org
- Snopes.com
- PolitiFact.com
- *The Washington Post* Fact Checker
- AllSides.com
- mediabiasfactcheck.com

526–38 ●
539–43

> **IF YOU NEED MORE HELP**
>
> See **QUOTING, PARAPHRASING, AND SUMMARIZING** for help in taking notes on your sources and deciding how to use them in your writing. See also **ACKNOWLEDGING SOURCES, AVOIDING PLAGIARISM** for advice on giving credit to the sources you use.

Synthesizing Ideas 50

To **ANALYZE** the works of a poet, you show how she uses similar images in three different poems to explore a recurring concept. To solve a crime, a detective studies several eyewitness accounts to figure out who did it. To trace the history of photojournalism, a professor **COMPARES** the uses of photography during the Civil War and during the Vietnam War. These are all cases where someone *synthesizes*—brings together material from two or more sources in order to generate new information or to support a new perspective. When you do research, you need to go beyond what your sources say; you need to use what they say to inspire and support *what you want to say*. This chapter focuses on how to synthesize ideas you find in other sources as the basis for your own ideas.

▲ 98–130

◆ 424–31

Reading for Patterns and Connections

Your task as a writer is to find as much information as you can on your topic—and then to sift through all that you have found to determine and support what you yourself will write. In other words, you'll need to synthesize ideas and information from the sources you've consulted to figure out first what arguments *you* want to make and then to provide support for those arguments.

When you synthesize, you group similar bits of information together, looking for patterns or themes or trends and trying to identify the key points. In the brief report on the following page, writer Jude Stewart synthesizes several pieces of research on boredom. Stewart's report originally appeared in *The Atlantic*, which uses an abbreviated documentation style.

Boredom has, paradoxically, become quite interesting to academics lately. The International Interdisciplinary Boredom Conference gathered humanities scholars in Warsaw for the fifth time in April. In early May, its less scholarly forerunner, London's Boring Conference, celebrated seven years of delighting in tedium. At this event, people flock to talks about toast, double yellow lines, sneezing, and vending-machine sounds, among other snooze-inducing topics.

This question allows Stewart to bring together four ways boredom can be measured.

What, exactly, is everybody studying? One widely accepted psychological definition of boredom is "the aversive experience of wanting, but being unable, to engage in satisfying activity." [1] But how can you quantify a person's boredom level and compare it with someone else's? In 1986, psychologists introduced the Boredom Proneness Scale, [2] designed to measure an individual's overall propensity to feel bored (what's known as "trait boredom"). By contrast, the Multidimensional State Boredom Scale, [3] developed in 2008, measures a person's feelings of boredom in a given situation ("state boredom"). A German-led team has since identified five types of state boredom: indifferent, calibrating, searching, reactant, and apathetic (indifferent boredom—characterized by low arousal—was the mellowest, least unpleasant kind; reactant—high arousal—was the most aggressive and unpleasant). [4] Boredom may be miserable, but let no one call it simple.

Stewart synthesizes seven different studies under one category, "behavior issues."

Boredom has been linked to behavior issues, including bad driving, [5] mindless snacking, [6] binge-drinking, [7] risky sex, [8] and problem gambling. [9] In fact, many of us would take pain over boredom. One team of psychologists discovered that two-thirds of men and a quarter of women would rather self-administer electric shocks than sit alone with their thoughts for 15 minutes. [10] Probing this phenomenon,

One study builds on a previous study.

another team asked volunteers to watch boring, sad, or neutral films, during which they could self-administer electric shocks. The bored volunteers shocked themselves more and harder than the sad or neutral ones did. [11]

Again, Stewart creates a category that includes two different studies.

But boredom isn't all bad. By encouraging contemplation and daydreaming, it can spur creativity. An early, much-cited study gave participants abundant time to complete problem-solving and word-association exercises. Once all the obvious answers were exhausted, participants gave more and more inventive answers to fend off boredom. [12] A British study took these findings one step further, asking subjects

Stewart shows how one study relates to an earlier one's findings.

to complete a creative challenge (coming up with a list of alternative

uses for a household item). One group of subjects did a boring activity first, while the others went straight to the creative task. Those whose boredom pumps had been primed were more prolific. [13]

In our always-connected world, boredom may be an elusive state, but it is a fertile one. Watch paint dry or water boil, or at least put away your smartphone for a while. You might unlock your next big idea.

Conclusion brings together all the research, creating a synthesis of the findings of all 13 sources.

The Studies

[1] Eastwood et al., "The Unengaged Mind" (*Perspectives on Psychological Science*, Sept. 2012)

[2] Farmer and Sundberg, "Boredom Proneness" (*Journal of Personality Assessment*, Spring 1986)

[3] Fahlman et al., "Development and Validation of the Multidimensional State Boredom Scale" (*Assessment*, Feb. 2013)

[4] Goetz et al., "Types of Boredom" (*Motivation and Emotion*, June 2014)

[5] Steinberger et al., "The Antecedents, Experience, and Coping Strategies of Driver Boredom in Young Adult Males" (*Journal of Safety Research*, Dec. 2016)

[6] Havermans et al., "Eating and Inflicting Pain Out of Boredom" (*Appetite*, Feb. 2015)

[7] Biolcati et al., "'I Cannot Stand the Boredom'" (*Addictive Behaviors Reports*, June 2016)

[8] Miller et al., "Was Bob Seger Right?" (*Leisure Sciences*, Jan. 2014)

[9] Mercer and Eastwood, "Is Boredom Associated with Problem Gambling Behaviour?" (*International Gambling Studies*, April 2010)

[10] Wilson et al., "Just Think: The Challenges of the Disengaged Mind" (*Science*, July 2014)

[11] Nederkoorn et al., "Self-Inflicted Pain Out of Boredom" (*Psychiatry Research*, March 2016)

[12] Schubert, "Boredom as an Antagonist of Creativity" (*Journal of Creative Behavior*, Dec. 1977)

[13] Mann and Cadman, "Does Being Bored Make Us More Creative?" (*Creativity Research Journal*, May 2014)

—Jude Stewart, "Boredom Is Good for You: The Surprising Benefits of Stultification"

Here are some tips for reading to identify patterns and connections:

- Read all your sources with an open mind. Withhold judgment, even of sources that seem wrong-headed or implausible. Don't jump to conclusions.

534–35 ⬤ Take notes and write a brief **SUMMARY** of each source to help you see relationships, patterns, and connections among your sources. Take notes on your own thoughts, too.

- Pay attention to your first reactions. You'll likely have many ideas to work with, but your first thoughts can often lead somewhere that you 331–34 ◯ will find interesting. Try **FREEWRITING**, **CLUSTERING**, or **LISTING** to see where they lead. How do these thoughts and ideas relate to your topic? 335–37 ◯ Where might they fit into your rough **OUTLINE**?

- Try to think creatively, and pay attention to thoughts that flicker at the edge of your consciousness, as they may well be productive.

- Be playful. Good ideas sometimes come when we let our guard down or take ideas to extremes just to see where they lead.

Ask yourself these questions about your sources:

- What sources make the strongest arguments? What makes them so strong?

- Do some arguments recur in several sources?

- Which arguments do you agree with? disagree with? Of those you disagree with, which ones seem strong enough that you need to 411 ◆ **ACKNOWLEDGE** them in your text?

- Are there any disagreements among your sources?

- Are there any themes you see in more than one source?

- Are any data—facts, statistics, examples—or experts cited in more than one source?

- Do several of your sources use the same terms? Do they use the terms similarly, or do they use them in different ways?

academic literacies | rhetorical situations | genres | fields | processes | strategies | research MLA / APA | media / design | readings | handbook

- What have you learned about your topic? How have your sources affected your thinking on your topic? Do you need to adjust your **THESIS**? If so, how?

387–89

- Have you discovered new questions you need to investigate?

- Keep in mind your **RHETORICAL SITUATION**—have you found the information you need that will achieve your purpose, appeal to your audience, and suit your genre and medium?

53

What is likely to emerge from this questioning is a combination of big ideas, including new ways of understanding your topic and insights into recent scholarship about it, and smaller ones, such as how two sources agree with each other but not completely and how the information in one source supports or undercuts the argument of another. These ideas and insights will become the basis for your own ideas and for what *you* have to say about the topic.

Synthesizing Ideas Using Notes

You may find that identifying connections among your sources is easier if you examine them together rather than reading them one by one. For example, taking notes on note cards and then laying the cards out on a desk or table (or on the floor) lets you see passages that seem related. Doing the same with photocopies or printouts of your sources can help you identify similarities as well.

In doing research for an essay arguing that the sale of assault weapons should be banned, you might find several sources that address the scope of U.S. citizens' right to bear arms. On the next page are notes taken on three such sources: Joe Klein, a journalist writing in *Time.com*; Antonin Scalia, a former U.S. Supreme Court justice, quoted in an online news article; and Drew Westen, a professor of psychology writing in a blog sponsored by the *New York Times*. Though the writers hold very different views, juxtaposing these notes and highlighting certain passages show a common thread running through the sources. In this example, all three sources might be used to support the thesis that restrictions on the owning of weapons—but not an outright ban—are both constitutional and necessary.

Source 1

Limits of gun ownership

Although the U.S. Constitution includes the right to bear arms, that right is not absolute. "No American has the right to own a stealth bomber or a nuclear weapon. Armor-piercing bullets are forbidden. The question is where you draw a reasonable bright line."
—Klein, "How the Gun Won" — quote

Source 4

Limits of gun ownership

Supreme Court Justice Antonin M. Scalia has noted that when the Constitution was written and ratified, some weapons were barred. So limitations could be put on owning some weapons, as long as the limits are consistent with those in force in 1789.
—Scalia, quoted in Woods — paraphrase

Source 3

Limits of gun ownership

Westen's "message consulting" research has shown that Americans are ambivalent about guns but react very positively to a statement of principle that includes both the right to own guns and restrictions on their ownership, such as prohibiting large ammunition clips and requiring all gun purchasers to undergo background checks for criminal behavior or mental illness.
—Westen — paraphrase

Synthesizing Information to Support Your Own Ideas

If you're doing research to write a **REPORT**, your own ideas will be communicated primarily through which information you decide to include from the sources you cite and how you organize that information. If you're writing a **TEXTUAL ANALYSIS**, your synthesis may focus on the themes, techniques, or other patterns you find. If you're writing a research-based **ARGUMENT**, on the other hand, your synthesis of sources must support the position you take in that argument. No matter what your genre, the challenge is to synthesize information from your research to develop ideas about your topic and then to support those ideas.

▲ 131–56

▲ 98–130

▲ 157–84

Entering the Conversation

As you read and think about your topic, you will come to an understanding of the concepts, interpretations, and controversies relating to your topic—and you'll become aware that there's a larger conversation going on. When you begin to find connections among your sources, you will begin to see your own place in that conversation, to discover your own ideas and your own stance on your topic. This is the exciting part of a research project, for when you write out your own ideas on the topic, you will find yourself entering that conversation. Remember that your **STANCE** as an author needs to be clear: simply stringing together the words and ideas of others isn't enough. You need to show readers *how* your source materials relate to one another and to your thesis.

■ 66–68

IF YOU NEED MORE HELP

See Chapter 51, QUOTING, PARAPHRASING, AND SUMMARIZING, for help in integrating source materials into your own text. See also Chapter 52 on ACKNOWL-EDGING SOURCES, AVOIDING PLAGIARISM for advice on giving credit to the sources you cite.

● 526–38
539–43

51 Quoting, Paraphrasing, and Summarizing

In an oral presentation about the rhetoric of Abraham Lincoln, you quote a memorable line from the Gettysburg Address. For an essay on the Tet Offensive in the Vietnam War, you paraphrase arguments made by several commentators and summarize some key debates about that war. When you work with the ideas and words of others, you need to clearly distinguish those ideas and words from your own and give credit to their authors. This chapter will help you with the specifics of quoting, paraphrasing, and summarizing source materials that you use in your writing.

Taking Notes

When you find material you think will be useful, take careful notes. How do you determine how much to record? You need to write down enough information so that when you refer to it later, you will be reminded of its main points and have a precise record of where it comes from.

- *Use a computer file, note cards, or a notebook,* labeling each entry with the information that will allow you to keep track of where it comes from—author, title, and the pages or the URL (or DOI [digital object identifier]). You needn't write down full bibliographic information (you can abbreviate the author's name and title) since you'll include that information in your **WORKING BIBLIOGRAPHY**.

  485–87

- *Take notes in your own words, and use your own sentence patterns.* If you make a note that is a detailed **PARAPHRASE**, label it as such so that you'll know to provide appropriate **DOCUMENTATION** if you use it.

  531–34
  544–47

526

academic literacies · rhetorical situations · genres · fields · processes · strategies · research MLA / APA · media / design · readings · handbook

- *If you find wording that you'd like to quote,* be sure to enclose it in quotation marks to distinguish your source's words from your own. Double-check your notes to be sure any quoted material is accurately quoted—and that you haven't accidentally **PLAGIARIZED** your sources.

539–43

- *Label each note with a number to identify the source and a subject heading* to relate the note to a subject, supporting point, or other element in your essay. Doing this will help you to sort your notes easily and match them up with your rough outline. Restrict each note to a single subject.

Here are a few examples of one writer's notes on a source discussing synthetic dyes, bladder cancer, and the use of animals to determine what causes cancers. Each note includes a subject heading and brief source information and identifies whether the source is quoted or paraphrased.

Source 3

Synthetic dyes

The first synthetic dye was mauve, invented in 1854 and derived from coal. Like other coal-derived dyes, it contained aromatic amines.
Steingraber, "Pesticides," 976 — paraphrase

Source 3

Synthetic dyes & cancer

Bladder cancer was common among textile workers who used dyes. Steingraber: "By the beginning of the twentieth century, bladder cancer rates among this group of workers had skyrocketed."
Steingraber, "Pesticides," 976 — paraphrase and quote

> **Source 3**
>
> Synthetic dyes & cancer
>
> In 1938, Wilhelm Hueper exposed dogs to aromatic amines and showed that the chemical caused bladder cancer. Steingraber, "Pesticides," 976 — paraphrase

Deciding Whether to Quote, Paraphrase, or Summarize

340–42 ◯
528–31 ●

When it comes time to **DRAFT**, you'll need to decide *how* to use any source you want to include—in other words, whether to quote, paraphrase, or summarize it. You might follow this rule of thumb: **QUOTE** texts when the wording is worth repeating or makes a point so well that no rewording will do it justice, when you want to cite the exact words of a known authority on your topic, when an authority's opinions challenge or disagree with those of others, or when the source is one you want to emphasize. **PARAPHRASE** sources that are not worth quoting but contain details you need to include. **SUMMARIZE** longer passages whose main points are important but whose details are not.

531–34 ●
534–35 ●

Quoting

Quoting a source is a way of weaving someone else's exact words into your text. You need to reproduce the source exactly, though you can modify it to omit unnecessary details (with ellipses) or to make it fit smoothly into your text (with brackets). You also need to distinguish quoted material from your own by enclosing short quotations in quotation marks, setting off longer quotes as a block, and using appropriate **SIGNAL PHRASES**.

535–38 ●

Incorporate short quotations into your text, enclosed in quotation marks. If you are following **MLA STYLE**, short quotations are defined as four typed

MLA 548–96 ●

academic literacies ✳ · rhetorical situations ■ · genres ▲ · fields ◆ · processes ◯ · strategies ◆ · research MLA / APA ● · media / design ▢ · readings ❚❚ · handbook ◺

lines or fewer; if using **APA STYLE**, as below, short means fewer than forty words.

APA 597–636

> Gerald Graff (2003) has argued that colleges make the intellectual life seem more opaque than it needs to be, leaving many students with "the misconception that the life of the mind is a secret society for which only an elite few qualify" (p. 1).

If you are quoting three lines or fewer of poetry, run them in with your text, enclosed in quotation marks. Separate lines with slashes and leave one space on each side of the slashes, as in this MLA style example:

> Emma Lazarus almost speaks for the Statue of Liberty with the words inscribed on its pedestal: "Give me your tired, your poor, / Your huddled masses yearning to breathe free, / The wretched refuse of your teeming shore" (lines 10–12).

Set off long quotations block style.   If you are using MLA style, set off quotations of five or more typed lines by indenting the quote one-half inch from the left margin. If you are using APA style, indent quotations of forty or more words one-half inch (or five to seven spaces) from the left margin. In either case, do not use quotation marks, and put any parenthetical documentation *after* any end punctuation.

> Nonprofit organizations such as Oxfam and Habitat for Humanity rely on visual representations of the poor. What better way to get our attention, asks rhetorician Diana George:
>
>> In a culture saturated by the image, how else do we convince Americans that—despite the prosperity they see all around them—there is real need out there? The solution for most nonprofits has been to show the despair. To do that they must represent poverty as something that can be seen and easily recognized: fallen down shacks and trashed out public housing, broken windows, dilapidated porches, barefoot kids with stringy hair, emaciated old women and men staring out at the camera with empty eyes. (210)

If you are quoting four or more lines of poetry, they need to be set off block style in the same way.

Indicate any omissions with ellipses.   You may sometimes delete words from a quotation that are unnecessary for your point. Insert three ellipsis marks (leaving a space before the first and after the last one) to indicate the deletion. If you omit a sentence or more in the middle of a quotation, put a period before the three ellipsis dots. Be careful not to distort the source's meaning, however.

> Faigley points out that Gore's "Information Superhighway" metaphor "associated the economic prosperity of the 1950s and . . . 1960s facilitated by new highways with the potential for vast . . . commerce to be conducted over the Internet" (253).

> According to Welch, "Television is more acoustic than visual. . . . One can turn one's gaze away from the television, but one cannot turn one's ears from it without leaving the area where the monitor leaks its aural signals into every corner" (102).

Indicate additions or changes with brackets.   Sometimes you'll need to change or add words in a quotation—to make the quotation fit grammatically within your sentence, for example, or to add a comment. In the following example, the writer changes the passage "one of our goals" to clarify the meaning of "our."

> Writing about the dwindling attention among some composition scholars to the actual teaching of writing, Susan Miller notes that "few discussions of writing pedagogy take it for granted that one of [writing teachers'] goals is to teach how to write" (480).

Here's an example of brackets used to add explanatory words to a quotation:

> Barbosa observes that Buarque's lyrics have long included "many a metaphor of *saudades* [yearning] so characteristic of *fado* music" (207).

Use punctuation correctly with quotations.   When you incorporate a quotation into your text, you have to think about the end punctuation in the quoted material and also about any punctuation you need to add when you insert the quote into your own sentence.

Periods and commas. Put periods or commas *inside* closing quotation marks, except when you have parenthetical documentation at the end, in which case you put the period or comma after the parentheses.

> "Country music," Tichi says, "is a crucial and vital part of the American identity" (23).

After long quotations set off block style with no quotation marks, however, the period goes *before* the documentation, as in the example on page 529.

Question marks and exclamation points. These go *inside* closing quotation marks if they are part of the quoted material but *outside* when they are not. If there's parenthetical documentation at the end of the quotation, any punctuation that's part of your sentence comes after it.

> Speaking at a Fourth of July celebration in 1852, Frederick Douglass asked, "What have I, or those I represent, to do with your national independence?" (35).

> Who can argue with W. Charisse Goodman's observation that media images persuade women that "thinness equals happiness and fulfillment" (53)?

Colons and semicolons. These always go *outside* closing quotation marks.

> It's hard to argue with W. Charisse Goodman's observation that media images persuade women that "thinness equals happiness and fulfillment"; nevertheless, American women today are more overweight than ever (53).

Paraphrasing

When you paraphrase, you restate information from a source in your own words, using your own sentence structures. Paraphrase when the source material is important but the original wording is not. Because it includes all the main points of the source, a paraphrase is usually about the same length as the original.

Here is a paragraph about synthetic dyes and cancer, followed by two paraphrases of it that demonstrate some of the challenges of paraphrasing:

ORIGINAL SOURCE

In 1938, in a series of now-classic experiments, exposure to synthetic dyes derived from coal and belonging to a class of chemicals called aromatic amines was shown to cause bladder cancer in dogs. These results helped explain why bladder cancers had become so prevalent among dyestuffs workers. With the invention of mauve in 1854, synthetic dyes began replacing natural plant-based dyes in the coloring of cloth and leather. By the beginning of the twentieth century, bladder cancer rates among this group of workers had skyrocketed, and the dog experiments helped unravel this mystery. The International Labor Organization did not wait for the results of these animal tests, however, and in 1921 declared certain aromatic amines to be human carcinogens. Decades later, these dogs provided a lead in understanding why tire-industry workers, as well as machinists and metalworkers, also began falling victim to bladder cancer: aromatic amines had been added to rubbers and cutting oils to serve as accelerants and antirust agents.

—Sandra Steingraber, "Pesticides, Animals, and Humans"

The following paraphrase borrows too much of the language of the original or changes it only slightly, as the highlighted words and phrases show:

UNACCEPTABLE PARAPHRASE: WORDING TOO CLOSE

Now-classic experiments in 1938 showed that when dogs were exposed to aromatic amines, chemicals used in synthetic dyes derived from coal, they developed bladder cancer. Similar cancers were prevalent among dyestuffs workers, and these experiments helped to explain why. Mauve, a synthetic dye, was invented in 1854, after which cloth and leather manufacturers replaced most of the natural plant-based dyes with synthetic dyes. By the early twentieth century, this group of workers had skyrocketing rates of bladder cancer, a mystery the dog experiments helped to unravel. As early as 1921, though, before the test results proved the connection, the International Labor Organization had labeled certain aromatic amines carcinogenic. Even so, decades later many metalworkers, machinists, and tire-industry workers began developing bladder cancer. The animal tests helped researchers understand that rubbers and cutting oils contained aromatic amines as accelerants and antirust agents (Steingraber 976).

The next paraphrase uses original language but follows the sentence structure of Steingraber's text too closely:

UNACCEPTABLE PARAPHRASE: SENTENCE STRUCTURE TOO CLOSE

In 1938, several pathbreaking experiments showed that being exposed to synthetic dyes that are made from coal and belong to a type of chemicals called aromatic amines caused dogs to get bladder cancer. These results helped researchers identify why cancers of the bladder had become so common among textile workers who worked with dyes. With the development of mauve in 1854, synthetic dyes began to be used instead of dyes based on plants in the dyeing of leather and cloth. By the end of the nineteenth century, rates of bladder cancer among these workers had increased dramatically, and the experiments using dogs helped clear up this oddity. The International Labor Organization anticipated the results of these tests on animals, though, and in 1921 labeled some aromatic amines carcinogenic. Years later these experiments with dogs helped researchers explain why workers in the tire industry, as well as metalworkers and machinists, also started dying of bladder cancer: aromatic amines had been put into rubbers and cutting oils as rust inhibitors and accelerants (Steingraber 976).

Patchwriting, a third form of unacceptable paraphrase, combines the other two. Composition researcher Rebecca Moore Howard defines it as "copying from a source text and then deleting some words, altering grammatical structures, or plugging in one-for-one synonym-substitutes." Here is a patchwrite of the first two sentences of the original source: (The source's exact words are shaded in yellow ; paraphrases are in blue .)

PATCHWRITE

Scientists have known for a long time that chemicals in the environment can cause cancer. For example, in 1938, in a series of important experiments, being exposed to synthetic dyes made out of coal and belonging to a kind of chemicals called aromatic amines was shown to cause dogs to develop bladder cancer. These experiments explain why this type of cancer had become so common among workers who handled dyes.

Here is an acceptable paraphrase of the entire passage:

ACCEPTABLE PARAPHRASE

Biologist Sandra Steingraber explains that pathbreaking experiments in 1938 demonstrated that dogs exposed to aromatic amines (chemicals used in coal-based synthetic dyes) developed cancers of the bladder that were similar to cancers common among dyers in the textile industry. After mauve, the first synthetic dye, was invented in 1854, leather and cloth manufacturers replaced most natural dyes made from plants with synthetic dyes, and by the early 1900s textile workers had very high rates of bladder cancer. The experiments with dogs proved the connection, but years before, in 1921, the International Labor Organization had labeled some aromatic amines carcinogenic. Even so, years later many metal-workers, machinists, and workers in the tire industry started to develop unusually high rates of bladder cancer. The experiments with dogs helped researchers understand that the cancers were caused by aromatic amines used in cutting oils to inhibit rust and in rubbers as accelerants (976).

Some guidelines for paraphrasing

- *Use your own words and sentence structure.* It is acceptable to use some words from the original, but as much as possible, the phrasing and sentence structures should be your own.

- *Introduce paraphrased text with* SIGNAL PHRASES.

- *Put in quotation marks any of the source's original phrasing that you use.*

- *Indicate the source.* Although the wording may be yours, the ideas and information come from another source; be sure to name the author and include DOCUMENTATION to avoid the possibility of PLAGIARISM.

535–38

MLA 551–57
APA 600–604
539–43

Summarizing

A summary states the main ideas in a source concisely and in your own words. Unlike a paraphrase, a summary does *not* present all the details, and it is generally as brief as possible. Summaries may boil down an entire

book or essay into a single sentence, or they may take a paragraph or more to present the main ideas. Here, for example, is a one-sentence summary of the Steingraber paragraph:

> Steingraber explains that experiments with dogs demonstrated that aromatic amines, chemicals used in synthetic dyes, cutting oils, and rubber, cause bladder cancer (976).

In the context of an essay, the summary might take this form:

> Medical researchers have long relied on experiments using animals to expand understanding of the causes of disease. For example, biologist and ecologist Sandra Steingraber notes that in the second half of the nineteenth century, the rate of bladder cancer soared among textile workers. According to Steingraber, experiments with dogs demonstrated that synthetic chemicals in dyes used to color the textiles caused the cancer (976).

Some guidelines for summarizing

- *Include only the main ideas; leave out the details.* A summary should include just enough information to give the reader the gist of the original. It is always much shorter than the original, sometimes even as brief as one sentence.

- *Use your own words.* If you quote phrasing from the original, enclose the phrase in quotation marks.

- *Indicate the source.* Although the wording may be yours, the ideas and information come from another source. Name the author, either in a signal phrase or parentheses, and include an appropriate **IN-TEXT CITATION** to avoid the possibility of **PLAGIARISM**.

MLA 551–57
APA 600–604
542–43

Introducing Source Materials Using Signal Phrases

You need to introduce quotations, paraphrases, and summaries clearly, usually letting readers know who the author is—and, if need be, something about their credentials. Consider this sentence:

> Professor and textbook author Elaine Tyler May argues that many high
> school history books are too bland to interest young readers (531).

The beginning ("Professor and textbook author Elaine Tyler May argues")
functions as a *signal phrase*, telling readers who is making the assertion and
why she has the authority to speak on the topic—and making clear that
everything between the signal phrase and the parenthetical citation comes
from that source. Since the signal phrase names the author, the parenthetical
citation includes only the page number; had the author not been identified
in the signal phrase, she would have been named in the parentheses:

> Even some textbook authors believe that many high school history
> books are too bland to interest young readers (May 531).

MLA and APA have different conventions for constructing signal
phrases. In MLA, the language you use in a signal phrase can be neutral—
like *X says* or *Y thinks* or *according to Z*. Or it can suggest something about

66–68 ■

the **STANCE**—the source's or your own. The example above referring to
the textbook author uses the verb *argues*, suggesting that what she says
is open to dispute (or that the writer believes it is). How would it change
your understanding if the signal verb were *observes* or *suggests*?

In addition to the names of sources' authors, signal phrases often give
readers information about institutional affiliations and positions authors
have, their academic or professional specialties, and any other information
that lets readers judge the credibility of the sources. You should craft each
signal phrase you use so as to highlight the credentials of the author. Here
are some examples:

> A study done by Anthony M. Armocida, professor of psychology at
> Duke University, showed that . . .

The signal phrase identifies the source's author, his professional position,
and his university affiliation, emphasizing his title.

> Science writer Isaac McDougal argues that . . .

This phrase acknowledges that the source's author may not have scholarly
credentials but is a published writer; it's a useful construction if the source
doesn't provide much information about the writer.

academic literacies | rhetorical situations | genres | fields | processes | strategies | research MLA / APA | media / design | readings | handbook

Writing in *Psychology Today*, Amanda Chao-Fitz notes that . . .

This is the sort of signal phrase you use if you have no information on the author; you establish credibility on the basis of the publication in which the source appears.

If you're writing using APA style, signal phrases are typically briefer, giving only the author's last name and the date of publication:

According to Benzinger (2010), . . .

Quartucci (2011) observed that . . .

SOME COMMON SIGNAL VERBS

acknowledges	claims	disagrees	observes
admits	comments	disputes	points out
advises	concludes	emphasizes	reasons
agrees	concurs	grants	rejects
argues	confirms	illustrates	reports
asserts	contends	implies	responds
believes	declares	insists	suggests
charges	denies	notes	thinks

Verb tenses. MLA and APA also have different conventions regarding the tenses of verbs in signal phrases. MLA requires present-tense verbs (*writes, asserts, notes*) in signal phrases to introduce a work you are quoting, paraphrasing, or summarizing.

In *Poor Richard's Almanack*, Benjamin Franklin <u>notes</u>, "He that cannot obey, cannot command" (739).

If, however, you are referring to the act of writing or saying something rather than simply quoting someone's words, you might not use the present tense. The writer of the following sentence focuses on the year in which the source was written—therefore, the verb is necessarily in the past tense:

Back in 1941, Kenneth Burke <u>wrote</u> that "the ethical values of work are in its application of the competitive equipment to cooperative ends" (316).

If you are following APA style, use the past tense to introduce sources composed in the past. If you are referring to a past action that didn't occur at a specific time or that continues into the present, you should use the present perfect.

Dowdall et al. (2020) <u>observed</u> that women attending women's colleges are less likely to engage in binge drinking than are women who attend coeducational colleges (p. 713).

Many researchers <u>have studied</u> drinking habits on college campuses.

APA requires the present tense, however, to discuss the results of an experiment or to explain conclusions that are generally agreed on.

The findings of this study <u>suggest</u> that excessive drinking has serious consequences for college students and their institutions.

The authors of numerous studies <u>agree</u> that smoking and drinking among adolescents are associated with lower academic achievement.

IF YOU NEED MORE HELP

See Chapter 52 for help **ACKNOWLEDGING SOURCES** and giving credit to the sources you use. See also the **SAMPLE RESEARCH PAPERS** to see how sources are cited in MLA and APA styles. And see Chapter 3 if you're writing a **SUMMARY/ RESPONSE** essay.

539–43 ●
MLA 589–96 ●
APA 628–36
33–44 ✳

Acknowledging Sources, **52**
Avoiding Plagiarism

Whenever you do research-based writing, you find yourself entering a conversation—reading what many others have had to say about your topic, figuring out what you yourself think, and then putting what you think in writing—"putting in your oar," as the rhetorician Kenneth Burke once wrote. As a writer, you need to *acknowledge* any words and ideas that come from others—to give credit where credit is due, to recognize the various authorities and many perspectives you have considered, to show readers where they can find your sources, and to situate your own arguments in the ongoing conversation. Using other people's words and ideas without acknowledgment is *plagiarism,* a serious academic and ethical offense. This chapter will show you how to acknowledge the materials you use and avoid plagiarism.

Acknowledging Sources

When you insert in your text information that you've obtained from others, your reader needs to know where your source's words or ideas begin and end. Therefore, you should usually introduce a source by naming the author in a **SIGNAL PHRASE** and then provide brief **DOCUMENTATION** of the specific material from the source in a parenthetical reference following the material. (Sometimes you can put the author's name in the parenthetical reference as well.) You need only brief documentation of the source here, since your readers will find full bibliographic information about it in your list of **WORKS CITED** or **REFERENCES**.

535–38
MLA 551–57
APA 600–604

MLA 558–87
APA 605–26

539

Sources that need acknowledgment. You almost always need to acknowledge any information that you get from a specific source. Material you should acknowledge includes the following:

- *Direct quotations.* Unless they are well known (see p. 542 for some examples), any quotations from another source must be enclosed in quotation marks, cited with brief bibliographic information in parentheses, and usually introduced with a signal phrase that tells who wrote or said it and provides necessary contextual information, as in the following sentence:

  > In a dissenting opinion on the issue of racial preferences in college admissions, Supreme Court justice Ruth Bader Ginsburg argues, "The stain of generations of racial oppression is still visible in our society, and the determination to hasten its removal remains vital" (*Gratz v. Bollinger*).

- *Arguable statements and information that may not be common knowledge.* If you state something about which there is disagreement or for which arguments can be made, cite the source of your statement. If in doubt about whether you need to give the source of an assertion, provide it. As part of an essay on "fake news" programs, for example, you might make the following assertion:

  > The satire of *The Daily Show* complements the conservative bias of FOX News, since both have abandoned the stance of objectivity maintained by mainstream news sources, contends Michael Hoyt, executive editor of the *Columbia Journalism Review* (43).

Others might argue with the contention that the FOX News Channel offers biased reports of the news, so the source of this assertion needs to be acknowledged. In the same essay, you might present information that should be cited because it's not widely known, as in this example:

> According to a report by the Pew Research Center, 12 percent of Americans under thirty got information about the 2012 presidential campaign primarily from "fake news" and comedy shows like *The Daily Show* and *Saturday Night Live* (2).

academic literacies | rhetorical situations | genres | fields | processes | strategies | research MLA / APA | media / design | readings | handbook

- *The opinions and assertions of others.* When you present the ideas, opinions, and assertions of others, cite the source. You may have rewritten the concept in your own words, but the ideas were generated by someone else and must be acknowledged, as they are here:

  > David Boonin, writing in the *Journal of Social Philosophy*, asserts that, logically, laws banning marriage between people of different races are not discriminatory since everyone of each race is affected equally by them. Laws banning same-sex unions are discriminatory, however, since they apply only to people with a certain sexual orientation (256).

- *Any information that you didn't generate yourself.* If you did not do the research or compile the data yourself, cite your source. This goes for interviews, statistics, graphs, charts, visuals, photographs—anything you use that you did not create. If you create a chart using data from another source, you need to cite that source.

- *Collaboration with and help from others.* In many of your courses and in work situations, you'll be called on to work with others. You may get help with your writing at your school's writing center or from fellow students in your writing courses. Acknowledging such collaboration or assistance, in a brief informational note, is a way of giving credit—and saying thank you. See guidelines for writing notes in the **MLA** and **APA** sections of this book.

MLA 557–58
APA 604–5

Sources that don't need acknowledgment. Widely available information and common knowledge do not require acknowledgment. What constitutes common knowledge may not be clear, however. When in doubt, provide a citation, or ask your instructor whether the information needs to be cited. You generally do not need to cite the following:

- *Information that most readers are likely to know.* You don't need to acknowledge information that is widely known or commonly accepted as fact. For example, in a literary analysis, you wouldn't cite a source saying that Harriet Beecher Stowe wrote *Uncle Tom's Cabin*; you can assume your readers already know that. On the other hand, you should cite the source from which you got the information that the book was first published in installments in a magazine and then, with revisions, in book form, because that information isn't common knowledge. As you do research in areas you're not familiar with, be aware that what constitutes common knowledge isn't always clear; the history of the novel's publication would be known to Stowe scholars and would likely need no acknowledgment in an essay written for them. In this case, too, if you aren't sure whether to acknowledge information, do so.

- *Information and documents that are widely available.* If a piece of information appears in several sources or reference works or if a document has been published widely, you needn't cite a source for it. For example, the date when astronauts Neil Armstrong and Buzz Aldrin landed a spacecraft on the moon can be found in any number of reference works. Similarly, the Declaration of Independence and the Gettysburg Address are reprinted in thousands of sources, so the ones where you found them need no citation.

- *Well-known quotations.* These include such famous quotations as Lady Macbeth's "Out, damned spot!" and John F. Kennedy's "Ask not what your country can do for you; ask what you can do for your country." Be sure, however, that the quotation is correct. Winston Churchill is said to have told a class of schoolchildren, "Never, ever, ever, ever, ever, ever, ever give up. Never give up. Never give up. Never give up." His actual words, however, are much different and begin "Never give in."

- *Material that you created or gathered yourself.* You need not cite photographs that you took, graphs that you composed based on your own findings, or data from an experiment or survey that you conducted—though you should make sure readers know that the work is yours.

A good rule of thumb: *when in doubt, cite your source.* You're unlikely to be criticized for citing too much—but you may invite charges of plagiarism by citing too little.

Avoiding Plagiarism

When you use the words or ideas of others, you need to acknowledge who and where the material came from; if you don't credit those sources, you

academic literacies   rhetorical situations   genres   fields   processes   strategies   research MLA / APA   media / design   readings   handbook

are guilty of plagiarism. Plagiarism is often committed unintentionally—as when a writer paraphrases someone else's ideas in language that is too close to the original. It is essential, therefore, to know what constitutes plagiarism: (1) using another writer's words or ideas without acknowledging the source, (2) using another writer's exact words without quotation marks, and (3) paraphrasing or summarizing someone else's ideas using language or sentence structures that are too close to theirs.

To avoid plagiarizing, take careful **NOTES** as you do your research, clearly labeling as quotations any words you quote directly and being careful to use your own phrasing and sentence structures in paraphrases and summaries. Be sure you know what source material you must **DOCUMENT**, and give credit to your sources, both in the text and in a list of **REFERENCES** or **WORKS CITED**.

526–28

544–47
APA 605–26
MLA 558–87

Be aware that it's easy to plagiarize inadvertently when you're working with online sources, such as full-text articles, that you've downloaded or cut and pasted into your notes. Keep careful track of these materials, since saving copies of your sources is so easy. Later, be sure to check your draft against the original sources to make sure your quotations are accurately worded—and take care, too, to include quotation marks and document the source correctly. Copying online material right into a document you are writing and forgetting to put quotation marks around it or to document it (or both) is all too easy to do. You must acknowledge information you find on the web just as you must acknowledge all other source materials.

And you must recognize that plagiarism has consequences. Scholars' work will be discredited if it too closely resembles another's. Journalists found to have plagiarized lose their jobs, and students routinely fail courses or are dismissed from their school when they are caught cheating—all too often by submitting as their own essays that they have purchased from online "research" sites. If you're having trouble completing an assignment, seek assistance. Talk with your instructor, or if your school has a writing center, go there for advice on all aspects of your writing, including acknowledging sources and avoiding plagiarism.

53 Documentation

In everyday life, we are generally aware of our sources: "I read it on Megan McArdle's blog." "Amber told me it's your birthday." "If you don't believe me, ask Mom." Saying how we know what we know and where we got our information is part of establishing our credibility and persuading others to take what we say seriously.

The goal of a research project is to study a topic, combining what we learn from sources with our own thinking and then composing a written text. When we write up the results of a research project, we cite the sources we use, usually by quoting, paraphrasing, or summarizing, and we acknowledge those sources, telling readers where the ideas came from. The information we give about sources is called documentation, and we provide it not only to establish our credibility as researchers and writers but also so that our readers, if they wish to, can find the sources themselves.

Understanding Documentation Styles

The Norton Field Guide covers the documentation styles of the Modern Language Association (MLA) and the American Psychological Association (APA). MLA style is used chiefly in the humanities; APA is used in the social sciences, sciences, education, and nursing. Both are two-part systems, consisting of (1) brief in-text parenthetical documentation for quotations, paraphrases, or summaries and (2) more-detailed documentation in a list of sources at the end of the text. MLA and APA require that the end-of-text documentation provide the following basic information about each source you cite:

- author, editor, or creator of the source
- title of source (and of publication or site where it appears)
- name of publisher
- date of publication
- retrieval information (for online sources)

MLA and APA are by no means the only documentation styles. Many other publishers and organizations have their own style, among them the University of Chicago Press and the Council of Science Editors. We focus on MLA and APA here because those are styles that college students are often required to use. On the following page are examples of how the two parts—the brief parenthetical documentation in your text and the more detailed information at the end—correspond in each of these systems.

The examples here and throughout this book are color-coded to help you see the crucial parts of each citation: tan for author and editor, yellow for title, and gray for publication information: place of publication, name of publisher, date of publication, page number(s), and so on.

As the examples of in-text documentation show, in either MLA or APA style you should name the author either in a signal phrase or in parentheses following the source information. But there are several differences between the two styles in the details of the documentation. In MLA, the author's full name is used in a signal phrase; in APA, only the last name is used. In APA, the abbreviation *p.* is used with the page number, which is provided only for a direct quotation; in MLA, a page number (if there is one) is always given, but with no abbreviation before it. Finally, in APA the date of publication always appears just after the author's name.

Comparing the MLA and APA styles of listing works cited or references also reveals some differences: MLA includes an author's first name while APA gives only initials; MLA puts the date near the end while APA places it right after the author's name; MLA capitalizes most of the words in a book's title and subtitle while APA capitalizes only the first words and proper nouns and proper adjectives in each.

MLA Style

IN-TEXT DOCUMENTATION

As Lester Faigley puts it, "The world has become a bazaar from which to shop for an individual 'lifestyle'" (12).

As one observer suggests, "The world has become a bazaar from which to shop for an individual 'lifestyle'" (Faigley 12).

WORKS-CITED DOCUMENTATION

Faigley, Lester. *Fragments of Rationality: Postmodernity and the Subject of Composition.* U of Pittsburgh P, 1992.

APA Style

IN-TEXT DOCUMENTATION

As Faigley (1992) suggested, "The world has become a bazaar from which to shop for an individual 'lifestyle'" (p. 12).

As one observer has noted, "The world has become a bazaar from which to shop for an individual 'lifestyle'" (Faigley, 1992, p. 12).

REFERENCE-LIST DOCUMENTATION

Faigley, L. (1992). *Fragments of rationality: Postmodernity and the subject of composition.* University of Pittsburgh Press.

Some of these differences are related to the nature of the academic fields in which the two styles are used. In humanities disciplines, the authorship of a text is emphasized, so both first and last names are included in MLA documentation. Scholarship in those fields may be several years old but still current, so the publication date doesn't appear in the in-text citation. In APA style, as in many documentation styles used in the sciences, education, and engineering, emphasis is placed on the date of publication because in these fields, more recent research is usually preferred over older studies. However, although the elements are arranged differently, both MLA and APA—and other documentation styles as well—require similar information about author, title, and publication.

54 MLA Style

MLA style calls for (1) brief in-text documentation and (2) complete bibliographic information in a list of works cited at the end of your text. The models and examples in this chapter draw on the ninth edition of the *MLA Handbook*, published by the Modern Language Association of America in 2021. For additional information, or if you're citing a source that isn't covered, visit style.mla.org.

A DIRECTORY TO MLA STYLE

In-Text Documentation   551

Notes   557

List of Works Cited   558

Formatting a Research Paper   587

Sample Research Paper   589

Throughout this chapter, you'll find models and examples that are color-coded to help you see how writers include source information in their texts and in their lists of works cited: tan for author, editor, translator, and other contributors; yellow for titles; gray for publication information—date of publication, page number(s), DOIs, and other location information.

IN-TEXT DOCUMENTATION

Whenever you quote, paraphrase, or summarize a source in your writing, you need to provide brief documentation that tells readers what you took from the source and where in the source you found that information. This brief documentation also refers readers to the full entry in your works-cited list, so begin with whatever comes first there: the author, the title, or a description of the source.

You can mention the author or title either in a signal phrase—"Toni Morrison writes," "In *Beowulf*," "According to the article 'Every Patient's Nightmare'"—or in parentheses—(Morrison). If relevant, include pages or other details about where you found the information in the parenthetical reference: (Morrison 67).

Shorten any lengthy titles or descriptions in parentheses by including the first noun with any preceding adjectives and omitting any initial articles (*Norton Field Guide* for *The Norton Field Guide to Writing*). If the title doesn't start with a noun, use the first phrase or clause (*How to Be* for *How to Be an Antiracist*). Use the full title if it's short.

The first two examples below show basic in-text documentation of a work by one author. Variations on those examples follow. The examples illustrate the MLA style of using quotation marks around titles of short works and italicizing titles of long works.

1. AUTHOR NAMED IN A SIGNAL PHRASE

535–38

If you mention the author in a **SIGNAL PHRASE**, put only the page number(s) in parentheses. Do not write *page* or *p.* The first time you mention the author, use their first and last names. You can usually omit any middle initials.

> David McCullough describes John Adams's hands as those of someone used to manual labor (18).

2. AUTHOR NAMED IN PARENTHESES

If you do not mention the author in a signal phrase, put their last name in parentheses along with any page number(s). Do not use punctuation between the name and the page number(s).

> Adams is said to have had "the hands of a man accustomed to pruning his own trees, cutting his own hay, and splitting his own firewood" (McCullough 18).

Whether you use a signal phrase and parentheses or parentheses only, try to put the parenthetical documentation at the end of the sentence or as close as possible to the material you've cited—without awkwardly interrupting the sentence. When the parenthetical reference comes at the end of the sentence, the period follows it.

3. TWO OR MORE WORKS BY THE SAME AUTHOR

If you cite multiple works by one author, include the title of the work you are citing either in the signal phrase or in parentheses.

> Robert Kaplan insists that understanding power in the Near East requires "Western leaders who know when to intervene, and do so without illusions" (*Eastward to Tartary* 330).

Put a comma between author and title if both are in the parentheses.

> Understanding power in the Near East requires "Western leaders who know when to intervene, and do so without illusions" (Kaplan, (*Eastward to Tartary* 330).

4. AUTHORS WITH THE SAME LAST NAME

Give each author's first and last names in any signal phrase, or add the author's first initial in the parenthetical reference.

> *Imaginative* applies not only to modern literature but also to writing of all periods, whereas *magical* is often used in writing about Arthurian romances (A. Wilson 25).

5. TWO OR MORE AUTHORS

For a work with two authors, name both. If you first mention them in a signal phrase, give their first and last names.

> Lori Carlson and Cynthia Ventura's stated goal is to introduce Julio Cortázar, Marjorie Agosín, and other Latin American writers to an audience of English-speaking adolescents (v).

For a work by three or more authors, that you mention in a signal phrase, you can either name them all or name the first author followed by *and others* or *and colleagues*. If you mention them in a parenthetical reference, name the first author followed by *et al*.

> Phyllis Anderson and colleagues describe British literature thematically (A54-A67).

6. ORGANIZATION OR GOVERNMENT AS AUTHOR

In a signal phrase, use the full name of the organization: American Academy of Arts and Sciences. In parentheses, use the shortest possible noun phrase, omitting any initial articles: American Academy.

> The US government can be direct when it wants to be. For example, it sternly warns, "If you are overpaid, we will recover any payments not due you" (Social Security Administration 12).

7. AUTHOR UNKNOWN

If you don't know the author, use the work's title in a signal phrase or in a parenthetical reference.

> A powerful editorial in *The New York Times* asserts that healthy liver donor Mike Hurewitz died because of "frightening" faulty postoperative care ("Every Patient's Nightmare").

8. LITERARY WORKS

When referring to common literary works that are available in many different editions, give the page numbers from the edition you are using, followed by information that will let readers of any edition locate the text you are citing.

NOVELS AND PROSE PLAYS. Give the page number followed by a semicolon and any chapter, section, or act numbers, separated by commas.

> In *Pride and Prejudice*, Mrs. Bennet shows no warmth toward Jane and Elizabeth when they return from Netherfield (Austen 105; ch. 12).

VERSE PLAYS. Give act, scene, and line numbers, separated with periods.

> Shakespeare continues the vision theme when Macbeth says, "Thou hast no speculation in those eyes / Which thou dost glare with" *(Macbeth* 3.3.96-97).

POEMS. Give the part and the line numbers, separated by periods. If a poem has only line numbers, use the word *line* or *lines* only in the first reference; after that, give only numbers.

> Walt Whitman sets up not only opposing adjectives but also opposing nouns in "Song of Myself" when he says, "I am of old and young, of the foolish as much as the wise, / . . . a child as well as a man" (16.330-32).

> One description of the mere in *Beowulf* is "not a pleasant place" (line 1372). Later, it is labeled "the awful place" (1378).

9. WORK IN AN ANTHOLOGY

Name the author(s) of the work, not the editor of the anthology.

> "It is the teapots that truly shock," according to Cynthia Ozick in her
> essay on teapots as metaphor (70).

> In *In Short: A Collection of Creative Nonfiction*, readers will find both an
> essay on Scottish tea (Hiestand) and a piece on teapots as metaphors (Ozick).

10. ENCYCLOPEDIA OR DICTIONARY

Acknowledge an entry in an encyclopedia or dictionary by giving the
author's name, if available. For an entry without an author, give the entry's
title.

> According to *Funk and Wagnall's New World Encyclopedia*, early
> in his career, most of Kubrick's income came from "hustling chess
> games in Washington Square Park" ("Kubrick, Stanley").

11. LEGAL DOCUMENTS

For legal cases, give whatever comes first in the works-cited entry. If you
are citing a government document in parentheses and multiple entries in
you works-cited list start with the same government author, give as much
of the name as you need to differentiate the sources.

> In 2015, for the first time, all states were required to license and recog-
> nize the marriages of same-sex couples (United States, Supreme Court).

12. SACRED TEXT

When citing a sacred text such as the Bible or the Qur'an for the first time,
give the title of the edition as well as the book, chapter, and verse (or their
equivalent), separated by periods. MLA recommends abbreviating the names
of the books of the Bible in parenthetical references. Later citations from the
same edition do not have to repeat its title.

> The wording from *The New English Bible* follows: "In the beginning of
> creation, when God made heaven and earth, the earth was without form
> and void . . ." (Gen. 1.1-2).

13. MULTIVOLUME WORK

If you cite more than one volume of a multivolume work, each time you cite one of the volumes, give the volume *and* the page number(s) in parentheses, separated by a colon and a space.

> Carl Sandburg concludes with the following sentence about those paying last respects to Lincoln: "All day long and through the night the unbroken line moved, the home town having its farewell" (4: 413).

If you cite an entire volume of a multivolume work in parentheses, give the author's last name followed by a comma and *vol.* before the volume number: (Sandburg, vol. 4). If your works-cited list includes only a single volume of a multivolume work, give just the page number in parentheses: (413).

14. TWO OR MORE WORKS CITED TOGETHER

If you're citing two or more works closely together, you will sometimes need to provide a parenthetical reference for each one.

> Dennis Baron describes singular *they* as "the missing word that's been hiding in plain sight" (182), while Benjamin Dreyer believes that "singular *they* is not the wave of the future; it's the wave of the present" (93).

If you are citing multiple sources for the same idea in parentheses, separate the references with a semicolon.

> Many critics have examined great works of literature from a cultural perspective (Tanner 7; Smith viii).

15. SOURCE QUOTED IN ANOTHER SOURCE

When you are quoting text that you found quoted in another source, use the abbreviation *qtd. in* in the parenthetical reference.

> Charlotte Brontë wrote to G. H. Lewes, "Why do you like Miss Austen so very much? I am puzzled on that point" (qtd. in Tanner 7).

16. WORK WITHOUT PAGE NUMBERS

For works without page or part numbers, including many online sources, no number is needed in a parenthetical reference.

> Studies show that music training helps children to be better at multitasking later in life ("Hearing the Music").

If you mention the author in a signal phrase, or if you mention the title of a work with no author, no parenthetical reference is needed.

> Arthur Brooks argues that a switch to fully remote work would have a negative effect on mental and physical health.

If the source has chapter, paragraph, or section numbers, use them with the abbreviations *ch.*, *par.*, or *sec.*: ("Hearing the Music," par. 2). Don't count lines or paragraphs on your own if they aren't numbered in the source. For an ebook, use chapter numbers. For an audio or video recording, give the hours, minutes, and seconds (separated by colons) as shown on the player: (00:05:21-31).

17. AN ENTIRE WORK OR A ONE-PAGE ARTICLE

If you cite an entire work rather than a part of it, or if you cite a single-page article, there's no need to include page numbers.

> Throughout life, John Adams strove to succeed (McCullough).

NOTES

Sometimes you may need to give information that doesn't fit into the text itself—to thank people who helped you, to provide additional details, to refer readers to other sources, or to add comments about sources. Such information can be given in a *footnote* (at the bottom of the page) or an *endnote* (on a separate page with the heading *Notes* or *Endnotes* just before your works-cited list). Put a superscript number at the appropriate point in your text, signaling to readers to look for the note with the corresponding number. If you have multiple notes, number them consecutively throughout your paper.

TEXT

This essay will argue that giving student athletes preferential treatment undermines educational goals.[1]

NOTE

    [1] I want to thank those who contributed to my thinking on this topic, especially my teacher Vincent Yu.

LIST OF WORKS CITED

A works-cited list provides full bibliographic information for every source cited in your text. See page 589 for guidelines on formatting this list and page 596 for a sample works-cited list.

Core Elements

The new MLA style provides a list of core elements for documenting sources, advising writers to list as many of them as possible in the order that MLA specifies. We've used these general principles to provide templates and examples for documenting fifty-three kinds of sources college writers most often need to cite and the following general guidelines for how to treat each of the core elements.

AUTHORS AND CONTRIBUTORS

- An author can be any kind of creator—a writer, a musician, an artist, and so on.
- If there is one author, list the name last name first: Morrison, Toni.
- If there are two authors, list the first author last name first and the second one first name first: Lunsford, Andrea, and Lisa Ede. Put their names in the order given in the work.
- If there are three or more authors, give the first author's name followed by *et al.*: Rose, Mike, et al.
- Include any middle names or initials: Heath, Shirley Brice; Toklas, Alice B.

- If there's no known author, start the entry with the title.
- If the author is a group or organization, use the full name, omitting any initial article: United Nations.
- If an author uses a handle that is significantly different from their name, include the handle in square brackets after the name: Ocasio-Cortez, Alexandria [@AOC].
- If there's an editor but no author, put the editor's name in the author position and specify their role: Lunsford, Andrea, editor.
- If you're citing someone in addition to an author—an editor, translator, director, or other contributors—specify their role. For works with multiple contributors, put the one whose work you wish to highlight before the title, and list any others you want to mention after the title. If you don't want to highlight one particular contributor, start with the title and include any contributors after the title. For contributors named before the title, put the label after the name: Fincher, David, director. For those named after the title, specify their role first: Directed by David Fincher.

TITLES

- Include any subtitles and capitalize all the words in titles and subtitles except for articles (*a, an, the*), prepositions (*to, at, from,* and so on), and coordinating conjunctions (*and, but, for, or, nor, so, yet*)—unless they are the first or last word of a title or subtitle.
- Italicize the titles of books, periodicals, websites, and other long whole works (*Pride and Prejudice, Wired*), even if they are part of a larger work.
- Enclose in quotation marks the titles of short works and sources that are part of larger works: "Letter from Birmingham Jail."
- To document a source that has no title, describe it without italics or quotation marks: Letter to the author, Photograph of a tree.
- For a short, untitled email, text message, tweet, or poem, you may want to include the text itself instead: Dickinson, Emily. "Immortal is an ample word." *American Poems*, www.americanpoems.com/poets /emilydickinson/immortal-is-an-ample-word.

PUBLICATION INFORMATION

- Write publishers', studios', and networks' names in full, but omit initial articles and words like *Company* or *Inc.*

- For academic presses, use *U* for *University* and *P* for *Press*: Princeton UP, U of California P. Spell out *Press* if the name doesn't include *University*: Running Press, MIT Press.

- Many publishers use an ampersand in their name: Simon & Schuster. MLA says to use *and* instead: Simon and Schuster.

- If the publisher is a division of an organization, list the organization and any divisions from largest to smallest: Stanford U, Center for the Study of Language and Information, Metaphysics Research Lab.

DATES

- Whether to give just the year or to include the month and day depends on the source. In general, give the full date that you find there.

- For books, give the publication date on the copyright page: 1948. If a book lists more than one date, use the most recent one.

- Periodicals may be published annually, monthly, seasonally, weekly, or daily. Give the full date that you find there: 2016, Apr. 2016, 16 Apr. 2016. Do not capitalize the names of seasons: spring 2021.

- Abbreviate the months except for May, June, and July: Jan., Feb., Mar., Apr., Aug., Sept., Oct., Nov., Dec.

- For online sources, use the copyright date or the full publication date that you find there, or a date of revision. If the source doesn't give a date, include the date you accessed the site: Accessed 6 June 2020. Give a date of access as well for online sources you think are likely to change, or for websites that have disappeared: Accessed 6 June 2017.

LOCATION

- For most print articles and other short works, help readers locate the source by giving a page number or range of pages: p. 24, pp. 24-35. For those that are not on consecutive pages, give the first page number with a plus sign: pp. 24+.

author　　　　title　　　　publication

- If it's necessary to specify a particular section of a source, give the section name before the page numbers: Sunday Review sec., p. 3.
- Indicate the location of an online source by giving a DOI if one is available; if not, give a URL—and use a permalink if one is available. MLA notes that URLs are not always reliable, so ask your instructor if you should include them. DOIs should start with *https://doi.org/*—but no need to include *https://* for a URL, unless you want the URL to be a hyperlink.
- For physical objects that you find in a museum, archive, or elsewhere, give the name of the place and enough information to identify it (city, city and state, or city and country): Menil Collection, Houston; Maine Jewish Museum, Portland, Maine; Biblioteca Pública, Manaus, Brazil.
- For performances or other live presentations, name the venue and its location: Mark Taper Forum, Los Angeles.

PUNCTUATION

- Use a period after the author name(s) that start an entry (Morrison, Toni.) and the title of the source you're documenting (*Beloved*.).
- Use a comma between the author's last and first names: Morrison, Toni.
- Sometimes you'll need to provide information about more than one work for a single source—for instance, when you cite an article from a periodical that you access through a database. MLA refers to the periodical and database (or any other entity that holds a source) as "containers." Use commas between elements within each container and put a period at the end of each container. For example:

> Semuels, Alana. "The Future Will Be Quiet." *The Atlantic,* Apr. 2016,
>   pp. 19-20. *ProQuest,* search.proquest.com/docview/1777443553
>   ?accountid+42654.

The guidelines below should help you document the kinds of sources you're likely to use. The first section shows how to acknowledge authors and other contributors and applies to all kinds of sources—print, online, or others. Later sections show how to treat titles, publication information, location, and access information for many specific kinds of sources. In general, provide as much information as possible for each source—enough to tell readers how to find a source if they wish to access it themselves.

Sources not covered　These guidelines will help you cite a variety of sources, but there may be sources you want to use that aren't mentioned here. If you're citing a source that isn't covered, consult the MLA style blog at style.mla.org, or ask them a question at style.mla.org/ask-a-question.

Authors and Contributors

When you name authors and other contributors in your citations, you are crediting them for their work and letting readers know who's in on the conversation. The following guidelines for citing authors and contributors apply to all sources you cite: in print, online, or in some other media.

1. ONE AUTHOR

Author's Last Name, First Name. *Title*. Publisher, Date.

Anderson, Chris. *The Long Tail: Why the Future of Business Is Selling Less of More.* Hyperion, 2006.

2. TWO AUTHORS

1st Author's Last Name, First Name, and 2nd Author's First and Last Names. *Title*. Publisher, Date.

Lunsford, Andrea, and Lisa Ede. *Singular Texts/Plural Authors: Perspectives on Collaborative Writing.* Southern Illinois UP, 1990.

3. THREE OR MORE AUTHORS

1st Author's Last Name, First Name, et al. *Title.* Publisher, Date.

Sebranek, Patrick, et al. *Writers INC: A Guide to Writing, Thinking, and Learning.* Write Source, 1990.

4. TWO OR MORE WORKS BY THE SAME AUTHOR

Give the author's name in the first entry, and then use three hyphens in the author slot for each of the subsequent works, listing them alphabetically by the first word of each title and ignoring any initial articles.

author　　　title　　　publication

Author's Last Name, First Name. *Title That Comes First Alphabetically.* Publisher, Date.

- - -. *Title That Comes Next Alphabetically.* Publisher, Date.

Kaplan, Robert D. *The Coming Anarchy: Shattering the Dreams of the Post Cold War.* Random House, 2000.

- - -. *Eastward to Tartary: Travels in the Balkans, the Middle East, and the Caucasus.* Random House, 2000.

5. AUTHOR AND EDITOR OR TRANSLATOR

Author's Last Name, First Name. *Title.* Role by First and Last Names, Publisher, Date.

Austen, Jane. *Emma.* Edited by Stephen M. Parrish, W. W. Norton, 2000.

Dostoevsky, Fyodor. *Crime and Punishment.* Translated by Richard Pevear and Larissa Volokhonsky, Vintage Books, 1993.

Start with the editor or translator, followed by their role, if you are focusing on their contribution rather than the author's. If there is a translator but no author, start with the title.

Pevear, Richard, and Larissa Volokhonsky, translators. *Crime and Punishment.* By Fyodor Dostoevsky, Vintage Books, 1993.

Beowulf. Translated by Kevin Crossley-Holland, Macmillan, 1968.

6. NO AUTHOR OR EDITOR

When there's no known author or editor, start with the title.

The Turner Collection in the Clore Gallery. Tate Publications, 1987.

"Being Invisible Closer to Reality." *The Atlanta Journal-Constitution,* 11 Aug. 2008, p. A3.

7. ORGANIZATION OR GOVERNMENT AS AUTHOR

Organization Name. *Title.* Publisher, Date.

Diagram Group. *The Macmillan Visual Desk Reference.* Macmillan, 1993.

For a government publication, give the name that is shown in the source.

> United States, Department of Health and Human Services, National Institute of Mental Health. *Autism Spectrum Disorders.* Government Printing Office, 2004.

When a nongovernment organization is both author and publisher, start with the title and list the organization only as the publisher.

> *Stylebook on Religion 2000: A Reference Guide and Usage Manual.* Catholic News Service, 2002.

If a division of an organization is listed as the author, give the division as the author and the organization as the publisher.

> Center for Workforce Studies. *2005-13: Demographics of the U.S. Psychology Workforce.* American Psychological Association, July 2015.

Articles and Other Short Works

Articles, essays, reviews, and other short works are found in journals, magazines, newspapers, other periodicals, and also in books—all of which you may find in print, online, or in a database. For most short works, you'll need to provide information about the author, the titles of both the short work and the longer work where it's found, any page numbers, and various kinds of publication information, all explained below.

8. ARTICLE IN A JOURNAL

PRINT

> Author's Last Name, First Name. "Title of Article." *Name of Journal,* Volume, Issue, Date, Pages.

> Cooney, Brian C. "Considering *Robinson Crusoe*'s 'Liberty of Conscience' in an Age of Terror." *College English,* vol. 69, no. 3, Jan. 2007, pp. 197-215.

ONLINE

> Author's Last Name, First Name. "Title of Article." *Name of Journal,* Volume, Issue, Date, DOI *or* URL.

Documentation Map (MLA)

Article in a Print Journal

Marge Simpson, Blue-Haired Housewife: ⬅ Title of article
Defining Domesticity on *The Simpsons*

JESSAMYN NEUHAUS ⬅ Author

MORE THAN TWENTY SEASONS AFTER ITS DEBUT AS A SHORT ON *THE Tracy Ullman Show* in 1989, pundits, politicians, scholars, journalists, and critics continue to discuss and debate the meaning and relevance of *The Simpsons* to American society. For academics and educators, the show offers an especially dense pop culture text, inspiring articles and anthologies examining *The Simpsons* in light of American religious life, the representation of homosexuality in cartoons, and the use of pop culture in the classroom, among many other topics (Dennis; Frank; Henry "The Whole World's Gone Gay"; Hobbs; Kristiansen). Philosophers and literary theorists in particular are intrigued by the quintessentially postmodern self-aware form and content of *The Simpsons* and the questions about identity, spectatorship, and consumer culture it raises (Alberti; Bybee and Overbeck; Glynn; Henry "The Triumph of Popular Culture"; Herron; Hull; Irwin et al.; Ott; Parisi).

Simpsons observers frequently note that this TV show begs one of the fundamental questions in cultural studies: can pop culture ever provide a site of individual or collective resistance or must it always ultimately function in the interests of the capitalist dominant ideology? Is *The Simpsons* a brilliant satire of virtually every cherished American myth about public and private life, offering dissatisfied Americans the opportunity to critically reflect on contemporary issues (Turner 435)? Or is it simply another TV show making money for the Fox Network? Is *The Simpsons* an empty, cynical, even nihilistic view of the world, lulling its viewers into laughing hopelessly at the pointless futility of

Volume

Name of journal ➡ *The Journal of Popular Culture*, Vol. 43, No. 4, 2010, pp. 761–81. ⬅ Pages
© 2010, Wiley Periodicals, Inc.

Issue

Date

Neuhaus, Jessamyn. "Marge Simpson, Blue-Haired Housewife: Defining Domesticity on *The Simpsons*." *The Journal of Popular Culture*, vol. 43, no. 4, 2010, pp. 761-81.

⬤ 564–71
for more on citing articles MLA style

Schmidt, Desmond. "A Model of Versions and Layers." *Digital Humanities Quarterly*, vol. 13, no. 3, 2019, www.digitalhumanities.org/dhq /vol/13/3/000430/000430.html.

9. ARTICLE IN A MAGAZINE

PRINT

Author's Last Name, First Name. "Title of Article." *Name of Magazine*, Volume (if any), Issue (if any), Date, Pages.

Burt, Tequia. "Legacy of Activism: Concerned Black Students' 50-Year History at Grinnell College." *Grinnell Magazine*, vol. 48, no. 4, summer 2016, pp. 32-38.

ONLINE

Author's Last Name, First Name. "Title of Article." *Name of Magazine*, Volume (if any), Issue (if any), Date, DOI *or* URL.

Brooks, Arthur C. "The Hidden Toll of Remote Work." *The Atlantic*, 1 Apr. 2021, www.theatlantic.com/family/archive/2021/04/zoom -remote-work-lonelinesshappiness/618473.

10. ARTICLE IN A NEWS PUBLICATION

PRINT

Author's Last Name, First Name. "Title of Article." *Name of Publication*, Date, Pages.

Saulny, Susan, and Jacques Steinberg. "On College Forms, a Question of Race Can Perplex." *The New York Times*, 14 June 2011, p. A1.

To document a particular edition of a newspaper, list the edition before the date. If a section name or number is needed to locate the article, put that detail after the date.

Burns, John F., and Miguel Helft. "Under Pressure, YouTube Withdraws Muslim Cleric's Videos." *The New York Times*, late ed., 4 Nov. 2010, sec. 1, p. 13.

author   title   publication

Documentation Map (MLA)

Article in an Online Magazine

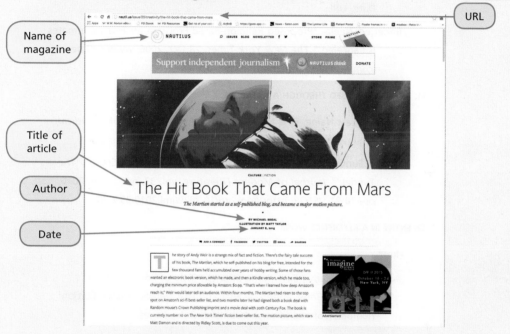

URL

Name of magazine

Title of article

Author

Date

Segal, Michael. "The Hit Book That Came from Mars." *Nautilus*, 8 Jan. 2015, nautil.us/issue/20/creativity/the-hit-book-that -came-from-mars.

577–81 for more on citing websites MLA style

ONLINE

Author's Last Name, First Name. "Title of Article." *Name of Publication*, Date, URL.

Banerjee, Neela. "Proposed Religion-Based Program for Federal Inmates Is Canceled." *The New York Times*, 28 Oct. 2006, www.nytimes .com/2006/10/28/us/28prison.html.

11. ARTICLE ACCESSED THROUGH A DATABASE

Author's Last Name, First Name. "Title of Article." *Name of Periodical*, Volume, Issue, Date, Pages. *Name of Database*, DOI or URL.

Stalter, Sunny. "Subway Ride and Subway System in Hart Crane's 'The Tunnel.'" *Journal of Modern Literature*, vol. 33, no. 2, Jan. 2010, pp. 70-91. *JSTOR*, https://doi.org/10.2979/jml.2010.33.2.70.

12. ENTRY IN A REFERENCE WORK

PRINT

Author's Last Name, First Name (if any). "Title of Entry." *Title of Reference Book*, edited by First and Last Names (if any), Edition number, Volume (if any), Publisher, Date, Pages.

Fritz, Jan Marie. "Clinical Sociology." *Encyclopedia of Sociology*, edited by Edgar F. Borgatta and Rhonda J. V. Montgomery, 2nd ed., vol. 1, Macmillan Reference USA, 2000, pp. 323-29.

"California." *The New Columbia Encyclopedia*, edited by William H. Harris and Judith S. Levey, 4th ed., Columbia UP, 1975, pp. 423-24.

ONLINE

Document online reference works the same as print ones, adding the URL after the date of publication.

"Baseball." *The Columbia Electronic Encyclopedia*, edited by Paul Lagassé, 6th ed., Columbia UP, 2012, www.infoplease.com/encyclopedia.

author   title   publication

Documentation Map (MLA)

Journal Article Accessed through a Database

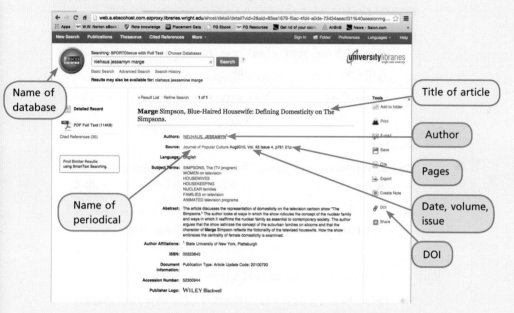

Name of database

Title of article

Author

Pages

Name of periodical

Date, volume, issue

DOI

Neuhaus, Jessamyn. "Marge Simpson, Blue-Haired Housewife: Defining
Domesticity on *The Simpsons*." *Journal of Popular Culture*, vol. 43,
no. 4, Aug. 2010, pp. 761-81. *EBSCOhost*, https://doi.org/10.1111
/j.1540-5931.2010.00769.x.

13. EDITORIAL OR OP-ED

EDITORIAL

Editorial Board. "Title." *Name of Periodical*, Date, Page or URL.

Editorial Board. "A New Look for Local News Coverage." *The Lakeville Journal*, 13 Feb. 2020, p. A8.

Editorial Board. "Editorial: Protect Reporters at Protest Scenes." *Los Angeles Times*, 11 Mar. 2021, www.latimes.com/opinion/story/2021 -03-11/reporters-protest-scenes.

OP-ED

Author's Last Name, First Name. "Title." *Name of Periodical*, Date, Page or URL.

Okafor, Kingsley. "Opinion: The First Step to COVID Vaccine Equity Is Overall Health Equity." *The Denver Post*, 15 Apr. 2021, www .denverpost.com/2021/04/15/covid-vaccine-equity-kaiser.

If it's not clear that it's an op-ed, add a label at the end.

Balf, Todd. "Falling in Love with Swimming." *The New York Times*, 17 Apr. 2021, p. A21. Op-ed.

14. LETTER TO THE EDITOR

Author's Last Name, First Name. "Title of Letter (if any)." *Name of Periodical*, Date, Page or URL.

Pinker, Steven. "Language Arts." *The New Yorker*, 4 June 2012, p. 10.

If the letter has no title, include *Letter* after the author's name.

Fleischmann, W. B. Letter. *The New York Review of Books*, 1 June 1963, www.nybooks.com/articles/1963/06/01/letter-21.

author   title   publication

15. REVIEW

PRINT

Reviewer's Last Name, First Name. "Title of Review." *Name of Periodical*,
Date, Pages.

Frank, Jeffrey. "Body Count." *The New Yorker*, 30 July 2007, pp. 86-87.

ONLINE

Reviewer's Last Name, First Name. "Title of Review." *Name of Periodical*,
Date, URL.

Donadio, Rachel. "Italy's Great, Mysterious Storyteller." *The New York
Review of Books*, 18 Dec. 2014, www.nybooks.com/articles/2014
/12/18/italys-great-mysterious-storyteller.

If a review has no title, include the title and author of the work being
reviewed after the reviewer's name.

Lohier, Patrick. Review of *Exhalation*, by Ted Chiang. *Harvard Review
Online*, 4 Oct. 2019, www.harvardreview.org/book-review
/exhalation.

16. COMMENT ON AN ONLINE ARTICLE

Commenter's Last Name, First Name *or* Username. Comment on "Title of
Article." *Name of Periodical*, Date posted, Time posted, URL.

Nick. Comment on "The Case for Reparations." *The Atlantic*, 22 May
2014, 3:04 p.m., www.theatlantic.com/business/archive/2014/05
/how-to-comment-on-reparations/371422/#article-comments.

Books and Parts of Books

For most books, you'll need to provide information about the author, the title, the publisher, and the year of publication. If you found the book inside a larger volume, a database, or some other work, be sure to specify that as well.

17. BASIC ENTRIES FOR A BOOK

PRINT

Author's Last Name, First Name. *Title*. Publisher, Year of publication.

Watson, Brad. *Miss Jane*. W. W. Norton, 2016.

EBOOK

Author's Last Name, First Name. *Title*. Ebook ed., Publisher, Year of publication.

Watson, Brad. *Miss Jane*. Ebook ed., W. W. Norton, 2016.

ON A WEBSITE

Author's Last Name, First Name. *Title*. Publisher, Year of publication, DOI *or* URL.

Ball, Cheryl E., and Drew M. Loewe, editors. *Bad Ideas about Writing*. West Virginia U Libraries, 2017, textbooks.lib.wvu.edu/badideas /badideasaboutwritingbook.pdf.

WHEN THE PUBLISHER IS THE AUTHOR

Title. Edition number (if any), Publisher, Year of publication.

MLA Handbook. 9th ed., Modern Language Association of America, 2021.

18. ANTHOLOGY OR EDITED COLLECTION

Last Name, First Name, editor. *Title*. Publisher, Year of publication.

Hall, Donald, editor. *The Oxford Book of Children's Verse in America*. Oxford UP, 1985.

Documentation Map (MLA)

Print Book

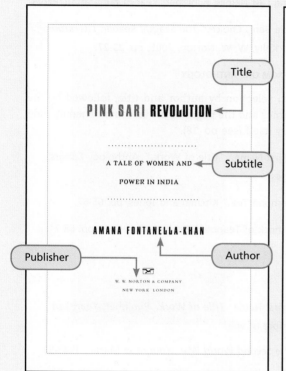

Year of publication

Title

Subtitle

Publisher

Author

Fontanella-Khan, Amana. *Pink Sari Revolution: A Tale of Women and Power in India.* W. W. Norton, 2013.

572–77 for more on citing books MLA style

19. WORK(S) IN AN ANTHOLOGY

> Author's Last Name, First Name. "Title of Work." *Title of Anthology*,
> edited by First and Last Names, Publisher, Year of publication, Pages.

> Achebe, Chinua. "Uncle Ben's Choice." *The Seagull Reader: Literature*,
> edited by Joseph Kelly, W. W. Norton, 2005, pp. 23-27.

TWO OR MORE WORKS FROM ONE ANTHOLOGY

Prepare an entry for each selection by author and title, followed by the anthology editors' last names and the pages of the selection. Then include an entry for the anthology itself (see no. 18).

> Author's Last Name, First Name. "Title of Work." Anthology Editors'
> Last Names, Pages.

> Hiestand, Emily. "Afternoon Tea." Kitchen and Jones, pp. 65-67.

> Ozick, Cynthia. "The Shock of Teapots." Kitchen and Jones, pp. 68-71.

20. MULTIVOLUME WORK

ALL VOLUMES

> Author's Last Name, First Name. *Title of Work.* Publisher, Year(s) of
> publication. Number of vols.

> Churchill, Winston. *The Second World War.* Houghton Mifflin, 1948-53.
> 6 vols.

SINGLE VOLUME

> Author's Last Name, First Name. *Title of Work.* Vol. number, Publisher,
> Year of publication.

> Sandburg, Carl. *Abraham Lincoln: The War Years.* Vol. 2, Harcourt, Brace
> and World, 1939.

If the volume has its own title, include it after the author's name, and indicate the volume number and series title after the year.

> Caro, Robert A. *Means of Ascent.* Vintage Books, 1990. Vol. 2 of *The Years of Lyndon Johnson.*

21. BOOK IN A SERIES

> Author's Last Name, First Name. *Title of Book.* Edited by First and Last Names, Publisher, Year of publication. Series Title.

> Walker, Alice. *Everyday Use.* Edited by Barbara T. Christian, Rutgers UP, 1994. Women Writers: Texts and Contexts.

22. GRAPHIC NARRATIVE OR COMIC BOOK

> Author's Last Name, First Name. *Title.* Publisher, Year of publication.

> Barry, Lynda. *One! Hundred! Demons!* Drawn and Quarterly, 2005.

If the work has both an author and an illustrator, start with the one you want to highlight, and label the role of anyone who's not an author.

> Pekar, Harvey. *Bob and Harv's Comics.* Illustrated by R. Crumb, Running Press, 1996.

> Crumb, R., illustrator. *Bob and Harv's Comics.* By Harvey Pekar, Running Press, 1996.

To cite several contributors, you can also start with the title.

> *Secret Invasion.* By Brian Michael Bendis, illustrated by Leinil Yu, inked by Mark Morales, Marvel, 2009.

23. SACRED TEXT

If you cite a specific edition of a religious text, you need to include it in your works-cited list.

> *The New English Bible with the Apocrypha.* Oxford UP, 1971.

> *The Torah: A Modern Commentary.* W. Gunther Plaut, general editor, Union of American Hebrew Congregations, 1981.

24. EDITION OTHER THAN THE FIRST

> Author's Last Name, First Name. *Title.* Edition name *or* number, Publisher, Year of publication.

> Smart, Ninian. *The World's Religions.* 2nd ed., Cambridge UP, 1998.

25. REPUBLISHED WORK

> Author's Last Name, First Name. *Title.* Year of original publication. Current publisher, Year of republication.

> Bierce, Ambrose. *Civil War Stories.* 1909. Dover, 1994.

26. FOREWORD, INTRODUCTION, PREFACE, OR AFTERWORD

> Part Author's Last Name, First Name. Name of Part. *Title of Book,* by Author's First and Last Names, Publisher, Year of publication, Pages.

> Tanner, Tony. Introduction. *Pride and Prejudice,* by Jane Austen, Penguin, 1972, pp. 7-46.

27. PUBLISHED LETTER

> Letter Writer's Last Name, First Name. "Title of letter." Day Month Year. *Title of Book,* edited by First and Last Names, Publisher, Year of publication, Pages.

author   title   publication

White, E. B. "To Carol Angell." 28 May 1970. *Letters of E. B. White,*
edited by Dorothy Lobrano Guth, Harper and Row, 1976, p. 600.

28. PAPER HEARD AT A CONFERENCE

Author's Last Name, First Name. "Title of Paper." Conference, Day
Month Year, Location.

Hern, Katie. "Inside an Accelerated Reading and Writing Classroom."
Conference on Acceleration in Developmental Education, 15 June
2016, Sheraton Inner Harbor Hotel, Baltimore.

29. DISSERTATION

Author's Last Name, First Name. *Title.* Year. Institution, PhD dissertation. *Name of Database,* URL.

Simington, Maire Orav. *Chasing the American Dream Post World War II:
Perspectives from Literature and Advertising.* 2003. Arizona State U,
PhD dissertation. *ProQuest,* search.proquest.com/docview/305340098.

For an unpublished dissertation, end with the institution and a description of the work.

Kim, Loel. *Students Respond to Teacher Comments: A Comparison of
Online Written and Voice Modalities.* 1998. Carnegie Mellon U, PhD
dissertation.

Websites

Many sources are available in multiple media—for example, a print periodical that is also on the web and contained in digital databases—but
some are published only on websites. A website can have an author, an
editor, or neither. Some sites have a publisher, and some do not. Include
whatever information is available. If the publisher and title of the site are
essentially the same, omit the name of the publisher.

30. ENTIRE WEBSITE

> Editor's Last Name, First Name, role. *Title of Site*. Publisher, Date, URL.

> Proffitt, Michael, chief editor. *The Oxford English Dictionary*. Oxford UP, 2021, www.oed.com.

PERSONAL WEBSITE

> Author's Last Name, First Name. *Title of Site*. Date, URL.

> Park, Linda Sue. *Linda Sue Park: Author and Educator*. 2021, lindasuepark.com.

If the site is likely to change, if it has no date, or if it no longer exists, include a date of access.

> *Archive of Our Own*. Organization for Transformative Works, archiveofourown.org. Accessed 23 Apr. 2021.

31. WORK ON A WEBSITE

> Author's Last Name, First Name (if any). "Title of Work." *Title of Site*, Publisher (if any), Date, URL.

> Cesareo, Kerry. "Moving Closer to Tackling Deforestation at Scale." *World Wildlife Fund*, 20 Oct. 2020, www.worldwildlife.org/blogs /sustainabilityworks/posts/moving-closer-to-tackling-deforestation-at-scale.

32. BLOG ENTRY

> Author's Last Name, First Name. "Title of Blog Entry." *Title of Blog*, Date, URL.

> Hollmichel, Stefanie. "Bring Up the Bodies." *So Many Books*, 10 Feb. 2014, somanybooksblog.com/2014/02/10/bring-up-the-bodies.

Document a whole blog as you would an entire website (no. 30) and a comment on a blog as you would a comment on an online article (no. 16).

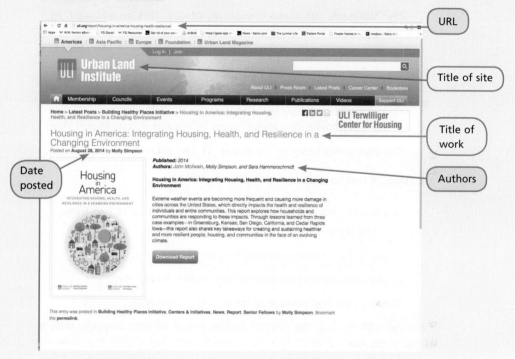

Documentation Map (MLA)

Work on a Website

McIlwain, John, et al. "Housing in America: Integrating Housing, Health, and Resilience in a Changing Environment." *Urban Land Institute*, 28 Aug. 2014, uli.org/report/housing-in-america-housing-health-resilience.

33. WIKI

"Title of Entry." *Title of Wiki*, Publisher, Date, URL.

"Pi." *Wikipedia*, Wikimedia Foundation, 28 Aug. 2013, en.wikipedia.org /wiki/Pi.

Personal Communication and Social Media

34. PERSONAL LETTER

Sender's Last Name, First Name. Letter to the author. Day Month Year.

Quindlen, Anna. Letter to the author. 11 Apr. 2017.

35. EMAIL OR TEXT MESSAGE

Sender's Last Name, First Name. Email *or* Text message to First Name Last Name *or* to the author. Day Month Year.

Smith, William. Email to Richard Bullock. 19 Nov. 2013.

Rombes, Maddy. Text message to Isaac Cohen. 4 May 2021.

O'Malley, Kit. Text message to the author. 2 June 2020.

You can also include the text of a short email or text message, with a label at the end.

Rust, Max. "Trip to see the cows tomorrow?" 27 Apr. 2021. Email.

36. POST TO *TWITTER*, *INSTAGRAM*, OR OTHER SOCIAL MEDIA

Author. "Title." *Title of Site*, Day Month Year, URL.

Oregon Zoo. "Winter Wildlife Wonderland." *Facebook*, 8 Feb. 2019, www.facebook.com/80229441108/videos/2399570506799549.

If there's no title, you can use a concise description or the text of a short post.

> Millman, Debbie. Photos of Roxane Gay. *Instagram*, 18 Feb. 2021, www .instagram.com/p/CLcT_EnhnWT.

> Obama, Barack [@POTUS44]. "It's been the honor of my life to serve you. You made me a better leader and a better man." *Twitter*, 20 Jan. 2017, twitter.com/POTUS44/status/822445882247413761.

Audio, Visual, and Other Sources

37. ADVERTISEMENT

PRINT

Description of ad. *Title of Periodical*, Date, Page.

Advertisement for Grey Goose. *Wine Spectator*, 18 Dec. 2020, p. 22.

VIDEO

"Title." *Title of Site*, uploaded by Company, Date, URL.

"First Visitors." *YouTube*, uploaded by Snickers, 20 Aug. 2020, www.youtube.com/watch?v=negeco0b1L0.

38. ART

ORIGINAL

Artist's Last Name, First Name. *Title of Art*. Year created, Location.

Van Gogh, Vincent. *The Potato Eaters.* 1885, Van Gogh Museum, Amsterdam.

IN A BOOK

Artist's Last Name, First Name. *Title of Art.* Year created, Location. *Title of Book,* by First and Last Names, Publisher, Year of publication, Page.

Van Gogh, Vincent. *The Potato Eaters.* 1885, Scottish National Gallery. *History of Art: A Survey of the Major Visual Arts from the Dawn of History to the Present Day,* by H. W. Janson, Prentice Hall / Harry N. Abrams, 1969, p. 508.

ONLINE

Artist's Last Name, First Name. *Title of Art.* Year created. *Title of Site,* URL.

Warhol, Andy. *Self-portrait.* 1979. *J. Paul Getty Museum,* www.getty .edu/art/collection/objects/106971/andy-warhol-self-portrait -american-1979.

39. CARTOON

PRINT

Author's Last Name, First Name. Cartoon *or* "Title of Cartoon." *Name of Periodical,* Date, Page.

Mankoff, Robert. Cartoon. *The New Yorker,* 3 May 1993, p. 50.

ONLINE

Author's Last Name, First Name. Cartoon *or* "Title of Cartoon." *Title of Site,* Date, URL.

Munroe, Randall. "Up Goer Five." *xkcd,* 12 Nov. 2012, xkcd.com/1133.

40. SUPREME COURT CASE

> United States, Supreme Court. *First Defendant v. Second Defendant*. Date
> of decision. *Title of Source Site*, Publisher, URL.

> United States, Supreme Court. *District of Columbia v. Heller*. 26 June
> 2008. *Legal Information Institute*, Cornell Law School, www.law
> .cornell.edu/supremecourt/text/07-290.

41. FILM

Name individuals based on the focus of your project—the director, the
screenwriter, or someone else.

> *Title of Film.* Role by First and Last Names, Production Company, Date.

> *Breakfast at Tiffany's.* Directed by Blake Edwards, Paramount, 1961.

ONLINE

> *Title of Film.* Role by First and Last Names, Production Company,
> Date. *Title of Site,* URL.

> *Interstellar.* Directed by Christopher Nolan, Paramount, 2014. *Amazon
> Prime Video*, www.amazon.com/Interstellar-Matthew-McConaughey
> /dp/B00TU9UFTS.

42. TV SHOW EPISODE

BROADCAST

> "Title of Episode." *Title of Show*, season, episode, role by First and Last
> Names (if any), Production Company, Date.

> "The Storm." *Avatar: The Last Airbender*, created by Michael Dante
> DiMartino and Bryan Konietzko, season 1, episode 12, Nickelodeon
> Animation Studios, 3 June 2005.

DVD

"Title of Episode." Broadcast Date. *Title of DVD*, role by First and Last
   Names (if any), season, episode, Production Company, Release Date,
   disc number. DVD.

"The Storm." 2005. *Avatar: The Last Airbender: The Complete Book 1 Collection*, created by Michael Dante DiMartino and Bryan Konietzko,
   episode 12, Nickelodeon Animation Studios, 2006, disc 3. DVD.

STREAMING ONLINE

"Title of Episode." *Title of Show*, season, episode, role by First and
   Last Names (if any), Production Company, Date. *Title of Site*, URL.

"The Storm." *Avatar: The Last Airbender*, season 1, episode 12,
   Nickelodeon Animation Studios, 2005. *Netflix*, www.netflix.com.

STREAMING ON AN APP

"Title of Episode." *Title of Show*, role by First and Last Names (if any),
   season, episode, Production Company, Date. *Name of* app.

"The Storm." *Avatar: The Last Airbender*, season 1, episode 12,
   Nickelodeon Animation Studios, 2005. *Netflix* app.

43. ONLINE VIDEO

"Title of Video." Name of Site, uploaded by Uploader's Name, Day
   Month Year, URL.

"Everything Wrong with *National Treasure* in 13 Minutes or Less."
   YouTube, uploaded by CinemaSins, 21 Aug. 2014, www.youtube
   .com/watch?v=1ul-_ZWvXTs.

44. PRESENTATION ON *ZOOM* OR OTHER VIRTUAL PLATFORM

MLA doesn't give specific guidance on how to cite a virtual presentation,
but this is what we recommend. See style.mla.org for more information.

> Author's Last Name, First Name. "Title." Sponsoring Institution, Day
> Month Year. *Name of Platform.*

Budhathoki, Thir. "Cross-Cultural Perceptions of Literacies in Student
Writing." Conference on College Composition and Communication,
9 Apr. 2021. *Zoom.*

45. INTERVIEW

If it's not clear that it's an interview, add a label at the end. If you are citing
a transcript of an interview, indicate that at the end as well.

PUBLISHED

> Subject's Last Name, First Name. Interview or "Title of Interview." Inter-
> view by First Name Last Name (if given). *Name of Publication,* Date,
> Pages *or* URL.

Whitehead, Colson. "Colson Whitehead: By the Book." *The New York
Times,* 15 May 2014, www.nytimes.com/2014/05/18/books/review
/colson-whitehead-by-the-book.html. Interview.

PERSONAL

> Subject's Last Name, First Name. Concise description. Day Month Year.

Bazelon, L. S. Telephone interview with the author. 4 Oct. 2020.

46. MAP

> *Title of Map.* Publisher, Date.

Brooklyn. J. B. Beers, 1874. Map.

47. MUSICAL SCORE

> Composer's Last Name, First Name. *Title of Composition.* Publisher,
> Year of publication.

Frank, Gabriela Lena. *Compadrazgo.* G. Schirmer, 2007.

48. ORAL PRESENTATION

Presenter's Last Name, First Name. "Title of Presentation." Sponsoring Institution, Date, Location.

Cassin, Michael. "Nature in the Raw—The Art of Landscape Painting." Berkshire Institute for Lifelong Learning, 24 Mar. 2005, Clark Art Institute, Williamstown, Massachusetts.

49. PODCAST

If you accessed a podcast on the web, give the URL; if you accessed it through an app, indicate that instead.

"Title of Episode." *Title of Podcast*, hosted by First Name Last Name, season, episode, Production Company, Date, URL.

"DUSTWUN." *Serial*, hosted by Sarah Koenig, season 2, episode 1, WBEZ / Serial Productions, 10 Dec. 2015, serialpodcast.org/season-two /1/dustwun.

"DUSTWUN." *Serial*, hosted by Sarah Koenig, season 2, episode 1, WBEZ / Serial Productions, 10 Dec. 2015. *Spotify* app.

50. RADIO PROGRAM

"Title of Episode." *Title of Program,* hosted by First Name Last Name, Station, Day Month Year.

"In Defense of Ignorance." *This American Life*, hosted by Ira Glass, WBEZ, 22 Apr. 2016.

51. SOUND RECORDING

If you accessed a recording on the web, give the URL; if you accessed it through an app, indicate that instead.

Artist's Last Name, First Name. "Title of Work." *Title of Album*, Label, Date, URL.

Beyoncé. "Pray You Catch Me." *Lemonade*, Parkwood Entertainment / Columbia Records, 2016, www.beyonce.com/album/lemonade -visual-album/songs.

Simone, Nina. "To Be Young, Gifted and Black." *Black Gold*, RCA Records, 1969. *Spotify* app.

ON A CD

Artist's Last Name, First Name. "Title of Work." *Title of Album*, Label, Date. CD.

Brown, Greg. "Canned Goods." *The Live One*, Red House, 1995. CD.

52. VIDEO GAME

Title of Game. Version, Distributor, Date of release.

Animal Crossing: New Horizons. Version 1.1.4, Nintendo, 6 Apr. 2020.

FORMATTING A RESEARCH PAPER

Name, course, title.   MLA does not require a separate title page, unless your paper is a group project. In the upper left-hand corner of your first page, include your name, your instructor's name, the course name and number, and the date. Center the title of your paper on the line after the date; capitalize it as you would a book title. If your paper is a group project, include all of that information on a title page instead, listing all the authors.

Page numbers.   In the upper right-hand corner of each page, one-half inch below the top of the page, include your last name and the page number. If it's a group project and all the names don't fit, include only the page number. Number pages consecutively throughout your paper.

Font, spacing, margins, and indents.   Choose a font that is easy to read (such as Times New Roman) and that provides a clear contrast between regular text and italic text. Set the font size between 11 and 13 points. Double-space the entire paper, including your works-cited list and any notes. Set one-inch margins at the top, bottom, and sides of your text; do not justify your text. The first line of each paragraph should be indented one-half inch from the left margin. End punctuation should be followed by one space.

Headings.   Short essays do not generally need headings, but they can be useful in longer works. Use a large, bold font for the first level of heading, and smaller fonts and italics to signal lower-level headings. MLA requires that headings all be flush with the left margin.

First-Level Heading

Second-Level Heading

Third-Level Heading

Long quotations.   When quoting more than three lines of poetry, more than four lines of prose, or dialogue between characters in a drama, set off the quotation from the rest of your text, indenting it one-half inch (or five spaces) from the left margin. Do not use quotation marks, and put any parenthetical documentation *after* the final punctuation.

> In *Eastward to Tartary*, Robert Kaplan captures ancient and contemporary Antioch for us:
>> At the height of its glory in the Roman-Byzantine age, when it had an amphitheater, public baths, aqueducts, and sewage pipes, half a million people lived in Antioch. Today the population is only 125,000. With sour relations between Turkey and Syria, and unstable politics throughout the Middle East, Antioch is now a backwater—seedy and tumbledown, with relatively few tourists. I found it altogether charming. (123)

> In the first stanza of Matthew Arnold's "Dover Beach," the exclamations make clear that the speaker is addressing someone who is also present in the scene:
>> Come to the window, sweet is the night air!
>> Only, from the long line of spray

Where the sea meets the moon-blanched land,
Listen! You hear the grating roar
Of pebbles which the waves draw back, and fling. (lines 6-10)

Be careful to maintain the poet's line breaks. If a line does not fit on one line of your paper, put the extra words on the next line. Indent that line an additional quarter inch (or two spaces). If a citation doesn't fit, put it on the next line, flush with the right margin.

Tables and illustrations.   Insert illustrations and tables close to the text that discusses them. For tables, provide a number (*Table* 1) and a title on separate lines above the table. Below the table, provide a caption with source information and any notes. Notes should be indicated with lower-case letters. For graphs, photos, and other figures, provide a figure number (*Fig.* 1) and caption with source information below the figure. Use a lowercase *f* when referring to a figure in your text: (fig. 1). If you give only brief source information, use commas between elements—Zhu Wei, *New Pictures of the Strikingly Bizarre #9*, print, 2004—and include full source information in your list of works cited. If you give full source information in the caption, don't include the source in your list of works cited. Punctuate as you would in the works-cited list, but don't invert the author's name: Berenice Sydney. *Fast Rhythm*. 1972, Tate Britain, London.

List of works cited.   Start your list on a new page, following any notes. Center the title, *Works Cited*, and double-space the entire list. Begin each entry at the left margin, and indent subsequent lines one-half inch (or five spaces). Alphabetize the list by authors' last names (or by editors' or translators' names, if appropriate). Alphabetize works with no author or editor by title, disregarding *A*, *An*, and *The*. To cite more than one work by a single author, list them as in no. 4 on page 562.

SAMPLE RESEARCH PAPER

The following report was written by Dylan Borchers for a first-year writing course. It's formatted according to the guidelines of the MLA (style.mla.org).

Dylan Borchers

Professor Bullock

English 102, Section 4

4 May 2018

Against the Odds:

Harry S. Truman and the Election of 1948

Just over a week before Election Day in 1948, a *New York Times* article noted "[t]he popular view that Gov. Thomas E. Dewey's election as President is a foregone conclusion" (Egan). This assessment of the race between incumbent Democrat Harry S. Truman and Dewey, his Republican challenger, was echoed a week later when *Life* magazine published a photograph whose caption labeled Dewey "The Next President" (Photograph). In a *Newsweek* survey of fifty prominent political writers, each predicted Truman's defeat, and *Time* correspondents declared Dewey would carry 39 of the 48 states (Donaldson 210). Nearly every major US media outlet endorsed Dewey.

The results of an election are not easily predicted, as is shown in the famous photograph in which Truman holds up a newspaper proclaiming Dewey the victor (fig. 1). Not only did Truman win, but he won by a significant margin: 303 electoral votes and 24,179,259 popular votes to Dewey's 189 electoral votes and 21,991,291 popular votes (Donaldson 204-07). In fact, many historians and political analysts argue that Truman would have won by an even greater margin had third-party candidates Henry

Annotations (margin notes):

Last name and page number.

Title centered.

Double-spaced throughout.

No page number needed for one-page source.

Borchers   2

Fig. 1. President Harry S. Truman holds up an edition of the *Chicago Daily Tribune* that mistakenly announced "Dewey Defeats Truman." Byron Rollins, *Dewey Defeats Truman*, photograph, 1948.

Illustration is positioned close to the text to which it relates, with figure number and caption with source information.

A. Wallace and Strom Thurmond not won votes (McCullough 711). Although Truman's defeat was predicted, those predictions themselves, Dewey's passiveness as a campaigner, and Truman's zeal turned the tide for a Truman victory.

In the months preceding the election, public opinion polls predicted that Dewey would win by a large margin. Pollster Elmo Roper stopped polling in September, believing there was no reason to continue, given a seemingly inevitable Dewey landslide. Although the margin narrowed as the election drew near, other pollsters predicted a Dewey win by at least 5 percent (Donaldson 209). Many historians believe that these predictions aided the president. Surveys showing Dewey in the lead may have prompted

No signal phrase; author and page number in parentheses.

some Dewey supporters to feel overconfident and therefore to stay home from the polls. Other analysts believe that the overwhelming predictions of a Truman loss kept home some Democrats who saw a Truman loss as inevitable. According to political analyst Samuel Lubell, those Democrats may have saved Dewey from an even greater defeat (Hamby, *Man* 465). Whatever the impact on the voters, the polls had a decided effect on Dewey.

Paragraphs indented ½ inch or 5 spaces.

Historians and political analysts alike cite Dewey's overly cautious campaign as a main reason Truman was able to win. Dewey firmly believed in public opinion polls. With all signs pointing to an easy victory, Dewey and his staff believed that all he had to do was bide his time and make no foolish mistakes. As the leader in the race, Dewey kept his remarks faultlessly positive, with the result that he failed to deliver a solid message or even mention Truman. Eventually, Dewey began to be perceived as aloof, stuffy, and out of touch with the public. One observer compared him to the plastic groom on top of a wedding cake

Two works cited within the same sentence.

(Hamby, "Harry S. Truman"), and others noted his stiff, cold demeanor (McCullough 671-74).

When fellow Republicans said he was losing ground, Dewey insisted that his campaign stay the course. Even *Time* magazine, though it endorsed and praised him, conceded that his speeches were dull (McCullough 696). Dewey's poll numbers slipped before the election, but he still held a comfortable lead. Truman's famous whistle-stop campaign would make the difference.

Borchers   4

Few candidates in US history have campaigned for the
presidency with more passion and faith than Harry Truman did in
1948. For thirty-three days, he traveled the nation, giving hundreds
of speeches from the back of the *Ferdinand Magellan* railroad car.
David McCullough writes of Truman's campaign:

> No President in history had ever gone so far in quest of
> support from the people, or with less cause for the effort,
> to judge by informed opinion. . . . As a test of his skills and
> judgment as a professional politician, not to say his stamina
> and disposition at age sixty-four, it would be like no other
> experience in his long, often difficult career, as he himself
> understood perfectly. (655)

Quotations of more than 4 lines indented $\frac{1}{2}$ inch and double-spaced.

Parenthetical reference after final punctuation.

He spoke in large cities and small towns, defending his
policies and attacking Republicans. As a former farmer, Truman
was able to connect with the public. He developed an energetic
style, usually speaking from notes rather than from a prepared
speech, and often mingled with the crowds, which grew larger as
the campaign progressed. In Chicago, over half a million people
lined the streets as he passed, and in St. Paul the crowd numbered
over 25,000. When Dewey entered St. Paul two days later, only 7,000
supporters greeted him (McCullough 842). By connecting directly
with the American people, Truman built the momentum needed to
surpass Dewey and win the election.

The legacy and lessons of Truman's whistle-stop campaign
continue to be studied, and politicians mimic his campaign methods

by scheduling multiple visits to key states, as Truman did. He visited California, Illinois, and Ohio 48 times, compared with 6 visits to those states by Dewey. Political scientist Thomas Holbrook concludes that his strategic campaigning in those states and others gave Truman the electoral votes he needed to win (61, 65).

The 1948 election also had an effect on pollsters, who, as Roper admitted, "couldn't have been more wrong." *Life* magazine's editors concluded that pollsters as well as reporters and commentators were too convinced of a Dewey victory to analyze the polls seriously, especially the opinions of undecided voters (Karabell 256). Pollsters assumed that undecided voters would vote in the same proportion as decided voters—and that turned out to be a false assumption (257). Such errors led pollsters to change their methods significantly after the 1948 election.

Many political analysts, journalists, and historians concluded that the Truman upset was in fact a victory for the American people. And Truman biographer Alonzo Hamby notes that "polls of scholars consistently rank Truman among the top eight presidents in American history" (*Man* 641). But despite Truman's high standing, and despite the fact that the whistle-stop campaign remains in our political landscape, politicians have increasingly imitated the style of the Dewey campaign, with its "packaged candidate who ran so as not to lose, who steered clear of controversy, and who made a good show of appearing presidential" (Karabell 266). The election of

Author named in signal phrase, page number in parentheses.

1948 shows that voters are not necessarily swayed by polls, but it may have presaged the packaging of candidates by public relations experts, to the detriment of public debate on the issues in future presidential elections.

1″

Works Cited

Donaldson, Gary A. *Truman Defeats Dewey*. UP of Kentucky, 1999.

Egan, Leo. "Talk Is Now Turning to the Dewey Cabinet." *The New York Times*, 20 Oct. 1948, p. E8.

Hamby, Alonzo L. "Harry S. Truman: Campaigns and Elections." *Miller Center*, U of Virginia, millercenter.org/president /biography/truman-campaigns-and-elections. Accessed 17 Mar. 2019.

- - -. *Man of the People: A Life of Harry S. Truman*. Oxford UP, 1995.

Holbrook, Thomas M. "Did the Whistle-Stop Campaign Matter?" *PS: Political Science and Politics*, vol. 35, no. 1, Mar. 2002, pp. 59-66.

Karabell, Zachary. *The Last Campaign: How Harry Truman Won the 1948 Election*. Alfred A. Knopf, 2000.

McCullough, David. *Truman*. Simon and Schuster, 1992.

Photograph of Truman. *Life*, 1 Nov. 1948, p. 37. *Google Books*, books .google.com/books?id=ekoEAAAAMBAJ&printsec =frontcover#v=onepage&q&f=false.

Rollins, Byron. *Dewey Defeats Truman*. 1948. *Harry S. Truman Library and Museum*, www.trumanlibrary.gov/photograph -records/95-187.

Roper, Elmo. "Roper Eats Crow; Seeks Reason for Vote Upset." *Evening Independent*, 6 Nov. 1948, p. 10. *Google News*, news.google.com/newspapers?nid=PZE8UkGerEcC&dat =19481106&printsec=frontpage&hl=en.

Heading centered.

Double-spaced.

Alphabetized by authors' last names.

Each entry begins at the left margin; subsequent lines are indented one-half inch.

Multiple works by a single author listed alphabetically by title. For second and subsequent works, replace author's name with three hyphens.

Every source used is in the list of works cited.

APA Style **55**

American Psychological Association (APA) style calls for (1) brief documentation in parentheses near each in-text citation and (2) complete documentation in a list of references at the end of your text. The models in this chapter draw on the *Publication Manual of the American Psychological Association*, 7th edition (2020). Additional information is available at www.apastyle.org.

A DIRECTORY TO APA STYLE

author   title   publication

Throughout this chapter, you'll find models and examples that are color-coded to help you see how writers include source information in their texts and reference lists: tan for author or editor, yellow for title, gray for publication information—publisher, date of publication, page number(s), DOI or URL, and so on.

IN-TEXT DOCUMENTATION

Brief documentation in your text makes clear to your readers precisely what you took from a source. If you are quoting, provide the page number(s) or other information that will help readers find the quotation in the source. You're not required to give the page number(s) with a paraphrase or summary, but you may want to do so if you are citing a long or complex work.

526–38

PARAPHRASES and **SUMMARIES** are more common than **QUOTATIONS** in APA-style projects. As you cite each source, you will need to decide whether to name the author in a signal phrase—"as McCullough (2020) wrote"—or in parentheses—"(McCullough, 2020)." Note that APA requires

535–38

you to use the past tense for verbs in **SIGNAL PHRASES**, or the present perfect if you are referring to a past action that didn't occur at a specific time or that continues into the present: "Moss (2019) argued," "Many authors have argued."

1. AUTHOR NAMED IN A SIGNAL PHRASE

Put the date in parentheses after the author's last name, unless the year is mentioned in the sentence. Put any page number(s) you're including in parentheses after the quotation, paraphrase, or summary. Parenthetical documentation should come *before* the period at the end of the sentence and *after* any quotation marks.

> McCullough (2001) described John Adams as having "the hands of a man accustomed to pruning his own trees, cutting his own hay, and splitting his own firewood" (p. 18).

> In 2001, McCullough noted that John Adams's hands were those of a laborer (p. 18).

John Adams had "the hands of a man accustomed to pruning his own trees," according to McCullough (2001, p. 18).

If the author is named after a quotation, as in this last example, put the page number(s) after the date within the parentheses.

2. AUTHOR NAMED IN PARENTHESES

If you do not mention an author in a signal phrase, put the name, the year of publication, and any page number(s) in parentheses at the end of the sentence or right after the quotation, paraphrase, or summary.

John Adams had "the hands of a man accustomed to pruning his own trees, cutting his own hay, and splitting his own firewood" (McCullough, 2001, p. 18).

3. AUTHORS WITH THE SAME LAST NAME

If your reference list includes more than one first author with the same last name, include initials in all documentation to distinguish the authors from one another.

Eclecticism is common in modern criticism (J. M. Smith, 1992, p. vii).

4. TWO AUTHORS

Always mention both authors. Use "and" in a signal phrase, but use an ampersand (&) in parentheses.

Carlson and Ventura (1990) wanted to introduce Julio Cortázar, Marjorie Agosín, and other Latin American writers to an audience of English-speaking adolescents (p. v).

According to the Peter Principle, "In a hierarchy, every employee tends to rise to his level of incompetence" (Peter & Hull, 1969, p. 26).

5. THREE OR MORE AUTHORS

When you refer to a work by three or more contributors, name only the first author followed by "et al.," Latin for "and others."

> Peilen et al. (1990) supported their claims about corporate corruption with startling anecdotal evidence (p. 75).

6. ORGANIZATION OR GOVERNMENT AS AUTHOR

If an organization name has a familiar abbreviation, give the full name and the abbreviation the first time you cite the source. In subsequent references, use only the abbreviation. If the organization does not have a familiar abbreviation, always use its full name.

FIRST REFERENCE

> The American Psychological Association (APA, 2020)
>
> (American Psychological Association [APA], 2020)

SUBSEQUENT REFERENCES

> The APA (2020)
>
> (APA, 2020)

7. AUTHOR UNKNOWN

Use the complete title if it's short; if it's long, use the first few words of the title under which the work appears in the reference list. Italicize the title if it's italicized in the reference list; if it isn't italicized there, enclose the title in quotation marks.

> According to *Feeding Habits of Rams* (2000), a ram's diet often changes from one season to the next (p. 29).

> The article noted that one donor died because of "frightening" postoperative care ("Every Patient's Nightmare," 2007).

author　　　title　　　publication

8. TWO OR MORE WORKS TOGETHER

If you document multiple works in the same parentheses, place the source information in alphabetical order, separated by semicolons.

> Many researchers have argued that what counts as "literacy" is not necessarily learned at school (Heath, 1983; Moss, 2003).

Multiple authors in a signal phrase can be named in any order.

9. TWO OR MORE WORKS BY ONE AUTHOR IN THE SAME YEAR

If your list of references includes more than one work by the same author published in the same year, order them alphabetically by title, adding lowercase letters ("a," "b," and so on) to the year.

> Kaplan (2000a) described orderly shantytowns in Turkey that did not resemble the other slums he visited.

10. SOURCE QUOTED IN ANOTHER SOURCE

When you cite a source that was quoted in another source, add the words "as cited in." If possible, cite the original source instead.

> Thus, Modern Standard Arabic was expected to serve as the "moral glue" holding the Arab world together (Choueri, 2000, as cited in Walters, 2019, p. 475).

11. WORK WITHOUT PAGE NUMBERS

Instead of page numbers, some works have paragraph numbers, which you should include (preceded by the abbreviation "para.") if you are referring to a specific part of such a source.

> Russell's dismissals from Trinity College at Cambridge and from City College in New York City have been seen as examples of the controversy that marked his life (Irvine, 2006, para. 2).

In sources with neither page nor paragraph numbers, point to a particular part of the source if possible: (Brody, 2020, Introduction, para. 2).

12. AN ENTIRE WORK

You do not need to give a page number if you are directing readers' attention to an entire work.

> Kaplan (2000) considered Turkey and Central Asia explosive.

When you're citing an entire website, give the URL in the text. You do not need to include the website in your reference list. To document a webpage, see no. 18 on page 614.

> Beyond providing diagnostic information, the website for the Alzheimer's Association (http://www.alz.org) includes a variety of resources for the families of patients.

13. PERSONAL COMMUNICATIONS

Document emails, telephone conversations, personal interviews, personal letters, messages from nonarchived online discussion sources, and other personal texts as "personal communication," along with the person's initial(s), last name, and the date. You do not need to include such personal communications in your reference list.

> L. Strauss (personal communication, December 6, 2013) told about visiting Yogi Berra when they both lived in Montclair, New Jersey.

NOTES

You may need to use footnotes to give an explanation or information that doesn't fit into your text. To signal a content footnote, place a superscript numeral at the appropriate point in your text. Include this information in a footnote, either at the bottom of that page or on a separate page with the heading "Footnotes" centered and in bold, after your reference list. If you have multiple notes, number them consecutively throughout your text. Here is an example from *In Search of Solutions: A New Direction in Psychotherapy* (2003).

author   title   publication

TEXT WITH SUPERSCRIPT

An important part of working with teams and one-way mirrors is taking the consultation break, as at Milan, BFTC, and MRI.[1]

FOOTNOTE

[1]It is crucial to note here that while working within a team is fun, stimulating, and revitalizing, it is not necessary for successful outcomes. Solution-oriented therapy works equally well when working solo.

REFERENCE LIST

A reference list provides full bibliographic information for every source cited in your text with the exception of entire websites, common computer software and mobile apps, and personal communications. See page 627 for guidelines on preparing such a list; for a sample reference list, see page 635.

Key Elements for Documenting Sources

To document a source in APA style, you need to provide information about the author, the date, the title of the work you're citing, and the source itself (who published it; volume, issue, and page numbers; any DOI or URL). The following guidelines explain how to handle each of these elements generally, but there will be exceptions. For that reason, you'll want to consult the entries for the specific kinds of sources you're documenting; these entries provide templates showing which details you need to include. Be aware, though, that sometimes the templates will show elements that your source doesn't have; if that's the case, just omit those elements.

AUTHORS

Most entries begin with the author's last name, followed by the first and any middle initials: Smith, Z. for Zadie Smith; Kinder, D. R. for Donald R. Kinder.

- If the author is a group or organization, use its full name: Black Lives Matter, American Historical Association.

- If there is no author, put the title of the work first, followed by the date.
- If the author uses a screen name, first give their real name, followed by the screen name in brackets: Scott, B. [@BostonScott2]. If only the screen name is known, leave off the brackets: AvalonGirl1990.

DATES

Include the date of publication, in parentheses right after the author. Some sources require only the year; others require the year, month, and day; and still others require something else. Consult the entry in this chapter for the specific source you're documenting.

- For a book, use the copyright year, which you'll find on the copyright page. If more than one year is given, use the most recent one.
- For most magazine or newspaper articles, use the full date that appears on the work, usually the year followed by the month and day.
- For a journal article, use the year of the volume.
- For a work on a website, use the date when the work was last updated. If that information is not available, use the date when the work was published.
- If a work has no date, use "n.d." for "no date."
- For online content that is likely to change, include the month, day, and year when you retrieved it. No need to include a retrieval date for materials that are unlikely to change.

TITLES

Capitalize only the first word and any proper nouns and adjectives in the title and subtitle of a work. But sometimes you'll also need to provide the title of a periodical or website where a source was found, and those are treated differently: capitalize all the principal words (excluding articles and prepositions).

- For books, reports, webpages, podcasts, and any other works that stand on their own, italicize the title: *White fragility*, *Radiolab*, *The 9/11 report*. Do not italicize the titles of the sources where you found them, however: NPR, ProQuest.

- For journal articles, book chapters, TV series episodes, and other works that are part of a larger work, do not italicize the title: The snowball effect, Not your average Joe. But do italicize the title of the larger work: *The Atlantic*, *Game of thrones*.

- If a work has no title, include a description in square brackets after the date: [Painting of sheep on a hill].

- If the title of a work you're documenting includes another title, italicize it: *Frog and Toad* and the self. If the title you're documenting is itself in italics, do not italicize the title within it: *Stay, illusion!: The Hamlet doctrine*.

- For untitled social media posts or comments, include the first twenty words as the title, in italics, followed by a bracketed description: *TIL pigeons can fly up to 700 miles in one day* [Tweet].

SOURCE INFORMATION

This indicates where the work can be found (in a database or on a website, for example, or in a magazine or on a podcast) and includes information about the publisher; any volume, issue, and page numbers; and, for some sources, a DOI or URL. DOIs and URLs are included in all the templates; if the work you are documenting doesn't have one, just leave it off.

- For a work that stands on its own (a book, a report, a webpage), the source might be the publisher, a database, or a website.

- For a work that's part of a larger work (an article, an episode in a TV series, an essay in a collection), the source might be a magazine, a TV series, or an anthology.

- Give the volume and issue for journals and magazines that include that information. No need to give them for newspapers.

- Include a DOI for any work that has one, whether you accessed the source in print or online. For an online work with no DOI, include a working URL unless the work is from an academic database. You can use a shortDOI (https://shortdoi.org/) or a URL shortened using an online URL shortener, as long as the shorter DOI or URL leads to the correct work. No need to include a URL for a print work with no DOI.

Authors and Other Contributors

Most entries begin with authors—one author, two authors, or twenty-five. And some include editors, translators, or others who've contributed. The following templates show you how to document the various kinds of authors and other contributors.

1. ONE AUTHOR

> Author's Last Name, Initials. (Year of publication). *Title*. Publisher. DOI *or* URL

> Lewis, M. (2003). *Moneyball: The art of winning an unfair game*. W. W. Norton.

2. TWO AUTHORS

> First Author's Last Name, Initials, & Second Author's Last Name, Initials. (Year of publication). *Title*. Publisher. DOI *or* URL

> Montefiore, S., & Montefiore, S. S. (2016). *The royal rabbits of London*. Aladdin.

3. THREE OR MORE AUTHORS

For three to twenty authors, include all names.

> First Author's Last Name, Initials, Next Author's Last Name, Initials, & Final Author's Last Name, Initials. (Year of publication). *Title*. Publisher. DOI *or* URL

> Greig, A., Taylor, J., & MacKay, T. (2013). *Doing research with children: A practical guide* (3rd ed.). Sage.

For a work by twenty-one or more authors, name the first nineteen authors, followed by three ellipsis points, and end with the final author.

> Gao, R., Asano, S. M., Upadhyayula, S., Pisarev, I., Milkie, D. E., Liu, T.-L., Singh, V., Graves, A., Huynh, G. H., Zhao, Y., Bogovic, J., Colonell, J., Ott, C. M., Zugates, C., Tappan, S., Rodriguez, A., Mosaliganti, K. R., Sheu, S.-H., Pasolli, H. A., . . . Betzig, E. (2019, January 18).

Cortical column and whole-brain imaging with molecular contrast and nanoscale resolution. *Science, 363*(6424). https://doi.org/10.1126/science.aau8302

4. TWO OR MORE WORKS BY THE SAME AUTHOR

If the works were published in different years, list them chronologically.

Lewis, B. (1995). *The Middle East: A brief history of the last 2,000 years.* Scribner.

Lewis, B. (2003). *The crisis of Islam: Holy war and unholy terror.* Modern Library.

If the works were published in the same year, list them alphabetically by title (ignoring "A," "An," and "The"), adding "a," "b," and so on to the year.

Kaplan, R. D. (2000a). *The coming anarchy: Shattering the dreams of the post Cold War.* Random House.

Kaplan, R. D. (2000b). *Eastward to Tartary: Travels in the Balkans, the Middle East, and the Caucasus.* Random House.

5. AUTHOR AND EDITOR

If a book has an author and an editor who is credited on the cover, include the editor in parentheses after the title.

Author's Last Name, Initials. (Year of publication). *Title* (Editor's Initials Last Name, Ed.). Publisher. DOI *or* URL (Original work published Year)

Dick, P. F. (2008). *Five novels of the 1960s and 70s* (J. Lethem, Ed.). Library of America. (Original works published 1964–1977)

6. AUTHOR AND TRANSLATOR

Author's Last Name, Initials. (Year of publication). *Title* (Translator's Initials Last Name, Trans.). Publisher. DOI *or* URL (Original work published Year)

Hugo, V. (2008). *Les misérables* (J. Rose, Trans.). Modern Library. (Original work published 1862)

7. EDITOR

> Editor's Last Name, Initials (Ed.). (Year of publication). *Title*. Publisher. DOI *or* URL

> Jones, D. (Ed.). (2007). *Modern love: 50 true and extraordinary tales of desire, deceit, and devotion*. Three Rivers Press.

8. UNKNOWN OR NO AUTHOR OR EDITOR

> *Title*. (Year of Publication). Publisher. DOI *or* URL

> *Feeding habits of rams*. (2000). Land's Point Press.

> Clues in salmonella outbreak. (2008, June 21). *The New York Times*, A13.

If the author is listed as "Anonymous," use that as the author's name in the reference list.

9. ORGANIZATION OR GOVERNMENT AS AUTHOR

Sometimes an organization or a government agency is both author and publisher. If so, omit the publisher.

> Organization Name *or* Government Agency. (Year of publication). *Title*. DOI *or* URL

> Catholic News Service. (2002). *Stylebook on religion 2000: A reference guide*.

Articles and Other Short Works

Articles, essays, reviews, and other short works are found in periodicals and books—in print, online, or in a database. For most short works, provide information about the author, the date, the titles of both the short work and the longer work, plus any volume and issue numbers, page numbers, and a DOI or URL if there is one.

10. ARTICLE IN A JOURNAL

Author's Last Name, Initials. (Year). Title of article. *Title of Journal,*
volume(issue), page(s). DOI *or* URL

Gremer, J. R., Sala, A., & Crone, E. E. (2010). Disappearing plants:
Why they hide and how they return. *Ecology, 91*(11), 3407–3413.
https://doi.org/10.1890/09-1864.1

11. ARTICLE IN A MAGAZINE

If a magazine is published weekly, include the year, month, and day. Put
any volume number and issue number after the title.

Author's Last Name, Initials. (Year, Month Day). Title of article.
Title of Magazine, volume(issue), page(s). DOI *or* URL

Klump, B. (2019, November 22). Of crows and tools. *Science, 366*(6468),
965. https://doi.org/10.1126/science.aaz7775

12. ARTICLE IN A NEWSPAPER

If page numbers are consecutive, separate them with an en dash. If not,
separate them with a comma.

Author's Last Name, Initials. (Year, Month Day). Title of article.
Title of Newspaper, page(s). URL

Schneider, G. (2005, March 13). Fashion sense on wheels. *The Washington
Post,* F1, F6.

13. ARTICLE ON A NEWS WEBSITE

Italicize the titles of articles on CNN, HuffPost, Salon, Vox, and other news
websites. Do not italicize the name of the website.

Author's Last Name, Initials. (Year, Month Day). *Title of article.*
Name of Site. URL

Travers, C. (2019, December 3). *Here's why you keep waking up at the
same time every night.* HuffPost. https://bit.ly/3drSwAR

14. JOURNAL ARTICLE FROM A DATABASE

> Author's Last Name, Initials. (Year). Title of article. *Title of Journal,*
> *volume*(issue), pages. DOI

> Simpson, M. (1972). Authoritarianism and education: A comparative
> approach. *Sociometry, 35*(2), 223–234. https://doi.org/10.2307/2786619

15. EDITORIAL

Editorials can appear in journals, magazines, and newspapers. If the editorial is unsigned, put the title in the author position.

> Author's Last Name, Initials. (Year, Month Day). Title of editorial
> [Editorial]. *Title of Periodical.* DOI or URL

> *The Guardian* view on local theatres: The shows must go on [Editorial].
> (2019, December 6). *The Guardian.* https://bit.ly/2VZHIUg

16. REVIEW

Use this general format to document a review that appears in a periodical or on a blog.

> Reviewer's Last Name, Initials. (Year, Month Day). Title of review
> [Review of the work *Title,* by Author's Initials Last Name]. *Title of*
> *Periodical* or *Name of Blog.* DOI or URL

> Joinson, S. (2017, December 15). Mysteries unfold in a land of minarets
> and magic carpets [Review of the book *The city of brass,* by S. A.
> Chakraborty]. *The New York Times.* https://nyti.ms/2kvwHFP

For a review published on a website that is not associated with a periodical or a blog, italicize the title of the review and do not italicize the website name.

Documentation Map (APA)

Article in a Journal with a DOI

Volume and issue

Title of journal

Pages

ETHICS & BEHAVIOR, 23(4), 324–337
Copyright © 2013 Taylor & Francis Group, LLC
ISSN: 1050-8422 print / 1532-7019 online
DOI: 10.1080/10508422.2013.787359

Routledge
Taylor & Francis Group

DOI

Publication year

Smart Technology and the Moral Life

Title of article

Author

Clifton F. Guthrie

Department of Science and Humanities
Husson University

Smart technology is recording and nudging our intuitive and behavioral reactions in ways that are not fully shaped by our conscious ethical reasoning and so are altering our social and moral worlds. Beyond reasons to worry, there are also reasons to embrace this technology for nudging human behavior toward prosocial activity. This article inquires about four ways that smart technology is shaping the individual moral life: the persuasive effect of promptware, our newly evolving experiences of embodiment, our negotiations with privacy, and our experiences of risk and serendipity.

Keywords: persuasive technology, morality, ethics, virtue

PERSUASIVE TECHNOLOGY

For some time, cars have worked to shape our behaviors, beeping to warn us when a door is unlocked or a seat belt unfastened, or giving us fuel efficiency feedback. These straightforward but persuasive sensor systems nudge us toward a repertoire of safe driving behaviors, and we often cannot override them even if we want to. Newer cars include an increasing number of smart technologies that interact with us more intelligently. Some detect the presence of electronic keys and make it impossible for drivers to lock themselves out. Others use sensors to monitor approaching obstacles or lane boundaries and give warnings or even apply the brakes. We are seeing the emergence of street intersections that communicate directly with cars and cars that can communicate with one another (Dean, Fletcher, Porges, & Ulrich, 2012). These are so-called smart technologies because they draw data from the environment and from us, and often make decisions on our behalf. A leading researcher in automated driving noted, "The driver is still in control. But if the driver is not doing the right thing, the technology takes over" (Markoff & Sengupta, 2013).

As cars become smarter they are helping to lead us into what technologists describe as a pervasive, ambient, or calm computing environment. In 1991, Mark Weiser of the Palo Alto Research Center presciently called it "ubiquitous computing" or "ubicomp" in a much-quoted article from *Scientific American*, in which he outlined what has come to be accepted as a standard interpretation of the history of human interaction with computers. This is the age in which computers are increasingly liberated from manual input devices like laptops and cell phones to become an invisible, interactive, computational sensorium. Early examples include motion sensors, smart

Correspondence should be addressed to Clifton F. Guthrie, Department of Science and Humanities, Husson University, 1 College Circle, Bangor, ME 04401. E-mail: cfguthrie@gmail.com

Guthrie, C. F. (2013). Smart technology and the moral life. *Ethics & Behavior, 23*(4), 324–337. https://doi.org/10.1080/10508422.2013.787359

610-14
for more on citing articles APA style

607
for more on DOIs

17. COMMENT ON AN ONLINE PERIODICAL ARTICLE OR BLOG POST

> Writer's Last Name, Initials [username]. (Year, Month Day). Text of
> comment up to 20 words [Comment on the article "Title of work"].
> *Title of Publication.* DOI or URL

> PhyllisSpecial. (2020, May 10). How about we go all the way again? It's
> about time . . . [Comment on the article "2020 Eagles schedule:
> Picking wins and losses for all 16 games"]. *The Philadelphia
> Inquirer.* https://rb.gy/iduabz

Link to the comment if possible; if not, include the URL of the article.

18. WEBPAGE

> Author's Last Name, Initials. (Year, Month Day). *Title of work.* Title of
> Site. URL

> Pleasant, B. (n.d.). *Annual bluegrass.* The National Gardening Association.
> https://garden.org/learn/articles/view/2936/

If the author and the website name are the same, use the website name
as the author. If the content of the webpage is likely to change and no
archived version exists, use "n.d." as the date and include a retrieval date.

> Worldometer. (n.d.). *World population.* Retrieved February 2, 2020, from
> https://www.worldometers.info/world-population/

Books, Parts of Books, and Reports

19. BASIC ENTRY FOR A BOOK

> Author's Last Name, Initials. (Year of publication). *Title.*
> Publisher. DOI or URL

PRINT BOOK

Schwab, V. E. (2018). *Vengeful.* Tor.

EBOOK

Jemisin, N. K. (2017). *The stone sky.* Orbit. https://amzn.com/B01N7EQOFA

Documentation Map (APA)

Webpage

URL

Title of site

Title of work

Date of publication

Author

Lazette, M. P. (2015, February 24). *A hurricane's hit to households.* Federal
Reserve Bank of Cleveland. https://www.clevelandfed.org/en
/newsroom-and-events/publications/forefront/ff-v6n01
/ff-20150224-v6n0107-a-hurricanes-hit-to-households.aspx

614
for more
on citing
webpages
APA style

Documentation Map (APA)
Book

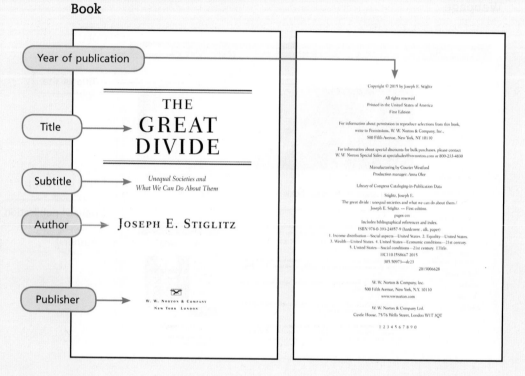

Year of publication

Title

Subtitle

Author

Publisher

THE
GREAT
DIVIDE

*Unequal Societies and
What We Can Do About Them*

JOSEPH E. STIGLITZ

W. W. NORTON & COMPANY
NEW YORK LONDON

614, 617–19
for more
on citing
books APA
style

Stiglitz, J. E. (2015). *The great divide: Unequal societies and what we can do about them.* W. W. Norton.

AUDIOBOOK

Obama, M. (2018). *Becoming* (M. Obama, Narr.) [Audiobook]. Random
    House Audio. http://amzn.com/B07B3JQZCL

Include the word "Audiobook" in brackets and the name of the narrator
only if the format and the narrator are something you've mentioned in
what you've written.

20. EDITION OTHER THAN THE FIRST

Author's Last Name, Initials. (Year). *Title* (Name *or* number
    ed.). Publisher. DOI *or* URL

Burch, D. (2008). *Emergency navigation: Find your position and shape
    your course at sea even if your instruments fail* (2nd ed.).
    International Marine/McGraw-Hill.

21. EDITED COLLECTION OR ANTHOLOGY

Editor's Last Name, Initials (Ed.). (Year). *Title* (Name *or* number ed., Vol.
    number). Publisher. DOI *or* URL

Gilbert, S. M., & Gubar, S. (Eds.). (2003). *The Norton anthology of literature
    by women: The traditions in English* (3rd ed., Vol. 2). W. W. Norton.

22. WORK IN AN EDITED COLLECTION OR ANTHOLOGY

Author's Last Name, Initials. (Year of edited edition). Title of work. In
    Editor's Initials Last Name (Ed.), *Title of collection* (Name *or*
    number ed., Vol. number, pp. pages). Publisher. DOI *or* URL (Original
    work published Year)

Baldwin, J. (2018). Notes of a native son. In M. Puchner, S. Akbari,
    W. Denecke, B. Fuchs, C. Levine, P. Lewis, & E. Wilson (Eds.), *The
    Norton anthology of world literature* (4th ed., Vol. F, pp. 728–743).
    W. W. Norton. (Original work published 1955)

23. CHAPTER IN AN EDITED BOOK

Author's Last Name, Initials. (Year). Title of chapter. In Editor's Initials Last Name (Ed.), *Title of book* (pp. pages). Publisher. DOI *or* URL

Amarnick, S. (2009). Trollope at fuller length: Lord Silverbridge and the manuscript of *The duke's children*. In M. Markwick, D. Denenholz Morse, & R. Gagnier (Eds.), *The politics of gender in Anthony Trollope's novels: New readings for the twenty-first century* (pp. 193–206). Routledge.

24. ENTRY IN A REFERENCE WORK (DICTIONARY, THESAURUS, OR ENCYCLOPEDIA)

If the entry has no author, use the name of the publisher as the author. If the reference work has an editor, include their name after the title of the entry. If the entry is archived or is not likely to change, use the publication date and do not include a retrieval date.

Author's Last Name, Initials. (Year). Title of entry. In Editor's Initials Last Name (Ed.), *Title of reference work* (Name *or* number ed., Vol. number, pp. pages). Publisher. URL

Merriam-Webster. (n.d.). Epoxy. In *Merriam-Webster.com dictionary*. Retrieved January 29, 2020, from https://www.merriam-webster.com /dictionary/epoxy

25. BOOK IN A LANGUAGE OTHER THAN ENGLISH

Author's Last Name, Initials. (Year). *Title of book* [English translation of title]. Publisher. DOI *or* URL

Ferrante, E. (2011). *L'amica geniale* [My brilliant friend]. Edizione E/O.

26. ONE VOLUME OF A MULTIVOLUME WORK

Author's Last Name, Initials. (Year). *Title of entire work* (Vol. number). Publisher. DOI *or* URL

Spiegelman, A. (1986). *Maus* (Vol. 1). Random House.

author   title   publication

If the volume has a separate title, include the volume number and title in italics after the main title.

> Ramazani, J., Ellmann, R., & O'Clair, R. (Eds.). (2003). *The Norton anthology of modern and contemporary poetry: Vol. 1. Modern poetry* (3rd ed.). W. W. Norton.

27. RELIGIOUS WORK

Do not include an author for most religious works. If the date of original publication is known, include it at the end.

> *Title.* (Year of publication). Publisher. URL (Original work published Year)

> *New American Bible.* (2002). United States Conference of Catholic Bishops. http://www.vatican.va/archive/ENG0839/_INDEX.HTM (Original work published 1970)

28. REPORT BY A GOVERNMENT AGENCY OR OTHER ORGANIZATION

> Author's Last Name, Initials. (Year). *Title* (Report No. number). Publisher. DOI *or* URL

> Centers for Disease Control and Prevention. (2009). *Fourth national report on human exposure to environmental chemicals.* US Department of Health and Human Services. https://www.cdc .gov/exposurereport/pdf/fourthreport.pdf

Include the year, month, and day if the report you're documenting includes that information. Omit the report number if one is not given. If more than one government department is listed as the publisher, list the most specific department as the author and the larger department as the publisher.

29. DISSERTATION

> Author's Last Name, Initials. (Year). *Title* (Publication No. number) [Doctoral dissertation, Name of School]. Database *or* Archive Name. URL

Solomon, M. (2016). *Social media and self-examination: The examination of social media use on identity, social comparison, and self-esteem in young female adults* (Publication No. 10188962) [Doctoral dissertation, William James College]. ProQuest Dissertations and Theses Global.

If the dissertation is in a database, do not include a URL. Include a URL if it is published elsewhere online. If it is unpublished, write "Unpublished doctoral dissertation" in brackets, and use the name of the school in place of the database.

30. PAPER OR POSTER PRESENTED AT A CONFERENCE

Presenter's Last Name, Initials. (Year, Month First Day–Last Day). *Title* [Paper or Poster presentation]. Name of Conference, City, State, Country. URL

Dolatian, H., & Heinz, J. (2018, May 25–27). *Reduplication and finite-state technology* [Paper presentation]. The 53rd Annual Meeting of the Chicago Linguistic Society, Chicago, IL, United States. http://shorturl.at/msuB2

Audio, Visual, and Other Sources

If you are referring to an entire website, do not include it in your reference list; simply mention the website's name in the body of your paper and include the URL in parentheses. Do not include email, personal communication, or other unarchived discussions in your list of references.

31. *WIKIPEDIA* ENTRY

Wikipedia has archived versions of its pages, so give the date when you accessed the page and the permanent URL of the archived page, which is found by clicking "View history."

Title of entry. (Year, Month Day). In *Wikipedia*. URL

author   title   publication

List of sheep breeds. (2019, September 9). In *Wikipedia*. https://en.wikipedia
.org/w/index.php?title=List_of_sheep_breeds&oldid=914884262

32. ONLINE FORUM POST

Author's Last Name, Initials [username]. (Year, Month Day). *Content of
the post up to 20 words* [Online forum post]. Name of Site. URL

Hanzus, D. [DanHanzus]. (2019, October 23). *GETCHA DAN HANZUS. ASK
ME ANYTHING!* [Online forum post]. Reddit. https://bit.ly/38WgmSF

33. BLOG POST

Author's Last Name, Initials [username]. (Year, Month Day). Title of post.
Name of Blog. URL

gcrepps. (2017, March 28). Shania Sanders. *Women@NASA*. https://blogs
.nasa.gov/womenatnasa/2017/03/28/shania-sanders/

If only the username is known, use it without brackets.

34. ONLINE STREAMING VIDEO

Uploader's Last Name, Initials [username]. (Year, Month Day). *Title*
[Video]. Name of Video Platform. URL

CinemaSins. (2014, August 21). *Everything wrong with* National treasure
in 13 minutes or less [Video]. YouTube. https://www
.youtube.com/watch?v=1ul-_ZWvXTs

Whoever uploaded the video is considered the author, even if someone else
created the content. If only the username is known, use it without brackets.

35. PODCAST

Host's Last Name, Initials (Host). (First Year–Last Year). *Podcast name*
[Audio podcast]. Production Company. URL

Poor, N., Woods, E., & Thomas, R. (Hosts). (2017–present). *Ear hustle*
[Audio podcast]. PRX. https://www.earhustlesq.com/

36. PODCAST EPISODE

> Host's Last Name, Initials (Host). (Year, Month Day). Episode title (No. number) [Audio podcast episode]. In *Podcast name*. Production Company. URL

> Tamposi, E., & Samocki, E. (Hosts). (2020, January 8). The year of the broads [Audio podcast episode]. In *The broadcast podcast*. Podcast One. https://podcastone.com/episode/the-year-of-the-broads

Omit the episode number if one is not given.

37. FILM

> Director's Last Name, Initials (Director). (Year). *Title* [Film]. Production Company. URL

> Jenkins, B. (Director). (2016). *Moonlight* [Film]. A24; Plan B; PASTEL.

> Cuarón, A. (Director). (2016). *Harry Potter and the prisoner of Azkaban* [Film; two-disc special ed. on DVD]. Warner Brothers.

List the director as the author of the film. Indicate how you watched the film only if the format is relevant to what you've written.

38. TELEVISION SERIES

> Executive Producer's Last Name, Initials (Executive Producer). (First Year–Last Year). *Title of series* [TV series]. Production Company. URL

> Iungerich, L., Gonzalez, E., & Haft, J. (Executive Producers). (2018–present). *On my block* [TV series]. Crazy Cat Lady Productions.

Indicate how you watched the TV series (two-disc DVD set, for example) only if the format is relevant to your essay.

39. TELEVISION SERIES EPISODE

> Writer's Last Name, Initials (Writer), & Director's Last Name, Initials (Director). (Year, Month Day). Title of episode (Season number, Episode number) [TV series episode]. In Executive Producer's Initials

Last Name (Executive Producer), *Title of series.* Production Company. URL

Siegal, J. (Writer), Morgan, D. (Writer), & Sackett, M. (Director). (2018, December 6). Janet(s) (Season 3, Episode 10) [TV series episode]. In M. Schur, D. Miner, M. Sackett, & D. Goddard (Executive Producers), *The good place*. Fremulon; 3 Arts Entertainment; Universal Television.

40. MUSIC ALBUM

Artist's Last Name, Initials. (Year). *Title of album* [Album]. Label. URL

Jonas Brothers. (2019). *Happiness begins* [Album]. Republic.

41. SONG

Artist's Last Name, Initials. (Year). Name of song [Song]. On *Title of album*. Label. URL

Giddens, R. (2015). Waterboy [Song]. On *Tomorrow is my turn*. Nonesuch.

42. *POWERPOINT* SLIDES

Author's Last Name, Initials. (Year, Month Day). *Title of presentation* [PowerPoint slides]. Publisher. URL

Pavliscak, P. (2016, February 21). *Finding our happy place in the internet of things* [PowerPoint slides]. Slideshare. https://bit.ly/3aOcfs7

43. RECORDING OF A SPEECH OR WEBINAR

Author's Last Name, Initials. (Year, Month Day *or* Year). *Title* [Speech audio recording *or* Webinar]. Publisher. URL

Kennedy, J. F. (1961, January 20). *Inaugural address* [Speech audio recording]. American Rhetoric. https://bit.ly/339Gc3e

For a speech, include the year, month, and day. For a webinar, include only the year.

44. PHOTOGRAPH

> Photographer's Last Name, Initials. (Year). *Title of photograph*
>   [Photograph]. Name of Site. URL

> Kudacki, P. (2013). [Photograph of Benedict Cumberbatch]. Time.
>   http://content.time.com/time/covers/asia/0,16641,20131028,00.html

Use this format to document a photograph that is not in a museum or on a museum website. For a photograph with no title, include a description of the photograph in brackets after the date.

45. MAP

> Mapmaker's Last Name, Initials. (Year). *Title of map* [Map].
>   Publisher. URL

> Daniels, M. (2018). *Human terrain: Visualizing the world's population, in*
>   *3D* [Map]. The Pudding. https://pudding.cool/2018/10/city_3d/

46. SOCIAL MEDIA POSTS

If only the username is known, do not use brackets. List any audiovisual content (e.g., videos, images, or links) in brackets. Replicate emoji or include a bracketed description. Follow the spelling and capitalization of the post.

> Author's Last Name, Initials [@username]. (Year, Month Day).
>   *Content of post up to 20 words* [Description of any audiovisual
>   content] [Type of post]. Platform. URL

TWEET

> Baron, D. [@DrGrammar]. (2019, November 11). *Gender conceal: Did you*
>   *know that pronouns can also hide someone's gender?* [Thumbnail
>   with link attached] [Tweet]. Twitter. https://bit.ly/2vaCcDc

INSTAGRAM PHOTOGRAPH OR VIDEO

> Jamil, J. [@jameelajamilofficial]. (2018, July 18). *Happy Birthday to our*
>   *leader. I steal all my acting faces from you.* @kristenanniebell [Face

with smile and sunglasses emoji] [Photograph]. Instagram.
    https://www.instagram.com/p/BlYX5F9FuGL/

FACEBOOK POST

Raptor Resource Project. (2020, May 8). *Happy Fri-yay, everyone! We'll
    keep the news short and sweet: today Decorah eaglets D34 and
    D35 turn 33 days* [Images attached]. Facebook. https://bit.ly/3icwFzN

47. DATA SET

Author's Last Name, Initials. (Year). *Title of data set* (Version number)
    [Data set]. Publisher. DOI *or* URL

Pew Research Center. (2019). *Core trends survey* [Data set]. https://www
    .pewresearch.org/internet/dataset/core-trends-survey/

Omit the version number if one is not given. If the publisher is the author,
no need to list it twice; omit the publisher.

48. SUPREME COURT CASE

Name of Case, volume US pages (Year). URL

Plessy v. Ferguson, 163 US 537 (1896). https://www.oyez.org/cases
    /1850-1900/163us537

Obergefell v. Hodges, 576 US ___ (2015). https://www.oyez.org
    /cases/2014/14-556

The source for most Supreme Court cases is the *United States Reports*, which
is abbreviated "US" in the reference list entry. If the case does not yet have
a page number, use three underscores instead.

Sources Not Covered by APA

To document a source for which APA does not provide guidelines, look at
models similar to the source you have cited. Give any information readers
will need in order to find the source themselves—author; date of publica-

tion; title; and information about the source itself (including who published it; volume, issue, and page numbers; and a DOI or URL). You might want to check your reference note to be sure it will lead others to your source.

FORMATTING A PAPER

Title page. APA generally requires a title page. The page number should go in the upper right-hand corner. Center the full title of the paper in bold in the top half of the page. Center your name, the name of your department and school, the course number and name, the instructor's name, and the due date on separate lines below the title. Leave one line between the title and your name.

Page numbers. Place the page number in the upper right-hand corner. Number pages consecutively throughout.

Fonts, spacing, margins, and indents. Use a legible font that will be accessible to everyone, either a serif font (such as Times New Roman or Bookman) or a sans serif font (such as Calibri or Verdana). Use a sans serif font within figure images. Double-space the entire paper, including any notes and your list of references; the only exception is footnotes at the bottom of a page, which should be single-spaced, and text within tables and images, the spacing of which will vary. Leave one-inch margins at the top, bottom, and sides of your text; do not justify the text. The first line of each paragraph should be indented one-half inch (or five to seven spaces) from the left margin. APA recommends using one space after end-of-sentence punctuation.

Headings. Though they are not required in APA style, headings can help readers follow your text. The first level of heading should be bold and centered; the second level of heading should be bold and flush with the left margin; the third level should be bold, italicized, and flush left. Capitalize all headings as you would any other title within the text.

First Level Heading

Second Level Heading

Third Level Heading

Abstract. An abstract is a concise summary of your paper that introduces readers to your topic and main points. Most scholarly journals require an abstract; an abstract is not typically required for student papers, so check your instructor's preference. Put your abstract on the second page, with the word "Abstract" centered and in bold at the top. Unless your instructor specifies a length, limit your abstract to 250 words or fewer.

Long quotations. Indent quotations of forty or more words one-half inch (or five to seven spaces) from the left margin. Do not use quotation marks, and place the page number(s) or documentation information in parentheses *after* the end punctuation. If there are paragraphs in the quotation, indent the first line of each paragraph another one-half inch.

> Kaplan (2000) captured ancient and contemporary Antioch:
>> At the height of its glory in the Roman-Byzantine age, when it had an amphitheater, public baths, aqueducts, and sewage pipes, half a million people lived in Antioch. Today the population is only 125,000. With sour relations between Turkey and Syria, and unstable politics throughout the Middle East, Antioch is now a backwater—seedy and tumbledown, with relatively few tourists. (p. 123)
>
> Antioch's decline serves as a reminder that the fortunes of cities can change drastically over time.

List of references. Start your list on a new page after the text but before any endnotes. Title the page "References," centered and in bold, and double-space the entire list. Each entry should begin at the left margin, and subsequent lines should be indented one-half inch (or five to seven spaces). Alphabetize the list by authors' last names (or by editors' names, if appropriate). Alphabetize works that have no author or editor by title, disregarding "A," "An," and "The." Be sure every source listed is cited in the text; do not include sources that you consulted but did not cite.

Tables and figures. Above each table or figure (charts, diagrams, graphs, photos, and so on), provide the word "Table" or "Figure" and a number, flush left and in bold (e.g., **Table 1**). On the following line, give a descriptive title, flush left and italicized. Below the table or figure, include a note with any necessary explanation and source information. Number tables and figures separately, and be sure to discuss them in your text so that readers know how they relate.

Table 1
Hours of Instruction Delivered per Week

	American classrooms	Japanese classrooms	Chinese classrooms
First grade			
Language arts	10.5	8.7	10.4
Mathematics	2.7	5.8	4.0
Fifth grade			
Language arts	7.9	8.0	11.1
Mathematics	3.4	7.8	11.7

Note. Adapted from *Peeking Out from Under the Blinders: Some Factors We Shouldn't Forget in Studying Writing* (Occasional Paper No. 25), by J. R. Hayes, 1991, National Center for the Study of Writing and Literacy (https://archive. nwp.org/cs/public/print/resource/720). Copyright 1991 by the Office of Educational Research and Improvement.

SAMPLE RESEARCH PAPER

The following sample pages are from "The Benefits of Prison Nursery Programs," a paper written by Analisa Johnson for a first-year writing course. It is formatted according to the guidelines of the *Publication Manual of the American Psychological Association,* 7th edition (2020). While APA guidelines are used widely in linguistics and the social sciences, exact requirements may vary from discipline to discipline and course to course. If you're unsure about what your instructor wants, ask for clarification.

1

Page number.

The Benefits of Prison Nursery Programs

Title bold and centered.

Analisa Johnson

Writing Program, Boston University

WR 150: Burning Questions: Human Expression

Samantha Myers

May 1, 2017

Author's name, school name and department, course number and name, instructor's name, and due date.

2

Abstract

The rising population of women in prisons has resulted in the births of some 2,000 babies per year to women behind bars. Female prisoners suffer from a number of inadequacies in their health care, but changes in birthing practices and the provision of nursery programs in prisons could yield important benefits. Currently, nine states offer such programs, and research conducted in these states has shown a number of positive effects. Fully 86.3% of women who have come through these programs remain in their communities after 3 years. Likewise, preschool performance of their children shows better emotional / behavioral adjustment than that of children who have been sent to foster care. Finally, estimates show that the annual costs of such programs are approximately 40% less than those of foster care.

    Keywords: birthing practices, correctional, foster care, health care, incarceration, nursery program, prenatal care, preschool, prison, recidivism, sentencing project, shackles

Heading bold and centered.

Limited to 250 words or fewer.

"Keywords:" in italics, indented.

1 inch   3

Title bold and centered.

The Benefits of Prison Nursery Programs

Double-spaced throughout.

Over the past 40 years or so, the United States has seen a steady increase in incarcerated individuals, with 2.2 million people currently in prisons and jails nationwide, according to statistics on prisons and the criminal justice system provided by the Sentencing Project (2017, p. 2). In particular, the number of incarcerated females has risen dramatically, at a rate 50% higher than that of men since the early 1980s. As recently as 2015, there were nearly 112,000 incarcerated women across the nation (Sentencing Project, 2017, p. 4). While there is a plethora of health care issues that women face when locked up, one of the most concerning is that of reproductive health, specifically pregnancy and birth in prison. Roughly 1 in 25 women entering prison or jail is pregnant (Yager, 2015). As a result, the number of babies born behind bars has also grown at an alarming rate. It is estimated that up to 2,000 infants are born to incarcerated mothers each year, only to be taken from them a scant 24 hours after birth and placed either with a family member or, more often, in the foster care system (Sufrin, 2012). Current scholarly sources have proven prison nursery programs—which allow mothers to keep their infants with them while they serve out their sentences—to be a very effective method in dealing with the issue of incarcerated mothers. Despite this fact, there are only nine nursery programs currently operational in America. In order to make prison nursery programs more prevalent, better education is needed for correctional administrators about the effectiveness of nursery programs.

1 inch

1 inch

1 inch

4

Inadequacies of Prison Health Care for Pregnant Women

When it comes to women's health care in the prison system, there are many inadequate areas, but two that are of great importance are prenatal care and birthing practices.

Prenatal Care

Hotelling (2008) discussed the lack of quality health care provided to expectant mothers behind bars. Despite adequate health care being mandated to all inmates through the Eighth Amendment to the Constitution, women still make up a lesser percentage of total incarcerated individuals than men—a fact that is used by correctional staff to justify providing scarcer health care and rehabilitative programs for incarcerated women. In addition, prisons are not subject to any sort of external review of their standards of inmate care, so they are not encouraged to improve health care services. As a result, many incarcerated women face unnecessarily high-risk pregnancies.

Birthing Practices

Another practice that increases the risk of complications in pregnancy in prison is the custom of shackling female inmates during labor, delivery, and postpartum. This practice is both degrading and inhumane and can pose a problem for health care providers in case of an emergency. In an official position statement, the Association of Women's Health, Obstetric and Neonatal Nurses (2011) noted that the unnecessary practice can interfere with the ability of nurses and health care providers to deliver the proper

5

care and treatment (p. 817). Only 18 states in the United States currently ban the shackling of expectant mothers in prison while they give birth (American Civil Liberties Union Foundation, 2012). The remaining 32 states are left to their own devices, in some cases shackling mothers with no regard to the recommendations of nurses and other health care providers.

Prison Nursery Programs

In order to effectively spread awareness of prison nursery programs, it must be clear exactly what they are and how they serve incarcerated mothers. Prison nursery programs offer women who become incarcerated while pregnant the option to keep and parent their child while they serve their sentences. Getting into these programs can be a rigorous process; with limited spots available, prospective mothers must have a nonviolent conviction, no record of child abuse, and be roughly within 18 months of completing their sentence—which is the maximum amount of time a child can stay with their mother behind bars (Stein, 2010, p. 11).

Author name in parentheses when no signal phrase is used.

Benefits

When mothers do get into these programs, there are many benefits to be had for both themselves and their children. For starters, mothers are provided with parenting classes, support groups, substance abuse counseling, and complementary day-care services to attend these classes. Many prisons also provide high school and college courses for those mothers who have not yet completed their education (Wertheimer, 2005). Lastly, vocational

6

programs are also offered, which aid in the job search once the women are released from prison.

Recidivism

As a result of the programs, many of the mothers have been shown to have a reduced recidivism rate. An astounding 86.3% of women exiting a prison nursery program remained in the community three years following their release (Goshin et al., 2013, Results section, para. 3). This is a proven positive for both the mothers and their children.

In-text citation of journal article without pagination.

Cost of Prison Nursery Programs

While it may seem as if implementing prison nursery programs across the country would be an expensive endeavor, it is important to consider by comparison the costs of putting children in foster care. On average, the total financial cost for one child to remain in foster care per year in Oregon is about $26,600 (Fixsen, 2011, p. 3). Conversely, based on an evaluation of Nebraska's prison nursery program, expenses for the nursery program would be roughly 40% less per year than foster care expenses would be for the same babies, and even more money would be saved if the nursery program reduced recidivism (Carlson, 1998, as cited in Yager, 2015, para. 34). Rapidly increasing the number of prison nursery programs across the country may result in some extra money spent in the short run, but it will provide benefits in the long run, both financially and socially.

Source quoted in another source identified with "as cited in."

7

References

American Civil Liberties Union Foundation. (2012). *The shackling of pregnant women & girls in U.S. prisons, jails & youth detention centers* [Briefing paper]. https://www.aclu.org/files/assets/anti-shackling_briefing_paper_stand_alone.pdf

Association of Women's Health, Obstetric and Neonatal Nurses. (2011). *Shackling incarcerated pregnant women* [Position statement]. http://www.jognn.org/article/S0884-2175(15)30763-2/pdf

Fixsen, A. (2011). *Children in foster care*. A Family for Every Child. http://www.afamilyforeverychild.org/wp=content/uploads/2018/04/children_in_foster_care.pdf

Goshin, L. S., Byrne, M. W., & Henninger, A. M. (2013). Recidivism after release from a prison nursery program. *Public Health Nursing, 33*(2), 109–117. https://doi.org/10.1111/phn.12072

Hotelling, B. A. (2008). Perinatal needs of pregnant incarcerated women. *The Journal of Perinatal Education, 17*(2), 37–44. https://doi.org/10.1624/105812408X298372

Sentencing Project. (2017). *Trends in U.S. corrections* [Fact sheet]. http://sentencingproject.org/wp-content/uploads/2016/01/Trends-in-US-Corrections.pdf

Stein, D. J. (2010, July/August). Babies behind bars: Nurseries for incarcerated mothers and their children. *Children's Voice, 19*(4), 10–13.

Heading bold and centered.

Alphabetized by authors' last names or first word of organization.

All lines after the first line of each entry indented.

8

Sufrin, C. (2012, July 1). *Incarcerated women and reproductive health care* [Video]. YouTube. https://www.youtube.com /watch?v=WNx1ntLyI2Q

Wertheimer, L. (2005, November 5). *Prenatal care behind bars* [Radio broadcast]. NPR. http://www.npr.org/templates/story/story .php?storyId=4990886

Yager, S. (2015, July/August). Prison born. *The Atlantic*. https://www .theatlantic.com/magazine/archive/2015/07/prison-born /395297/

All sources cited in the text are listed.

part 8

Media / Design

Consciously or not, we design all the texts we write, choosing typefaces, setting up text as lists or charts, deciding whether to add headings—and then whether to center them or align them on the left. Sometimes our genre calls for certain design elements—essays begin with titles, letters begin with salutations ("Dear Auntie Em"). Other times we design texts to meet the demands of particular audiences, formatting documentation in MLA or APA or some other style, setting type larger for young children, and so on. And our designs always depend upon our medium. A memoir might take the form of an essay in a book, be turned into a bulleted list for a slide presentation, or include links to images or other pages if presented on a website. The chapters in this part offer advice for CHOOSING MEDIA; working with DESIGN, IMAGES, and SOUND; WRITING ONLINE; and GIVING PRESENTATIONS.

Media / Design

Choosing Media 56

USA Today reports on contract negotiations between automakers and auto-workers with an article that includes a large photo and a colorful graph; the article on the same story on the *New York Times* website includes a video of striking workers. In your economics class, you give a presentation about the issue that includes *Prezi* slides.

These examples show how information about the same events can be delivered using three different media: print (*USA Today*), digital (*nytimes.com*), and spoken (the main medium for your class presentation). They also show how different media offer writers different modes of expressing meaning, ranging from words to images to sounds and hyperlinks. A print text can include written words and still visuals; online, the same text can also incorporate links to moving images and sound as well as to other written materials. A presentation with slides can include both spoken and written words, can incorporate video and audio elements—and can also include print handouts.

In college writing, the choice of medium often isn't up to you: your instructor may require a printed essay or a classroom talk, a website, or some combination of media. Sometimes, though, you'll be the one deciding. Because your medium will play a big part in the way your audience receives and reacts to your message, you'll need to think hard about what media best suit your audience, purpose, and message. This chapter will help you choose media when the choice is yours.

academic literacies

rhetorical situations

genres

fields

processes

strategies

research MLA / APA

media / design

readings

handbook

Print

When you have a choice of medium, print has certain advantages over spoken and digital text in that it's more permanent and doesn't depend on audience access to technology. Depending on your own access to technology, you can usually insert photos or other visuals and can present data and other information as graphs or charts. Obviously, though, print documents are more work than digital ones to update or change, and they don't allow for sound, moving images, or links to other materials.

Digital

Online writing is everywhere: on course learning management systems and class websites; in virtual discussion groups and wikis; in emails, text messages, tweets, and other social media. And when you're taking an online course, you are, by definition, always using a digital medium. Remember that this medium has advantages as well as limitations and potential pitfalls. You can add audio, video, and links—but your audience may not have the same access to technology that you do. These are just some of the things you'll need to keep in mind when deciding, say, whether to include or link to videos or a site that has restricted access. Also, digital texts that circulate online, through blogs, websites, email, or social media, can take on a life of their own; others may forward, like, retweet, or repost your text to much larger audiences than you originally considered.

Spoken

If you deliver your text orally, as a speech or presentation, you have the opportunity to use your tone of voice, gestures, and physical bearing to establish credibility. But you must write your text so that it's easy to understand when it is heard rather than read. Speaking from memory or from notecards, rather than reading a script or essay, often makes it easier for

academic literacies · rhetorical situations · genres · fields · processes · strategies · research MLA / APA · media / design · readings · handbook

the audience to follow your talk. The spoken medium can be used alone with a live, face-to-face audience, but it's often combined with print, in the form of handouts, or with digital media, in the form of presentation software like *PowerPoint* or *Prezi*, or designed for remote audiences in formats like webcasts, webinars, podcasts, or video-calling services such as *Skype*.

Multimedia

It's increasingly likely that you'll be assigned to create a multimedia text, one that includes some combination of print, oral, and digital elements. It's also possible that you'll have occasion to write a multimodal text, one that uses more than one mode of expression: words, images, audio, video, links, and so on. The words *multimedia* and *multimodal* are often used interchangeably, but *multimodal* is the term that's used most often in composition classes, whereas *multimedia* is the one used in other disciplines and in industry. In composition classes, the word generally refers to writing that includes more than just words.

For example, let's say that in a U.S. history class you're assigned to do a project about the effects of the Vietnam War on American society. You might write an essay using words alone to discuss such effects as increased hostility toward the military and government, generational conflict within families and society at large, and increased use of recreational drugs. But you could also weave such a text together with many other materials to create a multimodal composition.

If you're using print, for example, you could include photographs from the Vietnam era, such as of antiwar protests or military funerals. Another possibility might be a timeline that puts developments in the war in the context of events going on simultaneously elsewhere in American life, such as in fashion and entertainment or in the feminist and civil rights movements. If you're posting your project online, you might also incorporate video clips of TV news coverage of the war and clips from films focusing on it or its social effects, such as *Apocalypse Now* or *Easy Rider*. Audio elements could include recorded interviews with veterans who fought in the war, people who protested against it, or government officials who were involved in planning or overseeing it. Many of these elements could be inserted into your document as links.

If your assignment specifies that you give an oral presentation, you could play some of the music of the Vietnam era, show videos of government officials defending the war and demonstrators protesting it, maybe hang some psychedelic posters from the era.

361–70 ◯ You might do something similar with your own work by creating an electronic, or e-portfolio. Tips for compiling an **E-PORTFOLIO** may be found in Chapter 34.

Considering the Rhetorical Situation

55–56 ▣ **PURPOSE**   What's your purpose, and what media will best suit that purpose? A text or email may be appropriate for inviting a friend to lunch, but neither would be ideal for demonstrating to a professor that you understand a complex historical event; for that, you'd likely write a report, either in print or online—and you might include photos or maps or other such texts to provide visual context.

57–60 ▣ **AUDIENCE**   What media are your audience likely to expect—and be able to access? A blog may be a good way to reach people who share your interest in basketball or cupcakes, but to reach your grandparents, you may want to put a handwritten note in the mail. Some employers and graduate school admissions officers require applicants to submit résumés and applications online, while others prefer to receive them in print form.

61–65 ▣ **GENRE**   Does your genre require a particular medium? If you're giving an oral presentation, you'll often be expected to include slides. Academic essays are usually formatted to be printed out, even if they are submitted electronically. An online essay based on field research might include audio files of those you've interviewed, but if your essay were in print, you'd need to quote (or paraphrase or summarize) what they said.

STANCE If you have a choice of media, think about whether a particular medium will help you convey your stance. A print document in MLA format, for instance, will make you seem scholarly and serious. Tweeting or blogging, however, might work better for a more informal stance. Presenting data in charts will sometimes help you establish your credibility as a knowledgeable researcher.

66–68

Once you decide on the media and modes of expression you're using, you'll need to design your text to take advantage of their possibilities and to deal with their limitations. The next chapters will help you do that.

57 Designing Text

You're trying to figure out why a magazine ad you're looking at is so funny, and you realize that the text's font is deliberately intended to make you laugh. An assignment for a research paper in psychology specifies that you are to follow APA format. Your classmates complain that the *PowerPoint* slides you use for a presentation are hard to read because there's not enough contrast between the words and the background. Another says you include too many words on each slide. Whether you're putting together your résumé, creating a website for your intramural soccer league, or writing an essay for a class, you need to think about how you design what you write.

Sometimes you can rely on established conventions: in MLA and APA styles, for example, there are specific guidelines for margins, headings, and the use of single-, double-, or triple-spaced lines of text. But often you'll have to make design decisions on your own—and not just about words and spacing. If what you're writing includes photos, charts, tables, graphs, or other visuals, you'll need to integrate these with your written text in the most attractive and effective way; online, you may also need to decide where and how to include video clips and links. You might even use scissors, glue, and staples to attach objects to a poster or create pop-ups in a brochure.

No matter what your text includes, its design will influence how your audience responds to it and therefore how well it achieves your purpose. This chapter offers general advice on designing print and online texts.

Considering the Rhetorical Situation

As with all writing tasks, your rhetorical situation should affect the way you design a text. Here are some points to consider:

academic literacies · rhetorical situations · genres · fields · processes · strategies · research MLA / APA · media / design · readings · handbook

PURPOSE   How can you design your text to help achieve your purpose? If you're reporting information, for instance, you may want to present statistical data in a chart or table rather than in the main text to help readers grasp it more quickly. If you're trying to get readers to care about an issue, a photo or pull quote—a brief selection of text "pulled out" and reprinted in a larger font—might help you do so.   55–56

AUDIENCE   How can you make your design appeal to your intended audience? By using a certain font style or size to make your text look stylish, serious, or easy to read? What kind of headings—big and bold, simple and restrained?—would your readers expect or find helpful? What colors would appeal to them?   57–60

GENRE   Are you writing in a genre that has design conventions, such as an annotated bibliography, a lab report, or a résumé? Do you need to follow a format such as those prescribed in MLA or APA style?   61–65

STANCE   How can your design reflect your attitude toward your audience and subject? Do you need a businesslike font or a playful one? Would tables and graphs help you establish your credibility? How can illustrations help you convey a certain tone?   66–68

Some Basic Principles of Design

Be consistent. To keep readers oriented while reading documents or browsing multiple webpages, any design elements should be used consistently. In a print academic essay, that task may be as simple as using the same font throughout for your main text and using boldface or italics for headings. If you're writing for the web, navigation buttons and other major elements should be in the same place on every page. In a presentation, each slide should use the same background and the same font unless there's a good reason to introduce differences.

Keep it simple.   One of your main design goals should be to help readers see quickly—even intuitively—what's in your text and how to find specific information. Adding headings to help readers see the parts, using consistent colors and fonts to help them recognize key elements, setting off steps in lists, using white space to set off blocks of text or to call attention to certain elements, and (especially) resisting the temptation to fill pages with fancy graphics or unnecessary animations—these are all ways of making your text simple to read.

Look, for example, at a furniture store's simple, easy-to-understand webpage design on the next page. This webpage contains considerable information: a row of links across the top, directing readers to various products; a search option; a column down the right side that provides details about the chair shown in the wide left-hand column; thumbnail photos below the chair and ordering information; and more details across the bottom. Despite the wealth of content, the site's design is both easy to figure out and, with the generous amount of white space, easy on the eyes.

Aim for balance.   On the webpage on the following page, the photo takes up about a quarter of the screen and is balanced by a narrower column of text, and the product information tabs and text across the page bottom balance the company logo and search box across the top. For a page without images, balance can be created through the use of margins, headings, and spacing. In the journal page shown on page 564, notice how using white space around the article title and the author's name, as well as setting both in larger type and the author's name in all capital letters, helps to balance them vertically against the large block of text below. The large initial letter of the text also helps to balance the mass of smaller type that follows. MLA and APA styles have specific design guidelines for academic research papers that cover these elements. A magazine page might create a sense of balance by using pull quotes and illustrations to break up dense vertical columns of text.

Use color and contrast carefully.   Academic readers usually expect black text on a white background, with perhaps one other color for headings. Presentation slides and webpages are most readable with a plain, light-colored background and dark text that provides contrast. Remember that

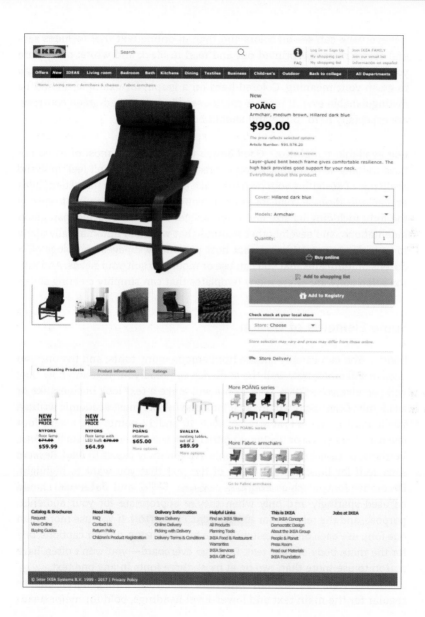

not everyone can see all colors and that an online text that includes several colors might be printed out and read in black and white; make sure your audience will be able to distinguish any color variations well enough to grasp your meaning. Colored lines on a graph, for example, should be distinguishable even if readers cannot see the colors. Red-green contrasts are especially hard to see and should be avoided.

Use available templates.   Good design takes time, and most of us do not have training as designers. If you're pressed for time or don't feel up to the challenge of designing your own text, take advantage of the many templates available. In *Microsoft Word*, for example, you can customize "styles" to specify the font, including its size and color; single- or double-spacing; paragraph indentations; and several other features that will then automatically apply to your document. Websites that host personal webpages and blogs offer dozens of templates that you can use or modify to suit your needs. And presentation software offers many templates that can simplify creating slides.

Some Elements of Design

Fonts.   You can usually choose from among many fonts, and the one you choose will affect how well the audience can read your text and how they will perceive your TONE. Times Roman will make a text look businesslike or academic; *Comic Sans* will make it look playful. For most academic writing, you'll want to use a font size between 10 and 12 points and a serif font (such as Times Roman or Bookman) rather than a sans serif font (such as Arial, Verdana, or Calibri) because serif fonts are generally easier to read. Reserve sans serif for headings and parts of the text that you want to highlight. Decorative fonts (such as *Magneto*, *Amaze*, Chiller, and **Jokerman**) should be used sparingly and only when they're appropriate for your audience, purpose, and the rest of your RHETORICAL SITUATION. If you use more than one font, use each one consistently: one for HEADINGS, one for captions, one for the main body of your text. Don't go overboard—you won't often have reason to use more than two or, at most, three fonts in any one text.

Every font has regular, **bold**, and *italic* forms. In general, choose regular for the main text and lower-level headings, bold for major head-

66–68 ▪

53 ▪
650–52 □

academic literacies   ·   rhetorical situations   ·   genres   ·   fields   ·   processes   ·   strategies   ·   research MLA / APA   ·   media / design   ·   readings   ·   handbook

ings, and italic within the main text to indicate titles of books and other long works and, occasionally, to emphasize words or brief phrases. Avoid italicizing or boldfacing entire sentences or paragraphs, especially in academic writing. If you are following **MLA**, **APA**, or some other style format, be sure your use of fonts conforms to its requirements.

MLA 548–96
APA 597–636

Finally, consider the line spacing of your text. Generally, academic writing is double-spaced, whereas **JOB LETTERS** and **RÉSUMÉS** are usually single-spaced. Some kinds of **REPORTS** may call for single-spacing; check with your instructor if you're not sure. You'll often need to add extra space to set off parts of a text—items in a list, for instance, or headings.

264–79
131–56

Layout.　Layout is the way text is arranged on a page. An academic essay, for example, will usually have a title centered at the top, one-inch margins all around, and double-spacing. A text can be presented in paragraphs— or in the form of **LISTS**, **TABLES**, **CHARTS**, **GRAPHS**, and so on. Sometimes you'll need to include other elements as well: headings, images and other graphics, captions, lists of works cited.

649–50
656

Paragraphs.　Dividing text into paragraphs focuses information for readers and helps them process it by dividing it into manageable chunks. If you're writing a story for a print newspaper with narrow columns, for example, you'll divide your text into shorter paragraphs than you would if you were writing an academic essay. In general, indent paragraphs five to seven spaces (one-half inch) when your text is double-spaced; either indent or skip a line between single-spaced paragraphs.

Lists.　Put into list form information that you want to set off and make easily accessible. Number the items in a list when the sequence matters (in instructions, for example); use bullets when the order is not important. Set off lists with an extra line of space above and below, and add extra space between the items if necessary for legibility. Here's an example:

> Darwin's theory of how species change through time derives from three postulates, each of which builds on the previous one:
>
> 1. The ability of a population to expand is infinite, but the ability of any environment to support populations is always finite.

2. Organisms within populations vary, and this variation affects the ability of individuals to survive and reproduce.

3. The variations are transmitted from parents to offspring.

—Robert Boyd and Joan B. Silk, *How Humans Evolved*

Do not set off text as a list unless there's a good reason to do so, however. Some lists are more appropriately presented in paragraph form, especially when they give information that is not meant to be referred to more than once. In the following example, there is no reason to highlight the information by setting it off in a list—and bad news is softened by putting it in paragraph form:

> I regret to inform you that the Scholarship Review Committee did not approve your application for a Board of Rectors scholarship for the following reasons: your grade-point average did not meet the minimum requirements; your major is not among those eligible for consideration; and the required letter of recommendation was not received before the deadline.

Presented as a list, that information would be needlessly emphatic.

Headings.   Headings make the structure of a text easier to follow and help readers find specific information. Some genres require standard headings—announcing an **ABSTRACT**, for example, or a list of **WORKS CITED**. Other times you will want to use headings to provide an overview of a section of text. You may not need any headings in brief texts, but when you do, you'll probably want to use one level at most, just to announce major topics. Longer texts, information-rich genres such as brochures or detailed **REPORTS**, and websites may require several levels of headings. If you decide to include headings, you will need to decide how to phrase them, what fonts to use, and where to position them.

Phrase headings concisely.   Make your headings succinct and parallel in structure. You might make all the headings nouns (**Mushrooms**), noun phrases (**Kinds of Mushrooms**), gerund phrases (**Recognizing Kinds of**

185–89 ▲
589 ●

131–56 ▲

Mushrooms), or questions (**How Do I Identify Mushrooms?**). Whatever form you decide on, use it consistently for each heading. Sometimes your phrasing will depend on your purpose. If you're simply helping readers find information, use brief phrases:

HEAD	**Forms of Social Groups among Primates**
SUBHEAD	*Solitary Social Groups*
SUBHEAD	*Monogamous Social Groups*

If you want to address your readers directly with the information in your text, consider writing your headings as questions:

How can you identify edible mushrooms?
Where can you find edible mushrooms?
How can you cook edible mushrooms?

Make headings visible.   Headings need to be visible, so if you aren't following an academic style like MLA or APA, consider making them larger than the regular text, putting them in **bold** or *italics*, or using <u>underlining</u>— or a different font. For example, you could use a serif font like Times Roman for your main text and a sans serif font like Arial for your headings. On the web, consider making headings a different color from the body text. When you have several levels of headings, use capitalization, bold, and italics to distinguish among the various levels:

First-Level Head
Second-Level Head
Third-level head

APA format requires that each level of heading appear in a specific style: centered bold uppercase and lowercase for the first level, flush-left bold uppercase and lowercase for the second level, and so on.

● APA 626

Position headings appropriately.   If you're following APA format, center first-level headings. If you are not following a prescribed format, you get to decide where to position your headings: centered, flush with the left margin, or even alongside the text in a wide left-hand margin. Position each level of head consistently throughout your text. Generally, online headings are positioned flush left.

White space.   Use white space to separate the various parts of a text. In general, use one-inch margins for the text of an essay or report. Unless you're following MLA or APA format, include space above headings, above and below lists, and around photos, graphs, and other visuals. See the two **SAMPLE RESEARCH PAPERS** in this book for examples of the formats required by MLA and APA.

MLA 589–96 ●
APA 628–36

Evaluating a Design

55–56 ▪

Does the design suit your PURPOSE?   Does the overall look of the design help convey the text's message, support its argument, or present information?

57–60 ▪

How well does the design meet the needs of your AUDIENCE?   Will the overall appearance of the text appeal to the intended readers? Is the font large enough for them to read? Are there headings to help them find their way through the text? Does the design help readers find the information they need?

61–65 ▪

How well does the text meet any GENRE requirements?   Can you tell by looking at the text that it is an academic essay, a lab report, a résumé, a blog? Do its fonts, margins, headings, and page layout meet the require-ments of **MLA**, **APA**, or whatever style is being followed?

MLA 587–89 ●
APA 626–28

66–68 ▪

How well does the design reflect your STANCE?   Do the page layout and fonts convey the appropriate tone—serious, playful, adventuresome, con-servative, or whatever other tone you intended?

academic literacies ✳
rhetorical situations ▪
genres ▲
fields ●
processes ○
strategies ◆
research MLA / APA ●
media / design ▫
readings ▮
handbook ◹

Using Visuals, Incorporating Sound

For an art history class, you write an essay comparing two paintings by Willem de Kooning. For a business class, you create a proposal to improve department communication in a small local firm and incorporate diagrams to illustrate the new procedure. For a visual rhetoric class, you take an autobiographical photograph and include a two-page analysis of how the picture distills something essential about you. For an engineering class project, you design a model of a bridge and give an in-class presentation explaining the structures and forces involved, which you illustrate with slides. For a psychology assignment, you interview several people who've suffered foreclosures on their homes in recent years about how the experience affected them—and then create an online text weaving together a slideshow of photos of the people outside their former homes, a graph of foreclosure rates, video and audio clips from the interviews, and your own insights.

All of these writing tasks require you to incorporate and sometimes to create visuals and sound. Many kinds of visuals can be included in print documents: photos, drawings, diagrams, graphs, charts, and more. And with writing that's delivered online or as a spoken presentation, your choices expand to include audio and video, voice-over narration, and links to other materials.

Visuals and sound aren't always appropriate, however, or even possible—so think carefully before you set out to include them. But they can help you make a point in ways that words alone cannot. Election polling results are easier to see in a bar graph than in a paragraph; photos of an event may convey its impact more powerfully than words alone; an audio clip can make a written analysis of an opera easier to understand. This chapter provides some tips for using visuals and incorporating sound in your writing.

Considering the Rhetorical Situation

53 ▪

Use visuals and sounds that are appropriate for your audience, purpose, and the rest of your **RHETORICAL SITUATION**. If you're trying to persuade voters in your town to back a proposal on an issue they don't know much about, for example, you might use dramatic pictures just to get their attention. But when it's important to come across as thoughtful and objective, maybe you need a more subdued look—or to make your points with written words alone. A newspaper article on housing prices might include a bar or line graph and also some photos. A report on that topic for an economics class would probably have graphs with no photos; a spoken presentation for a business class might use a dynamic graph that shows prices changing over time and an audio voice over for pictures of a neighborhood; a community website might have graphs, links to related sites, and a video interview with a home owner.

In your academic writing, especially, be careful that any visuals you use support your main point—and don't just serve to decorate the text. (Therefore, avoid clip art, which is primarily intended as decoration and comes off as unsophisticated and childish.) Images should validate or exemplify what you say elsewhere with written words and add information that words alone can't provide as clearly or easily.

Using Visuals

Photos, drawings, diagrams, videos, tables, pie charts, bar graphs—these are many kinds of visuals you could use. Visuals can offer support, illustration, evidence, and comparison and contrast in your document.

397–417
462–70
457–61

Photographs. Photos can support an **ARGUMENT**, illustrate **NARRATIVES** and **PROCESSES**, present other points of view, and help readers "place" your information in time and space. You may use photos you take yourself, or you can download photos and other images from the internet—within limits. Most downloadable photos are copyrighted, meaning that you can use them without obtaining permission from the copyright owner only if

An essay discussing the theme of mother and child might compare this painting from the Italian Renaissance (left) with a modern photograph such as Dorothea Lange's Migrant Mother *(right).*

you are doing so for academic purposes, to fulfill an assignment. If you are going to publish your text, either in print or on the web, you must have permission. You can usually gain permission by emailing the copyright holder, but that often entails a fee, so think carefully about whether you need the image. Consider, too, the file size of digital images; large files can clog readers' email in-boxes, take a long time to display on their screens, or be hard for you to upload in the first place, so you may have to compress an image in a zip file or reduce its resolution (which can diminish its sharpness).

Videos.   If you're writing online, you can include video clips for readers to play. If you're using a video already available online, such as on *YouTube*, you can show the opening image with an arrow for readers to click on to start the video, or you can simply copy the video's URL and paste it into your text as a **LINK**. In either case, you need to introduce the video in your text with a **SIGNAL PHRASE**. As with any other source, you need to provide an in-text citation and full documentation.

▢ 661–62
● 535–38

If you want to include a video you made yourself, you can edit it using such programs as *iMovie* or *Shotcut*. Once you're ready to insert it into your online document, the easiest way is to first upload it to *YouTube*, choosing the Private setting so only those you authorize may view it, and then create a link in your document.

Graphs, charts, and tables.　Statistical and other numerical information is often best presented in graphs, charts, and tables. If you can't find the right one for your purpose, you can create your own, as long as it's based on sound data from reliable sources. To do so, you can use various spreadsheet programs such as *Excel* or online chart and graph generators such as *Plot.ly* or *Venngage*.

645
646

In any case, remember to follow basic design principles: be **CONSISTENT**, label all parts clearly, and **KEEP THE DESIGN SIMPLE**, so readers can focus on the information and not be a distracted by a needlessly complex design. In particular, use color and contrast wisely to emphasize what's most significant. Choose **COLORS** that are easy to distinguish from one another—and that remain so if the graph or chart is printed out in black and white. (Using distinct gradations of color from light to dark will show well in black and white.) Some common kinds of graphs, charts, and tables are shown on the facing page.

646–48

Diagrams, maps, flowcharts, and timelines.　Information about place and time is often presented in diagrams, maps, flowcharts, and timelines. If you're using one of these infographics from the web or elsewhere, be sure to **DOCUMENT** it. Otherwise you can create one of these yourself. Make diagrams and maps as simple as possible for the point you're making. Unnecessarily complex maps can be more of a distraction than a help. To draw a flowchart, you can use the Shape tab on the Insert section of *Microsoft Word*. For timelines, make sure the scale accurately depicts the passage of time about which you are writing and avoids gaps and bunches.

544–47

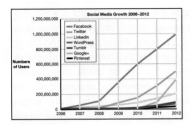

Line graphs are a good way of showing changes in data over time. Each line here represents a different social media platform. Plotting the lines together allows readers to compare the data at different points in time. Be sure to label the *x* and *y* axes and limit the number of lines to avoid confusion.

Bar graphs are useful for comparing quantitative data, measurements of how much or how many. The bars can be horizontal or vertical. This graph shows IKEA's earnings between 2000 and 2011. Some software offers 3-D and other special effects, but simple graphs are often easier to read.

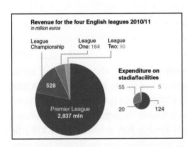

Pie charts can be used to show how a whole is divided into parts or how parts of a whole relate to one another. These two pie charts show and compare the revenue of four 2010–11 English soccer leagues and their expenditures. The segments in a pie should always add up to 100 percent, and each segment should be clearly labeled.

ECONOMY WATCH
A snapshot of key figures for the world's largest economies.

COUNTRY	GDP in billions in 2010	GDP GROWTH Y/year (%)	CURRENT ACC'T/GDP in 2010 (%)	INFLATION Year over year (%)	JOBLESS (%)
U.S.	$14,658	2.0‡	-3.2	3.5	8.6
Euro zone	12,474*	1.4	-0.2*	3.0	10.3
China	5,878	9.1	5.2	5.5	4.1§
Japan	5,459	5.6‡	3.6	-0.1	4.5
Germany	3,316	2.5	5.3	2.8‡	6.9
France	2,583	1.7	-2.1	2.5‡	9.7
Britain	2,247	0.5	-2.5	5.0	8.3
Italy	2,055	0.8	-2.1*	3.7‡	8.5
Brazil	1,601*	2.1	-1.5*	6.6	5.8
Canada	1,574	3.5‡	-3.1	2.9	7.4
India	1,538	6.9	-3.2	9.7	n.a.
Russia	1,222*	4.8	4.1*	6.8	6.4
Mexico	1,039	4.5	-0.7*	3.5	5.0
South Korea	833*	3.5	3.9*	4.2	3.1

* Actual figures of 2009   ** Harmonized figures   ‡ Quarter on quarter annualized   § Urban and September

Tables are useful for displaying numerical information concisely, especially when several items are being compared. The table here presents economic information for fourteen countries: 2010 GDP, GDP growth, current account GDP, inflation, and joblessness. Presenting information in columns and rows permits readers to find data and identify relationships among them.

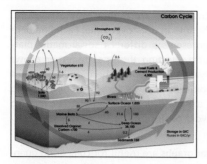

Diagrams and flowcharts are ways of showing relationships and processes. This diagram shows how carbon moves between the Earth and its atmosphere. Flowcharts can be made using widely available templates; diagrams, on the other hand, can range from simple drawings to works of art. Some simple flowcharts may be found in the genres chapters.

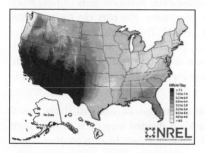

Maps show physical locations. This map shows the annual average direct solar resources for each of the U.S. states. Maps can be drawn to scale or purposefully out of scale to emphasize a point.

350–4

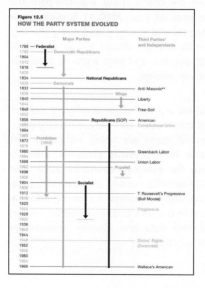

Figure 12.5
HOW THE PARTY SYSTEM EVOLVED

Timelines show change over time. These are useful to demonstrate **CAUSE** and **EFFECT** relationships or evolution. This timeline depicts how the American party system has evolved from 1788 to 2016. Timelines can be drawn horizontally or vertically.

 academic literacies

 rhetorical situations

 genres

 fields

 processes

 strategies

 research MLA / APA

 media / design

readings

handbook

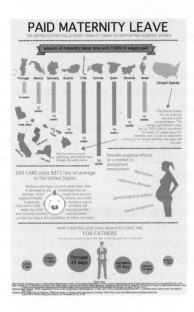

Infographics are eye-catching visual representations of information that help simplify a complicated subject. Infographics typically include an engaging title; a design that reflects the content being displayed; and a balance of charts, graphs, and other elements; readable fonts; and the sources of your information. Several websites offer templates to help you design and execute infographics, including *Piktochart*, *Infogram*, and several others.

SOME TIPS FOR USING VISUALS

- Position images as close as possible to the discussion to which they relate. In *Microsoft Word*, simply position your cursor where you want to insert an image; click the appropriate type of visual from the menu on the Insert tab; choose the appropriate image from your files; and click Insert. You may then need to adjust the way the text flows or wraps around the image: in the Page Layout tab, choose the appropriate option in Wrap Text.

- In academic writing, number all images, using separate sequences of numbers for figures (photos, graphs, diagrams, video clips, and drawings) and tables: Fig. 1, Fig. 2; Table 1, Table 2. Follow style guidelines (e.g., **MLA** or **APA**) for where to place the figure or table number and caption.

  MLA **589**
  APA **627–28**

- Explain in your written text whatever information you present in an image—don't expect it to speak for itself. Refer to the image before it appears, identifying it and summarizing its point. For example: "As Table 1 shows, Italy's economic growth rate has been declining for thirty years."

- Provide a title or caption for each image to identify it and explain its significance for your text. For example: "Table 1: Italy's Economic Growth Rate, 1985–2015."

- Label the parts of visuals clearly to ensure that your audience will understand what they show. For example, label each section of a pie chart to show what it represents.

- Cite the source of any images you don't create yourself. You need not document visuals you create, based on data from your own experimental or field research, but if you use data from a source to create a graph or chart, **CITE THE SOURCE** of the data.

539–42 ●

- In general, you may use visuals created by someone else in your academic writing as long as you include full **DOCUMENTATION**. If you post your writing online, however, you must first obtain permission from the copyright owner and include permission information. For example: Photo courtesy of Victoria and Albert Museum, London. Copyright holders will often tell you how they want the permission sentence to read.

544–47 ●

Incorporating Sound

Audio clips, podcasts, and other sound files can serve various useful purposes in online writing and spoken presentation. Music, for example, can create a mood for your text, giving your audience hints about how to interpret the meaning of your words and images or what emotional response you're evoking. Other types of sound effects—such as background conversations, passing traffic, birdsongs, crowd noise at sports events—can provide a sense of immediacy, of being part of the scene or event you're describing. Spoken words can serve as the primary way you present an online text or as an enhancement of or even a counterpoint to a written text. (And if your audience includes visually impaired people, an audio track can allow or help them to follow the text.)

You can download or link to various spoken texts online, or you can record voice and music as podcasts using programs such as *GarageBand* and *Audacity*. Remember to provide an **IN-TEXT CITATION** and full **DOCUMENTATION** of any sound material you obtain from another source.

MLA 551–57 ●
APA 600–604
544–47

Adding Links

If you're writing an online text in which you want to include images, video, or sound material available on the web, it's often easier and more effective to create links to them within the text than to embed them by copying and pasting. Rather than provide the URL for the link, use relevant words to make it easier for a reader to decide to click on the link. (See the example below where the links are marked by blue color and words such as "Francis Davis Millet and Millet family papers.") Such links allow readers to see the materials' original context and to explore it if they wish. Be selective in the number of links you include: too many links can dilute a text.

The example below shows a blog post from the Archives of American Art with links to additional detail and documentation.

John Singer Sargent

This lively caricature from the Francis Davis Millet and Millet family papers features an artist fervently painting his subject, just in the background. Most likely it is John Singer Sargent at work on his painting *Carnation, Lily, Lily, Rose*. His posture and the expression on his face suggest an exuberance that matches the action of the paint dripping and splashing as it prepares to meet the canvas with energetic strokes.

Caricature of an artist painting vigorously, ca. 1885-1886. Francis Davis Millet and Millet family papers. Archives of American Art, Smithsonian Institution.

535–38 ●

SOME TIPS FOR CREATING LINKS

- Indicate links with underlining and color (most often blue), and introduce them with a **SIGNAL PHRASE**.

- Don't include your own punctuation in a link. In the example on page 661, the period is not part of the link.

- Try to avoid having a link open in a new browser window. Readers expect links to open in the same window.

Editing Carefully—and Ethically

You may want to edit a photograph, cropping to show only part of it or using *Photoshop* or similar programs to enhance the colors or otherwise alter it. Similarly, you may want to edit a video, podcast, or other audio file to shorten it or remove irrelevant parts. If you are considering making a change of this kind, however, be sure not to do so in a way that misrepresents the content. If you alter a photo, be sure the image still represents the subject accurately; if you alter a recording of a speech or interview, be sure the edited version maintains the speaker's intent. Whenever you alter an image, a video, or a sound recording, tell your readers how you have changed it.

The same goes of editing charts and graphs. Changing the scale on a bar graph, for example, can change the effect of the comparison, making the quantities being compared seem very similar or very different, as shown in the two bar graphs of identical data in Figures 1 and 2.

Both charts show the increase in average housing costs in the United States between 2000 and 2015. However, by making the baseline in Figure 1 $200,000 instead of zero, the increase appears to be far greater than it was in reality. Just as you shouldn't edit a quotation or a photograph in a way that might misrepresent its meaning, you should not present statistical data in a way that could mislead readers.

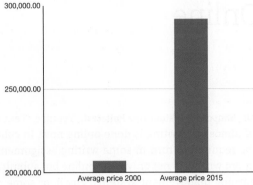

Fig. 1. Average housing prices in the United States, 2000–2015 (exaggerated).

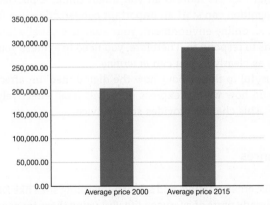

Fig. 2. Average housing prices in the United States, 2000–2015 (presented accurately).

59 Writing Online

Email. *Facebook. Snapchat, Instagram, Pinterest, Youtube.* Texts. Tweets. It may seem as if almost all writing is done online now. In college courses, you may still be required to turn in some writing assignments on paper, but more and more writing is not only done online but submitted that way too through learning management systems, email, or some other online system. You may rarely use email, but your professor may require you to do so. And many classes are being taught online, with little or no face-to-face communication between instructors and students.

Online, your instructor and classmates usually cannot see or hear you—and that matters more than you might think. A puzzled look or a smile of recognition can start an important conversation in a face-to-face class, but in an online environment, your audience usually has only your written words to respond to. Therefore, you need to express your thoughts and feelings as clearly as you can *in writing*.

So it's useful to think about how the digital medium affects the way we write—and how we can express ourselves most effectively when we write online. This chapter provides some advice.

Online Genres

For most of us, email, texting, and social networking sites like *Facebook* and *Twitter* are already parts of everyday life. But using them for academic purposes may require some careful attention. Following are some guidelines.

Email.   When emailing faculty members and school administrators, you are writing in an academic context, so your messages should reflect it: use an appropriate salutation ("Dear Professor Hagzanian"); write clearly

academic literacies · rhetorical situations · genres · fields · processes · strategies · research MLA / APA · media / design · readings · handbook

and concisely in complete sentences; use standard capitalization and punctuation; proofread; and sign your full name. If you are requesting something from your professor—to read a draft or to write a letter of recommendation—be sure to give enough notice well in advance of the deadline. If you're writing about a specific course or group work, identify the course or group explicitly. Also, craft a specific subject line; instead of writing "Question about paper," be specific: "Profile organization question." If you change topics, change your subject line as well rather than simply replying to an old email. And be careful before you hit Send—you want to be good and sure that your email neither says something you'll regret later (don't send an email when you're angry!) nor includes anything you don't want the whole world reading (don't put confidential or sensitive information in email).

Texts. Texting is inherently informal and often serves as an alternative to a phone call. Since texting often takes place as a conversation in real time (and phone keyboards can be hard to use), those who write texts often use acronyms, shorthand, and emoticons—ROTFL (rolling on the floor laughing), OST (on second thought), 2nite (tonight), 10Q (thank you), :) (happy)—to get their meaning across quickly and efficiently. If you use these abbreviations, though, be sure your readers will understand them!

Social media. You may take a course that involves using *Facebook* or another social media site as a way for class members to communicate or as part of a **LEARNING MANAGEMENT SYSTEM**. If so, you need to consider your rhetorical situation to make sure your course postings represent you as a respectful (and respectable) member of the class. Also, remember that many employers and graduate school administrators routinely check job applicants' social media pages, so don't post writing or photos that you wouldn't want a potential employer to see.

◻ 670–72

Websites. Websites are groups of webpages organized around a homepage and connected to one another (and to other websites) through links, which take users automatically from one page to another. While it's possible to create your own websites from scratch, free website builders such *as*

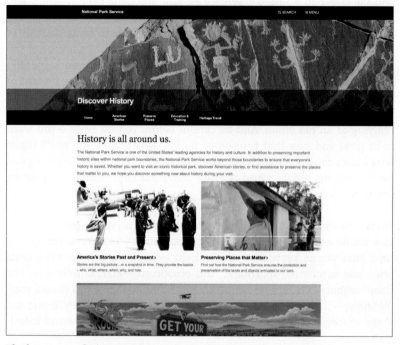

The homepage of Discover History, the National Park Service cultural resource program, provides a navigation menu that leads to various sections of the site. Links connect to pages describing Park Service programs.

Weebly, Google Sites, or Wix make it easy to create a site by providing templates for homepages, page designs, and navigation systems.

One key element in a website is the use of links to bring material from other sources into your text. You can link to the definition of a key term, for instance, rather than defining it yourself, or you can summarize a source and link to the full text rather than quoting or paraphrasing it. Providing links lets readers decide whether they need or want to see more detailed information—or not.

academic literacies   rhetorical situations   genres   fields   processes   strategies   research MLA / APA   media / design   readings   handbook

This blog, hosted by the Smithsonian Institution, focuses on marine biology and includes video, audio, slideshows, and written narratives.

Blogs. Blogs are websites that generally focus on a single topic—politics, celebrities, gaming, baseball, you name it. They're maintained and updated regularly by individuals or groups who post opinions, reflections, information, and more—with writing, photos, video and audio files, and links to other sites. Blogs are an easy way to share your writing with others—and to invite response. Free blog hosting sites such as *WordPress*, *Tumblr*, or *Blogger* offer templates that let you create a blog and post to it easily, and some learning management systems include blogging capability as well.

If your blog is public, anyone can read it, including potential employers, so just as with *Facebook* and other social media, you'll want to be careful about how you present yourself and avoid posting anything that others could see as offensive. (Think twice before posting when you're angry or upset.) You may want to activate privacy settings that let you restrict access to some of the content or that make your blog unsearchable by *Google* and other search tools. Also, assume that what you post in a blog is permanent: your friends, family, employer—anyone—may read a posting years in the future, even if the blog is no longer active.

Wikis. Wikis are websites that allow a group to work collaboratively, with all users free to add, edit, and delete content. *Wikipedia*, the online encyclopedia, is one of the most famous wikis: its content is posted and edited by people all over the world. You may be asked to contribute to a class wiki, such as the one below from a writing course at Bloomsburg University of Pennsylvania. Students post their work to the wiki, and everyone in the class has access to everyone else's writing and can comment on or revise it. When contributing to a wiki, you should be careful to write precisely, edit carefully, and make sure your research is accurate and appropriately cited—others may be quick to question and rewrite your work if it's sloppy or inaccurate. Free wiki apps include *MediaWiki*, *PmWiki*, and *DokuWiki*.

A writing-course wiki from Bloomsburg University of Pennsylvania.

Managing Online Course Work

Because so much of your college work will be done online—at the very least, you'll do most of your writing on a computer and submit some assignments via email—it's important to set up some procedures for yourself. In a single writing course, for example, you may write three or four drafts of four essays—that's twelve to sixteen documents. To keep track of your files, you'll need to create folders, establish consistent file names, and back up your work.

Creating folders.   Create a folder for each course, and name it with the course title or number and the academic term: ENG 101 Fall 2018. Within each course folder, create a folder for each major assignment. Save your work in the appropriate folder, so you can always find it.

Saving files.   Your word processor likely saves documents to a specific format identified by a three- or four-letter ending automatically added to the file name: .doc, .docx, .txt, and so on. However, this default format may not be compatible with other programs. If you're not sure what format you'll need, use the Save As command to save each document in Rich Text Format, or .rtf, which most word processors can read.

Naming files.   If you are expected to submit files electronically, your instructor may ask you to name them in a certain way. If not, devise a system that will let you easily find the files, including multiple drafts of your writing. For example, you might name your files using *Your last name + Assignment + Draft number + Date:* Jones Evaluation Draft 2 10-5-2018.docx. You'll then be able to find a particular file by looking for the assignment, the draft number, or the date. Saving all your drafts as separate files will make it easy to include them in a portfolio; also, if you lose a draft, you'll be able to use the previous one to reconstruct it.

Backing up your work.   Hard drives fail, laptops and tablets get dropped, flash drives are left in public computers. Because files stored in computers can be damaged or lost, you should save your work in several places: on your computer, on a flash drive or portable hard drive, in space supplied by your school, or online. You can also ensure that an extra copy of your work exists by emailing a copy to yourself.

Finding Basic Course Information

You'll need to learn some essential information about any online courses you take:

- *The phone number for the campus help desk* or technology center. Check the hours of operation, and keep the number handy.
- *The syllabus,* list of assignments, and calendar with deadlines.
- *Where to find tutorials* for your school's learning management system and other programs you may need help with.
- *How and when you can contact your instructor*—in person during office hours? by phone or email?—and how soon you can expect a response.
- *What file format you should use* to submit assignments—.doc, .docx, .rtf, .pdf, something else?—and how to submit them.
- *How to use the spellcheck function* on your word processor or learning management system.
- *How to participate in online discussions*—will you use a discussion board? a chat function in a learning management system? a blog? a social network? something else?

Using Learning Management Systems

Whether you're in a face-to-face, hybrid, or online class, you may be asked to do some or all of your classwork online using a learning management system such as *Blackboard, Moodle,* or *Canvas.* An LMS is a web-based educational tool that brings together all the course information your instructor wants you to have, along with features that allow you to participate in

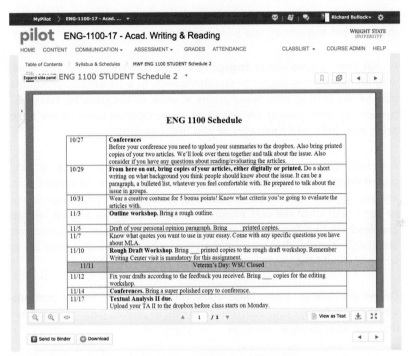

A course homepage from Wright State University's Pilot LMS.

the class in various ways. Your school's LMS likely includes the following features that you'll be expected to use:

A course homepage contains posts from your instructor; a calendar with due dates for assignments; and links to the course syllabus, other course content, and additional features available on the site.

A discussion board allows you to communicate with classmates even if everyone isn't logged in to the board at the same time. These conversations may be organized in "threads" so that posts on a particular topic appear together and may be read in order. When you contribute to a threaded discussion, treat it as an ongoing conversation: you need not introduce the topic but can simply add your comments.

A chat tool   allows you to engage in written conversations in real time, with all participants logged in simultaneously. In a classroom, doing this may be like texting with many others at once, so the rules for class discussion apply: be patient while waiting for a response; focus on the topic being discussed; avoid sarcasm or personal attacks.

A dropbox   is a place where you submit assignments online. If your course dropbox has folders for each assignment, be sure to upload your assignment into the correct folder. Keep in mind that systems go down, so don't wait until the last minute to submit a file. It's a good idea to double-check that the file you've submitted has been uploaded; often you can simply exit the dropbox and then return to it to see that your file is where it should be.

Online portfolios.   Many LMSs allow you to create an online portfolio where you may post your coursework as well as photos, personal information, and links to other websites.

Additional features.   An LMS may also include email; a space to keep a journal; a whiteboard for posting images, graphics, and presentations; a gradebook; a social network (sometimes called a Ning) for class members only; and other features that can help you keep track of your work in a class.

academic literacies · rhetorical situations · genres · fields · processes · strategies · research MLA / APA · media / design · readings · handbook

Giving Presentations **60**

In a marketing class, you give a formal presentation that includes slides and handouts as part of a research project on developing brand loyalty to clothing labels among college students. As a candidate for student government, you deliver several speeches to various campus groups that are simultaneously broadcast over the web. At a good friend's wedding, after you make a toast to the married couple, another friend who couldn't attend in person toasts them remotely using *Skype*; a third guest records both toasts on his cell phone and uploads them to *Facebook*. Whether or not you include digital and print media, whenever you are called on to give a spoken presentation, you need to make your points clear and memorable. This chapter offers guidelines to help you prepare and deliver effective presentations. We'll start with two good examples.

ABRAHAM LINCOLN

Gettysburg Address

Given by the sixteenth president of the United States, at the dedication of the Gettysburg battlefield as a memorial to those who died in the Civil War, this is one of the most famous speeches ever delivered in the United States.

> Four score and seven years ago our fathers brought forth on this continent, a new nation, conceived in Liberty, and dedicated to the proposition that all men are created equal.
>
> Now we are engaged in a great civil war, testing whether that nation, or any nation so conceived and so dedicated, can long endure.

673

We are met on a great battle-field of that war. We have come to dedicate a portion of that field, as a final resting place for those who here
gave their lives that that nation might live. It is altogether fitting and
proper that we should do this.

But, in a larger sense, we can not dedicate—we can not
consecrate—we can not hallow—this ground. The brave men, living
and dead, who struggled here, have consecrated it, far above our poor
power to add or detract. The world will little note, nor long remember
what we say here, but it can never forget what they did here. It is for
us the living, rather, to be dedicated here to the unfinished work which
they who fought here have thus far so nobly advanced. It is rather for
us to be here dedicated to the great task remaining before us—that
from these honored dead we take increased devotion to that cause for
which they gave the last full measure of devotion—that we here highly
resolve that these dead shall not have died in vain—that this nation,
under God, shall have a new birth of freedom—and that government
of the people, by the people, for the people, shall not perish from the
earth.

*You won't likely be called on to deliver such an address, but the techniques
Lincoln used—brevity, rhythm, recurring themes—are ones you can use in
your own spoken texts. The next example represents the type of spoken text
we are sometimes called on to deliver at important occasions in the lives of
our families.*

JUDY DAVIS

Ours Was a Dad . . .

*This short eulogy was given at the funeral of the writer's father, Walter Boock.
Judy Davis lives in Davis, California, where she was for many years the principal of North Davis Elementary School.*

Elsa, Peggy, David, and I were lucky to have such a dad. Ours was a
dad who created the childhood for us that he did not have for himself.

The dad who sent us airborne on the soles of his feet, squealing with delight. The dad who built a platform in the peach tree so we could eat ourselves comfortably into peachy oblivion. The dad who assigned us chores and then did them with us. The dad who felt our pain when we skinned our knees.

Ours was the dad who took us camping, all over the U.S. and Canada, but most of all in our beloved Yosemite. The one who awed us with his ability to swing around a full pail of water without spilling a drop and let us hold sticks in the fire and draw designs in the night air with hot orange coals.

Our dad wanted us to feel safe and secure. On Elsa's eighth birthday, we acquired a small camping trailer. One very blustery night in Minnesota, Mom and Dad asleep in the main bed, David suspended in the hammock over them, Peggy and Elsa snuggled in the little dinette bed, and me on an air mattress on the floor, I remember the most incredible sense of well-being: our family all together, so snug, in that little trailer as the storm rocked us back and forth. It was only in the morning that I learned about the tornado warnings. Mom and Dad weren't sleeping: they were praying that when morning came we wouldn't find ourselves in the next state.

Ours was the dad who helped us with homework at the round oak table. He listened to our oral reports, taught us to add by looking for combinations of 10, quizzed us on spelling words, and when our written reports sounded a little too much like the *World Book* encyclopedia, he told us so.

Ours was a dad who believed our round oak table that seated 5 twelve when fully extended should be full at Thanksgiving. Dad called the chaplain at the airbase, asked about homesick boys, and invited them to join our family. Or he'd call International House in Berkeley to see if someone from another country would like to experience an American Thanksgiving. We're still friends with the Swedish couple who came for turkey forty-five years ago. Many people became a part of our extended family around that table. And if twelve around the table was good, then certainly fourteen would be better. Just last fall, Dad commissioned our neighbor Randy to make yet another leaf for the table. There were fourteen around the table for Dad's last Thanksgiving.

Ours was a dad who had a lifelong desire to serve. He delivered Meals on Wheels until he was eighty-three. He delighted in picking up the day-old doughnuts from Mr. Rollen's shop to give those on his route an extra treat. We teased him that he should be receiving those meals himself! Even after walking became difficult for him, he continued to drive and took along an able friend to carry the meals to the door.

Our family, like most, had its ups and downs. But ours was a dad who forgave us our human failings as we forgave him his. He died in peace, surrounded by love. Elsa, Peggy, David, and I were so lucky to have such a dad.

This eulogy, in honor of the writer's father, provides concrete and memorable details that give the audience a clear image of the kind of man he was. The repetition of the phrase "ours was a dad" provides a rhythm and unity that moves the text forward, and the use of short, conventional sentences makes the text easy to understand—and deliver.

Key Features / Spoken Presentations

A clear structure. Spoken texts need to be clearly organized so that your audience can follow what you're saying. The **BEGINNING** needs to engage their interest, make clear what you will be talking about, and perhaps forecast the central parts of your talk. The main part of the text should focus on a few main points—only as many as your listeners can be expected to absorb and retain. (Remember, they can't go back to reread!) The **ENDING** is especially important: it should leave your audience with something, to remember, think about, or do. Davis ends as she begins, saying that she and her sisters and brother "were so lucky to have such a dad." Lincoln ends with a dramatic resolution: "that government of the people, by the people, for the people, shall not perish from the earth."

373–80

380–85

Signpost language to keep your audience on track. You may need to provide cues to help your listeners follow your text, especially **TRANSITIONS** that lead them from one point to the next. Sometimes you'll also want to stop and **SUMMARIZE** a complex point to help your audience keep track of your ideas and follow your development of them.

391

534–35

academic literacies / rhetorical situations / genres / fields / processes / strategies / research MLA / APA / media / design / readings / handbook

A tone to suit the occasion. Lincoln spoke at a serious, formal event, the dedication of a national cemetery, and his address is formal and even solemn. Davis's eulogy is more informal in **TONE**, as befits a speech given for friends and loved ones. In a presentation to a panel of professors, you probably would want to take an academic tone, avoiding too much slang and speaking in complete sentences. If you had occasion to speak on the very same topic to a neighborhood group, however, you would likely want to speak more casually.

66–68

Repetition and parallel structure. Even if you're never called on to deliver a Gettysburg Address, you will find that repetition and parallel structure can lend power to a presentation, making it easier to follow—and more likely to be remembered. "We can not dedicate—we can not consecrate—we can not hallow": the repetition of "we can not" and the parallel forms of the three verbs are one reason these words stay with us more than 150 years after they were written and delivered. These are structures any writer can use. See how the repetition of "ours was a dad" in Davis's eulogy creates a rhythm that engages listeners and at the same time unifies the text.

Slides and other media. Depending on the way you deliver your presentation, you will often want or need to use other media—*PowerPoint, Prezi,* or other presentation slides, video and audio clips, handouts, flip charts, whiteboards, and so on—to present certain information and to highlight key points.

Considering the Rhetorical Situation

As with any writing, you need to consider your rhetorical situation when preparing a presentation:

PURPOSE   Consider what your primary purpose is. To inform? persuade? entertain? evoke another kind of emotional response?

55–56

57–60   **AUDIENCE**   Think about whom you'll be addressing and how well you know them. Will they be interested, or will you need to get them interested? Are they likely to be friendly? How can you get and maintain their attention, and how can you establish common ground with them? How much will they know about your subject—will you need to provide background or define any terms?

61–65   **GENRE**   The genre of your text will affect the way you structure and present it. If you're making an argument, for instance, you'll need to consider counterarguments—and, depending on the way you're giving the presentation, perhaps to allow for questions and comments from members of the audience who hold other opinions. If you're giving a report, you may have reasons to prepare handouts with detailed information you don't have time to cover in your spoken text, or links to online documents or websites.

66–68   **STANCE**   Consider the attitude you want to express. Is it serious? thoughtful? passionate? well informed? humorous? something else? Choose your words and any other elements of your presentation accordingly. Whatever your attitude, your presentation will be received better by your listeners if they perceive you as comfortable and sincere.

A Brief Guide to Writing Presentations

Whether you're giving a poster presentation at a conference or an oral report in class, what you say will differ in important ways from what you might write for others to read. Here are some tips for composing an effective presentation.

Budget your time.   A five-minute presentation calls for about two and a half double-spaced pages of writing, and ten minutes means only four or five pages. Your introduction and conclusion should each take about one-tenth of the total time available; time for questions (if the format allows for them) should take about one-fifth; and the body of the talk, the rest. In a ten-minute presentation, then, allot one minute for your introduction, one minute for your conclusion, and two minutes for questions, leaving six minutes for the body of your talk.

Organize and draft your presentation.   Readers can go back and reread if they don't understand or remember something the first time through a text. Listeners can't. Therefore, it's important that you structure your presentation so that your audience can follow your text—and remember what you say.

- *Craft an introduction* that engages your audience's interest and tells them what to expect. Depending on your rhetorical situation, you may want to **BEGIN** with humor, with an anecdote, or with something that reminds them of the occasion for your talk or helps them see the reason for it. In any case, you always need to summarize your main points, provide any needed background information, and outline how you'll proceed.

  373–80

- *In the body of your presentation,* present your main points in more detail and support them with **REASONS** and **EVIDENCE**. As you draft, you may well find that you have more material than you can present in the time available, so you'll need to choose the most important points to focus on and leave out the rest.

  400–401
  401–8

- *Let your readers know you're concluding* (but try to avoid saying "in conclusion"), and then use your remaining time to restate your main points and to explain why they're important. End by saying "thank you" and offering to answer questions or take comments if the format allows for them.

Consider whether to use visuals.   You may want or need to include some visuals to help listeners follow what you're saying. Especially when you're presenting complex information, it helps to let them see it as well as hear it. Remember, though, that visuals should be a means of conveying information, not mere decoration.

DECIDING ON THE APPROPRIATE VISUALS

- *Slides* are useful for listing main points and for projecting illustrations, tables, and graphs.

- *Videos, animations, and sounds* can add additional information to your presentations.

- *Flip charts, whiteboards, or chalkboards* allow you to create visuals as you speak or to keep track of comments from your audience.

- *Posters* sometimes serve as the main part of a presentation, providing a summary of your points. You then offer only a brief introduction and answer any questions. You should be prepared to answer questions from any portion of your poster.

- *Handouts* can provide additional information, lists of works cited, or copies of any slides you show.

What visual tools (if any) you decide to use is partly determined by how your presentation will be delivered. Will you be speaking to a crowd or a class, delivering your presentation through a podcast, or creating an interactive presentation for a web conference? Make sure that any necessary equipment and programs are available—and that they work. If at all possible, check out any equipment in the place where you'll deliver your presentation before you go live. If you bring your own equipment for a live presentation, make sure you can connect to the internet if you need to and that electrical outlets are in reach of your power cords. Also, make sure that your visuals can be seen. You may have to rearrange the furniture or the screen to make sure everyone can see.

And finally, have a backup plan. Computers fail; projector bulbs burn out; marking pens run dry. Whatever your plan is, have an alternative in case any problems occur.

academic literacies rhetorical situations genres fields processes strategies research MLA / APA media / design readings handbook

Presentation software. *PowerPoint, Keynote,* and other presentation software can include images, video, and sound in addition to displaying written text. They are most useful for linear presentations that move audiences along one slide at a time. Cloud-based programs like *Prezi* also allow you to arrange words or slides in various designs, group related content together, and zoom in and out. Here are some tips for writing and designing slides:

- **Use LISTS or *images, not paragraphs*.** Use slides to emphasize your main points, not to reproduce your talk onscreen: keep your audience's attention focused on what you're saying. A list of brief points, presented one by one, reinforces your words. An image can provide additional information that your audience can take in quickly.

  □ 649–50

- **Make your text easy for your audience to read. FONTS** should be at least 18 points, and larger than that for headings. Projected slides are easier to read in sans serif fonts like Arial, Helvetica, and Tahoma than in serif fonts like Times New Roman. And avoid using all capital letters, which can be hard to read.

  □ 648–49

- ***Choose colors carefully.*** Your text and any illustrations must contrast with the background. Dark content on a light background is easier to read than the reverse. And remember that not everyone sees all colors; be sure your audience doesn't need to be able to see particular colors or contrasts in order to get your meaning. Red-green and blue-yellow contrasts are especially hard for some people to see and should be avoided.

- ***Use bells and whistles sparingly, if at all.*** Presentation software offers lots of decorative backgrounds, letters that fade in and out or dance across the screen, and sound effects. These features can be more distracting than helpful; use them only if they help to make your point.

- ***Mark your text.*** In your notes or prepared text, mark each place where you need to click a mouse to call up the next slide.

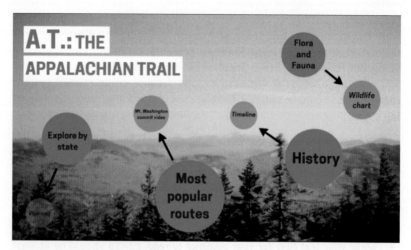

This Prezi presentation rotates, includes audio and video, and zooms in and out to let viewers take a closer look.

Truman

- Conducted whistle-stop campaign
- Made hundreds of speeches
- Spoke energetically
- Connected personally with voters
- Focused on key states

Truman's Whistle-Stop Campaign

Two PowerPoint slides on the U.S. presidential election of 1948. The slide on the left outlines the main points; the one on the right shows a map of Truman's whistle-stop campaign, providing a graphic illustration of the miles he traveled as he campaigned to be president.

academic literacies · rhetorical situations · genres · fields · processes · strategies · research MLA / APA · media / design · readings · handbook

Handouts.   When you want to give your audience information they can refer to later—reproductions of your visuals, bibliographic information about your sources, printouts of your slides—do so in the form of handouts. Refer to the handouts in your presentation, but unless they include material your audience needs to consult before or as you talk, wait until you are finished to distribute them so as not to distract listeners. Clearly label everything you give out, including your name and the date and title of the presentation.

Delivering a Presentation

The success of a presentation often hinges on how you deliver it. As you work on your spoken texts, bear in mind the following points:

Practice.   Practice, practice, and then practice some more. The better you know your talk, the more confident you will be, and your audience will respond positively to that confidence. If you're reading a prepared text, try to write it as if you were talking. Then practice by recording it as you read it; listen for spots that sound as if you're reading, and work on your delivery to sound more relaxed. As you practice, pay attention to keeping within your time limit. If possible, rehearse your talk with a small group of friends to test their response and to get used to speaking in front of an audience.

Speak clearly.   When you're giving a spoken presentation, your first goal is to be understood by your audience. If listeners miss important words or phrases because you don't pronounce them distinctly, your talk will not succeed. Make sure, too, that your pace matches your audience's needs. Often you'll need to make yourself speak more slowly than usual to explain complex material (or to compensate for nerves); sometimes you may need to speed up to keep your audience's attention. In general, though, strive for a consistent pace throughout, one that ensures you don't have to rush at the end.

Pause for emphasis.   In writing, you have white space and punctuation to show readers where an idea or discussion ends. When speaking, you need to pause to signal the end of a thought, to give listeners a moment to consider something you've said, or to get them ready for a surprising or amusing statement.

Stand up (or sit up) straight and look at your audience.   If you're in the same physical space as your audience, try to maintain some eye contact with them. If that's uncomfortable, fake it: pick a spot on the wall just above the head of a person in the back of the room, and focus on it. You'll appear as if you're looking at your audience even if you're not looking them in the eye. And if you stand or sit up straight, you'll project the sense that you have confidence in what you're saying. If you appear to believe in your words, others will, too. If you're speaking via an online forum like *Skype*, look at the computer's camera—not at the screen. Also, make sure the camera is positioned at your eye level, so you aren't looking down at it (and showing your viewers the ceiling behind you!).

Use gestures for emphasis.   If you're not used to speaking in front of a group, you may let your nervousness show by holding yourself stiffly, elbows tucked in. To overcome some of that nervousness, take some deep breaths, try to relax, and move your arms and the rest of your body as you would if you were talking to a friend. Use your hands for emphasis: most public speakers use one hand to emphasize specific points and both hands to make larger gestures. Watch politicians on C-SPAN to see how people who speak on a regular basis use gestures as part of their overall delivery.

part 9

Readings

"Read, read, read. Read everything—trash, classics, good and bad, and see how they do it." So said the American writer William Faulkner, and on the following pages you will find an anthology of readings that shows how Amy Tan, Lynda Barry, David Sedaris, Nicholas Carr, Judith Ortiz Cofer, and many other writers "do it." Read on, and pay attention to how these writers use the KEY FEATURES and STRATEGIES that you yourself are learning to use. The anthology includes readings in ten GENRES and a chapter of readings that mix genres; you'll find a menu of readings in the back of the book.

685

Readings

Literacy Narratives **61**

MATT DE LA PEÑA

Sometimes the "Tough Teen" Is Quietly Writing Stories

Matt de la Peña (b. 1973) is the author of six young adult novels, including Mexican WhiteBoy *(2008),* We Were Here *(2009), and* The Living *(2013), and five picture books. He won the 2016 Newbery Medal for his book* Last Stop on Market Street *(2015), and his debut novel,* Ball Don't Lie *(2005), was made into a feature film. In 2016, the National Council of Teachers of English awarded de la Peña the Intellectual Freedom Award. He has also written for newspapers and literary journals such as the* New York Times, George Mason Review, The Writer, Chiricú, *and* Pacific Review. *He teaches creative writing, and he gives talks and presentations at schools and libraries all over the country. The following literacy narrative was adapted from an NPR piece.*

I'M ASHAMED TO ADMIT THIS, but I didn't read a novel all the way through until after high school. Blasphemy, I know. I'm an author now. Books and words are my world. But back then I was too caught up in playing ball and running with the fellas. Guys who read books—especially for pleasure—were soft. Sensitive. And if there was one thing a guy couldn't be in my *machista*, Mexican family, it was sensitive. My old man didn't play that. Neither did my uncles or cousins or basketball teammates. And I did a good job fitting myself into the formula.

But there was something missing.

My world changed the day professor Heather Mayne sought me out in the middle of campus during my sophomore year in college. "I was rereading this last night," she said, holding out a book for me, "and I thought of *you*."

"Me?" I took the book and studied the cover.

"You." She made me promise to read it before I graduated. "And when 5
you finish," she said, "come talk to me. That's all I ask. Deal?"

That gave me 2½ years. "Deal," I told her.

I took the book with me on our next basketball road trip, to New Mexico State. The night before the game I cracked it open and read the first 10 or 15 pages. Why'd she give me this book? I wondered. It wasn't any good. The narrator couldn't even speak that good of English.

This was usually when I'd toss a book aside, telling myself it just wasn't my thing. But that wasn't an option in this case. I needed to find out why my professor had connected me to this one specific book.

By page 50 or so, I started caring about the character. She had a really tough life, far tougher than anything I'd experienced, and I tried to put myself in her shoes. The broken English, which seemed awkward at first, became poetic. I read a third of the novel that night and went to sleep.

After our game the next day, which we won on a buzzer-beater, I   10 hustled back to my hotel room to continue reading my book. I finished at 4 in the morning.

First of all, I'd never read a book in two days, and it made me feel smart (an important piece of the puzzle). Even more surprisingly, though, when I turned the last page I found myself on the verge of tears. I was shocked. How could black and white on a page make me feel so emotional? I was a tough kid from a tougher family. I hadn't shed a tear since elementary school. And here I was, choked up. From a book.

Before I reveal the title, I want all the guys reading this to know I *didn't* cry that night. I fought it off. Not everyone knows this, but it's not an official cry unless a tear exits the eye. And when I felt it coming on that night, I used an age-old trick. I looked up, allowing everything to soak back in. And it was all good.

The book I read that night was Alice Walker's *The Color Purple*.

My professor said something I will never forget when I went and talked to her the following week. Even in the harshest and ugliest of circumstances, she explained, there's still hope. That's what she loved most about *The Color Purple*.

It's what I loved most, too, I decided.   15

That hope.

I immediately went in search of other stories that might move me, too. I read all the novels I'd skipped in high school. I read novels by black female authors like Toni Morrison and Zora Neale Hurston. I read Ruth Forman's first poetry collection so many times I had every line memorized. And when I discovered Hispanic writers like Sandra Cisneros and Junot Díaz and Gabriel García Márquez, it was over. I was hooked. Novels became my secret place to "feel." My dad and uncles didn't need to know about it. Neither did my teammates. But I could sense something happening inside of me: reading was making me whole.

. . .

Back in my graduate school days, I used to drop by my folks' place once a week for dinner. I'd eat at the kitchen table talking to my mom and little sister while my dad ate in the living room watching his favorite TV show, *Cops.* We didn't usually interact a whole lot. But one night, my old man stopped me on my way out the door. He pointed at the book tucked under my arm and asked what I was reading.

"*One Hundred Years of Solitude,*" I said, holding it out for him to see. He nodded.

20

I assumed that was the end of it, so I waved to everyone and made my way through the front door. My dad followed me outside, though. "Hey, Matt," he said. "You think I could borrow that book when you're done?"

I'd never seen my dad read much of anything, and García Márquez seemed like a tough jumping-off point, but I handed over the book anyway, telling him: "It's all yours. I finished it on the ride up here."

It took him over a month to read the book. When he handed it back to me I tried to get his feedback on the multiple storylines and the magical realism, but all he'd say was that he liked it. He followed me outside the house that night, too. "I was thinking," he said, looking over his shoulder to make sure we were alone. "Maybe you could let me read whatever books you finish."

"Sure," I said, trying to hide my surprise.

Over the next two years, my old man read everything I put in front of him. Fiction, nonfiction, essays, plays. He even started reading books he found on his own. My mom pulled me aside one day and told me he

25

was becoming a completely different person. He was less angry now. He even talked about going back to school.

After my first novel came out, and I moved to New York, my dad enrolled at the local community college but kept it a secret. He struggled through a year of remedial courses but eventually got the hang of it and told his family what he was doing. He went on to earn his associate's degree, and we were all incredibly proud of him. But he didn't stop there. The following year he transferred to the University of California, Santa Cruz, where he studied literature.

My dad just recently finished his bachelor's degree, and he's now a bilingual teacher at an elementary school in Watsonville, California (where my mom teaches, too). He's still tough, and he doesn't show a whole lot of emotion. But you should see the guy's eyes light up when we start talking books. "You gotta read Roberto Bolaño, Matt. I'm serious. I don't know what's taking you so long."

"OK, OK," I say. "I'll read Bolaño."

"Start with *The Savage Detectives* and just go from there. Trust me."

Sometime when I have these kinds of conversations with my dad, 30 I find myself thinking: who the hell is this guy?

But it's like my dad always tells me. Reading changed his life.

Just like it changed mine.

Engaging with the Text

1. Matt de la Peña's literacy narrative can be read as two literacy narratives: his own and his father's. Who served as literacy sponsors (i.e., people who aid or hinder another in developing a literacy) for de la Peña and his father? How can you tell that these sponsorships were valuable to them?

2. Who do you think is the **AUDIENCE** for de la Peña's literacy narrative? How can you tell? Does he do a good job of appealing to that audience? Why or why not?

57–60

3. A key feature of a literacy narrative is an indication of the narrative's
   SIGNIFICANCE. For de la Peña, what is the significance of his introduction to the world of reading? Why do you think he includes the story
   of how his father came to love reading?

   87–88 ▲

4. What **STANCE** does de la Peña take toward his early experiences with
   reading? Is this stance effective? What other stances might he have
   taken?

   66–68 ■

5. *For Writing.* Did you have a literacy sponsor? Have you been a literacy
   sponsor for someone else? Write a **LITERACY NARRATIVE** that shows
   how your literacy sponsor helped you develop literacy in reading, writing, drawing, or something else, or how you helped someone else
   develop a literacy. Be sure to make the significance of that help clear
   in your essay.

   75–97 ▲

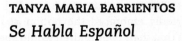

TANYA MARIA BARRIENTOS

Se Habla Español

Tanya Maria Barrientos (b. 1960) is director of executive communications for the Robert Wood Johnson Foundation, a former columnist and feature writer for the Philadelphia Inquirer, *and the author of two novels. The following essay appeared in* Latina, *a bilingual magazine published by and for Latinas. It was adapted from an essay of the same title that was published in* Border-Line Personalities: A New Generation of Latinas Dish on Sex, Sass, and Cultural Shifting *(2004). In this piece, Barrientos recounts her struggles as a Latina who is not fluent in Spanish. She takes her title from a phrase often seen in store windows, announcing that "Spanish is spoken" there.*

THE MAN ON THE OTHER END of the phone line is telling me the classes I've called about are first-rate: native speakers in charge, no more than six students per group. I tell him that will be fine and yes, I've studied a bit of Spanish in the past. He asks for my name and I supply it, rolling the double "r" in "Barrientos" like a pro. That's when I hear the silent snag, the momentary hesitation I've come to expect at this part of the exchange. Should I go into it again? Should I explain, the way I have to half a dozen others, that I am Guatemalan by birth but *pura gringa* by circumstance?

This will be the sixth time I've signed up to learn the language my parents speak to each other. It will be the sixth time I've bought workbooks and notebooks and textbooks listing 501 conjugated verbs in alphabetical order, in hopes that the subjunctive tense will finally take root in my mind. In class I will sit across a table from the "native speaker," who will wonder what to make of me. "Look," I'll want to say (but never do). "Forget the dark skin. Ignore the obsidian eyes. Pretend I'm a pink-cheeked, blue-eyed blonde whose name tag says 'Shannon.'" Because that is what a person who doesn't innately know the difference between *corre, corra,* and *corrí* is supposed to look like, isn't it?

I came to the United States in 1963 at age 3 with my family and immediately stopped speaking Spanish. College-educated and seamlessly bilingual when they settled in west Texas, my parents (a psychology professor and an artist) wholeheartedly embraced the notion of the American melting pot. They declared that their two children would speak nothing but *inglés*. They'd read in English, write in English, and fit into Anglo society beautifully.

It sounds politically incorrect now. But America was not a hyphenated nation back then. People who called themselves Mexican Americans or Afro-Americans were considered dangerous radicals, while law-abiding citizens were expected to drop their cultural baggage at the border and erase any lingering ethnic traits.

To be honest, for most of my childhood I liked being the brown girl 5 who defied expectations. When I was 7, my mother returned my older brother and me to elementary school one week after the school year had already begun. We'd been on vacation in Washington, DC, visiting the Smithsonian, the Capitol, and the home of Edgar Allan Poe. In the Volkswagen on the way home, I'd memorized "The Raven," and I would recite it with melodramatic flair to any poor soul duped into sitting through my performance. At the school's office, the registrar frowned when we arrived.

"You people. Your children are always behind, and you have the nerve to bring them in late?"

"My children," my mother answered in a clear, curt tone, "will be at the top of their classes in two weeks."

The registrar filed our cards, shaking her head.

I did not live in a neighborhood with other Latinos, and the public school I attended attracted very few. I saw the world through the clear, cruel vision of a child. To me, speaking Spanish translated into being poor. It meant waiting tables and cleaning hotel rooms. It meant being left off the cheerleading squad and receiving a condescending smile from the guidance counselor when you said you planned on becoming a lawyer or a doctor. My best friends' names were Heidi and Leslie and Kim. They told me I didn't seem "Mexican" to them, and I took it as a compliment. I enjoyed looking into the faces of Latino store clerks and waitresses and, yes, even our maid and saying "*Yo no hablo español.*" It made me feel superior. It made me feel American. It made me feel white. I thought if I stayed away from Spanish, stereotypes would stay away from me.

Then came the backlash. During the two decades when I'd worked 10 hard to isolate myself from the stereotype I'd constructed in my own head, society shifted. The nation changed its views on ethnic identity. College professors started teaching history through African American and Native American eyes. Children were told to forget about the melting pot and picture America as a multicolored quilt instead. Hyphens suddenly had muscle, and I was left wondering where I fit in.

The Spanish language was supposedly the glue that held the new Latino community together. But in my case it was what kept me apart. I felt awkward among groups whose conversations flowed in and out of Spanish. I'd be asked a question in Spanish and I'd have to answer in English, knowing this raised a mountain of questions. I wanted to call myself Latina, to finally take pride, but it felt like a lie. So I set out to learn the language that people assumed I already knew.

> If I stayed away from Spanish, stereotypes would stay away from me.

After my first set of lessons, I could function in the present tense. "*Hola, Paco. ¿Qué tal? ¿Qué color es tu cuaderno? El mío es azul.*" My vocabulary built quickly, but when I spoke, my tongue felt thick inside my mouth—and if I needed to deal with anything in the future or the past, I was sunk. I enrolled in a three-month submersion program in Mexico and emerged able to speak like a sixth-grader with a solid C average. I could read Gabriel García Márquez with a Spanish-English dictionary at my elbow, and I could follow 90 percent of the melodrama on any given telenovela. But true speakers discover my limitations the moment I stumble over a difficult construction, and that is when I get the look. The one that raises the wall between us. The one that makes me think I'll never really belong. Spanish has become a litmus test showing how far from your roots you've strayed.

My bilingual friends say I make too much of it. They tell me that my Guatemalan heritage and unmistakable Mayan features are enough to legitimize my membership in the Latin American club. After all, not all Poles speak Polish. Not all Italians speak Italian. And as this nation grows more and more Hispanic, not all Latinos will share one language. But I don't believe them.

There must be other Latinas like me. But I haven't met any. Or, I should say, I haven't met any who have fessed up. Maybe they are secretly struggling to fit in, the same way I am. Maybe they are hiring tutors and listening to tapes behind locked doors, just like me. I wish we all had the courage to come out of our hiding places and claim our rightful spot in the broad Latino spectrum. Without being called hopeless gringas. Without having to offer apologies or show remorse.

If it will help, I will go first.   15

Aquí estoy. Spanish-challenged and *pura* Latina.

Engaging with the Text

386–87 ◆ 1. Tanya Maria Barrientos gives her essay a Spanish **TITLE**. How does this prepare you for the subject of the essay? What does this title lead you to believe about Barrientos's feelings about Spanish? Is that impression supported by the rest of the essay? Why or why not?

373–80 ◆ 2. Barrientos **BEGINS** her essay with an anecdote about signing up for a Spanish class. What is the effect of beginning with this anecdote? Does it attract your interest? Why or why not? How does it prepare you for the rest of the essay?

87–88 ▲ 3. Barrientos tells of learning to read and write in Spanish. One key feature of a literacy narrative is an indication of the narrative's **SIGNIFICANCE**. For her, what is the significance of learning that language? Why is it so important to her?

66–68 ■ 4. Barrientos peppers her essay with Spanish words and phrases, without offering any English translation. What does this tell you about her **STANCE**? Would her stance seem different if she'd translated the Spanish? Why or why not?

5. *For Writing.* As Barrientos notes, language plays a big part in her identity. Think about the languages you speak. If you speak only English, think about what kind of accent you have. (If you think you don't have one, consider how you might sound to someone from a different region or social class.) Does the language you speak or accent you have change according to the situation? Does it change according to 256–63 ▲   how you perceive yourself? Write an essay **REFLECTING** on the way you speak and how it affects (or is affected by) your identity.

✳ academic literacies   ■ rhetorical situations   ▲ genres   ⬡ fields   ◯ processes   ◆ strategies   ⬤ research MLA / APA   ◻ media / design   ▮◀ readings   ◹ handbook

AMY TAN

Mother Tongue

Amy Tan (b. 1952) is the author of novels, children's books, essays, and a memoir. Her work has appeared in the New Yorker, National Geographic, *and other magazines. She is best known for her novel* The Joy Luck Club *(1989), which examines the lives of and the relationships between four Chinese American daughters and their mothers. The following selection was first delivered as a talk at a symposium on language in San Francisco in 1989. As you read, pay attention to how Tan describes the different Englishes she speaks.*

I AM NOT A SCHOLAR OF ENGLISH OR LITERATURE. I cannot give you much more than personal opinions on the English language and its variations in this country or others.

I am a writer. And by that definition, I am someone who has always loved language. I am fascinated by language in daily life. I spend a great deal of my time thinking about the power of language—the way it can evoke an emotion, a visual image, a complex idea, or a simple truth. Language is the tool of my trade. And I use them all—all the Englishes I grew up with.

Recently, I was made keenly aware of the different Englishes I do use. I was giving a talk to a large group of people, the same talk I had already given to half a dozen other groups. The nature of the talk was about my writing, my life, and my book, *The Joy Luck Club.* The talk was going along well enough, until I remembered one major difference that made the whole talk sound wrong. My mother was in the room. And it was perhaps the first time she had heard me give a lengthy speech, using the kind of English I have never used with her. I was saying things like, "The intersection of memory upon imagination" and "There is an aspect of my fiction that relates to thus-and-thus"—a speech filled with carefully wrought grammatical phrases, burdened, it suddenly seemed to me, with nominalized forms, past perfect tenses, conditional phrases, all the forms of standard English that I had learned in school and through books, the forms of English I did not use at home with my mother.

Just last week, I was walking down the street with my mother, and I again found myself conscious of the English I was using, the English I do use with her. We were talking about the price of new and used furniture and I heard myself saying this: "Not waste money that way." My husband was with us as well, and he didn't notice any switch in my English. And then I realized why. It's because over the twenty years we've been together I've often used the same kind of English with him, and sometimes he even uses it with me. It has become our language of intimacy, a different sort of English that relates to family talk, the language I grew up with.

So you'll have some idea of what this family talk I heard sounds   5
like, I'll quote what my mother said during a recent conversation which I videotaped and then transcribed. During this conversation, my mother was talking about a political gangster in Shanghai who had the same last name as her family's, Du, and how the gangster in his early years wanted to be adopted by her family, which was rich by comparison. Later, the gangster became more powerful, far richer than my mother's family, and one day showed up at my mother's wedding to pay his respects. Here's what she said in part:

"Du Yusong having business like fruit stand. Like off the street kind. He is Du like Du Zong—but not Tsung-ming Island people. The local people call putong, the river east side, he belong to that side local people. That man want to ask Du Zong father take him in like become own family. Du Zong father wasn't look down on him, but didn't take seriously, until that man big like become a mafia. Now important person, very hard to inviting him. Chinese way, came only to show respect, don't stay for dinner. Respect for making big celebration, he shows up. Mean gives lots of respect. Chinese custom. Chinese social life that way. If too important won't have to stay too long. He come to my wedding. I didn't see, I heard it. I gone to boy's side, they have YMCA dinner. Chinese age I was nineteen."

You should know that my mother's expressive command of English belies how much she actually understands. She reads the *Forbes* report, listens to *Wall Street Week*, converses daily with her stockbroker, reads all of Shirley MacLaine's books with ease—all kinds of things I can't begin to

academic literacies · rhetorical situations · genres · fields · processes · strategies · research MLA / APA · media / design · readings · handbook

understand. Yet some of my friends tell me they understand 50 percent of what my mother says. Some say they understand 80 to 90 percent. Some say they understand none of it, as if she were speaking pure Chinese. But to me, my mother's English is perfectly clear, perfectly natural. It's my mother tongue. Her language, as I hear it, is vivid, direct, full of observation and imagery. That was the language that helped shape the way I saw things, expressed things, made sense of the world.

Lately, I've been giving more thought to the kind of English my mother speaks. Like others, I have described it to people as "broken" or "fractured" English. But I wince when I say that. It has always bothered me that I can think of no way to describe it other than "broken," as if it were damaged and needed to be fixed, as if it lacked a certain wholeness and soundness. I've heard other terms used, "limited English," for example. But they seem just as bad, as if everything is limited, including people's perceptions of the limited English speaker.

I know this for a fact, because when I was growing up, my mother's "limited" English limited my perception of her. I was ashamed of her English. I believed that her English reflected the quality of what she had to say. That is, because she expressed them imperfectly her thoughts were imperfect. And I had plenty of empirical evidence to support me: the fact that people in department stores, at banks, and at restaurants did not take her seriously, did not give her good service, pretended not to understand her, or even acted as if they did not hear her.

My mother has long realized the limitations of her English as well. 10 When I was fifteen, she used to have me call people on the phone to pretend I was she. In this guise, I was forced to ask for information or even to complain and yell at people who had been rude to her. One time it was a call to her stockbroker in New York. She had cashed out her small portfolio and it just so happened we were going to go to New York the next week, our very first trip outside California. I had to get on the phone and say in an adolescent voice that was not very convincing, "This is Mrs. Tan."

And my mother was standing in the back whispering loudly, "Why he don't send me check, already two weeks late. So mad he lie to me, losing me money."

And then I said in perfect English, "Yes, I'm getting rather concerned. You had agreed to send the check two weeks ago, but it hasn't arrived."

Then she began to talk more loudly. "What he want, I come to New York tell him front of his boss, you cheating me?" And I was trying to calm her down, make her be quiet, while telling the stockbroker, "I can't tolerate any more excuses. If I don't receive the check immediately, I am going to have to speak to your manager when I'm in New York next week." And sure enough, the following week there we were in front of this astonished stockbroker, and I was sitting there red-faced and quiet, and my mother, the real Mrs. Tan, was shouting at his boss in her impeccable broken English.

We used a similar routine just five days ago, for a situation that was far less humorous. My mother had gone to the hospital for an appointment, to find out about a benign brain tumor a CAT scan had revealed a month ago. She said she had spoken very good English, her best English, no mistakes. Still, she said, the hospital did not apologize when they said they had lost the CAT scan and she had come for nothing. She said they did not seem to have any sympathy when she told them she was anxious to know the exact diagnosis, since her husband and son had both died of brain tumors. She said they would not give her any more information until the next time and she would have to make another appointment for that. So she said she would not leave until the doctor called her daughter. She wouldn't budge. And when the doctor finally called her daughter, me, who spoke in perfect English—lo and behold—we had assurances the CAT scan would be found, promises that a conference call on Monday would be held, and apologies for any suffering my mother had gone through for a most regrettable mistake.

I think my mother's English almost had an effect on limiting my 15 possibilities in life as well. Sociologists and linguists probably will tell you that a person's developing language skills are more influenced by peers. But I do think that the language spoken in the family, especially in immigrant families which are more insular, plays a large role in shaping the language of the child. And I believe that it affected my results on achievement tests, IQ tests, and the SAT. While my English skills were never judged as poor, compared to math, English could not be considered my strong suit. In grade school I did moderately well, getting perhaps B's, sometimes B-pluses, in English and scoring perhaps in the sixtieth or seventieth percentile on achievement tests. But those scores were not good enough to override the opinion that my true abilities lay in math and science, because in those areas I achieved A's and scored in the ninetieth percentile or higher.

This was understandable. Math is precise; there is only one correct answer. Whereas, for me at least, the answers on English tests were always a judgment call, a matter of opinion and personal experience. Those tests were constructed around items like fill-in-the-blank sentence completion, such as, "Even though Tom was _____, Mary thought he was _____." And the correct answer always seemed to be the most bland combinations of thoughts, for example, "Even though Tom was shy, Mary thought he was charming," with the grammatical structure "even though" limiting the correct answer to some sort of semantic opposites, so you wouldn't get answers like, "Even though Tom was foolish, Mary thought he was ridiculous." Well, according to my mother, there were very few limitations as to what Tom could have been and what Mary might have thought of him. So I never did well on tests like that.

The same was true with word analogies, pairs of words in which you were supposed to find some sort of logical, semantic relationship—for example, "*Sunset* is to *nightfall* as _____ is to _____." And here you would be presented with a list of four possible pairs, one of which showed the same kind of relationship: *red* is to *stoplight*, *bus* is to *arrival*, *chills* is to *fever*, *yawn* is to *boring*. Well, I could never think that way. I knew what the tests were asking, but I could not block out of my mind the images already created by the first pair, "*sunset* is to *nightfall*"—and I would see a burst of colors against a darkening sky, the moon rising, the lowering of a curtain of stars. And all the other pairs of words—red, bus, stoplight, boring—just threw up a mass of confusing images, making it impossible for me to sort out something as logical as saying: "A sunset precedes nightfall" is the same as "a chill precedes a fever." The only way I would have gotten that answer right would have been to imagine an associative situation, for example, my being disobedient and staying out past sunset, catching a chill at night, which turns into feverish pneumonia as punishment, which indeed did happen to me.

I have been thinking about all this lately, about my mother's English, about achievement tests. Because lately I've been asked, as a writer, why there are not more Asian Americans represented in American literature. Why are there few Asian Americans enrolled in creative writing programs? Why do so many Chinese students go into engineering? Well, these are broad sociological questions I can't begin to answer. But I have noticed in surveys—in fact, just last week—that Asian students, as a whole, always do significantly better on math achievement tests than in English. And this makes me think that there are other Asian-American students whose English spoken in the home might also be described as "broken" or "limited." And perhaps they also have teachers who are steering them away from writing and into math and science, which is what happened to me.

Fortunately, I happen to be rebellious in nature and enjoy the challenge of disproving assumptions made about me. I became an English major my first year in college, after being enrolled as pre-med. I started writing nonfiction as a freelancer the week after I was told by my former boss that writing was my worst skill and I should hone my talents toward account management.

But it wasn't until 1985 that I finally began to write fiction. And at first 20 I wrote using what I thought to be wittily crafted sentences, sentences that would finally prove I had mastery over the English language. Here's an example from the first draft of a story that later made its way into *The Joy Luck Club*, but without this line: "That was my mental quandary in its nascent state." A terrible line, which I can barely pronounce.

Fortunately, for reasons I won't get into today, I later decided I should envision a reader for the stories I would write. And the reader I decided upon was my mother, because these were stories about mothers. So with this reader in mind—and in fact she did read my early drafts—I began to write stories using all the Englishes I grew up with: the English I spoke to my mother, which for lack of a better term might be described as "simple"; the English she used with me, which for lack of a better term might be described as "broken"; my translation of her Chinese, which

academic literacies   rhetorical situations   genres   fields   processes   strategies   research MLA / APA   media / design   readings   handbook

could certainly be described as "watered down"; and what I imagined to be her translation of her Chinese if she could speak in perfect English, her internal language, and for that I sought to preserve the essence, but neither an English nor a Chinese structure. I wanted to capture what language ability tests can never reveal: her intent, her passion, her imagery, the rhythms of her speech and the nature of her thoughts.

Apart from what any critic had to say about my writing, I knew I had succeeded where it counted when my mother finished reading my book and gave me her verdict: "So easy to read."

Engaging with the Text

1. A literacy narrative needs **VIVID DETAIL** to bring it to life. What main kind of detail does Amy Tan use in her essay? Point to two of her details that strike you as especially interesting and revealing, and explain why they do.   ▲ 87

2. Tan **BEGINS** by announcing, "I am not a scholar of English. . . . I cannot give you much more than personal opinions on the English language and its variations in this country or others." How does this opening set up your expectations for the rest of the essay? Why do you think Tan chose to begin by denying her own authority?   ◆ 373–80

3. Tan writes about the different "Englishes" she speaks. What categories does she **DIVIDE** English into? Why are these divisions important to Tan? How does she say they affect her as a writer?   ◆ 419–20

4. How does writing for an academic **AUDIENCE** affect the language Tan primarily uses in the essay? What kind of English do you think she believes her audience speaks? Why? Support your answer with quotations from the text.   ■ 57–60

5. *For Writing.* Explore the differences between the language you speak at home and the languages you use with friends, teachers, employers, and so on. Write an essay that **REFLECTS** on the various languages you speak. If you speak only one language, consider the variations in the ways you speak it—at home, at work, at school, at church, wherever.   ▲ 256–63

NICOLE MILES

Formation of a Caribbean Illustrator

Nicole Miles (b. 1989) is a designer and illustrator living in the United Kingdom. She currently works as a designer for Hallmark UK on the Humour, Licensing & Properties team and as a freelance illustrator. Miles's work has appeared in Bust magazine, the New York Times, Bitch magazine, BuzzFeed, and other outlets. This graphic essay was created for U.S. Black History Month 2017 and appeared in BuzzFeed on February 24, 2017.

 academic literacies

 rhetorical situations

 genres

 fields

 processes

 strategies

research MLA / APA

media / design

readings

 handbook

EXCEPT ONE LITTLE QUESTION.

ONE BIG LITTLE QUESTION...

STUCK BETWEEN "BUT I DO!" AND "THEY'RE TOO HARD TO DRAW" I DON'T THINK I EVER HAD A REAL RESPONSE.

I GUESS YOU CAN'T IMAGINE THE SKIN COLOUR OF A LINE DRAWING...

IF ALL THE CHARACTERS LOOK EXACTLY THE SAME.

THERE WEREN'T REALLY ANY EXAMPLES IN MY BELOVED ANIME AND MANGA OF CHARACTERS WHO WERE UNMISTAKABLY BLACK THAT WEREN'T STRAIGHT UP GOLLIWOG.*

✳ A GOLLIWOG, "A HORRID SIGHT, THE BLACKEST GNOME", IS A CHARACTER CREATED IN THE HEYDAY OF MINSTREL SHOWS AND BLACKFACE. THE TERM HAS LONG BEEN USED AS A RACIAL SLUR. ONLY THE VERY IGNORANT OR THE VERY RACIST WOULD SEEK TO DEFEND THIS DOLL AS NOTHING MORE THAN AN INNOCENT TOY.

I WANTED TO DRAW BLACK PEOPLE IN A BEAUTIFUL WAY TO STAND UP AGAINST THE INSULTING COMIC DEPICTIONS.

academic literacies

rhetorical situations

genres

fields

processes

strategies

research MLA / APA

media / design

readings

handbook

IT FELT OK IF I TRIED AND FAILED AT DRAWING THE "DEFAULT" HUMAN – WHO IN ANIME IS ASIAN, BUT WHO MANY PEOPLE ASSUME IS WHITE BECAUSE OF HOW WIDELY REPRESENTED WHITE PEOPLE ARE IN POP CULTURE.

BUT EVERYTHING

IS HARD TO DRAW

...AT FIRST.

I COULDN'T ARTICULATE IT AT THE TIME, BUT THIS WAS THE START OF A REALISATION THAT THE LACK OF MEDIA REPRESENTATION OF PEOPLE WHO LOOKED LIKE ME AFFECTED ME EVEN IF I WASN'T INITIALLY AWARE OF IT.

AND IT WASN'T ENOUGH TO BE REPRESENTED IN JUST ONE WAY...

(REGARDLESS OF HOW POSITIVE THAT REPRESENTATION SEEMS.)

IT WAS NECESSARY TO HAVE VISUAL REPRESENTATION FROM LOTS OF DIFFERENT PERSPECTIVES.

AND MUCH LATER I STARTED TO APPRECIATE THE IMPORTANCE OF HEARING DIRECTLY FROM BLACK CREATORS AND FURTHER MARGINALISED VOICES WITHIN THE DIASPORA WHO SHOWED THAT YOU SHOULDN'T HAVE TO ACCEPT *ONLY* EVER BEING REPRESENTED BY THOSE FAR REMOVED FROM YOUR EXPERIENCE.

Engaging with the Text

1. Who is the **AUDIENCE** for Nicole Miles's graphic essay? Why do you think so? How does Miles appeal to this audience?

   57–60

2. A good literacy narrative includes **VIVID DETAILS** that help bring the story to life. In this essay, Miles uses both words and visuals to help readers picture the events of her story. Pick one panel of the essay and explain how the image strengthens or enhances your understanding of the text.

   87

3. Miles carefully **DEFINES** her terms. Why do you think she does this?

   432–42

4. Miles writes, "Growing up in the Caribbean, I loved illustrating my own manga comics. But learning how to draw people that looked like me took a little longer." Why did Miles have difficulty drawing black people? What was standing in her way?

5. *For Writing*. Create a cartoon strip about a literacy event in your life—learning to read, write, draw, play music, keep sports scores, read patterns, or something else. Make sure the visuals and the text work together to convey your message.

62 Textual Analyses

academic literacies   rhetorical situations   genres   fields   processes   strategies   research MLA / APA   media / design   readings   handbook

LAUREL THATCHER ULRICH

Well-Behaved Women Seldom Make History

Laurel Thatcher Ulrich (b. 1938) is a professor of history at Harvard University, where she was appointed the 300th Anniversary University Professor. She is author and editor of over a half-dozen books, including The Age of Homespun: Objects and Stories in the Creation of an American Myth *(2001),* A House Full of Females: Plural Marriage and Women's Rights in Early Mormonism, 1835–1870 *(2017), and* Well-Behaved Women Seldom Make History *(2007) from which the following essay was taken. Ulrich introduced the phrase "well-behaved women seldom make history" in a 1976 journal article titled "Vertuous Women Found: New England Ministerial Literature, 1668–1735," about how women were characterized in Puritan funeral sermons. Much to Ulrich's surprise, the phrase generated an explosion of cultural interest and now appears on greeting cards, T-shirts, bumper stickers, mugs, and plaques, among other places.*

SOME TIME AGO a former student emailed me from California: "You'll be delighted to know that you are quoted frequently on bumpers in Berkeley." Through a strange stroke of fate I've gotten used to seeing my name on bumpers. And on T-shirts, tote bags, coffee mugs, magnets, buttons, greeting cards, and websites.

I owe this curious fame to a single line from a scholarly article I published in 1976. In the opening paragraph, I wrote: "Well-behaved women seldom make history." That sentence, slightly altered, escaped into popular culture in 1995, when journalist Kay Mills used it as an epigraph for her informal history of American women, *From Pocahontas to Power Suits.* Perhaps by accident, she changed the word *seldom* to *rarely.* Little matter. According to my dictionary, *seldom* and *rarely* mean the same thing: "Well-behaved women *infrequently,* or on *few occasions,* make history." This may be one of those occasions. My original article was a study of the well-behaved women celebrated in Puritan funeral sermons.

In 1996, a young woman named Jill Portugal found the "rarely" version of the quote in her roommate's copy of *The New Beacon Book of Quotations by Women*. She wrote me from Oregon asking permission to print it on T-shirts. I was amused by her request and told her to go ahead; all I asked was that she send me a T-shirt. The success of her enterprise surprised both of us. A plain white shirt with the words "Well-behaved women rarely make history" printed in black roman type became a best-selling item. Portugal calls her company "one angry girl designs." Committed to "taking over the world, one shirt at a time," she fights sexual harassment, rape, pornography, and what she calls "fascist beauty standards."

Her success inspired imitators, only a few of whom bothered to ask permission. My runaway sentence now keeps company with anarchists, hedonists, would-be witches, political activists of many descriptions, and quite a few well-behaved women. It has been featured in *CosmoGirl*, the *Christian Science Monitor*, and *Creative Keepsake Scrapbooking Magazine*. According to news reports, it was a favorite of the pioneering computer scientist Anita Borg. The Sweet Potato Queens of Jackson, Mississippi, have adopted it as an "official maxim," selling their own pink-and-green T-shirt alongside another that reads "Never Wear Panties to a Party."

My accidental fame has given me a new perspective on American   5
popular culture. While some women contemplate the demise of feminism, others seem to have only just discovered it. A clerk in the Amtrak ticket office in D.C.'s Union Station told a fellow historian that all the women in her office wore the button. "I couldn't resist telling her that I was acquainted with you, and she just lit right up, and made me promise to tell you that the women at the Amtrak office thank you for all your 'words of wisdom.'"

. . .

The "well-behaved women" quote works because it plays into longstanding stereotypes about the invisibility and the innate decorum of the female sex. Many people think women are less visible in history than men because their bodies impel them to nurture. Their job is to bind the

academic literacies · rhetorical situations · genres · fields · processes · strategies · research MLA / APA · media / design · readings · handbook

wounds, stir the soup, and bear the children of those whose mission it is to fight wars, rule nations, and define the cosmos. Not all those who make this argument consider women unimportant—on the contrary, they often revere the contributions of women as wives, mothers, and caregivers—or at least they say so. But they also assume that domestic roles haven't changed much over the centuries, and that women who perform them have no history. A New Hampshire pastor captured this notion when he wrote in his commonplace book in 1650, "Woman's the center & lines are men." If women occupy the fixed center of life, and if history is seen as a linear progression of public events, a changing panorama of wars and kingdoms, then only those who through outrageous behavior, divine intervention, or sheer genius step into the stream of public consequence have a history.

The problem with this argument is not only that it limits women. It also limits history. Good historians are concerned not only with famous people and public events but with broad transformations in human behavior, things like falling death rates or transatlantic migration. Here seemingly small actions by large numbers of people can bring about profound change. But this approach runs up against another imperative of history—its reliance on written sources. Until recent times most women (and a great many men) were illiterate. As a consequence their activities were recorded, if at all, in other people's writing. People who caused trouble might show up in court records, newspapers, or their masters' diaries. Those who quietly went about their lives were either forgotten, seen at a distance, or idealized into anonymity. Even today, publicity favors those who make—or break—laws.

But the difficulty is bigger than that. History is an account of the past based on surviving sources, but it is also a way of making sense out of the present. In the heat and confusion of events, people on all sides of an issue mine old stories for inspiration, enlightenment, or confirmation. Their efforts add to the layers of understanding attached to the original events, shaping what later generations know and care about. Scholars sometimes call these popular reconstructions of the past "memory" to distinguish them from formal history. But serious history is also forged in the tumult of change. History is not just what happened in the past. It is what later generations choose to remember.

. . .

Historians don't own history. But we do have a lot of experience sifting through competing evidence. Historical research is a bit like detective work. We re-create past events from fragments of information, trying hard to distinguish credible accounts from wishful thinking. One of our jobs is to explore the things that get left out when a person becomes an icon. Recent scholarship on the Sweet Potato Queens' heroine, Mae West, is a good example. There is no question about West's reputation for misbehavior. She said it herself: "When I'm bad, I'm better." Beginning her stage career at the age of six, she moved from playing the saintly Little Eva in *Uncle Tom's Cabin* to shimmying her way to fame. In uptight Boston, theater owners cut off the lights "with West's first ripple." But in New York she was the darling of urban sophisticates who wanted

Mae West, photographed in the 1930s.

to explore the seamy side of life without leaving their theater seats. When she moved to Hollywood in the 1930s, censors tried to clean up her scripts, but she knew how to fill even the blandest lines with sexual innuendo. *Variety* complained that "Mae couldn't sing a lullaby without making it sexy."

That is how Mae West made history. But what sort of history did she make? Some recent studies focus on her debts to the male homosexuals whose outrageous impersonations defined *camp* in the 1920s. Others claim that her largest debt was to African American entertainers. West's shimmy, for example, ultimately derived from West African traditions adapted in rural dance halls, or "jooks." Her ballad "Honey let yo' drawers hang down low" (which may have inspired the Sweet Potato Queens' "Never Wear Panties to a Party") was a favorite in southern jooks. In the early twentieth century, West, the sexually active, streetwise girl from Brooklyn, gave middle-class audiences a glimpse of worlds that both fascinated and repelled. Like the legendary Godiva,* she allowed people to imagine the unimaginable. Because she was also a savvy business-woman, she was able to live off other people's fantasies.

A first-year student at a California university told me that to make history, people need to do the unexpected. She offered the example of civil rights activist Rosa Parks, "who would not leave her seat." I like her emphasis on the unexpected. It not only captures the sense of history as the study of how things change, it offers a somewhat more complex way of understanding the contribution of a woman like Parks.

Was Parks a well-behaved woman? The Montgomery, Alabama, bus company did not think so. As the student from California recognized, Parks made history precisely because she dared to challenge both social norms and the law. Her refusal to obey the statute that required her to give up her seat to a white passenger sparked the 361-day-long boycott that thrust Martin Luther King into the public eye and led to a historic Supreme Court decision outlawing segregation on public transportation.

Godiva: Lady Godiva, an eleventh-century Anglo-Saxon noblewoman who reportedly rode naked through the streets of Coventry, England, to protest taxes imposed by her husband. [Editor's note]

Yet Parks became an icon for the civil rights movement not only for her courage but because the media identified her as a hard-working seamstress who simply got tired of moving to the back of the bus. Few people outside Montgomery knew her as the politically conscious secretary of the local NAACP, nor understood how many years she and her husband had been working for social justice before that fateful day on the bus. In 1954 and 1955, Parks had attended workshops on desegregation sponsored by the radical Highlander Folk School in Tennessee, a public education project that Mississippi's Senator James Eastland excoriated as a "front for a conspiracy to overthrow this country."

Nor has popular history recorded the names of other Montgomery women—teenagers—whose arrests that year for refusing to give up their seats failed to ignite a movement. Years later, E. D. Nixon, president of the Montgomery NAACP, explained why he hadn't chosen any of these other women to make a historic stand against segregation. "OK, the case of Louise Smith. I found her daddy in front of his shack, barefoot, drunk. Always drunk. Couldn't use her. In that year's second case, the girl, very brilliant but she'd had an illegitimate baby. Couldn't use her. The last case before Rosa was the daughter of a preacher who headed a reform school for years. My interview of her convinced me that she wouldn't stand up to pressure. She were even afraid of me. When Rosa Parks was arrested, I thought, 'This is it!' 'Cause she's morally clean, she's reliable, nobody had nothing on her, she had the courage of her convictions." Parks's publicly acknowledged good behavior helped to justify her rebellion and win support for her cause. As one friend recalled, she "was too sweet to even say 'damn' in anger."

After Parks's death in the fall of 2005, the airways were filled with tributes celebrating the life of the "humble seamstress," the "simple woman" who sparked a revolution because her feet were tired. Reviewing these eulogies, syndicated columnist Ellen Goodman asked, "Is it possible we prefer our heroes to be humble? Or is it just our heroines?" She wondered if it wasn't time Americans got over the notion that women are "accidental heroines," unassuming creatures thrust into the public eye by circumstances beyond their control. Goodman noted that Parks and her compatriots spent years preparing for just such an opportunity.

Rosa Parks's mug shot, taken shortly after her arrest on December 1, 1955, for refusing to obey a bus driver's order to give up her seat to a white passenger.

She concluded: "Rosa Parks was 'unassuming'—except that she rejected all the assumptions about her place in the world. Rosa Parks was a 'simple woman'—except for a mind made up and fed up. She was 'quiet'—except, of course, for one thing. Her willingness to say 'no' changed the world."

The California student said that in contrast to Parks a "well-behaved woman" is "a quiet, subservient, polite, indoors, cooking, cleaning type of girl who would never risk shame by voicing her own opinion." There is a delicious irony in this part of her definition. Notice that it associates a particular kind of work—cooking and cleaning—with subservience and passivity. Yet the boycott that made Parks famous was sustained by hundreds of African American domestic servants—cooks and maids—who walked to work rather than ride segregated buses. They too did the unexpected.*

Serious history talks back to slogans. But in the contest for public attention, slogans usually win. Consider my simple sentence. It sat quietly for years in the folds of a scholarly journal. Now it honks its ambiguous wisdom from coffee mugs and tailgates.

. . .

In my scholarly work, my form of misbehavior has been to care about things that other people find predictable or boring. My second book is a case in point. At a distance, the life of Martha Moore Ballard was the stuff from which funeral sermons were made. She was a "good wife" in every sense of the word, indistinguishable from all the self-sacrificing and pious women celebrated in Puritan eulogies. In conventional terms,

---

*Awele Makeba's powerful one-woman show, "Rage Is Not a 1-Day Thing," dramatizes the lives of sixteen little-known participants, male and female, black and white. For details see her website, http://www.awele.com/programs.htm. For a list of resources prepared for the fiftieth anniversary of the boycott in 2005, see http://www.teachingforchange.org/busboycott/busboycott.htm. Additional documents can be found in Stewart Burns, ed., *Daybreak of Freedom: The Montgomery Bus Boycott* (Chapel Hill and London: University of North Carolina Press, 1997). Herbert Kohl, *She Would Not Be Moved: How We Tell the Story of Rosa Parks and the Montgomery Bus Boycott* (New York and London: The New Press, 2005), urges teachers to move from the theme "Rosa Was Tired" to the more historically accurate concept "Rosa Was Ready."

academic literacies   rhetorical situations   genres   fields   processes   strategies   research MLA / APA   media / design   readings   handbook

she did not make history. She cherished social order, respected authority, and abhorred violence. As a midwife and healer, she relied on home-grown medicines little different from those found in English herbals a century before her birth. Her religious sentiments were conventional; her reading was limited to the Bible, edifying pamphlets, and newspapers. Although she lived through the American Revolution, she had little interest in politics. She was a caregiver and a sustainer rather than a mover and shaker.

Ballard made history by performing a methodical and seemingly ordinary act—writing a few words in her diary every day. Through the diary we know her as a pious herbalist whose curiosity about the human body led her to observe and record autopsies as well as nurse the sick, whose integrity allowed her to testify in a sensational rape trial against a local judge who was her husband's employer, and whose sense of duty took her out of bed at night not only to deliver babies but to care for the bodies of a wife and children murdered by their own husband and father. The power of the diary is not only in its sensational stories, however, but in its patient, daily recording of seemingly inconsequential events, struggles with fatigue and discouragement, conflicts with her son, and little things—like the smell of a room where a dead body lay. In Ballard's case, the drama really was in the humdrum. The steadiness of the diary provided the frame for everything else that happened.

. . .

Although I have received mail addressed to Martha Ballard and have been identified on at least one college campus as a midwife, I am only a little bit like my eighteenth-century subject. Like her, I was raised to be an industrious housewife and a self-sacrificing and charitable neighbor, but sometime in my thirties I discovered that writing about women's work was a lot more fun than doing it. I remember thinking one winter day how ironic it was that I was wrapped in a bathrobe with the heat of a wood stove rising toward my loft as I wrote about a courageous woman who braved snowstorms and crossed a frozen river on a cake of ice to care for mothers in labor. I felt selfish, pampered, and decadent. But I did not stop what I was doing. I did not know why I needed to write Martha's story, and I could not imagine that anybody else would ever want to follow me through my meandering glosses on her diary. I was astonished at the reception of the book. Even more important than the prizes was the discovery of how important this long-dead midwife's story was to nurses, midwives, and anonymous caregivers dealing with quite different circumstances today. These readers helped me to see that history is more than an engaging enterprise. It is a primary way of creating meaning. The meaning I found in Martha Ballard's life had something to do with my own life experience, but perhaps a lot more to do with the collective experiences of a generation of Americans coping with dramatic changes in their own lives.

When I wrote that "well-behaved women seldom make history," 20 I was making a commitment to help recover the lives of otherwise obscure women. I had no idea that thirty years later, my own words would come back to me transformed. While I like some of the uses of the slogan more than others, I wouldn't call it back even if I could. I applaud the fact that so many people—students, teachers, quilters, nurses, newspaper columnists, old ladies in nursing homes, and mayors of western towns—think they have the right to make history.

Some history-making is intentional; much of it is accidental. People make history when they scale a mountain, ignite a bomb, or refuse to move to the back of the bus. But they also make history by keeping diaries, writing letters, or embroidering initials on linen sheets. History is a conversation and sometimes a shouting match between present and past, though often the voices we most want to hear are barely audible. People make history by passing on gossip, saving old records, and by naming rivers, mountains, and children. Some people leave only their bones, though bones too make history when someone notices.

Historian Gerda Lerner has written: "All human beings are practicing historians. . . . We live our lives; we tell our stories. It is as natural as breathing." But if no one cares about these stories, they do not survive. People do not only make history by living their lives, but by creating records and by turning other people's lives into books or slogans.

Engaging with the Text

1. What is the **PURPOSE** of Laurel Thatcher Ulrich's textual analysis of her slogan? What point is she trying to make with the analysis? How does her point relate to her purpose?

   55–56

2. How does Ulrich **BEGIN** her essay? How does the opening relate to how the essay **ENDS**? How effective is her beginning in drawing the reader to her analysis of the slogan "Well-behaved women seldom make history"?

   373–80
   380–85

3. Ulrich discusses the ambiguity of her slogan, noting that some read it as referring to the lack of women in histories or the lack of histories about women, whereas others read it as meaning that only by "misbehaving" do women make history. How does she relate this ambiguity to the broader issue of how history in general is written? Identify two examples she provides to illustrate the complexities of writing history.

4. What kind of **SUPPORT** does Ulrich offer as evidence of the points she makes? Select three pieces of evidence in the essay and discuss how effective each is in supporting the point it is intended to support.

   114

5. *For Writing.* Do a web search for "well-behaved women seldom [or rarely] make history" to identify three objects on which the slogan appears, and write an essay **ANALYZING** how its meaning might be understood by those who purchase them. Describe the objects and those—whether businesses, organizations, or individuals—who are promoting them. What meaning do you think the promoters assume potential buyers will perceive? How closely does that meaning relate to the point Ulrich originally made with this phrase? What does your analysis reveal about the role of slogans in history?

   98–130

DIANA GEORGE

Changing the Face of Poverty
Nonprofits and the Problem of Representation

Diana George (b. 1948) is professor emerita of English at Virginia Poly-technic Institute and State University. She has written widely on culture, writing, and visual representation. She is the editor of Kitchen Cooks, Plate Twirlers, and Troubadours *(1999), a collection of essays by writing program administrators, and a coauthor of* Reading Culture *(with John Trimbur, 2006) and* Picturing Texts *(with Lester Faigley, Anna Palchik, and Cynthia Selfe, 2004). The following analysis comes from* Popular Literacy: Studies in Cultural Practices and Poetics *(2001). The endnotes are presented according to* The Chicago Manual of Style, *as they appeared in the original publication.*

> Constructively changing the ways the poor are represented in every aspect of life is one progressive intervention that can challenge everyone to look at the face of poverty and not turn away.
> —BELL HOOKS, *OUTLAW CULTURE*

As I WRITE THIS, Thanksgiving is near. I am about to go out and fill a box with nonperishables for the annual St. Vincent de Paul food drive. Christmas lights already outline some porches. Each day my mailbox is stuffed with catalogs and bills and with appeals from the Native American Scholarship Fund, the Salvation Army, WOJB—Voice of the Anishinabe, the Navaho Health Foundation, the Barbara Kettle Gundlach Shelter Home for Abused Women, Little Brothers Friends of the Elderly, Habitat for Humanity, and more. One *New Yorker* ad for Children, Inc. reads, "You don't have to leave your own country to find third-world poverty." Underneath the ad copy, from a black-and-white photo, a young girl in torn and ill-fitting clothes looks directly at the viewer. The copy continues, "In Appalachia, sad faces of children, like Mandy's, will haunt you. There

> **ENCLOSED:** No Address Labels to Use Up.
> No Calendars to Look At.
> No Petitions to Sign.
>
> And No Pictures of Starving Children.

Text from the outer envelope of a 1998 Oxfam appeal.

are so many children like her—children who are deprived of the basic necessities right here in America."*

The Oxfam promise that I quote above—to use no pictures of starving children—is surely an attempt to avoid the emotional overload of such images as the one Children, Inc., offers. Still, those pictures—those representations of poverty—have typically been one way nonprofits have kept the poor before us. In a culture saturated by the image, how else do we convince Americans that—despite the prosperity they see all around them—there is real need out there? The solution for most nonprofits has been to show the despair. To do that they must represent poverty as something that can be seen and easily recognized: fallen down shacks and trashed out public housing, broken windows, dilapidated porches, barefoot kids with stringy hair, emaciated old women and men staring out at the camera with empty eyes. In such images, poverty is dirt and rags and helplessness. In mail, in magazines, and in newspapers, ads echoing these appeals must vie for our time, attention, and dollars with Eddie Bauer, Nordstrom's, The Gap, and others like them whose polished and attractive images fill our days.

In the pages that follow . . . I examine a particular representation of poverty—publicity videos produced by Habitat for Humanity—in order to suggest that reliance on stereotypes of poverty can, in fact, work against the aims of the organization producing them. . . .

---

*The copy here has been revised, with the author's permission, to reflect the more recent Children, Inc., ad. [Editor's note]

You don't have to leave your own country to find third-world poverty.

In Appalachia, sad faces of children, like Mandy's, will haunt you. There are so many children like her—children who are deprived of the basic necessities right here in America.

You can sponsor a boy or girl in need through Children, Inc. Just $24 a month will help provide clothing, shoes, school supplies and food as well as a feeling that someone cares. We'll send you the picture and story of the child you will be helping. Please write, call or visit our website to enroll. Your help will mean so much.

An ad for Children, Inc.

Habitat for Humanity: A Case in Point

I have chosen Habitat for Humanity publicity videos for my focus because Habitat is a popular and far-reaching nonprofit with affiliates not only in the United States but throughout the world. Its goal is not a modest one: Habitat for Humanity aims to eliminate poverty housing from the globe. More than that, Habitat puts housing into the hands of the people who will be housed—into the hands of the homeowners and their neighbors. This is not another program aimed at keeping people in what has become known as the poverty or welfare cycle.

To be very clear, then, I am not criticizing the work of Habitat   5 for Humanity. It is an organization that has done an amazing job of addressing what is, as cofounder Millard Fuller tells us again and again, a worldwide problem. What I would draw attention to, however, is how that problem of inadequate housing and its solution are represented,

academic literacies | rhetorical situations | genres | fields | processes | strategies | research MLA / APA | media / design | readings | handbook

Volunteers building a house with Habitat for Humanity.

especially in publicity material produced and distributed by the organization, and how those representations can feed into the troubles that Habitat continues to have as it attempts to change the ways Americans think of helping others. What's more, the kinds of visual arguments Habitat and other nonprofits use to advocate for action or change have become increasingly common tools for getting the message to the public, and yet, I would argue, these messages too often fail to overturn cultural commonplaces that represent poverty as an individual problem that can be addressed on an individual basis. Habitat's catch phrase—A Hand Up, Not a Hand-Out—appeals to a nation that believes anyone can achieve economic security with just the right attitude and set of circumstances.

Habitat's basic program has a kind of elegance. Applicants who are chosen as homeowners put in sweat equity hours to build their home and to help build the homes of others chosen by Habitat. The organization then sells the home to the applicant at cost (that cost held down through Habitat's ability to provide volunteer labor and donated materials) and charges a small monthly mortgage that includes no interest. Unlike public assistance, which is raised or lowered depending on the recipient's circumstances, most Habitat affiliates do not raise mortgage payments when homeowners get better jobs or find themselves in better financial shape. And once the house is paid for, it belongs to the homeowner.

Obviously, in order to run a program like this one, Habitat must produce publicity appeals aimed at convincing potential donors to give time, money, and material. Print ads, public service television and radio spots, commercial appeals linked to products like Maxwell House coffee, and publicity videos meant to be played for churches, volunteer organizations, and even in-flight video appeals on certain airlines are common media for Habitat.

Habitat publicity videos are typically configured as problem-solution arguments. The problem is that too many people have inadequate shelter. The solution is community involvement in a program like Habitat for Humanity. The most common setup for these productions is an opening sequence of images—a visual montage—in which we see black-and-white shots of rural shacks, of men and women clearly in despair, and of thin children in ragged clothing. The voice-over narrative of one such montage tells us the story:

> Poverty condemns millions of people throughout the world to live in deplorable and inhuman conditions. These people are trapped in a cycle of poverty, living in places offering little protection from the rain, wind, and cold. Terrible sanitary conditions make each day a battle with disease and death. And, for this, they often pay over half their income in rent because, for the poor, there are no other choices. Daily, these families are denied a most basic human need: a decent place to live. The reasons for this worldwide tragedy are many. They vary from city to city, country to country, but the result is painfully the same whether the families are in New York or New Delhi.[1]

It is a compelling dilemma.

Organizations like Habitat for Humanity, in order to convey the seriousness of this struggle and, of course, to raise funds and volunteer support for their efforts in addressing it, must produce all sorts of publicity. And in that publicity they must tell us quickly what the problem is and what we can do to help. To do that, Habitat gives us a visual representation of poverty, a representation that mirrors the most common understandings of poverty in America.

Now, there is nothing inherently wrong with that representation   10 unless, of course, what you want to do (as Habitat does) is convince the American people to believe in the radical idea that those who have must care for the needs of others, not just by writing a check, but by enabling an entirely different lifestyle. For Americans, it is truly radical to think that our poorer neighbors might actually be allowed to buy a home at no interest and with the donated time and materials of others. It is a radical notion that such a program means that these neighbors then own that house and aren't obliged to do more than keep up with payments in order to continue owning it. And it is a radical idea that Habitat does this work not only in our neighborhoods (not isolated in low-income housing developments) but throughout the world. Habitat International truly believes that we are all responsible for partnering with our neighbors throughout the world so that everyone might eventually have, at least, a simple decent place to live. Like the philosophy behind many nonprofits, Habitat's is not a mainstream notion.

Still, that representation of poverty—clinging as it does to commonplaces drawn from FSA photographs in this century, from Jacob Riis's nineteenth-century photos of urban poverty, and from documentaries of Third World hunger—has serious limitations, which must be obvious to those who remember the moment that the Bush administration* confidently announced that, after looking everywhere, they had discovered no real hunger in the United States. And that myth that poverty cannot/does not actually exist in the heart of capitalism has once again been reinforced in the 1998 Heritage Foundation report in which Robert Rector echoed the perennial argument that there is little true poverty in this country ("Myth").[2] Heritage Foundation's finding comes despite figures

---

Bush administration: the administration of George H. W. Bush (1989–93). FSA: the Farm Security Administration, a federal agency that hired such prominent photographers as Walker Evans and Dorothea Lange to document rural poverty in the 1930s. *Jacob Riis* (1849–1914): Danish American social reformer. [Editor's note]

from the National Coalition for the Homeless ("Myths and Facts About Homelessness"), which tell us that in 1997 nearly one in five homeless people in twenty-nine cities across the United States was employed in a full- or part-time job.[3]

In her call for a changed representation of poverty in America, bell hooks argues that in this culture poverty "is seen as synonymous with depravity, lack and worthlessness." She continues, "I talked with young black women receiving state aid, who have not worked in years, about the issue of representation. They all agree that they do not want to be identified as poor. In their apartments they have the material possessions that indicate success (a VCR, a color television), even if it means that they do without necessities and plunge into debt to buy these items."[4] Hers is hardly a noble image of poverty, but it is a true one and one that complicates the job of an organization like Habitat that must identify "worthy" applicants. This phenomenon of poverty in the center of wealth, in a country with its national mythology of hearty individuals facing the hardness of the Depression with dignity and pride, is certainly a part of what Manning Marable challenges when he asks readers not to judge poverty in the United States by the standards of other countries. Writing of poverty among black Americans, Marable reminds us that "the process of impoverishment is profoundly national and regional."[5] It does little good to compare the impoverished of this country with Third World poverty or, for that matter, with Depression Era poverty.

The solution in these Habitat videos is just as visible and compelling a representation as is the problem. The solution, it seems, is a modern-day barn raising. In clip after clip, Habitat volunteers are shown lined up to raise walls, to hammer nails, to cut boards, to offer each other the "hand up not a hand out," as these publicity messages tell us again and again. Like the barn-raising scene from Peter Weir's *Witness*, framed walls come together against blue skies. People who would normally live in very different worlds come together to help a neighbor. It is all finished in record time: a week, even a day. Volunteers can come together quickly. Do something. Get out just as quickly.

The real trouble with Habitat's representation, then, is twofold: it tells us that the signs of poverty are visible and easily recognized. And

academic literacies   rhetorical situations   genres   fields   processes   strategies   research MLA / APA   media / design   readings   handbook

it suggests that one of the most serious results of poverty (inadequate shelter) can be addressed quickly with volunteer efforts to bring individuals up and out of the poverty cycle.

Of course, if Habitat works, what could be wrong with the representation? It is an organization so popular that it receives support from diametrically opposed camps. Newt Gingrich and Jesse Jackson have both pounded nails and raised funds for Habitat. This is what Millard Fuller calls the "theology of the hammer." People might not agree on political parties and they might not agree on how to worship or even what to worship, Fuller says, but they can all agree on a hammer. All can come together to build houses. Or, can they?

As successful as Habitat has been, it is an organization that continues to struggle with such issues as who to choose for housing, how to support potential homeowners, and how to convince affiliates in the United States to tithe a portion of their funds to the real effort of Habitat: eliminating poverty housing throughout the world, not just in the United States. And, even in the United States, affiliates often have trouble identifying "deserving" applicants or convincing local residents to allow Habitat homes to be built in their neighborhoods. There are certainly many cultural and political reasons for these problems, but I would suggest that the way poverty continues to be represented in this country and on tapes like those videos limits our understanding of what poverty is and how we might address it.

That limitation holds true for those caught in poverty as well as those wanting to help. What if, as a potential Habitat applicant, you don't recognize yourself or you refuse to recognize yourself in those representations? As Stanley Aronowitz points out in *The Politics of Identity*, that can happen very easily as class identities, in particular, have become much more difficult to pin down since World War II, especially with an expansion of consumer credit that allowed class and social status to be linked to consumption rather than to professions or even wages. In his discussion of how electronic media construct the *social imaginary*, Aronowitz talks of the working class with few media representations available to them as having fallen into a kind of "cultural homelessness."[6] How much more true is that of the impoverished in this country who

15

may be neither homeless nor ragged, but are certainly struggling every day to feed their families, pay rent, and find jobs that pay more than what it costs for daycare?

I have been particularly interested in this last question because of a difficulty I mentioned earlier, that of identifying appropriate applicants for Habitat homes or even getting some of the most needy families of a given affiliate to apply for Habitat homes. When I showed the video *Building New Lives* to Kim Puuri, a Copper Country Habitat for Humanity homeowner and now member of the affiliate's Homeowner Selection Committee, and asked her to respond, she was very clear in what she saw as the problem:

> When I see those pictures I usually think of Africa or a third-world country and NOT the U.S. It's not that they can't be found here, it's just that you don't publicly see people that bad off other than street people. If they could gear the publicity more to the geographical areas, it may make more of an impact or get a better response from people. It would mean making several videos. It may not be so much of a stereotype, but an association between Habitat and the people they help. People viewing the videos and pictures see the conditions of the people and feel that their own condition may not be that bad and feel they probably wouldn't qualify.[7]

What this Habitat homeowner has noticed is very close to what Stuart Hall describes. That is, the problem with this image, this representation, is not that it is not real enough. The problem has nothing to do with whether or not these are images of poverty as it exists in the world. There is no doubt that this level of poverty does exist in this country and elsewhere despite the Heritage Foundation's attempts to demonstrate otherwise. The problem is that this representation of poverty is a narrow one and functions to narrow the ways we might respond to the poor who do not fit this representation.

The representation I have been discussing is one that insists on constructing poverty as an individual problem that can be dealt with by volunteers on an individual basis. That is the sort of representation common in this country, the sort of representation Paul Wellstone objects to in a recent call to action when he says "We can offer no single description of American poverty." What it takes to break through such a representation is first, as Hall suggests, to understand it as a representation, to understand it as a way of imparting meaning. And the only way to contest that representation, to allow for other meanings, other descriptions, is to know more about the many dimensions of poverty in America. "More than 35 million Americans—one out of every seven of our fellow citizens—are officially poor. More than one in five American children are poor. And the poor are getting poorer," Wellstone writes.[8] But we can be certain that much of that poverty is not the sort pictured in those black-and-white images. And if it doesn't *look* like poverty, then how do we address it? How do we identify those "deserving" our help?

Indeed, as Herbert Gans has suggested, the labels we have chosen to place on the poor in this country often reveal more than anything "an ideology of undeservingness," by which we have often elided poverty and immorality or laziness or criminality. "By making scapegoats of the poor for fundamental problems they have not caused nor can change," Gans argues, "Americans can also postpone politically difficult and divisive solutions to the country's economic ills and the need to prepare the economy and polity for the challenges of the twenty-first century."[9] These are tough issues to confront and certainly to argue in a twenty-minute video presentation aimed at raising funds and volunteer support, especially when every piece of publicity must make a complex argument visible.

Notes

1. *Building New Lives* (Americus, Ga.: Habitat for Humanity International). This and other Habitat videos are directed primarily at potential volunteers for the organization or might be used to inform local residents about the work of Habitat.

2. Robert Rector, "The Myth of Widespread American Poverty," *The Heritage Foundation Backgrounder* (18 Sept. 1998), no. 1221. This publication is available on-line at <http://www.heritage.org/library/backgrounder/bg1221es.html>.

3. Cited in Barbara Ehrenreich, "Nickel and Dimed: On (Not) Getting By in America," *Harper's* (January 1999), 44. See also Christina Coburn Herman's *Poverty Amid Plenty: The Unfinished Business of Welfare Reform,* NETWORK, A National Social Justice Lobby (Washington, D.C., 1999), from NETWORK's national Welfare Reform Watch Project, which reports that most studies of welfare use telephone surveys even though a substantial percentage of those needing aid do not have phone service (41 percent in the NETWORK survey had no operative phone) and, therefore, are not represented in most welfare reform reports. This report is available on-line at <http://www.network-lobby.org>.

4. bell hooks, "Seeing and Making Culture: Representing the Poor," *Outlaw Culture: Resisting Representations* (New York: 1994), 169.

5. Manning Marable, *How Capitalism Underdeveloped Black America* (Boston: South End Press, 1983), 54.

6. Stanley Aronowitz, *The Politics of Identity: Class, Culture, Social Movements* (New York: Routledge, 1992), 201.

7. Kim Puuri, personal correspondence with author.

8. Paul Wellstone, "If Poverty Is the Question," *Nation* (14 April 1997), 15.

9. Herbert J. Gans, *The War Against the Poor* (New York: Basic Books, 1995), 6–7.

Engaging with the Text

1. How, according to Diana George, is poverty represented by nonprofit agencies such as Habitat for Humanity? What problems does George identify as a result of such representation?

2. George opens her analysis with a bell hooks quote, followed by descriptions of how frequently she encounters charities near Thanksgiving. How do the quote and the description appeal to different **AUDIENCES**?

57–60 ◼

3. The Children, Inc., ad that George refers to is reprinted here on page 728. What does George mean by the "emotional overload" of this image? Why do you think the Oxfam envelope promises not to include images like this?

4. What main **PURPOSE** is George's textual analysis intended to serve? Where is that purpose made explicit? What other purposes might her essay serve?

55–56

5. *For Writing*. Identify a print, TV, or web ad aimed at influencing your opinion on a political or social issue. **ANALYZE** the visuals (drawings, pictures, photographs) and the accompanying words in the ad to describe how the issue is represented. How effectively does the ad meet its goals? Can you identify any problems with how the issue is represented that might undermine those goals?

98–130

ISABELLE GILL

Representation of Disney Princesses in the Media

Isabelle Gill (b. 1996) was a student in Dr. Angela Rounsaville's composition course at the University of Central Florida when she wrote this essay, which was subsequently published in Young Scholars in Writing in 2017. Gill graduated in 2018 with a degree in biomedical science, and she is currently a student at the University of Virginia School of Medicine. The in-text documentation and works-cited list follow MLA guidelines. As you read, pay attention to how Gill guides the reader to a clear interpretation and judgment.

DESPITE SIGNIFICANT STRIDES society has made toward combating sexism, media representations of women continue to be a problem. Numerous studies have identified gender bias in the ways media represent women (Fink and Kensicki; Niven and Zilber; Shacar; Wood). Media tend to favor representations of women who are "traditionally feminine" as well as not "too able, too powerful, or too confident" (Wood 33) over more complex representations. For example, research by Janet Fink and Linda Jean Kensicki shows that when media aimed at both men and women discuss female athletes, their focus is on sex appeal, fashion, and family rather than athletic accomplishment. Female scientists as well as female members of Congress also fall victim to this trend. Interviews with male scientists often portray them as primarily professionals while interviews with female scientists tend to reference their professionalism while highlighting domesticity and family life (Shacar). Similarly, media descriptions of the female members of Congress focus on domestic issues even though the congresswomen portray themselves as having diverse interests (Niven and Zilber). In sum, biased, gendered representations of women are common in various forms of media.

These misrepresentations can have significant social consequences. They can reinforce antiquated gender roles and diminish the perception of women's impact on society (England et al.; Fink and Kensicki; Graves; Niven and Zilber; Shacar; Wood). Since media have a powerful and pervasive influence on how society views men and women, their gendered representations have the potential to impact what is viewed as normal or appropriate for men and women in society (Wood 31–32).

Disney movies remain some of the most influential sources of gender role images for children, and these films have been heavily analyzed for their gendered content, especially their portrayal of princesses (England et al. 555). Researchers do not agree on the progressiveness of Disney princesses; some suggest the princesses are passive and promote stereotypical gender roles, while others see them as balanced role models embodying both feminine and masculine qualities (Bell et al.; Do Rozario; England et al.; Röhrich; Warner; Watsko; Westland). Many traditional feminist texts have "condemned . . . familiar fairy stories for encoding and therefore encouraging passive female behavior" and "reinforcing . . . restrictive images of girlhood and womanhood" (Westland 237). These critiques suggest that fairy tales imply women must be innocent, beautiful, and passive, and, as a result, many are hesitant to see Disney princess movies as positive for children.

However, other analysis of the first eight Disney princesses (Snow White through Mulan) has discovered that the princess often holds power in her film and that any passivity is more in response to "the ambitions of the femme fatale" (Do Rozario 42). For example, any fear or passivity shown by Snow White is directed toward the Evil Queen, another woman; similarly, the princesses Cinderella, Sleeping Beauty, and Ariel all face female villains. Analysis has also found that the princesses are often the ones making choices that drive the plot and outcome of the movie (Do Rozario 41). These findings suggest that Disney princesses do not conform to the standard male dominance / female submissiveness pattern common in antiquated fairy tales. Dawn Elizabeth England and colleagues code Disney princes' and princesses' actions and traits as traditionally masculine or feminine to find that although the original three princesses (Snow White, Cinderella, and Sleeping Beauty) represent more traditional feminine ideals, the newer princesses display both masculine and feminine characteristics in nearly equal numbers. Why, then, does the perception that Disney princesses only represent sexist ideals for women persist when the newer heroines display both feminine and masculine characteristics?

After studying media portrayals of the Disney princesses by examin- 5
ing film reviews of Disney princess movies from prominent publications,
I contend that entertainment media reinforce traditional gender roles
for the princesses, much as news media do with female athletes, scientists, and politicians. I further contend that false or misleading portrayals
of Disney princesses in film reviews have the potential to negatively
impact the creation of positive role models for young girls. While Disney
is often criticized for producing female heroines who fall short of being
strong feminist role models, my own research on film reviews paired
with existing scholarship on the movies demonstrates that, in fact, film
reviews, rather than the films themselves, might primarily create and
contribute to this perception. By describing the princesses using mostly
traditionally feminine vocabulary and degrading physical descriptions,
film reviews focus mainly on stereotypically female attributes of the
characters, ignoring their more masculine qualities. Additionally, even
when acknowledging the princesses' talents or empowered nature, film
reviews include critiques that serve to trivialize any accomplishments
and suggest that the characters are not fully empowered.

Findings and Discussion

Analysis of the diction and content of film reviews for the Disney princess movies suggests that it is entertainment news media, rather than
Disney, that characterize the heroines primarily in terms of their traditionally feminine traits. Through my analysis of the film reviews, I noticed
three recurring patterns that contribute to these inaccurate and problematic media portrayals of the Disney princesses—traditionally feminine
vocabulary, degrading physical descriptions, and critiques that serve to
trivialize accomplishments and suggest that the characters are not fully
empowered. These trends, as I demonstrate below, emphasize stereotypical female attributes of the characters and ignore their more masculine
strengths while belittling the characters in ways that suggest they are not
fit to be role models for young girls. Overall, I coded 95 instances of feminine vocabulary, 32 instances of masculine vocabulary, and 54 instances
of neutral vocabulary; 22 instances of degrading physical descriptions;

and 23 critiques that imply that the princesses are not fully empowered (see table 1).

Table 1
Results Summary

Discourse Pattern	Coded Instances
Vocabulary	95 female, 32 male, 54 neutral
Physical description	22
Not fully empowered	23

Vocabulary

One way film reviews construct inaccurate representations of the princesses is with the use of gendered vocabulary. Although my analysis of the films identifies the contemporary princesses as exhibiting almost as many masculine qualities as feminine characteristics, the vocabulary used to describe the princesses in reviews focuses on what would be considered stereotypically feminine descriptions—for example, "beautiful," "flirty," "sweet," and "kind." The diction used in the reviews is also often demeaning, such as "little princess," "wee lass," or "little nymph." While some terms traditionally used to describe boys and men are used, such as "independent," "brave," and "bold," these are included much more sparingly and generally only appear in one or two reviews per film. If the reviews accurately represented the princesses in the films, almost half of the vocabulary used to describe the heroines should have been masculine in nature; instead, 95 adjectives used are stereotypically feminine and only 32 are stereotypically masculine.

Additionally, there are 54 coded instances of reviewers choosing to include neutral terms that could be considered weakened versions of masculine language—for example, using "plucky" rather than "brave" when adjectives like "courageous," "gutsy," "heroic," or "valiant" could have been chosen. In another example, "spunky" and "feisty" are used over "courageous," "energetic," or "fearless." And in one final example, "intelligent" is often replaced with more modest phrases, such as reviews of *Mulan* that applaud her for "using quick thinking" and "using her wits" (Ebert, "Mulan"; Gleiberman, "Mulan"). Similarly, rather than clearly describing Belle's intellect and love of reading, reviews mention that she is "a bookworm" or "lived in the world of her favorite library books" (Ebert, "Beauty"; Gleiberman, "Beauty"). Thus, the reviews tend toward weaker language when describing any strength that does not fit into sexist ideals for women. The fact that the reviewers seem to recognize strong traits, typically used to describe men, in the princesses but still portray them in a weaker light suggests that reviewers are reluctant to acknowledge these characteristics, that they purposefully choose to emphasize the feminine traits, or that they are unable to recognize strong traits in women.

Analysis of word count reinforces this tendency toward negative characterizations—out of the thirty-eight film reviews analyzed, only nine devote more words to positive descriptions of the characters than negative ones. The reviews include an average of 4.12% of words based on positive descriptions but an average of 11.72% of words for negative descriptions. Overall, the reviews include much lengthier negative descriptions of the princesses or descriptions that are indicative of the three problematic trends mentioned earlier. Thus, the diction in the film reviews contributes to the misrepresentation of the princesses and exemplifies the tendency for reviewers to depict the characters in a more stereotypically feminine and/or negative manner.

Physical Descriptions

The inclusion of demeaning physical descriptions of the princesses 10 also serves to weaken their characters and perpetuate sexist ideals for women. About 20% of the reviews studied focus solely on the heroines' appearances rather than their personalities and do so in a way that is more demeaning than complimentary—for example, "sexy little honey-bunch," "Bambi with curves," "a babe," and "real housewife" (see table 2).

These descriptions are often lengthy and constitute most of the depictions of the heroine. For example, Gleiberman's racist and sexist review describes Pocahontas as "a strapping, high-cheekboned update

Table 2
Examples of Physical Descriptions of the Princesses[a]

Princess	Physical Descriptions
Ariel	"She's a **sexy little honey-bunch** with a double-scallop-shell bra and a mane of red hair tossed in tumble-out-of-bed Southern California salon style. She has no gills, but, when she smiles, she shows an acre of Farrah Fawcett teeth." (Wilmington)
Belle	"Provincial beauty Belle (**Bambi with curves**)" (Howe)
Pocahontas	"Pocahontas is a **babe**. She's the first Disney animated heroine since Tinker Bell with **great legs**—maybe with any legs. She wears form-fitting, off-the-shoulder buckskin that would be as much at home in Beverly Hills as in 17th-century Jamestown. She's got sloe eyes, a rosebud mouth, billowing black hair and terrific muscle tone." (Maslin, "History") "**A strapping, high-cheekboned** update of the usual Disney princess—she's an **aerobicized Native American superbabe**, with long, muscular brown legs, regal shoulder blades, and silky black hair flowing down to her waist. With her vacuous Asian doll eyes, she looks ready to host *Pocahontas' House of Style*." (Gleiberman, "Pocahontas")
Merida	"A nice girl in a **pretty green dress**." (Schwarzbaum)
Elsa	"Her flashy physical transformation from prim princess to ice queen does make her **resemble a real housewife** of some sort, however." (Lemire)

a. Boldface added for emphasis.

of the usual Disney princess—she's an aerobicized Native American superbabe, with long, muscular brown legs, regal shoulder blades, and silky black hair flowing down to her waist" but includes no attempts to characterize her personality. Not only does he focus exclusively on Pocahontas's physical appearance, but he does so in an extremely sexual way. This focus on appearance is evident in a second review for Pocahontas as well, which describes Pocahontas as "a babe" and "the first Disney animated heroine since Tinker Bell with great legs—maybe with any legs" (Maslin, "History"). The fact that several different reviews describe Pocahontas in this manner demonstrates a consistent attempt to sexualize this Disney princess. In another example, Elsa is described as looking like a "real housewife of some sort," which is degrading in a different sense—once again, the reviewer focuses on her physical appearance, but this time the implication is that she is not intelligent, the commonly held stereotype about the "Real Housewives" (Lemire). Portrayals such as these undermine the princesses as role models or authority figures by implying that their physical appearances are more important than anything else. Moreover, the highly sexualized nature of many of these descriptions is even more degrading as it perpetuates the view of women as little more than sexual objects for men.

The nature of the descriptions is actually more sexist and degrading for the 1990s princesses than for the older princesses, showing a lack of progress. Whereas the reviews of the princesses in *Snow White*, *Cinderella*, and *Sleeping Beauty* never say more than "beautiful," "doll-faced," or "voluptuous," the newer reviews use phrases like "sexy little honey-bunch" (Crowther; Nugent; Flinn; Wilmington). This trend is not represented in the reviews of *Mulan* or *The Princess and the Frog*, most likely because Mulan spends the film dressed as a man and Tiana, the princess in *The Princess and the Frog*, spends the film in the form of a frog. The lack of any physical descriptions of Mulan's male alter ego or Tiana's transformed state suggests reviewers do not find physical descriptions to be relevant to understanding the film, showing the prior descriptions to be not simply degrading but unnecessary as well.

Not Fully Empowered

Despite these consistent tendencies to portray strong heroines as weaker, more traditionally feminine characters, the reviews also regularly include criticisms suggesting the princesses are not empowered enough to qualify as role models—this pattern is recorded 23 times throughout analysis of the 38 reviews (see table 3).

Table 3
Examples of Critiques That Princesses Are Not Fully Empowered[a]

Princess	"Not Fully Empowered" Critiques
Jasmine	"Uses words like **'fabulous' and 'amazing' to express unre-markable thoughts.**" (Maslin, "Disney")
Pocahontas	"Only by aging the brave and precocious Pocahontas from 12 or 13 into the flirty, full grown vixen she becomes here, and **by making her so concerned with finding Mr. Right, does the film send any regrettable message.**" (Maslin, "History")
Mulan	"The message here is standard feminist empowerment: defy the matchmaker, dress as a boy, and choose your own career. **But 'Mulan' has it both ways, since inevitably Mulan's heart goes pitty-pat over Shang.**" (Ebert, "Mulan") "'Sign me up for the next war!' exclaims the heroine's grandmother, in a show of **what does not precisely qualify as progress for women.**" (Maslin, "Warrior") "For all of Mulan's courage and independence in rebelling against the matchmakers, this is **still enough of a fairy tale to need Mr. Right.**" (Maslin, "Warrior")
Tiana	"What she does have, like most Disney heroines, is a prince charming, Naveen." (Dargis, "Who") "**The prince, disappointingly if not surprisingly, becomes not only Tiana's salvation** but also that of the movie." (Dargis, "Who")
Merida	"Merida doesn't dream that her prince will come; she doesn't have to because . . . the alternative is comically unthinkable. It's no great surprise that she wins the struggle to determine her fate. **But hers is a contingent freedom won with smiles, acquiescence, and a literal needle and thread with which she neatly sews up the story, repairing a world where girls and women know exactly where they stand.**" (Dargis, "That Old Bayou Magic")
Anna & Elsa	"Flustered and fearful, Elsa dashes away in a fit of self-imposed exile—**which significantly weakens *Frozen*, since she's the film's most complicated and compelling figure.**" (Lemire)

a. Boldface added for emphasis.

These critiques usually misrepresent the film or suggest that a princess's promotion of feminist values is irrelevant if she falls in love. This not only suggests that the princesses shouldn't be role models but also seems to imply a woman is less of a feminist if she falls in love. For example, one review says, "For all of Mulan's courage and independence in rebelling against the matchmakers, this is still enough of a fairy tale to need Mr. Right" (Maslin, "Warrior"). This comment suggests that the fact that Mulan meets her "Mr. Right" somehow detracts from the "courage and independence" the reviewer previously acknowledges. Another review includes the passage, "Flustered and fearful, Elsa dashes away in a fit of self-imposed exile—which significantly weakens *Frozen*, since she's the film's most complicated and compelling figure" (Lemire). This description suggests that Elsa is less compelling since she experiences fear, a feminine trait under the coding system of England and colleagues—which in turn suggests that Elsa's display of fear weakens her character and the film by implying women cannot be afraid and still embody feminist values.

Compared to the other patterns of attempting to portray the characters in a more traditionally feminine light, this trend may seem contradictory. The other patterns seem to perpetuate stereotypical values for women, whereas critiques saying the princesses are not empowered enough would lead readers to assume that the reviewers do not wish these stereotypical values to be perpetuated. Nonetheless, it is an example of another way to prevent the creation of positive role models for girls by implying that none of the existing princesses are truly empowered.

Conclusions and Implications

Although Disney is often criticized for the stereotypically feminine nature of its princesses, my analysis demonstrates that film reviews contribute to this misperception. Misrepresentation of these heroines is a continuation of the aforementioned pattern wherein media use gender bias when discussing women, as identified in studies on media representations of female athletes, scientists, and politicians (Fink and Kensicki; Niven and Zilber; Shacar; Wood). Just as "journalists commonly

15

academic literacies   rhetorical situations   genres   fields   processes   strategies   research MLA / APA   media / design   readings   handbook

work with gendered frames to simplify ... events when covering women and men in public life" (Niven and Zilber 155), it would seem that these gendered frames apply to film reviews and entertainment media's presentations of Disney princesses as well. The result of these gendered frames is an inaccurate portrayal of women that serves to "perpetuate unrealistic, stereotypical, and limiting perceptions" of women (Wood 31). These perceptions, it seems, can lead to internal biases when examining the films and could even be a contributing factor to the disagreements regarding whether princesses are feminist figures or damsels in distress. It is possible that these gendered media representations of the princesses contribute to researchers' perceptions and could explain why some remain adamant that the princesses are negative influences for girls even when faced with evidence to the contrary.

Whether or not Disney heroines should be idols for young girls will most likely remain open to debate; however, researchers and the public cannot ignore gendered misrepresentations of the princesses in film reviews, and should consider the ways in which these misrepresentations influence internal biases or prejudices against the princesses. It is especially important that media influence is recognized because these distortions of Disney princesses likely have an important impact on young girls. As Julia Wood explains, "Because media pervade our lives, the ways they misrepresent genders may distort how we see ourselves and what we perceive as normal and desirable for men and women" (32). By taking characters that are often depicted as strong women and describing them as weak or only portraying stereotypical feminine qualities, these media distort the public's perception of these women. By subtly influencing society's views of Disney princesses in a way that implies they are stereotypically feminine, these media weaken the perception of the princess's strengths and focus instead on traits such as beauty and domesticity. These patterns could potentially impact the creation of positive role models for young girls by misrepresenting the characters children admire.

As children are likely to look up to Disney characters for years to come, it is critical that media misrepresentations of princesses be further studied. This research could be extended to analyze the portrayal of other female characters in Disney movies as well as media representations of female characters in other kinds of movies. Moreover, future research could examine children's perceptions of the Disney princesses at various age levels in order to determine whether or not adults are more likely to subscribe to these inaccurate portrayals than children. Regardless of what future research may discover, this analysis of media misrepresentations of Disney princesses contributes to the ongoing research on gender in media and identifies remaining disparities in gender equality.

Works Cited and Consulted

Aladdin. Directed by Ron Clements and John Musker, Walt Disney Pictures, 1992.

Beauty and the Beast. Directed by Gary Trousdale and Kirk Wise, Walt Disney Pictures, 1991.

Bell, Elizabeth, et al. *From Mouse to Mermaid: The Politics of Film, Gender, and Culture*. U of Indiana P, 1995.

Brave. Directed by Mark Andrews and Brenda Chapman, Walt Disney Pictures, 2012.

Cinderella. Directed by Clyde Geronimi, Wilfred Jackson, and Hamilton Luske, Walt Disney Productions, 1950.

Crowther, Bosely. "The Screen: Six Newcomers Mark Holiday." Review of *Cinderella*, directed by Clyde Geronimi, Wilfred Jackson, and Hamilton Luske. *The New York Times*, 23 Feb. 1950, timesmachine.nytimes.com/timesmachine/1950/02/23/issue.html.

Dargis, Manohla. "Who Needs a Prince When Fun's Afoot?" Review of *Brave*, directed by Mark Andrews and Brenda Chapman. *The New York Times*, 21 June 2012, www.nytimes.com/2012/06/22/movies/brave-pixars-new-animated-film.html.

\-\-\-. "That Old Bayou Magic: Kiss and Ribbit (and Sing)." Review of *The Princess and the Frog*, directed by Ron Clements and John Musker. *The New York Times*, 24 Nov. 2009, www.nytimes.com/2009/11/25/movies/25frog.html.

Do Rozario, Rebecca-Anne C. "The Princess and the Magic Kingdom: Beyond Nostalgia, the Function of the Disney Princess." *Women's Studies in Communication*, vol. 27, no. 1, 2010, pp. 35–49.

Ebert, Roger. "Beauty and the Beast." Review of *Beauty and the Beast*, directed by Gary Trousdale and Kirk Wise. *RogerEbert.com*, 22 Nov. 1991, www.rogerebert.com/reviews/beauty-and-the-beast-1991.

\-\-\-. "Mulan." Review of *Mulan*, directed by Tony Bancroft and Barry Cook. *RogerEbert.com*, 19 June 1998, www.rogerebert.com/reviews/mulan-1998.

England, Dawn Elizabeth, et al. "Gender Role Portrayal and the Disney Princesses." *Sex Roles: A Journal of Research*, vol. 64, nos. 7–8, 2011, pp. 555–76.

Fink, Janet S., and Linda Jean Kensicki. "An Imperceptible Difference: Visual and Textual Constructions of Femininity in Sports Illustrated and Sports Illustrated for Women." Women, Mass Communication and Society, vol. 5, no. 3, 2002, pp. 317–39.

Flinn, John C., Sr. "Review: 'Snow White and the Seven Dwarfs.'" Review of *Snow White and the Seven Dwarfs*, directed by William Cottrell, David Hand, Wilfred Jackson, Larry Morey, Perce Pearce, and Ben Sharpsteen. *Variety*, 28 Dec. 1937, variety.com/1937/film/reviews/snow-white-and-the-seven-dwarfs-1200411503/.

Frozen. Directed by Chris Buck and Jennifer Lee, Walt Disney Pictures, 2013.

Gleiberman, Owen. "Beauty and the Beast." Review of *Beauty and the Beast*, directed by Gary Trousdale and Kirk Wise. *Entertainment Weekly*, 15 Nov. 1991, ew.com/article/1991/11/15/beauty-and-beast-6/.

---. "Mulan." Review of *Mulan*, directed by Tony Bancroft and Barry Cook. *Entertainment Weekly*, 19 June 1998, ew.com/article /1998/06/19/mulan-3/.

---. "Pocahontas." Review of *Pocahontas*, directed by Mike Gabriel and Eric Goldberg. *Entertainment Weekly*, 16 June 1995, ew.com/article /1995/06/16/pocahontas-4/.

Graves, Sherryl Browne. "Television and Prejudice Reduction: When Does Television as a Vicarious Experience Make a Difference?" *Journal of Social Issues*, vol. 55, 1999, pp. 707–25.

Howe, Desson. "Beauty and the Beast." Review of *Beauty and the Beast*, directed by Gary Trousdale and Kirk Wise. *The Washington Post*, 22 Nov. 1991, www.washingtonpost.com/wp-srv/style/longterm /movies/videos/beautyandthebeastghowe_a0ae85.htm.

Lemire, Christy. "Frozen." Review of *Frozen*, directed by Chris Buck and Jennifer Lee. *RogerEbert.com*, 27 Nov. 2013, www.rogerebert.com /reviews/frozen-2013.

The Little Mermaid. Directed by Ron Clements and John Musker, Walt Disney Pictures, 1989.

Maslin, Janet. "Disney Puts Its Magic Touch on 'Aladdin.'" Review of *Aladdin*, directed by Ron Clements and John Musker. *The New York Times*, 11 Nov. 1992, www.nytimes.com/1992/11/11/movies/review -film-disney-puts-its-magic-touch-on-aladdin.html.

---. "History as Buckskin-Clad Fairy Tale." Review of *Pocahontas*, directed by Mike Gabriel and Eric Goldberg. *The New York Times*, 11 June 1995, www.nytimes.com/1995/06/11/nyregion/film-review -history-as-buckskin-clad-fairy-tale.html.

---. "A Warrior, She Takes On Huns and Stereotypes." Review of *Mulan*, directed by Tony Bancroft and Barry Cook. *The New York Times*, 19 June 1998, www.nytimes.com/1998/06/19/movies/film-review -a-warrior-she-takes-on-huns-and-stereotypes.html.

Mulan. Directed by Tony Bancroft and Barry Cook, Walt Disney Pictures, 1998.

Niven, David, and Jeremy Zilber. "'How Does She Have Time for Kids and Congress?' Views on Gender and Media Coverage from House Offices." *Women and Politics*, vol. 23, nos. 1–2, 2001, pp. 147–65.

Nugent, Frank S. "The Music Hall Presents Walt Disney's Delightful Fantasy, 'Snow White and the Seven Dwarfs.'" Review of *Snow White and the Seven Dwarfs*, directed by William Cottrell, David Hand, Wilfred Jackson, Larry Morey, Perce Pearce, and Ben Sharpsteen. *The New York Times*, 14 Jan. 1939, www.nytimes.com/1938/01/14 /archives/the-screen-in-review-the-music-hall-presents-walt -disneys.html.

Pocahontas. Directed by Mike Gabriel and Eric Goldberg, Walt Disney Pictures, 1995.

The Princess and the Frog. Directed by Ron Clements and John Musker, Walt Disney Pictures, 2009.

Röhrich, Lutz. Introduction. *Fairy Tales and Society: Illusion, Allusion, and Paradigm*, edited by Ruth B. Bottigheimer, U of Pennsylvania P, 1986, pp. 1–10.

Schwarzbaum, Lisa. "Brave." Review of *Brave*, directed by Mark Andrews and Brenda Chapman. *Entertainment Weekly*, 1 Aug. 2012, ew.com/article/2012/08/01/brave-2/.

Shacar, Orly. "Spotlighting Women Scientists in the Press: Tokenism in Science Journalism." *Public Understanding of Science*, vol. 9, 2000, pp. 347–58.

Sleeping Beauty. Directed by Clyde Geronimi, Walt Disney Productions, 1959.

Snow White and the Seven Dwarfs. Directed by William Cottrell, David Hand, Wilfred Jackson, Larry Morey, Perce Pearce, and Ben Sharpsteen, Walt Disney Productions, 1937.

Steedman, Carolyn. "The Tidy House." *Feminist Review*, vol. 6, 1980, pp. 1–24.

Warner, Marina. *From Beast to the Blonde: On Fairy Tales and Their Tellers*. Vintage Books, 1995.

Watsko, Janet. *Understanding Disney: The Manufacture of Fantasy*. Polity Press, 2001.

Westland, Ella. "Cinderella in the Classroom: Children's Responses to Gender Roles in Fairy Tales." *Gender and Education*, vol. 5, no. 3, 1993, pp. 237–49.

Wilmington, Michael. "Movie Review: 'Little Mermaid' Makes Big Splash." Review of *The Little Mermaid*, directed by Ron Clements and John Musker. *The Los Angeles Times*, 15 Nov. 1989, articles .latimes.com/1989-11-15/entertainment/ca-1802_1_big-leap.

Wood, Julia T. "Gendered Media: The Influence of Media on Views of Gender." Course pack for COMM45, U of Delaware, pp. 31–41. Originally published in *Gendered Lives: Communication, Gender, and Culture*, Wadsworth, 1994, pp. 231–44.

Engaging with the Text

387–89 ◆

1. What is the **THESIS** of Isabelle Gill's essay? Where in the text is this thesis stated?

114 ▲

2. Does Gill offer reasonable **SUPPORT** for her conclusions? Identify two reasons or pieces of evidence, and explain how they support her conclusions.

3. Why do you think Gill chose to analyze reviews of Disney movies as well as the movies themselves? Are you persuaded by her argument that Disney movies may have become less sexist over time but that Disney movie reviews have not? Why or why not?

656 ☐

4. Gill uses **TABLES** throughout her essay to help her present information. How effective are these tables? What purpose do they serve? What other visuals or design features might she have used?

98–130 ▲

5. *For Writing.* **ANALYZE** the portrayal of gender or race in four TV shows of the same genre (for example, four comedies or four dramas). Adapt Gill's gender coding scheme or develop a coding system of your own to help you in your analysis, and think about **LAYOUT**. Which design elements will allow you to present your information most clearly?

649–50 ☐

academic literacies · rhetorical situations · genres · fields · processes · strategies · research MLA / APA · media / design · readings · handbook

WILLIAM SAFIRE

A Spirit Reborn

William Safire (1929–2009) became an award-winning author and syndicated columnist after working as a speechwriter for President Richard Nixon and Vice President Spiro Agnew. His awards included a Pulitzer Prize for one of his political columns in 1978 and the Presidential Medal of Freedom in 2006, given by President George W. Bush. His last book, The Right Word in the Right Place at the Right Time *(2004), was a compilation of his weekly* On Language *columns published in the* New York Times Magazine. *For the first anniversary of the terrorist attacks of September 11, 2001, Safire published the following essay in the* Times, *analyzing what the Gettysburg Address meant to Americans after 9/11.*

ABRAHAM LINCOLN'S WORDS AT THE DEDICATION of the Gettysburg cemetery will be the speech repeated at the commemoration of September 11 by the governor of New York and by countless other speakers across the nation.

The lips of many listeners will silently form many of the famous phrases. "Four score and seven years ago"—a sonorous way of recalling the founding of the nation eighty-seven years before he spoke—is a phrase many now recite by rote, as is "the last full measure of devotion."

But the selection of this poetic political sermon as the oratorical centerpiece of our observance need not be only an exercise in historical evocation, nonpolitical correctness, and patriotic solemnity. What makes this particular speech so relevant for repetition on this first anniversary of the worst bloodbath on our territory since Antietam Creek's waters ran red is this: now, as then, a national spirit rose from the ashes of destruction.

Here is how to listen to Lincoln's all-too-familiar speech with new ears.

In those 236 words, you will hear the word *dedicate* five times. The first two times refer to the nation's dedication to two ideals mentioned in the Declaration of Independence, the original ideal of "liberty" and the ideal that became central to the Civil War: "that all men are created equal."

The third, or middle, *dedication* is directed to the specific consecration of the site of the battle of Gettysburg: "to dedicate a portion of that field as a final resting place." The fourth and fifth times Lincoln repeated *dedicate* reaffirmed those dual ideals for which the dead being honored fought: "to the unfinished work" and then "to the great task remaining before us" of securing freedom and equality.

Those five pillars of dedication rested on a fundament of religious metaphor. From a president not known for his piety—indeed, often criticized for his supposed lack of faith—came a speech rooted in the theme of national resurrection. The speech is grounded in conception, birth, death, and rebirth.

Consider the barrage of images of birth in the opening sentence. The nation was "conceived in liberty" and "brought forth"—that is, delivered into life—by "our fathers" with all "created" equal. (In the nineteenth century, both "men" and "fathers" were taken to embrace women and mothers.) The nation was born.

Then, in the middle dedication, to those who sacrificed themselves, come images of death: "final resting place" and "brave men, living and dead."

Finally, the nation's spirit rises from this scene of death: "that this nation, under God, shall have a new birth of freedom." Conception, birth, death, rebirth. The nation, purified in this fiery trial of war, is resurrected. Through the sacrifice of its sons, the sundered nation would be reborn as one. 10

An irreverent aside: all speechwriters stand on the shoulders of orators past. Lincoln's memorable conclusion was taken from a fine oration by the Reverend Theodore Parker at an 1850 Boston antislavery convention. That social reformer defined the transcendental "idea of freedom" to be "a government of all the people, by all the people, for all the people."

Lincoln, thirteen years later, dropped the "alls" and made the phrase his own. (A little judicious borrowing by presidents from previous orators shall not perish from the earth.) In delivering that final note, the Union's defender is said to have thrice stressed the noun "people" rather than the prepositions "of," "by," and "for." What is to be emphasized is not rhetorical rhythm but the reminder that our government's legitimacy springs from America's citizens; the people, not the rulers, are sovereign. Not all nations have yet grasped that.

academic literacies | rhetorical situations | genres | fields | processes | strategies | research MLA / APA | media / design | readings | handbook

Do not listen on September 11 only to Lincoln's famous words and comforting cadences. Think about how Lincoln's message encompasses but goes beyond paying "fitting and proper" respect to the dead and the bereaved. His sermon at Gettysburg reminds "us the living" of our "unfinished work" and "the great task remaining before us"—to resolve that this generation's response to the deaths of thousands of our people leads to "a new birth of freedom."

Engaging with the Text

1. William Safire's main point in his textual analysis is that after 9/11, as after the "bloodbath" of the Battle of Gettysburg, "a national spirit rose from the ashes of destruction." On the basis of your memories and experiences, do you agree with this point? Why or why not?

2. Who is the intended **AUDIENCE** for this analysis? Are they expected to be familiar with the Gettysburg Address? How can you tell? How did the intended audience affect how Safire wrote this essay?

   57–60

3. Of the ending of the Gettysburg Address, Safire observes that it is "the reminder that our government's legitimacy springs from America's citizens; the people, not the rulers, are sovereign." What **EVIDENCE** does Safire offer about the use of the word *dedicate* to support this conclusion?

   401–8

4. Safire ends his analysis by declaring that Lincoln's address "reminds 'us the living' of our 'unfinished work' and 'the great task remaining before us'—to resolve that this generation's response to the deaths of thousands of our people leads to 'a new birth of freedom.'" How do you react to this ending? Has Americans' response to 9/11 led to greater freedom? How, or why not? What "unfinished work," if any, remains?

5. *For Writing.* Famous speeches live on for a reason—for what they say, how they say it, or often both. Choose one that interests you, such as Julia Gillard's "Misogyny Speech," Barack Obama's "A More Perfect Union," Hillary Clinton's "Women's Rights Are Human Rights," or John F. Kennedy's Inaugural Address, and **ANALYZE** it as Safire has the Gettysburg Address. Look at how the speaker used particular language or rhetorical **STRATEGIES** to convey a message memorably.

   98–130

   371

63 Reports

academic literacies · rhetorical situations · genres · fields · processes · strategies · research MLA / APA · media / design · readings · handbook

JASON HASLER

An Ancient Remedy Reexamined

Jason Hasler (b. 1983) wrote the following essay in 2017 for a composition class at Genesee Community College. It was nominated for the Norton Writer's Prize by his instructor, Carol E. Geiselmann. The in-text documentation and reference list follow APA guidelines. As you read, notice how Hasler uses research to back up his ideas.

Abstract

In the years before penicillin, the practice of maggot debridement therapy (MDT) had been used to treat chronic and infectious wounds. With antibiotic-resistant wounds on the rise, the techniques of the past are playing a larger role in healing wounds. Medical doctors and researchers have studied the effectiveness of using maggots contained in a tea bag, using maggots free-roaming in a wound, and using conventional treatments such as hydrogel and bandages. Research shows that using maggots to clean a wound is more effective than conventional practices. The anatomy of the maggot, along with its ingestion of the necrotic tissue and the excretion of antibiotic and anti-inflammatory agents after digestion, have made this larva an effective wound healer. The use of maggots as a primary means of healing wounds has not been largely promoted due to lack of training in and knowledge of MDT and its proper application. With greater educational efforts for the use of maggot therapy, doctors could reduce the time it takes for patients' wounds to heal and reduce painful surgeries and amputations.

Keywords: maggot debridement therapy (MDT), larval therapy, chronic wounds, diabetic leg ulcers, necrotic tissue

The use of maggot debridement therapy (MDT), also known as larval therapy, as a technique for healing wounds dates back to ancient civilizations (Peck et al., 2015). When penicillin started being used on patients in the early 1940s, however, antibiotics replaced this ancient practice. Today, a crop of antibiotic-resistant wounds have created the need to reexamine the efficacy of MDT in the treatment of chronic wounds and wounds incurred on the battlefield. As of right now, MDT has been approved for medicinal purposes in the United States and the United Kingdom, but negative opinions about maggot medicine have stymied substantial gains in the medical field. These opinions would have to be remedied through education and training in order for MDT to be fully implemented in current medical practice.

The Maggot's Method

The method through which maggots heal wounds is truly astonishing. The maggots most commonly used for MDT are the *Lucilia sericata* larvae, which are also known as the blow fly or the common green bottle fly (Barnes et al., 2010, p. 234). Turkmen et al. (2008), doctors of plastic surgery in the United Kingdom and Turkey, stated that maggots "have beneficial effects on certain wounds, and their ability to satisfactorily debride necrotic tissue has been known by surgeons for many centuries" (p. 184). The effective way maggots eat necrotic tissue, secrete antibiotic and anti-inflammatory enzymes, and massage living tissue with their exteriors provides an exceptional healing method that surpasses conventional treatment. Arabloo et al. (2015) found that "[l]arva destroys the dead tissues and activates the live and healthy tissues, cleans the wound from bacteria, [but] does not damage the live and healthy tissues" (p. 2).

Barnes et al. (2010) tested the effectiveness of maggot excretion/ secretion against the three common types of bacteria normally found in a wound environment: *Staphylococcus aureus*, *E. coli*, and *P. aeruginosa* (p. 234). Barnes et al. (2010) concluded that *L. sericata* excretion/ secretions combatted *E. coli* below the level of detection (LOD) in 2 hours, *Staphylococcus aureus* below LOD in 4 hours, and *P. aeruginosa* below LOD in 24 hours (p. 235). The results of this clinical study support the fact that maggots are a natural, effective treatment against bacteria.   5

MDT versus Conventional Treatment

For the past century, doctors have been using antibiotics and hydrogel dressings and bandages to heal typical wounds. However, many chronic wounds and diabetic leg ulcers have been extremely difficult and time consuming to heal. The open wounds may become so infected that, despite the amount of medicine used, the limb will need to be amputated. MDT has been placed in clinical and medical facilities in order to combat these necrotic infections. Turkmen et al. (2008) conducted medical trials using larval therapy and traditional dressing; of the 34 patients, 29 (85%) found that all necrotic tissue was satisfactorily removed (p. 185). Turkmen et al. (2008) even described a particular case that showed the side-by-side effects of larval therapy and traditional methods:

> Two patients had multiple suppurative wounds on both legs. Larval therapy was applied to one leg; the other was treated with traditional dressing. Two weeks after application of larvae, the patients saw the difference between treatment methods and requested larval therapy to both legs. (p. 187)

The direct observation of both legs' healing progress provided significant positive feedback for MDT techniques. The ability for the doctors to recognize the fast healing process of MDT from one leg against the other proves that maggots are extremely effective in the fight against infectious wounds.

Other studies have shown positive results from using MDT to heal chronic wounds. Klaus and Steinwedel (2015) conducted a study that included 41 patients who used MDT; based on the 37 surveys returned, they found that 89% of the participants "indicated they would try MDT again and 94% would recommend it to others" (p. 409). These patients' treatments averaged 11 days before wounds were clear from infection. In another study that compared 61 ulcers treated with MDT to 84 ulcers treated conventionally, 80% of those treated with MDT were completely debrided, versus 48% of those treated conventionally (Sherman, 2002, as cited in Klaus & Steinwedel, 2015, p. 409). In addition, in a 3-week time period, wounds treated with maggot therapy had twice the granulation tissue and one-third the necrotic tissue of wounds treated with conventional methods (Sherman, 2002, as cited in Klaus & Steinwedel, 2015, p. 409).

Research from the Iran University of Medical Sciences has also found positive results of MDT versus traditional hydrogel dressings. Arabloo et al. (2016) found that "the mean debridement time for free larva was 14 days and 28 days for packed larva and 72 days for hydrogel" (p. 6). Arabloo et al. (2016) found that on average, wounds treated with MDT healed 2.42 days faster than wounds treated with hydrogel (p. 6). Clearly, these studies have demonstrated the effectiveness of maggots versus conventional methods.

Drawbacks of MT

Although it may seem that maggot therapy is the perfect solution to chronic and infected wounds, "MDT largely remains a therapy of last resort" (Peck et al., 2015, p. 595). One of the disadvantages of using maggots for wound care is the possibility of pain from the maggots moving around the wound. Arabloo et al. (2016) noted that patients treated with larvae experienced twice as much pain as patients treated with hydrogel (p. 6). Furthermore, Klaus and Steinwedel (2015) found that "40% of patients" have experienced pain with MDT, though these patients go on to say that using "tea-bag application versus placing the maggots directly in the wound" would reduce pain (p. 410).

The concept of using maggot therapy on the battlefield has triggered many other studies; however, certain factors need to be resolved. Military personnel who tested the survivability of maggots in a wartime environment found a low survival rate for *L. sericata* in military air transportation (Peck et al., 2015). Since maggot livelihood depends on certain temperature ranges and oxygen levels, Peck et al. (2015) suggested that maggots could have faced challenges while eating because of the vibrations in the planes and helicopters (p. 595).

The cost associated with maggot therapy has been another setback for widespread implementation of MDT. Conflicting figures have shown that maggot therapy tends to be more expensive than traditional methods. Arabloo et al. (2016) indicated that "[l]arval therapy costs are more

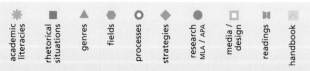

academic literacies · rhetorical situations · genres · fields · processes · strategies · research MLA / APA · media / design · readings · handbook

than hydrogel annually, 96.70 pounds for each participant on average" (p. 6). Klaus and Steinwedel (2015) also found that "MDT costs approximately $140 more per year than conventional debridement therapy with hydrocolloid dressings" (p. 409). However, the effectiveness of maggot therapy would likely offset the additional cost, rendering the practice cost-effective in the long run.

Nevertheless, the factor most responsible for defeating maggot therapy is lack of information and knowledge. Klaus and Steinwedel (2015) noted that society's perception of MDT remains a hurdle (p. 410). Turkmen et al. (2008) described the impact of society's perception of larval therapy on full implementation:

> Despite the fact that larval therapy accelerates wound healing, is cost-effective, and reduces nursing time, the nature of the larval therapy (as perceived by the patient and medical staff) engenders a continued reluctance to adopt this as a mainstream treatment in appropriate wounds. Educating medical staff about larval therapy may ensure that it is established in the management of certain difficult wounds. (p. 187)

The lack of training for the application and handling of maggots would need to be addressed and reconciled in order for MDT to become a primary choice for wound therapy and not just a last resort option. Klaus and Steinwedel (2015) discovered that of the 181 physicians surveyed, 80% have heard about MDT, 10% have practiced MDT, 25% knew someone who practiced MDT, and 60% knew that MDT was approved by the FDA (p. 409). This survey is an excellent portrayal of the lack of knowledge of MDT that exists among physicians.

In order to reverse the common misconceptions of MDT, further training and education will need to be administered. Up until the invention of antibiotics (penicillin), MDT was the tried and true process for healing wounds. However, the increasing number of antibiotic-resistant infections will render some of these modern antibiotic applications useless. A return to the therapies of the past will once again be necessary. Given that the effectiveness of MDT has been proven in tests, studies, and lab trials, it is only a matter of time before MDT enters the mainstream.

References

Arabloo, J., Grey, S., Mobinizadeh, M., Olyaeemanesh, A., Hamouazadeh, P., & Khamisabadi, K. (2016). Safety, effectiveness, and economic aspects of maggot debridement therapy for wound healing. *Medical Journal of the Islamic Republic of Iran, 30*(1), 1–7.

Barnes, K., Dixon, R., & Gennard, D. (2010). The antibacterial potency of the medicinal maggot, *Lucilia sericata* (Meigen): Variation in laboratory evaluation. *Journal of Microbiological Methods, 82,* 234–237. https://doi.org/10.1016/j.mimet.2010.06.005

Klaus, K., & Steinwedel, C. (2015). Maggot debridement therapy: Advancing to the past in wound care. *Medsurg Nursing, 24,* 407–411.

Peck, G., Helgeson, S., Powell, E., Roth, A., Flores, M., & Kirkup, B. (2015). Airworthiness testing of medical maggots. *Military Medicine, 180,* 591–596. https://doi.org/10.7205/MILMED-D-14-00548

Turkmen, A., Graham, K., & McGrouther, D. (2008). Therapeutic applications of the larvae for wound debridement. *Journal of Plastic, Reconstructive & Aesthetic Surgery, 63*(1), 184–188. https://doi.org/10.1016/j.bj.ps.2008.08.070

Engaging with the Text

55–56 ■

1. What is the **PURPOSE** of Jason Hasler's essay? What point is he trying to convey?

146 ▲

2. One of the key features of a report is a **TIGHTLY FOCUSED TOPIC**. Do you think Hasler's topic is tightly focused? Why or why not?

academic literacies • rhetorical situations • genres • fields • processes • strategies • research MLA / APA • media / design • readings • handbook

3. Reports usually avoid giving an opinion on their subject, but Hasler's opinion on the medicinal uses of maggots seems very clear. How would you describe Hasler's **STANCE** toward his subject? Identify one passage in the text in which his stance is clear.

66–68

4. What **EVIDENCE** does Hasler provide to support his claims in this report? Is the evidence convincing? Why or why not?

401–8

5. *For Writing.* Research an old-fashioned or obscure remedy for a medical problem (for example, potato for a spider bite, lemon juice for an earache, or olives for motion sickness). Find out to what degree this remedy has been shown to be effective, and then write a **REPORT** on this remedy to convince your readers of its effectiveness or lack thereof.

131–56

ELEANOR J. BADER

Homeless on Campus

Eleanor J. Bader (b. 1954) is a freelance writer and an instructor in the English Department at Kingsborough Community College in Brooklyn, New York. She is also the coauthor of Targets of Hatred: Anti-Abortion Terrorism *(2001). The following report appeared in the* Progressive, *a liberal political magazine, in 2004. As you read, notice how Bader effectively incorporates specific examples to support the information she reports.*

AESHA IS A TWENTY-YEAR-OLD at Kingsborough Community College in Brooklyn, New York. Until the fall of 2003, she lived with five people — her one-year-old son, her son's father, her sister, her mother, and her mother's boyfriend — in a three-bedroom South Bronx apartment. Things at home were fine until her child's father became physically abusive. Shortly thereafter, Aesha realized that she and her son had to leave the unit.

After spending thirty days in a temporary shelter, they landed at the city's emergency assistance unit (EAU). "It was horrible," Aesha says. "We slept on benches, and it was very crowded. I was so scared I sat on my bag and held onto the stroller day and night, from Friday to Monday." Aesha and her son spent several nights in the EAU before being sent to a hotel. Sadly, this proved to be a temporary respite. After a few days, they were returned to the EAU, where they remained until they were finally moved to a family shelter in Queens.

Although Aesha believes that she will be able to stay in this facility until she completes her associate's degree, the ordeal of being homeless has taken a toll on her and her studies. "I spend almost eight hours a day on the trains," she says. "I have to leave the shelter at 5:00 A.M. for the Bronx where my girlfriend watches my son for me. I get to her house around 7:00. Then I have to travel to school in Brooklyn — the last stop on the train followed by a bus ride — another two hours away."

Reluctantly, Aesha felt that she had no choice but to confide in teachers and explain her periodic absences. "They've all said that as long as I keep up with the work I'll be OK," she says. But that is not easy for Aesha or other homeless students.

Adriana Broadway lived in ten places, with ten different families, during high school. A native of Sparks, Nevada, Broadway told the LeTendre Education Fund for Homeless Children, a scholarship program administered by the National Association for the Education of Homeless Children and Youth, that she left home when she was thirteen. "For five years, I stayed here and there with friends," she wrote on her funding application. "I'd stay with whoever would take me in and allow me to live under their roof."

Johnny Montgomery also became homeless in his early teens. He told LeTendre staffers that his mother threw him out because he did not get along with her boyfriend. "She chose him over me," he wrote. "Hard days and nights have shaped me." Much of that time was spent on the streets.

Asad Dahir has also spent time on the streets. "I've been homeless more than one time and in more than one country," Dahir wrote on his scholarship application. Originally from Somalia, he and his family fled their homeland due to civil war and ended up in a refugee camp in neighboring Kenya. After more than a year in the camp, he and his thirteen-year-old brother were resettled, first in Atlanta and later in Ohio. There, high housing costs once again rendered the pair homeless.

Broadway, Montgomery, and Dahir are three of the forty-four homeless students from across the country who have been awarded LeTendre grants since 1999. Thanks, in part, to these funds, all three have been attending college and doing well.

But few homeless students are so lucky. "Each year at our national conference, homeless students come forward to share their stories," says Jenn Hecker, the organizing director of the National Student Campaign Against Hunger and Homelessness. "What often comes through is shame. Most feel as though they should be able to cover their costs." Such students usually try to blend in and are reluctant to disclose either their poverty or homelessness to others on campus, she says. Hecker blames rising housing costs for the problem and cites a 2003 survey that found the median wage needed to pay for a two-bedroom apartment in the United States to be $15.21, nearly three times the federal minimum.

Even when doubled up, students in the most expensive states— 10 Massachusetts, California, New Jersey, New York, and Maryland—are scrambling. "In any given semester, there are four or five families where the head of household is in college," says Beth Kelly, a family service counselor at the Clinton Family Inn, a New York City transitional housing program run by Homes for the Homeless.

Advocates for the homeless report countless examples of students sleeping in their cars and sneaking into a school gym to shower and change clothes. They speak of students who couch surf or camp in the woods—bicycling or walking to classes—during temperate weather. Yet, for all the anecdotes, details about homeless college students are hazy.

"I wish statistics existed on the number of homeless college students," says Barbara Duffield, executive director of the National Association for the Education of Homeless Children and Youth. "Once state and federal responsibility to homeless kids stops—at the end of high school—it's as if they cease to exist. They fall off the map."

Worse, they are neither counted nor attended to.

"Nobody has ever thought about this population or collected data on them because nobody thinks they are a priority to study," says Martha Burt, principal research associate at the Urban Institute.

Critics say colleges are not doing enough to meet—or even 15 recognize—the needs of this group.

"The school should do more," says Aesha. "They have a child care center on my campus, but they only accept children two and up. It would have helped if I could've brought my son to day care at school." She also believes that the college should maintain emergency housing for homeless students.

"As an urban community college, our students are commuters," responds Uda Bradford, interim dean of student affairs at Kingsborough Community College. "Therefore, our student support services are developed within that framework."

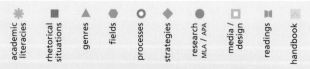

"As far as I know, no college has ever asked for help in reaching homeless students," says Mary Jean LeTendre, a retired Department of Education administrator and creator of the LeTendre Education Fund. "Individual colleges have come forward to help specific people, but there is nothing systematic like there is for students in elementary and high school."

"There is a very low awareness level amongst colleges," Duffield adds. "People have this 'you can pull yourself up by your bootstraps' myth about college. There is a real gap between the myth and the reality for those who are trying to overcome poverty by getting an education."

Part of the problem is that the demographics of college atten-   20 dance have changed. "Most educational institutions were set up to serve fewer, less diverse, more privileged students," says Andrea Leskes, a vice president with the Association of American Colleges and Universities. "As a result, we are not successfully educating all the students who come to college today. This means that nontraditional students — the older, returning ones as well as those from low income or other disenfranchised communities — often receive inadequate support services."

"It's not that colleges are not concerned, but attention today is not on serving the poor," says Susan O'Malley, chair of the faculty senate at the City University of New York. "It's not in fashion. During the 1960s, people from all over the country were going to Washington and making a lot of noise. The War on Poverty was influenced by this noise. Now the poor are less visible."

Mary Gesing, a counselor at Kirkwood Community College in Cedar Rapids, Iowa, agrees. "Nothing formal exists for this population, and the number of homeless students on campus is not tracked," she says. Because of this statistical gap, programs are not devised to accommodate homeless students or address their needs.

Despite these programmatic shortfalls, Gesing encounters two to three homeless students — often single parents — each semester. Some became homeless when they left an abuser. Others lost their housing because they could no longer pay for it due to a lost job, the termination of unemployment benefits, illness, the cessation of child support, or drug or alcohol abuse.

Kirkwood's approach is a "patchwork system," Gesing explains, and homeless students often drop out or fail classes because no one knows of their plight. "When people don't know who to come to for help they just fade away," she says.

"Without housing, access to a workspace, or access to a shower, students' lives suffer, their grades suffer, and they are more likely to drop classes, if not withdraw entirely from school. I've seen it happen," says Amit Rai, an English professor at a large, public university in Florida. "If seen from the perspective of students, administrators would place affordable housing and full access to health care at the top of what a university should provide."

Yet for all this, individual teachers—as well as administrators and counselors—can sometimes make an enormous difference.

B.R., a faculty member who asked that neither her name nor school be disclosed, has allowed several homeless students to sleep in her office during the past decade. "Although there is no institutional interest or involvement in keeping these students enrolled, a few faculty members really care about the whole student and don't shy away from helping," she says.

One of the students she sheltered lived in the space for three months, whenever she couldn't stay with friends. Like Aesha, this student was fleeing a partner who beat her. Another student had been kicked out of the dorm because her stepfather never paid the bill. She applied for financial assistance to cover the cost, but processing took months. "This student stayed in my office for an entire semester," B.R. says.

A sympathetic cleaning woman knew what was going on and turned a blind eye to the arrangement. "Both students showered in the dorms and kept their toothbrushes and cosmetics in one of the two department bathrooms which I gave them keys to," B.R. adds. "The administration never knew a thing. Both of the students finished school and went on to become social workers. They knew that school would be their saving grace, that knowledge was the only thing that couldn't be snatched."

academic literacies | rhetorical situations | genres | fields | processes | strategies | research MLA / APA | media / design | readings | handbook

Engaging with the Text

1. This piece reports on the general topic of homeless college students. What is Eleanor J. Bader's specific point? How do you know? How else could she have made her point explicit?

2. Bader's **PURPOSE** in this report is to make visible college students who are homeless and to report on some of the causes. How does this purpose affect the way the report is written? Point to specific examples from the text in your response.

   ■ 55–56

3. Bader **ENDS** her essay with a powerful quote from a teacher she calls B.R.: "[The students] knew that school would be their saving grace, that knowledge was the only thing that couldn't be snatched." What does B.R. mean by this observation? In what ways can an education help such students, and in what ways might it be misleading to think that an education alone will solve all of their problems?

   ◆ 380–85

4. Consider the number of **NARRATIVES** in this report. Why do you think Bader includes so many? What other kinds of **WELL-RESEARCHED INFORMATION** does she include, if any? What additional kinds of information might she have used to help accomplish her purpose?

   ◆ 462–70
   ▲ 146

5. *For Writing.* You may not be aware of some student services that are readily available on your campus. Choose one service your school provides, and do some research to learn who uses it and whether they're satisfied with it or think it could be improved. Write a **REPORT** on your findings. As an alternative, you may want to deliver your report as a website.

   ▲ 131–56

JONATHAN KOZOL

Fremont High School

An educator, activist, and award-winning writer, Jonathan Kozol (b. 1936) is known for his work as an advocate for social justice and public educa- tion. He is the author of over a dozen books, including Fire in the Ashes: Twenty-Five Years among the Poorest Children in America *(2012) and* The Shame of the Nation: The Restoration of Apartheid Schooling in America *(2005), from which the following selection is taken. In this piece, Kozol reports on one of the many schools he studied to write this book.*

FREMONT HIGH SCHOOL IN LOS ANGELES enrolls almost 5,000 students on a three-track schedule, with about 3,300 in attendance at a given time. The campus "sprawls across a city block, between San Pedro Street and Avalon Boulevard in South Central Los Angeles," the *Los Angeles Times* observes. A "neighborhood fortress, its perimeter protected by an eight-foot steel fence topped by spikes," the windows of the school are "shielded from gunfire by thick screens." According to teachers at the school, the average ninth grade student reads at fourth or fifth grade level. Nearly a third read at third grade level or below. About two thirds of the ninth grade students drop out prior to twelfth grade.

There were 27 homerooms for the first-year students, nine home- rooms for seniors at the time I visited in spring of 2003. Thirty-five to 40 classrooms, nearly a third of all the classrooms in the school, were located in portables. Some classes also took place in converted storage closets—"windowless and nasty," said one of the counselors—or in con- verted shop rooms without blackboards. Class size was high, according to a teacher who had been here for six years and who invited me into her tenth grade social studies class. Nearly 220 classes had enrollments ranging between 33 and over 40 students. The class I visited had 40 stu- dents, almost all of whom were present on the day that I was there.

Unlike the staggered luncheon sessions I observed at Walton High, lunch was served in a single sitting to the students in this school. "It's physically impossible to feed 3,300 kids at once," the teacher said. "The

academic literacies · rhetorical situations · genres · fields · processes · strategies · research MLA / APA · media / design · readings · handbook

The school's slogan at the front entrance projects a positive outlook.

line for kids to get their food is very long and the entire period lasts only 30 minutes. It takes them 15 minutes just to walk there from their classes and get through the line. They get 10 minutes probably to eat their meals. A lot of them don't try. You've been a teacher, so you can imagine what it does to students when they have no food to eat for an entire day. The schoolday here at Fremont is eight hours long."

For teachers, too, the schedule sounded punishing. "I have six classes every day, including my homeroom," she said. "I've had *more* than 40 students in a class some years. My average class this year is 36. I see more than 200 students every day. Classes start at seven-thirty. I don't usually leave until four or four-thirty. . . ."

High school students, when I meet them first, are often more reluc- 5 tant than the younger children are to open up their feelings and express their personal concerns; but hesitation on the part of students did not

The perimeter is protected by an eight-foot steel fence topped by spikes.

prove to be a problem in this class at Fremont High. The students knew I was a writer (they were told this by their teacher) and they took no time in getting down to matters that were on their minds.

"Can we talk about the bathrooms?" asked a student named Mireya.

In almost any classroom there are certain students who, by force of the directness or unusual sophistication of their way of speaking, tend to capture your attention from the start. Mireya later spoke insightfully of academic problems, at the school, but her observations on the physical and personal embarrassments she and her schoolmates had to undergo cut to the heart of questions of essential dignity or the denial of such dignity that kids in squalid schools like this one have to deal with.

Fremont High School, as court papers document, has "15 fewer bathrooms than the law requires." Of the limited number of bathrooms that are working in the school, "only one or two . . . are open and unlocked for girls to use." Long lines of girls are "waiting to use the bathrooms," which

are generally "unclean" and "lack basic supplies," including toilet paper. Some of the classrooms "do not have air-conditioning," so that students "become red-faced and unable to concentrate" during "the extreme heat of summer." The rats observed by children in their elementary schools proliferate at Fremont High as well. "Rats in eleven . . . classrooms," maintenance records of the school report. "Rat droppings" are recorded "in the bins and drawers" of the high school's kitchen. "Hamburger buns" are being "eaten off [the] bread-delivery rack," school records note.

No matter how many times I read these tawdry details in court filings and depositions, I'm always surprised again to learn how often these unsanitary physical conditions are permitted to continue in a public school even after media accounts describe them vividly. But hearing of these conditions in Mireya's words was even more unsettling, in part because this student was so fragile-seeming and because the need even to speak of these indignities in front of me and all the other students seemed like an additional indignity.

"The problem is this," she carefully explained. "You're not allowed to 10 use the bathroom during lunch, which is a 30-minute period. The only time that you're allowed to use it is between your classes." But "this is a huge building," she went on. "It has long corridors. If you have one class at one end of the building and your next class happens to be way down at the other end, you don't have time to use the bathroom and still get to class before it starts. So you go to your class and then you ask permission from your teacher to go to the bathroom and the teacher tells you, 'No. You had your chance between the periods. . . .'

"I feel embarrassed when I have to stand there and explain it to a teacher."

"This is the question," said a wiry-looking boy named Edward, leaning forward in his chair close to the door, a little to the right of where I stood. "Students are not animals, but even animals need to relieve themselves sometimes. We're in this building for eight hours. What do they think we're supposed to do?"

"It humiliates you," said Mireya, who went on to make the interesting statement that "the school provides solutions that don't actually work," and this idea was taken up by other students in describing course requirements within the school. A tall black student, for example, told me that she hoped to be a social worker or a doctor but was programmed into "Sewing Class" this year. She also had to take another course, called "Life Skills," which she told me was a very basic course—"a retarded class," to use her words—that "teaches things like the six continents," which she said she'd learned in elementary school.

When I asked her why she had to take these courses, she replied that she'd been told they were required, which reminded me of the response the sewing teacher I had met at Roosevelt Junior High School gave to the same question. As at Roosevelt, it turned out that this was not exactly so. What was required was that high school students take two courses in an area of study that was called "the Technical Arts," according to the teacher. At schools that served the middle class or upper middle class, this requirement was likely to be met by courses that had academic substance and, perhaps, some relevance to college preparation. At Beverly Hills High School, for example, the technical arts requirement could be fulfilled by taking subjects such as residential architecture, the designing of commercial structures, broadcast journalism, advanced computer graphics, a sophisticated course in furniture design, carving and sculpture, or an honors course in engineering research and design. At Fremont High, in contrast, this requirement was far more likely to be met by courses that were basically vocational.

Mireya, for example, who had plans to go to college, told me that she had to take a sewing class last year and now was told she'd been assigned to take a class in hair-dressing as well. When I asked the teacher why Mireya could not skip these subjects and enroll in classes that would help her to pursue her college aspirations, she replied, "It isn't a question of what students want. It's what the school may have available. If all the other elective classes that a student wants to take are full, she has to take one of these classes if she wants to graduate." 15

A very small girl named Obie who had big blue-tinted glasses tilted up across her hair interrupted then to tell me with a kind of wild gusto that she took hair-dressing *twice!* When I expressed surprise that this was possible, she said there were two levels of hair-dressing offered here at Fremont High. "One is in hair-styling," she said. "The other is in braiding."

Mireya stared hard at this student for a moment and then suddenly began to cry. "I don't *want* to take hair-dressing. I did not need sewing either. I knew how to sew. My mother is a seamstress in a factory. I'm trying to go to college. I don't need to sew to go to college. My mother sews. I hoped for something else."

"What would you rather take?" I asked.

"I wanted to take an AP class," she answered.

Mireya's sudden tears elicited a strong reaction from one of the boys who had been silent up to now. A thin and dark-eyed student, named Fortino, with long hair down to his shoulders who was sitting on the left side of the classroom, he turned directly to Mireya.

"Listen to me," he said. "The owners of the sewing factories need laborers. Correct?"

"I guess they do," Mireya said.

"It's not going to be their own kids. Right?"

"Why not?" another student said.

"So they can grow beyond themselves," Mireya answered quietly. "But we remain the same."

"You're ghetto," said Fortino, "so we send you to the factory." He sat low in his desk chair, leaning on one elbow, his voice and dark eyes loaded with a cynical intelligence. "You're ghetto—so you sew!"

"There are higher positions than these," said a student named Samantha.

"You're ghetto," said Fortino unrelentingly to her. "So sew!"

Mireya was still crying.

Several students spoke then of a problem about frequent substitute teachers, which was documented also in court papers. One strategy for staffing classes in these three- and four-track schools when substitutes could not be found was to assign a teacher who was not "on track"— that is, a teacher who was on vacation—to come back to school and fill in for the missing teacher. "Just yesterday I was subbing [for] a substitute who was subbing for a teacher who never shows up," a teacher told the ACLU lawyers. "That's one scenario. . . ."

Obie told me that she stopped coming to class during the previous semester because, out of her six teachers, three were substitutes. "Come on now! Like—hello? We live in a rich country? Like the richest country in the world? Hello?"

The teacher later told me that three substitutes in one semester, if the student's words were accurate, would be unusual. But "on average, every student has a substitute teacher in at least one class. Out of 180 teacher-slots, typically 25 or so cannot be filled and have to be assigned to substitutes."

Hair-dressing and sewing, it turned out, were not the only classes students at the school were taking that appeared to have no relevance to academic education. A number of the students, for example, said that they were taking what were known as "service classes" in which they would sit in on an academic class but didn't read the texts or do the lessons or participate in class activities but passed out books and did small errands for the teachers. They were given half-credits for these courses. Students received credits, too, for jobs they took outside of school, in fast-food restaurants for instance, I was told. How, I wondered, was a credit earned or grade determined for a job like this outside of school? "Best behavior and great customer service," said a student who was working in a restaurant, as she explained the logic of it all to ACLU lawyers in her deposition.

The teacher gave some other examples of the ways in which the students were shortchanged in academic terms. The year-round calendar, she said, gave these students 20 fewer schooldays than the students who attended school on normal calendars receive. In compensation, they attended classes for an extra hour, up until three-thirty, and students in the higher grades who had failed a course and had to take a make-up class remained here even later, until six, or sometimes up to nine.

"They come out of it just totally glassed-over," said the teacher, and, 35 as one result, most teachers could not realistically give extra homework to make up for fewer days of school attendance and, in fact, because the kids have been in school so long each day, she said, "are likely to give less."

Students who needed to use the library to do a research paper for a class ran into problems here as well, because, as a result of the tight scheduling of classes, they were given no free time to use the library except at lunch, or for 30 minutes after school, unless a teacher chose to bring a class into the library to do a research project during a class period. But this was fre-

quently impossible because the library was often closed when it was being used for other purposes such as administration of examinations, typically for "make-up tests," as I was told. "It's been closed now for a week because they're using it for testing," said Samantha.

"They were using it for testing last week also," said Fortino, who reported that he had a research paper due for which he had to locate 20 sources but had made no progress on it yet because he could not get into the library.

"You have to remember," said the teacher, "that the school's in session all year long, so if repairs need to be made in wiring or something like that in the library, they have to do it while the kids are here. So at those times the library is closed. Then, if there's testing taking place in there, the library is closed. And if an AP teacher needs a place to do an AP prep, the library is closed. And sometimes when the teachers need a place to meet, the library is closed." In all, according to the school librarian, the library is closed more than a quarter of the year.

During a meeting with a group of teachers later in the afternoon, it was explained to me in greater detail how the overcrowding of the building limited course offerings for students. "Even when students *ask* to take a course that interests them and teachers want to teach it," said one member of the faculty—she gave the example of a class in women's studies she said she would like to teach—"the physical shortages of space repeatedly prevent this." Putting students into service classes, on the other hand, did not require extra space. So, instead of the enrichment students might have gained from taking an elective course that had some academic substance, they were obliged to sit through classes in which they were not enrolled and from which they said that they learned virtually nothing.

Mireya had asked her teacher for permission to stay in the room 40
with us during my meeting with the other teachers and remained right to the end. At five P.M., as I was about to leave the school, she stood beside the doorway of the classroom as the teacher, who was giving me a ride, assembled all the work she would be taking home.

"Why is it," she asked, "that students who do not need what we need get so much more? And we who need it so much more get so much less?"

I told her I'd been asking the same question now for nearly 40 years and still had no good answer. She answered, maturely, that she did not think there was an answer.

Engaging with the Text

386–87 ◆

1. The **TITLE** of the book in which this essay appears is *The Shame of the Nation: The Restoration of Apartheid Schooling in America.* How does this piece illuminate and support the book title? Based on your reading of Jonathan Kozol's report, what is the "shame of the nation," and how is "apartheid schooling" taking place in the United States even though schools were legally desegregated over sixty years ago?

55–56 ■
57–60 ■

2. What is the **PURPOSE** of Kozol's report? What do you think Kozol hopes will happen because of it? Given this purpose, who is the most important **AUDIENCE** for this piece?

146 ▲
401–8 ◆

3. How does Kozol demonstrate that his information is **ACCURATE** and **WELL RESEARCHED**? What kinds of **EVIDENCE** does he use to support his points? To what degree do you find his information accurate?

380–85 ◆

4. Reread the final three paragraphs of Kozol's report. How effective is this **ENDING**? Do you think Kozol believes there is no answer to Mireya's question? Why or why not?

506–7 ●
131–56 ▲
424–31 ◆

5. *For Writing.* Research a public high school near where you live—the school you attended or one near your college. Get permission from the school principal to **INTERVIEW** several teachers and students about their experiences with the curriculum, recreation facilities, lunch room, school library, and class sizes. Locate any recent newspaper accounts or school reports to supplement and verify the information you obtain from your interviews. Write a **REPORT** that **COMPARES** what you find out about the high school you researched with what Kozol reports about Fremont High. In what ways are the problems similar and in what ways are they different?

❈ academic literacies   ■ rhetorical situations   ▲ genres   ● fields   ○ processes   ◆ strategies   ● research MLA / APA   □ media / design   ▮ readings   ⌃ handbook

ALINA TUGEND

Multitasking Can Make You Lose . . . Um . . . Focus

Alina Tugend (b. 1959) was a columnist for the Business section of the New York Times *from 2005 to 2015 and is the author of* Better by Mistake: The Unexpected Benefits of Being Wrong *(2011). Her work has also appeared in the* Los Angeles Times, *the* Atlantic, Worth *magazine, and other publications. This report on multitasking was published in the* New York Times *in 2008.*

As **YOU ARE READING THIS ARTICLE,** are you listening to music or the radio? Yelling at your children? If you are looking at it online, are you emailing or instant-messaging at the same time? Checking stocks?

Since the 1990s, we've accepted multitasking without question. Virtually all of us spend part or most of our day either rapidly switching from one task to another or juggling two or more things at the same time.

While multitasking may seem to be saving time, psychologists, neuroscientists and others are finding that it can put us under a great deal of stress and actually make us less efficient.

Although doing many things at the same time—reading an article while listening to music, switching to check email messages and talking on the phone—can be a way of making tasks more fun and energizing, "you have to keep in mind that you sacrifice focus when you do this," said Edward M. Hallowell, a psychiatrist and author of *CrazyBusy: Overstretched, Overbooked, and About to Snap!* (Ballantine, 2006). "Multitasking is shifting focus from one task to another in rapid succession. It gives the illusion that we're simultaneously tasking, but we're really not. It's like playing tennis with three balls."

Of course, it depends what you're doing. For some people, listening 5 to music while working actually makes them more creative because they are using different cognitive functions.

But despite what many of us think, you cannot simultaneously email and talk on the phone. I think we're all familiar with what

Dr. Hallowell calls "e-mail voice," when someone you're talking to on the phone suddenly sounds, well, disengaged.

"You cannot divide your attention like that," he said. "It's a big illusion. You can shift back and forth."

We all know that computers and their spawn, the smartphone and cellphone, have created a very different world from several decades ago, when a desk worker had a typewriter, a phone, and an occasional colleague who dropped into the office.

Think even of the days before the cordless phone. Those old enough can remember when talking on the telephone, which was stationary, meant sitting down, putting your feet up, and chatting—not doing laundry, cooking dinner, sweeping the floor, and answering the door.

That is so far in the past. As we are required, or feel required, to do   10 more and more things in a shorter period of time, researchers are trying to figure out how the brain changes attention from one subject to another.

A pedestrian walking and texting.

Earl Miller, the Picower professor of neuroscience at the Massachusetts Institute of Technology, explained it this way: human brains have a very large prefrontal cortex, which is the part of the brain that contains the "executive control" process. This helps us switch and prioritize tasks.

In humans, he said, the prefrontal cortex is about one-third of the entire cortex, while in dogs and cats, it is 4 or 5 percent and in monkeys about 15 percent.

"With the growth of the prefrontal cortex, animals become more and more flexible in their behavior," Professor Miller said.

We can do a couple of things at the same time if they are routine, but once they demand more cognitive process, the brain has "a severe bottleneck," he said.

Professor Miller conducted studies where electrodes were attached 15 to the head to monitor participants performing different tasks.

He found that "when there's a bunch of visual stimulants out there in front of you, only one or two things tend to activate your neurons, indicating that we're really only focusing on one or two items at a time."

David E. Meyer, a professor of psychology at the University of Michigan, and his colleagues looked at young adults as they performed tasks that involved solving math problems or classifying geometric objects.

Their 2001 study, published in *The Journal of Experimental Psychology*, found that for all types of tasks, the participants lost time when they had to move back and forth from one undertaking to another, and that it took significantly longer to switch between the more complicated tasks.

Although the time it takes for our brains to switch tasks may be only a few seconds or less, it adds up. If we're talking about doing two jobs that can require real concentration, like text-messaging and driving, it can be fatal.

The RAC Foundation, a British nonprofit organization that focuses 20 on driving issues, asked 17 drivers, age 17 to 24, to use a driving simulator to see how texting affects driving.

The reaction time was around 35 percent slower when writing a text message—slower than driving drunk or stoned.

All right, there are definitely times we should not try to multitask. But, we may think, it's nice to say that we should focus on one thing at a time, but the real world doesn't work that way. We are constantly interrupted.

A 2005 study, "No Task Left Behind? Examining the Nature of Fragmented Work," found that people were interrupted and moved from one project to another about every 11 minutes. And each time, it took about 25 minutes to circle back to that same project.

Interestingly, a study published last April, "The Cost of Interrupted Work: More Speed and Stress," found that "people actually worked faster in conditions where they were interrupted, but they produced less," said Gloria Mark, a professor of informatics at the University of California at Irvine and a co-author of both studies. And she also found that people were as likely to self-interrupt as to be interrupted by someone else.

"As observers, we'll watch, and then after every 12 minutes or so, for no apparent reasons, someone working on a document will turn and call someone or email," she said. As I read that, I realized how often I was switching between writing this article and checking my email. 25

Professor Mark said further research needed to be done to know why people work in these patterns, but our increasingly shorter attention spans probably have something to do with it.

Her study found that after only 20 minutes of interrupted performance, people reported significantly higher stress, frustration, workload, effort, and pressure.

"I also argue that it's bad for innovation," she said. "Ten and a half minutes on one project is not enough time to think in-depth about anything."

Dr. Hallowell has termed this effort to multitask "attention deficit trait." Unlike attention deficit disorder, which he has studied for years and has a neurological basis, attention deficit trait "springs entirely from the environment," he wrote in a 2005 *Harvard Business Review* article, "Overloaded Circuits: Why Smart People Underperform."

"As our minds fill with noise—feckless synaptic events signifying nothing—the brain gradually loses its capacity to attend fully and gradually to anything," he wrote. Desperately trying to keep up with a multitude of jobs, we "feel a constant low level of panic and guilt." 30

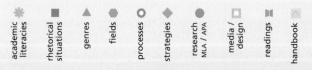

academic literacies · rhetorical situations · genres · fields · processes · strategies · research MLA / APA · media / design · readings · handbook

But Dr. Hallowell says that despite our belief that we cannot control how much we're overloaded, we can.

"We need to recreate boundaries," he said. That means training yourself not to look at your BlackBerry every 20 seconds, or turning off your cellphone. It means trying to change your work culture so such devices are banned at meetings. Sleeping less to do more is a bad strategy, he says. We are efficient only when we sleep enough, eat right, and exercise.

So the next time the phone rings and a good friend is on the line, try this trick: sit on the couch. Focus on the conversation. Don't jump up, no matter how much you feel the need to clean the kitchen. It seems weird, but stick with it. You, too, can learn the art of single-tasking.

Engaging with the Text

1. According to Alina Tugend's research, what are the **EFFECTS** of multitasking? Tugend doesn't say much about the causes of this practice. Why do you think she doesn't? What do you think are the causes?

   392–96

2. How well does Tugend maintain a **TIGHT FOCUS** on her topic in this report? Given the claim she makes in her title, why might a tightly focused topic be especially important for helping readers understand the issue?

   146

3. Tugend **DEFINES** several terms in her report. Locate one or more of these, and discuss what the definitions contribute to the report.

   432–42

4. What is Tugend's **STANCE** toward multitasking? Point out specific phrases that reveal her attitude. How appropriate is her stance, given her subject matter?

   66–68

5. *For Writing.* Undertake your own study of multitasking. Spend time observing students, faculty, and staff in common spaces on your campus—the library, the student union, the dorms, and so on—to see how much multitasking occurs. In addition, discuss with classmates, friends, and relatives their habits regarding multitasking. Write a **REPORT** on what you observe and what folks say about how beneficial or how detrimental multitasking can be.

   131–56

64 Arguments

academic
literacies

rhetorical
situations

genres

fields

processes

strategies

research
MLA / APA

media /
design

readings

handbook

ALEX WEISS

Should Gamers Be Prosecuted for Virtual Stealing?

Alex Weiss (b. 1990) was a student at Arizona State University when he wrote this essay as a blog posting for his Work and Play in Contemporary Fiction/Digital Narrative class. The online magazine Slate *published it in a section titled Future Tense, a partnership among* Slate, *Arizona State, and the New America Foundation. The purpose of this partnership, as noted by Future Tense, is to explore "how emerging technologies will change the way we live."*

T HE MASSIVELY MULTIPLAYER ONLINE VIDEO GAME *RuneScape* was the site of a "virtual theft."

Last week, the Dutch Supreme Court made a curious ruling: it convicted a teenage gamer of stealing something that doesn't exist. The defendant stole two virtual items while playing *RuneScape*, a free massively multiplayer online [MMO] video game. According to the Associated Press, the defendant's attorney argued that the stolen amulet and shield "were neither tangible nor material and, unlike for example electricity, had no economic value." The court, however, disagreed, ruling that the time the thirteen-year-old victim spent in the game trying to earn the objects gave them value.

As a reformed online-gaming thief, this ruling makes no sense to me. It places too much value on the time people spend playing video games. Video games are not work or investments for which people should be compensated; they are escapism.

During my disappointing teenage years, I played an MMO set in space-capitalist hell titled *EVE Online*. EVE is the rat race imploded upon itself, a game that brings out the worst of its subscribers' humanity. In EVE, players can spend months working toward a goal, anything from starting a small in-game business to the production of a massive ship that requires billions of EVE's in-game currency and months of man-hours.

The massively multiplayer online video game RuneScape *was the site of a "virtual theft."*

These projects may seem foolish to those outside of the gaming world, but they represent a great deal to their creators. And these hopes and dreams can be destroyed rapidly by another player who just wants to be a jerk. That's the whole point, actually.

EVE is one of the few MMOs that encourage players to use real money to purchase in-game currency, called *isk*, which in turn is used to build highly desirable objects in the virtual world. It is also the only game that actively allows thievery in the context of the game world. In fact, player satisfaction in *EVE* is based on taking chances and risking everything you've spent time building up. For instance, as *Kotaku* details, in 2010 pirates destroyed a ship that another player had filled with six years' worth of in-game subscription renewals. At the time, the six years' worth of play was valued at more than one thousand dollars in real money through *EVE*'s rather complicated financial system.

A few years ago, I could have been one of those pirates. In EVE, I enjoyed messing with people, making fake investments, engaging in corporation thievery, and even having an extended e-relationship with someone who thought I was a girl. I'd join corporations, running rainmaker scams by convincing the leadership that an antagonistic group was out to destroy everything we had built. Sometimes I even hired decoys to disrupt our supply lines just enough so that the monetary loss got their attention. After receiving the "bribe" money, they'd go away while I reaped the rewards of a now-trustworthy member of the target organization. After I had taken all I needed to take, I either blocked them or kept their enraged messages for posterity.

RuneScape, the game the Dutch minor was playing, is a bit different from both EVE, whose point is to engage in Bernie Madoff–esque shenanigans, and the more well-known *World of Warcraft*. WoW has a very strict policy against scamming, thievery, and even harsh language; violators can be banned, and victims' lost goods are refunded. The developers of *RuneScape*, however, didn't explicitly state that the thief couldn't do what he did, nor did they refund the victim his item. So here, we have a real-world court attempting to punish someone for behavior permitted within the realm. The real and virtual laws conflict, and it seems unfair to penalize the teenager for this. Reportedly, the player also beat up his victim, for which he should, of course, be punished. But attempting to bring real-world law into virtual realms—and putting monetary value on time spent immersed in a virtual world—seems dangerous.

Engaging with the Text

1. The **THESIS** of Alex Weiss's argument is "Video games are not work or investments for which people should be compensated; they are escapism." What **REASONS** and **EVIDENCE** does he offer to support this thesis? Do you agree with him? Why or why not? 387–89
    400–401
   401–8

2. At the end of his essay, Weiss writes that "attempting to bring real-world law into virtual realms—and putting monetary value on time

spent immersed in a virtual world—seems dangerous." Given the ruling in the case at the Dutch Supreme Court, what policies and issues regarding behavior in online games need to be legally ironed out in the next few years? Who should be involved in the debates over how online games are policed?

66–68

3. What is Weiss's **STANCE** toward gaming in this argument? How does he reveal his stance?

386–87

4. Weiss titles his argument "Should Gamers Be Prosecuted for Virtual Stealing?" How does the **TITLE** function in this argument? How would you respond to the question it poses?

5. *For Writing.* In an essay, explore one of the issues that emerging technologies (such as immersive virtual reality, driverless cars, and 3D printing) are giving rise to. Explain the issue and take a stand on it, **ARGUING** for how it should be addressed and who should be included in the debate. Be sure to provide **CONVINCING EVIDENCE** (for which you need to do some research), to adopt **A TRUSTWORTHY TONE**, and to **CONSIDER OTHER POSSIBLE POSITIONS** on the issue.

397–417
171–72

NICHOLAS CARR

Is Google Making Us Stupid?

Nicholas Carr (b. 1959) has written widely on technology, business, and culture. His books include The Shallows: What the Internet Is Doing to Our Brains *(2010),* The Glass Cage: Automation and Us *(2014), and* Utopia Is Creepy and Other Provocations *(2016). In addition to his blog* Rough Type, *in which he makes observations about the latest technologies and related issues, he regularly contributes to several periodicals. The following piece has been widely debated since its appearance as a cover article of the* Atlantic *in 2008. As you read, notice how Carr mixes in genres such as report and reflection to support his argument about the effects of the internet on literacy, cognition, and culture.*

"**D**AVE, STOP. STOP, WILL YOU?** Stop, Dave. Will you stop, Dave?" So the supercomputer HAL pleads with the implacable astronaut Dave Bowman in a famous and weirdly poignant scene toward the end of Stanley Kubrick's 2001: A *Space Odyssey.* Bowman, having nearly been sent to a deep-space death by the malfunctioning machine, is calmly, coldly disconnecting the memory circuits that control its artificial "brain." "Dave, my mind is going," HAL says, forlornly. "I can feel it. I can feel it."

I can feel it, too. Over the past few years I've had an uncomfortable sense that someone, or something, has been tinkering with my brain, remapping the neural circuitry, reprogramming the memory. My mind isn't going—so far as I can tell—but it's changing. I'm not thinking the way I used to think. I can feel it most strongly when I'm reading. Immersing myself in a book or a lengthy article used to be easy. My mind would get caught up in the narrative or the turns of the argument, and I'd spend hours strolling through long stretches of prose. That's rarely the case anymore. Now my concentration often starts to drift after two or three pages. I get fidgety, lose the thread, begin looking for something else to do. I feel as if I'm always dragging my wayward brain back to the text. The deep reading that used to come naturally has become a struggle.

Dave (Keir Dullea) removes HAL's "brain" in 2001: A Space Odyssey.

I think I know what's going on. For more than a decade now, I've been spending a lot of time online, searching and surfing and sometimes adding to the great databases of the internet. The web has been a godsend to me as a writer. Research that once required days in the stacks or periodical rooms of libraries can now be done in minutes. A few *Google* searches, some quick clicks on hyperlinks, and I've got the telltale fact or pithy quote I was after. Even when I'm not working, I'm as likely as not to be foraging in the web's info-thickets reading and writing emails, scanning headlines and blog posts, watching videos and listening to podcasts, or just tripping from link to link to link. (Unlike footnotes, to which they're sometimes likened, hyperlinks don't merely point to related works; they propel you toward them.)

For me, as for others, the internet is becoming a universal medium, the conduit for most of the information that flows through my eyes and ears and into my mind. The advantages of having immediate access to such an incredibly rich store of information are many, and they've been widely described and duly applauded. "The perfect recall of silicon memory," *Wired*'s Clive Thompson has written, "can be an enormous boon to thinking." But that boon comes at a price. As the media theorist Marshall McLuhan pointed out in the 1960s, media are not just passive channels of information. They supply the stuff of thought, but they also shape the process of thought. And what the internet seems to be doing is chipping away my capacity for concentration and contemplation. My mind now expects to take in information the way the internet distributes it: in a swiftly moving stream of particles. Once I was a scuba diver in the sea of words. Now I zip along the surface like a guy on a Jet Ski.

I'm not the only one. When I mention my troubles with reading to   5 friends and acquaintances—literary types, most of them—many say they're having similar experiences. The more they use the web, the more they have to fight to stay focused on long pieces of writing. Some of the bloggers I follow have also begun mentioning the phenomenon. Scott Karp, who writes a blog about online media, recently confessed that he has stopped reading books altogether. "I was a lit major in college, and used to be [a] voracious book reader," he wrote. "What happened?" He speculates on the answer: "What if I do all my reading on the web not so much because the way I read has changed, i.e., I'm just seeking convenience, but because the way I THINK has changed?"

Bruce Friedman, who blogs regularly about the use of computers in medicine, also has described how the internet has altered his mental habits. "I now have almost totally lost the ability to read and absorb a longish article on the web or in print," he wrote earlier this year. A pathologist who has long been on the faculty of the University of Michigan Medical School, Friedman elaborated on his comment in a telephone conversation with me. His thinking, he said, has taken on a "staccato" quality, reflecting the way he quickly scans short passages of text from many sources online. "I can't read *War and Peace* anymore," he admitted. "I've lost the ability to do that. Even a blog post of more than three or four paragraphs is too much to absorb. I skim it."

Anecdotes alone don't prove much. And we still await the long-term neurological and psychological experiments that will provide a definitive picture of how internet use affects cognition. But a recently published study of online research habits, conducted by scholars from University College London, suggests that we may well be in the midst of a sea change in the way we read and think. As part of the five-year research program, the scholars examined computer logs documenting the behavior of visitors to two popular research sites, one operated by the British Library and one by a UK educational consortium, that provide access to journal articles, ebooks, and other sources of written information. They found that people using the sites exhibited "a form of skimming activity," hopping from one source to another and rarely returning to any source they'd already visited. They typically read no more than one or two pages of an article or book before they would "bounce" out to another site. Sometimes they'd save a long article, but there's no evidence that they ever went back and actually read it. The authors of the study report:

> It is clear that users are not reading online in the traditional sense; indeed there are signs that new forms of "reading" are emerging as users "power browse" horizontally through titles, contents pages and abstracts going for quick wins. It almost seems that they go online to avoid reading in the traditional sense.

Thanks to the ubiquity of text on the internet, not to mention the popularity of text-messages on cell phones, we may well be reading more today than we did in the 1970s or 1980s, when television was our medium of choice. But it's a different kind of reading, and behind it lies a different kind of thinking—perhaps even a new sense of the self. "We are not only *what* we read," says Maryanne Wolf, a developmental psychologist at Tufts University and the author of *Proust and the Squid: The Story and Science of the Reading Brain*. "We are *how* we read." Wolf worries that the style of reading promoted by the internet, a style that puts "efficiency" and "immediacy" above all else, may be weakening our capacity for the kind of deep reading that emerged when an earlier technology, the printing press, made long and complex works of prose commonplace. When we read online, she says, we tend to become "mere decoders of information." Our ability to interpret text, to make the rich mental connections that form when we read deeply and without distraction, remains largely disengaged.

Reading, explains Wolf, is not an instinctive skill for human beings. It's not etched into our genes the way speech is. We have to teach our minds how to translate the symbolic characters we see into the language we understand. And the media or other technologies we use in learning and practicing the craft of reading play an important part in shaping the neural circuits inside our brains. Experiments demonstrate that readers of ideograms, such as the Chinese, develop a mental circuitry for reading that is very different from the circuitry found in those of us whose written language employs an alphabet. The variations extend across many regions of the brain, including those that govern such essential cognitive functions as memory and the interpretation of visual and auditory stimuli. We can expect as well that the circuits woven by our use of the internet will be different from those woven by our reading of books and other printed works.

Sometime in 1882, Friedrich Nietzsche* bought a typewriter—a Malling-Hansen Writing Ball, to be precise. His vision was failing, and keeping his eyes focused on a page had become exhausting and painful, often bringing on crushing headaches. He had been forced to curtail his writing, and he feared that he would soon have to give it up. The typewriter rescued him, at least for a time. Once he had mastered touch-typing, he was able to write with his eyes closed, using only the tips of his fingers. Words could once again flow from his mind to the page. 10

But the machine had a subtler effect on his work. One of Nietzsche's friends, a composer, noticed a change in the style of his writing. His already terse prose had become even tighter, more telegraphic. "Perhaps you will through this instrument even take to a new idiom," the friend wrote in a letter, noting that, in his own work, his "'thoughts' in music and language often depend on the quality of pen and paper."

Friedrich Nietzsche (1844–1900): nineteenth-century German philosopher whose work has been influential in several disciplines, including philosophy, literary studies, rhetoric, and linguistics. [Editor's note]

Friedrich Nietzsche and his Malling-Hansen Writing Ball.

"You are right," Nietzsche replied, "our writing equipment takes part in the forming of our thoughts." Under the sway of the machine, writes the German media scholar Friedrich A. Kittler, Nietzsche's prose "changed from arguments to aphorisms, from thoughts to puns, from rhetoric to telegram style."

The human brain is almost infinitely malleable. People used to think that our mental meshwork, the dense connections formed among the 100 billion or so neurons inside our skulls, was largely fixed by the time we reached adulthood. But brain researchers have discovered that that's not the case. James Olds, a professor of neuroscience who directs the Krasnow Institute for Advanced Study at George Mason University, says that even the adult mind "is very plastic." Nerve cells routinely break old connections and form new ones. "The brain," according to Olds, "has the ability to reprogram itself on the fly, altering the way it functions."

As we use what the sociologist Daniel Bell has called our "intellectual technologies"—the tools that extend our mental rather than our physical capacities—we inevitably begin to take on the qualities of those technologies. The mechanical clock, which came into common use in the 14th century, provides a compelling example. In *Technics and Civilization*, the historian and cultural critic Lewis Mumford described how the clock "disassociated time from human events and helped create the belief in an independent world of mathematically measurable sequences." The "abstract framework of divided time" became "the point of reference for both action and thought."

The clock's methodical ticking helped bring into being the scientific 15 mind and the scientific man. But it also took something away. As the late MIT computer scientist Joseph Weizenbaum observed in his 1976 book, *Computer Power and Human Reason: From Judgment to Calculation,* the conception of the world that emerged from the widespread use of timekeeping instruments "remains an impoverished version of the older one, for it rests on a rejection of those direct experiences that formed the basis for, and indeed constituted, the old reality." In deciding when to eat, to work, to sleep, to rise, we stopped listening to our senses and started obeying the clock.

The process of adapting to new intellectual technologies is reflected in the changing metaphors we use to explain ourselves to ourselves. When the mechanical clock arrived, people began thinking of their brains as operating "like clockwork." Today, in the age of software, we have come to think of them as operating "like computers." But the changes, neuroscience tells us, go much deeper than metaphor. Thanks to our brain's plasticity, the adaptation occurs also at a biological level.

The internet promises to have particularly far-reaching effects on cognition. In a paper published in 1936, the British mathematician Alan Turing proved that a digital computer, which at the time existed only as a theoretical machine, could be programmed to perform the function of any other information-processing device. And that's what we're seeing today. The internet, an immeasurably powerful computing system, is subsuming most of our other intellectual technologies. It's becoming our map and our clock, our printing press and our typewriter, our calculator and our telephone, and our radio and TV.

When the internet absorbs a medium, that medium is recreated in the internet's image. It injects the medium's content with hyperlinks, blinking ads, and other digital gewgaws, and it surrounds the content with the content of all the other media it has absorbed. A new email message, for instance, may announce its arrival as we're glancing over the latest headlines at a newspaper's site. The result is to scatter our attention and diffuse our concentration.

The internet's influence doesn't end at the edges of a computer screen, either. As people's minds become attuned to the crazy quilt of internet media, traditional media have to adapt to the audience's new expectations. Television programs add text crawls and pop-up ads, and magazines and newspapers shorten their articles, introduce capsule summaries, and crowd their pages with easy-to-browse info-snippets. When, in March of this year, the *New York Times* decided to devote the second and third pages of every edition to article abstracts, its design director, Tom Bodkin, explained that the "shortcuts" would give harried readers a quick "taste" of the day's news, sparing them the "less efficient" method of actually turning the pages and reading the articles. Old media have little choice but to play by the new-media rules.

Never has a communications system played so many roles in our lives — or exerted such broad influence over our thoughts — as the internet does today. Yet, for all that's been written about the internet, there's been little consideration of how, exactly, it's reprogramming us. The internet's intellectual ethic remains obscure.   20

About the same time that Nietzsche started using his typewriter, an earnest young man named Frederick Winslow Taylor carried a stopwatch into the Midvale Steel plant in Philadelphia and began a historic series of experiments aimed at improving the efficiency of the plant's machinists. With the approval of Midvale's owners, he recruited a group of factory hands, set them to work on various metalworking machines, and recorded and timed their every movement as well as the operations of

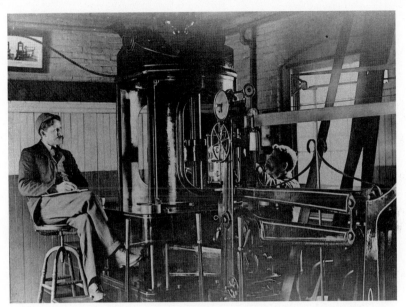

A testing engineer (possibly Taylor) observes a Midvale Steel worker c. 1885.

the machines. By breaking down every job into a sequence of small, discrete steps and then testing different ways of performing each one, Taylor created a set of precise instructions—an "algorithm," we might say today—for how each worker should work. Midvale's employees grumbled about the strict new regime, claiming that it turned them into little more than automatons, but the factory's productivity soared.

More than a hundred years after the invention of the steam engine, the Industrial Revolution had at last found its philosophy and its philosopher. Taylor's tight industrial choreography—his "system," as he liked to call it—was embraced by manufacturers throughout the country and, in time, around the world. Seeking maximum speed, maximum efficiency, and maximum output, factory owners used time-and-motion studies to organize their work and configure the jobs of their workers. The goal, as Taylor defined it in his celebrated 1911 treatise, *The Principles of Scientific Management*, was to identify and adopt, for every job, the "one best method" of work and thereby to effect "the gradual substitution of science for rule of thumb throughout the mechanic arts." Once his system was applied to all acts of manual labor, Taylor assured his followers, it would bring about a restructuring not only of industry but of society, creating a utopia of perfect efficiency. "In the past the man has been first," he declared; "in the future the system must be first."

Taylor's system is still very much with us; it remains the ethic of industrial manufacturing. And now, thanks to the growing power that computer engineers and software coders wield over our intellectual lives, Taylor's ethic is beginning to govern the realm of the mind as well. The internet is a machine designed for the efficient and automated collection, transmission, and manipulation of information, and its legions of programmers are intent on finding the "one best method"—the perfect algorithm—to carry out every mental movement of what we've come to describe as "knowledge work."

Google's headquarters, in Mountain View, California—the Googleplex— is the internet's high church, and the religion practiced inside its walls is Taylorism. Google, says its chief executive, Eric Schmidt, is "a company that's founded around the science of measurement," and it is striving to "systematize everything" it does. Drawing on the terabytes of behavioral data it collects through its search engine and other sites, it carries out thousands of experiments a day, according to the *Harvard Business Review*, and it uses the results to refine the algorithms that increasingly control how people find information and extract meaning from it. What Taylor did for the work of the hand, Google is doing for the work of the mind.

The company has declared that its mission is "to organize the world's information and make it universally accessible and useful." It seeks to develop "the perfect search engine," which it defines as something that "understands exactly what you mean and gives you back

The Googleplex.

exactly what you want." In Google's view, information is a kind of commodity, a utilitarian resource that can be mined and processed with industrial efficiency. The more pieces of information we can "access" and the faster we can extract their gist, the more productive we become as thinkers.

Where does it end? Sergey Brin and Larry Page, the gifted young men who founded Google while pursuing doctoral degrees in computer science at Stanford, speak frequently of their desire to turn their search engine into an artificial intelligence, a HAL-like machine that might be connected directly to our brains. "The ultimate search engine is something as smart as people—or smarter," Page said in a speech a few years back. "For us, working on search is a way to work on artificial intelligence." In a 2004 interview with *Newsweek*, Brin said, "Certainly if you had all the world's information directly attached to your brain, or an artificial brain that was smarter than your brain, you'd be better off." Last year, Page told a convention of scientists that Google is "really trying to build artificial intelligence and to do it on a large scale."

Such an ambition is a natural one, even an admirable one, for a pair of math whizzes with vast quantities of cash at their disposal and a small army of computer scientists in their employ. A fundamentally scientific enterprise, Google is motivated by a desire to use technology, in Eric Schmidt's words, "to solve problems that have never been solved before," and artificial intelligence is the hardest problem out there. Why wouldn't Brin and Page want to be the ones to crack it?

Still, their easy assumption that we'd all "be better off" if our brains were supplemented, or even replaced, by an artificial intelligence is unsettling. It suggests a belief that intelligence is the output of a mechanical process, a series of discrete steps that can be isolated, measured, and optimized. In Google's world, the world we enter when we go online, there's little place for the fuzziness of contemplation. Ambiguity is not an opening for insight but a bug to be fixed. The human brain is just an outdated computer that needs a faster processor and a bigger hard drive.

The idea that our minds should operate as high-speed data-processing machines is not only built into the workings of the internet, it is the network's reigning business model as well. The faster we surf across the web—the more links we click and pages we view—the more opportunities Google and other companies gain to collect information about us and to feed us advertisements. Most of the proprietors of the commercial internet have a financial stake in collecting the crumbs of data we leave behind as we flit from link to link—the more crumbs, the better. The last thing these companies want is to encourage leisurely reading or slow, concentrated thought. It's in their economic interest to drive us to distraction.

Maybe I'm just a worrywart. Just as there's a tendency to glorify techno-   30
logical progress, there's a countertendency to expect the worst of every new tool or machine. In Plato's *Phaedrus*, Socrates bemoaned the development of writing. He feared that, as people came to rely on the written word as a substitute for the knowledge they used to carry inside their

heads, they would, in the words of one of the dialogue's characters, "cease to exercise their memory and become forgetful." And because they would be able to "receive a quantity of information without proper instruction," they would "be thought very knowledgeable when they are for the most part quite ignorant." They would be "filled with the conceit of wisdom instead of real wisdom." Socrates wasn't wrong—the new technology did often have the effects he feared—but he was shortsighted. He couldn't foresee the many ways that writing and reading would serve to spread information, spur fresh ideas, and expand human knowledge (if not wisdom).

The arrival of Gutenberg's printing press,* in the 15th century, set off another round of teeth gnashing. The Italian humanist Hieronimo Squarciafico worried that the easy availability of books would lead to intellectual laziness, making men "less studious" and weakening their minds. Others argued that cheaply printed books and broadsheets would undermine religious authority, demean the work of scholars and scribes, and spread sedition and debauchery. As New York University professor Clay Shirky notes, "Most of the arguments made against the printing press were correct, even prescient." But, again, the doomsayers were unable to imagine the myriad blessings that the printed word would deliver.

So, yes, you should be skeptical of my skepticism. Perhaps those who dismiss critics of the internet as Luddites or nostalgists will be proved correct, and from our hyperactive, data-stoked minds will spring a golden age of intellectual discovery and universal wisdom. Then again, the internet isn't the alphabet, and although it may replace the printing press, it produces something altogether different. The kind of deep reading that a sequence of printed pages promotes is valuable not just for the knowledge we acquire from the author's words but for the intellectual vibrations those words set off within our own minds. In the quiet spaces opened up by the sustained, undistracted reading of a book, or

---

Johannes Gutenberg (1398–1468): a German goldsmith and printer credited with the invention of the printing press and the first mechanically printed Bible. [Editor's note]

by any other act of contemplation, for that matter, we make our own associations, draw our own inferences and analogies, foster our own ideas. Deep reading, as Maryanne Wolf argues, is indistinguishable from deep thinking.

If we lose those quiet spaces, or fill them up with "content," we will sacrifice something important not only in our selves but in our culture. In a recent essay, the playwright Richard Foreman eloquently described what's at stake:

> I come from a tradition of Western culture, in which the ideal (my ideal) was the complex, dense, and "cathedral-like" structure of the highly educated and articulate personality—a man or woman who carried inside themselves a personally constructed and unique version of the entire heritage of the West. [But now] I see within us all (myself included) the replacement of complex inner density with a new kind of self—evolving under the pressure of information overload and the technology of the "instantly available."

As we are drained of our "inner repertory of dense cultural inheritance," Foreman concluded, we risk turning into "'pancake people'—spread wide and thin as we connect with that vast network of information accessed by the mere touch of a button."

I'm haunted by that scene in 2001. What makes it so poignant, and so weird, is the computer's emotional response to the disassembly of its mind: its despair as one circuit after another goes dark, its childlike pleading with the astronaut—"I can feel it. I can feel it. I'm afraid"—and its final reversion to what can only be called a state of innocence. HAL's outpouring of feeling contrasts with the emotionlessness that characterizes the human figures in the film, who go about their business with an almost robotic efficiency. Their thoughts and actions feel scripted, as if they're following the steps of an algorithm. In the world of 2001, people have become so machinelike that the most human character turns out to be a machine. That's the essence of Kubrick's dark prophecy: as we come to rely on computers to mediate our understanding of the world, it is our own intelligence that flattens into artificial intelligence.

academic literacies   rhetorical situations   genres   fields   processes   strategies   research MLA / APA   media / design   readings   handbook

Engaging with the Text

1. According to Nicholas Carr, what has been the effect of the internet on the way we read, think, and live? What **EVIDENCE** does he offer to support his claims? How does his discussion of the changes wrought by other technologies help him make his argument?

2. Sergey Brin has noted, "Some say Google is God. Others say Google is Satan. But if they think Google is too powerful, remember that with search engines, unlike other companies, all it takes is a single click to go to another search engine." How does Carr's essay support or challenge this assertion? Why do you think this topic elicits such strong responses?

3. Where in his argument does Carr **INCORPORATE OTHER VIEWPOINTS**? How successfully does he deal with them?

 411–13

4. Why does Carr **BEGIN** and **END** by referring to HAL from the film *2001: A Space Odyssey*? How do the quotes he chooses from the film help him appeal to his **AUDIENCE**?

 373–85

57–60

5. *For Writing.* What is your view of how technology is affecting the way we think, read, write, and live? Write an **ARGUMENT** in which you support or challenge Carr's conclusion that "as we come to rely on computers to mediate our understanding of the world, it is our own intelligence that flattens into artificial intelligence." Consider mixing in some **REFLECTION** on your own use of computers to help make your argument.

157–84

 256–63

EVA DERZIC

In Defense of Writing Letters

Eva Derzic (b. 1992) was an undergraduate at the University of California, Berkeley, when she wrote this essay. It appeared in the UC Berkeley Comparative Literature Undergraduate Journal on December 3, 2013. As you read, notice how Derzic uses potential objections to letter writing to strengthen her argument that letter writing is valuable.

LETTER WRITING SEEMS TO BE A DYING ART, and I completely understand why. We live in a digital age—people are captivated by technology and speed. We can't be bothered to read the paper, so we get our news from tweets. Faxing takes too long; we prefer to send scans. Paging was cool in the 1990s, and then we decided that it took too long to wait for somebody to call us back and we started using cell phones. Phone calls take too much of our time: we prefer to circumvent the obligatory "Hello, how are you?" or the possibility that we might get forwarded to voicemail and simply text our friends and acquaintances when we need something from them. Instead of taking the time out of our day to chat with friends, we prefer to stalk them on *Facebook* and occasionally become passively involved in their lives by "liking" their status updates if we can find time away from broadcasting our own narcissism into the virtual ether. (Yes, I'm bashing *Facebook*, but I also recognize that it's practical and convenient, and I myself use it a lot.) Sadly, in such an age, letter writing falls to the wayside.

Now, here's why I think people should still write letters:

1. It takes time. It forces you to slow down and smell the proverbial roses. You have to sit down and collect your thoughts. You have to disconnect yourself from the fast-paced digital world for a moment and remember that there is life outside of the internet. If you want to write a good and thoughtful letter, you simply cannot do it in two minutes. You're probably going to be sitting there for at least twenty if you want to produce a piece

of writing that somebody else is going to want to read. And because it takes so much time, it shows that you truly do think and care about the recipient.

2. It's a mental exercise. Sure, you can still write a thoughtful note to somebody via email. There's a crucial difference between writing something on the computer and writing something on a piece of paper, however, and that is the delete button. You can fix an error on the computer very easily: a few key strokes, and voila! Not so when you're writing a letter with pen and paper—it turns into a very unpleasant and messy process involving gloopy, gunky, sticky, yucky correctional fluid. The fact that it's so hard to make changes to handwritten notes means you're more likely to try to get things right the first time—a practice that we don't seem to worry about much nowadays. (Just think of digital photography: once upon a time, taking crappy pictures cost a lot of money—you had to buy film and pay to have your pictures developed. Nowadays, you easily end up with megabytes upon megabytes of useless photos you've forgotten to delete from your hard drive.) Granted, it's great to be able to fix your mistakes on the computer, but it's so easy to do so that many people become complacent and slack off in terms of accuracy.

3. It's aesthetically pleasing. On many levels. There are numerous considerations that go into creating a letter: You have to select a paper, you have to select a pen, you get to show off your penmanship, and you have to choose a stamp. Paper alone is a difficult choice—there are different textures, colors, and watermarks from which to choose. You can even opt to have your paper scented. Pens pose another serious dilemma—do you prefer the elegance of a fountain pen, or are you going to go with the simpler and more practical ballpoint pen? What color ink will you choose? And then there's penmanship. The way you form your characters (cursive or print? are you writing quickly or are you taking time to make each letter perfect?) reveals a lot about your state of mind. If you're feeling super classy, you can give the envelope a wax seal and gild it. Finally, you have to choose a stamp. So there are many variables that show off various aspects of your personality and the degree of involvement that went into

creating the final document. With an email, you're limited to choosing a font, deciding how to format your paragraph breaks, and choosing whether or not you're going to insert images.

4. There's no immediate gratification. It takes time for the letter to reach the recipient, and it takes additional time for the recipient to draft a response. Depending on where you're sending the letter, this can be a few days or a few weeks. You don't get an immediate confirmation of receipt, or an immediate gleeful outburst of "THANK YOU! YOU'RE AN AWESOME PERSON FOR DOING THIS!" You simply have to hope that your efforts will be gratified with a response. This teaches you two things: patience and the suspension of expectation. Emails and text messages make us forget that people have lives outside of our own, and *Facebook* seems to have convinced us all that real-time status updates necessitate replies. Just think of how many times you've been angry at a person for not immediately replying to your text message, or how many times you've neurotically refreshed your inbox when you were expecting an urgent email. Mail is only delivered once daily, and checking your mailbox neurotically is futile and inherently idiotic (something you realize perhaps only when you catch yourself doing it).

Yes, writing a paper letter is an involved and time-consuming process. Yes, it's a bit old fashioned and definitely not a practical way of communicating urgent information. There are undeniably a thousand and one additional arguments you can make against the act. Nonetheless, I think letter writing still has a place in contemporary society.

Next time you're feeling bored, maybe log off *Facebook* for a moment and try walking into a paper store. They are actual places that do exist, and they are not merely havens for hipsters, snobs, and relics from another century. See what you end up walking out of there with. Or try walking into a post office. You'll quickly realize that the post office has many uses besides distributing bills and junk mail. I can guarantee you there's really no better feeling than opening your mailbox and finding a letter from a friend.

Engaging with the Text

1. What is Eva Derzic's **THESIS** in this essay? Where does she state it?

    387–89

2. Describe Derzic's **STANCE** toward her subject. How does her stance affect the way she comes across to her **AUDIENCE**? Is her tone appropriate for the audience she is trying to reach?

    66–68
    57–60

3. Derzic offers several **REASONS** for why people should write letters, and many of those reasons appeal to our senses: the opportunity to "smell the proverbial roses"; the need to write deliberately and with purpose in order to avoid "gloopy, gunky, sticky, yucky correctional fluid"; and the chance to select your pen and paper, to show off your penmanship, and to dress up your envelope. Why do you think Derzic chooses this approach?

    400–401

4. Where in her argument does Derzic **INCORPORATE OTHER VIEWPOINTS**? How successfully does she deal with them?

    411–13

5. *For Writing.* Derzic calls letter writing a "dying art." Can you think of other practices or technologies that aren't used as often as they once were but that might still serve a valuable purpose? Identify one such practice or technology and write an argument in which you support or challenge its use.

SARAH DZUBAY

An Outbreak of the Irrational

Sarah Dzubay (b. 1997) is an undergraduate at the University of Notre Dame. She is majoring in biological sciences and plans to go to medical school, which is what inspired her to write this essay in a first-year composition course. This essay appeared in 2017 in Fresh Writing, a Notre Dame journal devoted to first-year writing. As you read, notice how Dzubay uses evidence to support her argument.

IN THE SPRING OF 2015, a number of families who had visited Disneyland in the hopes of enjoying "the happiest place on Earth" returned home only to discover that their children had contracted measles. Measles, as well as diseases like polio and pertussis, are believed to be plagues of the past, which have not been encountered in over fifty years. So why have they reemerged in some of the most developed, wealthy, and educated countries in the world? These diseases were effectively eradicated through the discovery of vaccines. Before the measles vaccine was created in the 1960s, this disease had killed hundreds of millions of people throughout history. Measles wiped out any population who had not developed some form of resistance to it, especially native populations who came in contact with the foreign illness due to the arrival of European settlers and their domesticated animals. After the vaccine was produced and the majority of developed countries were inoculated with it, rates of infection for the measles were reduced to almost nothing. Now, after generations have lived life with no contact with anyone who has had measles, people are starting to lose their grasp on the severity of the disease. People who no longer fear the disease and are more concerned with the effects of the vaccine itself are opting out of vaccinating their children with the Measles, Mumps, and Rubella (MMR) vaccine (Lin and McGreevy). It is because of these choices that measles outbreaks are becoming more and more common around the United States, and in other countries as well.

The fear of vaccines is not unwarranted—the idea of injecting your child with some foreign substance, whose purpose, side effects, and origins you may not be educated about, is a frightening concept; but, as with many aspects of medicine, the costs must be weighed against the benefits. The fact of the matter is that without vaccines, our globe would be ravaged by disease and we would not be able to be as productive and successful as we are today. Vaccines have helped us overcome diseases that have haunted civilizations since the dawn of humanity; they protect us from the pathogens that fill our environments—deadly killers that we are able to forget about because of modern medical achievements. Vaccines are some of the most important medical discoveries in history because they have allowed us to break through those barriers that, in the past, prevented humans from being more productive due to the abundance of life-threatening illnesses. With our life expectancies vastly lengthened and our daily lives less affected by sickness, it has become easy for first-world citizens to forget the true importance of getting vaccinated. The movement to opt out of vaccination is irrational and dangerous. Individuals advocating for their right to exercise their personal freedom are looking in the wrong places for justification and ignoring the threat they present to society as a whole.

One of the most important concepts behind the effectiveness of inoculation is that of herd immunity. Herd immunity refers to the idea that by vaccinating a majority, the small population who cannot get vaccinated will still be protected from the disease. Epidemiologists, who study the spread of disease, try to determine something called a *basic reproduction number* (R_0) for a disease, which is the number of people that one infected individual can likely spread their disease to (Sadava). This number then helps to determine the percentage of people who must be vaccinated for the protection to be strong enough to protect those who cannot be vaccinated for medical reasons, like infants, elderly people, or those with compromised immune systems. This is called the *immunity threshold* (Willingham and Helft). At this level, the general population is safe because those who have had their vaccinations are not only directly protecting themselves, but also indirectly aiding those who have not been vaccinated, because it is much more difficult for the disease to spread. However, when the levels of vaccination drop below this threshold level, diseases can come back with a vengeance, just as the measles have begun to. Families choosing to opt out of the MMR and other vaccines are a threat to the protection that we have built against disease as a national and international community. Electing to refuse the vaccines that the majority of the population are provided with, based solely on unfounded personal interest, is selfish, because these individuals become free riders in a vaccinated community whose herd immunity they are counting on to protect them. Vaccine refusal is also dangerous, as it puts herd immunity at risk by lowering the number of vaccinated individuals below the immunity threshold.

One may ask who these people are and why they are choosing to threaten the safety of the greater population. Perhaps surprisingly, the people in developed countries who are refusing to get vaccinated are not the underprivileged or uneducated, but rather the opposite. Generally, wealthy, privileged people are more inclined to question what their doctors recommend, do their own investigation online, and be more confident in their own beliefs and findings. When faced with the decision of whether to vaccinate their kids or not, these middle- and upper-class families are searching high and low for reasons to say no. Being curious and asking questions about the effectiveness or safety of a vaccine is not an issue; it is, in fact, prudent and advisable. However, many times the sources these people are consulting are not reputable and have little scientific validity. One of the biggest concerns today about vaccinations is that they cause autism. Many celebrities and politicians, such as Jenny McCarthy and Donald Trump, have spoken out against vaccines because they believe they are to be blamed for the rise of autism in the modern world. The root of this issue is a paper published in 1998 by Andrew Wakefield that claimed a correlation between vaccines and autism in young children. This paper was read widely and still, to this day, scares people out of vaccinating their children, despite the fact that this paper has been completely invalidated by follow-up research and Mr. Wakefield has been tried for misconduct ("Case").

academic literacies   rhetorical situations   genres   fields   processes   strategies   research MLA / APA   media / design   readings   handbook

Another, more complex issue presented by anti-vaccine advocates 5 is that vaccines cause children to have seizures, along with other dangerous reactions that result in long-term disabilities. One family, featured in a NOVA television episode about the vaccine controversy, were horrified when their infant son began to have terrible seizures hours after he received his first round of vaccines (*Vaccines*). Initially, they, like a number of other families who have had similar experiences, blamed the vaccines for their child's health problems. However, as they began to delve deeper into the issue and consulted more medical professionals and researchers, they discovered that their son's devastating epilepsy had not been caused by a vaccine, but rather triggered by it. While watching their child have seizures was a terrible experience for this family, they came to understand that this underlying genetic problem would have resulted in their son's having seizures no matter what. Herein lies the difficulty with the argument that vaccines cause children to have life-long health problems because of a negative reaction—many times this reaction is the result of a previously unobserved health problem that the child already possessed at birth ("Infant Immunizations"). Because babies get their first vaccines so quickly after their birth, it can be exceedingly difficult to differentiate between a vaccine-related issue and a birth defect. It is true that vaccines can sometimes cause unpleasant reactions or even illness, but this does not validate choosing to avoid any vaccines whatsoever. Rather, people should use their account of a negative experience with a vaccine to try and advocate for an improvement in that inoculation, so that the problem is solved and progress can be made for the benefit of all.

Political and ethical values can also play a role in a person's decision to vaccinate or not. Many people fear that because companies are attempting to make a profit off of the vaccines they are producing, these pharmaceutical corporations are pressuring the CDC and other regulatory agencies to approve their vaccines before they are truly effective or safe (Fadda et al.). Anti-vaccine activists argue that vaccines are not really necessary, but are instead the product of doctors having been paid off by medical corporations to force families to use their products.

Besides being scientifically incorrect, this argument falls short because our medical system is essentially an economic marketplace. Vaccines are not a profitable or lucrative investment for companies. At most, one type of vaccine is administered three times to an individual, not two or three times daily like some heart or pain medications. Without subsidization or incentives from the government, companies would not be able to make any money off of vaccines, and there would simply be no economic reason for them to produce these products ("Key Concepts"). The way in which our economic system is set up, it is necessary that companies be able to make money off of medicines, or there would be no drive for companies to innovate and provide these necessities.

Discussion and research are vital parts of any society. They allow for progress and innovation, relationships to be strengthened, and cooperation to flourish. However, the way in which upper-class families are attacking the issue of vaccination is hardly a real discussion at all. By basing their arguments off of outdated and unfounded scientific evidence, as well promoting a high level of paranoia about the conventional medical community, their arguments fail to bring any benefit to society. Instead of helping to improve our nation's discourse on the subject of medicinal standards and patient-physician relations, these people are obstinately refusing to see reason, thereby showing their own selfishness. When people live in a community, it is their duty to think not only of what is best for them and their closest kin, but also of the greater good. By losing sight of this fundamental responsibility to help provide protection for all of those around us, people are threatening the safe environment the scientific and medical communities have worked to build, while simultaneously depending on others to do the work for them. It is time for anti-vaccination advocates to open their minds and not only discuss their fears about vaccination with the medical community, but also listen to the hard evidence. We must all claim our roles as responsible protectors of our nation's health.

Works Cited

"A Case of Junk Science, Conflict, and Hype." *Nature Immunology*, 1 Dec. 2008, https://doi.org/10.1038/ni1208-1317.

Fadda, Marta, et al. "Addressing Issues of Vaccination Literacy and Psychological Empowerment in the Measles-Mumps-Rubella (MMR) Vaccine Decision-Making: A Qualitative Study." *BMC Public Health*, vol. 15, no. 1, 2015, p. 836.

"Infant Immunizations FAQs." Centers for Disease Control and Prevention, 2016, www.cdc.gov/vaccines/parents/parent-questions.html.

"Key Concepts: Economics of Vaccine Production." World Health Organization, www.who.int/immunization/programmes_systems /financing/analyses/en.

Lin, Rong-Gong, II, and Patrick McGreevy. "California's Measles Outbreak Is Over, but Vaccine Fight Continues." *Los Angeles Times*, 17 Apr. 2015, www.latimes.com/local/california/la-me-measles -20150418-story.html.

Sadava, David E. *The Science of Biology*. 10th ed., W. H. Freeman, 2013.

Vaccines—Calling the Shots. Directed by Sonya Pemberton, WGBH, 26 Aug. 2015, www.pbs.org/wgbh/nova/body/vaccines-calling-shots .html.

Willingham, Emily, and Laura Helft. "What Is Herd Immunity?" NOVA, WGBH, 5 Sept. 2014, www.pbs.org/wgbh/nova/body /herd-immunity.html.

Engaging with the Text

1. What is Sarah Dzubay's **POSITION** on vaccines? How well does she argue her position?

   ▲ 170

2. One of the key features of an argument is that it gives careful consideration to other **VIEWPOINTS**. How does Dzubay acknowledge—and refute—other viewpoints?

   ◆ 411–13

401–8 ◆
114 ▲

3. What **EVIDENCE** does Dzubay provide to **SUPPORT** her argument? Point to two pieces of evidence she uses. Do you find this evidence convincing? Why or why not?

4. What are your views on vaccines? Why do you hold these views? How would you respond to someone who holds opposing views? What kinds of evidence would you use to try to convince them?

5. *For Writing.* At the end of her essay, Dzubay observes that "[w]hen people live in a community, it is their duty to think not only of what is best for them and their closest kin, but also of the greater good." Identify an issue that people have very strong and opposing views on in health care, criminal justice, politics, education, the workforce, or some other area. Research the issue, pick a side, and then write an **ARGUMENT** for that side based on the idea that one must think of the greater good.

157–84 ▲

✳ academic literacies
■ rhetorical situations
▲ genres
● fields
○ processes
◆ strategies
● research MLA / APA
□ media / design
▮▮ readings
∧ handbook

Evaluations **65**

DANAH BOYD

Wikipedia *as a Site of Knowledge Production*

danah boyd (b. 1977) is a visiting professor at New York University, a principal researcher at Microsoft Research, and a founder and the president of the Data & Society research institute. An award-winning researcher, boyd is the author of Hanging Out, Messing Around, and Geeking Out: Kids Living and Learning with New Media *(2009),* Participatory Culture in a Networked Era *(2015), and* It's Complicated: The Social Lives of Networked Teens *(2014) from which this evaluation is taken. She blogs both at* DML Central *blog and on her own site,* Apophenia, *which means "seeing patterns or meaning in apparently random or meaningless data."*

WIKIPEDIA HAS A BAD RAP in American K–12 education. The de facto view among many educators is that a free encyclopedia that anyone can edit must be filled with inaccuracies and misleading information. Students' tendency to use the service as their first and last source for information only reinforces their doubts. Ignoring the educational potential of *Wikipedia*, teachers consistently tell students to stay clear of *Wikipedia* at all costs. I heard this sentiment echoed throughout the United States.

In Massachusetts, white fifteen-year-old Kat told me that "*Wikipedia* is a really bad thing to use because they don't always cite their sources. . . . You don't know who's writing it." Brooke, a white fifteen-year-old from Nebraska, explained that "[teachers] tell us not to [use *Wikipedia*] because a lot of—some of the information is inaccurate." These comments are nearly identical to the sentiments I typically hear from parents and teachers. Although it is not clear whether students are reproducing their teachers' beliefs or have come to the same conclusion independently, students are well aware that most teachers consider *Wikipedia* to have limited accuracy.

When people dismiss *Wikipedia*, they almost always cite limited trust and credibility, even though analyses have shown that *Wikipedia*'s content is just as credible as, if not more reliable than, more traditional resources like *Encyclopaedia Britannica*.[1] Teachers continue to prefer famil-

academic literacies · rhetorical situations · genres · fields · processes · strategies · research MLA / APA · media / design · readings · handbook

iar, formally recognized sources. Educators encourage students to go to the library. When they do recommend digital sources, they view some as better than others without explaining why.[2] As Aaron, a white fifteen-year-old from Texas explained, "A lot of teachers don't want you to use [Wikipedia] as a source in a bibliography because it's not technically accredited. And they'd rather you use a university professor's website or something." Although Aaron didn't know what it meant for a source to be accredited, he had a mental model of which sources his teachers viewed as legitimate and which they eschewed. Similarly, Heather, a white sixteen-year-old from Iowa, explained, "Our school says not to use *Wikipedia* as our main source. You can use it as like a second or third source but not as a main source. They say *MSN Encarta*. . . . They say to use that because it's more reliable." When I asked students why they should prefer sites like *Encarta* and professors' webpages, they referenced trust and credibility, even though students couldn't explain what made those particular services trustworthy.

Although nearly every teenager I met told me stories about teachers who had forbidden them from using *Wikipedia* for schoolwork, nearly all of them used the site anyhow. Some used the site solely as a starting point for research, going then to Google to find sources they could cite that their teachers considered more respectable. Others knowingly violated their teachers' rules and worked to hide their reliance on *Wikipedia.* In Boston, I met a teen boy who told me that his teachers never actually checked the sources, so he used *Wikipedia* to get information he needed. When he went to list citations, he said they came from more credible sources like *Encarta,* knowing that his teachers would never check to see whether a particular claim *actually* came from *Encarta.* In other words, he faked his sources because he believed his teachers wouldn't check. Although he had found a way of working around his teachers' rules, he had failed to learn why they wanted citations in the first place. All he had learned was that his teachers' restrictions on using *Wikipedia* were "stupid."

Because many adults assume that youth are digitally savvy—and 5 because they themselves do not understand many online sources—they often end up giving teens misleading or inaccurate information about what they see online. A conflict emerges as teens turn to *Wikipedia* with uncritical eyes while teachers deride the site without providing a critical lens with which to look at the information available.

 Wikipedia can be a phenomenal educational tool, but few educators I met knew how to use it constructively. Unlike other sources of information, including encyclopedias and books by credible authors, the entire history of how users construct a *Wikipedia* entry is visible. By looking at the "history" of a page, a viewer can see when someone made edits, who did the editing, and what that user edited. By looking at the discussion, it's possible to read the debates that surround the edits. *Wikipedia* isn't simply a product of knowledge; it's also a record of the process by which people share and demonstrate knowledge.

 In most educational institutions, publishers and experts vet much of the content that teens encounter and there is no discussion about why something is accurate or not. Some teachers deem certain publications trustworthy and students treat that content as fact. Reading old history books and encyclopedias can be humorous — or depressing, depending on the content and your point of view — because of what the writers assumed to be accurate at one point in time or in one cultural context. Just like today, past students who were given those materials were also taught that all of the information they were receiving was factual.

 Although many students view textbooks as authoritative material, the content is neither neutral nor necessarily accurate. Textbooks often grow outdated more quickly than schools can replace them. The teens I interviewed loved finding inaccuracies in their own textbooks, such as lists of planets that included Pluto. Of course, not all inaccuracies are the product of mistakes or outdated facts. Some writers insert biases into texts because they reinforce certain social or political beliefs. In the United States, Texas is notorious for playing a significant role in shaping the content of textbooks in all states.[3] So when educators in Texas insist on asserting that America's "founding fathers" were all Christian, it creates unease among historians who do not believe this to be accurate. What goes into a textbook is highly political.

 History, in particular, differs depending on perspective. I grew up hearing examples of this in my own family. Born to a British father

and a Canadian mother, my mother moved to New York as a young girl. She recalls her confusion when my grandfather complained about her American history lessons and threatened to destroy her textbook. Compared to the British narratives my patriotic British veteran grandfather had learned, the American origin story was outright offensive. American and British high schools teach events like the American Revolutionary War very differently—and rarely do schools in either country consider such things as the role of women or the perspectives of slaves or Native Americans. This is a topic of deep interest to historians and the driving force behind books like Howard Zinn's *A People's History of the United States*, which tells American history through the perspective of those who "lost." Although many people believe that the winner gets to control the narrative, accounts also diverge when conflicting stories don't need to be resolved. When countries like the United States and the United Kingdom produce their own textbooks, they don't need to arrive at mutually agreeable narratives. However, when people like my mother cross the ocean and must face conflicting perspectives, there's often little room for debating these perspectives. In my mother's childhood household, there was a right history and a wrong history. According to my grandfather, my mother's textbook was telling the wrong history.

Wikipedia often, but not always, forces resolution of conflicting 10 accounts. Critics may deride *Wikipedia* as a crowdsourced, user-generated collection of information of dubious origin and accuracy, but the service also provides a platform for seeing how knowledge evolves and is contested. The *Wikipedia* entry on the American Revolution is a clear product of conflicting ideas of history, with information that stems from British and American textbooks interwoven and combined with information on the role of other actors that have been historically marginalized in standard textbooks.

What makes the American Revolution *Wikipedia* entry interesting is not simply the output in the form of a comprehensive article but the extensive discussion pages and edit history. On the history pages, those who edit *Wikipedia* entries describe why they made a change. On discussion pages, participants debate how to resolve conflicts between editors. There's an entire section on the American Revolution discussion page dedicated to whether colonists should be described as "patriots"—the American term—or "insurgents"—the British term. In the discussion, one user suggests a third term: "revolutionaries." Throughout the *Wikipedia* entry, the editors collectively go to great lengths to talk about "American patriots" or use terms like "revolutionaries" or simply describe the colonists as "Americans." The American Revolution discussion page on *Wikipedia* is itself a lesson about history. Through archived debate, the editors make visible just how contested simple issues are, forcing the reader to think about why writers present information in certain ways. I learned more about the different viewpoints surrounding the American Revolution by reading the *Wikipedia* discussion page than I learned in my AP American history class.

Although most teens that I met who used the internet knew of *Wikipedia* and most of those who had visited the site knew it was editable, virtually none knew about the discussion page or the history of edits. No one taught them to think of *Wikipedia* as an evolving document that reveals how people produce knowledge. Instead they determined whether an article was "good" or "bad" based on whether they thought that their teachers could be trusted when they criticized *Wikipedia*. This is a lost opportunity. *Wikipedia* provides an ideal context for engaging youth to interrogate their sources and understand how information is produced.

Wikipedia is, by both its nature and its commitments, a work in progress. The content changes over time as users introduce new knowledge and raise new issues. The site has its share of inaccuracies, but the community surrounding *Wikipedia* also has a systematic approach to addressing them. At times, people actively and intentionally introduce false information, either as a hoax or for personal gain. *Wikipedia* acknowledges these problems and maintains a record for observers. *Wikipedia* even maintains a list of hoaxes that significantly affected the site.[4]

Many digital technologies undermine or destabilize institutions of authority and expertise, revealing alternative ways of generating and curating content.[5] Crowdsourced content—such as what is provided to *Wikipedia*—is not necessarily better, more accurate, or more compre-

academic literacies · rhetorical situations · genres · fields · processes · strategies · research MLA / APA · media / design · readings · handbook

hensive than expert-vetted content, but it can, and often does, play a valuable role in making information accessible and providing a site for reflection on the production of knowledge. The value of *Wikipedia* would be minimal if it weren't for sources that people could use in creating entries. Many of *Wikipedia's* history articles, for example, rely heavily on content written by historians. What *Wikipedia* does well is combine and present information from many sources in a free, publicly accessible, understandable way while also revealing biases and discussions that went into the production of that content. Even with their limitations and weaknesses, projects like *Wikipedia* are important for educational efforts because they make the production of knowledge more visible. They also highlight a valuable way of using technology to create opportunities for increased digital literacy.

Notes

1. Jim Giles, "Special Report: Internet Encyclopaedias Go Head to Head," *Nature* 438 (2005): 900–901.

2. Although educators often dismiss *Wikipedia* over issues of credibility, they also tend to downplay the educational value of using the service. In "Writing, Citing, and Participatory Media: Wikis as Learning Environments in the High School Classroom" (*International Journal of Learning and Media* 1, no. 4 [2010]: 23–44), Andrea Forte and Amy Bruckman found that engaging with wikis was a learning-rich experience for high school students that contributed to both writing and information assessment skills.

3. Texas's undue influence on the US textbook market is discussed in Gail Collins, "How Texas Inflicts Bad Textbooks on Us," *New York Review of Books*, June 21, 2012. For examples of how Texan Christianity shapes textbooks, see Michael Birnbaum, "Historians Speak Out Against Proposed Texas Textbook Changes," *Washington Post*, March 18, 2010.

4. See http://en.wikipedia.org/wiki/Wikipedia:List_of_hoaxes_on_Wikipedia.241.

5. The potential of social media and other recent technologies for helping address issues in information flow and curation—including

crowd-sourcing, classification, and cooperation—has been the topic of numerous books in recent years. See David Weinberger, *Everything Is Miscellaneous: The Power of the New Digital Disorder* (New York: Holt, 2007); Clay Shirky, *Cognitive Surplus: Creativity and Generosity in a Connected Age* (New York: Penguin, 2010); and Yochai Benkler, *The Penguin and the Leviathan: How Cooperation Triumphs over Self-Interest* (New York: Crown, 2011).

Engaging with the Text

1. Why does danah boyd think *Wikipedia*'s "bad rap in American K–12 education" is undeserved? What crucial advantage does she think the site provides? How much had you thought about this issue before you read this essay? Do you agree with boyd about its importance? Why or why not?

57–60 ■

2. The primary **AUDIENCE** for boyd's evaluation is teachers, though parents and students would also benefit from it. Is her evaluation effective for this audience? Why or why not? How might it change if she were targeting students instead, or parents who don't want their children "confused" by conflicting interpretations of historical events?

373–80 ◆
380–85 ◆

3. This essay does not **BEGIN** with boyd's own assessment of *Wikipedia*. Instead, she starts out with its general reputation and only gradually leads up to her own judgment, stating it most fully in her **ENDING** paragraph. What are the advantages of this strategy? What might be the disadvantages? Was it a good choice for this topic? Why or why not?

206 ▲

4. A strong evaluation requires a **BALANCED AND FAIR** assessment of a subject. Is boyd's assessment of *Wikipedia* balanced and fair? Identify two passages that support your answer, and explain how.

5. *For Writing.* Select an information website other than *Wikipedia* that offers definitions or encyclopedic information. Compare and contrast several entries on that site with their counterparts on *Wikipedia*, and offer an **EVALUATION** of the site based on that comparison.

202–10 ▲

✳ academic literacies   ■ rhetorical situations   ▲ genres   ⬥ fields   ○ processes   ◆ strategies   ● research MLA / APA   ▢ media / design   ▮ readings   ⌃ handbook

ADRIENNE GREEN

The Boldness of Roxane Gay's Hunger

Adrienne Green is the managing editor of the Atlantic, *as well as a frequent writer for the magazine. Prior to joining the* Atlantic *in 2015, she was the editor-in-chief of* FANGLE Magazine, *an Ohio University student magazine. This book review essay appeared in the* Atlantic *on June 13, 2017.*

WHAT IS OFTEN DEEMED THE MOST INTOXICATING PART of weight-loss stories is the moment of triumph. Think, confetti showering the winning contestant on a reality show, a newly svelte celebrity swimming inside their "fat" jeans, or Oprah underscoring in a Weight Watchers ad that she can, in fact, eat bread *every* day. At a time when there is no shortage of recommendations for women on how to discipline or make peace with their bodies, Roxane Gay's book, *Hunger: A Memoir of (My) Body*, stands out precisely because she begins it by declaring that she hasn't overcome her "unruly body and unruly appetites."

Hunger is about weight gained and lost and gained—at her heaviest Gay weighed 577 pounds. It's also about so much more: the body she built to shield herself from the contempt of men and her own sense of shame, her complex relationship with parents who took great interest in solving her weight "problem," and what it has meant for her to be highly visible and yet feel unseen. She describes much of her ongoing struggle with weight and trauma as a result of being gang-raped at the age of 12 in the woods near her home in Nebraska. "People see bodies like mine and make their assumptions. They think they know the why of my body. They do not," she writes. "I ate and ate and ate in the hopes that if I made myself big, my body would be safe." The story of Roxane Gay's body did not begin with this violation of her innocence, but it was the fracture that would come to define her relationship with food, desire, and denial for decades.

Hunger builds on Gay's writing about feminism, women's bodies, and rape culture to unflinchingly tackle personal experiences. Paradox is a recurrent theme: she uses it to illustrate her complicated efforts to face her body, accept it and what it has endured, and still desire to change it. Her unadorned writing style communicates the strain of confronting her weight and her life as they've changed. Lines like "I do not know why I turned to food. Or I do" and "I do not have an answer to that question, or I do," imply that Gay understands all too well a broader culture that refuses to accommodate fat bodies and the restraint required to describe the slights she's experienced within it.

While Gay is grappling with a painful, first-person story, she gracefully weaves in the sharp commentary that she's come to be known for. She notes how coming to terms with her own size afforded her empathy for people with differently abled bodies. She denounces reality shows like *The Biggest Loser*, *Fit to Fat to Fit*, *Revenge Body*, and *Extreme Makeover: Weight Loss Edition*, among others, that market themselves as advocating empowerment through exercise, but that "treat fat as an enemy that must be destroyed, a contagion that must be eradicated." And while she takes the thinspiration industrial complex—from commercials on women's networks to Oprah's wheelbarrow of animal fat—to task with heartening doses of sarcasm, she also adeptly pinpoints how impossible it is for women to simply exist in a culture that equates obesity with misery and within which their own self-determination will never be enough.

Gay is sometimes referred to as an "overnight sensation." Those most familiar with her work are quick to point to the roughly 20 years of writing online that led to her recent successes, from the novel, *An Untamed State*, to the collections *Bad Feminist* and *Difficult Women*. But what *Hunger* illuminates is that food and the anonymity of writing on the internet were two of the salves for the loneliness and anxiety that enveloped Gay into her 20s. Its short, intimate chapters follow Gay through the brokenness of her teens, the recklessness of the following decade, and her current, ongoing struggle to reconcile the fact that being an overweight black woman at times makes her body a site for commentary

5

academic literacies · rhetorical situations · genres · fields · processes · strategies · research MLA / APA · media / design · readings · handbook

and her humanity invisible. She mercilessly describes the way this rudeness gets couched as concern:

> When you're overweight, your body becomes a matter of public record in many respects. Your body is constantly and prominently on display. . . . Fat, much like skin color, is something you cannot hide, no matter how dark the clothing you wear, or how diligently you avoid horizontal stripes. . . . People are quick to offer statistics and information about the dangers of obesity, as if you are not only fat but incredibly stupid, unaware, and delusional about your body and a world that is vigorously inhospitable to that body. . . . You are your body, nothing more, and your body should damn well become less.

This is not the first time Gay has written about her weight, the assault she experienced in her youth, and the ways that society assigns value to women of her size. *An Untamed State*, a novel that in some ways parallels Gay's own experiences, follows a protagonist who is brutally kidnapped and then raped. *Bad Feminist* included an essay about Gay's trip to fat camp, and countless essays she's previously published online—including "Breaking Uniform," and "My Body Is Wildly Undisciplined and I Deny Myself Nearly Everything I Desire"—are reprinted in *Hunger*. Last year she appeared on *This American Life*, where she noted the difference between being "Lane Bryant fat" and super-morbidly obese (the latter the clinical term for Gay's size).

In *Hunger*, she repeatedly juxtaposes an inherent, internal conflict: the survival mechanism of making herself bigger in the years following her rape and the ways in which that very act has made her life difficult in a new way. In one revealing section, Gay describes the kinds of exhausting considerations that she makes daily because of her size—from googling event venues to see if there are stairs, to worrying about airport seating, to dressing in mostly jeans and cotton shirts, to wondering whether a restaurant's chairs will have arms that will pinch her. The catalog of small anxieties that interrupt her days is moving, even as it highlights the ways the world doesn't accommodate women like Gay.

Her descriptions of violence are both specific—down to the scent of the beer on the breath of her rapists—and omnipresent. Trauma reverberates through the short chapters, even as she appears to accept what happened, and to rebuild. There are countless permutations of the sentence, "When I was twelve years old I was raped and then I ate and ate and ate to build my body into a fortress," and descriptions of herself as "a mess." She relies on the repetitive descriptions of her rape and her brokenness in a way that might in other circumstances seem gratuitous, but which in *Hunger* serves to give readers some emotional insight into the unrelenting nature of trauma.

Woven into this repetition is a ruminative preoccupation with strength, in all its varieties. In a 2012 article for *The Rumpus,* Gay wrote that she is "always interested in the representations of strength in women . . . and what it costs for a woman to be strong. All too often, representations of a woman's strength overlook that cost." What makes *Hunger* emotionally resonant is her ability to make the cost of survival—her moving forward from the rape and the challenge of her size—so transparent.

Gay occasionally nods to her identity as a black woman—for example, describing growing up Haitian American, or noting the white classmate who hurled "affirmative action" at her as an insult when he was not admitted to the school of his choice. But she leaves for just a few moments her explicit comments on the ways that black women's bodies are read in popular culture—which result in some of the most powerful lines in the book. "Black women are rarely allowed their femininity," she notes at one point, when talking about how people misgender her because of her size. And when she says that she doesn't want to allow her body to dictate her existence, part of that determination involves negotiating space as a black woman in places that she describes as "inhospitable" to blackness. 10

Observations such as these help make *Hunger* a gripping book, with vivid details that linger long after its pages stop. In addressing unwieldy topics such as weight, sexual violence, and trauma, Gay's takeaways are many and her ending impossible to classify as a destination. And by writing this memoir she's exposed imperfections—in culture, feminism, and herself—that require any claims to humanity and dignity to make room for inconsistency. She doesn't try to reconcile how her critiques

academic literacies | rhetorical situations | genres | fields | processes | strategies | research MLA / APA | media / design | readings | handbook

and failures intersect in ways that might seem contradictory; she allows herself to fall short of those aspirations and forms her own conception of her body and of healing. She began her memoir by warning that it would not inspire motivation, though her ability to reject society's judgment of and contempt for overweight people, while being vulnerable enough to admit that she struggles with body positivity, inspires hopefulness nonetheless. *Hunger* is arresting and candid. At its best, it affords women, in particular, something so many other accounts deny them — the right to take up space they are entitled to, and to define what that means.

Engaging with the Text

1. Adrienne Green does not **BEGIN** her essay with a discussion of Roxane Gay's book, but rather with a general comment on how society reacts to weight-loss stories. Why do you think she chooses to begin this way? Is this an effective way to begin? Why or why not?

   373–80

2. A good evaluation is balanced and fair, often pointing out both the good and the bad. Green's evaluation of *Hunger*, however, is overwhelmingly positive. How does Green **SUPPORT** her assessment? Is the support she provides adequate? Why or why not?

   114

3. Green is evaluating *Hunger* specifically, but she discusses other books and essays written by Roxane Gay throughout the evaluation. Why do you think Green does this? One of the features of an evaluation is a **KNOWLEDGEABLE** discussion of the subject. How does Green's knowledge of Gay's other works strengthen her assessment of *Hunger*?

   206

4. What is your opinion of weight-loss reality shows? What role do you think these kinds of shows play in how people — especially women — view their bodies?

5. *For Writing*. Select a book in a specific genre — for example, memoir, science fiction, or graphic novel — and write an **EVALUATION** of it. Consider what features readers would expect to see in a book of that genre so that you can identify those features as evaluation criteria, and then use these criteria to offer a balanced review of the book.

   202–10

NATALIE STANDIFORD
The Tenacity of Hope

Natalie Standiford (b. 1961) is author of numerous books for children and young adults, including How to Say Goodbye in Robot *(2009),* The Only Girl in School *(2016), and* The Secret Tree *(2012), which the* New York Times *named a Notable Children's Book of 2012. She worked as an assistant editor in the children's book division of the publisher Random House before leaving to become a full-time writer. Standiford is also a musician, playing bass with fellow authors in the band Tiger Beat. The following book review appeared in the* New York Times *in 2012.*

"**I AM NOT A MATHEMATICIAN, BUT I KNOW THIS,**" says Hazel Grace Lancaster, the narrator of *The Fault in Our Stars*, the latest novel by John Green, a Michael L. Printz medalist and author of several best-selling novels for young adults. "There are infinite numbers between zero and one. There's .1 and .12 and .112 and an infinite collection of others." The trouble, she says, is, "I want more numbers than I'm likely to get."

This is a problem faced by the heroines in both *The Fault in Our Stars* and *The Probability of Miracles,* two young adult novels about 16-year-old girls who have cancer: their days are numbered. At the outset, the two books are remarkably similar. Both begin by bluntly describing the harsh realities of life as a cancer patient through the wry sensibility of a smart, sarcastic teenage girl. They are both surprisingly funny and entertaining, given the subject matter, and both are at heart teenage love stories. About halfway through, though, *The Probability of Miracles* veers off in one direction—toward the miracles of the title—while *The Fault in Our Stars* stays the course of tragic realism. And that's where the difference lies.

Campbell Cooper, the heroine of Wendy Wunder's first novel, is a child of Disney World: her parents were both fire dancers in the "Spirit of Aloha" show at the Polynesian Hotel. Growing up in a manufactured fantasy world has made Cam understandably cynical. When her doctor reports that her cancer has spread and medical science has done all it can, Cam resigns herself to dying.

Then she comes across a "Flamingo List" she made a year earlier, a list of everything she wants to do before she dies, things she imagines to be part of a normal adolescence, like "Lose my virginity at a keg party," "Kill my little sister's dreams" and "Experiment with petty shoplifting." It's time to start crossing things off the Flamingo List, and so she starts with the easiest one: shoplifting.

Cam has accepted that she's going to die. But her mother and little 5 sister want her to keep fighting, to believe in miracles. Hoping Cam will learn to "trust how the universe unfolds," her mother insists on a road trip to Promise, Me., a mystical town known for its healing powers.

Promise, a sparkling New England village, is as much of a fantasy—if a less plasticized version—as the world Cam left behind in Florida. Upon their arrival, a handsome boy named Asher invites her and her family to stay in his gorgeous mansion overlooking the ocean. And though Cam resists the idea, Promise does appear to be full of miracles. The sunsets last for hours. Orcas improbably leap out of the bay in the evening. There are purple dandelions, a rainbow at night, snow in July and an unlikely flock of flamingoes. And Cam feels better. She can eat again; she has energy. Though she is "hope-resistant," that begins to change.

Cam has setbacks, but eventually she succumbs to the spell of Promise and Asher, a hunky football star who reads James Joyce for fun. Even Cam says, "A person can be too perfect, you know." By the end of the summer, she has crossed everything off her Flamingo List. Meanwhile, her sarcasm has lost its edge, and alas, so has the book. When Cam's story, which starts out so gritty and real, devolves into fantasy, the sense of what dying young of cancer is really like is lost.

The grim reality is always present, however, in Hazel Lancaster, the heroine of *The Fault in Our Stars*, who narrates her story in a hip, angry, funny tone similar to Cam's. Hazel has thyroid cancer that has spread calamitously to her lungs when she meets Augustus Waters, a former basketball player who has lost a leg to osteosarcoma, at a support group for cancer kids in Indianapolis. Augustus lends Hazel his favorite book, *The Price of Dawn*, the "brilliant and haunting novelization of my favorite video game," so she lends him hers: *An Imperial Affliction* by Peter Van Houten, about a girl who has cancer. Van Houten ends his novel abruptly in the middle of a sentence, and Hazel is obsessed with finding out what happened to the characters. Augustus, too, becomes riveted by *An Imperial Affliction,* and uses his "wish" from "The Genie Foundation," an organization devoted to the cheering up of sick children, to send himself and Hazel to Amsterdam to meet Van Houten.

At first Augustus, like Asher, seems too good to be true. He's sexy and smart, and he appears to want nothing more than to do nice things for Hazel. But we come to understand how Gus's illness has forced him to confront the big questions of life and death. Over the course of the narrative, his appealing exterior breaks down; his flaws, fears, and humiliations are exposed, yet he is all the more lovable for his frailty and heartbreaking humanity.

Like *The Probability of Miracles,* this is a love story, but it is also a book 10 by John Green, author of *Looking for Alaska* and *Paper Towns,* and it is written in his signature tone, a blend of melancholy, sweet, philosophical, and funny. When Hazel decides to give away her childhood swing set because the sight of it depresses her, she considers this headline for the Craigslist ad: "Lonely, Vaguely Pedophilic Swing Set Seeks the Butts of Children." Green's characters may be improbably witty, but even under the direst circumstances they are the kind of people you wish you knew.

If the story takes a grimmer turn than that of *The Probability of Miracles,* the characters compel the reader to stick with them. *The Fault in Our Stars* is all the more heart-rending for its bluntness about the medical realities of cancer. There are harrowing descriptions of pain, shame, anger, and bodily fluids of every type. It is a narrative without rainbows or flamingoes; there are no magical summer snowstorms. Instead, Hazel has to lug a portable oxygen tank with her wherever she goes, and Gus has a prosthetic leg. Their friend Isaac is missing an eye and later goes blind. These unpleasant details do nothing to diminish the romance; in Green's hands, they only make it more moving. He shows us true love—two teenagers helping and accepting each other through the most humiliating physical and emotional ordeals—and it is far more romantic than any sunset on the beach.

As Hazel and Gus often remind each other, the world is not a wish-granting factory. Nevertheless, "a forever within the numbered days" can be found, and as Hazel shows us, maybe that's all we can ask for.

Engaging with the Text

1. At first, Natalie Standiford seems to maintain the same objective **STANCE** toward both novels she is reviewing. When she begins to give a negative evaluation of one and a positive evaluation of the other, does her stance—as reflected in her tone—change accordingly? Why do you think she does or does not shift her tone in this way?

   66–68

2. A writer of an evaluation must offer a **KNOWLEDGEABLE** discussion of her subject. How does Standiford reveal she is knowledgeable about the books she is reviewing? Point to one passage that makes clear that she knows what she is writing about—not only these books but others by their authors as well.

   206

3. On the basis of what **CRITERIA** does Standiford compare and contrast the two novels? Are her criteria appropriate? Why or why not? What other criteria might she have used?

   206

4. Standiford uses **TRANSITIONS** between her paragraphs to connect the ideas. For example, she refers back to the subject of the last sentence of the previous paragraph, as in "This is a problem . . ." and "Promise . . ."; she also links ideas chronologically using "Then" and "At first" and by comparison using "Like." Are these transitions clear and effective? Why or why not? How else might Standiford have helped readers move from one paragraph to another?

   391

5. *For Writing.* Different writers often deal with the same subject from different perspectives. Select two short stories or brief nonfiction narratives (such as newspaper stories) that deal with the same subject. **COMPARE AND CONTRAST** the presentation of the storylines, the characters, and the settings in the two works, and write an **EVALUATION** that explains which you found more successful and why (or why both failed or succeeded equally).

   424–31
202–10

ASHLEY FOSTER

Polyvore.com: An Evaluation of How Fashion Is Consumed Online

Ashley Foster (b. 1994) is an undergraduate at Arizona State University where she is majoring in writing, rhetorics, and literacies in the Department of English. After graduation, she plans to find a job in technical writing, and she hopes to go on to law school. She wrote this essay in 2017 while enrolled in a course on research methods in rhetoric. Since this essay was written, the website Foster is evaluating has been replaced by SSENSE, a different fashion and shopping platform. As you read, notice how Foster uses images to give her readers a better sense of the website she's evaluating.

In a world where advertisements drive consumers to buy, sell, trade, and barter for goods, there are online sites that strive to be different. One of these is *Polyvore*, a database of clothing, accessories, beauty products, and home decor that caters to the fashion-forward who seek to express themselves creatively in an online space. The idea of a website in which one could catalogue and collage brands, stores, trends, and celebrities was conceived of in 2006 by Pasha Sadri, whose initial goal was to create a mood board that would help him decorate his home. A year later, the idea turned into *Polyvore*, which had $2.5 million in funding from Benchmark and Harrison Metal to launch the official website. Since its release in 2007, *Polyvore* has had an estimated twenty million unique visitors each month as of 2012 (Hamanaka). The "About" page on *Polyvore* explains that "*Polyvore* disrupts the traditional e-commerce model by giving everyone everywhere a voice in shaping today's trends and influencing purchases."

The structure of the web-based campaign is sophisticated yet simple, allowing users to rely on their own fashion judgment to lead them where the trends go. On the home page, tabs route to information on what's trending in outfits for men and women, further broken down into subcategories such as beauty and accessories. From the "Create" tab, users can create "sets," or picture collages, centered around fashion

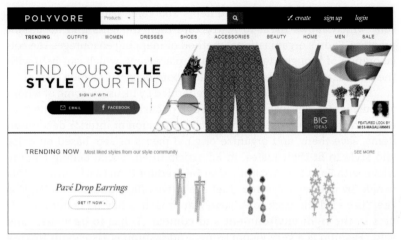

Screenshot of Polyvore's home page.

and room design using items they have saved while browsing the website or other fashion websites. Functionality includes dragging, dropping, resizing, and cropping, with categories like tops, skirts, and bags, and users can create sets using pre-made templates or start from scratch. This method is useful for organizing virtual data, as there is no physical

Screenshot of the "Create" tab on Polyvore.

way of doing so. Users can save items and come back to their drafted sets, which allows them to restructure their thoughts and document progress. Sadri's organizational method of mapping encourages the collaboration of thought, taste, style, and placement, which can help with the visualization of a set, whether for room decor or fashion design.

Polyvore is made up of content generated by its users, some of whom are businesses. Because users share and publish this content to the general database, other users can search for fashion or interior decoration items, save them, and organize original pieces or sets based on color and style to fit their tastes. In an article titled "Social Selling Finding Niche with Polyvore," *Women's Wear Daily* editor Evan Clark outlines this benefit by quoting *Polyvore's* chief executive officer and cofounder, Jess Lee: "Lee said the trick to *Polyvore's* approach is having fashion products in the right environment and context. 'It has to be visual,' she said. 'Fashion is a very visual thing. And fashion is also about mixing and matching. People are in the right mind-set when they come to the site.'"

The home page is a place where praise and recognition are paid to the work of *Polyvore* users. There are sections dedicated to "top sets," winners of design contests, and sets that are featured in the community spotlight. These highlights are a nice touch to help blend user content with trending and upcoming fashion statements.

One of *Polyvore's* most appealing features is that most of the items available for use in sets or designs are also available for purchase. Not only is this site an archive for past fashion staples, it is also an inspiration for use in real-time online shopping. Items for sale can vary in terms of pricing, but are generally affordable, depending on the type of look and product. In *Women's Wear Daily*, tech editor Kari Hamanaka, discussing the correlation between price and the shopper in her article entitled "Polyvore Reveals Most-Searched Fashion Brands," writes:

> Fast-fashion retailers Topshop, H&M, and Forever 21 claimed the number one, two, and three spots, respectively, on the list of the top-10 brands users searched for during the year. "They're all super-trendy, all very fashion-forward, but they're affordable," pointed out

Polyvore editorial curator Amy Hicks. "Our members—who are 18 to 34 [years old]—they love a trend, but they love it at a great price."

This website is great for those interested in fashion, because of the affordances allowed in terms of creativity, materials for use in the set, usability, and options for additions from other parts of the internet. The clean format in which users are able to search for items is also appealing; the site's creator focuses on simplicity. The site's simple black-and-white backdrop focuses attention on the fashion pieces on the home page; it serves as a clean slate, opening up space for creativity.

An example of another online style database with a similar design is *Pinterest*, which does a great job of collecting data but does not allow space for users to create original sets. Instead of just having users save items to a board that they may never look at again, *Polyvore*'s website design allows users to look back on their sets and use their imagination or personal preferences to create an online personality. This online personality not only reflects the style of a *Polyvore* user, but also allows this same user to document their capabilities as a contributor to social fashion.

Nevertheless, *Polyvore* has a couple of shortcomings. Because the website's content is provided by business and non-business users, not all products are available for purchase, which means that some only serve the purpose of being an artistic presence in a set. I have often hovered over an interactive set to check the price on a sweater or shirt only to find that it was pulled straight from a blog page with no link to a store website. Other issues to take into consideration are that the quality of an item and an item's availability cannot be guaranteed by *Polyvore*.

In sum, *Polyvore* is a valuable, though not perfect, site that belongs to all its users, promotes the growth of a social knowledge regarding fashion trends, and provides a collaborative environment where such fashion can be documented. The website itself caters to fashion, which can be seen in the variety of options one can use when building sets and fashion collages, and it is a great tool for people who want to stay on top of style trends.

Works Cited

Clark, Evan. "Social Selling Finding Niche with Polyvore." *WWD: Women's Wear Daily*, 21 Dec. 2012, wwd.com/business-news/financial/social-selling-finding-niche-with-polyvore-6552356/.

Hamanaka, Kari. "Polyvore Reveals Most-Searched Fashion Brands." *WWD: Women's Wear Daily*, 12 Dec. 2014, wwd.com/business-news/media/polyvore-reveals-most-searched-fashion-brands-8072153/.

Polyvore. Yahoo Lifestyle, 2007–18, www.polyvore.com.

Engaging with the Text

206 ▲

1. An evaluation should be **BALANCED AND FAIR**. Is Ashley Foster's evaluation a balanced and fair assessment of the website *Polyvore*? Why or why not?

55–56 ■

2. What is the **PURPOSE** of Foster's evaluation? How do you know? What do you think she wants readers to take away from her essay?

3. Foster includes two images, both screenshots of *Polyvore* pages. What is the purpose of these images? Do you find them helpful? Why or why not?

391 ◆
380–85

4. The final paragraph of Foster's essay begins with the **TRANSITION** "In sum . . ." Why do you think Foster **ENDS** her essay that way? Is this ending effective? Why or why not? How else might she have chosen to end her essay?

202–10 ▲

5. *For Writing.* Select a website you frequent and write an **EVALUATION** of it for people who know little or nothing about it. What information would the **AUDIENCE** need to help them decide whether or not to visit the website? Make sure to keep your assessment balanced and fair.

57–60 ■

Literary Analyses **66**

BAILEY BASINGER

Tension, Contradiction, and Ambiguity: Gender Roles in "A Rose for Emily"

Bailey Basinger (b. 1996) wrote this literary analysis of William Faulkner's "A Rose for Emily" when she was a student at Arizona State University, Tempe. She now attends Sandra Day O'Connor College of Law. As you read, notice how Basinger draws on literary critics to enrich her analysis.

IN "**A ROSE FOR EMILY**," William Faulkner creates Emily Grierson and Homer Barron as characters whose gender identity and sexuality are ambiguous. Faulkner leaves subtle and often contradictory clues throughout that hint at possible definitions of their sexuality, setting up an unsettling tension. Moreover, through the narration of a collective "we" representing the community of the fictional Jefferson, Mississippi, Faulkner illustrates the community's—and, by extension, society's—persistent attempts to fit the two characters into an unequivocal sexual binary. Yet critics have been less certain about Emily's and Homer's sexuality. Hal Blythe, for example, argues that Homer may be best understood as a homosexual (49–50), but Blythe's perspective has been criticized by other literary scholars such as James Wallace (105–07) and Judith Caesar (195–98). This essay argues that Faulkner presents an ambiguous perspective on both Homer's and Emily's sexuality, despite the town's relentless attempts to attribute a clear gender identity and sexuality to both, in order to make a point about society's insistence on defining gender and sexuality even when they are undefinable. The town's desire to assign Homer and Emily clear gender identities and sexualities, even in the face of ambiguous evidence, reveals more about the prejudices in the town than it does about Emily and Homer, but the ambiguities help create tension in the story that contributes to its surprise ending.

In the first physical description given of Emily, Faulkner sets her up as a character whose gender identity and sexuality are clearly ambigu-

academic literacies · rhetorical situations · genres · fields · processes · strategies · research MLA / APA · media / design · readings · handbook

ous. The narrator describes her as "a small, fat woman in black, with a thin gold chain descending to her waist and vanishing into her belt, leaning on an ebony cane with a tarnished gold head" (Faulkner 852). In his essay "Horror and Perverse Delight," Dennis Allen discusses Emily's adoption of masculine accessories, noting that "mediating the distinction between male and female, Emily has equipped herself with a good deal of phallic paraphernalia. In fact, the only details of her costume mentioned in the passage are the cane she holds before her and the watch suspended from the gold chain that vanishes beneath her belt" (686). These phallic symbols clash with Emily's supposed femininity.

Emily's hair is also an important symbol of the tensions around her gender identity. The importance of her hair as a symbol is underscored through the narrator's use of nearly identical introductory phrases — "when we next saw Emily" and "when we saw her again" — to open the descriptions of her hair. For example, after her seclusion following her father's death, the narrator explains, "When we saw her again, her hair was cut short, making her look like a girl" (Faulkner 855). The use of the word *girl* signifies Emily's haircut gave her a more youthful appearance. But the haircut was uncommon for women at the end of the nineteenth century. Women, young and old, had long hair until the early years of the twentieth century. Hair was only cut due to illness. While the short hair signifies perhaps illness (possibly even mental illness, "with insanity in the family" [854]), it is also likely to suggest a masculine appearance. Faulkner makes this contradiction more explicit later in the story when the narrator again mentions Emily's hair, noting, "When we next saw Emily, she had grown fat and her hair was turning gray. . . . Up to the day of her death at seventy-four it was still that vigorous iron-gray, like the hair of an active man" (858). The narrator describes the natural graying of Emily's hair as suggesting masculinity. Through illustrating Emily's appearance as both feminine and masculine, Faulkner again emphasizes Emily's ambiguous gender. Her identity overall is impossible to define in binary "either-or" terms; her hair is pointed to as a sign that she is potentially both young and old, male and female.

The tension created by these contradictions is reinforced by the community's continued attempts to define Emily as a heterosexual woman. In attempting to explain why Emily had not yet married, the town first agrees that "[n]one of the young men were ever quite good enough for Miss Emily" (Faulkner 854). The town chooses to blame her failure to get married on her family's perceived high social status and her father's rejection of suitors. However, when Emily remains single into her thirties, the town changes its theory, claiming that "even with insanity in the family she wouldn't have turned down all of her chances if they had really materialized" (854). The town contradicts its earlier statement that Emily's family's perceived high social status had ruined her chances at marriage, instead claiming she never had any serious suitors at all. Again, the town chooses to believe Emily is a heterosexual woman and creates evidence to support their beliefs regardless of Emily's seeming androgyny and apparent refusal to marry. Even after her death, certain members of the community are willing to invent memories of Emily. At her funeral the narrator describes "the very old men—some in their brushed Confederate uniforms—on the porch and the lawn, talking of Miss Emily as if she had been a contemporary of theirs, believing that they had danced with her and courted her perhaps" (859). The men in their Confederate uniforms create memories to prove Emily's heterosexuality even when the rest of the community recognizes these memories are false. The town is so determined to define Emily's sexuality and gender that they are willing to use contradictory and clearly fabricated evidence to support their definition.

Just as Faulkner emphasizes Emily's androgyny through phallic accessories, he also equips Homer with violent phallic images. As the town of Jefferson watches Emily and Homer drive around in his buggy, they observe "Homer Barron with his hat cocked and a cigar in his teeth, reins and whip in a yellow glove" (Faulkner 857). The use of this hypermasculine imagery—the word *cocked* paired with the phallic objects of a cigar and whip—is paired with Homer's own remarks that "he liked men, and . . . drank with the younger men in the Elks' Club—that he was not a marrying man" (857). Thomas Bonner, Jr., explains the "not a marrying man" phrase in his article on "The Functions of Ambiguity":

5

> The phrase "not a marrying man," as Homer is described by Faulkner, is one of those spaces for interpretation. . . . Ample evidence suggests its ambiguity—homosexual or confirmed bachelor, perhaps a conscious choice of words as the term has frequency in nineteenth and twentieth century American writing. (493)

In other words, explaining his preference for men and his distaste for marriage, it is possible that Homer is attempting to tell the town he is not a heterosexual, but the town is refusing to listen. Choosing to overlook his visits with the younger men at the Elks' Club, the town claims, "[W]e were sure that they [Homer and Emily] were to be married" (Faulkner 857). Just as the town refuses to acknowledge Emily's ambiguous sexual traits, they ignore Homer's.

Although Faulkner seems to hint at Homer's attraction to men, Homer's sexuality is never explicitly stated and is therefore still ambiguous. Indeed, Bonner suggests, "While there may be some possibility of seeing Homer as homosexual, more evidence exists to indicate otherwise" (494). However, Faulkner purposefully makes Homer's sexuality unclear. It is unclear, for example, whether Emily and Homer were ever intimate, though there is clearly some sort of relationship between them. After Emily's death, the town notices that the room in which Homer's body laid was "decked and furnished as for a bridal" (Faulkner 860) and filled with items Emily had bought him such as the monogrammed toilet set and the suit of clothes. The care with which the room was decorated for a wedding and the personal touches on the objects she bought him implies a closeness between them. Furthermore, on the pillow next to Homer's body, the townspeople saw "the indentation of a head" and "a long strand of iron gray hair" (860), the hair that reminded the town of "an active man" (857). Homer's body "had apparently once lain in the attitude of an embrace" (860). The indentation, the gray hair, and the body's pose suggest that Emily had lain in bed with Homer, again suggesting some affection between them, but whether that affection was sexual cannot be determined. The close relationship between Emily and Homer could have been sexual, but, if so, the dramatic reveal of the final scene would suggest that the intimacy was after death.

Faulkner never gives definitive proof of Emily's or Homer's sexual preferences and purposefully makes both ambiguous. Rather, Faulkner cleverly and subtly leaves clues that could be used to support a variety of ways of defining their sexuality. Like the townspeople of Jefferson, many readers and scholars have attempted to pin down both characters' sexuality. Many scholars have argued for motives surrounding Emily's possible murder of Homer that support one stagnant understanding of Emily's sexuality. For example, in "Emily Grierson's Oedipus Complex," Jack Scherting employs Freud to explain Emily's relationship with men:

> Deliberately and with consummate skill Faulkner employed the Freudian principle of Oedipal fixation as a means of depicting Emily's character and informing the story with its powerful theme, a theme intimately connected with the incestuous nature of Emily's love for Homer. Emily Grierson was possessed by an unresolved Oedipal complex. Her libidinal desires for her father were transferred, after his death, to a male surrogate—Homer Barron. (399)

Scherting supports this claim for Emily's Oedipal complex by citing her father's rejection of her suitors as one of the causes for her development of a fixation on her father. However, even the fact that Emily had suitors cannot be stated with any certainty. Additionally, Scherting cites Emily's affair with Homer as a reenactment of her Oedipal complex, but neither the town nor the reader can ever confirm if Homer and Emily were intimate or desired to be so.

Another scholar, Hal Blythe, argues, "A closer examination of Miss Emily's 'lover,' Homer Barron, reveals . . . Miss Emily's 'beau' ideal is homosexual" (49), citing as evidence Homer's claimed preference for men and the use of the name *Homer* as a reference to ancient Greek homosexuality. Blythe also might have pointed out the name *Barron* as signifying "noble fighter," a masculine trait. Therefore, Homer's preference for surrounding himself with men could be used as evidence of his homosexuality; however, because Faulkner never explicitly states Homer's sexual preferences, one cannot say with any certainty what they were. Although Blythe seems to at least recognize Homer's ambiguous sexuality, he, like Scherting, assumes that Emily is heterosexual and argues that Emily killed Homer out of rage for her unrequited love. While that is a possibility, Faulkner keeps the death itself ambiguous as well.

Throughout "A Rose for Emily," there is an incongruity between the town's relentless attempts to define Homer and Emily as a traditional couple and their physical descriptions, which raise questions about their gender and sexuality. In this way, Faulkner is providing commentary on society's inclination to define sexuality and gender identity in binary terms even when they are fluid and undefinable. As Faulkner scholar Max Putzel notes, "'A Rose for Emily' tells more about the town than about the victims of its malice—including Miss Emily" (222). Bonner agrees: "Max Putzel is right. . . . In the end more can be said with certitude about the nature of the townspeople than can be said about Emily" (498). The same could be said for the townspeople and Homer. By giving the reader more insight into the town than into Homer or Emily, Faulkner demonstrates—and criticizes—society's real and continued tendency to look for a rigid definition of individuals' gender and sexuality even when none may exist.

Works Cited

Allen, Dennis W. "Horror and Perverse Delight: Faulkner's 'A Rose for Emily.'" *Modern Fiction Studies*, vol. 30, no. 4, 1984, pp. 685–95. EBSCOhost, accession no.: 24576493.

Blythe, Hal. "Faulkner's 'A Rose for Emily.'" *The Explicator*, vol. 47, no. 2, 1989, pp. 49–50, https://doi.org/10.1080/00144940.1989.9933908.

Bonner, Thomas, Jr. "The Functions of Ambiguity: A Response to 'Miss Emily after Dark.'" *Mississippi Quarterly*, vol. 64, nos. 3–4, 2011, pp. 491–99, www.thefreelibrary.com/The+functions+of+ambiguity%3A+a+response+to+%22Miss+Emily+After+Dark%22.-a0290112236.

Caesar, Judith. "Faulkner's Gay Homer, Once More." *The Explicator*, vol. 68, no. 3, 2010, pp. 195–98. *Taylor and Francis Online*, https://doi.org/10.1080/00144940.2010.499087.

Faulkner, William. "A Rose for Emily." *The Norton Field Guide to Writing with Readings*, edited by Richard Bullock and Maureen Daly Goggin. 5th ed., W. W. Norton, 2019, pp. 851–60.

Putzel, Max. *Genius of Place: William Faulkner's Triumphant Beginnings.* Louisiana State UP, 1985.

Scherting, Jack. "Emily Grierson's Oedipus Complex: Motif, Motive, and Meaning in Faulkner's 'A Rose for Emily.'" *Studies in Short Fiction*, vol. 17, no. 4, Sept. 1980, pp. 397–405. *EBSCOhost*, accession no.: 7134648.

Wallace, James. "Faulkner's 'A Rose for Emily.'" *The Explicator*, vol. 50, no. 2, 1992, pp. 105–07. *Taylor and Francis Online*, https://doi.org /10.1080/00144940.1992.9937918.

Engaging with the Text

387–89

1. What is Bailey Basinger's **THESIS**? Restate it in your own words. Read "A Rose for Emily" (on pp. 851–60) yourself. Are you convinced by Basinger's argument? Why or why not? Point to three pieces of evidence she uses and explain why you do or do not find them convincing.

528–31

2. How does Basinger use **QUOTATIONS** from Faulkner's short story? Is her use of quotations effective? Why or why not? What other quotations might she have used?

519–25

3. How does Basinger **SYNTHESIZE OTHER SCHOLARSHIP** on Faulkner's story in her analysis? How does this synthesis support her analysis of the story?

4. Basinger focuses on gender and sexuality in "A Rose for Emily." Should she have broadened her focus? narrowed it? Why?

98–130

477

5. *For Writing.* **ANALYZE** some facet of a literary work that intrigues you: its theme, its characters, its setting, its narrator, or its structure. You should **RESEARCH** scholarship on the literary piece, and write an essay that both presents your own analysis and responds to what others have said about the same work. You can agree with what they say, disagree, or both; the important thing is to think about what others say, and to

526–38

QUOTE, **PARAPHRASE**, or **SUMMARIZE** their views in your text.

academic literacies · rhetorical situations · genres · fields · processes · strategies · research MLA / APA · media / design · readings · handbook

LIZ MOORE

Abuse of an Unnamed Wife: Is She Familiar?

Liz Moore (b. 1998) is a student at Sam Houston State University in Huntsville, Texas. She wrote the following literary analysis of Charlotte Perkins Gilman's short story "The Yellow Wallpaper" in a first-year writing class. As you read, notice how Moore uses both textual evidence as well as outside research about psychological abuse in her analysis.

"THE YELLOW WALLPAPER" BY CHARLOTTE PERKINS GILMAN is a warning about the damage that can be done when a vulnerable person is isolated by an abuser and when a woman is treated as lesser because of her gender. The story was published in 1892, but the narrator's description of mental abuse could be the story of the vast number of women who suffer domestic abuse today. By focusing on the psychological factors involved in domestic abuse, the author introduces the idea that abuse is not limited to physical violence—possibly an unusual position in its day but widely recognized today. In fact, the tactics used by our unnamed narrator's husband, John, are now included in definitions of domestic abuse. The unnamed wife in the story could be anyone—then or now—and in this way the story shines a light on what would otherwise be an invisible injustice.

The National Domestic Abuse Hotline defines domestic violence as "a pattern of behavior used by one partner to maintain power and control over another partner in an intimate relationship." While many people think of abuse as physical harm, the more common, and insidious, version is emotional manipulation resulting in mental abuse. Examples of abuse include separating the victim from friends and family, preventing them from making decisions, shaming them, controlling the finances, and preventing them from working ("What Is Domestic Violence?"). All these alarming behaviors are found in the dynamic between John and his wife. That the wife is lonely is apparent, for she tells the reader, "I cry at nothing, and cry most of the time. . . . I don't when John is here, or anybody else, but when I am alone. And I am alone a good deal just now"

(Gilman 250). This is an indisputable canon of isolation. John, however, manipulates the narrator out of going on "a visit to Cousin Henry and Julia," telling her she "wasn't able to go, nor able to stand it after [she] got there" (251). John now becomes the only solid presence in her life, and her reliance on him grows as a result.

One of John's frequent tactics in manipulating the narrator is gaslighting, defined by the *Oxford English Dictionary* as an attempt to "manipulate a person by psychological means into questioning his or her own sanity" ("Gaslight"). When John tells others, "'Bless her little heart! . . . she shall be as sick as she pleases!'" (Gilman 252), he dismisses her concerns, trivializing them to the point that even she believes she "never used to be so sensitive" and that she "think[s] it is due to this nervous condition" (247). By discounting her symptoms, John creates an uncertainty in his wife that eventually leads to the complete destruction of her ability to regulate her senses. John gaslights his wife to shift the dynamic of their relationship and take control.

Modern psychologists have also determined that abusers have an exaggerated sense of entitlement and lack a sense of accountability. Lack of accountability translates to "abuse happen[ing] in the context of a world that says that it's okay to hurt others when we are hurt" (Askin). John is used to being seen as an authority by others because of his status as a doctor. His wife says in her diary, "John is a physician, and *perhaps*—(I would not say it to a living soul, of course, but this is dead paper and a great relief to my mind)—*perhaps* that is one reason I do not get well faster. You see, he does not believe I am sick! And what can one do?" (Gilman 246). She is obviously aware that his disregard prolongs her illness, but she has no available recourse. John's entitled belief that his authority is irrefutable fuels the inferno of his wife's insanity. The narrator expresses her discomfort that he "ask[s] Jennie [John's sister] a lot of professional questions" about the narrator (255). This is a blatant invasion of privacy, and yet John's sister complies willingly. Jennie is possibly the only person to whom the wife could look for help; nonetheless, Jennie does nothing. Her reaction proves to John that there are no consequences for his actions and is symbolic of how the world viewed husband-wife relations when the story was written. When first reading

academic literacies · rhetorical situations · genres · fields · processes · strategies · research MLA / APA · media / design · readings · handbook

through the story, a reader may mistake the narrator's restriction for her husband's care, but this is exactly why cases of emotional abuse are so easy to overlook. Being forced to comply with a scheduled regime could drive anyone mad, and this woman is no exception.

Healthy relationships are meant to build up, not tear down, intimate 5 partners. The National Domestic Violence Hotline indicates that "[h]ealthy relationships allow both partners to feel supported and connected but still feel independent. Communication and boundaries are the two major components of a healthy relationship" ("What Is a Healthy Relationship?"). In "The Yellow Wallpaper," the fragile narrator, whose thoughts exist only on the pages of her diary, is desperate for communication. However, anytime she tries to express her inner worries, her husband brushes her off as another "hysterical" female: "If a physician of high standing, and one's own husband, assures friends and relatives that there really is nothing the matter with one but temporary nervous depression—a slight hysterical tendency—what is one to do?" (Gilman 246). The wife feels that she has no options. She never experiences the relief that her opinions are heard on any level. Boundaries are nonexistent. John has complete control of his wife, forcing her to endure the yellow wallpaper that is slowly driving her to madness. In no way could any person familiar with the traits of abusive relationships believe that the bond between the wife and husband in Charlotte Perkins Gilman's tragedy is healthy.

Not so long ago, to be female meant to have no control, as Kim Swanson elaborates in "Crime against Women—A Brief History of Laws in the US": "From early childhood, [women] were raised without rights, some barely treated better than slaves; while others may have had the appearance of freedom they were often kept under the control of a male family member." Swanson goes on to describe the legal status of women in the 1800s:

> [A] woman's legal status in life was directly connected to her husband, brother, or father. . . . [The public] believed that husbands had the God given right to correct their wives through the use of physical punishment in various forms . . . [and] the laws offered little to no protection from crime against women.

Gilman herself was forced to undergo treatment for hysteria after she sought help for what we now know to be postpartum depression. The so-called rest cure prescribed to her worsened the symptoms. Gilman never really recovered, but she did use her first-hand experience in "The Yellow Wallpaper" "to criticize [her] doctor's patriarchal approach as well as society's efforts to keep women passive" (Schilb and Clifford 245). She also exposed the abuse that women of this time suffered due to their inferior status. Her outcry against such abuses made her a valuable activist for women's rights.

The abuse in the tale told by the pitiful wife has been observed by many. Such abuse is common even today. According to the National Coalition against Domestic Violence, "On average, nearly 20 people per minute are physically abused by an intimate partner in the United States. During one year, this equates to more than 10 million women and men" ("Statistics"). Though Charlotte Perkins Gilman was one of the first women to tell the world a story about abuse, she is not the last. Novels today like *The Girl on the Train* by Paula Hawkins and *The Wife between Us* by Greer Hendricks and Sarah Pekkanen also help readers empathize with the disorienting and destructive effects of abuse. If her circumstances had been different, perhaps the mysterious narrator in "The Yellow Wallpaper" could have remained intact and sane, but Gilman had another story to tell.

Works Cited

Askin, Carrie. "Five Reasons People Abuse Their Partners." *Psychology Today*, 27 Oct. 2015, www.psychologytoday.com/blog/hurt-people -hurt-people/201510/five-reasons-people-abuse-their-partners.

"Gaslight, *v*." *Oxford English Dictionary*, Oxford UP, 2004, www.oed.com /viewdictionaryentry/Entry/11125.

Gilman, Charlotte Perkins. "The Yellow Wallpaper." *Arguing about Literature: A Guide and Reader*, edited by John Schilb and John Clifford. 2nd ed., Bedford/St. Martin's, 2017, pp. 245–59.

Schilb, John, and John Clifford. Brief Biographical Headnote for Charlotte Perkins Gilman's "The Yellow Wallpaper." *Arguing about Literature: A Guide and Reader*, edited by John Schilb and John Clifford. 2nd ed., Bedford/St. Martin's, 2017, p. 245.

"Statistics." National Coalition against Domestic Violence, ncadv.org/statistics. Accessed 15 Mar. 2018.

Swanson, Kim. "Crime against Women—A Brief History of Laws in the US." Get Inclusive, 28 Mar. 2014, www.getinclusive.com/blog/crime-women-brief-history-laws-us.

"What Is a Healthy Relationship?" National Domestic Violence Hotline, www.thehotline.org. Accessed 15 Mar. 2018.

"What Is Domestic Violence?" National Domestic Violence Hotline, www.thehotline.org. Accessed 15 Mar. 2018.

Engaging with the Text

1. What is the **THESIS** of Liz Moore's essay? Restate the thesis in your own words. Read "The Yellow Wallpaper" (pp. 862–78) yourself. Do you agree with Moore's analysis? Why or why not?

   387–89

2. A key feature of a literary analysis is **CAREFUL ATTENTION TO THE LANGUAGE OF THE TEXT**. How much attention does Moore pay to the language of the text? Point out one or two places where she analyzes the language of the text in order to make a larger point about Gilman's story.

   216

3. Who do you think is the intended **AUDIENCE** of Moore's analysis? How can you tell?

   57–60

4. Moore could have chosen to analyze "The Yellow Wallpaper" using only the language of the text and other scholars' analyses of the story, but instead she chose to include **RESEARCH** about the psychological effects of domestic abuse. Why do you think she does this? Do you think this research strengthens her analysis? Why or why not?

   477

211–23 ▲
477 ●

5. *For Writing.* Select one of the poems or stories in Chapter 66 and write a **LITERARY ANALYSIS** of that piece. Make sure to do some **RESEARCH** on the author, the context in which the piece was written, any outside scholarship, and anything else you think might be relevant. Write an essay that presents your own analysis of the piece, using outside research where appropriate.

❋ academic literacies
■ rhetorical situations
▲ genres
● fields
○ processes
◆ strategies
● research MLA / APA
▢ media / design
❚❚ readings
◿ handbook

WILLIAM FAULKNER

A Rose for Emily

William Faulkner (1897–1962) was the author of twenty novels, including The Sound and the Fury *(1929), As I Lay Dying (1930), and Absalom! Absalom! (1936), as well as many short stories and six books of poetry. He received the Nobel Prize for Literature in 1949 and Pulitzer Prizes in 1954 and 1962. The story "A Rose for Emily" was first published in 1931.*

WHEN MISS EMILY GRIERSON DIED, our whole town went to her funeral: the men through a sort of respectful affection for a fallen monument, the women mostly out of curiosity to see the inside of her house, which no one save an old man-servant—a combined gardener and cook—had seen in at least ten years.

It was a big, squarish frame house that had once been white, decorated with cupolas and spires and scrolled balconies in the heavily lightsome style of the seventies,* set on what had once been our most select street. But garages and cotton gins had encroached and obliterated even the august names of that neighborhood; only Miss Emily's house was left, lifting its stubborn and coquettish decay above the cotton wagons and the gasoline pumps—an eyesore among eyesores. And now Miss Emily had gone to join the representatives of those august names where they lay in the cedar-bemused cemetery among the ranked and anonymous graves of Union and Confederate soldiers who fell at the battle of Jefferson.

Alive, Miss Emily had been a tradition, a duty, and a care; a sort of hereditary obligation upon the town, dating from that day in 1894 when Colonel Sartoris, the mayor—he who fathered the edict that no Negro woman should appear on the streets without an apron—remitted her taxes, the dispensation dating from the death of her father on into

---

*Seventies: the 1870s, the decade after the Civil War (1861–65). [Editor's note]

perpetuity. Not that Miss Emily would have accepted charity. Colonel Sartoris invented an involved tale to the effect that Miss Emily's father had loaned money to the town, which the town, as a matter of business, preferred this way of repaying. Only a man of Colonel Sartoris' generation and thought could have invented it, and only a woman could have believed it.

When the next generation, with its more modern ideas, became mayors and aldermen, this arrangement created some little dissatisfaction. On the first of the year they mailed her a tax notice. February came, and there was no reply. They wrote her a formal letter, asking her to call at the sheriff's office at her convenience. A week later the mayor wrote her himself, offering to call or to send his car for her, and received in reply a note on paper of an archaic shape, in a thin, flowing calligraphy in faded ink, to the effect that she no longer went out at all. The tax notice was also enclosed, without comment.

They called a special meeting of the Board of Aldermen. A deputa-   5
tion waited upon her, knocked at the door through which no visitor had passed since she ceased giving china-painting lessons eight or ten years earlier. They were admitted by the old Negro into a dim hall from which a stairway mounted into still more shadow. It smelled of dust and disuse—a close, dank smell. The Negro led them into the parlor. It was furnished in heavy, leather-covered furniture. When the Negro opened the blinds of one window, a faint dust rose sluggishly about their thighs, spinning with slow motes in the single sun-ray. On a tarnished gilt easel before the fireplace stood a crayon portrait of Miss Emily's father.

They rose when she entered—a small, fat woman in black, with a thin gold chain descending to her waist and vanishing into her belt, leaning on an ebony cane with a tarnished gold head. Her skeleton was small and spare; perhaps that was why what would have been merely plumpness in another was obesity in her. She looked bloated, like a body long submerged in motionless water, and of that pallid hue. Her eyes, lost in the fatty ridges of her face, looked like two small pieces of coal pressed into a lump of dough as they moved from one face to another while the visitors stated their errand.

She did not ask them to sit. She just stood in the door and listened quietly until the spokesman came to a stumbling halt. Then they could hear the invisible watch ticking at the end of the gold chain.

Her voice was dry and cold. "I have no taxes in Jefferson. Colonel Sartoris explained it to me. Perhaps one of you can gain access to the city records and satisfy yourselves."

"But we have. We are the city authorities, Miss Emily. Didn't you get a notice from the sheriff, signed by him?"

"I received a paper, yes," Miss Emily said. "Perhaps he considers 10 himself the sheriff. . . . I have no taxes in Jefferson."

"But there is nothing on the books to show that, you see. We must go by the—"

"See Colonel Sartoris. I have no taxes in Jefferson."

"But, Miss Emily—"

"See Colonel Sartoris." (Colonel Sartoris had been dead almost ten years.) "I have no taxes in Jefferson. Tobe!" The Negro appeared. "Show these gentlemen out."

II

So she vanquished them, horse and foot, just as she had vanquished 15 their fathers thirty years before about the smell. That was two years after her father's death and a short time after her sweetheart—the one we believed would marry her—had deserted her. After her father's death she went out very little; after her sweetheart went away, people hardly saw her at all. A few of the ladies had the temerity to call, but were not received, and the only sign of life about the place was the Negro man—a young man then—going in and out with a market basket.

"Just as if a man—any man—could keep a kitchen properly," the ladies said; so they were not surprised when the smell developed. It was another link between the gross, teeming world and the high and mighty Griersons.

A neighbor, a woman, complained to the mayor, Judge Stevens, eighty years old.

"But what will you have me do about it, madam?" he said.

"Why, send her word to stop it," the woman said. "Isn't there a law?"

"I'm sure that won't be necessary," Judge Stevens said. "It's probably   20
just a snake or a rat that nigger of hers killed in the yard. I'll speak to
him about it."

The next day he received two more complaints, one from a man
who came in diffident deprecation. "We really must do something about
it, Judge. I'd be the last one in the world to bother Miss Emily, but we've
got to do something." That night the Board of Aldermen met—three
gray-beards and one younger man, a member of the rising generation.

"It's simple enough," he said. "Send her word to have her place
cleaned up. Give her a certain time to do it in, and if she don't . . ."

"Dammit, sir," Judge Stevens said, "will you accuse a lady to her face
of smelling bad?"

So the next night, after midnight, four men crossed Miss Emily's
lawn and slunk about the house like burglars, sniffing along the base of
the brickwork and at the cellar openings while one of them performed
a regular sowing motion with his hand out of a sack slung from his
shoulder. They broke open the cellar door and sprinkled lime there, and
in all the outbuildings. As they recrossed the lawn, a window that had
been dark was lighted and Miss Emily sat in it, the light behind her, and
her upright torso motionless as that of an idol. They crept quietly across
the lawn and into the shadow of the locusts that lined the street. After
a week or two the smell went away.

That was when people had begun to feel really sorry for her. People   25
in our town, remembering how old lady Wyatt, her great-aunt, had gone
completely crazy at last, believed that the Griersons held themselves a
little too high for what they really were. None of the young men were
quite good enough for Miss Emily and such. We had long thought of
them as a tableau; Miss Emily a slender figure in white in the background, her father a spraddled silhouette in the foreground, his back to
her and clutching a horsewhip, the two of them framed by the back-flung
front door. So when she got to be thirty and was still single, we were
not pleased exactly, but vindicated; even with insanity in the family
she wouldn't have turned down all of her chances if they had really
materialized.

When her father died, it got about that the house was all that was left to her; and in a way, people were glad. At last they could pity Miss Emily. Being left alone, and a pauper, she had become humanized. Now she too would know the old thrill and the old despair of a penny more or less.

The day after his death all the ladies prepared to call at the house and offer condolence and aid, as is our custom. Miss Emily met them at the door, dressed as usual and with no trace of grief on her face. She told them that her father was not dead. She did that for three days, with the ministers calling on her, and the doctors, trying to persuade her to let them dispose of the body. Just as they were about to resort to law and force, she broke down, and they buried her father quickly.

We did not say she was crazy then. We believed she had to do that. We remembered all the young men her father had driven away, and we knew that with nothing left, she would have to cling to that which had robbed her, as people will.

III

She was sick for a long time. When we saw her again, her hair was cut short, making her look like a girl, with a vague resemblance to those angels in colored church windows — sort of tragic and serene.

The town had just let the contracts for paving the sidewalks, and 30 in the summer after her father's death they began to work. The construction company came with niggers and mules and machinery, and a foreman named Homer Barron, a Yankee — a big, dark, ready man, with a big voice and eyes lighter than his face. The little boys would follow in groups to hear him cuss the niggers, and the niggers singing in time to the rise and fall of picks. Pretty soon he knew everybody in town. Whenever you heard a lot of laughing anywhere about the square, Homer Barron would be in the center of the group. Presently we began to see him and Miss Emily on Sunday afternoons driving in the yellowwheeled buggy and the matched team of bays from the livery stable.

At first we were glad that Miss Emily would have an interest, because the ladies all said, "Of course a Grierson would not think serously of a Northerner, a day laborer." But there were still others, older people, who said that even grief could not cause a real lady to forget *noblesse oblige*—without calling it *noblesse oblige*.* They just said, "Poor Emily. Her kinsfolk should come to her." She had some kin in Alabama; but years ago her father had fallen out with them over the estate of old lady Wyatt, the crazy woman, and there was no communication between the two families. They had not even been represented at the funeral.

And as soon as the old people said, "Poor Emily," the whispering began. "Do you suppose it's really so?" they said to one another. "Of course it is. What else could . . ." This behind their hands; rustling of craned silk and satin behind jalousies† closed upon the sun of Sunday afternoon as the thin, swift clop-clop-clop of the matched team passed: "Poor Emily."

She carried her head high enough—even when we believed that she was fallen. It was as if she demanded more than ever the recognition of her dignity as the last Grierson; as if it had wanted that touch of earthiness to reaffirm her imperviousness. Like when she bought the rat poison, the arsenic. That was over a year after they had begun to say "Poor Emily," and while the two female cousins were visiting her.

"I want some poison," she said to the druggist. She was over thirty then, still a slight woman, though thinner than usual, with cold, haughty black eyes in a face the flesh of which was strained across the temples and about the eyesockets as you imagine a lighthouse-keeper's face ought to look. "I want some poison," she said.

"Yes, Miss Emily. What kind? For rats and such? I'd recom—"   35

"I want the best you have. I don't care what kind."

The druggist named several. "They'll kill anything up to an elephant. But what you want is—"

"Arsenic," Miss Emily said. "Is that a good one?"

"Is . . . arsenic? Yes ma'am. But what you want—"   40

Noblesse oblige: the traditional obligation of the nobility to treat the lower classes with respect and generosity (French). [Editor's note]

†*Jalousies*: slatted window blinds. [Editor's note]

"I want arsenic."

The druggist looked down at her. She looked back at him, erect, her face like a strained flag. "Why, of course," the druggist said. "If that's what you want. But the law requires you to tell what you are going to use it for."

Miss Emily just stared at him, her head tilted back in order to look him eye for eye, until he looked away and went and got the arsenic and wrapped it up. The Negro delivery boy brought her the package; the druggist didn't come back. When she opened the package at home there was written on the box, under the skull and bones: "For rats."

IV

So the next day we all said, "She will kill herself"; and we said it would be the best thing. When she had first begun to be seen with Homer Barron, we had said, "She will marry him." Then we said, "She will persuade him yet," because Homer himself had remarked—he liked men, and it was known that he drank with the younger men in the Elk's Club—that he was not a marrying man. Later we said, "Poor Emily," behind the jalousies as they passed on Sunday afternoon in the glittering buggy, Miss Emily with her head high and Homer Barron with his hat cocked and a cigar in his teeth, reins and whip in a yellow glove.

Then some of the ladies began to say that it was a disgrace to the town and a bad example to the young people. The men did not want to interfere, but at last the ladies forced the Baptist minister—Miss Emily's people were Episcopal—to call upon her. He would never divulge what happened during that interview, but he refused to go back again. The next Sunday they again drove about the streets, and the following day the minister's wife wrote to Miss Emily's relations in Alabama.

So she had blood-kin under her roof again and we sat back to watch developments. At first nothing happened. Then we were sure that they were to be married. We learned that Miss Emily had been to the jeweler's and ordered a man's toilet set in silver, with the letters H. B. on each piece. Two days later we learned that she had bought a complete outfit of men's clothing, including a nightshirt, and we said, "They are married." We were really glad. We were glad because the two female cousins were even more Grierson than Miss Emily had ever been.

So we were not surprised when Homer Barron—the streets had been finished some time since—was gone. We were a little disappointed that there was not a public blowing-off, but we believed that he had gone on to prepare for Miss Emily's coming, or to give her a chance to get rid of the cousins. (By that time it was a cabal, and we were all Miss Emily's allies to help circumvent the cousins.) Sure enough, after another week they departed. And, as we had expected all along, within three days Homer Barron was back in town. A neighbor saw the Negro man admit him at the kitchen door at dusk one evening.

And that was the last we saw of Homer Barron. And of Miss Emily for some time. The Negro man went in and out with the market basket, but the front door remained closed. Now and then we would see her at a window for a moment, as the men did that night when they sprinkled the lime, but for almost six months she did not appear on the streets. Then we knew that this was to be expected too; as if that quality of her father which had thwarted her woman's life so many times had been too virulent and too furious to die.

When we next saw Miss Emily, she had grown fat and her hair was turning gray. During the next few years it grew grayer and grayer until it attained an even pepper-and-salt iron-gray, when it ceased turning. Up to the day of her death at seventy-four it was still that vigorous iron gray, like the hair of an active man.

From that time on her front door remained closed, save for a period of six or seven years, when she was about forty, during which she gave lessons in china-painting. She fitted up a studio in one of the downstairs rooms, where the daughters and grand-daughters of Colonel Sartoris' contemporaries were sent to her with the same regularity and in the same spirit that they were sent on Sundays with a twenty-five cent piece for the collection plate. Meanwhile her taxes had been remitted.

Then the newer generation became the backbone and the spirit of 50 the town, and the painting pupils grew up and fell away and did not send their children to her with boxes of color and tedious brushes and pictures cut from the ladies' magazines. The front door closed upon the last one and remained closed for good. When the town got free postal delivery Miss Emily alone refused to let them fasten the metal numbers above her door and attach a mailbox to it. She would not listen to them.

Daily, monthly, yearly we watched the Negro grow grayer and more stooped, going in and out with the market basket. Each December we sent her a tax notice, which would be returned by the post office a week later, unclaimed. Now and then we would see her in one of the downstairs windows—she had evidently shut up the top floor of the house—like the carven torso of an idol in a niche, looking or not looking at us, we could never tell which. Thus she passed from generation to generation—dear, inescapable, impervious, tranquil, and perverse.

And so she died. Fell ill in the house filled with dust and shadows, with only a doddering Negro man to wait on her. We did not even know she was sick; we had long since given up trying to get any information from the Negro. He talked to no one, probably not even to her, for his voice had grown harsh and rusty, as if from disuse.

She died in one of the downstairs rooms, in a heavy walnut bed with a curtain, her gray head propped on a pillow yellow and moldy with age and lack of sunlight.

V

The Negro met the first of the ladies at the front door and let them in, with their hushed, sibilant voices and their quick, curious glances, and then he disappeared. He walked right through the house and out the back and was not seen again.

The two female cousins came at once. They held the funeral on the second day, with the town coming to look at Miss Emily beneath a mass of bought flowers, with the crayon face of her father musing profoundly above the bier and the ladies sibilant and macabre; and the very old men—some in their brushed Confederate uniforms—on the porch and the lawn, talking of Miss Emily as if she had been a contemporary of theirs, believing that they had danced with her and courted her perhaps, confusing time with its mathematical progression, as the old do, to whom all the past is not a diminishing road, but, instead, a huge meadow which no winter ever quite touches, divided from them now by the narrow bottleneck of the most recent decade of years.

Already we knew that there was one room in that region above stairs which no one had seen in forty years, and which would have to be forced. They waited until Miss Emily was decently in the ground before they opened it.

The violence of breaking down the door seemed to fill this room with pervading dust. A thin, acrid pall as of the tomb seemed to lie everywhere upon this room decked and furnished as for a bridal: upon the valance curtains of faded rose color, upon the rose-shaded lights, upon the dressing table, upon the delicate array of crystal and the man's toilet things backed with tarnished silver, silver so tarnished that the monogram was obscured. Among them lay a collar and tie, as if they had just been removed, which, lifted, left upon the surface a pale crescent in the dust. Upon a chair hung the suit, carefully folded; beneath it the two mute shoes and the discarded socks.

The man himself lay in the bed.

For a long while we just stood there, looking down at the profound and fleshless grin. The body had apparently once lain in the attitude of an embrace, but now the long sleep that outlasts love, that conquers even the grimace of love, had cuckolded him. What was left of him, rotted beneath what was left of the nightshirt, had become inextricable from the bed in which he lay; and upon him and upon the pillow beside him lay that even coating of the patient and biding dust.

Then we noticed that in the second pillow was the indentation of a 60 head. One of us lifted something from it, and leaning forward, that faint and invisible dust dry and acrid in the nostrils, we saw a long strand of iron-gray hair.

RITA DOVE

The First Book

Rita Dove (b. 1952) served as poet laureate of the United States from 1993 to 1995 and as poet laureate of Virginia from 2004 to 2006. Dove is the author of ten books of poetry, a book of short stories, a novel, a book of essays, and a play. She has won numerous awards, including, in 1987, the Pulitzer Prize for her poetry collection Thomas and Beulah. *The following poem was first published in 1999 in Dove's collection* On the Bus with Rosa Parks.

Open it.

Go ahead, it won't bite.
Well . . . maybe a little.

More a nip, like. A tingle.
It's pleasurable, really.   5

You see, it keeps on opening.
You may fall in.

Sure, it's hard to get started;
remember learning to use

knife and fork? Dig in: 10
you'll never reach bottom.

It's not like it's the end of the world—
just the world as you think

you know it.

CHARLOTTE PERKINS GILMAN

The Yellow Wallpaper

Charlotte Perkins Gilman (1860–1935) was a writer, a feminist, and a social activist. She wrote numerous short stories, novels, and works of nonfiction. One of her most famous works is "The Yellow Wallpaper," a fictional account of a woman whose husband insists she is sick and keeps her locked in a room with yellow wallpaper, causing her to lose her grip on reality. It was inspired by Gilman's own experiences with her controlling husband and with the doctor who prescribed a "rest cure" for her postpartum depression, a course of treatment that made her depression exponentially worse. "The Yellow Wallpaper" is often read as a commentary on psychological abuse and on the oppression of women in the late nineteenth century.

IT IS VERY SELDOM that mere ordinary people like John and myself secure ancestral halls for the summer.

A colonial mansion, a hereditary estate, I would say a haunted house, and reach the height of romantic felicity—but that would be asking too much of fate!

Still I will proudly declare that there is something queer about it.

Else, why should it be let so cheaply? And why have stood so long untenanted?

John laughs at me, of course, but one expects that in marriage.   5

John is practical in the extreme. He has no patience with faith, an intense horror of superstition, and he scoffs openly at any talk of things not to be felt and seen and put down in figures.

John is a physician, and *perhaps*—(I would not say it to a living soul, of course, but this is dead paper and a great relief to my mind)—*perhaps* that is one reason I do not get well faster.

You see he does not believe I am sick!

And what can one do?

If a physician of high standing, and one's own husband, assures   10 friends and relatives that there is really nothing the matter with one

but temporary nervous depression—a slight hysterical tendency—what is one to do?

My brother is also a physician, and also of high standing, and he says the same thing.

So I take phosphates or phosphites—whichever it is, and tonics, and journeys, and air, and exercise, and am absolutely forbidden to "work" until I am well again.

Personally, I disagree with their ideas.

Personally, I believe that congenial work, with excitement and change, would do me good.

But what is one to do?   15

I did write for a while in spite of them; but it *does* exhaust me a good deal—having to be so sly about it, or else meet with heavy opposition.

I sometimes fancy that in my condition if I had less opposition and more society and stimulus—but John says the very worst thing I can do is to think about my condition, and I confess it always makes me feel bad.

So I will let it alone and talk about the house.

The most beautiful place! It is quite alone, standing well back from the road, quite three miles from the village. It makes me think of English places that you read about, for there are hedges and walls and gates that lock, and lots of separate little houses for the gardeners and people.

There is a *delicious* garden! I never saw such a garden—large and   20 shady, full of box-bordered paths, and lined with long grape-covered arbors with seats under them.

There were greenhouses, too, but they are all broken now.

There was some legal trouble, I believe, something about the heirs and coheirs; anyhow, the place has been empty for years.

That spoils my ghostliness, I am afraid, but I don't care—there is something strange about the house—I can feel it.

I even said so to John one moonlight evening, but he said what I felt was a *draught*, and shut the window.

I get unreasonably angry with John sometimes. I'm sure I never used   25 to be so sensitive. I think it is due to this nervous condition.

But John says if I feel so, I shall neglect proper self-control; so I take pains to control myself—before him, at least, and that makes me very tired.

I don't like our room a bit. I wanted one downstairs that opened on the piazza and had roses all over the window, and such pretty old-fashioned chintz hangings! but John would not hear of it.

He said there was only one window and not room for two beds, and no near room for him if he took another.

He is very careful and loving, and hardly lets me stir without special direction.

I have a schedule prescription for each hour in the day; he takes all 30 care from me, and so I feel basely ungrateful not to value it more.

He said we came here solely on my account, that I was to have perfect rest and all the air I could get. "Your exercise depends on your strength, my dear," said he, "and your food somewhat on your appetite; but air you can absorb all the time." So we took the nursery at the top of the house.

It is a big, airy room, the whole floor nearly, with windows that look all ways, and air and sunshine galore. It was nursery first and then playroom and gymnasium, I should judge; for the windows are barred for little children, and there are rings and things in the walls.

The paint and paper look as if a boys' school had used it. It is stripped off—the paper—in great patches all around the head of my bed, about as far as I can reach, and in a great place on the other side of the room low down. I never saw a worse paper in my life.

One of those sprawling flamboyant patterns committing every artistic sin.

It is dull enough to confuse the eye in following, pronounced 35 enough to constantly irritate and provoke study, and when you follow the lame uncertain curves for a little distance they suddenly commit suicide—plunge off at outrageous angles, destroy themselves in unheard of contradictions.

The color is repellent, almost revolting; a smoldering unclean yellow, strangely faded by the slow-turning sunlight.

It is a dull yet lurid orange in some places, a sickly sulphur tint in others.

academic literacies / rhetorical situations / genres / fields / processes / strategies / research MLA / APA / media / design / readings / handbook

No wonder the children hated it! I should hate it myself if I had to live in this room long.

There comes John, and I must put this away—he hates to have me write a word.

We have been here two weeks, and I haven't felt like writing before, 40 since that first day.

I am sitting by the window now, up in this atrocious nursery, and there is nothing to hinder my writing as much as I please, save lack of strength.

John is away all day, and even some nights when his cases are serious.

I am glad my case is not serious!

But these nervous troubles are dreadfully depressing.

John does not know how much I really suffer. He knows there is no 45 *reason* to suffer, and that satisfies him.

Of course it is only nervousness. It does weigh on me so not to do my duty in any way!

I meant to be such a help to John, such a real rest and comfort, and here I am a comparative burden already!

Nobody would believe what an effort it is to do what little I am able—to dress and entertain, and order things.

It is fortunate Mary is so good with the baby. Such a dear baby!

And yet I *cannot* be with him, it makes me so nervous. 50

I suppose John never was nervous in his life. He laughs at me so about this wallpaper!

At first he meant to repaper the room, but afterwards he said that I was letting it get the better of me, and that nothing was worse for a nervous patient than to give way to such fancies.

He said that after the wallpaper was changed it would be the heavy bedstead, and then the barred windows, and then that gate at the head of the stairs, and so on.

"You know the place is doing you good," he said, "and really, dear, I don't care to renovate the house just for a three months' rental."

"Then do let us go downstairs," I said, "there are such pretty rooms 55 there."

Then he took me in his arms and called me a blessed little goose, and said he would go down to the cellar, if I wished, and have it white-washed into the bargain.

But he is right enough about the beds and windows and things.

It is an airy and comfortable room as any one need wish, and, of course, I would not be so silly as to make him uncomfortable just for a whim.

I'm really getting quite fond of the big room, all but that horrid paper.

Out of one window I can see the garden, those mysterious deep-shaded arbors, the riotous old-fashioned flowers, and bushes and gnarly trees.   60

Out of another I get a lovely view of the bay and a little private wharf belonging to the estate. There is a beautiful shaded lane that runs down there from the house. I always fancy I see people walking in these numerous paths and arbors, but John has cautioned me not to give way to fancy in the least. He says that with my imaginative power and habit of story-making, a nervous weakness like mine is sure to lead to all manner of excited fancies, and that I ought to use my will and good sense to check the tendency. So I try.

I think sometimes that if I were only well enough to write a little it would relieve the press of ideas and rest me.

But I find I get pretty tired when I try.

It is so discouraging not to have any advice and companionship about my work. When I get really well, John says we will ask Cousin Henry and Julia down for a long visit; but he says he would as soon put fireworks in my pillowcase as to let me have those stimulating people about now.

I wish I could get well faster.   65

But I must not think about that. This paper looks to me as if it *knew* what a vicious influence it had!

There is a recurrent spot where the pattern lolls like a broken neck and two bulbous eyes stare at you upside down.

I get positively angry with the impertinence of it and the everlasting-ness. Up and down and sideways they crawl, and those absurd, unblink-ing eyes are everywhere. There is one place where two breadths didn't match, and the eyes go all up and down the line, one a little higher than the other.

I never saw so much expression in an inanimate thing before, and we all know how much expression they have! I used to lie awake as a child and get more entertainment and terror out of blank walls and plain furniture than most children could find in a toy store.

I remember what a kindly wink the knobs of our big, old bureau 70 used to have, and there was one chair that always seemed like a strong friend.

I used to feel that if any of the other things looked too fierce I could always hop into that chair and be safe.

The furniture in this room is no worse than inharmonious, however, for we had to bring it all from downstairs. I suppose when this was used as a playroom they had to take the nursery things out, and no wonder! I never saw such ravages as the children have made here.

The wallpaper, as I said before, is torn off in spots, and it sticketh closer than a brother—they must have had perseverance as well as hatred.

Then the floor is scratched and gouged and splintered, the plaster itself is dug out here and there, and this great heavy bed which is all we found in the room, looks as if it had been through the wars.

But I don't mind it a bit—only the paper.   75

There comes John's sister. Such a dear girl as she is, and so careful of me! I must not let her find me writing.

She is a perfect and enthusiastic housekeeper, and hopes for no better profession. I verily believe she thinks it is the writing which made me sick!

But I can write when she is out, and see her a long way off from these windows.

There is one that commands the road, a lovely shaded winding road, and one that just looks off over the country. A lovely country, too, full of great elms and velvet meadows.

This wallpaper has a kind of sub-pattern in a different shade, a 80 particularly irritating one, for you can only see it in certain lights, and not clearly then.

But in the places where it isn't faded and where the sun is just so—I can see a strange, provoking, formless sort of figure, that seems to skulk about behind that silly and conspicuous front design.

There's sister on the stairs!

Well, the Fourth of July is over! The people are gone and I am tired out. John thought it might do me good to see a little company, so we just had mother and Nellie and the children down for a week.

Of course I didn't do a thing. Jennie sees to everything now.

But it tired me all the same.   85

John says if I don't pick up faster he shall send me to Weir Mitchell in the fall.

But I don't want to go there at all. I had a friend who was in his hands once, and she says he is just like John and my brother, only more so!

Besides, it is such an undertaking to go so far.

I don't feel as if it was worthwhile to turn my hand over for anything, and I'm getting dreadfully fretful and querulous.

I cry at nothing, and cry most of the time.   90

Of course I don't when John is here, or anybody else, but when I am alone.

And I am alone a good deal just now. John is kept in town very often by serious cases, and Jennie is good and lets me alone when I want her to.

So I walk a little in the garden or down that lovely lane, sit on the porch under the roses, and lie down up here a good deal.

I'm getting really fond of the room in spite of the wallpaper. Perhaps *because* of the wallpaper.

It dwells in my mind so!   95

I lie here on this great immovable bed—it is nailed down, I believe—and follow that pattern about by the hour. It is as good as gymnastics, I assure you. I start, we'll say, at the bottom, down in the corner over there where it has not been touched, and I determine for the thousandth time that I *will* follow that pointless pattern to some sort of a conclusion.

academic literacies · rhetorical situations · genres · fields · processes · strategies · research MLA / APA · media / design · readings · handbook

I know a little of the principle of design, and I know this thing was not arranged on any laws of radiation, or alternation, or repetition, or symmetry, or anything else that I ever heard of.

It is repeated, of course, by the breadths, but not otherwise.

Looked at in one way each breadth stands alone, the bloated curves and flourishes—a kind of "debased Romanesque" with *delirium tremens*—go waddling up and down in isolated columns of fatuity.

But, on the other hand, they connect diagonally, and the sprawling outlines run off in great slanting waves of optic horror, like a lot of wallowing seaweeds in full chase. 100

The whole thing goes horizontally, too, at least it seems so, and I exhaust myself in trying to distinguish the order of its going in that direction.

They have used a horizontal breadth for a frieze, and that adds wonderfully to the confusion.

There is one end of the room where it is almost intact, and there, when the crosslights fade and the low sun shines directly upon it, I can almost fancy radiation after all—the interminable grotesques seem to form around a common center and rush off in headlong plunges of equal distraction.

It makes me tired to follow it. I will take a nap I guess.

I don't know why I should write this. 105

I don't want to.

I don't feel able.

And I know John would think it absurd. But I *must* say what I feel and think in some way—it is such a relief!

But the effort is getting to be greater than the relief.

Half the time now I am awfully lazy, and lie down ever so much. 110

John says I musn't lose my strength, and has me take cod liver oil and lots of tonics and things, to say nothing of ale and wine and rare meat.

Dear John! He loves me very dearly, and hates to have me sick. I tried to have a real earnest reasonable talk with him the other day, and tell him how I wish he would let me go and make a visit to Cousin Henry and Julia.

But he said I wasn't able to go, nor able to stand it after I got there; and I did not make out a very good case for myself, for I was crying before I had finished.

It is getting to be a great effort for me to think straight. Just this nervous weakness I suppose.

And dear John gathered me up in his arms, and just carried me 115 upstairs and laid me on the bed, and sat by me and read to me till it tired my head.

He said I was his darling and his comfort and all he had, and that I must take care of myself for his sake, and keep well.

He says no one but myself can help me out of it, that I must use my will and self-control and not let any silly fancies run away with me.

There's one comfort, the baby is well and happy, and does not have to occupy this nursery with the horrid wallpaper.

If we had not used it, that blessed child would have! What a fortunate escape! Why, I wouldn't have a child of mine, an impressionable little thing, live in such a room for worlds.

I never thought of it before, but it is lucky that John kept me here 120 after all, I can stand it so much easier than a baby, you see.

Of course I never mention it to them any more—I am too wise— but I keep watch of it all the same.

There are things in that paper that nobody knows but me, or ever will.

Behind that outside pattern the dim shapes get clearer every day.

It is always the same shape, only very numerous.

And it is like a woman stooping down and creeping about behind 125 that pattern. I don't like it a bit. I wonder—I begin to think—I wish John would take me away from here!

It is so hard to talk with John about my case, because he is so wise, and because he loves me so.

But I tried it last night.

It was moonlight. The moon shines in all around just as the sun does.

I hate to see it sometimes, it creeps so slowly, and always comes in by one window or another.

academic literacies   rhetorical situations   genres   fields   processes   strategies   research MLA / APA   media / design   readings   handbook

John was asleep and I hated to waken him, so I kept still and watched 130
the moonlight on that undulating wallpaper till I felt creepy.

The faint figure behind seemed to shake the pattern, just as if she
wanted to get out.

I got up softly and went to feel and see if the paper *did* move, and
when I came back John was awake.

"What is it, little girl?" he said. "Don't go walking about like that—
you'll get cold."

I thought it was a good time to talk, so I told him that I really was
not gaining here, and that I wished he would take me away.

"Why darling!" said he, "our lease will be up in three weeks, and I 135
can't see how to leave before.

"The repairs are not done at home, and I cannot possibly leave town
just now. Of course if you were in any danger, I could and would, but
you really are better, dear, whether you can see it or not. I am a doctor,
dear, and I know. You are gaining flesh and color, your appetite is better,
I feel really much easier about you."

"I don't weigh a bit more," said I, "nor as much; and my appetite
may be better in the evening when you are here, but it is worse in the
morning when you are away!"

"Bless her little heart!" said he with a big hug, "she shall be as sick
as she pleases! But now let's improve the shining hours by going to sleep,
and talk about it in the morning!"

"And you won't go away?" I asked gloomily.

"Why, how can I, dear? It is only three weeks more and then we 140
will take a nice little trip of a few days while Jennie is getting the house
ready. Really, dear, you are better!"

"Better in body perhaps—" I began, and stopped short, for he sat
up straight and looked at me with such a stern, reproachful look that I
could not say another word.

"My darling," said he, "I beg of you, for my sake and for our child's
sake, as well as for your own, that you will never for one instant let that
idea enter your mind! There is nothing so dangerous, so fascinating, to
a temperament like yours. It is a false and foolish fancy. Can you not
trust me as a physician when I tell you so?"

So of course I said no more on that score, and we went to sleep before long. He thought I was asleep first, but I wasn't, and lay there for hours trying to decide whether that front pattern and the back pattern really did move together or separately.

On a pattern like this, by daylight, there is a lack of sequence, a defiance of law, that is a constant irritant to a normal mind.

The color is hideous enough, and unreliable enough, and infuriating enough, but the pattern is torturing. 145

You think you have mastered it, but just as you get well under way in following, it turns a back-somersault and there you are. It slaps you in the face, knocks you down, and tramples upon you. It is like a bad dream.

The outside pattern is a florid arabesque, reminding one of a fungus. If you can imagine a toadstool in joints, an interminable string of toadstools, budding and sprouting in endless convolutions—why, that is something like it.

That is, sometimes!

There is one marked peculiarity about this paper, a thing nobody seems to notice but myself, and that is that it changes as the light changes.

When the sun shoots in through the east window—I always watch for that first long, straight ray—it changes so quickly that I never can quite believe it. 150

That is why I watch it always.

By moonlight—the moon shines in all night when there is a moon—I wouldn't know it was the same paper.

At night in any kind of light, in twilight, candlelight, lamplight, and worst of all by moonlight, it becomes bars! The outside pattern I mean, and the woman behind it is as plain as can be.

I didn't realize for a long time what the thing was that showed behind, that dim subpattern, but now I am quite sure it is a woman.

By daylight she is subdued, quiet. I fancy it is the pattern that keeps her so still. It is so puzzling. It keeps me quiet by the hour. 155

I lie down ever so much now. John says it is good for me, and to sleep all I can. Indeed he started the habit by making me lie down for an hour after each meal.

It is a very bad habit I am convinced, for you see I don't sleep.

And that cultivates deceit, for I don't tell them I'm awake—O no!

The fact is I am getting a little afraid of John.

He seems very queer sometimes, and even Jennie has an inexplicable look. 160

It strikes me occasionally, just as a scientific hypothesis—that perhaps it is the paper!

I have watched John when he did not know I was looking, and come into the room suddenly on the most innocent excuses, and I've caught him several times *looking at the paper*! And Jennie too. I caught Jennie with her hand on it once.

She didn't know I was in the room, and when I asked her in a quiet, a very quiet voice, with the most restrained manner possible, what she was doing with the paper—she turned around as if she had been caught stealing, and looked quite angry—asked me why I should frighten her so!

Then she said that the paper stained everything it touched, that she had found yellow smooches on all my clothes and John's, and she wished we would be more careful!

Did not that sound innocent? But I know she was studying that 165 pattern, and I am determined that nobody shall find it out but myself!

Life is very much more exciting now than it used to be. You see I have something more to expect, to look forward to, to watch. I really do eat better, and am more quiet than I was.

John is so pleased to see me improve! He laughed a little the other day, and said I seemed to be flourishing in spite of my wallpaper.

I turned it off with a laugh. I had no intention of telling him it was *because* of the wallpaper—he would make fun of me. He might even want to take me away.

I don't want to leave now until I have found it out. There is a week more, and I think that will be enough.

I'm feeling ever so much better! I don't sleep much at night, for it is 170 so interesting to watch developments; but I sleep a good deal in the daytime.

In the daytime it is tiresome and perplexing.

There are always new shoots on the fungus, and new shades of yellow all over it. I cannot keep count of them, though I have tried conscientiously.

It is the strangest yellow, that wallpaper! It makes me think of all the yellow things I ever saw—not beautiful ones like buttercups, but old, foul, bad yellow things.

But there is something else about that paper—the smell! I noticed it the moment we came into the room, but with so much air and sun it was not bad. Now we have had a week of fog and rain, and whether the windows are open or not, the smell is here.

It creeps all over the house.

I find it hovering in the dining room, skulking in the parlor, hiding in the hall, lying in wait for me on the stairs.

It gets into my hair.

Even when I go to ride, if I turn my head suddenly and surprise it— there is that smell!

Such a peculiar odor, too! I have spent hours in trying to analyze it, to find what it smelled like.

It is not bad—at first, and very gentle, but quite the subtlest, most enduring odor I ever met.

In this damp weather it is awful, I wake up in the night and find it hanging over me.

It used to disturb me at first. I thought seriously of burning the house—to reach the smell.

But now I am used to it. The only thing I can think of that it is like is the *color* of the paper! A yellow smell.

There is a very funny mark on this wall, low down, near the mopboard. A streak that runs round the room. It goes behind every piece of furniture, except the bed, a long, straight, even *smooch*, as if it had been rubbed over and over.

I wonder how it was done and who did it, and what they did it for. Round and round and round—round and round and round—it makes me dizzy!

I really have discovered something at last.

academic literacies · rhetorical situations · genres · fields · processes · strategies · research MLA / APA · media / design · readings · handbook

Through watching so much at night, when it changes so, I have finally found out. The front pattern *does* move—and no wonder! The woman behind shakes it!

Sometimes I think there are a great many women behind, and sometimes only one, and she crawls around fast, and her crawling shakes it all over.

Then in the very bright spots she keeps still, and in the very shady spots she just takes hold of the bars and shakes them hard.

And she is all the time trying to climb through. But nobody could 190 climb through that pattern—it strangles so; I think that is why it has so many heads.

They get through, and then the pattern strangles them off and turns them upside down, and makes their eyes white!

If those heads were covered or taken off it would not be half so bad.

I think that woman gets out in the daytime!

And I'll tell you why—privately—I've seen her!

I can see her out of every one of my windows!   195

It is the same woman, I know, for she is always creeping, and most women do not creep by daylight.

I see her in that long shaded lane, creeping up and down. I see her in those dark grape arbors, creeping all around the garden.

I see her on that long road under the trees, creeping along, and when a carriage comes she hides under the blackberry vines.

I don't blame her a bit. It must be very humiliating to be caught creeping by daylight!

I always lock the door when I creep by daylight. I can't do it at night, 200 for I know John would suspect something at once.

And John is so queer now, that I don't want to irritate him. I wish he would take another room! Besides, I don't want anybody to get that woman out at night but myself.

I often wonder if I could see her out of all the windows at once.

But, turn as fast as I can, I can only see out of one at one time.

And though I always see her, she *may* be able to creep faster than I can turn!

I have watched her sometimes away off in the open country, creep- 205
ing as fast as a cloud shadow in a high wind.

If only that top pattern could be gotten off from the under one! I mean
to try it, little by little.

I have found out another funny thing, but I shan't tell it this time!
It does not do to trust people too much.

There are only two more days to get this paper off, and I believe
John is beginning to notice. I don't like the look in his eyes.

And I heard him ask Jennie a lot of professional questions about
me. She had a very good report to give.

She said I slept a good deal in the daytime. 210

John knows I don't sleep very well at night, for all I'm so quiet!

He asked me all sorts of questions, too, and pretended to be very
loving and kind.

As if I couldn't see through him!

Still, I don't wonder he acts so, sleeping under this paper for three
months.

It only interests me, but I feel sure John and Jennie are secretly 215
affected by it.

Hurrah! This is the last day, but it is enough. John is to stay in town over
night, and won't be out until this evening.

Jennie wanted to sleep with me—the sly thing! but I told her I should
undoubtedly rest better for a night all alone.

That was clever, for really I wasn't alone a bit! As soon as it was
moonlight and that poor thing began to crawl and shake the pattern, I
got up and ran to help her.

I pulled and she shook, I shook and she pulled, and before morning
we had peeled off yards of that paper.

A strip about as high as my head and half around the room. 220

And then when the sun came and that awful pattern began to laugh
at me, I declared I would finish it today!

We go away tomorrow, and they are moving all my furniture down
again to leave things as they were before.

Jennie looked at the wall in amazement, but I told her merrily that I did it out of pure spite at the vicious thing.

She laughed and said she wouldn't mind doing it herself, but I must not get tired.

How she betrayed herself that time! 225

But I am here, and no person touches this paper but me—not *alive*!

She tried to get me out of the room—it was too patent! But I said it was so quiet and empty and clean now that I believed I would lie down again and sleep all I could; and not to wake me even for dinner—I would call when I woke.

So now she is gone, and the servants are gone, and the things are gone, and there is nothing left but that great bedstead nailed down, with the canvas mattress we found on it.

We shall sleep downstairs tonight, and take the boat home tomorrow.

I quite enjoy the room, now it is bare again. 230

How those children did tear about here!

This bedstead is fairly gnawed!

But I must get to work.

I have locked the door and thrown the key down into the front path.

I don't want to go out, and I don't want to have anybody come in, 235 till John comes.

I want to astonish him.

I've got a rope up here that even Jennie did not find. If that woman does get out, and tries to get away, I can tie her!

But I forgot I could not reach far without anything to stand on!

This bed will *not* move!

I tried to lift and push it until I was lame, and then I got so angry I 240 bit off a little piece at one corner—but it hurt my teeth.

Then I peeled off all the paper I could reach standing on the floor. It sticks horribly and the pattern just enjoys it! All those strangled heads and bulbous eyes and waddling fungus growths just shriek with derision!

I am getting angry enough to do something desperate. To jump out of the window would be admirable exercise, but the bars are too strong even to try.

Besides I wouldn't do it. Of course not. I know well enough that a step like that is improper and might be misconstrued.

I don't like to *look* out of the windows even—there are so many of those creeping women, and they creep so fast.

I wonder if they all come out of that wallpaper as I did?   245

But I am securely fastened now by my well-hidden rope—you don't get *me* out in the road there!

I suppose I shall have to get back behind the pattern when it comes night, and that is hard!

It is so pleasant to be out in this great room and creep around as I please!

I don't want to go outside. I won't, even if Jennie asks me to.

For outside you have to creep on the ground, and everything is green   250
instead of yellow.

But here I can creep smoothly on the floor, and my shoulder just fits in that long smooch around the wall, so I cannot lose my way.

Why there's John at the door!

It is no use, young man, you can't open it!

How he does call and pound!

Now he's crying for an axe.   255

It would be a shame to break down that beautiful door!

"John dear!" said I in the gentlest voice, "the key is down by the front steps, under a plantain leaf!"

That silenced him for a few moments.

Then he said—very quietly indeed, "Open the door, my darling!"

"I can't," said I. "The key is down by the front door under a plantain   260
leaf!"

And then I said it again, several times, very gently and slowly, and said it so often that he had to go and see, and he got it of course, and came in. He stopped short by the door.

"What is the matter?" he cried. "For God's sake, what are you doing!"

I kept on creeping just the same, but I looked at him over my shoulder.

"I've got out at last," said I, "in spite of you and Jane. And I've pulled off most of the paper, so you can't put me back!"

Now why should that man have fainted? But he did, and right across   265
my path by the wall, so that I had to creep over him every time!

LANGSTON HUGHES

Theme for English B

Langston Hughes (1901–67) was a social activist and a prolific writer known for his poems, novels, and plays. He was one of the most influential people in the Harlem Renaissance in the 1920s and was also one of the first to write jazz poetry, a kind of poetry that uses jazz-like rhythms or recreates the improvisational feel of jazz. The following poem was first published in 1949 in the literary magazine Common Ground.

The instructor said,

> *Go home and write*
> *a page tonight.*
> *And let that page come out of you—*
> *Then, it will be true.*   5

I wonder if it's that simple?
I am twenty-two, colored, born in Winston-Salem.
I went to school there, then Durham, then here
to this college on the hill above Harlem.
I am the only colored student in my class.   10
The steps from the hill lead down into Harlem,
through a park, then I cross St. Nicholas,
Eighth Avenue, Seventh, and I come to the Y,
the Harlem Branch Y, where I take the elevator
up to my room, sit down, and write this page: 15

It's not easy to know what is true for you or me
at twenty-two, my age. But I guess I'm what
I feel and see and hear. Harlem, I hear you:
hear you, hear me—we two—you, me, talk on this page.
(I hear New York, too.) Me—who?   20

Well, I like to eat, sleep, drink, and be in love.
I like to work, read, learn, and understand life.
I like a pipe for a Christmas present,
or records—Bessie, bop, or Bach.
I guess being colored doesn't make me *not* like   25
the same things other folks like who are other races.
So will my page be colored that I write?
Being me, it will not be white.
But it will be
a part of you, instructor.   30
You are white—
yet a part of me, as I am a part of you.
That's American.
Sometimes perhaps you don't want to be a part of me.
Nor do I often want to be a part of you.   35
But we are, that's true!
As I learn from you,
I guess you learn from me—
although you're older—and white—
and somewhat more free.   40

This is my page for English B.

academic literacies   rhetorical situations   genres   fields   processes   strategies   research MLA / APA   media / design   readings   handbook

EMILY DICKINSON
A word is dead

Emily Dickinson (1830–86) wrote almost 1,800 poems but during her lifetime published only a few of them, remaining mostly secluded in her family home in Amherst, Massachusetts, and little known to the public. Through her family's and friends' efforts after her death, her work became widely read and celebrated, and today she is considered one of the most prominent nineteenth-century American poets. "A word is dead" was first published in 1894.

A word is dead
When it is said,
    Some say.
I say it just
Begins to live   5
    That day.

67 Memoirs

academic literacies

rhetorical situations

genres

fields

processes

strategies

research MLA / APA

media / design

readings

handbook

DAVID SEDARIS

Us and Them

Humorist David Sedaris (b. 1956) is the author of several collections of personal essays and stories, including Squirrel Seeks Chipmunk: A Modest Bestiary *(2010),* Let's Explore Diabetes with Owls *(2013),* Calypso *(2018), and* Theft by Finding: Diaries, 1977–2002 *(2017). A frequent contributor to the* New Yorker, *he is also a playwright whose works include* SantaLand Diaries *and* Seasons Greetings *(1998), as well as works coauthored with his sister Amy Sedaris. The following essay comes from Sedaris's book-length memoir* Dress Your Family in Corduroy and Denim *(2005).*

W**HEN MY FAMILY FIRST MOVED** to North Carolina, we lived in a rented house three blocks from the school where I would begin the third grade. My mother made friends with one of the neighbors, but one seemed enough for her. Within a year we would move again and, as she explained, there wasn't much point in getting too close to people we would have to say good-bye to. Our next house was less than a mile away, and the short journey would hardly merit tears or even good-byes, for that matter. It was more of a "see you later" situation, but still I adopted my mother's attitude, as it allowed me to pretend that not making friends was a conscious choice. I could if I wanted to. It just wasn't the right time.

Back in New York State, we had lived in the country, with no sidewalks or streetlights; you could leave the house and still be alone. But here, when you looked out the window, you saw other houses, and people inside those houses. I hoped that in walking around after dark I might witness a murder, but for the most part our neighbors just sat in their living rooms, watching TV. The only place that seemed truly different was owned by a man named Mr. Tomkey, who did not believe in television. This was told to us by our mother's friend, who dropped by one afternoon with a basketful of okra. The woman did not editorialize—rather, she just presented her information, leaving her listener to make of it what she might. Had my mother said, "That's the craziest thing I've ever heard in my life," I assume that the friend would have agreed, and had she said, "Three cheers for Mr. Tomkey," the friend likely would have agreed as well. It was a kind of test, as was the okra.

To say that you did not believe in television was different from saying that you did not care for it. Belief implied that television had a master plan and that you were against it. It also suggested that you thought too much. When my mother reported that Mr. Tomkey did not believe in television, my father said, "Well, good for him. I don't know that I believe in it, either."

"That's exactly how I feel," my mother said, and then my parents watched the news, and whatever came on after the news.

Word spread that Mr. Tomkey did not own a television, and you began 5 hearing that while this was all very well and good, it was unfair of him to inflict his beliefs upon others, specifically his innocent wife and children. It was speculated that just as the blind man develops a keener sense of hearing, the family must somehow compensate for their loss. "Maybe they read," my mother's friend said. "Maybe they listen to the radio, but you can bet your boots they're doing *something*."

I wanted to know what this something was, and so I began peering through the Tomkeys' windows. During the day I'd stand across the street from their house, acting as though I were waiting for someone, and at night, when the view was better and I had less chance of being discovered, I would creep into their yard and hide in the bushes beside their fence.

Because they had no TV, the Tomkeys were forced to talk during dinner. They had no idea how puny their lives were, and so they were not ashamed that a camera would have found them uninteresting. They did not know what attractive was or what dinner was supposed to look like or even what time people were supposed to eat. Sometimes they wouldn't sit down until eight o'clock, long after everyone else had finished doing the dishes. During the meal, Mr. Tomkey would occasionally pound the table and point at his children with a fork, but the moment he finished, everyone would start laughing. I got the idea that he was imitating someone else, and wondered if he spied on us while we were eating.

When fall arrived and school began, I saw the Tomkey children marching up the hill with paper sacks in their hands. The son was one grade lower than me, and the daughter was one grade higher. We never spoke, but I'd pass them in the halls from time to time and attempt to view the world through their eyes. What must it be like to be so ignorant and alone? Could a normal person even imagine it? Staring at an Elmer Fudd lunch box, I tried to divorce myself from everything I already knew: Elmer's inability to pronounce the letter r, his constant pursuit of an intelligent and considerably more famous rabbit. I tried to think of him as just a drawing, but it was impossible to separate him from his celebrity.

One day in class a boy named William began to write the wrong answer on the blackboard, and our teacher flailed her arms, saying, "Warning, Will. Danger, danger." Her voice was synthetic and void of emotion, and we laughed, knowing that she was imitating the robot in a weekly show about a family who lived in outer space. The Tomkeys, though, would have thought she was having a heart attack. It occurred to me that they needed a guide, someone who could accompany them through the course of an average day and point out all the things they were unable to understand. I could have done it on weekends, but friendship would have taken away their mystery and interfered with the good feeling I got from pitying them. So I kept my distance.

In early October the Tomkeys bought a boat, and everyone seemed greatly 10 relieved, especially my mother's friend, who noted that the motor was definitely secondhand. It was reported that Mr. Tomkey's father-in-law owned a house on the lake and had invited the family to use it whenever they liked. This explained why they were gone all weekend, but it did not make their absences any easier to bear. I felt as if my favorite show had been canceled.

Halloween fell on a Saturday that year, and by the time my mother took us to the store, all the good costumes were gone. My sisters dressed as witches and I went as a hobo. I'd looked forward to going in disguise to the Tomkey's door, but they were off at the lake, and their house was dark. Before leaving, they had left a coffee can full of gumdrops on the front porch, alongside a sign reading DON'T BE GREEDY. In terms of Halloween candy, individual gumdrops were just about as low as you could get. This was evidenced by the large number of them floating in an adjacent dog bowl. It was disgusting to think that this was what a gumdrop might look like in your stomach, and it was insulting to be told not to take too much of something you didn't really want in the first place. "Who do these Tomkeys think they are?" my sister Lisa said.

The night after Halloween, we were sitting around watching TV when the doorbell rang. Visitors were infrequent at our house, so while my father stayed behind, my mother, sisters, and I ran downstairs in a group, opening the door to discover the entire Tomkey family on our front stoop. The parents looked as they always had, but the son and daughter were dressed in costumes—she as a ballerina and he as some kind of a rodent with terry-cloth ears and a tail made from what looked to be an extension cord. It seemed they had spent the previous evening isolated at the lake and had missed the opportunity to observe Halloween. "So, well, I guess we're trick-or-treating *now*, if that's okay," Mr. Tomkey said.

I attributed their behavior to the fact that they didn't have a TV, but television didn't teach you everything. Asking for candy on Halloween was called trick-or-treating, but asking for candy on November first was called begging, and it made people uncomfortable. This was one of the things you were supposed to learn simply by being alive, and it angered me that the Tomkeys did not understand it.

"Why of course it's not too late," my mother said. "Kids, why don't you . . . run and get . . . the candy."

"But the candy is gone," my sister Gretchen said. "You gave it away last night." 15

"Not *that* candy," my mother said. "The other candy. Why don't you run and go get it?"

"You mean *our* candy?" Lisa said. "The candy that we *earned*?"

This was exactly what our mother was talking about, but she didn't want to say this in front of the Tomkeys. In order to spare their feelings, she wanted them to believe that we always kept a bucket of candy lying around the house, just waiting for someone to knock on the door and ask for it. "Go on, now," she said. "Hurry up."

academic literacies · rhetorical situations · genres · fields · processes · strategies · research MLA / APA · media / design · readings · handbook

My room was situated right off the foyer, and if the Tomkeys had looked in that direction, they could have seen my bed and the brown paper bag marked MY CANDY. KEEP OUT. I didn't want them to know how much I had, and so I went into my room and shut the door behind me. Then I closed the curtains and emptied my bag onto the bed, searching for whatever was the crummiest. All my life chocolate has made me ill. I don't know if I'm allergic or what, but even the smallest amount leaves me with a blinding headache. Eventually, I learned to stay away from it, but as a child I refused to be left out. The brownies were eaten, and when the pounding began I would blame the grape juice or my mother's cigarette smoke or the tightness of my glasses—anything but the chocolate. My candy bars were poison but they were brand-name, and so I put them in pile no. 1, which definitely would not go to the Tomkeys.

Out in the hallway I could hear my mother straining for something 20 to talk about. "A boat!" she said. "That sounds marvelous. Can you just drive it right into the water?"

"Actually, we have a trailer," Mr. Tomkey said. "So what we do is back it into the lake."

"Oh, a trailer. What kind is it?"

"Well, it's a *boat* trailer," Mr. Tomkey said.

"Right, but is it wooden, or you know . . . I guess what I'm asking is what *style* trailer do you have?"

Behind my mother's words were two messages. The first and most 25 obvious was "Yes, I am talking about boat trailers, but also I am dying." The second, meant only for my sisters and me, was "If you do not immediately step forward with that candy, you will never again experience freedom, happiness, or the possibility of my warm embrace."

I knew that it was just a matter of time before she came into my room and started collecting the candy herself, grabbing indiscriminately, with no regard to my rating system. Had I been thinking straight, I would have hidden the most valuable items in my dresser drawer, but instead, panicked by the thought of her hand on my doorknob, I tore off the wrappers and began cramming the candy bars into my mouth, desperately, like someone in a contest. Most were miniature, which made them easier to accommodate, but still there was only so much room, and it was hard to chew and fit more in at the same time. The headache began immediately, and I chalked it up to tension.

My mother told the Tomkeys she needed to check on something, and then she opened the door and stuck her head inside my room. "What the *hell* are you doing?" she whispered, but my mouth was too full to answer. "I'll just be a moment," she called, and as she closed the door behind her and moved toward my bed, I began breaking the wax lips and candy necklaces pulled from pile no. 2. These were the second-best things I had received, and while it hurt to destroy them, it would have hurt even more to give them away. I had just started to mutilate a miniature box of Red Hots when my mother pried them from my hands, accidentally finishing the job for me. BB-size pellets clattered onto the floor, and as I followed them with my eyes, she snatched up a roll of Necco wafers.

"Not those," I pleaded, but rather than words, my mouth expelled chocolate, chewed chocolate, which fell onto the sleeve of her sweater. "Not those. Not those."

She shook her arm, and the mound of chocolate dropped like a horrible turd upon my bedspread. "You should look at yourself," she said. "I mean, *really* look at yourself."

Along with the Necco wafers she took several Tootsie pops and half a dozen caramels wrapped in cellophane. I heard her apologize to the Tomkeys for her absence, and then I heard my candy hitting the bottom of their bags. 30

"What do you say?" Mrs. Tomkey asked.

And the children answered, "Thank you."

While I was in trouble for not bringing my candy sooner, my sisters were in more trouble for not bringing theirs at all. We spent the early part of the evening in our rooms, then one by one we eased our way back upstairs, and joined our parents in front of the TV. I was the last to arrive, and took a seat on the floor beside the sofa. The show was a Western, and even if my head had not been throbbing, I doubt I would have had the wherewithal to follow it. A posse of outlaws crested a rocky hilltop, squinting at a flurry of dust advancing from the horizon,

academic literacies   rhetorical situations   genres   fields   processes   strategies   research MLA / APA   media / design   readings   handbook

and I thought again of the Tomkeys and of how alone and out of place they had looked in their dopey costumes. "What was up with that kid's tail?" I asked.

"Shhhh," my family said.

For months I had protected and watched over these people, but now, with one stupid act, they had turned my pity into something hard and ugly. The shift wasn't gradual, but immediate, and it provoked an uncomfortable feeling of loss. We hadn't been friends, the Tomkeys and I, but still I had given them the gift of my curiosity. Wondering about the Tomkey family had made me feel generous, but now I would have to shift gears and find pleasure in hating them. The only alternative was to do as my mother had instructed and take a good look at myself. This was an old trick, designed to turn one's hatred inward, and while I was determined not to fall for it, it was hard to shake the mental picture snapped by her suggestion: here is a boy sitting on a bed, his mouth smeared with chocolate. He's a human being, but also he's a pig, surrounded by trash and gorging himself so that others may be denied. Were this the only image in the world, you'd be forced to give it your full attention, but fortunately there were others. This stagecoach, for instance, coming round the bend with a cargo of gold. This shiny new Mustang convertible. This teenage girl, her hair a beautiful mane, sipping Pepsi through a straw, one picture after another, on and on until the news, and whatever came on after the news.

Engaging with the Text

1. David Sedaris **TITLES** his essay "Us and Them." Whom does this title refer to? Whom are we meant to sympathize with—"us" or "them"? How do you know?

◆ 386–87

2. Successful memoirs tell a **GOOD STORY**. Do you think "Us and Them" meets that requirement? Why or why not? Refer to specific details from the text in your response.

▲ 228

3. Sedaris describes two handwritten signs from Halloween night. The first is attached to a "coffee can full of gumdrops" telling trick or treaters "DON'T BE GREEDY." The second graces young Sedaris's bag of candy: "MY CANDY. KEEP OUT." What significance do these two signs have in the story? What do they tell us about Sedaris?

66–68 4. How would you characterize Sedaris's **STANCE**? What specific passages indicate his attitude about the events he recalls?

5. *For Writing.* Recall a time when a person or event taught you something about yourself, something that perhaps you could not fully 224–32 understand until now. Write a **MEMOIR** that describes the person or 228 narrates the event. Include **VIVID DETAIL** and be sure to make clear 229 what **SIGNIFICANCE** the person or event had in your life.

* academic literacies
■ rhetorical situations
▲ genres
⬟ fields
○ processes
◆ strategies
● research MLA / APA
□ media / design
📖 readings
⟋ handbook

ANDRE DUBUS III

My Father Was a Writer

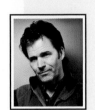

Andre Dubus III (b. 1959), who teaches at the University of Massachusetts Lowell, is a 2012 recipient of the American Academy of Arts and Letters Award in Literature. He is the author of six works of fiction, most recently Gone So Long (2018). His novel House of Sand and Fog (1999), a finalist for the National Book Award, was turned into an Academy Award–nominated film released in 2003. The following is an excerpt from his nonfiction book, Townie: A Memoir *(2011).*

IT WAS THE SIX OF US: my young parents and all four of us kids born in a five year period beginning in 1958. We were each born on Marine bases, delivered by Marine doctors, Suzanne at Quantico in Virginia, me and Jeb on Camp Pendleton in California, and Nicole on Whidbey Island in Washington State. During these years, our father spent a lot of time aboard the USS *Ranger* off the coast of Japan. When we did see him, it was for brief stretches in cramped Marine base housing. His head was shaved, his face smooth and clean, but he was a man who didn't smile much, a man who seemed locked into a car on a road he didn't want to be on. But then my father's father died in 1963, and almost immediately after that Dad retired from the Marines as a captain and was accepted into the Iowa Writers' Workshop in Iowa City.

Though I didn't have words for it, I'd never seen him happier; he laughed often and loud; he hugged and kissed our mother at every turn; he'd let his hair grow out long enough you could actually see some on his head, thick and brown. He'd grown a mustache, too. At night before bed, he'd sit me, my brother, and two sisters down at the kitchen table or on the couch in the living room and he'd tell us stories he made up himself—adventure stories where the hero and heroine were Indians defending their families and their people from the white man. One of them was Running Blue Ice Water, a kind and brave warrior who lingered in my imagination long after we'd been tucked in upstairs in a large room all four of us children shared.

My memory of that time is the memory of parties, though we were so broke we ate canned meat and big blocks of government cheese. Once a month Pop sold blood. But the parties went on. They happened at night, the house filled with talk and laughter and cigarette smoke. There were parties during the day, too. Blankets laid out on grass under the sun. Men and women eating sandwiches and sipping wine and reading poems out loud to each other.

Some parties were at the Vonneguts' house next door. All the Vonnegut kids were older than we were, but the father, Kurt, would walk down to our house every afternoon and sit with us four kids in the living room and watch *Batman* on the small black-and-white. He smoked one cigarette after the other. He laughed a lot and made jokes, and once he squinted down at me through the smoke and said: "Who's your favorite bad guy?"

"Um, False Face."

He smiled, his face a warm mix of mustache and round eyes and curly hair. "I like the Riddler."

In our bedroom floor was an air vent that overlooked the living room, and sometimes on party nights we kids would huddle around it and spy on our mother and father and their friends below, watch them dance and drink and argue and laugh, the men always louder than the women, their cigarette smoke curling up through the grate into our faces. I remember hearing a lot of dirty words then but also ones like *story, novel,* and *poem. Hemingway* and *Chekhov.*

In the morning we'd be up long before our parents. We'd get cereal and poke around in the party ruins, the table and floors of our small house littered with empty beer bottles, crushed potato chips, overflowing ashtrays, half the butts brushed with lipstick. If there was anything left in a glass, and if there wasn't a cigarette floating in it, Suzanne and I would take a few sips because we liked the taste of watered-down whiskey or gin. Once we found a carrot cake in the living room. Its sides were covered with white frosting, but the middle was nothing but a mashed crater. I remembered the cake from the night before, a mouthwatering three-layer with frosted writing on the top. I asked my mother who it

5

was for and she said it was for one of their friends who'd just sold his novel to a publisher; they were going to celebrate. And now the cake was unrecognizable, and when my mother came down that morning looking young and beautiful, probably in shorts and one of my father's shirts, smoking a cigarette, only twenty-five or -six, I asked her what had happened to the cake. She dug her finger into the frosting, then smiled at me. "Just your father and his crazy writer friends, honey." Did that mean he was a crazy writer, too? I wasn't sure.

It was another party at our house that confirmed it for me, though, one that began with jazz on the record player, a platter of cucumbers and carrots and horseradish dip on the kitchen table, glasses set out on the counter, and in his front room on his black wooden desk were two lit candles on either side of something rectangular and about two or three inches high covered with a black cloth. As my father's friends showed up one or two couples at a time, he'd walk them into his room with a drink or bottle of beer in his hand, and he'd point at what he told them was the failed novel he was holding a funeral for. He'd laugh and they'd laugh and one of his writer friends put his hand on his shoulder and squeezed, both of them looking suddenly pained and quite serious. I knew then my father was a writer too.

When our father's first book was published in 1967, he got a job 10 teaching at a small college in Massachusetts. We loaded up our rusted Chevrolet and drove east. For a year we lived in the woods of southern New Hampshire in a rented clapboard house on acres of pine and pasture. We had a swimming pool and a herd of sheep. There were fallen pine needles and a brook along whose banks Jeb and I found arrowheads, smooth pebbles, the bleached bones of rabbits or squirrels. We felt rich; we had all that land to play on, we had that big old house—its dark inviting rooms, its fireplaces, its fading wallpaper and floorboards fastened with square-cut nails from before the Civil War; we had that *pool*.

In 1968 we moved again, this time to a cottage on a pond on the Massachusetts–New Hampshire border. I was nine, and so it seemed like a house, but it was really a summer camp. Downstairs was the kitchen and its worn linoleum floor, the small living room with the black-and-white TV where we heard of the killing of Martin Luther King Jr.; it's where we saw X-ray photos of Robert Kennedy's brain and the .22 caliber bullet shot into it; it's where the following summer we watched a man walk on the moon, my mother sitting on the arm of the couch in shorts and one of Pop's button-down shirts, saying, "We're on the moon, you guys. We're on the fucking *moon*."

My father, thirty-two years old then, was earning seven thousand dollars a year teaching. He had a brown beard he kept trimmed, and he ran five miles a day, a ritual he had begun in the Marine Corps a few years earlier. My mother and father rarely had money to go out to a restaurant, but they still hosted a lot of parties at our house, usually on Friday or Saturday nights, sometimes both; my mother would set out saltine crackers and dip, sliced cheese and cucumbers and carrots; they'd open a jug of wine and a bucket of ice and wait for their friends to bring the rest: more wine, beer, bottles of gin and bourbon. Most of their friends came from the college where Pop taught: there was an art professor, a big man who wore black and had a clean-shaven handsome face and laughed loudly and looked to me like a movie actor; there were bearded poets and bald painters and women who taught pottery or literature or dance. There were students, too, mainly women, all of them beautiful, as I recall, with long shiny hair and straight white teeth, and they dressed in sleeveless sweaters or turtlenecks and didn't wear bras, their bell-bottoms hugging their thighs and flaring out widely over their suede boots.

The house would be filled with talk and laughter, jazz playing on the record player—a lot of Brubeck, Gerry Mulligan, and Buddy Rich. From my bed upstairs I could smell pot and cigarette smoke. I could hear music and the animated voices of my mother and father and their loud, intriguing friends. Sometimes there'd be yelling, and there'd be words like *Saigon, Viet Cong*, and *motherfucking Nixon*.

One weeknight on the news, there was a story about Marines killed in battle. I was lying on the floor under the coffee table as the camera panned over the bodies of soldiers lying on the ground, most of them on their stomachs, their arms splayed out beside them. Pop sat straight on the couch. His hands were on his knees, and his eyes were shining. "Pat, those are boys. Oh, goddamnit, those are eighteen-year-old *boys*."

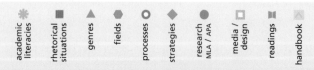

academic literacies · rhetorical situations · genres · fields · processes · strategies · research MLA / APA · media / design · readings · handbook

Later, sleeping in the bed beside my brother's, there was a weight 15 on my chest and I woke to my father holding me, crying into the pillow beside my ear. "My son, my son, oh, my son." He smelled like bourbon and sweat. It was hard to breathe. I couldn't pull my arms free of the blankets to hug Pop back. Then he was off me, crying over Jeb on his bed, and there was my mother's whisper from the doorway, her shadowed silhouette. Her arm reached for our father, and he stood and looked down at us both a long while, then he was gone. The house was quiet, my room dark and still. I lay awake and thought of all the good men on TV who'd been shot in the head. I saw again the dead soldiers lying on the ground, and until Pop had cried over us, I hadn't thought much about Jeb and me having to go and fight, too. But in only nine years I'd be as old as the dead, and it'd be my turn, wouldn't it?

But soldiers have to be brave, and I was not; I was a new kid in school again, something I would be over and over for many years, trying to find a solitary desk away from the others, dreading recess because everybody knew everyone else and threw balls back and forth and chased after each other grabbing and laughing, and I just didn't have the courage to jump in. Then some kid would see me looking and yell, "What're you lookin' at? You got a *problem?*"

Sometimes I'd get shoved and kicked and pushed to the ground. I was still trying to figure out what I'd done to make them mad, I had not yet learned that cruelty was cruelty and you don't ask why, just hit first and hit hard.

There was more fighting at home. My parents must've tried to keep it from us because it seemed to happen only late at night, both of them screaming at each other, swearing, sometimes throwing things—pots or pans, a plate or glass or ashtray, anything close by. When they fought, their Southern accents were easier to hear, especially my mother's, "God-damn you, you sonofa*bitch.*" Pop's voice would get chest-deep and he'd yell back at her as if she were a Marine under his command.

Many nights my brother and two sisters and I would listen from the stairs in our pajamas, not because we enjoyed it but because it was easier to bear when we weren't hearing it alone in our beds.

But by morning, the sun shone through the trees and most of the 20 thrown or broken dishes in the living room would be picked up, the kitchen smelling like bacon and eggs, grits and toast and coffee, the night before a bad dream already receding into the shadows where it belonged. . . .

One sunlit afternoon in the early fall our parents sat us down in the living room and told us they were getting separated. My father stood in the kitchen doorway. My mother leaned against the wall on the other side of the room. *Separated*. It was a word I'd never thought much about before, but now I pictured them being cut one from the other with a big, sharp knife. I sat in my father's chair, and I couldn't stop crying.

Then Pop was gone for weeks. One night, after Suzanne and Jeb and Nicole were asleep, I lay in bed listening to my mother crying in her room. It sounded like she was doing it into her pillow, but I could still hear it, and I got up and walked down the creaking floorboards of the hallway and knocked on her door. Her bedside lamp was on. She lifted her head, wiped her eyes, and smiled at me. I asked her if she was all right. She sat up and looked me up and down. She said, "I'm going to tell you because you're old enough to hear it. Your father left me for Betsy Armstrong. That's where he is right now, staying with her."

Betsy was one of the rich girls from the college. She had long straight hair and a pretty face. I remembered her laughing once in the kitchen with my mother. Now my mother got out of bed and leaned down and hugged me. I hugged her back.

Then Pop was home again. I woke one morning and heard his voice downstairs. I ran down there, and he hugged me. Later that day he was in the bathroom shaving. I went in there just to watch. I was ten years old, he was thirty-three. He turned from the mirror and said, "So you know about Betsy then?"

The air in the room felt thicker somehow. "Yeah." 25

He reached into his wallet and pulled out a small photograph. He handed it to me. "That's her."

It was of a girl I barely remembered seeing before, not the one I'd thought she was. "She's pretty."

"Yes, she is." Pop took the photo and slid it back into his wallet. I left the bathroom and walked straight to the kitchen where Mom stood at the sink washing dishes. I looked up at her face. She smiled down at me.

"Dad's girlfriend is prettier than you are, Mom." Her smile faded and she looked into the dishwater and kept scrubbing. I walked back to the bathroom and told my father what I'd said.

He was wiping shaving cream from his face with a towel. He stopped, 30 the towel still pressed to his cheek. "No, go apologize to her. Go tell her you're sorry right now."

I ran outside and into the woods. I don't remember ever apologizing to my mother, but Pop was back, girlfriend or not, and for a while things seemed to get back to normal, and there was less fighting than before. Each night when Pop came home from teaching, Mom would be cooking in the kitchen and they'd have cocktail hour, which meant none of us kids was allowed in there while they sipped Jim Beam and our father unwound and told Mom his day and she told him hers.

Soon the hour would be over, and the six of us would sit at the rickety table in that small, hot kitchen and we'd eat. We lived in New England, but at suppertime our house smelled like any in South Louisiana: Mom fried chicken, or simmered smothered breakfast steak or cheap cuts of pork, all served up with rice and gravy and baking powder biscuits. On the side there'd be collard greens or sliced tomatoes, cucumbers, and onions she'd put ice cubes on to keep crisp. She baked us hot tamale pies, and macaroni and cheese, or vegetable soup she'd cook for hours in a chicken stock, then serve in a hollowed-out crust of French bread, its top a steaming layer of melted cheddar. But while the food was wonderful, my mother and father hardly even looked at one another anymore and instead kept their attention on us, asking about school, about the tree fort Jeb and I were building out in the woods, about the Beatles album Suzanne listened to, the drawings Nicole did each afternoon. We rarely left the table hungry, but there was a hollowness in the air, a dark unspeakable stillness, one my father would soon drive into, and away.

It happened early on a Sunday in November. Pop was so much taller than the four of us, and we were following him down the porch stairs and along the path, Suzanne behind him in her cotton nightgown, then me and Jeb in our pajamas, Nicole last, her thick red hair and small face. We were eleven, ten, nine, and six. Ahead of us, there was the glint of frost on the gravel driveway and our car, the old Lancer, packed now with Pop's things: his clothes, his books, his shaving kit. The house was surrounded by tall pines and it was too cold to smell them, the air so clear and bright. Inside the house Mom was crying as if her pain were physical, as if someone were holding her down and doing something bad to her.

Daddy! Nicole ran past us over the gravel and she leapt and Pop turned, his eyes welling up, and he caught her, her arms around his neck, her face buried under his chin. I tried to ignore our mother's cries coming from the house. When my father looked down at me over Nicole's small shoulder, I stood as straight as I could and I hoped I looked strong.

Pop kissed Nicole's red hair. He lowered her to the gravel. His beard 35 was thick and dark, his cheeks and throat shaved clean. He was wearing a sweatshirt and corduroy pants, and he glanced up at our house. There was only the sound of our mother's cries, so maybe he would change his mind. Maybe he would stay.

Becoming a writer helped Andre Dubus III forge a relationship with his father, but making himself completely whole took more.

He looked down at us. "I'll see you soon. We'll go out to eat."

He hugged Suzanne, squeezed my shoulder. He tousled Jeb's hair, then he was in his car driving down the hill through the pines, blue exhaust coughing out its pipe. Jeb scooped up a handful of gravel and ran down the hill after him, "You bum! You bum! You bum!" He threw it all at once, the small rocks scattering across the road and into the woods like shrapnel.

Pop drove across the short bridge, then up a rise through more trees. Mom would need to be comforted now. Nicole too. There was food to think about. How to get it with no car. I tried to keep standing as straight as I could.

Engaging with the Text

1. How would you sum up what Andre Dubus III is saying in this memoir? Try to express in a sentence or two the **SIGNIFICANCE** to him of the events he relates.

    ▲ 229

2. Dubus's memoir is saturated in **VIVID DETAILS**. Select three paragraphs from different parts of the essay, and discuss what the details in them add to the story.

    ▲ 228

3. Dubus's **STANCE** toward his father in this memoir is respectful but somewhat distant. Identify two passages that make his stance clear. Is the stance appropriate for the story he is telling? Why or why not? What does his stance reveal about his feelings toward his father at the time he wrote the memoir?

    ■ 66–68

4. Dubus **TITLES** his memoir *My Father Was a Writer*. What is the significance of this title? Think of another title Dubus could have used, and explain what would be lost or gained by doing so.

    ◆ 386–87

5. *For Writing.* Write a **MEMOIR** about an event or several related events from your childhood that focuses on the significance of a particular person in your life. Use **VIVID DETAILS** to put your reader into the **NARRATIVE**.

    ▲ 224–32

    ▲ 228
    ◆ 462–70

MALALA YOUSAFZAI

Who Is Malala?

Malala Yousafzai (b. 1997) is an influential advocate for the education of girls and women. In 2012, Yousafzai was shot by the Taliban in Pakistan while on a school bus, and she has gone on to become one of the most important activists of her generation. In 2014, she became the youngest person ever to win the Nobel Peace Prize for her activism. In 2017, she was accepted into Oxford's Lady Margaret Hall to study politics, philosophy, and economics. The following essay, which recalls the story of the Taliban attack, is excerpted from her memoir I Am Malala: The Girl Who Stood Up for Education and Was Shot by the Taliban *(2013).*

ONE MORNING IN LATE SUMMER when my father was getting ready to go to school he noticed that the painting of me looking at the sky which we had been given by the school in Karachi had shifted in the night. He loved that painting and had hung it over his bed. Seeing it crooked disturbed him. "Please put it straight," he asked my mother in an unusually sharp tone.

That same week our math teacher, Miss Shazia, arrived at school in a hysterical state. She told my father that she'd had a nightmare in which I came to school with my leg badly burned and she had tried to protect it. She begged him to give some cooked rice to the poor, as we believe that if you give rice, even ants and birds will eat the bits that drop to the floor and will pray for us. My father gave money instead and she was distraught, saying that wasn't the same.

We laughed at Miss Shazia's premonition, but then I started having bad dreams too. I didn't say anything to my parents, but whenever I went out I was afraid that Taliban with guns would leap out at me or throw acid in my face, as they had done to women in Afghanistan. I was particularly scared of the steps leading up to our street where the boys used to hang out. Sometimes I thought I heard footsteps behind me or imagined figures slipping into the shadows.

Unlike my father, I took precautions. At night I would wait until everyone was asleep—my mother, my father, my brothers, the other family in our house and any guests we had from our village—then I'd check every single door and window. I'd go outside and make sure the front gate was locked. Then I would check all the rooms, one by one. My room was at the front with lots of windows and I kept the curtains open. I wanted to be able to see everything, though my father told me not to. "If they were going to kill me they would have done it in 2009," I said. But I worried someone would put a ladder against the house, climb over the wall, and break in through a window.

Then I'd pray. At night I used to pray a lot. The Taliban think we are   5 not Muslims but we are. We believe in God more than they do and we trust him to protect us. I used to say the *Ayat al-Kursi*, the Verse of the Throne from the second *surah* of the Quran, the Chapter of the Cow. This is a very special verse and we believe that if you say it three times at night your home will be safe from *shayatin* or devils. When you say it five times your street will be safe, and seven times will protect the whole area. So I'd say it seven times or even more. Then I'd pray to God, "Bless us. First our father and family, then our street, then our whole *mohalla*, then all Swat." Then I'd say, "No, all Muslims." Then, "No, not just Muslims; bless all human beings."

The time of year I prayed most was during exams. It was the one time when my friends and I did all five prayers a day like my mother was always trying to get me to do. I found it particularly hard in the afternoon, when I didn't want to be dragged away from the TV. At exam time I prayed to Allah for high marks though our teachers used to warn us, "God won't give you marks if you don't work hard. God showers us with his blessings, but he is honest as well."

So I studied hard too. Usually I liked exams as a chance to show what I could do. But when they came around in October 2012 I felt under pressure. I did not want to come second to Malka-e-Noor again as I had in March. Then she had beaten me by not just one or two marks, the usual difference between us, but by five marks! I had been taking extra lessons with Sir Amjad, who ran the boys' school. The night before the exams began I stayed up studying until 3 o'clock in the morning and reread an entire textbook.

The first paper, on Monday, 8 October, was physics. I love physics because it is about truth, a world determined by principles and laws—no messing around or twisting things like in politics, particularly those in my country. As we waited for the signal to start the exam, I recited holy verses to myself. I completed the paper, but I knew I'd made a mistake filling in the blanks. I was so cross with myself I almost cried. It was just one question worth only one mark, but it made me feel that something devastating was going to happen.

When I got home that afternoon I was sleepy, but the next day was Pakistan Studies, a difficult paper for me. I was worried about losing even more marks, so I made myself coffee with milk to drive away the devils of sleep. When my mother came she tried it and liked it and drank the rest. I could not tell her, "*Bhabi*, please stop it, that's my coffee." But there was no more coffee left in the cupboard. Once again I stayed up late, memorizing the textbook about the history of our independence.

In the morning my parents came into my room as usual and woke me up. I don't remember a single school day on which I woke up early by myself. My mother made our usual breakfast of sugary tea, chapatis, and fried egg. We all had breakfast together—me, my mother, my father, Khushal, and Atal. It was a big day for my mother, as she was going to start lessons that afternoon to learn to read and write with Miss Ulfat, my old teacher from kindergarten.

My father started teasing Atal, who was eight by then and cheekier than ever. "Look, Atal, when Malala is prime minister, you will be her secretary," he said.

Atal got very cross. "No, no, no!" he said. "I'm no less than Malala. I will be prime minister and she will be my secretary." All the banter meant I ended up being so late I only had time to eat half my egg and no time to clear up.

The Pakistan Studies paper went better that I thought it would. There were questions about how Jinnah had created our country as the first Muslim homeland and also about the national tragedy of how Bangladesh came into being. It was strange to think that Bangladesh was once part of Pakistan despite being a thousand miles away. I answered all the questions and was confident I'd done well. I was happy when the

10

exam was over, chatting and gossiping with my friends as we waited for Sher Mohammad Baba, a school assistant, to call for us when the bus arrived.

The bus did two trips every day, and that day we took the second one. We liked staying on at school and Moniba said, "As we're tired after the exam, let's stay and chat before going home." I was relieved that the Pakistan Studies exam had gone well, so I agreed. I had no worries that day. I was hungry, but because we were fifteen we could no longer go outside to the street, so I got one of the small girls to buy me a corn cob. I ate a little bit of it then gave it to another girl to finish.

At 12 o'clock Baba called us over the loudspeaker. We all ran down   15 the steps. The other girls all covered their faces before emerging from the door and climbed into the back of the bus. I wore my scarf over my head but never over my face.

I asked Usman Bhai Jan to tell us a joke while we were waiting for two teachers to arrive. He has a collection of extremely funny stories. That day instead of a story he did a magic trick to make a pebble disappear. "Show us how you did it!" we all clamored, but he wouldn't.

When everyone was ready he took Miss Rubi and a couple of small children in the front cab with him. Another little girl cried, saying she wanted to ride there too. Usman Bhai Jan said no, there was no room; she would have to stay in the back with us. But I felt sorry for her and persuaded him to let her in the cab.

Atal had been told by my mother to ride on the bus with me, so he walked over from the primary school. He liked to hang off the tailboard at the back, which made Usman Bhai Jan cross, as it was dangerous. That day Usman Bhai Jan had had enough and refused to let him. "Sit inside, Atal Khan, or I won't take you!" he said. Atal had a trantrum and refused, so he walked home in a huff with some of his friends.

Usman Bhai Jan started the *dyna* and we were off. I was talking to Moniba, my wise, nice friend. Some girls were singing, I was drumming rhythms with my fingers on the seat.

Moniba and I liked to sit near the open back so we could see out.   20 At that time of day Haji Baba Road was always a jumble of colored rickshaws, people on foot and men on scooters, all zigzagging and honking.

An ice-cream boy on a red tricycle painted with red and white nuclear missiles rode up behind waving at us, until a teacher shooed him away. A man was chopping off chickens heads, the blood dripping onto the street. I drummed my fingers. Chop, chop, chop. Drip, drip, drip. Funny, when I was little we always said Swatis were so peace-loving it was hard to find a man to slaughter a chicken.

The air smelled of diesel, bread, and kebab mixed with the stink from the stream where people still dumped their rubbish and were never going to stop despite all my father's campaigning. But we were used to it. Besides, soon the winter would be here, bringing the snow, which would cleanse and quieten everything.

The bus turned right off the main road at the army checkpoint. On a kiosk was a poster of crazy-eyed men with beards and caps or turbans under big letters saying WANTED TERRORISTS. The picture at the top of a man with a black turban and beard was Fazlullah. More than three years had passed since the military operation to drive the Taliban out of Swat had begun. We were grateful to the army but couldn't understand why they were still everywhere, in machine-gun nests on roofs and manning checkpoints. To even enter our valley people needed official permission.

The road up the small hill is usually busy, as it is a shortcut, but that day it was strangely quiet. "Where are all the people?" I asked Moniba. All the girls were singing and chatting and our voices bounced around inside the bus.

Around that time my mother was probably just going through the doorway into our school for her first lesson since she had left school at age six.

I didn't see the two young men step out into the road and bring the van to a sudden halt. I didn't get a chance to answer their question "Who is Malala?" or I would have explained to them why they should let us girls go to school as well as their own sisters and daughters.

The last thing I remember is that I was thinking about the revision I needed to do for the next day. The sounds in my head were not the *crack, crack, crack* of three bullets, but the *chop, chop, chop, drip, drip, drip* of the man severing the heads of chickens, and them dropping into the dirty street, one by one.

Engaging with the Text

1. Identify two **VIVID DETAILS** Malala Yousafzai includes in her memoir. How do these details enrich Yousafzai's story?

   ▲ 228

2. What purpose does the **TITLE** serve? How is it appropriate for this memoir?

   ◆ 386–87

3. What is Yousafzai's **STANCE** in this essay? Does her stance align with her **PURPOSE**? Why or why not?

   ■ 66–68
   55–56

4. Yousafzai spends a lot of time building up to the main event of her story—the moment when she is shot by the Taliban. Why do you think she does this? Is this approach effective? Why or why not?

5. *For Writing.* Think back to a day that did not go as you expected and write a brief **MEMOIR** about it. Include specific **DETAILS** so your readers can imagine exactly what happened.

   ▲ 224–32
   228

JUDITH ORTIZ COFER

The Myth of the Latin Woman

Judith Ortiz Cofer (1952–2016) retired in 2013 from the University of Georgia, where she was the Regents' and Franklin Professor of English and Creative Writing. She was a prolific writer, known as a poet, a short-story writer, a novelist, an essayist, and an autobiographer. Her works, some intended for a young-adult audience, include the novels The Meaning of Consuelo *(2003) and* If I Could Fly *(2011), the books of poems* Terms of Survival *(1987) and* Reaching for the Mainland *(1995), and the bilingual picture book* ¡A Bailar! Let's Dance! *(2011). The following essay comes from her memoir* The Latin Deli: Prose and Poetry *(1993).*

ON A BUS TRIP TO LONDON FROM OXFORD UNIVERSITY where I was earning some graduate credits one summer, a young man, obviously fresh from a pub, spotted me and as if struck by inspiration went down on his knees in the aisle. With both hands over his heart he broke into an Irish tenor's rendition of "María" from *West Side Story.* My politely amused fellow passengers gave his lovely voice the round of gentle applause it deserved. Though I was not quite as amused, I managed my version of an English smile: no show of teeth, no extreme contortions of the facial muscles—I was at this time of my life practicing reserve and cool. Oh, that British control, how I coveted it. But María had followed me to London, reminding me of a prime fact of my life: you can leave the Island, master the English language, and travel as far as you can, but if you are a Latina, especially one like me who so obviously belongs to Rita Moreno's gene pool, the Island travels with you.

This is sometimes a very good thing—it may win you that extra minute of someone's attention. But with some people, the same things can make you an island—not so much a tropical paradise as an Alcatraz, a place nobody wants to visit. As a Puerto Rican girl growing up in the United States and wanting like most children to "belong," I resented the stereotype that my Hispanic appearance called forth from many people I met.

Our family lived in a large urban center in New Jersey during the sixties, where life was designed as a microcosm of my parents' casas on the island. We spoke in Spanish, we ate Puerto Rican food bought at the bodega, and we practiced strict Catholicism complete with Saturday confession and Sunday mass at a church where our parents were accommodated into a one-hour Spanish mass slot, performed by a Chinese priest trained as a missionary for Latin America.

As a girl I was kept under strict surveillance, since virtue and modesty were, by cultural equation, the same as family honor. As a teenager I was instructed on how to behave as a proper señorita. But it was a conflicting message girls got, since the Puerto Rican mothers also encouraged their daughters to look and act like women and to dress in clothes our Anglo friends and their mothers found too "mature" for our age. It was, and is, cultural, yet I often felt humiliated when I appeared at an American friend's party wearing a dress more suitable to a semiformal than to a playroom birthday celebration. At Puerto Rican festivities, neither the music nor the colors we wore could be too loud. I still experience a vague sense of letdown when I'm invited to a "party" and it turns out to be a marathon conversation in hushed tones rather than a fiesta with salsa, laughter, and dancing—the kind of celebration I remember from my childhood.

I remember Career Day in our high school, when teachers told us to   5 come dressed as if for a job interview. It quickly became obvious that to the barrio girls, "dressing up" sometimes meant wearing ornate jewelry and clothing that would be more appropriate (by mainstream standards) for the company Christmas party than as daily office attire. That morning I had agonized in front of my closet, trying to figure out what a "career girl" would wear because, essentially, except for Marlo Thomas on TV, I had no models on which to base my decision. I knew how to dress for school: at the Catholic school I attended we all wore uniforms; I knew how to dress for Sunday mass, and I knew what dresses to wear for parties at my relatives' homes. Though I do not recall the precise details of my Career Day outfit, it must have been a composite of the above choices. But I remember a comment my friend (an Italian-American) made in later years that coalesced my impressions of that day. She said that at the business school she was attending the Puerto Rican girls always stood out for wearing "everything at once." She meant, of course, too much jewelry, too many accessories. On that day at school, we were simply made the negative models by the nuns who were themselves not credible fashion experts to any of us. But it was painfully obvious to me that to the others, in their tailored skirts and silk blouses, we must have seemed "hopeless" and "vulgar." Though I now know that most adolescents feel out of step much of the time, I also know that for the Puerto Rican girls of my generation that sense was intensified. The way our teachers and classmates looked at us that day in school was just a taste of the culture clash that awaited us in the real world, where prospective employers and men on the street would often misinterpret our tight skirts and jingling bracelets as a come-on.

Mixed cultural signals have perpetuated certain stereotypes—for example, that of the Hispanic woman as the "Hot Tamale" or sexual firebrand. It is a one-dimensional view that the media have found easy to promote. In their special vocabulary, advertisers have designated "sizzling" and "smoldering" as the adjectives of choice for describing not only the foods but also the women of Latin America. From conversations in my house I recall hearing about the harassment that Puerto Rican women endured in factories where the "boss men" talked to them as if sexual innuendo was all they understood and, worse, often gave them the choice of submitting to advances or being fired.

It is custom, however, not chromosomes, that leads us to choose scarlet over pale pink. As young girls, we were influenced in our decisions about clothes and colors by the women—older sisters and mothers who had grown up on a tropical island where the natural environment was a riot of primary colors, where showing your skin was one way to keep cool as well as to look sexy. Most important of all, on the island, women perhaps felt freer to dress and move more provocatively, since, in most cases, they were protected by the traditions, mores, and laws of a Spanish / Catholic system of morality and machismo whose main rule was: *You may look at my sister, but if you touch her I will kill you.* The extended family and church structure could provide a young woman with a circle of safety in her small pueblo on the island; if a man "wronged" a girl, everyone would close in to save her family honor.

This is what I have gleaned from my discussions as an adult with older Puerto Rican women. They have told me about dressing in their best party clothes on Saturday nights and going to the town's plaza to promenade with their girlfriends in front of the boys they liked. The males were thus given an opportunity to admire the women and to express their admiration in the form of *piropos*: erotically charged street poems they composed on the spot. I have been subjected to a few piropos while visiting the Island, and they can be outrageous, although custom dictates that they must never cross into obscenity. This ritual, as I understand it, also entails a show of studied indifference on the woman's part; if she is "decent," she must not acknowledge the man's impassioned words. So I do understand how things can be lost in translation. When a Puerto Rican girl dressed in her idea of what is attractive meets a man from the mainstream culture who has been trained to react to certain types of clothing as a sexual signal, a clash is likely to take place. The line I first heard based on this aspect of the myth happened when the boy who took me to my first formal dance leaned over to plant a sloppy overeager kiss painfully on my mouth, and when I didn't respond with sufficient passion said in a resentful tone: "I thought you Latin girls were supposed to mature early"—my first instance of being thought of as a fruit or vegetable—I was supposed to *ripen*, not just grow into womanhood like other girls.

It is surprising to some of my professional friends that some people, including those who should know better, still put others "in their place." Though rarer, these incidents are still commonplace in my life. It happened to me most recently during a stay at a very classy metropolitan hotel favored by young professional couples for their weddings. Late one evening after the theater, as I walked toward my room with my new colleague (a woman with whom I was coordinating an arts program), a middle-aged man in a tuxedo, a young girl in satin and lace on his arm, stepped directly into our path. With his champagne glass extended toward me, he exclaimed, "Evita!"

Our way blocked, my companion and I listened as the man half-recited, half-bellowed "Don't Cry for Me, Argentina." When he finished, the young girl said: "How about a round of applause for my daddy?" We

<!-- 10 -->

complied, hoping this would bring the silly spectacle to a close. I was becoming aware that our little group was attracting the attention of the other guests. "Daddy" must have perceived this too, and he once more barred the way as we tried to walk past him. He began to shout-sing a ditty to the tune of "La Bamba"—except the lyrics were about a girl named María whose exploits all rhymed with her name and gonorrhea. The girl kept saying "Oh, Daddy" and looking at me with pleading eyes. She wanted me to laugh along with the others. My companion and I stood silently waiting for the man to end his offensive song. When he finished, I looked not at him but at his daughter. I advised her calmly never to ask her father what he had done in the army. Then I walked between them and to my room. My friend complimented me on my cool handling of the situation. I confessed to her that I really had wanted to push the jerk into the swimming pool. I knew that this same man— probably a corporate executive, well educated, even worldly by most standards—would not have been likely to regale a white woman with a dirty song in public. He would perhaps have checked his impulse by assuming that she could be somebody's wife or mother, or at least some-body who might take offense. But to him, I was just an Evita or a María: merely a character in his cartoon-populated universe.

Because of my education and my proficiency with the English lan-guage, I have acquired many mechanisms for dealing with the anger I experience. This was not true for my parents, nor is it true for the many Latin women working at menial jobs who must put up with stereotypes about our ethnic group such as: "They make good domestics." This is another facet of the myth of the Latin woman in the United States. Its origin is simple to deduce. Work as domestics, waitressing, and factory jobs are all that's available to women with little English and few skills. The myth of the Hispanic menial has been sustained by the same media phenomenon that made "Mammy" from *Gone with the Wind* America's idea of the black woman for generations; María, the housemaid or coun-ter girl, is now indelibly etched into the national psyche. The big and the little screens have presented us with the picture of the funny Hispanic maid, mispronouncing words and cooking up a spicy storm in a shiny California kitchen.

This media-engendered image of the Latina in the United States has been documented by feminist Hispanic scholars, who claim that such portrayals are partially responsible for the denial of opportunities for upward mobility among Latinas in the professions. I have a Chicana friend working on a Ph.D. in philosophy at a major university. She says her doctor still shakes his head in puzzled amazement at all the "big words" she uses. Since I do not wear my diplomas around my neck for all to see, I too have on occasion been sent to that "kitchen," where some think I obviously belong.

One such incident that has stayed with me, though I recognize it as a minor offense, happened on the day of my first public poetry reading. It took place in Miami in a boat-restaurant where we were having lunch before the event. I was nervous and excited as I walked in with my notebook in my hand. An older woman motioned me to her table. Thinking (foolish me) that she wanted me to autograph a copy of my brand new slender volume of verse, I went over. She ordered a cup of coffee from me, assuming that I was the waitress. Easy enough to mistake my poems for menus, I suppose. I know that it wasn't an intentional act of cruelty, yet of all the good things that happened that day, I remember that scene most clearly, because it reminded me of what I had to overcome before anyone would take me seriously. In retrospect I understand that my anger gave my reading fire, that I have almost always taken doubts in my abilities as a challenge—and that the result is, most times, a feeling of satisfaction at having won a convert when I see the cold, appraising eyes warm to my words, the body language change, the smile that indicates that I have opened some avenue for communication. That day I read to that woman and her lowered eyes told me that she was embarrassed at her little faux pas, and when I willed her to look up at me, it was my victory, and she graciously allowed me to punish her with my full attention. We shook hands at the end of the reading, and I never saw her again. She has probably forgotten the whole thing but maybe not.

Yet I am one of the lucky ones. My parents made it possible for me to acquire a stronger footing in the mainstream culture by giving me the chance at an education. And books and art have saved me from the harsher forms of ethnic and racial prejudice that many of my Hispanic *compañeras* have had to endure. I travel a lot around the United States, reading from my books of poetry and my novel, and the reception I most often receive is one of positive interest by people who want to know more about my culture. There are, however, thousands of Latinas without the privilege of an education or the entree into society that I have. For them life is a struggle against the misconceptions perpetuated by the myth of the Latina as whore, domestic, or criminal. We cannot change this by legislating the way people look at us. The transformation, as I see it, has to occur at a much more individual level. My personal goal in my public life is to try to replace the old pervasive stereotypes and myths about Latinas with a much more interesting set of realities. Every time I give a reading, I hope the stories I tell, the dreams and fears I examine in my work, can achieve some universal truth which will get my audience past the particulars of my skin color, my accent, or my clothes.

I once wrote a poem in which I called us Latinas "God's brown   15
daughters."This poem is really a prayer of sorts, offered upward, but also, through the human-to-human channel of art, outward. It is a prayer for communication, and for respect. In it, Latin women pray "in Spanish to an Anglo God / with a Jewish heritage," and they are "fervently hoping / that if not omnipotent / at least He be bilingual."

Engaging with the Text

1. A strong memoir includes **VIVID DETAILS** to bring the past back to
   228
   387–89
   life. How do the details Judith Ortiz Cofer includes support her **THESIS** that Latinas are poorly understood and grossly stereotyped? Identify two of these details and explain how they help her make her case.

2. How does Cofer **END** her essay? What is the significance of the ending?
   380–85

3. What is the **PURPOSE** of this memoir? What do you think Cofer hopes
   55–56
   it to achieve? Where in the essay does she make that hope explicit?

academic literacies | rhetorical situations | genres | fields | processes | strategies | research MLA / APA | media / design | readings | handbook

4. Cofer explains that the way Puerto Rican women dress in Puerto Rico is "read" very differently by other people than when they dress in the same way elsewhere in the United States. What is the difference between the two responses? What does she say to explain why in one place the young women are respected and revered and in the other are disrespected and treated rudely? What role do you think dress should play in how people read other people?

5. **For Writing.** Think about the way you dress. What image are you trying to create through your clothing and accessories? How do others *read* your image? Do they read it in ways you mean it to be read or in other ways that go against your intentions? Write a **MEMOIR**, one that reflects on both the past and the present, that addresses these questions.

▲ 224–32

68 Profiles

academic literacies   rhetorical situations   genres   fields   processes   strategies   research MLA / APA   media / design   readings   handbook

JAMES HAMBLIN

Living Simply in a Dumpster

James Hamblin (b. 1983), a former radiologist at the UCLA Medical Center, left medical practice to join the Atlantic *as editor of its health channel. Today, he is a senior editor there, writing about health and hosting a video series titled* If Our Bodies Could Talk *that he started in 2013. The following profile appeared in the* Atlantic *in 2014.*

TUCKED BEHIND THE WOMEN'S RESIDENCE HALLS in a back corner of Huston-Tillotson University's campus in Austin, Texas, sits a green dumpster. Were it not for the sliding pitched roof and weather station perched on top, a reasonable person might dismiss the box as "just another dumpster"—providing this person did not encounter the dean of the University College Jeff Wilson living inside.

The current exterior.

Professor Wilson went to the dumpster not just because he wished to live deliberately, and not just to teach his students about the environmental impacts of day-to-day life, and not just to gradually transform the dumpster into "the most thoughtfully-designed, tiniest home ever constructed." Wilson's reasons are a tapestry of these things.

Until this summer, the green dumpster was even less descript than it is now. There was no sliding roof; Wilson kept the rain out with a tarp. He slept on cardboard mats on the floor. It was essentially, as he called it, "dumpster camping." The goal was to establish a baseline experience of the dumpster without any accoutrements, before adding them incrementally.

Not long ago, Wilson was nesting in a 2,500-square-foot house. After going through a divorce ("nothing related to the dumpster," he told me, unsolicited), he spun into the archetypal downsizing of a newly minted bachelor. He moved into a 500-square-foot apartment. Then he began selling clothes and furniture on *Facebook* for almost nothing. Now he

Professor Wilson at home.

says almost everything he owns is in his 36-square-foot dumpster, which is sanctioned and supported by the university as part of an ongoing sustainability-focused experiment called The Dumpster Project. "We could end up with a house under $10,000 that could be placed anywhere in the world," Wilson said at the launch, "[fueled by] sunlight and surface water, and people could have a pretty good life."

Wilson, known around town as Professor Dumpster, recounted 5 in another recent interview that he now owns four pairs of pants, four shirts, three pairs of shoes, three hats, and, in keeping with his hipsteresque aesthetic, "eight or nine" bow ties. (That's an exceptional bow-tie-to-shirt ownership ratio.) He keeps all of this in cubbies under a recently installed false floor, along with some camping cooking equipment.

Customization of the space really began in July. Wilson asked Twitter what was the first thing he needed, and the response was almost unanimous: air conditioning. In the Austin heat, the dumpster was getting up to 130 degrees Fahrenheit during the day. On some nights it did not fall below the high 80s. So on his six-month anniversary of living in a human-sized convection oven, Wilson procured a modest air conditioner.

"We didn't want to make it too easy," Wilson said. "I wanted to see how elastic my sleeping habits would be relative to temperature and humidity. I found that I could actually get to sleep pretty well as long as I went to bed at about 11:00 P.M."

With the weather station now strapped to the top, Wilson tracks his personal climate in real time. Pulling up data on his computer from inside his centrally cooled office as we spoke, he announced that the dumpster was currently 104 degrees. During the spring, when Austin was a little cooler, he was able to pass some daytime hours in the dumpster. With the arrival of summer, that became unbearable. "But some interesting things happened because of that," he explained. He spent a lot more time out in the community, just walking around. "I almost feel like East Austin is my home and backyard," he said. He is constantly thinking about what sorts of things a person really needs in a house, and what can be more communal.

"What if everybody had to go to some sort of laundromat?" Wilson posited. "How would that shift how we have to, or get to, interact with others? I know I have met a much wider circle of people just from going to laundromats and wandering around outside of the dumpster when I would've been in there if I had a large flat screen and a La-Z-Boy."

Perks like insulation will come, allowing the small air conditioner to   10
keep pace with the Texas sun. The second phase of The Dumpster Project, which Wilson and collaborators call the "average American dumpster studio," will incorporate more amenities including a bed, a lamp, and a classic home-evoking pitched roof that will slide back and forth to allow ventilation, weather stripping, and locks (making this possibly the only dumpster in the world with interior locks). Eventually, the dumpster will have a dome to catch rainwater and provide shade, as well as a (tiny) sink and kitchen.

"Actually," he said as we spoke by phone, "it is starting to rain right now, and my roof's open on the dumpster."

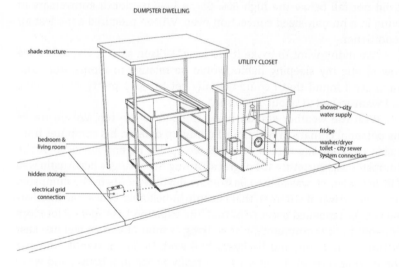

DUMPSTER DWELLING

shade structure

UTILITY CLOSET

shower - city
water supply

fridge

bedroom &
living room

washer/dryer
toilet - city sewer
system connection

hidden storage

electrical grid
connection

Phase two, currently in progress.

academic literacies
rhetorical situations
genres
fields
processes
strategies
research MLA / APA
media / design
readings
handbook

"Oh my god."

"Can I call you right back? It's a downpour. I'll be back in about a minute."

He called me back a minute later, sounding less distressed than one might expect from a person whose home had been drenched. The disposition that might make a person amenable to dumpster life is not one easily troubled by a little rain. His dumpster-home once looked like this:

The interior of the dumpster on Wilson's first night there.

He's also welcoming of anyone who wants to stop by the dumpster and talk sustainability any time. In addition to teaching courses in environmental change, global health and welfare, and environmental science at the college, Wilson describes The Dumpster Project primarily as an educational initiative that just happened to dovetail with his current life-downsizing. On some nights, Wilson will stay with a friend, and students from the ecology-focused campus group Green Is the New Black will get a night to stay in the dumpster.

"What does home look like in a world of 10 billion people?" the project's site implores, referring to the projected 40 percent increase in the human population by the end of the century. "How do we equip current and future generations with the tools they need for sustainable living practices?"

Unfortunately the site does not answer those questions in concrete terms. But with only 39 percent of Americans identifying as "believers" in global warming, just raising questions and promoting consciousness of sustainability might be a lofty enough aspiration.

Wilson's most anticipated upcoming boon is a toilet. "I'm not as concerned about the shower," he said, "but getting to the toilet sometimes requires kind of a midnight run." Currently, he uses facilities at the university's gym. A toilet and shower will soon connect to the dumpster externally. "You don't really want to have a composting toilet inside of a closed-up 36 square feet," he explained.

In four months Wilson will enter the third phase of the project, the "uber dumpster home." That will involve installing solar panels and

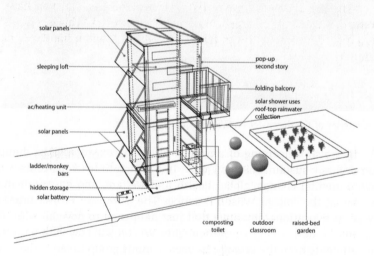

Phase three, beginning this winter.

unplugging from the energy grid, as well as completing aesthetic work that will essentially remove any semblance of dumpsterdom. "We kind of want to do the outside in a modern *Dwell* look," he said, including windows and reused lumber siding. "We want it basically to be such that if you were blindfolded and placed inside it, you'd just think you were in a very tiny house."

Wilson already goes around to local elementary and middle 20 schools recounting his experience in the context of talking about using less space, less energy, and less water, and creating less waste. There is a K–12 curriculum built around the dumpster experiment, and eventually the finished dumpster will be transported to these schools for display.

For Professor Dumpster, the undertaking is at once grand and diminutive, selfless and introspective, silly and gravely important, even dark. "We bring everything into the home these days," Wilson said. "You don't really need to leave the home for anything, even grocery shopping, anymore. What's interesting about this is it's really testing the limits of what you need in a home."

"The big hypothesis we're trying to test here is, can you have a pretty darn good life on much, much less?" He paused. "This is obviously an outlier experiment. But so far, I have, I'd say. A better life than I had before."

Engaging with the Text

1. James Hamblin's main point in this profile is that "Professor Wilson went to the dumpster not just because he wished to live deliberately, and not just to teach his students about the environmental impacts of day-to-day life, and not just to gradually transform the dumpster into 'the most thoughtfully-designed, tiniest home ever constructed.' Wilson's reasons are a tapestry of these things." How well does the rest of the profile support this **THESIS STATEMENT**?

387–89

2. A good profile typically covers an **INTERESTING SUBJECT**. What caught your attention as you read this profile? How interesting did you find the subject?

239 ▲

3. Although downsizing one's home is becoming more common, especially among those concerned with sustainability, Wilson's thirty-six-square-foot dumpster dwelling takes the trend to an extreme. How comfortable would you be in such a space? Explain how much space you believe you need to live a good life—either alone or as part of a multiperson household or both—and why.

653–63 ▢

4. **VISUALS** in a profile should be appropriate for the rhetorical situation. What do the visuals contribute to this profile? How well would you comprehend it without them? For this subject, what other visuals (including other kinds) might be helpful—or just interesting and engaging?

240 ▲

5. *For Writing.* Select an unusual subject—person, place, or thing—to profile. You will need a **FIRSTHAND ACCOUNT** of the subject, so it needs to be one you can easily visit, probably nearby your home or campus. If you are not profiling a person, try to speak with or research people involved with the subject to offer your readers a close-up view of it from a perspective besides your own.

ANA PACHECO

Street Vendors: *Harvest of Dreams*

Ana Pacheco (b. 1997) was a student at the University of California, Riverside, when she wrote this profile. It was nominated for the Norton Writer's Prize by her instructor. As you read, notice how she uses direct quotations from her subject to make the profile come alive.

JUST A FEW BLOCKS AWAY from the mainstream Glendale area in Los Angeles lie the headquarters of LA's greatest entrepreneurs. Although their attire is ragged, their business sense and determination are sharp. Among the crowd, a woman dressed in a bright lime skirt and vest stands out. Her name is Victoria Perez, and she is well known for walking around the streets carrying a matching lime green bucket on her head. Every morning, this *canasta* is filled with fresh-baked Salvadorian sweet bread, or *marquesotes*—a dollar each, or three for two.

Victoria Perez became a street vendor in 2006 after the death of her daughter. Victoria and her then three-month-old grandson were left alone in America with funeral debts and an empty refrigerator. For nearly two months, Victoria searched ceaselessly for a job. However, being a female middle-aged undocumented immigrant, she was never hired. Desperate to bring food to the table, Victoria used the last of her savings to fund her "Bucket-Bread Business." Now, eleven years later, she calls her business a "booming success." In these neighborhoods, Victoria is a household name when it comes to the best Salvadorian sweet bread.

It is not uncommon to hear stories like Victoria's among street vendors. According to the website *streetvendor.org*, street vendors are "small business people struggling to make ends meet. Most are immigrants and people of color. They work long hours under harsh conditions, asking for nothing more than a chance to sell their goods on the public sidewalk" ("About SVP"). However, in Los Angeles, street vendors have a bad reputation, and, according to Victoria and her colleagues, they face any number of obstacles to success. Even though LA is a so-called sanctuary city with an extremely diverse population, street vendors of color are often victims of harassment, racism, and discrimination.

When I mention to Victoria that many people do not acknowledge street vendors as valuable members of society, she immediately says, "Why not? Valuable members of society are those who are lawful, who work for a living, who participate in political affairs, and who contribute to the welfare of our society. I am all of those things. I might have a humble job and a small home but that doesn't make me any less valuable in this world."

Street vendors, Victoria points out, are job creators, who help push 5 the economy and generate revenue for cities through payments for licenses and permits, fees and fines, and certain kinds of taxes. According to Women in Informal Employment: Globalizing and Organizing (WIEGO), an organization that seeks to shine a light on the hardships faced by poor working women, "Street vendors are an integral part of urban economies around the world." In addition to the economic contributions of street vendors, WIEGO acknowledges that "street trade adds vibrancy to urban life and in many places is considered a cornerstone of historical and cultural heritage" ("Street Vendors"). Street trade is a multicultural phenomenon that allows people of different ethnic backgrounds to interact with foreign traditions, foods, and customs.

Victoria also believes that street vendors help globalize popular ethnic foods and customs. After all, America is the only place where a middle-aged woman can get up at four in the morning to beat up a few dozen eggs to make nearly four dozen *marquesotes*, and head out by seven with her matching *canasta* and skirt to sell them next to Javier, the lovely man in flannel with the Mexican curios and *rompope* (Mexican eggnog). As Victoria puts it, the melting pot of our country "is all thanks to immigration, and it is what makes this country great. Just think about it. In El Salvador, they don't have a taco bowl for lunch, pho for dinner, and then buy one of my *marquesotes* for dessert. I believe that diversity and freedom are America's pillars. They are what make us a great nation."

But none of that prevents the harassment and bad treatment of street vendors. Shop owners, unhappy when vendors set up shop in front

of their businesses, are often the cause of this aggression. They believe that street vendors steal their customers, or scare potential clients away.

"It's like the shop owners believe they have a right to mistreat us. Besides, the police rarely get involved," Victoria says. "Many times I have seen the people in the store kick out my friends from the sidewalk. I tell them that it is a public area and that they cannot kick us out. They don't care. One time a man intentionally knocked over my bread bucket. That day I didn't have anything to eat, but I did get to hit him in the head."

Despite her short stature, Victoria is one of the most respected street vendors in the area, and she is known for her wit and sass. She is also one of the most active members of the community, often voicing the concerns of her people and defending their rights. She is a supporter of and has been an active participant in the gay rights movement, the fight for female reproductive rights, the Black Lives Matter movement, and other social justice causes. Victoria sees these events as excellent opportunities to exercise her voice. In addition to this, she claims large crowds are wonderful for the business.

Victoria fled El Salvador with her two children after her husband—a high-ranking general for the country's national force—was murdered in the Salvadoran civil war. Since retaliation against a militant's family was common, Victoria thought it best to leave the country, but the road to the United States was long and hard. 10

"It took me about two years to get to California," she tells me. "I traveled with my one-year-old son and my four-year-old daughter. My boy never made it. My girl and I had to bury him on a rocky mountain in Guatemala near the Mexican border. It was one of the hardest things I have ever had to do." Tears stream down her face as she remembers her son's death. "I have never visited his grave. You know, I don't even remember where it is. I never got to say goodbye."

After twenty-seven months of anguish, Victoria and her surviving daughter made it to California. But their struggles had only just begun. Back home in El Salvador, Victoria was an upper-class lady. She was married to a well-respected general and her parents were wealthy ranch owners. Victoria's kids were heirs to her family's haciendas and her husband's riches. Here, she has had to work long hours in harsh conditions just to earn enough money to survive. Upon hearing this, I can't help but wonder if Victoria has ever regretted coming to America.

"Sometimes," she says. "I won't lie, at times I wonder what my life would have been back home, but it is what it is. There is violence here too, but at least here my little girl and I were innocent bystanders and not targets. Our lifestyle was not lavish, but at least we had each other, and we didn't live in constant fear of being attacked."

Before saying goodbye to Victoria, I ask her to debunk a common stereotype of immigrants. She tells me that she sees all immigrants as bound by a sort of "universal immigrant experience" that is widely misunderstood. She says: "Back home, I had a future that was largely truncated by our country's poisoned political system and the crime surrounding it. It's not easy leaving behind everything one holds dear. It's not easy immigrating to a country where your education and knowledge have no value. Many people think of us as failed people. That is wrong. Most of us are here for very specific reasons. We have a goal or a purpose. I want my boy to go to college. Danny over there, partially blind and everything, bought himself that ice cream cart to be able to work. Bills don't pay themselves. Linda unexpectedly took over her husband's magazine cart after he fell ill and Lilyanna began selling bracelets after her husband left her and her two sons. You see, there might be tragedy in our stories but that doesn't make us failed people. We are fighters."

Works Cited

"About SVP." *The Street Vendor Project*, Urban Justice Center, www.streetvendor.org/about/. Accessed 6 Feb. 2017.

"Street Vendors." Women in Informal Employment: Globalizing and Organizing, www.wiego.org/informal-economy/occupational -groups/street-vendors. Accessed 6 Feb. 2017.

academic literacies   rhetorical situations   genres   fields   processes   strategies   research MLA / APA   media / design   readings   handbook

Engaging with the Text

1. Who is the **AUDIENCE** for Ana Pacheco's profile of Victoria Perez? How can you tell?

2. Pacheco uses many **QUOTATIONS** in her profile, letting the subject of the profile speak for herself. Why do you think Pacheco does this? What would be lost if she hadn't used quotations?

3. Pacheco **ENDS** her profile with Perez's views on immigration. Why do you think she chose to end this way? Is this an effective ending? Why or why not?

4. One of the key features of a profile is a **FIRSTHAND ACCOUNT**. Is Pacheco's firsthand account effective? Why or why not?

5. *For writing.* Select a specific group of people, such as student workers, supermarket cashiers, cowboys, or ranchers, and identify a member of that group to interview. Write a **PROFILE** of that person as a member of the larger group they belong to, using the person's own words as well as outside research on the group as a whole.

57–60

528–31

380–85

240

233–45

STEVEN KURUTZ

Can a $300 Cooler Unite America?

Steven Kurutz (b. 1976) is a features reporter for the New York Times, *where this essay appeared in September 2017. Before joining the* Times, *Kurutz was a staff writer at the* Wall Street Journal *and at* Details. *The author of* Like a Rolling Stone: The Strange Life of a Tribute Band *(2008), his writing has also appeared in the* Southern Review, Lit Hub, Beloit Fiction Journal, *and* Creative Nonfiction's True Story.

IN A COUNTRY WHERE WE CAN'T seem to agree on anything, one opinion has lately reached a broad consensus across diverse groups of people: Yeti is pretty awesome.

Miranda Lambert loves her Yeti. Jason Momoa, the beefy actor from *Game of Thrones*, considers his Yeti essential technology. The hit country song "Buy Me a Boat" by Chris Janson is, in part, an ode to Yeti, or rather, an ode to money because, as Mr. Janson sings, "It could buy me a Yeti 110 iced down with some Silver Bullets."

Yeti is wildly popular in liberal Portland, Oregon, and in the conservative South, beloved by grizzled dads who hunt and fish and their beach-going daughters. If you are not yet initiated into the cult, it may surprise you to learn that a Yeti is a plastic cooler.

Think of those hard coolers you buy at Walmart for $30 and use for family picnics and road trips and toss in the garage in between. Yeti coolers are sim-

Credit Jason Raish

ilar, but better-constructed and way more expensive. They are made using a technology called rotomolding (short for rotational molding and involving resin and an oven), and, as home tests have proved, keep cold for days. They cost $380 for the medium-size Tundra 50, topping out at $1,300 for the Tundra 350.

It's now peak Yeti time, because football tailgating season is in high 5 gear. But every day is peak Yeti time, because as Matt Reintjes, the company's chief executive, said, the coolers are "pursuit agnostic." Anywhere people are gathered together and stuff needs to stay cold, he argues (a golf outing with your buddies, a bachelorette weekend, a beer bash in the woods, the parking lot outside a Springsteen concert), is an occasion to bring your Yeti.

"We talk about being 'built for the wild,' but we don't want to define what the wild means," Mr. Reintjes said.

The Yeti Tank 85 at a tailgating event in Tuscaloosa, Alabama, this month. The Yeti may have its biggest fan base in the South. Credit Claire Middlebrooks/Yeti

It's this wide-ranging usefulness that has made Yeti coolers perhaps the only product ever endorsed in the pages of both *Cosmopolitan* and Petersen's *Bowhunting*, which told its readers that a Yeti is key when you have "a pack overflowing with fresh elk meat."

The fact that some Yetis are nearly the cost of a designer suit or Chanel flats has improbably elevated the humble cooler to a luxury status accessory. Onward Reserve, a preppy men's store, sells Yeti coolers alongside Smathers & Branson needlepoint belts and Barbour jackets in its Washington, DC, location. And stylish young women have taken to monogramming and customizing with stickers their Yeti Rambler Lowball tumblers, which cost around $20 for the 10-ounce cup and come in a variety of colors including seafoam.

Carter Coyle, a 29-year-old investigative reporter for WCSC in Charleston, South Carolina, thought Yeti coolers were "completely ridiculous" when she first heard about them "because they're so expensive," she said. But after her fiancé got her a tumbler for Christmas, she became a big fan of the brand. "They're awesome," she said, explaining how when she was out covering Hurricane Irma for the TV station the tumbler "kept my iced coffee cool all day"—a steadying reminder of human progress in the face of nature's chaos.

Ms. Coyle and her fiancé haven't yet splurged on a cooler. But they did include the blue Tundra 45 in their wedding registry and hope to progress to the next rank in the Yeti tribe. "You see everyone with their Yeti cups or coolers or both," Ms. Coyle said. "It's become part of beach culture here. Just like, 'Hey, bring your bathing suit, bring your Yeti.'" 10

The company was founded by Roy and Ryan Seiders, brothers from Texas, who didn't set out to make the Rolex of beer chillers. In 2005, they were avid fishermen and middling businessmen in the outdoors space (Ryan manufactured and sold high-end fishing rods; Roy customized aluminum boats for fishing the Gulf Coast).

Roy was putting coolers on the boats he built, but found the ones on the market wouldn't hold up to the abuse that fishermen put them through. When Ryan discovered a more durable cooler made in Thailand, Roy switched his focus to the cooler business and became a distributor for this model. But he decided he could do even better, and soon Ryan joined him in the business venture.

academic literacies | rhetorical situations | genres | fields | processes | strategies | research MLA / APA | media / design | readings | handbook

The brothers used the same rotomolding process that forms the rigid plastic of kayaks, and they didn't focus on keeping the price low, only making the sturdiest cooler possible. The $300 Yeti was born.

For several years, the coolers were one of the best-kept secrets of hunters and anglers, who bought them at independent hardware stores and outdoors retailers like Cabelas.

But in 2014, Yeti introduced its lower-priced drinkware, along with a range of colors beyond matte white. Then came a stylish soft cooler that could be slung over the shoulder, the original Hopper, priced at $300 at the time. Soon, the brand found favor with a wider range of outdoors enthusiasts and consumers interested in premium goods. Now even city slickers with no obvious need for immediate refrigeration are getting into Yeti, just as they embraced Timberland boots and Canada Goose jackets. 15

At Hatchet Outdoor Supply Co., in Brooklyn Heights, Yeti hard coolers in a range of colors and sizes fill the display window. The store started carrying the coolers in spring 2017, said Matthew Young, a sales associate. "I wasn't sure how they'd sell here," he said. "But they're one of the biggest sellers. We're on our third or fourth shipment. People buy them for camping. Some people want to use them as a backup in case the power goes out."

People have found all sorts of uses for their Yetis. Mr. Reintjes, the CEO, recently heard about a guy walking through the Detroit airport with a Yeti Hopper; he was an American expat businessman, taking a cooler loaded with Chick-fil-A back to his family in Hong Kong. Photographers use the coolers to store equipment.

In a truly strange social media trend that the company has distanced itself from, Yeti fans, mostly college-age women, post photos of themselves to *Instagram* wearing bikinis and sitting on coolers using the hashtag #yetibutts.

The brand seems to have its biggest fan base in the Gulf States and the South, where the coolers are so popular that in Mobile, Alabama, a man broke into an Ace Hardware store in July and made off with $5,000 worth of Yeti merchandise. The local news media called him the "cooler crook."

Meredith Tannehill, who runs Mish Mash Interiors, a gift shop in Augusta, Georgia, has owned a Yeti Roadie 20 cooler for three years, 20 along with several tumblers. She said in the humid South, Yeti is less a trendy fashion accessory than a necessity.

"Down here it's hot, what, 80 percent of the year?" Ms. Tannehill said. "They're expensive, but they're worth it."

Before Yeti came along with its coolers and tumblers, she doesn't know how she dealt with melting ice and drinks gone tepid. As far as she's concerned, the Yeti is a divine invention.

"It was kind of like all of a sudden there was Yeti," Ms. Tannehill said. "God dropped the Yeti down: 'Here you go, South, it's hot, I see you're struggling.'"

Engaging with the Text

239 ▲
240–41
401–8 ◆

1. Do you find the **SUBJECT** of this profile interesting? Why or why not? What **ENGAGING DETAILS** does Kurutz use to bring his subject to life?

2. What **EVIDENCE** does Kurutz offer to make the case that the Yeti is extremely popular today? Do you find the evidence convincing? Why or why not?

57–60 ■

3. This piece was published in the *New York Times*, which means it was probably written for a wide **AUDIENCE**. How does Kurutz shape his profile to appeal to a wide range of people? How might his profile be different if he had written it for an audience of hunters? college students? seniors?

4. What is your opinion of the Yeti cooler? What are the pros and cons? Would you purchase a Yeti if you could? Why or why not?

233–45 ▲
528–31 ●

5. *For Writing.* Choose a popular product that appeals to a wide range of people, interview several people who use this product, and write a **PROFILE** of it, using **QUOTATIONS** from the product users where appropriate. Be sure to include engaging details to help bring your subject to life.

TATIANA SCHLOSSBERG

At This Academy, the Curriculum Is Garbage

Tatiana Schlossberg (b. 1990) is an environmental journalist, formerly with the New York Times, where this profile appeared in 2014. She previously wrote for the Yale Herald, an undergraduate newspaper at Yale University where she also served as editor, and the Bergen Record, a newspaper in northern New Jersey where she primarily covered crime and police work.

R OSE-GOLD LIGHT WAS FALLING ONTO JAMAICA BAY and sea gulls passed overhead on another beautiful morning at Floyd Bennett Field in Brooklyn, a far reach of New York City mostly devoid of New Yorkers and cars.

It was a perfect setting, then, for learning how to drive a garbage truck, which is why some of the world's least graceful vehicles were groaning and screeching their way through a narrow trail of orange traffic cones. Nearby, where Sanitation Department trainees were learning how to both load the trucks and dump them, the air was filled with sounds familiar to any New Yorker—the crashing of cans and crushing of garbage in the early morning hours, so loud it might as well be happening inside one's bedroom.

"Hey!" an instructor called out to his students. "You have to make sure the hopper's closed before you drive off!"

Police academies are famous enough to have earned their own movie franchise, and stories about firefighters learning how to slide down a firehouse pole as a loyal Dalmatian watches nearby, and hop on a blaring truck are easy enough to imagine. But sanitation workers must be trained too—to pick up trash, recyclables and, now, compost every day; to sweep the streets and clear them after a snowstorm, and remove fallen trees after a hurricane; and to operate the half-dozen types of trucks needed to keep the city's streets and sidewalks tidy.

From the summer to the start of snow season, the Sanitation 5 Department will train 450 new workers at its academy, bringing the

Students practiced driving a garbage truck by navigating an obstacle course set up at the Sanitation Department academy at Floyd Bennett Field in Brooklyn.

force to 6,000 uniformed workers. A class of 125 that graduated on Friday is the first of four that will go through the four-week training this year.

On a recent day at the academy, after roll call and calisthenics, the trainees separated into groups. One learned about snow, though not a flake was around. Another practiced driving and dumping, and a third focused on changing tires, operating forklifts and washing the trucks.

At a session devoted to cleaning up litter, an instructor was teaching his students about one of the department's biggest occupational hazards: syringes in trash bags.

"Do you have X-ray vision?" he asked. He warned the trainees to hold the bags away from their bodies. "There could be needles in there!"

Another instructor showed his group how to line up the end of a snow chain with a forward-facing ridge on the tire, and then wind it

Without a flake to be seen, Edward Leccese, 36, and James Maggiore, 31, both from Staten Island, learned how to attach chains to the tires of snowplows.

around clockwise. He explained that once they went to work, the trainees would need to learn how to do it quickly, because hunching over the tire of a truck carrying 16 tons of salt "isn't somewhere you want to be for too long." His students practiced putting the chains on three more times.

No one was learning how to hang off the back of a truck. The 10 department put a stop to the practice about four years ago after deciding it was too risky.

"I'm horrified when I see the private carters doing that," said Kathryn Garcia, the city's sanitation commissioner. "It's already a dangerous job."

To cut down on injuries further, Ms. Garcia has introduced a stretching program for workers to follow before heading out on their trucks in the morning.

The training does not cover how to deal with rats. When asked if he had any advice for avoiding rodent-related injuries, Steven Harbin, a department chief who runs the training academy, paused and then said, "Get a broom and tap the can."

The Sanitation Department's training academy was created in 1950, but there have been formal efforts to train new workers since the early 20th century, when the agency was known as the Department of Street Cleaning, said Robin Nagle, the department's resident anthropologist.

Picking up dead horses and stopping cholera are no longer concerns. 15 More recently the department, which has a budget of $1.4 billion, has taken on a role as the city's environmental brigade, gathering up separated plastics, paper and food waste; and as the agency that redeems or bedevils the mayor, depending on how fast the streets are cleared of snow.

Despite what some would consider drawbacks of the job, it is in high demand. Applicants must first pass a written exam, which was last given in 2007 because of hiring freezes. A new test is scheduled for the fall, a spokesman for the department said.

When new hires are finally called, but before they enter the academy, they must pass a physical evaluation, which mostly involves lifting and throwing garbage bags and cans of various weights in a specified amount of time. The physical test used to be harder and was widely known within the Civil Service as the "Superman" test for the number of feats of strength it entailed.

After criticism that the exam was unnecessarily difficult and an obstacle for women hoping to join the department, it was made somewhat easier—workers no longer had to try to vault over an eight-foot wall, for example—and in 1986, the city hired its first garbagewomen.

Now about 3 percent of the sanitation force, and five of the 125 current trainees, are women, including Valerie Albanese, a former school safety officer from Staten Island. Ms. Albanese, 43, said she had switched jobs because she liked physical labor.

"I'm also very excited to work with maggots," she joked. 20

Though most of the students in the current class said they considered the pay and benefits good, there was, not surprisingly, some envy of graduates of the police and fire academies, who earn more money and get all the glory.

After five and a half years, a sanitation worker can earn up to $69,933, not including overtime, about $20,000 less than police officers with the same experience. And sanitation veterans joke stoically that while the police get to ride their horses in parades, the garbage workers get to clean up after them.

"Maybe one day, when the New York Rangers are in the playoffs, we'll be able to have our honor guard standing behind them for the national anthem, instead of the Fire Department," said Patrick Siliato, 29, an academy instructor whose father is also a sanitation worker. (The Sanitation Department does indeed have an honor guard.)

The equipment that sanitation workers use, though, can be every bit as intricate as the gear on a fire engine. At the academy, one group of students was being trained in how to work a front-end loader, which is used to move heavy materials, like snow, salt, dirt and other debris. Operating the vehicle requires manipulating three pedals, two levers and a steering wheel that controls the body and front axle at once.

George Wilmer, a trainee from Crown Heights, Brooklyn, who was   25 eating an Italian combo sandwich during a midmorning break, was learning on the garbage truck. He said he used to work in shipping and receiving before finally getting the call from the Sanitation Department this year, seven years after taking the written test.

Mr. Wilmer, 43, said that he had knocked over a few cones when he was going through the obstacle course, but that it was "to be expected."

Another trainee, Anthony Olivieri, 27, a member of the New York National Guard whose mother is a sanitation worker, disagreed. He said he had not knocked over a single cone.

Mr. Wilmer said, "I used to have trucks like these ones under my Christmas tree when I was little.

"Now I get to play with the real thing."

Engaging with the Text

64–67

1. Tatiana Schlossberg maintains a lighthearted yet respectful **STANCE** toward her subject of garbage school. How is this stance appropriate given the subject? What other stance might she have taken?

386–87

2. The **TITLE** of Schlossberg's profile can be read in two ways: either the curriculum is bad or it is devoted to garbage. Newspapers often use clever headlines of this kind to draw readers into an article. Suggest two other ways the profile might be titled—one simply informative and the other using a play on words or some other form of humor, like the actual title.

528–31

3. Schlossberg includes many **QUOTATIONS**. Choose two of them that strike you as especially interesting, and explain what they add to the profile.

380–85

4. Schlossberg **ENDS** her profile with a quotation from one of the students: "Mr. Wilmer said, 'I used to have trucks like these ones under my Christmas tree when I was little. Now I get to play with the real thing.'" Is this an effective way to end? Why or why not? Why do you think Schlossberg chose to end this way?

5. *For Writing.* Schlossberg focuses on a subject that most of her readers have probably never thought about, namely, how sanitation workers are trained. Select a person whose job does not get much public notice yet is crucial to helping a community or an institution to function well, such as an administrator or an assistant at your school or a telephone repair person. Write a **PROFILE** on a day in the life of this worker that reveals how important the job is.

233–45

Proposals 69

MICHAEL CHABON

Kids' Stuff

Michael Chabon (b. 1963) has published a dozen books, about half of them novels, including The Yiddish Policemen's Union (2007), *the serialized novel* Gentlemen of the Road (2007), *and most recently* Moonglow: A Novel (2016). *In 2001, he was awarded a Pulitzer Prize for Fiction for his novel* The Amazing Adventures of Kavalier & Clay, *which explores the lives of two Jewish comic-book artists in the 1940s. In addition to his novels, Chabon has written short-story and essay collections, newspaper serials, screenplays, children's and young-adult books, and comics. "Kids' Stuff" originated as a keynote speech at the 2004 Eisner Awards, known as the "Oscar awards of the comics industry."*

FOR AT LEAST THE FIRST FORTY YEARS OF THEIR EXISTENCE, from the Paleo-zoic pre-Superman era of *Famous Funnies* (1933) and *More Fun Comics* (1936), comic books were widely viewed, even by those who adored them, as juvenile: the ultimate greasy kids' stuff.* Comics were the lit-erary equivalent of bubblegum cards, to be poked into the spokes of a young mind, where they would produce a satisfying—but entirely bogus—rumble of pleasure. But almost from the first, fitfully in the early days, intermittently through the fifties, and then starting in the mid-sixties with increasing vigor and determination, a battle has been waged by writers, artists, editors, and publishers to elevate the medium, to expand the scope of its subject matter and the range of its artistic styles, to sharpen and increase the sophistication of its language and visual grammar, to probe and explode the limits of the sequential panel, to give free rein to irony, tragedy, autobiography, and other grown-up-type modes of expression.

Also from the first, a key element—at times the central element—of this battle has been the effort to alter not just the medium itself but the

---

*Greasy kids' stuff: a phrase used in 1960s advertisements for Vitalis, a men's hair-care product, to disparage competing brands. [Editor's note]

public perception of the medium. From the late, great Will Eisner's lonely insistence, in an interview with the *Baltimore Sun* back in 1940 (1940!), on the artistic credibility of comics, to the nuanced and scholarly work of recent comics theorists, both practitioners and critics have been arguing passionately on behalf of comics' potential to please—in all the aesthetic richness of that term—the most sophisticated of readers.

The most sophisticated, that is, of *adult* readers. For the adult reader of comic books has always been the holy grail, the promised land, the imagined lover who will greet the long-suffering comic-book maker, at the end of the journey, with open arms, with acceptance, with approval.

A quest is often, among other things, an extended bout of inspired madness. Over the years this quest to break the chains of childish readership has resulted, like most bouts of inspired madness, in both folly and stunning innovation. Into the latter category we can put the work of Bernard Krigstein or Frank Miller, say, with their attempts to approximate, through radical attack on the conventions of panel layouts, the fragmentation of human consciousness by urban life; or the tight, tidy, miniaturized madness of Chris Ware. Into the former category—the folly—we might put all the things that got Dr. Frederic Wertham so upset about EC Comics in the early fifties, the syringe-pierced eyeballs and baseball diamonds made from human organs; or the short-lived outfitting of certain Marvel titles in 1965 with a label that boasted "A Marvel Pop Art Production"; or the hypertrophied, tooth-gnashing, blood-letting quote unquote heroes of the era that followed Miller's *The Dark Knight Returns*. An excess of the desire to appear grown up is one of the defining characteristics of adolescence. But these follies were the inevitable missteps and overreaching in the course of a campaign that was, in the end, successful.

Because the battle has now, in fact, been won. Not only are comics 5 appealing to a wider and older audience than ever before, but the idea of comics as a valid art form on a par at least with, say, film or rock and roll is widely if not quite universally accepted. Comics and graphic novels are regularly reviewed and debated in *Entertainment Weekly*, the *New York Times Book Review*, even in the august pages of the *New York Review of Books*. Ben Katchor won a MacArthur Fellowship, and Art Spiegelman a Pulitzer Prize.

A vintage Spider-Man cover.

academic literacies   rhetorical situations   genres   fields   processes   strategies   research MLA / APA   media / design   readings   handbook

But the strange counterphenomenon to this indisputable rise in the reputation, the ambition, the sophistication, and the literary and artistic merit of many of our best comics over the past couple of decades is that over roughly the same period comics readership has declined. Some adults are reading better comics than ever before; but fewer people overall are reading any—far fewer, certainly, than in the great sales heyday of the medium, the early fifties, when by some estimates* as many as 650 million comic books were sold annually (compared to somewhere in the neighborhood of 80 million today). The top ten best-selling comic books in 1996, primarily issues making up two limited series, Marvel's *Civil Wars* and DC's *Infinite Crisis*, were all superhero books, and, like the majority of superhero books in the post–*Dark Knight*, post-*Watchmen* era, all of them dealt rather grimly, and in the somewhat hand-wringing fashion that has become obligatory, with the undoubtedly grown-up issues of violence, freedom, terrorism, vigilantism, political repression, mass hysteria, and the ambivalent nature of heroism. Among the top ten best-selling titles in 1960 (with an aggregate circulation, for all comics, of 400 million) one finds not only the expected *Superman* and *Batman* (decidedly sans ambivalence) but *Mickey Mouse*, *Looney Tunes*, and the classic sagas of *Uncle Scrooge*. And nearly the whole of the list for that year, from top to bottom, through *Casper the Friendly Ghost* (#14) and *Little Archie* (#25) to *Felix the Cat* (#47), is made up of kids' stuff, more or less greasy.

To recap—Days when comics were aimed at kids: huge sales. Days when comics are aimed at adults: not so huge sales, and declining.

The situation is more complicated than that, of course. Since 1960 there have been fundamental changes in a lot of things, among them the way comics are produced, licensed, marketed, and distributed. But maybe it is not too surprising that for a while now, fundamental changes and all, some people have been wondering: what if there were comic books for children?

---

*See, for example, www.comichron.com.

Leaving aside questions of creator's rights, paper costs, retail consolidation, the explosive growth of the collector market, and direct-market sales, a lot of comic-book people will tell you that there is simply too much competition for the kid dollar these days and that, thrown into the arena with video games, special-effects-laden films, the internet, iPods, etc., comics will inevitably lose out. I find this argument unconvincing, not to mention a cop-out. It is, furthermore, an example of our weird naïveté, in this generation, about how sophisticated we and our children have become vis-à-vis our parents and grandparents, of the misguided sense of retrospective superiority we tend to display toward them and their vanished world. As if in 1960 there was not a *ton* of cool stuff besides comic books on which a kid could spend his or her considerably less constricted time and considerably more limited funds. In the early days of comics, in fact, unlike now, a moderately adventuresome child could find all kinds of things to do that were not only fun (partly because they took place with no adult supervision or mediation), but absolutely free. The price of fun doesn't get any more competitive than that.

I also refuse to accept as explanation for anything the often-tendered argument that contemporary children are more sophisticated, that the kind of comics that pleased a seven-year-old in 1960 would leave an ultracool kid of today snickering with disdain. Even if we accept this argument with respect to "old-fashioned" comics, it would seem to be invalidated by the increasing sophistication of comic books over the past decades. But I reject its very premise. The supposed sophistication—a better term would be *knowingness*—of modern children is largely, I believe, a matter of style, a pose which they have adapted from and modeled on the rampant pose of knowingness, of being wised up, that characterizes the contemporary American style, and has done at least since the late fifties–early sixties heyday of *Mad* magazine (a publication largely enjoyed, from the beginning, by children). Even in their irony and cynicism there is something appealingly insincere, maladroit, and, well, *childish* about children. What is more, I have found that even my own children, as knowing as they often like to present themselves, still take profound pleasure in the old

10

comics that I have given them to read. My older son has still not quite recovered from the heartbreak he felt, when he was seven, reading an old "archive edition" of *Legion of Superheroes*, at the tragic death of Ferro Lad.

Children did not abandon comics; comics, in their drive to attain respect and artistic accomplishment, abandoned children. And for a long time the lovers and partisans of comics were afraid, after so many years of struggle and hard work and incremental gains, to pick up that old jar of greasy kid stuff again, and risk undoing all the labor of so many geniuses and revolutionaries and ordinary, garden-variety artists. Comics have always been an arriviste art form, and all upstarts are to some degree ashamed of their beginnings. But shame, anxiety, the desire to preserve hard-won gains—such considerations no longer serve to explain the disappearance of children's comics. The truth is that comic-book creators have simply lost the habit of telling stories to children. And how sad is that?

When commentators on comics address this question, in the hope of encouraging publishers, writers, and artists to produce new comic books with children in mind, they usually try formulating some version of the following simple equation: create more child readers now, and you will find yourselves with more adult readers later on. Hook them early, in other words. But maybe the equation isn't so simple after all. Maybe what we need, given the sophistication of children (if we want to concede that point) and the competition for their attention and their disposable income (which has always been a factor), is not simply *more* comics for kids, but more *great* comics for kids.

Easy, I suppose, for me to say. So although I am certain that there are many professional creators of comics—people with a good ear and a sharp eye for and a natural understanding of children and their enthusiasms—who would be able to do a far better job of it, having thrown down the finned, skintight gauntlet, I now feel obliged to offer, at the least, a few tentative principles and one concrete suggestion on how more great comics for kids might be teased into the marketplace, even by amateurs like me. I have drawn these principles, in part, from my memories of the comics I loved when I was young, but I think they hold true as well for the best and most successful works of children's literature.

1. Let's not tell stories that we think "kids of today" might like. That is a route to inevitable failure and possible loss of sanity. *We should tell stories that we would have liked as kids.* Twist endings, the unexpected usefulness of unlikely knowledge, nobility and bravery where it's least expected, and the sudden emergence of a thread of goodness in a wicked nature, those were the kind of stories told by the writers and artists of the comic books that I liked.

2. Let's tell stories that, over time, build up an intricate, involved, involving mythology that is also accessible and comprehensible at any point of entry. The intricacy, the accretion of lore over time, should be both inventive and familiar, founded in old mythologies and fears but fully reinterpreted, reimagined. It will demand, it will ache, to be mastered by a child's mythology-mastering imagination. The accessibility will come from our making a commitment to tell a full, complete story, or a complete piece of a story, in every issue. This kind of layering of intricate lore and narrative completeness was a hallmark of the great "Superman-family" books (Adventure, Jimmy Olsen, Superboy) under the editorship of Mort Weisinger.   15

3. Let's cultivate an unflagging readiness as storytellers to retell the same stories *with endless embellishment.* Anybody who thinks that kids get bored by hearing the same story over and over again has never spent time telling stories to kids. The key, as in baroque music, is repetition with *variation.* Again the Mort Weisinger–edited *Superman* books, written by unflagging storytellers like Edmond Hamilton and Otto Binder, were exemplary in this regard. The proliferation of theme and variation there verges, at times, on sheer, splendid madness.

4. Let's blow their little minds. A mind is not blown, in spite of whatever Hollywood seems to teach, merely by action sequences, things exploding, thrilling planetscapes, wild bursts of speed. Those are all good things; but a mind is blown when something that you always feared but knew to be impossible turns out to be true; when the world turns out to be far vaster,

far more marvelous or malevolent than you ever dreamed; when you get proof that everything is connected to everything else, that everything you know is wrong, that you are both the center of the universe and a tiny speck sailing off its nethermost edge.

So much for my principles: here is my concrete suggestion. If it seems a little obvious, or has already been tried and failed, then I apologize. But I cannot help noticing that in the world of children's *literature*, an over-whelming preponderance of stories are stories *about* children. The same is true of films for children: the central characters are nearly always a child, or a pair or group of children. Comic books, however, even those theoretically aimed at children, are almost always about adults or teen-agers. Doesn't that strike you as odd? I suggest that a publisher should try putting out a truly thrilling, honestly observed and remembered, richly imagined, involved and yet narratively straightforward comic book for children, *about children*.

My oldest son is ten now, and he likes comic books. In 1943, if you were a ten-year-old, you probably knew a dozen other kids your age who were into Captain Marvel and the Submariner and the Blue Beetle. When I was ten, in 1973, I knew three or four. But in his class, in his world, my son is all but unique; he's the only one he knows who reads them, studies them, seeks to master and be worthy of all the rapture and strangeness they still contain. Now, comic books are so important to me—I have thought, talked, and written about them so much—that if my son did not in fact like them, I think he would be obliged to loathe them. I have pretty much *forced* comics on my children. But those of us who grew up loving comic books can't afford to take this handcrafted, one-kid-at-a-time approach anymore. We have to sweep them up and carry them off on the flying carpets of story and pictures on which we ourselves, in entire generations, were borne aloft, on carpets woven by Curt Swan and Edmond Hamilton, Jack Kirby and Stan Lee, Chris Claremont and John Byrne. Those artists did it for us; we who make comics today have a solemn debt to pass it on, to weave bright carpets of our own. It's our duty, it's our opportunity, and I really do believe it will be our pleasure.

Engaging with the Text

_249_ ▲

1. Good proposals present a **WELL-DEFINED PROBLEM** so that readers understand the need for a solution. What problem does Michael Chabon present? How persuasively does he make the case for its existence and seriousness?

2. Chabon does not accept the argument made by comic-book people that the reason comic books today are being published more for adults than for children is that "there is simply too much competition for the kid dollar these days and that, thrown into the arena with video games, special-effects-laden films, the internet, iPods, etc., comics will inevitably lose out." Why does he find this position unconvincing? What is your opinion on why the sales of comic books are declining and why so few are for children?

_400–401_ ◆

3. What are the four principles Chabon offers for creating great comics for kids? What **REASONS** does he offer for these principles?

_57–60_ ■

4. What aspects of Chabon's proposal seem aimed particularly at his intended **AUDIENCE**—the kinds of "writers, artists, editors, and publishers" who attend the Eisner Awards? What parts might they find flattering? challenging? What parts might they be especially sympathetic to? Why?

_246–55_ ▲

5. **For Writing.** Research some children's pastimes—such as card games, board games, or jigsaw puzzles—to identify one that has declined in popularity over the last fifty years. How would you propose bringing it back? What would it take to get kids interested in this pastime today? Write a **PROPOSAL** that outlines your ideas for reinvigorating the pastime.

DENNIS BARON

Don't Make English Official—Ban It Instead

Dennis Baron (b. 1944) is a professor of English and linguistics at the University of Illinois at Urbana-Champaign. His essays on the history of English usage, language legislation, and technology and literacy have been widely published in newspapers and magazines. His books include The English-Only Question: An Official Language for Americans? *(1992),* A Better Pencil: Reading, Writers, and the Digital Revolution *(2009), and* The Wit of William Shakespeare *(2012). He also serves as a consultant to policy makers, lawyers, and journalists on questions concerning language. The following proposal originally appeared in the* Washington Post *in 1996.*

CONGRESS IS CONSIDERING, and may soon pass, legislation making English the official language of the United States. Supporters of the measure say that English forms the glue that keeps America together. They deplore the dollars wasted translating English into other languages. And they fear a horde of illegal aliens adamantly refusing to acquire the most powerful language on earth.

On the other hand, opponents of official English remind us that without legislation we have managed to get over ninety-seven percent of the residents of this country to speak the national language. No country with an official language law even comes close. Opponents also point out that today's non-English-speaking immigrants are picking up English faster than earlier generations of immigrants did, so instead of official English, they favor "English Plus," encouraging everyone to speak both English and another language.

I would like to offer a modest proposal to resolve the language impasse in Congress. Don't make English official, ban it instead.

That may sound too radical, but proposals to ban English first surfaced in the heady days after the American Revolution. Anti-British sentiment was so strong in the new United States that a few superpatriots wanted to get rid of English altogether. They suggested replacing English with Hebrew,

thought by many in the eighteenth century to be the world's first language, the one spoken in the garden of Eden. French was also considered,
because it was thought at the time, and especially by the French, to be
the language of pure reason. And of course
there was Greek, the language of Athens, the
world's first democracy. It's not clear how
serious any of these proposals were, though
Roger Sherman* of Connecticut supposedly
remarked that it would be better to keep
English for ourselves and make the British speak Greek.

**Proposals to ban
English first surfaced
shortly after the
American Revolution.**

Even if the British are now our allies, there may be some benefit to   5
banning English today. A common language can often be the cause of
strife and misunderstanding. Look at Ireland and Northern Ireland, the
two Koreas, or the Union and the Confederacy. Banning English would
prevent that kind of divisiveness in America today.

Also, if we banned English, we wouldn't have to worry about whose
English to make official: the English of England or America? of Chicago
or New York? of Ross Perot or William F. Buckley?†

We might as well ban English, too, because no one seems to read it
much lately, few can spell it, and fewer still can parse it. Even English
teachers have come to rely on computer spell checkers.

Another reason to ban English: it's hardly even English anymore.
English started its decline in 1066, with the unfortunate incident at Hastings.‡ Since then it has become a polyglot conglomeration of French,
Latin, Italian, Scandinavian, Arabic, Sanskrit, Celtic, Yiddish and Chinese,
with an occasional smiley face thrown in.

More important, we should ban English because it has become a
world language. Remember what happened to all the other world lan-

---

Roger Sherman (1721–93): American revolutionary leader and signer of the Declaration of Independence and the U.S. Constitution. [Editor's note]

†*William F. Buckley Jr.* (1925–2008): conservative political commentator. *Ross Perot*:
American industrialist and independent presidential candidate. [Editor's note]

‡*Hastings*: port on south coast of England, site of Saxon army's defeat by the invading
Norman forces led by William of Normandy (c. 1028–87). [Editor's note]

academic literacies | rhetorical situations | genres | fields | processes | strategies | research MLA / APA | media / design | readings | handbook

guages: Latin, Greek, Indo-European? One day they're on everybody's tongue; the next day they're dead. Banning English now would save us that inevitable disappointment.

Although we shouldn't ban English without designating a replacement for it, there is no obvious candidate. The French blew their chance when they sold Louisiana. It doesn't look like the Russians are going to take over this country anytime soon—they're having enough trouble taking over Russia. German, the largest minority language in the U.S. until recently, lost much of its prestige after two world wars. Chinese is too hard to write, especially if you're not Chinese. There's always Esperanto, a language made up a hundred years ago that is supposed to bring about world unity. We're still waiting for that. And if you took Spanish in high school you can see that it's not easy to get large numbers of people to speak another language fluently.

> **We might as well ban English . . . no one seems to read it much lately.**

In the end, though, it doesn't matter what replacement language we pick, just so long as we ban English instead of making it official. Prohibiting English will do for the language what Prohibition did for liquor. Those who already use it will continue to do so, and those who don't will want to try out what has been forbidden. This negative psychology works with children. It works with speed limits. It even worked in the Garden of Eden.

Engaging with the Text

1. Dennis Baron signals that his proposal is meant as satire when he writes, "I would like to offer a modest proposal to resolve the language impasse in Congress. Don't make English official, ban it instead." Here Baron alludes to Jonathan Swift's "A Modest Proposal," an essay that is a tour de force of satire. If we aren't meant to take his proposal at face value—and we aren't—what is its **PURPOSE**? What, in other words, is the real argument Baron is making?

55–56

373–80

2. Baron **BEGINS** his essay by presenting two views on whether or not English should be the official language of the United States. What is the central problem that both sides are trying to address? Is this an effective beginning? Why or why not? How else might he have begun?

400–401

3. Baron offers six **REASONS** for accepting his "solution." What are they? What is the central point that holds these different reasons together?

4. If Baron's purpose is not actually to propose banning English in America, why do you think he chose to use the proposal genre to put forth his argument? What other **GENRES** might he have used?

73

246–55

5. *For Writing.* Identify a current hotly debated issue in the country, your state, your town, or your school. **PROPOSE** an outlandish solution for the problem and provide a plausible, if ironic, argument for your solution. Be sure to anticipate—and respond to—possible objections to your proposed solution.

academic literacies   rhetorical situations   genres   fields   processes   strategies   research MLA / APA   media / design   readings   handbook

JOHNNA S. KELLER

The Politics of Stairs

Johnna S. Keller (b. 1973) is an architect who specializes in sustainable design and currently works at M+A Architects in Columbus, Ohio. Keller has written and presented on sustainability and social equity at a number of conferences, and is a co-facilitator of the Living Building Challenge Collaborative in Columbus. This essay appeared in 2016 in Design Equilibrium, *a magazine published by the Atlanta chapter of the American Institute of Architects (AIA Atlanta).*

A FEW MONTHS AGO, a friend sent me an image on *Facebook*. It shows a wheelchair user facing an elevator confronted with the words, "Today is the day we take the stairs."

This example demonstrates how the concept of "human-powered living" fails to include all humans, and unfortunately, this example is part of a growing trend in architecture. Stairs have been reborn as the energy-conserving and health-promoting sister to the elevator, especially in sustainable design. However, if stairs and stair users have been reimagined as the preferred sustainable building occupant, then it appears that occupants with mobility impairments, relegated to using an energy-consuming elevator, have become marginalized as undesirable occupants. Ironically, this is occurring at a time when social equity is reemerging as an integral part of the triple bottom line of sustainability, which inspires the question: how can we best bring together sustainability with social equity?

In a growing number of new building projects, energy conservation measures are implemented via rigorous design strategies and energy-saving programs. In a Seattle project that has been called "the greenest commercial building in the world," the design team created the "irresistible stairway" with panoramic views of the city in the name of health and energy conservation, meanwhile locating the elevator at the back of the building and making it accessible only via keycard. In

A sign urging people to take the stairs instead of the elevator so they will burn more calories.

addition, the tenants must abide by strict energy usage budgets and are fined for any overages. Imagine an employee in a wheelchair in a building like this, or an important client who uses a cane, or a parent with a sick toddler in a stroller visiting a doctor's office, and you begin to see how a tucked-away elevator with controlled access can be problematic.

Preferred stairways, like the "irresistible stairway," incorporate the design approach called the "pull strategy," which promotes desired behavior via information, aesthetic quality, or sensory appeal. For example, by locating the main stairway in a visually more prominent location than any motorized vertical circulation elements (i.e., elevators and escalators), providing increased lighting or sensory stimulation elements, like artwork and music, and installing motivational signage, building users are "pulled" or encouraged to use the stairs rather than hunting down the elevator. The intent of these pull strategies is to improve occupant health through physical activity and to reduce environmental impacts associated with energy consumption. Pull strategies such as these are integrated into the Leadership in Energy and Environmental Design (LEED) green building program as the pilot credit, "Design for Active Occupants," and were recently introduced as a requirement for the "Human Powered Living" Imperative in the Living Building Challenge (LBC) 3.0 and the "Interior Fitness Circulation" Precondition in the newly introduced WELL Building Standard v1.0.

However, these growing programs have imagined pull strategies that 5 benefit only one type of user—those who want to and are able to climb stairs—and in this way, these programs have created an unequal stan-

The bottom floor of the Stedelijk Museum in Amsterdam, which offers three modes of vertical transport: an elevator, an escalator, and a flight of stairs. The designer has chosen to integrate these three into a triptych, so that each mode of transport is visible from a single vantage point on the floor. Photo © Margaret Price.

dard of access. In such situations, architects are applying accessibility in a "check-the-box" way; that is, they are attempting to comply with the bare minimum of ADA Standards for Accessible Design, and nothing further. At times, this creates architectural designs that border on the nonsensical—for example, locating accessible restrooms on the second floor of a building with no elevator. The ADA Standards do not detail how to create equal access, which is why we often find the accessible entrance in the rear of a building or, as in the case of "the greenest commercial building in the world," elevators hidden in the back. If we are not creating sustainable buildings that are equally accessible by all occupants, then there is a fundamental flaw with our sustainable building standards and their future within our field.

The foundation of sustainability is built on best practices, rather than minimum guidelines. It is about going above and beyond to create better buildings for the occupants and our environment. For instance, the LEED rating system's bare minimum requirements, or prerequisites, are already based on achieving percentages beyond minimum design requirements for water and energy use, and earning points towards

Moving sidewalk roped off with the words "Saving Energy for the Future" in the Denver International Airport.

certification requires going above and beyond that. The LBC goes even further than the LEED rating system in almost every respect, even social equity. If that is the case, then why are we "checking a box" when it comes to accessibility, especially if it marginalizes a portion of our building occupants? What might happen to the way our buildings look if we reimagined access as the priority end use, allowing that goal to inspire new and creative design strategies?

For example, what if we incorporate more passive heating and cooling strategies to accommodate less available energy, or if we have different user expectations of what conditioned spaces feel like? Or what if we encourage manufacturers of elevators and escalators to use less energy, or possibly even no energy, the way we are transforming the marketplace for building materials? What if we install different vertical circulation elements, like ramps—not as an afterthought, but as a central design strategy? There are many what-if questions that we could ask ourselves as creative designers of the built environment, but perhaps a foundational question is: what is sustainability without equity?

Architects might benefit from rethinking equal access and designing user choice among vertical circulation elements. What if, instead of signs that read "Take the stairs!" there were signs that read "The temperature in this building is set to x degrees in order to prioritize our energy use for access to everyone."

Engaging with the Text

1. Keller's essay originally appeared in *Design Equilibrium,* a magazine for architects. What other **AUDIENCES** might be interested in this proposal? Why?

   57–60

2. Keller's proposal begins with an anecdote about a wheelchair user confronting a sign on an elevator urging people to use the stairs. How does this beginning help **DEFINE THE PROBLEM** Keller proposes to solve? How does Keller combine accessibility and sustainability in the discussion of the problem?

   249

386–87 ◆

3. The **TITLE** of Keller's essay is "The Politics of Stairs." Since "politics" can be thought of as the ways in which power is used in a society, what does this title imply about the role of power in the design of public places? What kinds of power is Keller alluding to? Who has it? Who doesn't?

432–42 ◆

4. How does Keller **DEFINE** "pull strategy"? According to Keller, what are the shortcomings of this strategy in current building design?

5. *For Writing*. Identify another issue related to sustainability (actions or policies that meet current needs while making sure future generations' needs are also met) or accessibility (ease of use or entry for everyone) that concerns you. Describe the problem and write a **PROPOSAL** for how it might be solved.

246–55 ▲

**ANDREAS GHABRIAL, ALANA HARDY,
and OGDEN PLAYGROUND COMMITTEE**

Proposal for Ogden Playground Project

Andreas Ghabrial, Alana Hardy, and the Ogden Playground Committee were members of the Ogden Junior Public School community in Toronto, Canada, when this proposal was written. Ghabrial was the school's principal and Hardy its vice-principal. This proposal was published on April 25, 2013; in August 2015, work began on the construction of a new playground for the school community.

I. Summary

We are inviting you to participate in an ambitious and much-needed playground revitalization project taking place in downtown Toronto at Ogden Junior Public School.

Ogden Junior Public School is a vibrant inner-city learning community committed to providing a safe and caring learning environment for our Junior Kindergarten to Grade 6 students. Nestled between Chinatown and the Financial District in downtown Toronto, our history dates back to 1855. We are lucky to have a naturalized setting for part of our yard, yet there is a lack of playground equipment, since our most recent structure was torn down over fifteen years ago due to safety issues. Our school yard contains a broken asphalt surface with one meager basketball net, one set of monkey bars that are too high for our students to utilize, and one old climber.

Our mission is to create a beautiful space where families can gather, play, share ideas, and build a sense of community. We envision new recreational facilities including a safe and inclusive playground, a soft grass playing field, and a running track that will help our young athletes participate in various sports. We envision a greener space for more native trees, perennial plantings, and a vegetable/flower garden that can be enjoyed by everyone, as well as chess tables and a badminton court to bring together our neighbors and community.

As a small inner city school with limited fundraising abilities, the Ogden community has worked hard to raise $10,000 over a four year period, but unfortunately we are still well short of our ultimate goal of $200,000. As it is virtually impossible for us to raise the required amount internally, we are imploring our local community for support.

We are hoping that you would consider supporting our community venture by donating generously toward our fundraising goal. This would create a positive collaborative relationship between you and your local school and community. We look forward to hearing from you in the near future so that we can begin our journey together.

Andreas Ghabrial, Principal
Alana Hardy, Vice-Principal
Ogden Playground Committee

II. Introduction

Our mission statement is to create a beautiful space where families can gather, play, share ideas, and build a sense of community. We want a safe, beautiful place for children to run, jump, and explore the

Ogden Junior Public School courtyard

natural world around them. Ogden Jr. PS is a vibrant inner-city learning community. Our JK to Grade 6 public elementary school is situated in Toronto, just north of Queen Street and east of Spadina Avenue. We are lucky enough to have a naturalized setting for part of our yard, but our kids and our community want to expand and revitalize the existing play space.

Ogden Junior Public School has a proud history. Phoebe Street School, one of Toronto's first six schools, opened in April of 1855. Within 20 years, it boasted the largest enrollment of any elementary school in Toronto. In 1905 several classrooms were damaged by fire, and a decision was made to rebuild a newer, larger school. The new school was named Ogden Public School, in honor of Dr. W. W. Ogden, who served as Trustee for 45 years.

By 1957, the second Ogden School was opened, located on the original site of Phoebe Street School. By 1967, Ogden Public School had an enrollment of 500 students.

Today, there are approximately 200 students enrolled at Ogden Junior Public School, with 25 teaching and support staff. We are committed to providing a safe and caring learning environment within our diverse, inclusive community. The Ogden Day Care provides before- and after-school care as well as day care to over 50 Ogden families. A number of community partners also support our families: University Settlement, St. Felix Centre, and Scadding Court. Together we are able to provide additional support to families, such as English as a Second Language programs, referrals to Toronto Health Services, and recreational programs such as swimming, fitness classes, and homework clubs.

Ogden Junior Public School offers focused literacy and numeracy 10 curriculum for all JK to Grade 6 students, additional supports for learners with special needs, additional supports for students who are new English Language Learners, and daily Cantonese language instruction for all students.

Woven throughout our rigorous curriculum is a focus on arts education, healthy and active living, character education, development of social responsibility, and teambuilding opportunities such as ballroom dance lessons, chess club, school teams, and extracurricular activities.

III. Needs/Problems

Our current building was built in 1957 and our most recent play structure was torn down over 15 years ago due to safety issues. We are so appreciative of what we have, yet we are still lacking in basic playground facilities. Our school yard contains an asphalt surface with one junior basketball net, a small naturalized area, one climber, and one set of monkey bars.

As a small school with limited fundraising abilities, the Ogden community has been working very hard to raise the necessary funds for our project. Thanks to our neighboring community members and businesses, last summer we have reached the initial deposit amount required by our school board to draft a master landscape plan. This deposit will fund some of our capital costs once a work plan is put in place. But our dream needs over $200,000!

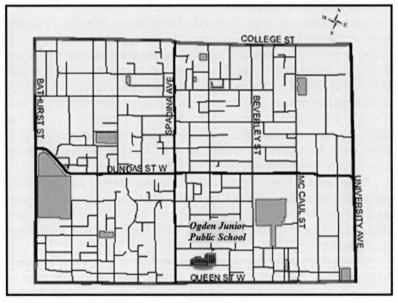

Map of the area surrounding Ogden Junior Public School

academic literacies ☀ | rhetorical situations ■ | genres ▲ | fields ◆ | processes ○ | strategies ◆ | research MLA / APA ● | media / design ☐ | readings ▮ | handbook ◿

Without equipment to play on, our young students turn to other unsafe areas of our school grounds for play. Our March 2012 parent survey results indicate that of the 10% of the total Ogden families who answered, over 70% have safety concerns with Ogden School grounds, 30% having had injuries on the property and 90% wanting improvements. Safety concerns of our school grounds expressed by the Ogden Community include:

- Lack of fencing and gates around the school grounds, especially on Phoebe Street on the northwest corner where heavy public traffic on Spadina Avenue is only 80 feet away. This ease of public accessibility, not visible from the school building, compromises the security of our students and leads to the unwanted activities mentioned above. Throughout the school day, we also have a stream of public traffic travelling to and from Phoebe Street through our grounds to our back alley that connects onto heavy traffic on Queen Street. In the spring of 2011, our school had to go into lock-down mode because a thief and a merchant in pursuit from Queen Street entered our grounds and our building.

- The boulders and the four mounds averaging 10 feet high, two of which are asphalt surface, were installed when the current building was built in 1957. Over the years there have been a multitude of injures as a direct result of the asphalt, mounds, and boulders on the existing playground. Some of these injuries were minor, but some required medical attention, including concussions, broken arms, severe sprains, head abrasions, fractured clavicle, fractured back, back injuries, contusion to the eyes, stitches to the knees, facial stitches, and badly sprained ankles. The mounds also create blind spots, thus compromising security and supervision of students during recess and lunch breaks. For decades, because our location is close to the downtown club district, the hidden areas of our school ground have been a target location for unwanted activities, including drug use, sex, and alcohol consumption, during the after-school hours, which has a direct impact on our community neighbors as well as the school population.

- Deteriorating brick tree planters, which were installed when the current building was built in 1957, have been a cause of injuries for our young students over the last 10 years. The temporary fencing installed around the perimeter of the planters over five years ago has collected garbage and limited our space use. It has also sent a message to our community of lack of maintenance, inviting vandalism and unwanted activities common to a downtown neighborhood.
- Uneven, cracked asphalt, on which our students play sports, has caused many scrapes, cuts, and bruises throughout the year.
- Uneven, often slippery paths and public sidewalk in front of the school used for long distance running for our cross-country and track & field teams.

IV. Ogden School Ground Photographs

The school grounds

A rendering of a playground

V. Goals/Objectives

1. Our first priority for our Ogden Community is to address safety con-   15
cerns of our school grounds. Our primary goal of increasing safety is to
install fencing and gates around the school grounds with access points
visible to the school and our neighbors for better security for our students,
parents, staff, and community. Secondly, we would like to eliminate or
relocate the boulders in a safer configuration and eliminate or modify the
mounds by making them smaller or installing a safer surface. This would
help to minimize the injuries from falls for young children when falls do
happen, to increase visibility and security of our students, and to discourage unwanted activities during after-school hours. Thankfully, the removal
of the deteriorating brick tree planters and the temporary fencing around
it was achieved by the TDSB Facilities Department March 12–16, 2012. They
installed wooden tree planters in its place to preserve the two mature
trees on our property. Temporary fencing was installed a few weeks later
to separate the parking lot and around a planter on the northwest corner.

2.   Our second priority is to promote a healthy lifestyle, in a safe area, for our whole community. Our students are dedicated, hardworking, and enthusiastic youngsters who would benefit from a safe place to play under the watchful eyes of our staff, parents, and childcare providers. We envision an inclusive playground equipped with climbers, slides, connecting walkways, and other features that will meet the needs of many students who reside in high-rise apartments and homes near the downtown core. With the play structure, students will be less inclined to spend time on the asphalt mounds, therefore minimizing injuries. Secondly, we would like to install a grass playing field. An even, soft playing field will help our young athletes play soccer, baseball, lacrosse, and other team sports without the fear of injuries from falls on concrete. A field space will benefit our community as well by building partnerships with local organizations and groups such as University Settlement Recreation Centre, St. Felix Community Centre, Chinese seniors' groups, and tai chi schools to do their activities during after-school hours. Our third goal is to install a running track to help promote cardiovascular exercise for all and provide a safe place for our cross-country and track & field teams to train.

3.   Our third priority is to increase green space and beautify our neighborhood. We strive to be environmental stewards! Our naturalized area consists primarily of conifer trees like pine that have no foliage and dirt with small trace of grass that has been trampled on by little feet. Our primary goal of greening is to plant more indigenous deciduous trees that produce more oxygen to help improve the air quality of our downtown neighborhood. We would also like to plant native perennial plants on our naturalized area to be enjoyed by our school and our community. Our third goal is to plant a community garden. We want to celebrate our cultural diversity through community plantings reflecting our inclusive philosophy: bok choy and tomatoes, coriander and potatoes! Most of our students do not have an opportunity to grow seeds for vegetables, flowers, or plants. Our inner-city kids would be able to experience the joys of growing flowers and plants that specifically attract birds and butterflies.

4.   Our fourth priority is to engage our community. Our first goal for community engagement is to install outdoor seating with permanent chess tables. Chess has been a great community builder for Ogden Jr. PS. Our

students learn to play chess in the primary grades and continue to hone their skills by playing in tournaments with friends and family members! Our second goal is to install an outdoor badminton court: on any given night in the spring or fall you will discover young children and their families engaged in a lively badminton match. We would like to work with our community to outline the boundaries of a court on our grounds, including poles for a net and accessibility to badminton racquets and birds.

VI. Evaluation

Our progress on our playground project will be monitored and evalu- 20 ated by our principal, our vice-principal, and the playground committee. Our school community consisting of students, staff, and parents are regularly invited for input, in particular at our bi-monthly playground project meetings. At points when major decisions are required, TDSB facilities managers, consultants, superintendent, trustees, and our community neighbors will also be consulted to oversee our project development.

VII. Next Steps

Step 1:

Contact Ogden Playground Committee to endorse our project or to find out more about it. You are also welcome to contact our school administration.

Step 2:

Please help spread the word about our project! If you have contacts, resources, or time to contribute, we would be delighted.

Step 3:

Donate money! Contributions over $25 are eligible for a tax receipt.

Engaging with the Text

1. A key feature of a proposal is a **CONVINCING ARGUMENT** for the pro-   ▲ 249
   posed solution. Does the authors' solution seem feasible to you? Why
   or why not?

380–85 ◆

2. How does the proposal **END**? Why do you think the authors chose to end it this way? Is this an effective ending?

644–52 ☐

3. This proposal has several **DESIGN** features, including a bullet point list, a numbered list, and pictures. Why do you think the authors chose to include these features? How does the design help the authors achieve their **PURPOSE**?

55–56 ■
392–96 ◆

4. The authors identify several **EFFECTS** of not having playground facilities. What are those effects? Why do you think the authors chose to discuss those effects in their proposal?

5. *For Writing.* Identify a place in your community or school that could be improved. Write a **PROPOSAL** that explains the problem and recommends a feasible solution. Consider also including a call to action.

246–55 ▲

Reflections 70

DAVE BARRY

Guys vs. Men

Dave Barry (b. 1947) is a humorist who is the author of over thirty books and countless columns. Two of his books—Dave Barry Turns 40 (1990) and Dave Barry's Greatest Hits (1988)—served as the basis for the TV sitcom Dave's World, which ran for four seasons from 1993 to 1997. In 1988, Barry was awarded a Pulitzer Prize for Commentary. Formerly a syndicated columnist, he has had writing published in over 500 newspapers in the United States and abroad. The following reflection is from his book Dave Barry's Complete Guide to Guys (1996).

MEN ITSELF IS A SERIOUS WORD, not to mention *manhood* and *manly.* Such words make being male sound like a very important activity, as opposed to what it primarily consists of, namely, possessing a set of minor and frequently unreliable organs.

But men tend to attach great significance to Manhood. This results in certain characteristically masculine, by which I mean stupid, behavioral patterns that can produce unfortunate results such as violent crime, war, spitting, and ice hockey. These things have given males a bad name.* And the "Men's Movement," which is supposed to bring out the more positive aspects of Manliness, seems to be densely populated with loons and goobers.

So I'm saying that there's another way to look at males: not as aggressive macho dominators; not as sensitive, liberated, hugging drummers; but as *guys.*

And what, exactly, do I mean by "guys"? I don't know. I haven't thought that much about it. One of the major characteristics of guyhood is that we guys don't spend a lot of time pondering our deep innermost feelings. There is a serious question in my mind about whether guys

---

*Specifically, "asshole."

actually *have* deep innermost feelings, unless you count, for example, loyalty to the Detroit Tigers, or fear of bridal showers.

But although I can't define exactly what it means to be a guy, I can   5 describe certain guy characteristics, such as:

Guys Like Neat Stuff

By "neat," I mean "mechanical and unnecessarily complex." I'll give you an example. Right now I'm typing these words on an *extremely* powerful computer. It's the latest in a line of maybe ten computers I've owned, each one more powerful than the last. My computer is chock-full of RAM and ROM and bytes and megahertzes and various other items that enable a computer to kick data-processing butt. It is probably capable of supervising the entire U.S. air-defense apparatus while simultaneously processing the tax return of every resident of Ohio. I use it mainly to write a newspaper column. This is an activity wherein I sit and stare at the screen for maybe ten minutes, then, using only my forefingers, slowly type something like:

Henry Kissinger looks like a big wart.

I stare at this for another ten minutes, have an inspiration, then amplify the original thought as follows:

Henry Kissinger looks like a big fat wart.

Then I stare at that for another ten minutes, pondering whether   10 I should try to work in the concept of "hairy."

This is absurdly simple work for my computer. It sits there, humming impatiently, bored to death, passing the time between keystrokes via brain-teaser activities such as developing a Unified Field Theory of the universe and translating the complete works of Shakespeare into rap.*

In other words, this computer is absurdly overqualified to work for me, and yet soon, I guarantee, I will buy an *even more powerful* one. I won't be able to stop myself. I'm a guy.

---

*To be or not? I got to *know*.
Might kill myself by the end of the *show*.

Probably the ultimate example of the fundamental guy drive to have neat stuff is the Space Shuttle. Granted, the guys in charge of this program *claim* it has a Higher Scientific Purpose, namely to see how humans function in space. But of course we have known for years how humans function in space: They float around and say things like: "Looks real good, Houston!"

No, the real reason for the existence of the Space Shuttle is that it is one humongous and spectacularly gizmo-intensive item of hardware. Guys can tinker with it practically forever, and occasionally even get it to work, and use it to place *other* complex mechanical items into orbit, where they almost immediately break, which provides a great excuse to send the Space Shuttle up *again*. It's Guy Heaven.

Other results of the guy need to have stuff are Star Wars, the   15
recreational boating industry, monorails, nuclear weapons, and wristwatches that indicate the phase of the moon. I am not saying that women haven't been involved in the development or use of this stuff. I'm saying that, without guys, this stuff probably would not exist; just as, without women, virtually every piece of furniture in the world would still be in its original position. Guys do not have a basic need to rearrange furniture. Whereas a woman who could cheerfully use the same computer for fifty-three years will rearrange her furniture on almost a weekly basis, sometimes in the dead of night. She'll be sound asleep in bed, and suddenly, at 2 A.M., she'll be awakened by the urgent thought: *The blue-green sofa needs to go perpendicular to the wall instead of parallel, and it needs to go there RIGHT NOW.* So she'll get up and move it, which of course necessitates moving other furniture, and soon she has rearranged her entire living room, shifting great big heavy pieces that ordinarily would require several burly men to lift, because there are few forces in Nature more powerful than a woman who needs to rearrange furniture. Every so often a guy will wake up to discover that, because of his wife's overnight efforts, he now lives in an entirely different house.

(I realize that I'm making gender-based generalizations here, but my feeling is that if God did not want us to make gender-based generalizations, She would not have given us genders.)

Guys Like a Really Pointless Challenge

Not long ago I was sitting in my office at the *Miami Herald*'s Sunday magazine, *Tropic*, reading my fan mail,* when I heard several of my guy coworkers in the hallway talking about how fast they could run the forty-yard dash. These are guys in their thirties and forties who work in journalism, where the most demanding physical requirement is the ability to digest vending-machine food. In other words, these guys have absolutely no need to run the forty-yard dash.

But one of them, Mike Wilson, was writing a story about a star high-school football player who could run it in 4.38 seconds. Now if Mike had written a story about, say, a star high-school poet, none of my guy coworkers would have suddenly decided to find out how well they could write sonnets. But when Mike turned in his story, they became *deeply* concerned about how fast they could run the forty-yard dash. They were so concerned that the magazine editor, Tom Shroder, decided that they should get a stopwatch and go out to a nearby park and find out. Which they did, a bunch of guys taking off their shoes and running around barefoot in a public park on company time.

This is what I heard them talking about, out in the hall. I heard Tom, who was thirty-eight years old, saying that his time in the forty had been 5.75 seconds. And I thought to myself: This is ridiculous. These are middle-aged guys, supposedly adults, and they're out there *bragging* about their performance in this stupid juvenile footrace. Finally I couldn't stand it anymore.

"Hey!" I shouted. "I could beat 5.75 seconds."   20

So we went out to the park and measured off forty yards, and the guys told me that I had three chances to make my best time. On the first try my time was 5.78 seconds, just three-hundredths of a second slower than Tom's, even though, at forty-five, I was seven years older than he. So I just *knew* I'd beat him on the second attempt if I ran really, really hard, which I did for a solid ten yards, at which point my left hamstring

---

*Typical fan letter: "Who cuts your hair? Beavers?"

muscle, which had not yet shifted into Spring Mode from Mail-Reading Mode, went, and I quote, "pop."

I had to be helped off the field. I was in considerable pain, and I was obviously not going to be able to walk right for weeks. The other guys were very sympathetic, especially Tom, who took the time to call me at home, where I was sitting with an ice pack on my leg and twenty-three Advil in my bloodstream, so he could express his concern.

"Just remember," he said, "*you didn't beat my time.*"

There are countless other examples of guys rising to meet pointless challenges. Virtually all sports fall into this category, as well as a large part of U.S. foreign policy. ("I'll bet you can't capture Manuel Noriega!"* "Oh YEAH??")

Guys Do Not Have a Rigid and Well-Defined Moral Code

This is not the same as saying that guys are bad. Guys *are* capable of   25 doing bad things, but this generally happens when they try to be Men and start becoming manly and aggressive and stupid. When they're being just plain guys, they aren't so much actively *evil* as they are lost. Because guys have never really grasped the Basic Human Moral Code, which I believe was invented by women millions of years ago when all the guys were out engaging in some other activity, such as seeing who could burp the loudest. When they came back, there were certain rules that they were expected to follow unless they wanted to get into Big Trouble, and they have been trying to follow these rules ever since, with extremely irregular results. Because guys have never *internalized* these rules. Guys are similar to my small auxiliary backup dog, Zippy, a guy dog[†] who has been told numerous times that he is *not* supposed to (1) get into the kitchen garbage or (2) poop on the floor. He knows that these are the rules, but he has never really understood *why*, and some-times he gets to thinking: Sure, I am *ordinarily* not supposed to get into

---

*Manuel Noriega: former military dictator in Panama; he was removed from power by the United States in 1989. [Editor's note]

[†]I also have a female dog, Earnest, who *never* breaks the rules.

academic literacies ・ rhetorical situations ・ genres ・ fields ・ processes ・ strategies ・ research MLA / APA ・ media / design ・ readings ・ handbook

the garbage, but obviously this rule is not meant to apply when there are certain extenuating* circumstances, such as (1) somebody just threw away some perfectly good seven-week-old Kung Pao Chicken, and (2) I am home alone.

And so when the humans come home, the kitchen floor has been transformed into GarbageFest USA, and Zippy, who usually comes rushing up, is off in a corner disguised in a wig and sunglasses, hoping to get into the Federal Bad Dog Relocation Program before the humans discover the scene of the crime.

When I yell at him, he frequently becomes so upset that he poops on the floor.

Morally, most guys are just like Zippy, only taller and usually less hairy. Guys are *aware* of the rules of moral behavior, but they have trouble keeping these rules in the forefronts of their minds at certain times, especially the present. This is especially true in the area of faithfulness to one's mate. I realize, of course, that there are countless examples of guys being faithful to their mates until they die, usually as a result of being eaten by their mates immediately following copulation. Guys outside of the spider community, however, do not have a terrific record of faithfulness.

I'm not saying guys are scum. I'm saying that many guys who consider themselves to be committed to their marriages will stray if they are confronted with overwhelming temptation, defined as "virtually any temptation."

Okay, so maybe I *am* saying guys are scum. But they're not *mean-spirited* scum. And few of them—even when they are out of town on business trips, far from their wives, and have a clear-cut opportunity—will poop on the floor. 30

---

*I am taking some liberties here with Zippy's vocabulary. More likely, in his mind, he uses the term *mitigating*.

Engaging with the Text

1. Dave Barry claims that he isn't able to say what he means by the term "guys" because "one of the major characteristics of guyhood is that we guys don't spend a lot of time pondering our deep innermost feelings." Yet in this piece—indeed even this sentence—he identifies specific characteristics of "guys" that suggest he has indeed pondered this state of maleness thoroughly. How do you account for this contradiction?

2. Despite his assertion that he can't define the term, Barry essentially provides an **EXTENDED DEFINITION** of the term "guy," detailing several characteristics. What are they? Do you agree with his description of them? Why or why not? What other characteristics would you add, if any?

   434–40

3. Barry includes several **EXAMPLES** of the behavior he identifies as characteristic of guys. Identify several passages that include such examples and discuss what these contribute to his reflection.

   439–40

4. What is Barry's **STANCE** toward his topic? Point to specific passages that reveal that stance. Is this stance appropriate for Barry's **PURPOSE**? Why or why not?

   66–68
55–56

5. *For Writing.* Identify a specific group of people, animals, things, or places, and reflect on what distinguishing characteristics are shared by its members. Write a **REFLECTION** on the group that identifies those major characteristics. Study Barry's reflection to see what techniques he uses to elicit a smile or chuckle. Try your hand at one or more of these.

   256–63

academic literacies   rhetorical situations   genres   fields   processes   strategies   research MLA / APA   media / design   readings   handbook

GEETA KOTHARI

If You Are What You Eat, Then What Am I?

Geeta Kothari (b. 1962) has published stories and essays in numerous newspapers, journals, and anthologies. She teaches writing at the University of Pittsburgh, where she is director of the Writing Center, and is the nonfiction editor at the Kenyon Review, *a literary journal published at Kenyon College. Her debut short story collection,* I Brake for Moose and Other Stories, *was published in 2017. The following reflection first appeared in 1999 in the* Kenyon Review. *As you read, notice how Kothari incorporates vivid anecdotes to illustrate the competing cultural experiences that complicate her sense of identity.*

> To belong is to understand the tacit codes of the people you live with.   —MICHAEL IGNATIEFF, BLOOD AND BELONGING

THE FIRST TIME MY MOTHER and I open a can of tuna, I am nine years old. We stand in the doorway of the kitchen, in semidarkness, the can tilted toward daylight. I want to eat what the kids at school eat: bologna, hot dogs, salami—foods my parents find repugnant because they contain pork and meat byproducts, crushed bone and hair glued together by chemicals and fat. Although she has never been able to tolerate the smell of fish, my mother buys the tuna, hoping to satisfy my longing for American food.

Indians, of course, do not eat such things.

The tuna smells fishy, which surprises me because I can't remember anyone's tuna sandwich actually smelling like fish. And the tuna in those sandwiches doesn't look like this, pink and shiny, like an internal organ. In fact, this looks similar to the bad foods my mother doesn't want me to eat. She is silent, holding her face away from the can while peering into it like a half-blind bird.

"What's wrong with it?" I ask.

She has no idea. My mother does not know that the tuna everyone 5
else's mothers made for them was tuna *salad*.

"Do you think it's botulism?"

I have never seen botulism, but I have read about it, just as I have read about but never eaten steak and kidney pie.

There is so much my parents don't know. They are not like other parents, and they disappoint me and my sister. They are supposed to help us negotiate the world outside, teach us the signs, the clues to proper behavior: what to eat and how to eat it.

We have expectations, and my parents fail to meet them, especially my mother, who works full-time. I don't understand what it means, to have a mother who works outside and inside the home; I notice only the ways in which she disappoints me. She doesn't show up for school plays. She doesn't make chocolate-frosted cupcakes for my class. At night, if I want her attention, I have to sit in the kitchen and talk to her while she cooks the evening meal, attentive to every third or fourth word I say.

We throw the tuna away. This time my mother is disappointed. I go to school with tuna eaters. I see their sandwiches, yet cannot explain the discrepancy between them and the stinking, oily fish in my mother's hand. We do not understand so many things, my mother and I.   10

When we visit our relatives in India, food prepared outside the house is carefully monitored. In the hot, sticky monsoon months in New Delhi and Bombay, we cannot eat ice cream, salad, cold food, or any fruit that can't be peeled. Definitely no meat. People die from amoebic dysentery, unexplained fevers, strange boils on their bodies. We drink boiled water only, no ice. No sweets except for jalebi, thin fried twists of dough in dripping hot sugar syrup. If we're caught outside with nothing to drink, Fanta, Limca, Thums Up (after Coca-Cola is thrown out by Mrs. Gandhi) will do. Hot tea sweetened with sugar, served with thick creamy buffalo milk, is preferable. It should be boiled, to kill the germs on the cup.

My mother talks about "back home" as a safe place, a silk cocoon frozen in time where we are sheltered by family and friends. Back home, my sister and I do not argue about food with my parents. Home is where they know all the rules. We trust them to guide us safely through the maze of city streets for which they have no map, and we trust them to feed and take care of us, the way parents should.

academic literacies   rhetorical situations   genres   fields   processes   strategies   research MLA / APA   media / design   readings   handbook

Finally, though, one of us will get sick, hungry for the food we see our cousins and friends eating, too thirsty to ask for a straw, too polite to insist on properly boiled water.

At my uncle's diner in New Delhi, someone hands me a plate of aloo tikki, fried potato patties filled with mashed channa dal and served with a sweet and a sour chutney. The channa, mixed with hot chilies and spices, burns my tongue and throat. I reach for my Fanta, discard the paper straw, and gulp the sweet orange soda down, huge drafts that sting rather than soothe.

When I throw up later that day (or is it the next morning, when a   15 stomachache wakes me from deep sleep?), I cry over the frustration of being singled out, not from the pain my mother assumes I'm feeling as she holds my hair back from my face. The taste of orange lingers in my mouth, and I remember my lips touching the cold glass of the Fanta bottle.

At that moment, more than anything, I want to be like my cousins.

In New York, at the first Indian restaurant in our neighborhood, my father orders with confidence, and my sister and I play with the silverware until the steaming plates of lamb biryani arrive.

What is Indian food? my friends ask, their noses crinkling up.

Later, this restaurant is run out of business by the new Indo-Pak-Bangladeshi combinations up and down the street, which serve similar food. They use plastic cutlery and Styrofoam cups. They do not distinguish between North and South Indian cooking, or between Indian, Pakistani, and Bangladeshi cooking, and their customers do not care. The food is fast, cheap, and tasty. Dosa, a rice flour crepe stuffed with masala potato, appears on the same trays as chicken makhani.

Now my friends want to know, Do you eat curry at home?   20

One time my mother makes lamb vindaloo for guests. Like dosa, this is a South Indian dish, one that my Punjabi mother has to learn from a cookbook. For us, she cooks everyday food—yellow dal, rice, chapati, bhaji. Lentils, rice, bread, and vegetables. She has never referred to anything on our table as "curry" or "curried," but I know she has made chicken curry for guests. Vindaloo, she explains, is a curry too. I understand then that curry is a dish created for guests, outsiders, a food for people who eat in restaurants.

I look around my boyfriend's freezer one day and find meat: pork chops, ground beef, chicken pieces, Italian sausage. Ham in the refrigerator, next to the homemade bolognese sauce. Tupperware filled with chili made from ground beef and pork.

He smells different from me. Foreign. Strange.

I marry him anyway.

He has inherited blue eyes that turn gray in bad weather, light brown 25
hair, a sharp pointy nose, and excellent teeth. He learns to make chili with ground turkey and tofu, tomato sauce with red wine and portobello mushrooms, roast chicken with rosemary and slivers of garlic under the skin.

He eats steak when we are in separate cities, roast beef at his mother's house, hamburgers at work. Sometimes I smell them on his skin. I hope he doesn't notice me turning my face, a cheek instead of my lips, my nose wrinkled at the unfamiliar, musky smell.

I have inherited brown eyes, black hair, a long nose with a crooked bridge, and soft teeth with thin enamel. I am in my twenties, moving to a city far from my parents, before it occurs to me that jeera, the spice my sister avoids, must have an English name. I have to learn that haldi = turmeric, methi = fenugreek. What to make with fenugreek, I do not know. My grandmother used to make methi roti for our breakfast, cornbread with fresh fenugreek leaves served with a lump of homemade butter. No one makes it now that she's gone, though once in a while my mother will get a craving for it and produce a facsimile ("The cornmeal here is wrong") that only highlights what she's really missing: the smells and tastes of her mother's house.

I will never make my grandmother's methi roti or even my mother's unsatisfactory imitation of it. I attempt chapati; it takes six hours, three phone calls home, and leaves me with an aching back. I have to write translations down: jeera = cumin. My memory is unreliable. But I have always known garam = hot.

academic literacies · rhetorical situations · genres · fields · processes · strategies · research MLA / APA · media / design · readings · handbook

If I really want to make myself sick, I worry that my husband will one day leave me for a meat-eater, for someone familiar who doesn't sniff him suspiciously for signs of alimentary infidelity.

Indians eat lentils. I understand this as absolute, a decree from an   30 unidentifiable authority that watches and judges me.

So what does it mean that I cannot replicate my mother's dal? She and my father show me repeatedly, in their kitchen, in my kitchen. They coach me over the phone, buy me the best cookbooks, and finally write down their secrets. Things I'm supposed to know but don't. Recipes that should be, by now, engraved on my heart.

Living far from the comfort of people who require no explanation for what I do and who I am, I crave the foods we have shared. My mother convinces me that moong is the easiest dal to prepare, and yet it fails me every time: bland, watery, a sickly greenish yellow mush. These imperfect limitations remind me only of what I'm missing.

But I have never been fond of moong dal. At my mother's table it is the last thing I reach for. Now I worry that this antipathy toward dal signals something deeper, that somehow I am not my parents' daughter, not Indian, and because I cannot bear the touch and smell of raw meat, though I can eat it cooked (charred, dry, and overdone), I am not American either.

I worry about a lifetime purgatory in Indian restaurants where I will complain that all the food looks and tastes the same because they've used the same masala.

Engaging with the Text

1. Geeta Kothari uses food as a way to explore the larger issue of cultural identity. How does she **DESCRIBE** Indian and American food? What **SPECIFIC DETAILS** does she include to help her readers understand the pulls of both American and Indian culture?

443–51
260

2. A good **TITLE** indicates what the piece is about and makes readers want to read it. How well does this title do those things? How does Kothari answer the question her title asks?

386–87

373–80 ◆

3. How does Kothari **BEGIN** her reflection? Is this an effective beginning? Why or why not? How does it signal to readers what Kothari will address in the rest of the piece?

4. For Kothari, cultural identity shapes, and is shaped by, the foods one eats and the ways one eats them. Her reflection reveals a struggle over two cultures—Indian and American—and she worries that she cannot locate herself fully in either. At the end of her text, she notes: "I worry that this antipathy toward dal signals something deeper, that somehow I am not my parents' daughter, not Indian, and because I cannot bear the touch and smell of raw meat . . . I am not American either." What does it mean to live on the border between two cultures in the ways Kothari describes?

256–63 ▲

5. *For Writing.* Think about the kinds of foods you grew up with and the ways they were similar or dissimilar to those of your peers. Write an essay **REFLECTING** on the role food has played in your own sense of your identity—whether it be your cultural heritage, your identification (or not) with your generation, your individual or family identity, or some other form.

✳ academic literacies
■ rhetorical situations
▲ genres
⬣ fields
○ processes
◆ strategies
● research MLA / APA
□ media / design
◗◖ readings
⌃ handbook

VANN R. NEWKIRK II

When Picture-Day Combs Don't Actually Comb

Vann R. Newkirk II (b. 1962) is a staff writer at the Atlantic. He writes about politics and policy, focusing especially on health policy. He is also a co-founder of and contributing editor for Seven Scribes, a website "where Black and allied young writers and artists can offer commentary and analysis on politics, pop culture, literature, and art." This essay was published in the Atlantic on February 22, 2017.

Lᴵᴋᴇ Sᴜɴᴅᴀʏ school ᴀɴᴅ Fʀɪᴅᴀʏ ɴɪɢʜᴛ football ɢᴀᴍᴇs, Picture Days are rituals in the South. I went to a lot of different schools in different cities and towns, and had to memorize new customs, traditions, mascots, and slogans at each one, but the anchors that made the experience of school cohesive were the days we did the duck-walk to school in uncreased penny loafers to spend 30 seconds in front of a camera and get envelopes full of our faces three weeks later.

Picture Days are theater and pageantry, one of the small ways we established order in our own chaotic lives. We all got dressed to the nines—to the tens if they exist—all patent leather and starched slacks and vests and fresh haircuts and pomade. Also, a little Blue Magic and white stockings for the girls. Mamas kissed us on the forehead and doted on us even as they hissed, "Don't you ruin them clothes before you get your picture taken!" My warnings from my mama were more precise: it took 20 years for my face to realize the difference between a grimace and a smile, and my glasses have never been clean.

We behaved on Picture Day—only the worst monsters among us would ever disobey direct orders from our mamas—and did our little duck walks in little duckling lines to the photographer's room. We sat in the hallway in advance, and students eagerly awaited the final accoutrement that made Picture Day whole. Our teacher gave us each one small, cheap black comb—the most spartan of designs. The final directions were simple. Each of us went to the bathroom mirror to "fix ourselves," and use the comb to make sure our hair was just right for the photo. Mama's orders.

All good, except for one thing: those combs were absolutely useless for my hair in any hairstyle I wore. My low fades and Caesar haircuts were best maintained with brushes. The teeth of the comb would simply graze over my hair with no effect at best, or actually disrupt my carefully maintained waves at worst. When I wore my hair higher, the teeth would snag in my dense curls immediately. Picture Day combs always made my situation worse. The ritual glamour of unison inevitably flickered for me in this one step.

Combs like those have never really been a hair utensil of choice for me—I mostly use brushes and picks—and I was never more aware that this is a somewhat uncommon position than at Picture Day. The combs' symbolic importance gave them a strange real-world value that lasted even after our close-ups were done. In our grade-school bartering markets, children traded the combs like currency—and many kids went home hungry after trading lunches or lunch money to accumulate the most little black combs.

With an outsider's eye and fully detached from their significance, I became a broker of black combs in the mold of Dutch tulip merchants. My biggest score came from trading a handful of black combs for a slightly wobbly X-Brain yo-yo, quite the haul for a pocketful of nothing. But at the back of my mind, the absurdity of it all never quite left me. I was trading something that was absolutely worthless to me, and nobody seemed to understand why I didn't value it. And I was always aware that the other children in my neighborhood and family who went to different schools didn't seem to have the same experience with black-comb mania.

Now listen, this isn't some sepia-colored essay about realizing I was different, and embracing a conflicted racial identity through the experience of receiving a single comb. Little combs certainly ain't colored water fountains, and I wasn't exactly Ruby Bridges. I've never really had

academic literacies · rhetorical situations · genres · fields · processes · strategies · research MLA / APA · media / design · readings · handbook

a moment of questioning who I am in the broader scope of America. My father studies black history, and I've always known it. I'm black, I always knew that I was black, and I always knew that my blackness manifested in ways that made me different in mostly white spaces. One of those happened to be how my hair grew. I was never mystified by the fact that people often wanted to touch it, but I never allowed them to, either. My detachment was colored by knowing amusement more so than bemusement. "White people," so the black mantra goes.

Still, the memories of Picture Days and of black combs brings to mind just how fundamentally our differences shape our rituals and our blind spots. How many teachers that organized Picture Days thought that combs might not be universal hair-care items? How many photography companies in our southern towns thought to offer little black soft-bristled brushes or afro picks or dreadlock grease and beeswax and beads to black and brown boys and girls, or white kids with "difficult" hair?

I hate the Picture Day combs and I love the Picture Day combs. They are maybe the earliest beauty product I remember, which is a strange thing since they had no purpose for me. I still have the X-Brain yo-yo, and I do relish the arcade time I earned with my classmates' lunch money. And I do recall that after each Picture Day I'd go home and brush my hair a little harder. In our envelopes three weeks later, the boys had their parts done just right and the girls had every strand in place. My smile always looked like a grimace.

Engaging with the Text

1. What is Newkirk's **STANCE** toward his topic? Is his stance appropriate for his **PURPOSE**? Why or why not?

    66–68

    55–56

2. Newkirk writes, "I hate the Picture Day combs and I love the Picture Day combs." How are we supposed to make sense of these opposing ideas? What do you think Newkirk means by this statement?

259–60 ▲

3. How is Newkirk's reflection **STRUCTURED**? In what ways does the structure allow him to relate all of his ideas to one another? How else might he have organized his essay?

260 ▲

4. One key feature of a reflection is the inclusion of **SPECIFIC DETAILS**. Identify two specific details that Newkirk offers and explain how they contribute to his essay.

5. *For Writing.* Newkirk reflects on a very common object—the comb. What other common objects would make good subjects for a reflection? Select a common object that you use or are familiar with and write a **REFLECTION** about it, making sure to choose an appropriate structure and include specific details that will help your reader connect with your subject.

256–63 ▲

BETH NGUYEN

American Stories Are Refugee Stories

Beth Nguyen (b. 1974), also known as Bich Minh Nguyen, is a writer and professor who currently directs the MFA program in writing at the University of San Francisco. Her memoir, Stealing Buddha's Dinner *(2007), won the PEN/Jerard Fund Award, and her novel* Short Girls *(2009) was an American Book Award winner. Her latest novel,* Pioneer Girl *(2014), explores the connection between a Vietnamese immigrant family and Laura Ingalls Wilder. This essay was published in* Literary Hub *on May 1, 2017.*

FOR MOST OF MY LIFE, I could pretend I was not a refugee. I grew up in the Midwest, in a mostly white town in the 1980s, and back then the idea was to forget the past and move along. Stay out of trouble. Don't talk about the war. Don't react to racist taunts. Behave well enough not to get noticed. And that's what I did. But every April, I remembered. My family had left Saigon on April 29, 1975, the day before the fall of the city and the end of the war. I was a baby, carried by my father and uncles and grandmother, brought by motorcycle, boat, ship, and airplane to refugee camps and eventually the United States, and given an American childhood. I grew up with sitcoms and suburbs, crosswalks and sugar cones. No one in my family wanted to talk about the leaving. Still, every April, I tried to imagine what had happened, how we had fled in the night without knowing where we would end up or if we would even make it. I knew that this was a gift: to have not the experience, but the imagining.

Refugees don't quite fit in to the romantic immigrant narrative in America. Their arrival is less about opportunity and more about survival. Refugees are a more obvious, uncomfortable reminder of war and loss. But America is ruthless to newcomers. Refugees—those who are even allowed in this country at all—are expected to become relatively self-sufficient in eight months. They are supposed to pay back the cost of travel to get to the United States. And they are expected to be absolutely grateful.

I watched my father and uncles and grandmother struggle with English, struggle with the strange habits of Americans. Always there was a sense of not knowing how things were supposed to be done. Who would even think to tell us? In your first experience of winter and snow, how would you know what to do with an iced-over windshield? In a pre-internet world, how would you know there was a thing called a scraper? What if you threw boiling water on the car, thinking this would surely melt the ice, having no idea the glass would explode? What if in trying to navigate this new cold world you tried to ask questions at stores but people just stared and said, I can't understand you. Speak up. Speak English. What if people told you, go back to where you came from, as if you could?

Growing up, I was afraid all the time. It was a low-lying fear that I couldn't explain to myself or dare admit out loud. It kept me awake at night, made me feel both too visible and invisible. I think now that I was afraid of all that my family didn't know about American life—how far from being settled or self-sufficient we actually were. It's why I learned to read early and copied inflected dialogue from TV shows. I memorized words, perfected my English. I tried to live in libraries. In school, I watched and learned whatever my white friends did. What they wore. What they brought for lunch. Their idioms and slang. I could be almost just like them, so long as I avoided the mirror and used powerful forms of denial whenever I was in my Vietnamese home. I thought I could transcend my origins, as if I were never a refugee, as if I were American-born, as I sometimes pretended to be. As if that would keep me safe.

My father has a photograph of him in Saigon, leaning against his prized Yamaha motorcycle. He is so young—he was 28 when we left Vietnam—his hair full and wavy. His smile is a gambler's smile. Later, that motorcycle would get us from our house to the Saigon River, where we found passage on a boat that found its way to a US naval ship on the sea. My father had abandoned the motorcycle, of course, leaving it on the riverbank with the key because someone else would need it. 5

April 30th marks the anniversary of the fall of Saigon, when North Vietnamese forces took over the city and crashed tanks through the gates of the presidential palace. *Fall* is always the word people use, and whenever I heard that, growing up, I imagined bodies and buildings in slow-motion collapse. I still imagine it, because I cannot really know it. Not that day, nor the day before it—the chaos and darkness, families deciding to leave because there was no other choice.

Gallup polls from 1975 show that most Americans were not in favor of Vietnamese resettlement. Maybe this is why, for most of my life, the word *refugee* has seemed suffused with shame. The only narratives I saw about the Vietnam war came from white people and their movies. Their gaze, their versions, made the story that most Americans knew. And in this current era of increased xenophobia, with an administration that refuses to help people who need help the most, refugees are still a source of suspicion and resentment. Why help them when we could help US citizens?

The message to refugees and immigrants is a demand for value: prove that you belong here, prove that you have any right to exist here. And while you're doing so, stay quiet and don't make a fuss. If refugees are lauded, it's for what they might accomplish: look at those who became doctors, scientists, inventors. The good refugee is invariably described as gracious, which is to say grateful.

It's nearly impossible not to absorb these demands, or at least feel the weight of them. For most of my life I have behaved accordingly, well enough that I could pretend I wasn't a refugee at all. Because I was afraid and because I thought I would be safer. But silence has never been a protection. And increasingly, there is no safety.

When I say I am a refugee, a daughter and granddaughter of refugees, I mean I carry my family's story with me. My father and uncles fought in the war and lost; we left; we didn't know where we would end up. I mean, I am an American citizen not by birth but by need. I took the tests and paid the fees. And every April my father and uncles remember 1975 and I try to imagine. I look at that photo of my father with his motorcycle and am astonished by how far it has traveled, intact, across so much water and land. It is an artifact. Like our bodies and our faces, it is proof of our history and of how we got here.

Engaging with the Text

1. Beth Nguyen writes, "I am an American citizen not by birth but by need." What does she mean by that statement? What point is she trying to make?

259 ▲

2. One of the key features of a reflection is a **TOPIC** that is intriguing to the writer. How can you tell that Nguyen is intrigued by her topic? Identify two sentences that reveal that Nguyen finds her topic interesting.

3. What is the significance of the photograph of Nguyen's father and his motorcycle? Why is this **SPECIFIC DETAIL** so important to Nguyen?

260 ▲
386–87 ◆
387–89

4. The **TITLE** of this reflection, "American Stories Are Refugee Stories," can almost be thought of as a **THESIS** statement. Do you agree with the idea that American stories are refugee stories? Why or why not?

5. *For Writing.* Think back on your own childhood. Are there any events or activities that were meaningful to you when you were young that are still meaningful to you now? Pick one of these events or activities and write a **REFLECTION** on it, explaining why it is important to you.

256–63 ▲

Texts That Mix Genres 71

See also:

ANNA QUINDLEN
Write for Your
Life   280

LYNDA BARRY

Lost and Found

Lynda Barry (b. 1956) is an award-winning cartoonist and author. Well known for her weekly comic strip Ernie Pook's Comeek, *Barry is the author of nineteen books, the latest of which is* Syllabus: Notes from an Accidental Professor *(2014). As the title suggests, Barry teaches workshops around the country on comic writing. Her graphic novel* What It Is *(2008) received the comics industry's 2009 Eisner Award for Best Reality-Based Work. This work is part memoir; Barry often writes about her life, as she does in* One! Hundred! Demons! *(2002), from which this excerpt is taken.*

academic literacies | rhetorical situations | genres | fields | processes | strategies | research MLA / APA | media / design | readings | handbook

EACH QUARTER-INCH AD WAS LIKE A CHAPTER IN A BOOK. I'D IMAGINE THE WHOLE STORY: THE FREAKED-OUT PEOPLE, THE FREAKED-OUT ANIMALS, AND ME, ALWAYS COMING TO THE RES-CUE AND NEVER ACCEPTING THE REWARD.

NO, KEEP THE FIVE HUNDRED DOLLARS, SIR. ALL I CARE ABOUT IS THAT HENRY IS HOME.

PLEASE, MA'AM, WHAT MY NAME IS DOESN'T MATTER. AND NEITHER DOES THE TEN THOUSAND DOLLARS. ALL THAT MAT-TERS IS JINGLES.

LIKE MOST WRITERS, I LOVED TO READ WHEN I WAS LITTLE, BUT UNTIL RECENTLY, I NEVER REALLY THOUGHT ABOUT SOME OF THE THINGS I ENJOYED READING MOST. THE CLASSI-FIED ADS FASCINATED ME.

CRYPT IN MAUSOLEUM. PRIME LOC. EYE-LEVEL. BEST OFFER. EVENINGS.

SZ.12 WEDDING DRESS. NEVER WORN. MUST SACRIFICE.

FILL DIRT, VERY CLEAN.

PARTY PIANIST. MY PIANO OR YOURS.

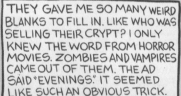

THEY GAVE ME SO MANY WEIRD BLANKS TO FILL IN. LIKE WHO WAS SELLING THEIR CRYPT? I ONLY KNEW THE WORD FROM HORROR MOVIES. ZOMBIES AND VAMPIRES CAME OUT OF THEM. THE AD SAID "EVENINGS." IT SEEMED LIKE SUCH AN OBVIOUS TRICK.

DING DONG.

WHO IS IT?

UH, I'M HERE ABOUT THE CRYPT?

AAHHHH!!

SAME WITH THE WEDDING DRESS AD. WHO ELSE WAS GOING TO CALL ABOUT IT EXCEPT A MAIDEN? IT SAID "MUST SACRI-FICE." WHO ELSE GOT SACRIFICED BUT MAIDENS? THE POLICE WOULD BE BAFFLED BY HOW MAIDENS KEPT DISAPPEARING.

HELLO?

YES?

YOU'VE GOT TO BE KIDDING.

OK.

NOT ANOTHER MAIDEN!

I'M AFRAID SO.

DANG!

academic literacies rhetorical situations genres fields processes strategies research MLA / APA media / design readings handbook

WHEN I CAME FORWARD WITH THE SOLUTION TO THESE CRIMES, AT FIRST NO ONE WOULD BELIEVE ME. I EXPECTED THAT. I WATCHED A LOT OF MOVIES. NO ONE EVER BELIEVES KIDS AT FIRST. YOU HAVE TO WAIT UNTIL ALMOST THE END. YOU HAVE TO WAIT 'TIL YOUR LIFE IS IN DANGER.

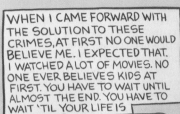

CALLING ALL CARS! THAT KID WAS RIGHT ABOUT THE WANT ADS!

BUT NOW THE CRYPT-VAMPIRE AND THE WEDDING DRESS-ZOMBIE HAVE HER IN THEIR CLUTCHES! WE WERE SO STUPID! REPEAT! VERY STUPID!

MOSTLY I DIED IN MY CLAS-SIFIED STORIES. EVEN THEN I LOVED TRAGIC ENDINGS. PEO-PLE WOULD BE CRYING SO HARD. THEY'D COVER MY COFFIN WITH FILL DIRT, VERY CLEAN. THE PARTY PIANIST WOULD PLAY.

CHERISH IS THE WORD I USE TO DIS-CRI-IBE..

WHEN I READ ABOUT WRITER'S LIVES, THERE ARE USUALLY STORIES ABOUT WRITING FROM THE TIME THEY WERE LITTLE. I NEVER WROTE ANYTHING UN-TIL I WAS A TEENAGER, AND THEN IT WAS ONLY A DIARY THAT SAID THE SAME THING OVER AND OVER.

I thought Bill liked me but turns out he doesn't. I'm so depressed about Bill. He didn't call me. I can't stop thinking about Bill.

WRITERS TALK ABOUT ALL THE BOOKS THEY LOVED WHEN THEY WERE CHILDREN. CLASSIC STORIES I NEVER READ, BUT I LIED ABOUT BECAUSE I WAS SCARED IT WAS PROOF I WASN'T REALLY A WRITER.

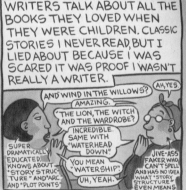

AND WIND IN THE WILLOWS? AMAZING.

"THE LION, THE WITCH AND THE WARDROBE?" INCREDIBLE. SAME WITH "WATERHEAD DOWN"

AH, YES.

YOU MEAN "WATERSHIP".

UH, YEAH.

SUPER DRAMATICALLY EDUCATED. KNOWS ABOUT "STORY STRUC-TURE" AND "ARC" AND "PLOT POINTS"

JIVE-ASS FAKER WHO CAN'T SPELL AND HAS NO IDEA WHAT "STORY STRUCTURE" EVEN MEANS

 academic literacies

 rhetorical situations

 genres

 fields

 processes

 strategies

 research MLA / APA

 media / design

 readings

 handbook

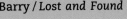

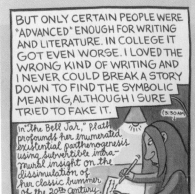

BUT ONLY CERTAIN PEOPLE WERE "ADVANCED" ENOUGH FOR WRITING AND LITERATURE. IN COLLEGE IT GOT EVEN WORSE. I LOVED THE WRONG KIND OF WRITING AND I NEVER COULD BREAK A STORY DOWN TO FIND THE SYMBOLIC MEANING, ALTHOUGH I SURE TRIED TO FAKE IT.

(3:30 AM)

In "The Bell Jar," Plath profounds her enumerated existential parthenogenesis using subvertible intra-mural insight on the dissimulation of her classic bummer of the 20th century.

MY TROUBLE ENDED WHEN I STARTED MAKING COMIC-STRIPS. IT'S NOT SOMETHING A PERSON HAS TO BE VERY "ADVANCED" TO DO. AT LEAST NOT IN THE MINDS OF LITERARY TYPES.

SO YOU'RE A CARTOONIST! HOW ADORABLE!

POLITICAL?
NO.
HUMOROUS?
KINDA.
WE'RE BOTH WRITERS.

SAY, MAYBE WE COULD COLLABORATE! WE WRITE IT AND YOU DRAW IT! HOW FUN!

NOBODY FEELS THE NEED TO PROVIDE DEEP CRITICAL IN-SIGHT TO SOMETHING WRITTEN BY HAND. MOSTLY THEY KEEP IT AS SHORT AS A WANT AD. THE WORST I GET IS, "TOO MANY WORDS. NOT FUNNY. DON'T GET THE JOKE." I CAN LIVE WITH THAT.

GALS, EVER FELT SO intimidated by the IDEA OF writing THAT you've never even given it a try? Think writing IS only FOR "writers"? Sure IS common!

ESPECIALLY BECAUSE I'M SURE THAT THE NINE-YEAR-OLD VERSION OF ME WHO MADE UP ALL THOSE "CLASSI-FIED STORIES" WOULD THINK THAT THIS ONE HAD A VERY HAPPY ENDING.

(and YES, Gals- the first thing I read in the paper IS still the "lost and found")

LOST. SOMEWHERE AROUND PUBERTY. ABILITY TO MAKE UP STORIES. HAPPINESS DEPENDS ON IT. PLEASE WRITE.

Engaging with the Text

87

1. Lynda Barry uses both text and images to provide **VIVID DETAILS** in her narrative. Choose two details that include both an image and verbal text, and explain how Barry makes these two modes of expression work together effectively.

452–56

2. In a number of places, Barry uses (or invents) **DIALOGUE** between herself and various other people, including another writer, the creative-writing teacher "Mrs. Snobaroo," and people at a party who find out that Barry is a cartoonist. How does this dialogue—which seems to focus on the lack of connection or understanding between Barry and the people she's talking with—help Barry **SUPPORT** the larger point she's making in her narrative?

114

66–68

3. How would you describe the **STANCE** Barry takes toward her early experiences with literacy? What other kind of stance might she have taken? What would have been the advantages and disadvantages, if any, of that other stance versus the one she actually takes?

4. Given that we know Barry is a highly successful author and cartoonist, why do you suppose she wrote about her lack of success in getting into creative writing classes and dealing with literature classes in high school and college? What point is she making by recalling these failures?

5. *For Writing.* Select an early memory of reading and/or writing that continues to feel relevant and important for you today. Create a cartoon strip about this experience, telling the story by drawing pictures and writing supporting text (or writing the text first and drawing pictures to illustrate it). If possible, choose a title related to what you were reading or writing about during this experience, as Barry does with "Lost and Found."

academic literacies · rhetorical situations · genres · fields · processes · strategies · research MLA / APA · media / design · readings · handbook

ANU PARTANEN

Finland's School Success

What Americans Keep Ignoring

Anu Partanen (b. 1975) is a Finnish writer who lives in the United States and writes for both Finnish- and English-language magazines and newspapers, including the Atlantic, *the* New York Times, *and* Fortune. *She is the author of* The Nordic Theory of Everything *(2016), which suggests ways in which Americans could improve their lives by learning from Nordic practices. The following essay appeared in the* Atlantic *in 2011.*

EVERYONE AGREES the United States needs to improve its education system dramatically, but how? One of the hottest trends in education reform lately is looking at the stunning success of the West's reigning education superpower, Finland. Trouble is, when it comes to the lessons that Finnish schools have to offer, most of the discussion seems to be missing the point.

The small Nordic country of Finland used to be known—if it was known for anything at all—as the home of Nokia, the mobile phone giant. But lately Finland has been attracting attention on global surveys of quality of life—*Newsweek* ranked it number one last year—and Finland's national education system has been receiving particular praise, because in recent years Finnish students have been turning in some of the highest test scores in the world.

Finland's schools owe their newfound fame primarily to one study: the PISA survey, conducted every three years by the Organization for Economic Co-operation and Development (OECD). The survey compares 15-year-olds in different countries in reading, math, and science. Finland has ranked at or near the top in all three competencies on every survey since 2000, neck and neck with superachievers such as South Korea and Singapore. In the most recent survey in 2009 Finland slipped slightly, with students in Shanghai, China, taking the best scores, but

Finnish schools assign less homework and engage children in more creative play.

the Finns are still near the very top. Throughout the same period, the PISA performance of the United States has been middling, at best.

Compared with the stereotype of the East Asian model—long hours of exhaustive cramming and rote memorization—Finland's success is especially intriguing because Finnish schools assign less homework and engage children in more creative play. All this has led to a continuous stream of foreign delegations making the pilgrimage to Finland to visit schools and talk with the nation's education experts, and constant coverage in the worldwide media marveling at the Finnish miracle.

So there was considerable interest in a recent visit to the U.S. by one of the leading Finnish authorities on education reform, Pasi Sahlberg, director of the Finnish Ministry of Education's Center for International Mobility and author of the new book *Finnish Lessons: What Can the World Learn from Educational Change in Finland?* Earlier this month, Sahlberg stopped by the Dwight School in New York City to speak with educators and students, and his visit received national media attention and generated much discussion.

academic literacies
rhetorical situations
genres
fields
processes
strategies
research MLA / APA
media / design
readings
handbook

And yet it wasn't clear that Sahlberg's message was actually getting through. As Sahlberg put it to me later, there are certain things nobody in America really wants to talk about.

During the afternoon that Sahlberg spent at the Dwight School, a photographer from the *New York Times* jockeyed for position with Dan Rather's TV crew as Sahlberg participated in a roundtable chat with students. The subsequent article in the *Times* about the event would focus on Finland as an "intriguing school-reform model."

Yet one of the most significant things Sahlberg said passed practically unnoticed. "Oh," he mentioned at one point, "and there are no private schools in Finland."

This notion may seem difficult for an American to digest, but it's true. Only a small number of independent schools exist in Finland, and even they are all publicly financed. None is allowed to charge tuition fees. There are no private universities, either. This means that practically every person in Finland attends public school, whether for pre-K or a Ph.D.

The irony of Sahlberg's making this comment during a talk at the 10 Dwight School seemed obvious. Like many of America's best schools, Dwight is a private institution that costs high-school students upward of $35,000 a year to attend—not to mention that Dwight, in particular, is run for profit, an increasing trend in the U.S. Yet no one in the room commented on Sahlberg's statement. I found this surprising. Sahlberg himself did not.

Sahlberg knows what Americans like to talk about when it comes to education, because he's become their go-to guy in Finland. The son of two teachers, he grew up in a Finnish school. He taught mathematics and physics in a junior high school in Helsinki, worked his way through a variety of positions in the Finnish Ministry of Education, and spent years as an education expert at the OECD, the World Bank, and other international organizations.

Now, in addition to his other duties, Sahlberg hosts about a hundred visits a year by foreign educators, including many Americans, who want to know the secret of Finland's success. Sahlberg's new book is partly an attempt to help answer the questions he always gets asked.

From his point of view, Americans are consistently obsessed with certain questions: How can you keep track of students' performance if you don't test them constantly? How can you improve teaching if you have no accountability for bad teachers or merit pay for good teachers? How do you foster competition and engage the private sector? How do you provide school choice?

The answers Finland provides seem to run counter to just about everything America's school reformers are trying to do.

For starters, Finland has no standardized tests. The only exception   15
is what's called the National Matriculation Exam, which everyone takes at the end of a voluntary upper-secondary school, roughly the equivalent of American high school.

Instead, the public school system's teachers are trained to assess children in classrooms using independent tests they create themselves. All children receive a report card at the end of each semester, but these reports are based on individualized grading by each teacher. Periodically, the Ministry of Education tracks national progress by testing a few sample groups across a range of different schools.

As for accountability of teachers and administrators, Sahlberg shrugs. "There's no word for accountability in Finnish," he later told an audience at the Teachers College of Columbia University. "Accountability is something that is left when responsibility has been subtracted."

For Sahlberg what matters is that in Finland all teachers and administrators are given prestige, decent pay, and a lot of responsibility. A master's degree is required to enter the profession, and teacher training programs are among the most selective professional schools in the country. If a teacher is bad, it is the principal's responsibility to notice and deal with it.

And while Americans love to talk about competition, Sahlberg points out that nothing makes Finns more uncomfortable. In his book Sahlberg quotes a line from a Finnish writer named Samuli Paronen: "Real winners do not compete." It's hard to think of a more un-American idea, but when it comes to education, Finland's success shows that the Finnish attitude might have merits. There are no lists of best schools or teachers in Finland. The main driver of education policy is not competition between teachers and between schools, but cooperation.

Finally, in Finland, school choice is noticeably not a priority, nor is engaging the private sector at all. Which brings us back to the silence after Sahlberg's comment at the Dwight School that schools like Dwight don't exist in Finland.

"Here in America," Sahlberg said at the Teachers College, "parents can choose to take their kids to private schools. It's the same idea of a marketplace that applies to, say, shops. Schools are a shop and parents can buy what ever they want. In Finland parents can also choose. But the options are all the same."

Herein lay the real shocker. As Sahlberg continued, his core message emerged, whether or not anyone in his American audience heard it.

Decades ago, when the Finnish school system was badly in need of reform, the goal of the program that Finland instituted, resulting in so much success today, was never excellence. It was equity.

Since the 1980s, the main driver of Finnish education policy has been the idea that every child should have exactly the same opportunity to learn, regardless of family background, income, or geographic location. Education has been seen first and foremost not as a way to produce star performers, but as an instrument to even out social inequality.

In the Finnish view, as Sahlberg describes it, this means that schools should be healthy, safe environments for children. This starts with the basics. Finland offers all pupils free school meals, easy access to health care, psychological counseling, and individualized student guidance.

In fact, since academic excellence wasn't a particular priority on the Finnish to-do list, when Finland's students scored so high on the first PISA survey in 2001, many Finns thought the results must be a mistake. But subsequent PISA tests confirmed that Finland—unlike, say, very similar countries such as Norway—was producing academic excellence through its particular policy focus on equity.

That this point is almost always ignored or brushed aside in the U.S. seems especially poignant at the moment, after the financial crisis and Occupy Wall Street movement have brought the problems of inequality in America into such sharp focus. The chasm between those who can afford $35,000 in tuition per child per year—or even just the price of a house in a good public school district—and the other "99 percent" is painfully plain to see.

Pasi Sahlberg goes out of his way to emphasize that his book *Finnish Lessons* is not meant as a how-to guide for fixing the education systems of other countries. All countries are different, and as many Americans point out, Finland is a small nation with a much more homogeneous population than the United States.

Yet Sahlberg doesn't think that questions of size or homogeneity should give Americans reason to dismiss the Finnish example. Finland is a relatively homogeneous country—as of 2010, just 4.6 percent of Finnish residents had been born in another country, compared with 12.7 percent in the United States. But the number of foreign-born residents in Finland doubled during the decade leading up to 2010, and the country didn't lose its edge in education. Immigrants tended to concentrate in certain areas, causing some schools to become much more mixed than others, yet there has not been much change in the remarkable lack of variation between Finnish schools in the PISA surveys across the same period.

Samuel Abrams, a visiting scholar at Columbia University's Teachers College, has addressed the effects of size and homogeneity on a nation's education performance by comparing Finland with another Nordic country: Norway. Like Finland, Norway is small and not especially diverse overall, but unlike Finland it has taken an approach to education that is more American than Finnish. The result? Mediocre performance in the PISA survey. Educational policy, Abrams suggests, is probably more important to the success of a country's school system than the nation's size or ethnic makeup.

Indeed, Finland's population of 5.4 million can be compared to many an American state—after all, most American education is managed at the state level. According to the Migration Policy Institute, a research organization in Washington, there were 18 states in the U.S. in 2010 with an identical or significantly smaller percentage of foreign-born residents than Finland.

30

academic literacies · rhetorical situations · genres · fields · processes · strategies · research MLA / APA · media / design · readings · handbook

What's more, despite their many differences, Finland and the U.S. have an educational goal in common. When Finnish policymakers decided to reform the country's education system in the 1970s, they did so because they realized that to be competitive, Finland couldn't rely on manufacturing or its scant natural resources and instead had to invest in a knowledge-based economy.

With America's manufacturing industries now in decline, the goal of educational policy in the U.S.—as articulated by most everyone from President Obama on down—is to preserve American competitiveness by doing the same thing. Finland's experience suggests that to win at that game, a country has to prepare not just some of its population well, but all of its population well, for the new economy. To possess some of the best schools in the world might still not be good enough if there are children being left behind.

Is that an impossible goal? Sahlberg says that while his book isn't meant to be a how-to manual, it is meant to be a "pamphlet of hope."

"When President Kennedy was making his appeal for advancing American science and technology by putting a man on the moon by the end of the 1960's, many said it couldn't be done," Sahlberg said during his visit to New York. "But he had a dream. Just like Martin Luther King a few years later had a dream. Those dreams came true. Finland's dream was that we want to have a good public education for every child regardless of where they go to school or what kind of families they come from, and many even in Finland said it couldn't be done." 35

Clearly, many were wrong. It is possible to create equality. And perhaps even more important—as a challenge to the American way of thinking about education reform—Finland's experience shows that it is possible to achieve excellence by focusing not on competition, but on cooperation, and not on choice, but on equity.

The problem facing education in America isn't the ethnic diversity of the population but the economic inequality of society, and this is precisely the problem that Finnish education reform addressed. More equity at home might just be what America needs to be more competitive abroad.

Engaging with the Text

1. According to this essay, what are some of the major differences between how schools are run in the United States and how they are run in Finland? Identify at least three differences, pointing to the sentences that reveal them.

386–87 ◆

2. What is the answer to the implied question in the **TITLE** of this essay? What do Americans keep ignoring about Finland's school success? Why do you think Americans have not adopted the Finnish system of education? How would a similar system fare in the United States?

380–85 ◆

3. Anu Partanen **ENDS** her essay by saying that "the problem facing education in America . . . [is] the economic inequality of society. . . . More equity at home might just be what America needs to be more competitive abroad." Do you agree with her conclusion? Why or why not?

401–8 ◆
489–510 ●

4. What kind of **EVIDENCE** does Partanen provide to support her argument? How does she use **SOURCES**? How convincing is the evidence and the sources of it?

5. *For Writing.* Write an essay responding to Partanen's argument. Do you believe the Finnish system would improve education in the United States, or not? For another perspective, you might read Jonathan Kozol's essay "Fremont High School" on page 770. In your essay, you might mix several genres—to **ARGUE** your own position, **EVALUATE** schools you've attended, and **REFLECT** on your own education.

157–84 ▲
202–10
256–63

academic literacies · rhetorical situations · genres · fields · processes · strategies · research MLA / APA · media / design · readings · handbook

JEREMY DOWSETT

What My Bike Has Taught Me about White Privilege

Jeremy Dowsett (b. 1979) is a writer and a pastor at a church in Lansing, Michigan. He has written on topics such as white privilege, racism, and religion. Many of his pieces echo points made in his Western Michigan University honors thesis, "Toward an Authentically Anti-Racist Curriculum." The following essay was originally posted in 2014 on his blog, A Little More Sauce, and it later appeared in Quartz, a digital business news publication.

THE PHRASE "WHITE PRIVILEGE" is one that rubs a lot of white people the wrong way. It can trigger something in them that shuts down conversation or at least makes them very defensive. (Especially those who grew up relatively less privileged than other folks around them.) And I've seen more than once where this happens and the next move in the conversation is for the person who brought up white privilege to say, "The reason you're getting defensive is because you're feeling the discomfort of having your privilege exposed."

I'm sure that's true sometimes. And I'm sure there are a lot of people, white and otherwise, who can attest to a kind of a-ha moment or paradigm shift where they "got" what privilege means and they did realize they had been getting defensive because they were uncomfortable at having their privilege exposed. But I would guess that more often than not, the frustration and the shutting down is about something else. It comes from the fact that nobody wants to be a racist. And the move "you only think that because you're looking at this from the perspective of privilege" or the more terse and confrontational "check your privilege!" kind of sound like an accusation that someone is a racist (if they don't already understand privilege). And the phrase "white privilege" kind of sounds like, "You are a racist and there's nothing you can do about it because you were born that way."

And if this were what "white privilege" meant— which it is not—defensiveness and frustration would be the appropriate response. But privilege talk is not intended to make a moral assessment or a moral claim about the privileged at all. It is about systemic imbalance. It is about injustices that have arisen because of the history of racism that birthed the way things are now. It's not saying, "You're a bad person because you're white." It's saying, "The system is skewed in ways that you maybe haven't realized or had to think about precisely because it's skewed in YOUR favor."

I am white. So I have not experienced racial privilege from the "under" side firsthand. But my children (and a lot of other people I love) are not white. And so I care about privilege and what it means for racial justice in our country. And one experience I have had firsthand, which has helped me to understand privilege and listen to privilege talk without feeling defensive, is riding my bike.

Now, I know, it sounds a little goofy at first. But stick with me. 5 Because I think that this analogy might help some white people understand privilege talk without feeling like they're having their character attacked.

About five years ago I decide to start riding my bike as my primary mode of transportation. As in, on the street, in traffic. Which is enjoyable for a number of reasons (exercise, wind in yer face, the cool feeling of going fast, etc.). But the thing is, I don't live in Portland or Minneapolis. I live in the capital city of the epicenter of the auto industry: Lansing, Michigan. This is not, by any stretch, a bike-friendly town. And often, it is downright dangerous to be a bike commuter here.

Now sometimes it's dangerous for me because people in cars are just blatantly a**holes to me. If I am in the road—where I legally belong—people will yell at me to get on the sidewalk. If I am on the sidewalk—which is sometimes the safest place to be—people will yell at me to get on the road. People in cars think it's funny to roll down their window and yell something right when they get beside me. Or to splash me on purpose. People I have never met are angry at me for just being on a bike in "their" road and they let me know with colorful language and other acts of aggression.

I can imagine that for people of color life in a white-majority context feels a bit like being on a bicycle in midst of traffic. They have the
right to be on the road, and laws on the books to make it equitable, but
that doesn't change the fact that they are on a bike in a world made for
cars. Experiencing this when I'm on my bike in traffic has helped me to
understand what privilege talk is really about.

Now most people in cars are not intentionally aggressive toward me.
But even if all the jerks had their licenses revoked tomorrow, the road
would still be a dangerous place for me. Because the whole transportation infrastructure privileges the automobile. It is born out of a history
rooted in the auto industry that took for granted that everyone should
use a car as their mode of transportation. It was not built to be convenient or economical or safe for me.

And so people in cars—nice, non-aggressive people—put me in dan- 10
ger all the time because they see the road from the privileged perspective
of a car. E.g., I ride on the right side of the right lane. Some people fail
to change lanes to pass me (as they would for another car) or even give
me a wide berth. Some people fly by just inches from me not realizing
how scary/dangerous that is for me (like if I were to swerve to miss some
roadkill just as they pass). These folks aren't aggressive or hostile toward
me, but they don't realize that a pothole or a buildup of gravel or a broken
bottle, which they haven't given me enough room to avoid—because in
a car they don't need to be aware of these things—could send me flying
from my bike or cost me a bent rim or a flat tire.

So the semi driver who rushes past throwing gravel in my face in
his hot wake isn't necessarily a bad guy. He could be sitting in his cab
listening to Christian radio and thinking about nice things he can do for
his wife. But the fact that "the system" allows him to do those things
instead of being mindful of me is a privilege he has that I don't. (I have
to be hyper-aware of him.)

This is what privilege is about. Like drivers, nice, non-aggressive
white people can move in the world without thinking about the "pot-
holes" or the "gravel" that people of color have to navigate, or how things
that they do—not intending to hurt or endanger anyone—might actually be making life more difficult or more dangerous for a person of color.

Nice, non-aggressive drivers that don't do anything at all to endanger me are still privileged to pull out of their driveway each morning and know that there are roads that go all the way to their destination. They don't have to wonder if there are bike lanes and what route they will take to stay safe. In the winter, they can be certain that the snow will be plowed out of their lane into my lane and not the other way around.

And it's not just the fact that the whole transportation infrastructure is built around the car. It's the law, which is poorly enforced when cyclists are hit by cars, the fact that gas is subsidized by the government and bike tires aren't, and just the general mindset of a culture that is in love with cars after a hundred years of propaganda and still thinks that bikes are toys for kids and triathletes.

So when I say the semi driver is privileged, it isn't a way of calling him a bad person or a man-slaughterer or saying he didn't really earn his truck, but just a way of acknowledging all that—infrastructure, laws, government, culture—and the fact that if he and I get in a collision, I will probably die and he will just have to clean the blood off of his bumper. In the same way, talking about *racial* privilege isn't a way of telling white people they are bad people or racists or that they didn't really earn what they have.

It's a way of trying to make visible the fact that the system is not neutral, it is not a level playing field, it's not the same experience for everyone. There are biases and imbalances and injustices built into the warp and woof of our culture. (The recent events in Ferguson, Missouri, should be evidence enough of this.) Not because you personally are a racist, but because the system has a history and was built around this category "race" and that's not going to go away overnight (or even in 100 years). To go back to my analogy: bike lanes are relatively new, and still just kind of an appendage on a system that is inherently car-centric.

So—white readers—the next time someone drops the p-word, try to remember they aren't calling you a racist or saying you didn't really earn your college degree, they just want you to try to empathize with how scary it is to be on a bike sometimes (metaphorically speaking).

One last thing: Now, I know what it is like to be a white person engaged in racial reconciliation or justice work and to feel like privilege

academic literacies   rhetorical situations   genres   fields   processes   strategies   research MLA / APA   media / design   readings   handbook

language is being used to silence you or to feel frustrated that you are genuinely trying to be a part of the solution not the problem but every time you open your mouth someone says, "Check your privilege." (Even though privilege language doesn't mean "You are one of the bad guys," some people do use it that way.) So if you'll permit me to get a few more miles out of this bike analogy (ya see what I did there?), I think it can help encourage white folks who have felt that frustration to stay engaged and stay humble.

I have a lot of "conversations" with drivers. Now, rationally, I know that most drivers are not jerks. But I have a long and consistent history of bad experiences with drivers and so, when I've already been honked at or yelled at that day, or when I've read a blog post about a fellow cyclist who's been mowed down by a careless driver, it's hard for me to stay civil.

But when I'm not so civil with a "privileged" driver, it's not because 20 I hate him/her, or think s/he is evil. It's because it's the third time that day I got some gravel in the face. So try to remember that even if you don't feel like a "semi driver," a person of color might be experiencing you the way a person on a bike experiences being passed by a semi. Even if you're listening to Christian radio.

Engaging with the Text

1. Jeremy Dowsett **DEFINES** "privilege talk" as "not intended to make   ◆ 432–42
a moral assessment or a moral claim about the privileged at all. It is about systemic imbalance. It is about injustices that have arisen because of the history of racism that birthed the way things are now. It's not saying, 'You're a bad person because you're white.' It's saying, 'The system is skewed in ways that you maybe haven't realized or had to think about precisely because it's skewed in YOUR favor.'" Does this definition help you understand the concept of "white privilege"? Do you think his definition is correct? Why or why not?

2. A successful text that mixes genres offers a **CLEAR FOCUS**. What is   ▲ 283
Dowsett's focus? How clear and successful is it?

3. Dowsett is clearly writing for an audience that doesn't understand the concept of "white privilege." Identify two specific passages that reveal this intended **AUDIENCE**.

57–60

4. To help his audience understand the concept of "white privilege," Dowsett compares it to the experience of car drivers who both see and don't see bike riders and as a consequence don't treat them respectfully on the road. Readers have had mixed reactions to this comparison, with some claiming it is helpful and others claiming the opposite. How successful do you find this **COMPARISON** for Dowsett's purpose? Why? What other comparison might he have made?

424–31

5. *For Writing.* Select a concept involving relationships between people, such as patriarchy, political correctness, or helicopter parenting, and **COMPARE** it to a subject with which your targeted audience would be more familiar to help them understand your perspective on the concept. Be sure to offer a **DEFINITION** of your concept and clearly explain your **ANALOGY** for it.

424–31

432–42

430

SNEHA SAHA
The Wedding Carriage

Sneha Saha (b. 1995) wrote the "The Wedding Carriage" in the spring of 2017 for an undergraduate writing course on the narrative essay at Johns Hopkins University. It was nominated for the Norton Writer's Prize by her instructor. As you read, notice how she uses features of several different genres to tell one coherent story.

MS. COCHRAN BECKONS TO KAREN, her twelve-year-old daughter, who has just come down from her bedroom.

"Why aren't you wearing socks?" she chides her. "You're going to catch a cold if you leave the house like that. Go back to your room and put on some socks."

Stubborn as she is, Karen does not budge.

"I'm already wearing them, Mom. Look!" she insists, pointing down to her feet.

In no mood for another one of her daughter's tantrums, Ms. Cochran   5
calls out to her husband, "TOMMMM! Where are you? Get down here!"

It appears to be an average morning in the Cochran household.

Or at least that's how I imagine the scene plays out in Ms. Cochran's mind. In reality, it is two o'clock in the afternoon, and Ms. Cochran is lying on a bed at St. Francis Hospital in Hartford. There is no one else in the room besides me, a college student volunteering for the summer. I have just entered Ms. Cochran's room, and she is reprimanding me for not wearing my socks. My initial reaction is to look down and confirm that my shoes and socks are, in fact, still on my feet. This is my first time meeting Ms. Cochran, and it takes me several seconds to realize that she likely suffers from dementia and has mistaken me for someone named Karen.

As a volunteer, I am not allowed to access a patient's records before visiting a room. The surprise of each encounter is one of the parts I enjoy most about my position. It is the reason I have been coming back to St.

Francis for most summers since I was fifteen. And yet this is one of those moments when I desperately wish I had some prior knowledge of Ms. Cochran's history. I wonder who Karen and Tom are, and whether Ms. Cochran ever experiences moments of clarity. How can I connect with someone who appears to be in a world of her own?

As a volunteer, I have had no formal training in communicating with dementia patients. Until this point, my only experience with the disease has come from interacting with my maternal grandfather in India, who suffered from dementia and who passed away when I was fifteen. Even then, I communicated with him exclusively via *Skype*, exchanging a few words each week in broken Bengali. The last time I saw him in person was seven years ago, before his health began to deteriorate. In this moment at St. Francis, I find myself rummaging through vague memories of him in search of insight, anything really, to help me reach Ms. Cochran. Perhaps, I think, I can excuse myself and ask a nurse for assistance. But the nurses are already overloaded with work, and Ms. Cochran is becoming more and more impatient with me. It seems I will have to find a way to navigate this situation alone.

Naturally, I assume that the best approach is to reason with Ms. Cochran. Three years on the high school debate team taught me how to collect evidence, craft an argument, and persuade my listeners. Armed with these skills, I prepare to articulate my contentions and draw Ms. Cochran toward my point of view. Starting with the obvious, I point down and explain to her that I am wearing my shoes and socks. Though her gaze follows my finger, she seems to be looking past my feet at some distant object. At once, she resumes her tirade against my footwear, and I decide to shift gears. Perhaps I can convince Ms. Cochran that socks are not necessary because it is eighty-five degrees and sunny outside. I cross the room to the window and raise the blinds. As sunlight pours in, Ms. Cochran turns to me and scowls. 10

"What do you think you're doing, young lady? You're not leaving this house until you clean your room."

At least it's not the socks this time, I think, breathing a small sigh of relief. But I know I am still far from a breakthrough, and my powers of reasoned persuasion are failing me. While I have no doubt that Ms.

academic literacies · rhetorical situations · genres · fields · processes · strategies · research MLA / APA · media / design · readings · handbook

Cochran can hear and see me, she appears to have conjured up a reality that only she is privy to—a reality in which my logic does not apply.

In this moment, I recall my grandfather, who, during his early stages of dementia, held certain fixed beliefs about his own reality. Similar to Ms. Cochran, he would resist his family's attempts to reason with him, which further provoked him and made him cling more tightly to his delusions. For a long time, he was convinced that his two daughters were stealing from him and trusted only his caregivers. Ironically, as my aunt would later discover, there had been a caregiver who was caught stealing from the house. Despite this revelation, my grandfather continued to distrust my mother and aunt and remained loyal to his caregivers. Standing next to Ms. Cochran, I wonder how my mother managed to remain calm through her father's outbursts. How do you cope with a loved one who has seemingly turned his back on a forty-year relationship? I am barely ten minutes into meeting Ms. Cochran, and my frustration is already brewing. Back then, my mother told me that she understood the basis of my grandfather's delusion: she visited him once a year, whereas his caregivers took care of him every day. From this perspective, it made sense that my grandfather would trust them more than his family. While his caregivers were present in the moment, his family was fading into the past. Instead of denying my grandfather's accusations, my mother rationalized them, and in time she learned to accept his version of reality.

Perhaps it is time for me to try the same. Ms. Cochran calls again for Tom: "Come down and look at this!" She is beaming, as if preparing to reveal a surprise to her husband. "They're passing by again. It's so beautiful, don't you think?"

I follow Ms. Cochran's gaze to the wall in front of her bed. At first, I 15 see nothing but a TV, whiteboard, and hand sanitizer dispenser. "What is it? Who's passing by?" I begin to probe Ms. Cochran's visions.

"It's the carriage! Just look at them. Aren't they gorgeous?" she asks. Against the backdrop of the wall, I build a window into Ms. Cochran's mind. Through it, I see a horse-drawn carriage carrying two people, a young Ms. Cochran and her husband. She appears as a young woman in her late twenties, dressed in a white lace gown and surrounded by a crowd of people throwing kisses and flowers. Tom curls an arm around Ms. Cochran's shoulder, and the two exchange a kiss. Just then, the carriage sets in motion and drives off the screen.

"They're beautiful," I reply, turning back to Ms. Cochran. "It's like a scene straight out of a movie."

Whether or not Ms. Cochran is actually reliving her wedding day is beyond my knowledge. Her descriptions of the scene are vague, and at times I struggle to decipher her jumbled speech. The most elegant interpretation, it seems, is that Tom is Ms. Cochran's deceased husband, whose memory she keeps alive by living in the past. However, it is entirely possible that Tom was a son or a brother or a friend. Seeing the elation on Ms. Cochran's face, I realize that Tom's actual identity is not important. What matters is that this man, real or imagined, is very much a part of Ms. Cochran's reality. By entering her world, I have finally found a way to connect with her.

An apparent calm washes over Ms. Cochran as she leans back against the headboard and loses herself in her visions. I take this as my cue to excuse myself from the room. "Please let me know if there's anything else you need today. It was very nice to meet you, Ms. Cochran." I deliver the standard farewell, knowing full well that she still doesn't know who I am.

"You better be putting on those socks, missy!" she retorts.   20

"Yes, of course. I'm going to grab a pair from my room." I smile and exit the room.

As I would later learn, my acceptance of Ms. Cochran's reality was actually the basis for validation therapy, a management tool used by geriatric psychiatrists, social workers, and other people who deal with dementia patients. Historically, it was believed that patients who lost touch with reality should be "reoriented to the real world" (Bursack). In 1982, however, the publication of Naomi Feil's book *Validation: The Feil Method* gave rise to a new way of thinking, in which validating a patient's reality was found to "reduce stress and . . . [enhance] dignity by reinforcing

self-esteem" (Bursack). This strategy has been shown to foster trust and empathy between dementia patients and their caretakers.

Although Feil's theory emphasizes the benefits of "therapeutic fibbing" to patients, my own experience with Ms. Cochran—like my mother's experience with her father—showed me how this method can offer relief to a caretaker as well (Bursack). By coming to terms with her father's false accusations, my mother better understood the nature of his illness and the ways in which it influenced his perception of the world. Her empathy helped her gain closure with him towards the end of his life, when multiple strokes left him bedridden and unable to speak. As for me, my initial frustration with Ms. Cochran dissipated once I let go of the urge to prove to her that I was correct. As it turned out, entering into Ms. Cochran's reality, a false reality to me, was the key to establishing a real connection and ultimately calming her.

I wonder how things would have turned out if I were a physician or someone more familiar with Ms. Cochran's case. In some sense, my inexperience proved to be an asset rather than a limitation. It allowed me to overcome my early stubbornness and let go of the need to "fix" Ms. Cochran's perceptions. By contrast, the field of modern medicine is built on the principle of identifying a problem and applying science to fix it. But what if the solution to some of these apparent problems lies not in scientific rationality but in our ability to redefine the issue? Instead of pathologizing a person's reality, what if we embraced it? Practicing empathy, I learned, does not require special training or expertise. And yet with patience—and a little bit of imagination—it can play a powerful role in a person's healing process.

Work Cited

Bursack, Carol Bradley. "Validation Therapy for Dementia: Calming or Condescending?" *Aging Care*, 27 July 2018, www.agingcare.com /articles/validation-therapy-for-dementia-166707.htm.

Engaging with the Text

386–87
55–56
283
528–31
282–83

1. What does Sneha Saha's **TITLE** refer to? What **PURPOSE** does the title serve? Is it fitting for this essay? Why or why not?

2. Do you believe Saha's essay has a **CLEAR FOCUS**? Why or why not? If so, what is that focus?

3. How does Saha use **QUOTATIONS**? What do they add to her essay?

4. What would you say is the **PRIMARY GENRE** of this essay? Why do you think so? What other supporting genres are mixed in? How might Saha's essay be different if she had used one of the supporting genres as her primary genre?

5. *For Writing.* Visit an older relative or acquaintance. Interview that person about something important to them—for example, a disease they are coping with, a former occupation, or a favorite hobby. Write an essay about your visit with the person, focusing especially on the topic that is important to them. Do some outside research on the topic as well, and incorporate what you learn into your essay.

academic literacies
rhetorical situations
genres
fields
processes
strategies
research MLA / APA
media / design
readings
handbook

part 10

Handbook

"Pfft, English, who needs that? I'm never going to England." So says the illustrious Homer Simpson on an early episode called "The Way We Was." Maybe Homer can ignore the conventions of English grammar and usage, but that's not the case for the rest of us. If we want the world to take seriously what we think and say, we need to pay attention to our grammar and language. We need to edit our SENTENCES so they're clear, choose our LANGUAGE carefully, and use PUNCTUATION purposefully. This handbook provides guidelines to help you edit what you write.

Handbook

Sentences   **S**

academic literacies | rhetorical situations | genres | fields | processes | strategies | research MLA / APA | media / design | readings | handbook

S-1 Elements of a Sentence

In casual situations, we often use a kind of shorthand, because we know our audience will fill in the gaps. When we say "Coffee?" to a dinner guest, he knows we mean, "Would you like some coffee?" When we text "7 @ Starbucks?" to a friend, she'll understand that we're asking, "Should we meet at 7:00 at Starbucks?" In more formal writing or speaking situations, though, our audience may not share the same context; to be sure we're understood, we usually need to present our ideas in complete sentences. This chapter reviews the parts of a sentence.

S-1a Subjects and Predicates

Glossary
HB-29–34
HB-12–24

A sentence contains a subject and a predicate. The subject, which usually includes a **NOUN** or **PRONOUN**, names the topic of the sentence; the predicate, which always includes a **VERB**, says what the subject is or does.

> S P
> ▶ Birds fly.

> S ┌─────P─────┐
> ▶ Birds are feathered vertebrates.

Sometimes the subject and the predicate contain only one word. Usually, however, both contain more than one word.

> ┌──────S──────┐┌────P────┐
> ▶ Birds of many kinds fly south in the fall.

> ┌────────S────────┐┌──────P──────┐
> ▶ Flying in a V formation is characteristic of geese.

> ┌─────S─────┐┌────P────┐
> ▶ One of the flock leads the others.

A sentence may contain more than one subject or verb.

> S   S   V
> ▶ Birds and butterflies fly south in the fall.

> S V   V
> ▶ Birds fly south in the fall and return north in the spring.

academic literacies · rhetorical situations · genres · fields · processes · strategies · research MLA / APA · media / design · readings · handbook

At times, the subject comes after the verb.

▶ Here comes the sun.

▶ In the attic were old photographs and toys.

Expressing subjects explicitly

English requires an explicit subject in every **CLAUSE**, even if all of the clauses in a sentence are about the same subject.

HB-6

▶ Although the dinner cost too much, it impressed my guests.

The only exception is commands, in which the subject is understood to be *you*.

▶ Eat smaller portions at each meal.

In informal conversation, speakers sometimes emphasize a noun subject by repeating it as a pronoun: *My friend Jing she changed her name to Jane.* In academic writing, though, don't repeat a subject this way.

▶ The visiting students ~~they~~ were detained at the airport.

Sentences beginning with *there* or *it*. In some cases where the subject comes after the verb, an **EXPLETIVE** — *there* or *it* — is required before the verb.

Glossary

▶ There is Is no place like home.

▶ It is Is both instructive and rewarding to work with young children.

You can often rephrase the sentence to avoid using the expletive.

▶ Working with young children It is both instructive and rewarding. ~~to work with young children.~~

HB-8 ⌃

S-1b Clauses

A clause is a group of words containing a subject and a predicate. An independent clause can function alone as a sentence: *Birds fly.* A subordinate clause begins with a **SUBORDINATING WORD** such as *because, as,* or *which* and cannot stand alone as a sentence: *because birds fly.* (See p. HB-8 for a list of common subordinating words.)

⌐INDEPENDENT CLAUSE¬ ⌐————— SUBORDINATE CLAUSE —————¬
▶ My yard is now quiet because most of the birds flew south.

⌐————— SUBORDINATE CLAUSE —————¬ ⌐————— INDEPENDENT CLAUSE —————¬
▶ Although they travel really far, the birds always find their way back.

S-1c Phrases

A phrase is a word group that makes sense but lacks a subject, a verb, or both and thus cannot stand alone as a sentence. Some common ones are prepositional, appositive, participial, gerund, and infinitive phrases.

HB-56–57 ⌃

A prepositional phrase starts with a **PREPOSITION** such as *at, from, of,* or *in* and usually ends with a noun or pronoun: *at school, from home, in bed.* It usually functions as an adjective or adverb.

▶ The day *after the World Series* everyone *in San Francisco* celebrated.

An appositive phrase follows and gives additional information about a noun or pronoun. It functions as a noun.

▶ We all know that computers and their spawn, *the smartphone and cellphone,* have created a very different world from several decades ago.
— Alina Tugend,
"Multitasking Can Make You Lose . . . Um . . . Focus"

Glossary ⌃

A participial phrase contains the **PRESENT PARTICIPLE** or **PAST PARTICIPLE** of a verb plus any **OBJECTS**, **MODIFIERS**, and **COMPLEMENTS**. It functions as an adjective.

▶ *Brimming with optimism,* I headed over to the neighborhood watering hole and waited.
— Hal Niedzviecki, "Facebook in a Crowd"

▶ A study from Princeton *issued at the same times as the Duke study* showed that women in the sciences reported less satisfaction in their jobs and less of a sense of belonging than their male counterparts.
— Anna Quindlen, "Still Needing the F Word"

A gerund phrase includes the -*ing* form of a verb plus any objects, modifiers, and complements. It functions as a noun.

▶ *Asking for candy on Halloween* was called trick-or-treating, but *asking for candy on November first* was called begging.
— David Sedaris, "Us and Them"

An infinitive phrase includes an infinitive (*to* plus the base form of a verb: *to read, to write*) and any objects, modifiers, and complements. It functions as a noun, an adjective, or an adverb.

▶ The plan *to commit more troops* requires top-level approval.

▶ The point of ribbon decals is *to signal that we support our troops*.

S-2 Sentence Fragments

Sentence fragments often show up in advertising: "Got milk?" "Good to the last drop." "Not bad for something that tastes good too." We use them in informal speech and text messages as well. In other kinds of writing, though, some readers consider fragments too informal, and in many academic writing situations, it's better to avoid them altogether. This chapter helps you identify and edit out fragments.

S-2a Identifying Fragments

A sentence fragment is a group of words that is capitalized and punctuated as a sentence but is not a sentence. A sentence needs at least one **INDEPENDENT CLAUSE**, which contains a **SUBJECT** and a **VERB** and does not start with a **SUBORDINATING WORD**.

HB-6
HB-4–5
HB-12–24
HB-8

NO SUBJECT	The catcher batted fifth. Fouled out, ending the inning. *Who fouled out?*
NO VERB	The first two batters walked. Manny Ramirez again. *What did Ramirez do again?*
SUBORDINATING WORD	Although the Yankees loaded the bases. *There is a subject (Yankees) and a verb (loaded), but although is a subordinating word. What happened after the Yankees loaded the bases?*

SOME SUBORDINATING WORDS

after	because	so that	until	while
although	before	that	when	who
as	if	though	where	which
as if	since	unless	whether	why

S-2b Editing Fragments

Since some readers regard fragments as errors, it's generally better to write complete sentences. Here are four ways to make fragments into sentences.

Add a subject

▶ The catcher batted fifth. ~~Fouled out,~~ ending the inning.
                  He fouled out,

Add a verb

▶ The first two batters walked. Manny Ramirez again.
                         walked

Sometimes, a fragment contains a verb form, such as a present participle or past participle, that cannot function as the main verb of a sentence. In these cases, you can either substitute an appropriate verb form or add a **HELPING VERB**.

HB-17–19

▶ As the game went on, the fans started to lose interest. The pitcher's arm ~~weakening,~~ and the fielders ~~making~~ a number of errors.
       weakened,   made

▶ The media influence the election process. Political commercials ^{are} appearing on television more frequently than in years past.

Remove the subordinating word

▶ I'm thinking about moving to a large city. ~~Because~~ I dislike the lack of privacy in my country town of three thousand residents.

Attach the fragment to a nearby sentence

▶ Some candidates spread nasty stories, ^{about} ~~About~~ their opponents.

▶ These negative stories can deal with many topics, ^{such} ~~Such~~ as marital infidelity, sources of campaign funds, and drug use.

▶ Put off by negative campaigning, ^{some} ~~Some~~ people decide not to vote at all.

Note that using a semicolon to attach a fragment to a nearby sentence *isn't* a good solution. See **P–2** for tips on using semicolons.

⋀ HB-84–85

S-2c Intentional Fragments

Writers sometimes use fragments intentionally.

FOR EMPHASIS	Throughout my elementary and middle school years, I was a strong student, always on the honor roll. I never had a GPA below 3.0. I was smart, and I knew it. *That is, until I got the results of the proficiency test.*
	—Shannon Nichols, " 'Proficiency' "
TO BE INFORMAL	The SAT writing test predicts how successful a student will be in college. *Since when?*
TO LIST SEVERAL EXAMPLES	The small details stand out. *The bathrooms with green stalls and mirrors with painted Ducks slugging conference foes. The extra-large furniture tested to withstand 500 pounds. The elevators decorated with famous plays in Oregon football history, the actual plays, drawn up in Xs and Os by a*

> *coach. The room for professional scouts to watch footage of*
> *Oregon players. The ticker running sports scores.*
>   —Greg Bishop, "We Are the University of Nike."

Though fragments are common in informal contexts, they are often considered errors in academic writing.

S-3 Comma Splices, Fused Sentences

You'll sometimes see a comma splice in ads or literary works: "He dropped the bucket, the paint spilled on his feet." Or the comma may be omitted, forming a fused sentence: "He dropped the bucket the paint spilled on his feet." A comma splice or a fused sentence is generally regarded as an error in academic writing. This chapter shows how to recognize comma splices and fused sentences and edit them out of your writing.

S-3a Identifying Comma Splices and Fused Sentences

HB-6 △

A comma splice occurs when two or more **INDEPENDENT CLAUSES** follow one another with only a comma between them.

COMMA SPLICE	T. S. Eliot is best known for his poetry, he also wrote several plays.

A fused sentence occurs when two or more independent clauses follow one another with no punctuation in between.

FUSED SENTENCE	The school board debated the issue for three days they were unable to reach an agreement.

S-3b Editing Comma Splices and Fused Sentences

There are several ways to edit out comma splices and fused sentences.

academic literacies | rhetorical situations | genres | fields | processes | strategies | research MLA / APA | media / design | readings | handbook

Make the clauses two sentences

▶ T. S. Eliot is best known for his poetry/. ~~he~~ He also wrote several plays.

Use a comma and a **COORDINATING CONJUNCTION**

∧ HB-38

▶ The school board debated the issue for three days, but they were unable to reach an agreement.

Use a semicolon

If the relationship between the two clauses is clear without a coordinating conjunction, you can simply join them with a semicolon.

▶ Psychologists study individuals' behavior/; sociologists focus on group-level dynamics.

When clauses are linked by a **TRANSITION** such as *therefore* or *as a result*, the transition needs to be preceded by a semicolon and should generally be followed by a comma.

✳ 14

▶ The hill towns experienced heavy spring and summer rain/; therefore, the fall foliage fell far short of expectations.

Recast one clause as a subordinate clause

Add a **SUBORDINATING WORD** to clarify the relationship between the two clauses.

∧ HB-8

▶ Although initial ~~Initial~~ critical responses to *The Waste Land* were mixed, the poem has been extensively anthologized, read, and written about.

S-3c Intentional Comma Splices

Writers sometimes use only a comma between clauses that are very brief or closely parallel in structure, as in proverbs like *Marry in haste, repent at leisure.* In academic writing, though, such sentences may be seen as mistakes.

S-4 Verbs

Verbs are the engines of sentences, giving energy, action, and life to writing. "I Googled it" is much more vivid than "I found it on the Internet"—and the difference is the verb. Sometimes, however, our use of verbs can obscure our meaning, as when a politician avoids taking responsibility by saying, "Mistakes were made." Our choice of verbs shapes our writing in important ways, and this chapter reviews ways of using verbs appropriately and effectively.

S-4a Verb Tenses

To express time, English verbs have three simple tenses—present, past, and future. In addition, each of these verb tenses has perfect and progressive forms that indicate more complex time frames. The present perfect, for example, can be used to indicate an action that began in the past but is continuing into the present. The lists that follow show each of these tenses for the regular verb *talk* and the irregular verb *write*.

Simple tenses

PRESENT	PAST	FUTURE
I talk	I talked	I will talk
I write	I wrote	I will write

Use the simple present to indicate actions that take place in the present or that occur habitually. Use the simple past to indicate actions that were completed in the past. Use the simple future to indicate actions that will take place in the future.

▶ Most wealthy industrialized countries *operate* national health-insurance systems.

▶ In 2010, Congress *approved* the Affordable Care Act.

▶ Prohibiting English *will do* for the language what Prohibition *did* for liquor.   —Dennis Baron, "Don't Make English Official—Ban It Instead"

Use the present tense to express a scientific fact or a general truth even when the rest of the sentence is in the past tense.

> ▶ The security study showed that taxis and planes are the top places
> where people ~~lost~~ *lose* their phones.

In general, use the present tense to write about literature.

> ▶ In the first book of the series, Rowling *introduces* us to eleven-year-old Harry Potter; in the seventh and final volume, Harry *enters* full adulthood.

In **APA STYLE**, use the past tense to report results of an experiment, the present perfect to refer to a past action that didn't occur at a specific time or that continues into the present, and the present tense to give your own insights into or conclusions about the results.

● APA 597–636

> ▶ The bulk of the data collected in this study *validated* the research of Neal Miller; the subjects *appeared* to undergo operant conditioning of their smooth muscles in order to relax their frontalis muscles and increase their skin temperatures. Subjects 3 and 6 each *failed* to do this in one session; subject 7 *failed* several times. This finding *is* difficult to explain precisely.
> —Sarah Thomas, "The Effect of Biofeedback Training on Muscle Tension and Skin Temperature"

Perfect tenses

PRESENT PERFECT	PAST PERFECT	FUTURE PERFECT
I have talked	I had talked	I will have talked
I have written	I had written	I will have written

Use the present perfect to indicate actions that took place at unspecified times in the past or that began in the past and continue into the present (or have relevance in the present).

> ▶ Many teachers and parents *have resisted* the increasing pressure for more standardized testing of students.

Use the past perfect for an action that was completed before another past action began.

> ▶ By the time I was born, the Gulf War *had* already ended.
> *The war ended before the writer was born.*

Use the future perfect to indicate actions that will be completed at a specific time in the future.

▶ By this time next year, you *will have graduated*.

Progressive tenses

PRESENT PROGRESSIVE	PAST PROGRESSIVE	FUTURE PROGRESSIVE
I am talking	I was talking	I will be talking
I am writing	I was writing	I will be writing

PRESENT PERFECT PROGRESSIVE	PAST PERFECT PROGRESSIVE	FUTURE PERFECT PROGRESSIVE
I have been talking	I had been talking	I will have been talking
I have been writing	I had been writing	I will have been writing

Use progressive tenses to indicate continuing action.

▶ The Heat *are having* a great year, but the Spurs *are leading* the league.

▶ We *were watching* TV when the doorbell rang.

▶ During the World Cup, soccer fans around the world *will be watching* on TV or online.

▶ Willie joined the Grace Church Boy Choir when he was ten, and he *has been singing* ever since.

S-4b Verb Forms

There are four forms of a verb: the base form, the past, the past participle, and the present participle. Samples of each appear in the lists below. All of the various tenses are generated with these four forms.

The past tense and past participle of all regular verbs are formed by adding -ed or -d to the base form (*talked, lived*). Irregular verbs are not as predictable; see the list of some common ones below. The present participle consists of the base form plus -ing (*talking, living*).

BASE FORM	On Thursdays, we *visit* a museum.
PAST TENSE	Last week, we *visited* the Museum of Modern Art.

PAST PARTICIPLE	I have also *visited* the Metropolitan Museum, but I've not yet *been* to the Cloisters.
PRESENT PARTICIPLE	We will be *visiting* the Cooper-Hewitt Museum tomorrow to see the cutlery exhibit.

Some common irregular verbs

BASE FORM	PAST TENSE	PAST PARTICIPLE	PRESENT PARTICIPLE
be	was/were	been	being
bring	brought	brought	bringing
choose	chose	chosen	choosing
come	came	come	coming
do	did	done	doing
eat	ate	eaten	eating
find	found	found	finding
fly	flew	flown	flying
give	gave	given	giving
go	went	gone	going
hang (suspend)	hung	hung	hanging
have	had	had	having
know	knew	known	knowing
make	made	made	making
prove	proved	proved, proven	proving
rise	rose	risen	rising
set	set	set	setting
sit	sat	sat	sitting
teach	taught	taught	teaching
write	wrote	written	writing

It's easy to get confused about when to use the past tense and when to use a past participle. One simple guideline is to use the past tense if there is no helping verb and to use a past participle if there is one.

▶ For vacation last summer, my family ~~gone~~ *went* to the Outer Banks.

▶ After a week at the beach, we had ~~ate~~ *eaten* a lot of seafood.

Gerunds and infinitives

A gerund is a verb form ending in -*ing* that functions as a noun: *hopping, skipping, jumping.*

▶ Although many people like *driving*, some prefer *walking.*

An infinitive is a verb form made up of *to* plus the base form of a verb: *to hop, to skip, to jump.*

▶ Although many people like *to drive*, some prefer *to walk.*

In general, use infinitives to express intentions or desires, and use gerunds to express plain facts.

▶ I planned *to learn* Spanish, Japanese, and Arabic.

▶ I also wanted ~~studying~~ Russian.
  ^ to study

▶ Unfortunately, I ended up *studying* only Spanish and Arabic—and *speaking* only Spanish.

▶ Just in time for Thanksgiving, the painters finished ~~to put~~ up the wallpaper.
  ^ putting

Some verbs—*begin, continue, like, prefer,* and a few others—can be followed by either a gerund or an infinitive with little if any difference in meaning. But with several verbs—*forget, remember, stop,* and a few others—the choice of an infinitive or a gerund changes the meaning.

▶ I stopped *to eat* lunch.
  In other words, I took a break so that I could eat lunch.

▶ I stopped *eating* lunch.
  In other words, I no longer ate lunch.

HB-56–57 ∧

Always use a gerund after a **PREPOSITION**.

▶ The water is too cold for ~~to swim.~~
  ^ swimming.

S-4c Helping Verbs

Do, *have*, *be*, and **MODALS** such as *can* and *may* all function as helping verbs that are used with **MAIN VERBS** to form certain **TENSES** and **MOODS**. *Do*, *have*, and *be* change form to indicate different tenses; modals do not.

HB-18–19
HB-12–14
HB-20–21

FORMS OF *DO*	do, does, did
FORMS OF *HAVE*	have, has, had
FORMS OF *BE*	be, am, is, are, was, were, been
MODALS	can, could, may, might, must, shall, should, will, would, ought to

Do, *does*, and *did* require the base form of the main verb.

▶ That professor *did take* class participation into account when calculating grades.

▶ Sometimes even the smartest students *do* not *like* to answer questions out loud in class.

Have, *has*, and *had* require the past participle of the main verb.

▶ I *have applied* for insurance through one of the new exchanges.

▶ When all of the visitors *had gone*, the security guards locked the building for the night.

Forms of *be* are used with a present participle to express a continuing action or with a past participle to express the **PASSIVE VOICE**.

HB-19–20

CONTINUING ACTION

▶ The university *is considering* a change in its policy on cell phone use.

▶ I *was studying* my notes from last week as I walked to class.

PASSIVE VOICE

▶ Six classes per semester *is considered* a heavy course load.

▶ Ancient Greek *was studied* by many university students in the early twentieth century, but it is not a popular major today.

Modals

Can, could, may, might, must, ought to, shall, should, will, and would: these are modals, a kind of helping verb used with the base form of a main verb to express whether an action is likely, possible, permitted, or various other conditions. Modals don't take the third–person –s or the –ed or –ing endings that ordinary verbs do.

Likelihood *will, could, ought to, may, might*

▶ The Spurs *will* win tomorrow. [*very certain*]

▶ The Lakers *could* defeat the Heat. [*somewhat certain*]

▶ It *ought to* be a very close series between the Warriors and the Cavaliers. [*moderately certain*]

▶ The Rockets *may* win their game tonight. [*less certain*]

▶ The Knicks *might* make the playoffs someday. [*much less certain*]

Assumption *must*

▶ The dog just started barking; he *must* hear our guests arriving.

Expectation *should, ought to*

▶ Two large onions *should* be enough for this recipe.

▶ The potatoes *ought to* be ready in twenty minutes.

Ability *can, could*

▶ Mick Jagger *can* still put on quite a performance, but years ago he *could* sing and throw himself around the stage more dramatically.
How much longer *will* he *be able to* keep rocking?

Necessity or obligation *must, should, ought to*

▶ Travelers *must* have a passport for foreign travel.

▶ We *should* leave early tomorrow because of the holiday traffic.

▶ You *ought to* get to the airport at least two hours before your scheduled departure.

Permission and requests *may, can, could, would, will*

▶ People traveling with small children *may* board the plane first.

▶ The hotel's check-in time is 4:00 PM, but travelers *can* often check in earlier.

▶ *Would* someone help me put my suitcase in the overhead rack?

▶ *Will* you please turn off your phone?

Advice *should, ought to*

▶ You *should* never text while driving.

▶ You *ought to* be careful about using wi-fi networks in public places.

Intention *will, shall*

▶ Marianna *will* bring an apple pie for Thanksgiving dinner.

▶ We *shall* overcome.

S-4d Active and Passive Voice

Verbs can sometimes be active or passive. In the active voice, the subject performs the action of the verb (*Becky solved the problem*). In the passive voice, the subject receives the action (*the problem was solved by Becky*).

ACTIVE   One year ago, almost to the day, I *asked* my hairdresser to cut off 16 inches of my hair.
　　　　　—Suleika Jaouad, "Finding My Cancer Style"

PASSIVE   As a teenager I *was instructed* on how to behave as a proper señorita. —Judith Ortiz Cofer, "The Myth of the Latin Woman"

Active verbs tend to be more direct and easier to understand, but the passive voice can be useful when you specifically want to emphasize the recipient of the action.

▶ In a sense, little girls *are urged* to please adults with a kind of coquettishness, while boys *are enjoined* to behave like monkeys toward each other.　　　　　—Paul Theroux, "Being a Man"

The passive voice is also appropriate in scientific writing when you want to emphasize the research itself, not the researchers.

▶ The treatment order was random for each subject, and it *was reversed* for his or her second treatment.
—Sarah Thomas, "The Effect of Biofeedback Training on Muscle Tension and Skin Temperature"

S-4e Mood

English verbs have three moods: indicative, imperative, and subjunctive. The indicative is used to state facts, opinions, or questions.

▶ Habitat for Humanity *has built* twelve houses in the region this year.

▶ What other volunteer opportunities *does* Habitat *offer*?

The imperative is used to give commands or directions.

▶ *Sit* up straight, and *do* your work.

The subjunctive is used to indicate unlikely or hypothetical conditions or to express wishes, requests, or requirements.

▶ We would be happier if we *had* less pressure at work.

▶ My mother wishes my brother *were* more responsible with his money.

▶ Most colleges require that each applicant *write* an essay.

The subjunctive has two types—one that is the same form as the past tense and one that is the same as the base form.

Conditional sentences

The subjunctive is used most often in conditional sentences, ones that include a clause beginning with *if* or another word that states a condition. Use the indicative in the *if* clause to show that you are confident the condition is posssible; use the subjunctive to show that it's doubtful or impossible.

academic literacies · rhetorical situations · genres · fields · processes · strategies · research MLA / APA · media / design · readings · handbook

If it's a fact or a possibility. When there's no doubt that the condition in the *if* clause is true or possible, use the indicative in both clauses.

▶ If an earthquake *strikes* that region, forecasters *expect* a tsunami.

▶ A century ago, if a hurricane *struck*, residents *had* very little warning.

▶ If you *follow* that diet for two weeks, you *will lose* about ten pounds.

If it's unlikely, impossible, or hypothetical. When the condition in the *if* clause is not likely or possible, use the subjunctive (same as the past form) in the *if* clause and *would* (or *could* or *might*) + the base form of a verb in the other clause. For *be*, use *were* in the *if* clause, not *was*.

▶ If I *won* the lottery, I *could pay off* my student loans.

▶ If Martin Luther King Jr. *were* alive, he *would acknowledge* progress in race relations, but he *would* also *ask* significant questions.

Because the subjunctive can sound rather formal, it's often not used in informal contexts. In formal and most academic writing, however, it's best to do so.

> **INFORMAL** I *wish* I *was* in Paris.
>
> **ACADEMIC** In *The Three Sisters,* Masha *wishes* she *were living* in Moscow.

When the *if* clause is about an event in the past that never happened, use the past perfect in the *if* clause and *would have* (or *could have* or *might have*) + a past participle in the other clause.

▶ If the police officer *had separated* the witnesses, their evidence *would have been* admissible in court.

Requests, recommendations, and demands

In *that* clauses following verbs such as *ask, insist,* or *suggest,* use the subjunctive to express a request, a recommendation, or a demand. Use the base form of the verb in the *that* clause.

▶ I recommended that Hannah *study* French as an undergraduate.

▶ The CEO will insist that you *be* at your desk before nine each morning.

S-4f Phrasal Verbs

Act up. Back down. Carry on. These are all phrasal verbs, composed of more than one word—usually a verb and a preposition. You know what *act* means. You know what *up* means. If English is not your primary language, however, you may need to check a dictionary to find out that *act up* means to "misbehave" (or to say that using another phrasal verb, you may need to *look it up*). With phrasal verbs, knowing the meaning of each part does not always help you to know what the phrasal verb itself means.

Phrasal verbs can be divided into two categories, separable and inseparable. With separable verbs, the parts can be separated by an **OBJECT**; with inseparable ones, the parts can never be separated.

Glossary

> **SEPARABLE**   I used to *look up* words in a dictionary; now I *look* them *up* on my phone.
>
> **INSEPARABLE**   Jim and his family are *caring for* his elderly mother.

With separable phrasal verbs, you have a choice: you can put the object between the parts, or after the complete phrasal verb.

▶ With a hurricane forming nearby, NASA *called off* tomorrow's lunar launch.

▶ Darn! They *called* the launch *off?*

When the object is a long phrase, however, it almost always follows the complete verb.

▶ NASA engineers called the launch of the lunar mission scheduled for tomorrow ~~off~~ . ^off

The personal pronouns *me, you, him, her, it, us,* and *them* are almost always placed between the parts.

▶ The launch was scheduled for yesterday, but NASA called off ~~it~~ because of the weather. ^it

Some phrasal verbs never take an object—for example, *come over* (meaning to "visit") and *catch on* (meaning to "become popular").

▶ Why don't you *come over* and see us sometime?

▶ Even the developers of *Pinterest* were astonished by how quickly it *caught on.*

academic literacies · rhetorical situations · genres · fields · processes · strategies · research MLA / APA · media / design · readings · handbook

With some phrasal verbs, the meaning changes depending on whether or not there is an object. To look *something* *up*, for instance, means to "find information"; without an object, to look *up* means to "get better."

▶ When in doubt, *look up* phrasal verbs in a dictionary.

▶ The sun's out and the roses are in bloom; things are *looking up!*

Go to **wwnorton.com/write/fieldguidelinks** for a glossary of phrasal verbs.

Some common phrasal verbs

SEPARABLE

back up   means to "support": *Dodson's hypothesis is well stated, but the data do not back it up.*

break down   means to "divide into smaller parts": *Their analysis might be clearer if it broke the data down state by state.*

carry out   means to "fulfill" or "complete": *We plan to carry out a survey on what the students in our dorm are reading.*

find out   means to "learn" or "get information": *Some parents decide not to find out the gender before their baby is born because they want to be surprised; others just want to annoy relatives.*

point out   means to "call attention to": *The lizards blend in with the leaves so well that they were hard to see until the guide pointed them out.*

INSEPARABLE

call for   means to "require" or "deserve": *Our current economic situation calls for bold and innovative thinking.*

get over   means to "recover": *Grandma always insisted that the best way to get over a cold was to eat chicken soup.*

look into   means to "investigate": *GAO investigators are looking into allegations of fraud by some college recruiters.*

settle on   means to "decide on" or "choose": *We considered Elizabeth, Margaret, Jane, and many other names for our baby, but finally we settled on Susanna.*

touch on   means to "mention briefly": *The Wall Street Journal article focused on productivity and barely touched on issues of worker safety.*

DO NOT TAKE AN OBJECT

come about   means to "happen" or "occur": *How did the dispute come about in the first place?*

get by   means to "survive" or "manage," usually with few resources: *Many retired workers can't get by on just their pensions; they have to find part-time work as well.*

give in   means to "yield" or "agree": *After much discussion, members of the union voted not to give in to management's demands for a reduction in benefits.*

show up   means to "arrive": *Did everyone show up for the rehearsal?*

take off   means to "leave the ground": *The JetBlue flight took off an hour late because of thunderstorms in the Midwest.* It also means to "make great progress": *Sales of Anna Karenina took off in 2004, after it was recommended by Oprah Winfrey.*

S-5 Subject-Verb Agreement

Subjects and verbs should agree: if the subject is in the third-person singular, the verb should be in the third-person singular—"Dinner is on the table." Yet sometimes context affects subject-verb agreement, as when we say that "macaroni and cheese *make* a great combination" but that "macaroni and cheese *is* our family's favorite comfort food." This chapter focuses on subject-verb agreement.

S-5a Agreement in Number and Person

Subjects and verbs should agree with each other in number (singular or plural) and person (first, second, or third). To make a present-tense verb agree with a third-person singular subject, add -s or -es to the base form.

▶ A 1922 *ad* for Resinol soap *urges* women to "make that dream come true" by using Resinol. —Doug Lantry, "'Stay Sweet as You Are'"

To make a present-tense verb agree with any other subject, simply use the base form without any ending.

▶ *I listen* to NPR every morning while *I brush* my teeth.

▶ *Drunk drivers cause* thousands of preventable deaths each year.

Be and *have* have **IRREGULAR** forms and so do not follow the -s/-es rule.   HB-15

▶ The test of all knowledge *is* experiment.
                              —Richard Feynman, "Atoms in Motion"

▶ The scientist *has* a lot of experience with ignorance and doubt and uncertainty, and this experience *is* of great importance.
                              —Richard Feynman, "The Value of Science"

In questions, a helping verb is often necessary. The subject, which generally goes between the helping verb and the main verb, should agree with the helping verb.

▶ How long *does an air filter last* on average?

▶ *Have the 10 ml pipettes arrived* yet?

S-5b Subjects and Verbs Separated

A verb should agree with its subject, not with another word that falls in between.

▶ In the backyard, the *leaves* of the apple tree *rattle* across the lawn.
                              —Gary Soto, "The Guardian Angel"

                              fluctuates
▶ The *price* of soybeans fluctuate according to demand.
                              ^

S-5c Compound Subjects

Two or more subjects joined by *and* are generally plural.

▶ Swiss cheese and shrimp *are* both high in vitamin B12.

However, if the parts of the subject form a single unit, they take a singular verb.

>   *is*
> ▶ Forty acres and a mule ~~are~~ what General William T. Sherman promised each
> freed slave.

If the subjects are joined by *or* or *nor*, the verb should agree with the closer subject.

>   *is*
> ▶ Either you or she ~~are~~ mistaken.

>   *were*
> ▶ Neither the teacher nor his students ~~was~~ able to solve the equation.

S-5d Subjects That Follow the Verb

English verbs usually follow their subjects. Be sure the verb agrees with the subject even when the subject follows the verb, such as when the sentence begins with *there is* or *there are*.

>   *are*
> ▶ There ~~is~~ too many unresolved problems for the project to begin.

>   *were*
> ▶ In the middle of the room ~~was~~ a desk and a floor lamp.

S-5e Collective Nouns

Collective nouns such as *group, team, audience,* or *family* can take singular or plural verbs, depending on whether the noun refers to the group as a single unit or to the individual members of the group.

>   *sings*
> ▶ The choir ~~sing~~ Handel's *Messiah* every Christmas.

> ▶ Gregor's family *keep* reassuring themselves that things will be just fine
> again.   —Scott Russell Sanders, "Under the Influence"
> *The word* themselves *shows that* family *refers to its individual members.*

S-5f *Everyone* and Other Indefinite Pronouns

Most **INDEFINITE PRONOUNS**, such as *anyone, anything, each, either, everyone, everything, neither, nobody, no one, one, somebody, someone,* and *something,* take a singular verb, even if they seem plural or refer to plural nouns.

Glossary

▶ Everyone in our dorm *has* already *signed* the petition.

▶ Each of the candidates ~~agree~~ ^{*agrees*} with the president.

Both, few, many, others, and *several* are always plural.

▶ Although there are many great actors working today, few *are* as versatile as Meryl Streep.

All, any, enough, more, most, none, and *some* are singular when they refer to a singular noun, but they are plural when they refer to a plural noun.

▶ Don't assume that all of the members of a family ~~votes~~ ^{*vote*} the same way.

▶ Most of the music we heard last night ~~come~~ ^{*comes*} from the baroque period.

S-5g *Who, That, Which*

The **RELATIVE PRONOUNS** *who, that,* and *which* take a singular verb when they refer to a singular noun and a plural verb when they refer to a plural noun.

Glossary

▶ In these songs, Lady Gaga draws on a tradition of camp that *extends* from drag queen cabaret to Broadway and disco.
—Jody Rosen, review of *Born This Way*

▶ Scott Karp, who *writes* a blog about online media, recently confessed that he has stopped reading books altogether.
—Nicholas Carr, "Is *Google* Making Us Stupid?"

One of the is always followed by a plural noun, and when the noun is followed by *who* or *that*, the verb should be plural.

>   ask
> ▶ Jaime is one of the speakers who ~~asks~~ provocative questions.
>
> *Several speakers ask provocative questions. Jaime is one. Who refers to speakers, so the verb is plural.*

If the phrase begins with *the only one*, however, the verb should be singular.

>   asks
> ▶ Jaime is the only one of the speakers who ~~ask~~ provocative questions.
>
> *Only one speaker asks provocative questions: Jaime. Who thus refers to one, so the verb is singular.*

S-5h Words Such as *News* and *Physics*

Words like *news*, *athletics*, and *physics* seem plural but are usually singular in meaning and take singular verb forms.

> ▶ The *news* of widespread layoffs *alarms* everyone in the company.

Some of these words, such as *economics*, *mathematics*, *politics*, and *statistics*, have plural meanings in some uses and take plural verbs.

> ▶ For my roommate, mathematics *is* an endlessly stimulating field.

> ▶ The complex mathematics involved in this proof *are* beyond the scope of this lecture.

S-5i Titles and Words Used as Words

Titles and words that are discussed as words are singular.

>   depicts
> ▶ *The Royal Tenenbaums* ~~depict~~ three talented siblings who are loosely based on characters created by J. D. Salinger.

>   is
> ▶ *Man-caused disasters* ~~are~~ a term favored by some political analysts as a substitute for the term *terrorist attacks*.

S-6 Pronouns

We use pronouns to take the place of nouns so that we don't have to write or say the same word or name over and over. Imagine how repetitive our writing would be without pronouns: *Little Miss Muffet sat on a tuffet eating Little Miss Muffet's curds and whey.* Luckily, we have pronouns, and this chapter demonstrates how to use them clearly.

S-6a Pronoun-Antecedent Agreement

Antecedents are the words that pronouns refer to. Most of the time, a pronoun must agree with its antecedent in gender and number.

IN GENDER   *Grandma* took *her* pie out of the oven.

IN NUMBER   *My grandparents* spent weekends at *their* cabin on White Bear Lake.

Generic nouns

Generic nouns refer to a type of person or thing (*a farmer, a mom*). In casual writing, you'll often see plural pronouns used to refer to singular generic nouns. This usage is increasingly common in academic writing too, although many writers still prefer to use pronouns that agree with their antecedents.

▶ Every lab technician should always wear goggles to protect *his or her* eyes while working with chemicals.

▶ Every lab technician should always wear goggles to protect *their* eyes while working with chemicals.

Indefinite pronouns like everyone and each

INDEFINITE PRONOUNS such as *anyone, each, everyone,* and *someone* are singular even if they seem to be plural or refer to plural nouns.

▶ Everyone in the class did *his or her* best.

Glossary

If you find *his or her* awkward, you can rewrite the sentence to make the antecedents plural.

>   All of the students
> ▶ ~~Everyone~~ in the class did their best.
>   ^

In conversation and informal writing, and increasingly in academic writing as well, *they* and other plural pronouns are often used to refer to indefinite pronouns that are grammatically singular.

> ▶ Somebody may beat me, but *they* are going to have to bleed to do it.
>   —Steve Prefontaine

Collective nouns like audience and team

Collective nouns such as *audience*, *committee*, or *team* take a singular pronoun when they refer to the group as a whole and a plural pronoun when they refer to members of the group as individuals.

>   its
> ▶ The winning team drew ~~their~~ inspiration from the manager.
>   ^

>   their
> ▶ The winning team threw ~~its~~ gloves in the air.
>   ^

He, his, and other masculine pronouns

HB-67–68 ⌃

To avoid **SEXIST LANGUAGE**, use *he*, *him*, *his*, or *himself* only when you know that the antecedent is male.

>   or her.
> ▶ Before meeting a new doctor, many people worry about not liking him/
>   ^

Many writers have begun using *they*, *them*, and *their* to refer to a person whose gender is unknown or not relevant to the context.

> ▶ Someone in my building is selling *their* laptop; *they* put up a sign by the mailboxes.

Glossary

Acceptance for this usage, known as **SINGULAR THEY**, is growing. In addition, some people prefer to use pronouns other than *he* or *she*, such as *they* or *ze*. You should refer to people using the pronouns they'd use to refer to themselves in the third person.

S-6b Pronoun Reference

A pronoun usually needs a clear antecedent, a specific word to which it refers.

▶ *My grandmother* spent a lot of time reading to me. *She* mostly read

the standards, like *The Little Engine That Could.*

          —Richard Bullock, "How I Learned about the Power of Writing"

Ambiguous reference

If there is more than one word that a pronoun could refer to, rewrite the sentence to clarify which one is the antecedent.

                            the printer
▶ After I plugged the printer into the computer, ~~it~~ sputtered and died.

What sputtered and died—the computer or the printer? The edit makes the reference clear.

Implied reference

If a pronoun does not refer clearly to a specific word, rewrite the sentence to omit the pronoun or insert an antecedent.

Unclear reference of *this*, *that*, and *which*. These three pronouns must refer to specific antecedents.

                                 an oversight that
▶ Ultimately, the Justice Department did not insist on the breakup of Microsoft, ~~which~~ set the tone for a liberal merger policy.

Indefinite use of *they*, *it*, and *you*. Except in expressions like *it is raining* or *it seems that*, *they* and *it* should be used only to refer to people or things that have been specifically mentioned. *You* should be used only to address your reader.

    Many
▶ ~~In many~~ European countries, ~~they~~ don't allow civilians to carry handguns.

    The
▶ ~~On the~~ Weather Channel, ~~it~~ said that storms would hit Key West today.

► Many doctors argue that age should not be an impediment to
  for people who
physical exercise ~~if you~~ have always been active.

Both in conversation and in writing, antecedents are often left unstated if the audience will easily grasp the meaning. For academic writing, however, it's better not to use implied or indefinite antecedents.

S-6c Pronoun Case

Pronouns change case according to how they function in a sentence. There are three cases: subject, object, and possessive. Pronouns functioning as subjects or subject **COMPLEMENTS** are in the subject case; those functioning as **OBJECTS** are in the object case; those functioning as possessives are in the possessive case.

Glossary

SUBJECT	*We* lived in a rented house three blocks from the school.
OBJECT	I went to my room and shut the door behind *me*.
POSSESSIVE	All *my* life chocolate has made me ill.

—David Sedaris, "Us and Them"

SUBJECT	OBJECT	POSSESSIVE
I	me	my / mine
we	us	our / ours
you	you	your / yours
he / she / it	him / her / it	his / her / hers / its
they	them	their / theirs
who / whoever	whom / whomever	whose

In subject complements

Glossary

Use the subject case for pronouns that follow **LINKING VERBS** such as *be*, *seem*, *become*, and *feel*.

                                                              I.
► In fact, Li was not the one who broke the code; it was ~~me.~~

If It was I *sounds awkward, revise the sentence further:* I broke it.

In compound structures

When a pronoun is part of a compound subject, it should be in the subject case. When it's part of a compound object, it should be in the object case.

> ▶ On our vacations, my grandfather and ~~me~~ ^I^ went fishing together.
>
> ▶ There were never any secrets between ~~he~~ ^him^ and ~~I~~ ^me.^

After than *or* as

Often comparisons with *than* or *as* leave some words out. When such comparisons include pronouns, your intended meaning determines the case of the pronoun.

> ▶ You trust John more than *me.*
> *This sentence means* You trust John more than you trust me.

> ▶ You trust John more than *I.*
> *This sentence means* You trust John more than I trust him.

Before or after infinitives

Pronouns that come before or after an **INFINITIVE** are usually in the object case.

Glossary

> ▶ The professor asked Scott and ~~I~~ ^me^ to tell our classmates and ~~she~~ ^her^ about our project.

Before gerunds

Pronouns that come before a **GERUND** are usually in the possessive case.

◢ HB-16

> ▶ Savion's fans loved ~~him~~ ^his^ tap dancing to classical music.

With who *or* whom

There's strong evidence that *whom* is disappearing from use in both formal and informal contexts, but some instructors may expect you to use it. Use *who* (and *whoever*) where you would use *he* or *she*, and use *whom* (and *whomever*) where you would use *him* or *her*. These words appear most often in questions and in **SUBORDINATE CLAUSES**.

In questions. It can be confusing when one of these words begins a question. To figure out which case to use, try answering the question using *she* or *her*. If *she* works, use *who*; if *her* works, use *whom*.

Whom
▶ ~~Who~~ do the critics admire most?
   ^
They admire her, so change who *to* whom.

Who
▶ ~~Whom~~ will begin the discussion on this thorny topic?
  ^
She will begin the discussion, so change whom *to* who.

In subordinate clauses. To figure out whether to use *who* or *whom* in a subordinate clause, you need to determine how it functions in the clause. If it functions as a subject, use *who*; if it functions as an object, use *whom*.

         whomever
▶ You may invite ~~whoever~~ you like.
        ^
Whomever is the object of you like.

      whoever
▶ I will invite ~~whomever~~ is free that night.
      ^
Whoever is the subject of is free that night. *The clause* whoever is free that night *is the object of the whole sentence.*

When we *or* us *precedes a noun*

If you don't know whether to use *we* or *us* before a noun, choose the pronoun that you would use if the noun were omitted.

▶ *We* students object to the recent tuition increases.
Without students, *you would say* We object, *not* Us object.

▶ The state is solving its budget shortfall by unfairly charging *us* students.
Without students, *you would say* unfairly charging us, *not* unfairly charging we.

S-7 Parallelism

Been there, done that. Eat, drink, and be merry. For better or for worse. Out of sight, out of mind. All of these common sayings are parallel in structure, putting related words in the same grammatical form. Parallel structure emphasizes the connection between the elements and can make your writing rhythmic and easy to read. This chapter offers guidelines for maintaining parallelism in your writing.

S-7a In a Series or List

Use the same grammatical form for all items in a series or list—all nouns, all gerunds, all prepositional phrases, and so on.

▶ The seven deadly sins—*avarice, sloth, envy, lust, gluttony, pride,* and *wrath*—were all committed Sunday during the twice-annual bake sale at St. Mary's of the Immaculate Conception Church.   —*The Onion*

▶ After fifty years of running, biking, swimming, weight lifting, and _{playing} tennis to stay in shape, Aunt Dorothy was unhappy to learn she needed knee surgery.

S-7b With Paired Ideas

One way to emphasize the connection between two ideas is to put them in identical grammatical forms. When you connect ideas with *and, but,* or another **COORDINATING CONJUNCTION** or with *either . . . or* or another **CORRELATIVE CONJUNCTION**, use the same grammatical structure for each idea.

△ HB-38
HB-38

▶ Many rural residents are voting on conservation issues and ~~agree~~ ^{agreeing} to pay higher taxes to keep community land undeveloped.

▶ General Electric paid millions of dollars to dredge the river and ^{to remove} ~~for removing~~ carcinogens from backyards.

▶ Sweet potatoes are highly nutritious, providing both dietary fiber and ~~as a good source of~~ vitamins A and C.

▶ Information on local cleanup efforts can be obtained not only from the town government but also ~~by going to~~ at the public library.

S-7c On Presentation Slides

PowerPoint and other presentation tools present most information in lists. Entries on these lists should be in parallel grammatical form.

During the 1946 presidential race, Truman
- Conducted a whistle-stop campaign
- Made hundreds of speeches
- Spoke energetically
- Connected personally with voters

S-7d On a Résumé

Entries on a résumé should be grammatically and typographically parallel. Each entry in the example below has the date on the left; the job title in bold followed by the company on the first line; the city and state on the second line; and the duties performed on the remaining lines, each starting with a verb.

2012–present **INTERN**, Benedetto, Gartland, and Company
New York, NY
Assist in analyzing data for key accounts.
Design *PowerPoint* slides and presentations.

2011, summer **SALES REPRESENTATIVE**, Vector Marketing Corporation
New York, NY
Sold high-quality cutlery, developing client base.

2010, summer **TUTOR**, Grace Church Opportunity Project
New York, NY
Tutored children in math and reading.

academic literacies · rhetorical situations · genres · fields · processes · strategies · research MLA / APA · media / design · readings · handbook

S-7e In Headings

When you add headings to a piece of writing, put them in parallel form—all nouns, all prepositional phrases, and so on. Consider, for example, the following three headings in two of the research chapters.

Acknowledging Sources
Avoiding Plagiarism
Understanding Documentation Styles

S-7f With All the Necessary Words

Be sure to include all the words necessary to make your meaning clear and your grammar parallel.

▶ Voting gained urgency in cities, ^in^ suburbs, and on farms.

▶ She loved her son more than ^she loved^ her husband.

The original sentence was ambiguous; it could also mean that she loved her son more than her husband did.

▶ A cat's skeleton is more flexible than ^that of^ a dog.

The original sentence compared one animal's skeleton to a whole animal rather than to another animal's skeleton.

S-8 Coordination, Subordination

When we combine two or more ideas in one sentence, we can use coordination to give equal weight to each idea or subordination to give more emphasis to one of the ideas. Assume, for example, that you're writing about your Aunt Irene. Aunt Irene made great strawberry jam. She did not win a blue ribbon at the Iowa State Fair.

COORDINATION	Aunt Irene made great strawberry jam, but she did not win a blue ribbon at the Iowa State Fair.
SUBORDINATION	Though Aunt Irene made great strawberry jam, she did not win a blue ribbon at the Iowa State Fair.

S-8a Linking Equal Ideas

To link ideas that you consider equal in importance, use a coordinating conjunction, a pair of correlative conjunctions, or a semicolon.

COORDINATING CONJUNCTIONS

and	or	so	yet
but	nor	for	

▶ The line in front of Preservation Hall was very long, *but* a good tenor sax player was wandering up and down the street, *so* I took my place at the end of the line.   —Fred Setterberg, "The Usual Story"

▶ New models of coursework may need to be developed, *and* instructors may need to be hired.
                              —Megan Hopkins, "Training the Next Teachers for America"

Be careful not to overuse *and*. Try to use the coordinating conjunction that best expresses your meaning.

▶ Mosquitoes survived the high-tech zapping devices, ~~and~~ *but* bites were a small price for otherwise pleasant evenings in the country.

CORRELATIVE CONJUNCTIONS

either . . . or	not only . . . but also	whether . . . or
neither . . . nor	just as . . . so	

▶ *Just as* the summer saw endless rain, *so* the winter brought many snowstorms.

While a semicolon alone can signal equal importance, you might use a **TRANSITION** such as *therefore* or *in fact* to make the relationship between the ideas especially clear.

* 14

▶ Snowplows could not get through; trains stopped running.

▶ The 1996 film *Space Jam* stars Bugs Bunny and Michael Jordan, an unlikely pairing; *however,* the two are well matched in heroic status and mythic strengths.

S-8b Emphasizing One Idea over Others

To emphasize one idea over others, put the most important one in an **INDEPENDENT CLAUSE** and the less important ones in **SUBORDINATE CLAUSES** or **PHRASES**.

HB-6–7

▶ ─────PHRASE─────
Wanting to walk to work, LeShawn rented a somewhat expensive apartment downtown.

▶ ─────SUBORDINATE CLAUSE─────
His monthly expenses were actually lower because he saved so much money in transportation costs.

S-9 Shifts

You're watching the news when your brother grabs the remote and changes the channel to a cartoon. The road you're driving on suddenly changes from asphalt to gravel. These shifts are jarring and sometimes disorienting. Similarly, shifts in writing—from one tense to another, for example—can confuse your readers. This chapter explains how to keep your writing consistent in verb tense, point of view, and number.

S-9a Shifts in Tense

HB-12–14 ⌃

Only when you want to emphasize that actions take place at different times should you shift verb **TENSE**.

▶ My plane *will arrive* in Albuquerque two hours after it *leaves* Portland.

Otherwise, keep tenses consistent.

▶ As the concert ended, several people ~~are~~ ^{were} already on their way up the aisle, causing a distraction.

In writing about literary works, use the present tense. Be careful not to shift to the past tense.

▶ The two fugitives start down the river together, Huck fleeing his abusive father and Jim running away from his owner. As they ~~traveled,~~ ^{travel,} they ~~met~~ ^{meet} with many colorful characters, including the Duke and King, two actors and con artists who involve Huck and Jim in their schemes.

S-9b Shifts in Point of View

Do not shift between first person (*I, we*), second person (*you*), and third person (*he, she, it, they, one*).

▶ When ~~one has~~ ^{you have} a cold, you should stay home to avoid infecting others.

S-9c Shifts in Number

Unnecessary shifts between singular and plural subjects can confuse readers.

▶ Because of late frosts, oranges have risen dramatically in price. But since ~~the orange is~~ ^{oranges are} such a staple, they continue to sell.

academic literacies · rhetorical situations · genres · fields · processes · strategies · research MLA / APA · media / design · readings · handbook

Language L

L-1 Appropriate Words

Cool. Sweet. Excellent. These three words can mean the same thing, but each has a different level of formality. We usually use informal language when we're talking with friends, and we use slang and abbreviations when we send text messages, but we choose words that are more formal for most of our academic and professional writing. Just as we wouldn't wear an old T-shirt to most job interviews, we wouldn't write in a college essay that *Beloved* is "an awesome book." This chapter offers you help in choosing words that are appropriate for different audiences and purposes.

L-1a Formal and Informal Words

55–56
57–60

Whether you use formal or informal language depends on your **PURPOSE** and **AUDIENCE**.

> **FORMAL**   Four score and seven years ago our fathers brought forth on this continent, a new nation, conceived in Liberty, and dedicated to the proposition that all men are created equal.
> —Abraham Lincoln, Gettysburg Address

> **INFORMAL**   Our family, like most, had its ups and downs.
> —Judy Davis, "Ours Was a Dad"

The first, more formal sentence was delivered in 1863 to twenty thousand people, including many officials and prominent citizens. The second, less formal sentence was spoken in 2004 to a small gathering of family and friends at a funeral.

Colloquial language (*What's up? No clue*) and slang (*A-list, S'up?*) are not appropriate for formal speech and most academic and professional writing.

▶ ~~A lot of~~ high school ~~kids~~ have so little time for lunch that they end up ~~gobbling down their food~~ as they race to class.

Many ... *students* ... *eating*

L-1b Pretentious Language

Long or complicated words might seem to lend authority to your writing, but often they make it sound pretentious and stuffy. Use such words sparingly and only when they best capture your meaning and suit your **WRITING CONTEXT**.

53

> *After*
> ▶ ~~Subsequent to~~ adopting the new system, managers ~~averred~~ *claimed* that their
>   ^   ^
>   *together*   *better than expected.*
> staff worked ~~synergistically in a way that exceeded parameters.~~
>   ^   ^

L-1c Jargon

Jargon is a specialized vocabulary of a profession, trade, or field and should be used only when you know your audience will understand what you are saying. A computer enthusiast might easily understand the following paragraph, but most readers would not be familiar with terms like *HDMI*, *DVI*, and *1080p*.

> ▶ HDMI is the easiest and most convenient way to go about high-def. Why? Because you get [video] and sound in a single, USB-like cable, instead of a nest of component cables or the soundless garden hose of DVI. Also, unless you're trying to run 1080p over 100 feet or somesuch, stay away from premium brands. Any on-spec cheapie HDMI cable will be perfect for standard living room setups.
> —Rob Beschizza, "Which Is Better, HDMI or Component?"

When you are writing for an audience of nonspecialists, resist the temptation to use overly technical language.

> *small incision*
> ▶ The ~~mini-sternotomy~~ at the lower end of the ~~sternum resulted in~~ *breastbone preserved*
>   ^   ^
> *her appearance.*
> ~~satisfactory cosmesis.~~
> ^

L-1d Clichés

Steer clear of clichés, expressions so familiar that they have become trite (*white as snow, the grass is always greener*).

▶ The company needs a recruiter who thinks ~~outside the box.~~ *unconventionally.*

▶ After canoeing all day, we all slept ~~like logs.~~ *soundly.*

▶ Nita ~~is a team player,~~ *collaborates well,* so we hope she will be assigned to the project.

L-2 Precise Words

Serena Overpowers Sloane. Mariano Finishes Off the Sox. In each case, the writer could have simply used the word *beats*. But at least to sports fans, these newspaper headlines are a bit more precise and informative as a result of the words chosen. This chapter offers guidelines for editing your own writing to make it as precise as it needs to be.

L-2a *Be* and *Do*

Try not to rely too much on *be* or *do*. Check your writing to see where you can replace forms of these words with more precise verbs.

▶ David Sedaris's essay "Us and Them" ~~is about~~ *focuses on* his love/hate relationship with his family.

▶ Some doctors no longer believe that ~~doing~~ *solving* crossword puzzles can delay the onset of senility or Alzheimer's disease.

Sometimes using a form of *be* or *do* is the right choice, such as when you are describing something or someone.

▶ Most critics agree that *Citizen Kane, Casablanca,* and *The Shawshank Redemption are* some of the finest movies ever made.

L-2b Abstract and Concrete Words

Abstract words refer to general qualities or ideas (*truth, beauty*), whereas concrete words refer to specific things that can be perceived with our senses (*books, lipstick*). You'll often need to use words that are general or abstract, but remember that specific, concrete words can make your writing more precise and more vivid—and can make an abstract concept easier to understand.

▶ In Joan Didion's work, there has always been a fascination with what she once called "the unspeakable peril of the everyday"—the coyotes by the interstate, the snakes in the playpen, the fires and Santa Ana winds of California.
　　　　　　　—Michiko Kakutani, "The End of Life as She Knew It"

The concrete words coyotes, snakes, fires, *and* winds *help explain the abstract* peril of the everyday.

L-2c Figurative Language

Glossary

Figures of speech such as **SIMILES** and **METAPHORS** are words used imaginatively rather than literally. They can help readers understand an abstract point by comparing it to something they are familiar with or can easily imagine.

SIMILE　　His body is in almost constant motion—rolling those cigarettes, rubbing an elbow, reaching for a glass—but the rhythm is tranquil and fluid, *like a cat licking its paw.*
　　　　　　　—Sean Smith, "Johnny Depp: Unlikely Superstar"

METAPHOR　And so, before the professor had even finished his little story, *I had become a furnace of rage.*
　　　　　　　—Shelby Steele, "On Being Black and Middle Class"

L-3 Idioms

A piece of cake. Walking on air. Cute as a button. These are just three of the thousands of English idioms and idiomatic expressions that are used every day. Most idioms are phrases (and sometimes whole sentences) whose meaning cannot be understood by knowing the meanings of the individual words. We use idioms because they give a lot of information in few words and add color and texture to what we say or write. If you're learning English, a well-chosen idiom also demonstrates your fluency in the language. Some idioms appear more often in conversation than in formal writing, but many will be useful to you in your academic work.

L-3a Recognizing Idioms

When you read or hear a phrase that seems totally unrelated to the topic, you have probably encountered an idiom.

▶ Influencing Hollywood is a little *like herding cats.*
　　　　　　　　　　　　　　—Jane Alexander, *Command Performance*
　　Cats are notoriously independent and indifferent to following directions; thus a difficult, maybe impossible task is said to be "like herding cats."

▶ As the economy contracts, we Americans are likely to find that we have been living too *high on the hog.*　　　　　　　　　　　—*Los Angeles Times*
　　Ham, ribs, bacon, and other meats that are considered the most tasty and desirable are from the upper parts of the hog. People who live extravagantly or luxuriously are sometimes said to be living "high on the hog."

▶ This internship is not just about class credit. This is about really getting a *leg up* for when you graduate.
　　　　　　　　　　　　　　—Morgan to Chelsea, *Days of Our Lives*
　　When a rider is mounting a horse, another person often supports the rider's left leg while the right one swings over the horse's back. Having "a leg up" means you've been given extra help or certain advantages.

▶ I love to see a young girl go out and *grab* the world *by the lapels.*
                                                                —Maya Angelou

Grabbing the front of a jacket, or "grabbing someone by the lapels," is a firm and aggressive move that aims to take charge of a situation.

L-3b Understanding Idioms

Idioms may seem peculiar or even nonsensical if you think about their literal meanings, but knowing where they originated can help you figure out what they mean. Many idioms, for example, originate in sports, music, and animal contexts, where their meanings are literal. Used in other contexts, their meanings are similar, if not exactly literal.

▶ When the senator introduced the bill, she thought passage would be a *slam dunk* since public opinion was strongly favorable.

In basketball, a player scores a "slam dunk" by shoving the ball through the basket in a dramatic way. As an idiom, a "slam dunk" refers to a victory gained easily or emphatically.

▶ George Saunders' commencement speech really *struck a chord* with the Syracuse graduates.

A chord is a group of musical notes that harmonize; to "strike a chord" with an audience means to make a connection by bringing up something interesting or relevant to them.

▶ Some members of Congress think that limiting food stamps will get more Americans back to work; I think they're *barking up the wrong tree.*

This idiom refers to a dog in pursuit of an animal that has disappeared into a group of trees; the dog is barking at one tree, but its prey has climbed up another. To "bark up the wrong tree" means to pursue the wrong course of action.

You can sometimes figure out the meaning of an idiom based on its context; but if you're not sure what it means or how to use it properly, look it up online—go to **wwnorton.com/write/fieldguidelinks** for links to some good sources. The *Cambridge Dictionary of American Idioms* is a good print source.

14 ✳

L-3c Common Idiomatic Expressions in Academic and Professional Writing

Idiomatic expressions are words that go together like peanut butter and jelly—you often find them together. You've probably encountered expressions such as *with respect to, insofar as,* or *as a matter of fact* in academic or professional writing. Many of these expressions function as **TRANSITIONS**, helping readers follow your reasoning and understand how your ideas relate to one another. You're expected to signal the connections among your ideas explicitly in academic writing, and the following idiomatic expressions can help you do so.

To shift to a narrower focus

with respect to, with regard to indicate the precise topic you are addressing: *The global economic situation is much more complicated with respect to certain nations' high levels of debt.*

insofar as sets a limit or scope for a statement: *Despite her short stature, Bates is the team leader insofar as direction and determination are concerned.*

in particular points to something especially true within a generalization: *Cosmetic surgery procedures for men have increased tremendously in the last decade; liposuction and eyelid surgery, in particular, showed dramatic increases.*

To give examples

a case in point frames an example that illustrates a point: *Recent business activity shows a clear trend toward consolidation. The merger of two airlines last year is a case in point.*

for instance indicates an example that illustrates an idea: *Green vegetables are highly nutritious; one serving of kale, for instance, provides the full daily recommended value of vitamins A and C.*

To add information

in addition introduces a new but related point: *Locally grown tomatoes are available nearly everywhere; in addition, they are rich in vitamin C.*

along the same lines connects two similar ideas: *Many cities are developing parking meter plans along the same lines as the system in Chicago.*

academic literacies   rhetorical situations   genres   fields   processes   strategies   research MLA / APA   media / design   readings   handbook

by the same token signals a point that follows the logic of the previous point: *Insider trading has damaged the reputation of the financial industry in general; by the same token, high-profile embezzlers like Bernie Madoff have eroded the public's confidence in many investment advisers.*

as a matter of fact, in fact signal a statement that explains or contrasts with a previous point: *Wind power is an increasingly common energy source; as a matter of fact, wind energy generation quadrupled between 2000 and 2006.*

To emphasize something

of course emphasizes a point that is (or should be) obvious: *Fresh foods are preferable to processed foods, of course, but fresh foods are not always available.*

in any case, in any event introduce something that is true regardless of other conditions: *The city has introduced new precautions to ensure the election goes smoothly; the results will be closely scrutinized in any event.*

To signal alternatives or conflicting ideas

on the one hand . . . on the other hand introduces contrasting ideas or conditions: *On the one hand, some critics have loudly rejected reality television; on the other hand, unscripted shows are often received well by the public.*

up to a point signals acceptance of part but not all of an argument or idea: *The senator's statement is correct up to a point, but her conclusions are misguided.*

have it both ways to benefit from two conflicting positions: *Tech companies want to have it both ways, asking the government to be more transparent about its use of user data while not disclosing that they are using these data for their own commercial purposes.*

of two minds signals ambivalence, validates conflicting ideas: *On the question of whether organic food is worth the extra cost, I am of two minds: I like knowing that the food is grown without chemicals, but some studies suggest that the health benefits are questionable.*

in contrast signals a change in direction or a different idea on the same subject: *Large birds such as crows can live for more than ten years; in contrast, tiny hummingbirds generally live less than three years.*

on the contrary signals an opposite idea or opposing position: *Some bankers claim that the proposed mortgage regulations would harm the economy; on the contrary, the new rules would be the most effective means of reinvigorating it.*

in fact, as a matter of fact   signal a statement that challenges or refutes a previous statement: *Nicholas Carr suggests that Google is making us stupid; in fact, some argue that by giving us access to more information, it's making us better informed.*

To summarize or restate something

in brief, in short   introduce a short summary of points already established: *In brief, the accident was caused by a combination of carelessness and high winds.*

in other words   signals a restatement or explanation of the preceding idea: *Our opposition to the proposal is firm and unequivocal; in other words, we emphatically decline.*

in conclusion, in sum   signal the final statement or section of a text: *In conclusion, the evidence points to a clear and simple solution to the problem.*

Sports idioms in business writing. You'll encounter and use many idioms in business writing, especially ones that come from sports—probably because the competitiveness of the business world makes it easily comparable to sports. Following are some idioms that often come up in business contexts.

a team player   someone who acts in the interest of a whole team or group rather than for individual gain: *The best managers are team players, making sure that the credit for a success is shared among everyone who contributed to the effort.*

to cover all the bases   an expression that comes from baseball, where the fielders must protect all four bases against the other team's runners; as an idiom, it means to be thorough—to deal with all aspects of a situation and consider all possibilities: *Her report was well executed; it covered all the bases and anticipated all possible counterproposals.*

across the board   a large board at a racetrack displays the names of all the horses in a race; to place an equal bet on every horse is to bet "across the board," so the idiom refers to something affecting all items in a group equally: *Proponents of the new health-care policy insist that it will reduce costs across the board, from doctor visits to medical procedures to prescription medicines.*

Considering context. Many idiomatic expressions are quite informal. These can be used effectively in casual conversation or social media, but they are rarely if ever appropriate in academic or professional writing. As

with all writing, you need to consider your **AUDIENCE** and **PURPOSE** when you use idiomatic expressions.

57–60
55–56

In a conversation with a friend or family member, you might say *let's cut to the chase;* with a business colleague, however, it may be more appropriate to suggest that you *get right to the point,* or *focus on what's most important.*

In an email to a friend, you might say something sounds *like a piece of cake;* with your boss, it would be more appropriate to say it sounds *doable* or *easy to do.*

On Facebook, you might describe an improv show as *over the top;* in a review for a class, it would be more appropriate to say it was *excessive* or *outrageous.*

L-4 Words Often Confused

When you're tired, do you *lay* down or *lie* down? After dinner, do you eat *desert* or *dessert?* This chapter's dual purpose is to alert you to everyday words that can trip you up and to help you understand the differences between certain words that people tend to confuse.

accept, except *Accept* means "to receive willingly": *accept an award. Except* as a preposition means "excluding": *all languages except English.*

adapt, adopt *Adapt* means "to adjust": *adapt the recipe to be dairy free. Adopt* means "to take as one's own": *adopt a pet from a shelter.*

advice, advise *Advice* means "recommendation": *a lawyer's advice. Advise* means "to give advice": *We advise you to learn your rights.*

affect, effect *Affect* is usually a verb that means "to produce a change in": *Stress can affect health. Effect* is a noun that means "result": *The effects of smoking are well known.* As a verb, it means "to cause": *A mediator works to effect a compromise.*

all right, alright *All right* is the preferred spelling.

allusion, illusion *Allusion* means "indirect reference": *an allusion to Beowulf. Illusion* means "false appearance": *an optical illusion.*

a lot Always two words, *a lot* means "a large number or amount" or "to a great extent": *a lot of voters; he misses her a lot.* The phrase is too informal for most academic writing.

among, between   Use *among* for three or more items: *among the fifty states.* Use *between* for two items: *between you and me.*

amount, number   Use *amount* for things you can measure but not count: *a large amount of water.* Use *number* for things you can count: *a number of books.*

as, as if, like   *Like* introduces a noun or noun phrase: *It feels like silk.* To begin a subordinate clause, use *as* or *as if: Do as I say, not as I do; It seemed as if he had not prepared at all for the briefing.*

bad, badly   Use *bad* as an adjective following a linking verb: *I feel bad.* Use *badly* as an adverb following an action verb: *I play piano badly.*

capital, capitol   A *capital* is a city where the government of a state, province, or country is located: *Kingston was the first state capital of New York.* A *capitol* is a government building: *the dome of the capitol.*

cite, sight, site   *Cite* means "to give information from a source by quoting, paraphrasing, or summarizing": *Cite your sources. Sight* is the act of seeing or something that is seen: *an appalling sight.* A *site* is a place: *the site of a famous battle.*

compose, comprise   The parts *compose* the whole: *Fifty states compose the Union.* The whole *comprises* the parts: *The Union comprises fifty states.*

could of   In writing, use *could have (could've).*

council, counsel   *Council* refers to a body of people: *the council's vote. Counsel* means "advice" or "to advise": *her wise counsel; she counseled victims of domestic abuse.*

criteria, criterion   *Criteria* is the plural of *criterion* and takes a plural verb: *Certain criteria have been established.*

data   *Data,* the plural of *datum,* technically should take a plural verb (*The data arrive from many sources*), but some writers treat it as singular (*The data is persuasive*).

desert, dessert   *Desert* as a noun means "arid region": *Mojave Desert.* As a verb it means "to abandon": *He deserted his post. Dessert* is a sweet served toward the end of a meal.

disinterested, uninterested   *Disinterested* means "fair" or "unbiased": *a disinterested jury. Uninterested* means "bored" or "indifferent": *uninterested in election results.*

academic literacies | rhetorical situations | genres | fields | processes | strategies | research MLA / APA | media / design | readings | handbook

emigrate (from), immigrate (to)   *Emigrate* means "to leave one's country": *emigrate from Slovakia.* *Immigrate* means "to move to another country": *immigrate to Canada.*

etc.   The abbreviation *etc.* is short for the Latin *et cetera,* "and other things." *Etc.* is fine in notes and bibliographies, but avoid using it in your writing in general. Substitute *and so on* if necessary.

everyday, every day   *Everyday* is an adjective meaning "ordinary": *After the holidays, we go back to our everyday routine.* *Every day* means "on a daily basis": *Eat three or more servings of fruit every day.*

fewer, less   Use *fewer* when you refer to things that can be counted: *fewer calories.* Use *less* when you refer to an amount of something that cannot be counted: *less fat.*

good, well   *Good* is an adjective: *She looks good in that color; a good book.* *Well* can be an adjective indicating physical health after a linking verb (*She looks well despite her recent surgery*) or an adverb following an action verb (*He speaks Spanish well*).

hopefully   In academic writing, avoid *hopefully* to mean "it is hoped that"; use it only to mean "with hope": *to make a wish hopefully.*

imply, infer   *Imply* means "to suggest": *What do you mean to imply? Infer* means "to conclude": *We infer that you did not enjoy the trip.*

its, it's   *Its* is a possessive pronoun: *The movie is rated R because of its language.* *It's* is a contraction of "it is" or "it has": *It's an action film.*

lay, lie   *Lay,* meaning "to put" or "to place," always takes a direct object: *She lays the blanket down. Lie,* meaning "to recline" or "to be positioned," never takes a direct object: *She lies on the blanket.*

lead, led   The verb *lead* (rhymes with *bead*) means "to guide": *I will lead the way. Led* is the past tense and past participle of *lead: Yesterday I led the way.* The noun *lead* (rhymes with *head*) is a type of metal: *Use copper pipes instead of lead pipes.*

literally   Use *literally* only when you want to stress that you don't mean *figuratively: While sitting in the grass, he realized that he literally had ants in his pants.*

loose, lose   *Loose* means "not fastened securely" or "not fitting tightly": *a pair of loose pants. Lose* means "to misplace" or "to not win": *lose an earring; lose the race.*

man, mankind   Use *people, humans, humanity,* or *humankind* instead.

many, much   Use *many* when you refer to things that can be counted: *many books.* Use *much* to refer to something that cannot be counted: *much knowledge.*

may of, might of, must of   In writing, use *may have, might have,* or *must have.*

media   *Media,* a plural noun, takes a plural verb: *Many political scientists believe that the media have a huge effect on voting behavior.* The singular form is *medium: TV is a popular medium for advertising.*

percent, percentage   Use *percent* after a number: *80 percent.* Use *percentage* after an adjective or article: *an impressive percentage; the percentage was impressive.*

principal, principle   As a noun, *principal* means "a chief official" or "a sum of money": *in the principal's office; raising the principal for a down payment.* As an adjective, it means "most important": *the principal cause of death. Principle* means "a rule by which one lives" or "a basic truth or doctrine": *Lying is against her principles; the principles of life, liberty, and the pursuit of happiness.*

raise, rise   Meaning "to grow" or "to cause to move upward," *raise* always takes a direct object: *He raised his hand.* Meaning "to get up," *rise* never takes a direct object: *The sun rises at dawn.*

the reason . . . is because   Use *because* or *the reason . . . is (that),* but not both: *The reason for the price increase was a poor growing season* or *prices increased because of a poor growing season.*

reason why   Instead of this redundant phrase, use *the reason* or *the reason that: Psychologists debate the reasons that some people develop depression and others do not.*

respectfully, respectively   *Respectfully* means "in a way that shows respect": *Speak to your elders respectfully. Respectively* means "in the order given": *George H. W. Bush and George W. Bush were the forty-first president and the forty-third president, respectively.*

sensual, sensuous   *Sensual* suggests sexuality: *a sensual caress. Sensuous* involves pleasing the senses through art, music, and nature: *the violin's sensuous solo.*

set, sit   *Set,* meaning "to put" or "to place," takes a direct object: *Please set the vase on the table. Sit,* meaning "to take a seat," does not take a direct object: *She sits on the bench.*

should of   In writing, use *should have* (*should've*).

stationary, stationery   *Stationary* means "staying put": *a stationary lab table. Stationery* means "writing paper": *the college's official stationery.*

than, then   *Than* is a conjunction used for comparing: *She is taller than her mother. Then* is an adverb used to indicate a sequence: *Finish your work, and then reward yourself.*

that, which   Use *that* to add information that is essential for identifying something: *The wild horses that live on this island are endangered.* Use *which* to give additional but nonessential information: *Abaco Barb horses, which live on an island in the Bahamas, are endangered.*

their, there, they're   *Their* signifies possession: *their canoe. There* tells where: *Put it there. They're* is a contraction of "they are": *They're busy.*

to, too, two   *To* is either a preposition that tells direction (*Give it to me*) or part of an infinitive (*To err is human*). *Too* means "also" or "excessively": *The younger children wanted to help, too; It's too cold to sit outside. Two* is a number: *tea for two.*

unique   Because *unique* suggests that something is the only one of its kind, avoid adding comparatives or superlatives (*more, most, less, least*), intensifiers (such as *very*), or qualifiers (such as *somewhat*).

weather, whether   *Weather* refers to atmospheric conditions: *dreary weather. Whether* refers to a choice between options: *whether to stay home or go out.*

who's, whose   *Who's* is a contraction for "who is" or "who has": *Who's the best candidate for the job? Who's already eaten? Whose* refers to ownership: *Whose keys are these? Tom, whose keys were on the table, had left.*

would of   In writing, use *would have* (*would've*).

your, you're   *Your* signifies possession: *your diploma. You're* is a contraction for "you are": *You're welcome.*

L-5 Prepositions

A great session with your favorite video game. You've finally reached the cave of the dying wise man who will tell you the location of the key that you need. He points a long, bony finger toward a table and struggles to rasp out one word, "jar." You're down to your last life. You only have one chance. Is the key *in the jar? under* it? *behind* it? Oh, that one little preposition makes all the difference!

Real life is seldom this dramatic, but correct prepositions do make a difference. Prepositions are words like *at, from, in,* and *with* that describe relationships, often in time and space: *at work, in an hour, with your mom.* English has a large number of prepositions compared to other languages, and sometimes it's difficult to choose the right one.

Glossary

Prepositions are always followed by noun or pronoun **OBJECTS**. (You can't just "write about"; you have to write about something.) Together a preposition and its object form a prepositional phrase. In the following examples, the prepositions are underlined and the prepositional phrases are italicized.

▶ This is a book *about writing.*

▶ We're *in the midst of a literacy revolution.* —Andrea Lunsford

▶ Research is formalized curiosity. It is poking and prying *with a purpose.*
—Zora Neale Hurston

▶ *In the years between 1969 and 1978,* I lived, worked, and played *with the children and their families in Roadville and Trackton.*
—Shirley Brice Heath

The table and lists on the following page summarize the basic differences in the ways to use three common prepositions—*at, on,* and *in.*

AT	a specific point	●	at home at the gym at noon
ON	a line	——————	on the avenue on the table on a specific day
IN	a shape or enclosure	⬭	in a container in the park in two hours

Prepositions of place

AT *a specific address or business:* at 33 Parkwood Street, at McDonald's
a public building or unnamed business: at the library, at the gym
a general place: at home, at work

ON *a surface:* on the floor, on the grass, on the wall
a street: on Ninth Street, on Western Avenue
an electronic medium: on the radio, on the web
public transportation: on the bus, on an airplane

IN *a container, room, or area:* in the jar, in my office, in the woods
a geographic location: in San Diego, in the Midwest
a printed work: in the newspaper, in Chapter 3

Prepositions of time

AT *a specific time:* at 4:30 PM, at sunset, at lunchtime

ON *a day of the week:* on Friday
an exact date: on September 12
a holiday: on Thanksgiving, on Veteran's Day

IN *a defined time period:* in an hour, in three years
a month, season, or year: in June, in the fall, in 2011
a part of the day: in the morning, in the evening

L-6 Unnecessary Words

At *this point in time. Really unique. In a manner of speaking.* Each of these phrases includes words that are unnecessary or says something that could be expressed more concisely. This chapter shows you how to edit your own writing to make every word count.

L-6a *Really, Very,* and Other Empty Words

Intensifiers such as *really* and *very* are used to strengthen what we say. Qualifiers such as *apparently, possibly, seem,* or *tend to* are a way to soften what we say. It's fine to use words like these when they are necessary. Sometimes, however, they are not. You shouldn't say that something is "very unique," because things either are unique or they're not; there's no need to add the intensifier. And why say that someone is "really smart" when you could say that they are "brilliant"?

▶ Accepted by five colleges, Jackson ~~seems to be facing an apparently very~~ ^{is facing a} difficult decision.

L-6b *There Is, It Is*

Glossary

EXPLETIVE constructions like *there is* and *it is* can be useful ways to introduce and emphasize an idea, but sometimes they only add unnecessary words. Eliminating them in such cases can make the sentence more concise and also make its verb stronger.

▶ ~~It is necessary for~~ Americans today ^{must} to learn to speak more than one language.

▶ ^{Four} ~~There are four~~ large moons and more than thirty small ones ~~that~~ orbit Jupiter.

In certain contexts, however, expletives can be the best choices. Imagine the ending of *The Wizard of Oz* if Dorothy had said "No place is like home" instead of the more emphatic—and sentimental—"There's no place like home."

L-6c Wordy Phrases

Many common phrases use several words when a single word will do. Editing out such wordy phrases will make your writing more concise and easier to read.

WORDY	CONCISE
as far as . . . is concerned	concerning
at the time that	when
at this point in time	now
in spite of the fact that	although, though
in the event that	if
in view of the fact that	because, since

▶ ~~Due to the fact that~~ _{Because} Professor Lee retired, the animal sciences department now lacks a neurology specialist.

L-6d Redundancies

Eliminate words and phrases that are unnecessary for your meaning.

▶ Painting the house purple ~~in color~~ will make it stand out from the many white houses in town.

▶ Dashing ~~quickly~~ into the street to retrieve the ball, the young girl was almost hit by a car.

▶ Campers should know how much wood is ~~sufficient~~ enough for a fire to burn all night.

L-7 Adjectives and Adverbs

Adjectives and adverbs are words that describe other words, adding important information and detail. When Dave Barry writes that the Beatles "were the *coolest* thing you had ever seen" and that "they were *smart*; they were *funny*; they didn't take themselves *seriously*," the adjectives and adverbs (italicized here) make clear why he "wanted *desperately* to be a Beatle." This chapter will help you use adjectives and adverbs in your own writing.

L-7a Choosing between Adjectives and Adverbs

Glossary
HB-29–34

Adjectives are words used to modify **NOUNS** and **PRONOUNS**. They usually answer one of these questions: Which? What kind? How many?

▶ *Two* rows of *ancient oak* trees lined the *narrow* driveway.

▶ *Many* years of testing will be needed to determine whether the *newest* theories are *correct*.

▶ If you are craving something *sweet*, have a piece of fruit.

HB-12–24

Adverbs are words used to modify **VERBS**, adjectives, and other adverbs. They usually answer one of these questions: How? When? Where? Why? Under what conditions? To what degree? Although many adverbs end in -ly (*tentatively*, *immediately*), many do not (*now*, *so*, *soon*, *then*, *very*).

▶ Emergency personnel must respond *quickly* when an ambulance arrives.

▶ Environmentalists are *increasingly* worried about Americans' consumption of fossil fuels.

▶ If the senator had known that the news cameras were on, she would not have responded *so angrily*.

Well *and* good

Use *well* as an adjective to describe physical health; use *good* to describe emotional health or appearance.

▶ Some herbs can keep you feeling ~~good~~ *well* when everyone else has the flu.

▶ Staying healthy can make you feel *good* about yourself.

Good should not be used as an adverb; use *well*.

▶ Because both Williams sisters play tennis so ~~good,~~ *well,* they've frequently competed against each other in major tournaments.

Bad *and* badly

Use the adjective *bad* after a **LINKING VERB** to describe an emotional state or feeling. In such cases, the adjective describes the subject.

Glossary

▶ Arguing with your parents can make you feel *bad*.

Use the adverb *badly* to describe an **ACTION VERB**.

Glossary

▶ Arguing with your parents late at night can make you sleep *badly*.

L-7b Using Comparatives and Superlatives

Most adjectives and adverbs have three forms: the positive, the comparative, and the superlative. The comparative is used to compare two things, and the superlative is used to compare three or more things.

COMPARATIVE	Who's the *better* quarterback, Eli Manning or his brother?
SUPERLATIVE	Many Colts fans still consider Peyton Manning to be the *best* quarterback ever.

The comparative and superlative of most adjectives are formed by adding the endings *-er* and *-est*: *slow, slower, slowest*. Longer adjectives and most adverbs use *more* and *most* (or *less* and *least*): *clearly, more clearly, most clearly*.

If you add -er or -est to an adjective or adverb, do not also use *more* or *most* (or *less* and *least*).

▶ The ~~most~~ lowest point in the United States is in Death Valley.

A few adjectives and adverbs have irregular comparatives and superlatives.

	COMPARATIVE	SUPERLATIVE
good, well	better	best
bad, badly	worse	worst
far (distance)	farther	farthest
far (time or amount)	further	furthest
little (amount)	less	least
many, much, some	more	most

L-7c Placing Modifiers Carefully

Glossary

Place adjectives, adverbs, and other **MODIFIERS** so that readers clearly understand which words they modify.

▶ The doctor explained advances in cancer treatment to the families of patients. ~~at the seminar.~~
at the seminar

The doctor, not the patients, is at the seminar.

▶ ~~The~~ surgeons assured the patient that they intended to make only two small incisions. ~~before the anesthesiologist arrived.~~
Before the anesthesiologist arrived, the

The original sentence suggests that the incisions will be made without anesthesia, surely not the case.

To avoid ambiguity, position limiting modifiers such as *almost, even, just, merely,* and *only* next to the word or phrase they modify—and be careful that your meaning is clear. See how the placement of *only* can result in two completely different meanings.

▶ A triple-threat athlete, Martha ~~only~~ played soccer in college.
only

▶ A triple-threat athlete, Martha ~~only~~ played soccer in college.
only

academic literacies · rhetorical situations · genres · fields · processes · strategies · research MLA / APA · media / design · readings · handbook

Be careful that your placement of *not* doesn't result in a meaning you don't intend.

> ▶ When I attended college, every student was ~~not~~ using a laptop.
> *not*

Dangling modifiers

Modifiers are said to be dangling when they do not clearly modify any particular word in the sentence. You can usually fix a dangling modifier by adding a **SUBJECT** that the modifier clearly refers to, either in the rest of the sentence or in the modifier itself.

Glossary

> ▶ Speaking simply and respectfully, many people ~~felt comforted by the doctor's~~ presentation.
> *the doctor comforted with his*
>
> *The doctor was speaking, not the other people.*

> ▶ While running to catch the bus, the shoulder strap on my bag broke.
> *I was*

Split infinitives

When you place a modifier between *to* and the base form of the verb in an **INFINITIVE**, you create a split infinitive: *to deliberately avoid*. When a split infinitive is awkward or makes a sentence difficult to follow, put the modifier elsewhere in the sentence.

Glossary

> ▶ Professional soccer players are expected to ~~rigorously~~ train every day.
> *rigorously*

Sometimes, however, a split infinitive is easier to follow.

> ▶ One famous split infinitive appears in the opening sequence of *Star Trek*: "to boldly go where no man has gone before."

L-8 Articles

A, *an*, and *the* are articles, words used before a noun to indicate whether something is general or specific. Use *a* or *an* with nouns whose specific identity is not known to your audience: *I'm reading a great book.* Use *the* with nouns whose specific identity is known to your audience, whether the noun describes something specific: *the new book by Dave Eggers*—or is something you've mentioned: *Beverly is almost finished writing her book. The book will be published next year.* Sometimes no article is needed: *Books are now available in print and online.*

L-8a When to Use *A* or *An*

Use *a* or *an* before singular count nouns referring to something that's not specific or that you're mentioning to your audience for the first time. Count nouns name things that can be counted: *one book, two books.* Use *a* before consonant sounds: *a tangerine, a university;* use *an* before vowel sounds: *an orange, an hour.*

▶ *An apartment* near campus might be rather expensive.

Any apartment near campus would be expensive, not just a specific one.

▶ I put *a carrot*, some tomatoes, and a little parsley in the salad.

This carrot is being mentioned for the first time.

Do not use *a* or *an* before a noncount noun. Noncount nouns name abstract items (*respect, curiosity*) and liquids and masses that cannot be measured with numbers (*milk, sand, rice*).

▶ Our team could use *some encouragement* from the coach.

▶ The last thing Portland needs this week is *more rain.*

L-8b When to Use *The*

Use *the* before any nouns whose identity is clear to your audience and before superlatives.

▶ Mando ordered a cheeseburger and french fries and asked for *the burger* to be well done.

The article the is used because it refers to a cheeseburger that's already been mentioned: the one that Mando ordered.

▶ His friends had raved about *the fries* at this restaurant.

The specific fries are identified: they are the ones at this restaurant.

▶ His friends were right; these were *the best fries* he'd ever eaten.

The is used before a superlative: these were the best fries ever.

Use *the* with most plural proper nouns (*the Adirondack Mountains, the Philippines, the Dallas Cowboys*) and with singular proper nouns in the following categories.

LARGER BODIES OF WATER   the Arctic Ocean, the Mississippi River

GOVERNMENT BODIES   the U.S. Congress, the Canadian Parliament

HISTORICAL PERIODS   the Renaissance, the Tang Dynasty

LANDMARKS   the Empire State Building, the Taj Mahal

REGIONS   the East Coast, the Middle East, the Mojave Desert

RELIGIOUS ENTITIES, TEXTS, AND LEADERS   the Roman Catholic Church, the Qur'an, the Dalai Lama

L-8c When No Article Is Needed

No article is needed before noncount nouns (*salt, imagination, happiness*) and plural count nouns (*ideas, puppies*) when they refer to something "in general."

▶ *Milk* and *eggs* are on sale this week.

▶ *Information* wants to be free.   —Stewart Brand, *Whole Earth Review*

▶ Be less curious about people and more curious about *ideas.*
                                               —Marie Curie

Brand and Curie refer to information and ideas in general, not a specific kind of information or specific ideas.

No article is needed with most singular proper nouns: *Barack Obama, Lake Titicaca, Yosemite.*

L-9 Words for Building Common Ground

A secretary objects to being called one of "the girls." The head of the English department finds the title "chairman" offensive. Why? The secretary is male, the department head is a woman, and those terms don't include them. We can build common ground with others—or not—through the words we choose, by including others or leaving them out. This chapter offers tips for using language that is positive and inclusive and that will build common ground with those we wish to reach.

L-9a Avoiding Stereotypes

Stereotypes are generalizations about groups of people and as such can offend because they presume that all members of a group are the same. The writer Geeta Kothari explains how she reacts to a seemingly neutral assumption about Indians: "Indians eat lentils. I understand this as an absolute, a decree from an unidentifiable authority that watches and judges me."

We're all familiar with stereotypes based on sex or race, but stereotypes exist about other characteristics as well: age, body type, education, income, occupation, physical ability, political affiliation, region, religion, sexual orientation, and more. Be careful not to make any broad generalizations about any group—even neutral or positive ones (that Asian students work especially hard, for example, or that Republicans are particularly patriotic).

Also be careful not to call attention to a person's group affiliation if that information is not relevant.

▶ The ~~gay~~ physical therapist who worked the morning shift knew when to let patients rest and when to push them.

L-9b Using Preferred Terms

When you are writing about a group of people, try to use terms that members of that group use themselves. This advice is sometimes easier said than done, because language changes—and words that were commonly used ten years ago may not be in wide use today. Americans of African

ancestry, for example, were referred to many years ago as "colored" or "Negro" and then as "black"; today, the preferred terminology is "African American."

When you are referring to ethnicities, especially of individuals, it's usually best to be as specific as possible. Instead of saying that someone is Latina, Latino, or Hispanic, for instance, say that they are Puerto Rican or Dominican or Cuban, as appropriate. The same is true of religions; specify a denomination or branch of religion when you can (a Sunni Muslim, an Episcopalian, an Orthodox Jew). And while "Native American" and "American Indian" are both acceptable as general terms, it's often better to refer to a particular tribal nation (Dakota, Chippewa).

It is becoming more common for people to specify (or ask one another about) their preferred pronouns, in person and in email signatures and social media bios, a practice that is in response to increasing flexibility about gender identity. A person's appearance may not always be an accurate predictor of gender identity or pronoun preference. Some individuals opt to be referred to as *they*, a usage that transforms *they* from its conventional usage as plural to a singular pronoun of unspecified gender. Other people may use other pronouns, such as *ze/hir/hirs*. See **S-6a** for more information about preferred pronouns.

⌃ HB-29–30

L-9c Editing Out Sexist Language

Sexist language is language that stereotypes or ignores women or men—or that unnecessarily calls attention to someone's gender. Try to eliminate such language from your writing. In particular, avoid nouns that include *man* when you're referring to people who may be either men or women.

INSTEAD OF	USE
man, mankind	humankind, humanity, humans, people
salesman	salesperson
fireman	firefighter
congressman	representative, member of Congress
male nurse	nurse
woman truck driver	truck driver

He, she, they

Writers once used *he, him,* and other masculine pronouns as a default to refer to people whose sex was unknown to them. Today such usage is not widely accepted—and it is no way to build common ground. Here are some alternatives.

Use *he or she* or singular *they* (Note, however, that using *he or she* repeatedly may become awkward.)

> ▶ Before anyone can leave the country, he *or she* must have a passport or some other official documentation.

Replace a singular noun or pronoun with a plural noun

> ▶ Before ~~anyone~~ *travelers* can leave the country, ~~he~~ *they* must have a passport or some other official documentation.

Eliminate the pronoun altogether

> ▶ Before ~~anyone can leave~~ *leaving* the country, ~~he~~ *a traveler* must have a passport or some other official documentation.

Increasingly, *they* is being used to refer to a person whose gender is unknown or not relevant to the context. This usage may not be acceptable in academic writing; check with your instructor about whether it's appropriate in your writing.

> ▶ Someone left *their* clothes in the washing machine overnight.

L-10 Englishes

"English? Who needs that? I'm never going to England," declares Homer in an early episode of *The Simpsons.* Sorry, Homer. Anyone using this book does need English. In fact, most of us need a variety of Englishes—the "standard" English we're expected to use at school, the specialized English we use in particular academic and professional fields, and the colloquial English we use in

various other communities we belong to. This chapter offers some guidance in using these many varieties of English effectively and appropriately in academic writing.

L-10a Standard Edited English

This is the variety used—and expected—in most academic and professional contexts, and one you need to be able to use comfortably and competently. "Standard" means that it is nearly uniform throughout the English-speaking world. Despite some minor differences—in England and Canada, for example, *labor* is *labour* and an *elevator* is a *lift*—the uniformity means that your writing has the potential to be understood by millions of people. "Edited" means that it is carefully written and polished. And "English"—well, you already know what that is.

L-10b Formal and Informal English

Some of the variation in English comes from levels of formality. Academic writing is usually formal. The tone is crisp and serious; information is stated directly. These characteristics display your competence and authority. The most informal language, on the other hand, tends to be found in the ways we talk with our close friends and relatives; those conversations are full of **IDIOMS** and slang.

HB-46–51

Words with the same basic meaning can convey very different messages when they have different levels of formality—and so the words you choose should always be guided by what's appropriate to your **AUDIENCE**, **TOPIC**, and the larger context.

57–60

387–89

See, for example, two headlines that appeared in two different newspapers on the day that Pope Benedict XVI announced his resignation:

▶ Pope Resigns in Historic Move   *—Wall Street Journal*

▶ I'M OUTTA HERE, GUYS: Pope Gives God 2 Weeks' Notice

—New York Post

The first headline is from the *Wall Street Journal*, a newspaper dedicated to business news, with an audience of corporate and government executives. Its tone is professional and businesslike, and its English is formal. The second is from the *New York Post*, a daily tabloid newspaper known for its sensationalist headlines; its English is informal, going for laughs and marking a sharp contrast with the pomp and majesty of the papal office.

In the cartoon below the adult understands quite well what the child is saying; she's merely suggesting a more formal and polite — and appropriate — way to express his judgment of the painting.

"Instead of 'It sucks' you could say, 'It doesn't speak to me.'"

Mixing formal and informal

Occasionally mixing in an informal element — a playful image, an unexpected bit of slang — can enliven formal writing. For example, in a book about the alimentary canal, science writer Mary Roach gives detailed, well-researched descriptions of all aspects of digestion, including the anatomy of the digestive system. Although her topic is serious, she stirs in some irreverent **METAPHORS** and surprising comparisons along the way, as this description of the esophagus shows.

Glossary

> ▶ The esophagus is a thin, pink stretchable membrane, a biological bubble gum.   —Mary Roach, *Gulp: Adventures on the Alimentary Canal*

Such everyday imagery makes a potentially dry subject come to life. What's more, the information is easier to remember. Quick: what color is your esophagus? You remembered, didn't you?

L-10c English across Fields

If you've ever listened in on a group of nurses, software designers, lawyers, or taxi drivers, you probably heard words you didn't understand, jokes you didn't think were funny. All professional fields have their own specialized language.

Restaurant staff, for example, have a shorthand for relaying food orders and seating information. In this example from an essay about blue-collar work, UCLA professor Mike Rose describes a restaurant where his mother was a waitress:

> ▶ *Fry four on two*, my mother would say as she clipped a check onto the metal wheel. Her tables were *deuces*, *four-tops*, or *six-tops* according to their size; seating areas also were nicknamed. The *racetrack*, for instance, was the fast-turnover front section. Lingo conferred authority and signaled know-how.   —Mike Rose, "Blue Collar Brilliance"

You might not know what *deuces* or *four-tops* are (or maybe you do), but it's language Rose's mother knows her colleagues will understand. On the one hand, specialized language allows professionals to do their work with greater ease and efficiency; on the other hand, it marks and helps construct a community around a certain field of work.

L-10d English across Regions

Have you ever wished that British TV shows had subtitles? The characters are definitely speaking English, but you may have a hard time understanding them. Every region has its own accent, of course, but there may also be words and expressions that are unfamiliar or mean something different to those who don't live there. In Australia (and parts of Wisconsin), for example, a *bubbler* is a drinking fountain. In India, the *hall* is the part of the house known in the United States as the living room.

In the U.S. South, *y'all* is the way many folks say *you all*. Country singer Miranda Lambert, a native of Texas, uses *y'all* frequently in her *Twitter* feed, such as in this tweet thanking a North Dakota audience after a performance:

▶ Thanks New Town ND! Y'all were so fun! And LOUD! Came to party and did it right! —Miranda Lambert, @mirandalambert, June 8, 2013

In choosing to use *y'all* rather than the more standard *you*, Lambert emphasizes her southern heritage and establishes a friendly, down-home tone.

Other regions as well have their own forms of the second person plural. In Chicago and New York you might hear *youse*, and in Pittsburgh it's *yinz*. Such local language is widely understood in the regions where it is used, though it may sound strange to people from other places. Using regional language in your writing can be a good way to evoke a place—and, like Lambert, can demonstrate pride in your own regional roots.

L-10e Englishes across Cultures and Communities

Some varieties of English are associated with a particular social, ethnic, or other community. African American English is perhaps the best-known of these Englishes. Not all African Americans use it, and those who do may not use it exclusively. Not all of its users are African Americans themselves.

All of its users, however, follow the conventions and rules that make this variety of English consistent and recognizable.

Linguist Geneva Smitherman has written extensively on this variety of English, often using the language itself to support her points. See how she shifts from standard edited English into African American English to establish her authority as an insider and drive home her point with a stylistic punch.

> ▶ Think of black speech as having two dimensions: language and style. . . . Consider [this example]. Nina Simone sing: "It bees dat way sometime." Here the language aspect is the use of the verb *be* to indicate a recurrent event or habitual condition, rather than a one-time-only occurrence. But the total expression—"It bees dat way sometime"—also reflects Black English style, for the statement suggests a point of view, a way of looking at life, and a method of adapting to life's realities. To live by the philosophy of "It bees dat way sometime" is to come to grips with the changes that life bees puttin us through, and to accept the changes and bad times as a constant, ever-present reality.   —Geneva Smitherman, *Talkin and Testifyin: The Language of Black America*

Many other communities develop their own Englishes as well. Ethnic communities often use an English that includes words from another language. Men and women often speak differently, as Deborah Tannen and other linguists have shown. Even young people use an English that might sound very strange coming from a gray-haired elder (imagine your grandfather greeting you with "Dude!").

The differences can be subtle but sometimes a single word can make someone sound young, or old, or Texan, or Canadian—and can establish credibility with an audience. See how a simple "OMG" is enough to establish hipness with young readers of a newspaper article about a fashion show for puppies:

> ▶ If your pup has been good this year, it deserves a treat from Ware of the Dog, a line of luxury knits from the designer Tom Scott and his friend Jackie Rosenthal. The collection includes OMG-cute alpaca sweaters, cable-knit turtlenecks, hoodies and a geometric-pattern merino jacquard pullover.   —"Shopping Snapshots," *New York Times*

Speaking to the article's young audience, the phrase *OMG-cute* not only shows off knowledge of youth culture but also puts a little zest into an otherwise lifeless list of items.

L-10f Mixing Englishes

As a writer, you can use different varieties of English or even different languages for various purposes. Here are some examples and suggestions for doing so effectively and appropriately.

To evoke a person or represent speech

When you are describing people, you may want to quote their words, to let readers "hear" them talk—and to let them speak for themselves. Some multilingual authors flavor their English writing with words or phrases from another language to give readers an authentic sense of someone's words or thoughts. Even if some readers don't understand the non-English words, they usually add more flavor than meaning. See, for example, how Sandra Cisneros mixes English and Spanish in relating an exchange between her parents as they bicker about a trip to visit relatives. Using two languages in the dialogue adds flavor and realism, and the context makes the meaning clear even for readers who don't speak Spanish.

> ► "Zoila, why do you insist on being so stubborn?" Father shouts into the mirror, clouding the glass. "*Ya verás.* You'll see, *vieja*, it'll be fun."
> "And stop calling me *vieja*," Mother shouts back. "I hate that word! Your mother's old; I'm not old."   —Sandra Cisneros, *Caramelo*

When writing dialogue, you may sometimes want to use nonstandard spelling to mimic dialect or sound, as Flannery O'Connor does with the speech of a young boy questioning an outlaw.

> ► "What you got that gun for?" John Wesley asked. "Whatcha gonna do with that gun?"   —Flannery O'Connor, "A Good Man Is Hard to Find"

To evoke a place or an event

In certain settings or situations—sports, auctions, math class—you will hear language you wouldn't hear anywhere else. In some cases, the topics require specialized words. There's no way to talk about golf without mentioning *par* or *putting* or *a hole in one*, or to teach math without words like *variable* or *function*. In other cases, people tend to use a certain kind of language. Think about the conversations you'd hear in a board meeting, or the ones you'd hear in a sports bar.

Such language can be used to evoke a place or an event, as in this recap of a 2013 NBA playoff game between the Los Angeles Lakers and the Dallas Mavericks.

> ▶ The Mavericks played Bryant aggressively, trapping him out of the pick and roll and forcing him into tough shots. He had his moments, he made his share of shots despite great defensive strategy, and ended the night right. Bryant picked up his tenth rebound to seal his triple-double and put up a beautiful hook shot to cap it off and send it home.
> —Drew Garrison, *Silver Screen and Roll*

The writer can assume that his readers are familiar with the language he uses; in fact, many readers probably watched the game and just read the recap in order to relive it. His use of basketball **JARGON** helps put them back in the action. But for an audience unfamiliar with basketball, he'd need to explain terms like *pick and roll* and *triple double*.

▲ HB-43

To build common ground with an audience

Language is one good way to establish credibility and build common ground with readers. For example, in a feature article about how letters to the editor are chosen for publication in the daily newspaper of a city in Minnesota, the writer included the word *uff-da*, a purely local touch:

> ▶ We don't publish mass produced letters. There are people in these United States who like to send letters to every newspaper in the country on a weekly basis. *Uff-da!* These are easy to catch. There are also some lobbying organizations who provide forms for supporters where writers don't actually pen their own thoughts.   —Tim Engstrom, *Albert Lea Tribune*

Uff-da is a Norwegian expression that is widely used in the region. It means *wow!, whew!, no kidding!,* or even *OMG!* depending on the situation. The writer doesn't need it to convey his meaning, but using it demonstrates a sense of local knowledge and pride—and helps build common ground with his readers.

Think carefully, however, before using words from a language or variety of language that you don't speak yourself; you may offend some readers. And if by chance you use words incorrectly, you could even damage your credibility.

✳ academic literacies
■ rhetorical situations
▲ genres
⬢ fields
○ processes
◆ strategies
● research MLA / APA
▢ media / design
▮▮ readings
◿ handbook

Punctuation / Mechanics

P

P-1 Commas

Commas matter. Consider the title of the best-selling book *Eats, Shoots & Leaves*. The cover shows two pandas, one with a gun in its paw, one whitewashing the comma. Is the book about a panda that dines, then fires a gun and exits? Or about the panda's customary diet? In fact, it's a book about punctuation; the ambiguity of its title illustrates how commas affect meaning. This chapter shows when and where to use commas in your writing.

P-1a To Join Independent Clauses with *And, But,* and Other Coordinating Conjunctions

HB-38

HB-6

Put a comma before the **COORDINATING CONJUNCTIONS** *and, but, for, nor, or, so,* and *yet* when they connect two **INDEPENDENT CLAUSES**. The comma signals that one idea is ending and another is beginning.

▶ I do not love Shakespeare, but I still have those books.
—Rick Bragg, "All Over But the Shoutin' "

▶ Most people think the avocado is a vegetable, yet it is actually a fruit.

▶ The blue ribbon went to Susanna, and Sarah got the red ribbon.

Without the comma, readers might first think both girls got blue ribbons.

Although some writers omit the comma, especially with short independent clauses, you'll never be wrong to include it.

▶ I was smart, and I knew it.   —Shannon Nichols, " 'Proficiency' "

No comma is needed between the verbs when a single subject performs two actions.

▶ Many fast-food restaurants now give calorie counts on menus and offer a variety of healthy meal options.

▶ Augustine wrote extensively about his mother/ but mentioned his father only briefly.

P-1b To Set Off Introductory Words

Use a comma after an introductory word, **PHRASE**, or **CLAUSE** to mark the
end of the introduction and the start of the main part of the sentence.

HB-6–7

> ▶ Typically, a girl has a best friend with whom she sits and talks, frequently
> telling secrets.   —Deborah Tannen, "Gender in the Classroom"

> ▶ In terms of wealth rather than income, the top 1 percent control 40
> percent.   —Joseph E. Stiglitz, "Of the 1%, by the 1%, for the 1%"

> ▶ Even ignoring the extreme poles of the economic spectrum, we find
> enormous class differences in the life-styles among the haves, the have-
> nots, and the have-littles.
> —Gregory Mantsios, "Class in America—2003"

> ▶ When Miss Emily Grierson died, our whole town went to her funeral.
> —William Faulkner, "A Rose for Emily"

Some writers don't use a comma after a short introductory word, phrase,
or clause, but it's never wrong to include one.

P-1c To Separate Items in a Series

Use a comma to separate the items in a series. The items may be words,
PHRASES, or **CLAUSES**.

HB-6–7

> ▶ I spend a great deal of time thinking about the power of language
> —the way it can evoke an emotion, a visual image, a complex idea, or a
> simple truth.   —Amy Tan, "Mother Tongue"

Though some writers leave out the comma between the final two items
in a series, this omission can confuse readers. It's never wrong to include
the final comma.

> ▶ Nadia held a large platter of sandwiches—egg salad, peanut butter, ham,
> and cheese.
>
> *Without the last comma, it's not clear whether there are three or four kinds of
> sandwiches on the platter.*

P-1d To Set Off Nonessential Elements

A nonessential (or nonrestrictive) element is one that could be deleted without changing the basic meaning of the sentence; it should be set off with commas. An essential (or restrictive) element is one that is needed to understand the sentence; therefore, it should not be set off with commas.

NONESSENTIAL

▶ Spanish, which is a Romance language, is one of six official languages at the United Nations.

The detail about being a Romance language adds information, but it is not essential to the meaning of the sentence and so is set off with commas.

ESSENTIAL

▶ Navajo is the Athabaskan language that is spoken in the Southwest by the Navajo people.

The detail about where Navajo is spoken is essential: Navajo is not the only Athabaskan language; it is the Athabaskan language that is spoken in the Southwest.

Note that the meaning of a sentence can change depending on whether or not an element is set off with commas.

▶ My sister, Mary, just published her first novel.
The writer has only one sister.

▶ My sister Mary just published her first novel.
The writer has more than one sister; the one named Mary just published a novel.

Essential and nonessential elements can be clauses, phrases, or words.

CLAUSES

▶ He always drove Chryslers, which are made in America.

▶ He always drove cars that were made in America.

PHRASES

▶ I fumble in the dark, trying to open the mosquito netting around my bed.

▶ I see my mother clutching my baby sister.
　　　　　　　　　　　　　　—Chanrithy Him, "When Broken Glass Floats"

WORDS

▶ At 8:59, Flight 175 passenger Brian David Sweeney tried to call his wife, Julie.

▶ At 9:00, Lee Hanson received a second call from his son Peter.
—The 9/11 Commission, "The Hijacking of United 175"

Sweeney had only one wife, so her name provides extra but nonessential information. Hanson presumably had more than one son, so it is essential to specify which son called.

P-1e To Set Off Parenthetical Information

Information that interrupts the flow of a sentence needs to be set off with commas.

▶ Bob's conduct, most of us will immediately respond, was gravely wrong.
—Peter Singer, "The Singer Solution to World Poverty"

▶ With as little as two servings of vegetables a day, it seems to me, you can improve your eating habits.

P-1f To Set Off Transitional Expressions

TRANSITIONS such as *thus, nevertheless, for example,* and *in fact* help connect sentences or parts of sentences. They are usually set off with commas.

✳ 14

▶ The real world, *however,* is run by money.
—Joanna MacKay, "Organ Sales Will Save Lives"

When a transition connects two **INDEPENDENT CLAUSES** in the same sentence, it is preceded by a semicolon and is followed by a comma.

HB-6

▶ There are few among the poor who speak of themselves as lower class; *instead,* they refer to their race, ethnic group, or geographic location.
—Gregory Mantsios, "Class in America—2003"

P-1g To Set Off Direct Quotations

Use commas to set off quoted words from the speaker or source.

▶ Pa shouts back, "I just want to know where the gunfire is coming from."
      —Chanrithy Him, "When Broken Glass Floats"

▶ "You put a slick and a con man together," she said, "and you have predatory lenders."
      —Peter Boyer, "Eviction: The Day They Came for Addie Polk's House"

▶ "Death and life are in the power of the tongue," says the proverb.

P-1h To Set Off Direct Address, *Yes* or *No*, Interjections, and Tag Questions

DIRECT ADDRESS	"Yes, Virginia, there really is a Santa Claus."
YES OR NO	No, you cannot replace the battery on your iPhone.
INTERJECTION	Oh, a PS4. How long did you have to wait to get it?
TAG QUESTION	That wasn't so hard, was it?

P-1i With Addresses, Place Names, and Dates

▶ Send contributions to Human Rights Campaign, 1640 Rhode Island Ave., Washington, DC 20036.

▶ Athens, Georgia, is famous for its thriving music scene.

▶ Amelia Earhart disappeared over the Pacific Ocean on July 2, 1937, while trying to make the first round-the-world flight at the equator.

Omit the commas, however, if you invert the date (on 2 July 1937) or if you give only the month and year (in July 1937).

P-1j Checking for Unnecessary Commas

Commas have so many uses that it's easy to add them unnecessarily. Here are some situations when you should not use a comma.

Between a subject and a verb

▶ What the organizers of the 1969 Woodstock concert did not anticipate/was the turnout.

▶ The event's promoters/turned down John Lennon's offer to play with his Plastic Ono Band.

Between a verb and its object or complement

▶ Pollsters wondered/how they had so poorly predicted the winner of the 1948 presidential election.

▶ Virtually every prediction indicated/that Thomas Dewey would defeat Harry Truman.

▶ The *Chicago Tribune*'s famous wrong headline was/an embarassment to the newspaper.

After a coordinating conjunction

▶ The College Board reported a decline in SAT scores and/attributed the decline to changes in "student test-taking patterns."

▶ The SAT was created to provide an objective measure of academic potential, but/studies in the 1980s found racial and socioeconomic biases in some test questions.

After *like* or *such as*

▶ Many American-born authors, such as/Henry James, Ezra Pound, and F. Scott Fitzgerald, lived as expatriates in Europe.

After a question mark or an exclamation point

▶ Why would any nation have a monarch in an era of democracy?⁄you might ask yourself.

▶ "O, be some other name!⁄" exclaims Juliet.

P-2 Semicolons

Semicolons offer one way to connect two closely related thoughts. Look, for example, at Martha Stewart's advice about how to tell if fruit is ripe: "A perfectly ripened fruit exudes a subtle but sweet fragrance from the stem end, appears plump, and has deeply colored skin; avoid those that have wrinkles, bruises, or tan spots." Stewart could have used a period, but the semicolon shows the connection between what to look for and what to avoid when buying peaches or plums.

P-2a Between Independent Clauses

HB-38 ⌃

Closely related independent clauses are most often joined with a comma plus *and* or another **COORDINATING CONJUNCTION**. If the two clauses are closely related and don't need a conjunction to signal the relationship, they may be linked with a semicolon.

▶ The silence deepened; the room chilled.

—Wayson Choy, "The Ten Thousand Things"

▶ The life had not flowed out of her; it had been seized.

—Valerie Steiker, "Our Mother's Face"

A period would work in either of the examples above, but the semicolon suggests a stronger connection between the two independent clauses.

14 ✳

Another option is to use a semicolon with a **TRANSITION** that clarifies the relationship between the two independent clauses. Put a comma after the transition.

▶ There are no secret economies that nourish the poor; on the contrary, there are a host of special costs. —Barbara Ehrenreich,
Nickel and Dimed: On (Not) Getting By in America

P-2b In a Series with Commas

Use semicolons to separate items in a series when one or more of the items contain commas.

▶ There are images of a few students: Erwin Petschaur, a muscular German boy with a strong accent; Dave Sanchez, who was good at math; and Sheila Wilkes, everyone's curly-haired heartthrob.

—Mike Rose, "Potato Chips and Stars"

P-2c Checking for Mistakes with Semicolons

Use a comma, not a semicolon, to set off an introductory clause.

▶ When the sun finally sets;, everyone gathers at the lake to watch the fireworks.

Use a colon, not a semicolon, to introduce a list.

▶ Every American high school student should know that the U.S. Constitution contains three sections;: preamble, articles, and amendments.

P-3 End Punctuation

She married him. She married him? She married him! In each of these three sentences, the words are the same, but the end punctuation completely changes the meaning—from a simple statement to a bemused question to an emphatic exclamation. This chapter will help you use periods, question marks, and exclamation points in your writing.

P-3a Periods

Use a period to end a sentence that makes a statement.

▶ Rose Emily Meraglio came to the United States from southern Italy as a little girl in the early 1920s and settled with her family in Altoona, Pennsylvania.

—Mike Rose, "The Working Life of a Waitress"

An indirect question, which reports something that someone else has asked, ends with a period, not a question mark.

▶ Presidential candidates are often asked how they will expand the economy and create jobs?.

HB-105–7

When a sentence ends with an **ABBREVIATION** that has its own period, do not add another period.

▶ The Rat Pack included Frank Sinatra and Sammy Davis Jr./

HB-105–7

See **P-10** for more on periods with abbreviations.

P-3b Question Marks

Use a question mark to end a direct question.

▶ Did I think that because I was a minority student jobs would just come looking for me? What was I thinking?
—Richard Rodriguez, "None of This Is Fair"

Use a period rather than a question mark to end an indirect question.

▶ Aunt Vivian often asked what Jesus would do?.

P-3c Exclamation Points

Use an exclamation point to express strong emotion or add emphasis to a statement or command. Exclamation points should be used sparingly, however, or they may undercut your credibility.

▶ "Keith," we shrieked as the car drove away, "Keith, we love you!"
—Susan Jane Gilman, "Mick Jagger Wants Me"

When the words themselves are emotional, an exclamation point is often unnecessary, and a period is sufficient.

▶ It was so close, so low, so huge and fast, so intent on its target that I swear to you, I swear to you, I felt the vengeance and rage emanating from the plane.
—Debra Fontaine, "Witnessing"

academic literacies | rhetorical situations | genres | fields | processes | strategies | research MLA / APA | media / design | readings | handbook

P-4 Quotation Marks

"Girls Just Want to Have Fun" "Two thumbs up!" "Frankly, my dear, I don't give a damn." These are just some of the ways that quotation marks are used—to indicate a song title, to cite praise for a movie, to set off dialogue. In college writing, you will use quotation marks frequently to acknowledge when you've taken words from others. This chapter will show you how to use quotation marks correctly and appropriately.

P-4a Direct Quotations

Use quotation marks to enclose words spoken or written by others.

> ▶ "Nothing against Tom, but Johnny may be the bigger star now," says director John Waters.
> —Sean Smith, "Johnny Depp: Unlikely Superstar"

> ▶ Newt Gringrich and Jesse Jackson have both pounded nails and raised funds for Habitat for Humanity. This is what Millard Fuller calls the "theology of the hammer."
> —Diana George, "Changing the Face of Poverty"

When you introduce quoted words with *he said, she claimed*, or another such **SIGNAL PHRASE**, put a comma after the verb and capitalize the first word of the quote if it's a complete sentence. When you follow a quote with such an expression, use a comma before the closing quotation mark (unless the quote is a question or an exclamation).

Glossary

> ▶ When my mother reported that Mr. Tomkey did not believe in television, my father said, "Well, good for him. I don't know that I believe in it either."
> "That's exactly how I feel," my mother said, and then my parents watched the news, and whatever came on after the news.
> —David Sedaris, "Us and Them"

You do not need any punctuation between *that* and a quotation, nor do you need to capitalize the first word of the quote.

> ▶ We were assigned to write one essay agreeing or disagreeing with George Orwell's statement that/"the slovenliness of our language makes it easier for us to have foolish thoughts."

In dialogue, insert a new paragraph and a new pair of quotation marks to signal each change of speaker.

> ▶   "What's this?" the hospital janitor said to me as he stumbled over my right shoe.
>   "My shoes," I said.
>   "That's not a shoe, brother," he replied, holding it to the light. "That's a brick."   —Henry Louis Gates Jr., "A Giant Step"

HB-102

See **P-8c** for help with capitalization in a direct quotation.

P-4b Long Quotations

529

MLA 588–89

APA 627

Long quotations should be set off without quotation marks as **BLOCK QUOTATIONS**. Each documentation style has distinct guidelines for the length and formatting of block quotations; you'll find more on long quotations in **MLA STYLE** and **APA STYLE**. The following example uses MLA style, which calls for setting off quotations of five or more typed lines of prose by indenting them five spaces (or half an inch) from the left margin. Note that in the following example, the period precedes the parenthetical documentation.

> Biographer David McCullough describes Truman's railroad campaign as follows:
>> No president in history had ever gone so far in quest of support from the people, or with less cause for the effort, to judge by informed opinion. . . . As a test of his skills and judgment as a professional politician, not to say his stamina and disposition at age sixty-four, it would be like no other experience in his long, often difficult career, as he himself understood perfectly. (655)

P-4c Titles of Short Works

Use quotation marks to enclose the titles of articles, chapters, essays, short stories, poems, songs, and episodes of television series. Titles of books, films, newspapers, and other longer works should be in italics (or underlined) rather than enclosed in quotation marks.

▶ In "Unfriendly Skies Are No Match for El Al," Vivienne Walt, a writer for *USA Today,* describes her experience flying with this airline.
—Andie McDonie, "Airport Security"

Note that the title of the newspaper is italicized, whereas the newspaper article title takes quotation marks.

▶ With every page of Edgar Allan Poe's story "The Tell-Tale Heart," my own heart beat faster.

▶ Rita Dove's poem "Dawn Revisited" contains vivid images that appeal to the senses of sight, sound, smell, and taste.

P-4d Single Quotation Marks

When you quote a passage that already contains quotation marks, whether they enclose a quotation or a title, change the inner ones to single quotation marks.

▶ Debra Johnson notes that according to Marilyn J. Adams, "effective reading instruction is based on 'direct instruction in phonics, focusing on the orthographic regularities of English.' "

▶ Certain essays are so good (or so popular) that they are included in almost every anthology. *The Norton Reader* notes, "Some essays—Martin Luther King Jr.'s 'Letter from Birmingham Jail' and Jonathan Swift's 'Modest Proposal,' for example—are constant favorites" (xxiii).

P-4e With Other Punctuation

When other punctuation follows material in quotation marks, it should go inside the closing quotation mark in some cases and outside in others. The following guidelines are those that are conventional in the United States; they differ from those in many other countries.

Commas and periods

Put commas and periods inside closing quotation marks.

▶ "On the newsstand, the cover is acting as a poster, an ad for what's inside," she said. "The loyal reader is looking for what makes the magazine exceptional."

　　　　　　　　—Katharine Q. Seelye, "Lurid Numbers on Glossy Pages!"

Semicolons and colons

Put semicolons and colons outside closing quotation marks.

▶ No elder stands behind our young to say, "Folks have fought and died for your right to pierce your face, so do it right"; no community exists that can model for a young person the responsible use of the "right"; for the right, even if called self-expression, comes from no source other than desire.

　　　　　　　　—Stephen L. Carter, "Just Be Nice"

▶ According to James Garbarino, author of *Lost Boys: Why Our Sons Turn Violent and How We Can Save Them*, it makes no sense to talk about violent media as a direct cause of youth violence. Rather, he says, "it depends": Media violence is a risk factor that, working in concert with others, can exacerbate bad behavior.

　　　　　　　　—Maggie Cutler, "Whodunit—The Media?"

Question marks and exclamation points

Put question marks and exclamation points inside closing quotation marks if they are part of the quotation but outside if they apply to the whole sentence.

▶ Then she began to talk more loudly. "What he want, I come to New York tell him front of his boss, you cheating me?"

　　　　　　　　—Amy Tan, "Mother Tongue"

▶ How many people know the words to "Louie, Louie"?

P-4f With Parenthetical Documentation

When you provide parenthetical **DOCUMENTATION** for a quotation, put it after the closing quotation mark, and put any end punctuation that's part of your sentence after the parentheses.

● 544–47

▶ An avid baseball fan, Tallulah Bankhead once said, "There have been only two geniuses in the world: Willie Mays and Willie Shakespeare" (183).

P-4g Checking for Mistakes with Quotation Marks

Avoid using quotation marks to identify **SLANG** or to emphasize a word. Remove the quotation marks, or substitute a better word.

△ HB-69–71

SLANG	Appearing ⁄hip⁄ is important to many parents in New York.
EMPHASIS	The woman explained that she is ⁄only⁄ the manager, not the owner, of the health club.

Do not put quotation marks around indirect quotations, those that do not quote someone's exact words.

▶ Grandmother always said that ⁄meat that was any good didn't need seasoning.⁄

P-5 Apostrophes

McDonald's: "I'm *lovin'* it" proclaims an ad, demonstrating two common uses of the apostrophe: to show ownership (*McDonald's*) and to mark missing letters (*I'm, lovin'*). This chapter offers guidelines on these and other common uses for apostrophes.

P-5a Possessives

Use an apostrophe to make a word possessive: *Daniel Craig's eyes, someone else's problem, the children's playground.*

Singular nouns

To make most singular nouns possessive, add an apostrophe and -s.

▶ The challenge now will be filling the park's seats.
—Michael Kimmelman, "A Ballpark Louder Than Its Fans"

▶ In Plato's *Phaedrus*, Socrates bemoaned the development of writing.
—Nicholas Carr, "Is *Google* Making Us Stupid?"

▶ Bill Gates's philanthropic efforts focus on health care and education.

If adding -'s makes pronunciation awkward, some writers use only an apostrophe with singular nouns that end in -s: *Euripides', George Saunders'*.

Plural nouns

To form the possessive of a plural noun not ending in -s, add an apostrophe and -s. For plural nouns that end in -s, add only an apostrophe.

▶ Are women's minds different from men's minds?
—Evelyn Fox Keller, "Women in Science"

▶ The neighbors' complaints about noise led the club owner to install soundproof insulation.

▶ Did you hear that Laurence Strauss is getting married? The reception will be at the Strausses' home.

Personal pronouns

HB-32 ⬉

Personal pronouns such as *we, she*, and *you* have their own possessive forms, which never take an apostrophe. See **S-6c** for a complete list.

▶ The graduates let out a cheer as they tossed *their* hats in the air—and later got a good chuckle when the valedictorian accidentally stepped on *hers*.

Something, everyone, *and other indefinite pronouns*

HB-27 ⬉

To form the possessive of an **INDEFINITE PRONOUN**, add an apostrophe and -s.

▶ Clarabelle was everyone's favorite clown.

academic literacies · rhetorical situations · genres · fields · processes · strategies · research MLA / APA · media / design · readings · handbook

Joint possession

To show that two or more individuals possess something together, use the possessive form for the last noun only.

▶ Carlson and Ventura's book is an introduction to Latino writers for English-speaking adolescents.

To show individual possession, make each noun possessive.

▶ Jan's and Al's heart transplants inspired me to become an organ donor.

Compound nouns

For nouns made up of more than one word, make the last word possessive.

▶ The surgeon general's report persuaded many people to stop smoking.

P-5b Contractions

An apostrophe in a contraction indicates where letters have been omitted.

▶ I've learned that sometimes friends and business don't mix.
                                        —Iliana Roman, "First Job"
I've *is a contraction of* I have; don't *is a contraction of* do not.

P-5c Plurals

You'll often see apostrophes used to pluralize numbers, letters, abbreviations, and words discussed as words: 7's, A's, NGO's, *thank you's*. Usage is changing, however, and in the case of numbers, abbreviations, and words discussed as words, you should leave out the apostrophe in your own writing.

Plural of numbers

▶ The winning hand had three 8s.

▶ We were astonished to hear Grandma Eleanor say she loved the 1950s.

Plural of abbreviations and words discussed as words

▶ How many TV**s** does the average American family have in its home?

▶ The resolution passed when there were more *aye***s** than *nay***s**.
See that words discussed as words are italicized but the -s ending is not.

Plural of letters

Italicize the letter but not the -s ending: ABCs. To avoid confusion, use an apostrophe with lowercase letters and uppercase A and I.

▶ Mrs. Duchovny always reminded us to dot our *i*'s and cross our *t*'s.

▶ The admissions officers spoke enthusiastically about the college's no-grades option—and then said we'd need mostly *A*'s to get in.

P-5d Checking for Mistakes with Apostrophes

Do not use an apostrophe in the following situations.

With plural nouns that are not possessive

▶ Both ~~cellist's~~ cellists played encores.

With his, hers, ours, yours, and theirs

▶ Look at all the lettuce. ~~Our's~~ Ours is organic. Is ~~your's~~ yours?

With the possessive its

▶ It's an unusual building; ~~it's~~ its style has been described as postmodern, but it fits beautifully with the Gothic buildings on our campus.
It's is a contraction meaning "it is" or "it has"; its is the possessive form of it.

P-6 Other Punctuation

Some carpenters can do their jobs using only a hammer and a saw, but most rely on additional tools. The same is true of writers: you can get along with just a few punctuation marks, but having some others in your toolbox—colons, dashes, parentheses, brackets, ellipses, and slashes—can help you say what you want to more precisely—and can help readers follow what you write more easily. This chapter can help you use these other punctuation marks effectively.

P-6a Colons

Colons are used to direct attention to words that follow the colon: an explanation or elaboration, a list, a quotation, and so on.

▶ What I remember best, strangely enough, are the two things I couldn't understand and over the years grew to hate: grammar lessons and mathematics.   —Mike Rose, "Potato Chips and Stars"

▶ I sized him up as fast as possible: tight black velvet pants pulled over his boots, black jacket, a red-green-yellow scarf slashed around his neck.
                              —Susan Jane Gilman, "Mick Jagger Wants Me"

▶ She also voices some common concerns: "The product should be safe, it should be easily accessible, and it should be low-priced."
                              —Dara Mayers, "Our Bodies, Our Lives"

▶ Fifteen years after the release of the Carnegie report, College Board surveys reveal data are no different: test scores still correlate strongly with family income.   —Gregory Mantsios, "Class in America—2003"

Colons are also used after the salutation in a business letter, in ratios, between titles and subtitles, between city and publisher in bibliographies, between chapter and verse in biblical references, and between numbers that indicate hours, minutes, and seconds.

▶ Dear President Michaels:

▶ For best results, add water to the powder in a 3:1 ratio.

▶ *The Last Campaign: How Harry Truman Won the 1948 Election*

▶ New York: Norton, 2014.

▶ "Death and life are in the power of the tongue" (Proverbs 18:21).

▶ The morning shuttle departs at 6:52 AM.

P-6b Dashes

You can create a dash by typing two hyphens (--) with no spaces before or after or by selecting the em dash from the symbol menu of your word-processing program.

Use dashes to set off material you want to emphasize. Unlike colons, dashes can appear not only after an independent clause but also at other points in a sentence. To set off material at the end of a sentence, place a dash before it; to set off material in the middle of the sentence, place a dash before and after the words you want to emphasize.

▶ After that, the roller coaster rises and falls, slowing down and speeding up—all on its own.
　　　　　　　　　—Cathi Eastman and Becky Burrell, "The Science of Screams"

▶ It did not occur to me—possibly because I am an American—that there could be people anywhere who had never seen a Negro.
　　　　　　　　　—James Baldwin, "Stranger in the Village"

Dashes are often used to signal a shift in tone or thought.

▶ The best way to keep children home is to make the home atmosphere pleasant—and let the air out of the tires.　　　　　—Dorothy Parker

Keep in mind that dashes are most effective if they are used only when material needs particular emphasis. Too many dashes can interfere with the flow and clarity of your writing.

P-6c Parentheses

Use parentheses to enclose supplemental details and digressions.

▶ When I was a child, attending grade school in Washington, DC, we took classroom time to study manners. Not only the magic words "please" and

"thank you" but more complicated etiquette questions, like how to answer the telephone ("Carter residence, Stephen speaking") and how to set the table (we were quizzed on whether knife blades point in or out).
—Stephen L. Carter, "Just Be Nice"

▶ In their apartments they have the material possessions that indicate success (a VCR, a color television), even if it means that they do without necessities and plunge into debt to buy these items.
—Diana George, "Changing the Face of Poverty"

▶ Before participating in the trials, Seeta and Ratna (not their real names) knew nothing about H.I.V.   —Dara Mayers, "Our Bodies, Our Lives"

P-6d Brackets

Put brackets around words that you insert in a **QUOTATION**.

528–31

▶ As Senator Reid explained, "She [Nancy Pelosi] realizes that you cannot make everyone happy."

If you are quoting a source that contains an error, put the Latin word *sic* in brackets after the error to indicate that the mistake is in the original source.

▶ Warehouse has been around for 30 years and has 263 stores, suggesting a large fan base. The chain sums up its appeal thus: "styley [*sic*], confident, sexy, glamorous, edgy, clean and individual, with it's [*sic*] finger on the fashion pulse."   —Anne Ashworth, "Chain Reaction: Warehouse"

P-6e Ellipses

Ellipses are three spaced dots that indicate an omission or a pause. Use ellipses to show that you have omitted words within a **QUOTATION**. If you omit a complete sentence or more in the middle of a quoted passage, add the three dots after the period.

528–31

ORIGINAL

▶ The Lux ad's visual content, like Resinol's, supports its verbal message. Several demure views of Irene Dunne emphasize her "pearly-smooth skin," the top one framed by a large heart shape. In all the photos, Dunne wears a feathery, feminine collar, giving her a birdlike appearance: she is a bird of

paradise or an ornament. At the bottom of the ad, we see a happy Dunne
being cuddled and admired by a man.

—Doug Lantry, " 'Stay Sweet as You Are' "

WITH ELLIPSES

▶ The Lux ad's visual content . . . supports its verbal message. Several demure
views of Irene Dunne emphasize her "pearly-smooth skin," the top one
framed by a large heart shape. . . . At the bottom of the ad, we see a happy
Dunne being cuddled and admired by a man.

If you use parenthetical documentation after quoted material, place
ellipses *before* the parentheses to indicate the deletion of words, but put
the end punctuation *after* the parentheses.

▶ According to Kathleen Welch, "One can turn one's gaze away from
television, but one cannot turn one's ears from it without leaving the
area . . . " (102).

P-6f Slashes

When you quote two or three lines of poetry and run them in with the
rest of your text, use slashes to show where one line ends and the next
begins. Put a space before and after each slash.

▶ In the opening lines of the poem, he warns the reader to "Lift not the
painted veil which those who live / Call Life" (1-2).

—Stephanie Huff, "Metaphor and Society in Shelley's 'Sonnet'"

P-7 Hyphens

If your mother gives you much needed advice, has she given you a great deal
of advice that you needed, or advice that you needed badly? What about a
psychiatry experiment that used thirty five year old subjects? Were there
thirty-five subjects who were a year old? thirty subjects who were five years
old? or an unspecified number of thirty-five-year-old subjects? Hyphens
could clear up the confusion. This chapter provides tips for when to use
hyphens and when to omit them.

P-7a Compound Words

Compound words can be two words (*ground zero*), a hyphenated word (*self-esteem*), or one word (*outsource*). Check a dictionary, and if a compound is not there, assume that it is two words.

Compound adjectives

A compound adjective is made up of two or more words. Most compound adjectives take a hyphen before a noun.

▶ a little-known trombonist

▶ a foul-smelling river

Do not use a hyphen to connect an -ly adverb and an adjective.

▶ a carefully executed plan

A compound adjective after a noun is usually easy to read without a hyphen; add a hyphen only if the compound is unclear without it.

▶ The river has become foul smelling in recent years.

Prefixes and suffixes

A hyphen usually isn't needed after a prefix or before a suffix (*preschool, antislavery, counterattack, catlike, citywide*). However, hyphens are necessary in the following situations.

WITH *GREAT-, SELF-, -ELECT*   great-aunt, self-hatred, president-elect

WITH CAPITAL LETTERS   anti-American, post-Soviet literature

WITH NUMBERS   post-9/11, the mid-1960s

TO AVOID DOUBLE AND TRIPLE LETTERS   anti-intellectualism, ball-like

FOR CLARITY   re-cover (cover again) *but* recover (get well)

Numbers

Hyphenate fractions and compound numbers from twenty-one to ninety-nine.

▶ three-quarters of their income

▶ thirty-five subjects

P-7b At the End of a Line

Use a hyphen to divide a multisyllabic word that does not fit on one line. (A one-syllable word is never hyphenated.) Divide words between syllables as shown in a dictionary, after a prefix, or before a suffix. Divide compound words between the parts of the compound, if possible. Do not leave only one letter at the end or the beginning of a line.

op-er-a-tion   knot-ty   main-stream

Dividing internet addresses

Do not insert a hyphen in a URL or DOI that you break at the end of a line. It's standard practice to break URLs or DOIs that won't fit on a line after a double slash or before any other punctuation mark.

P-8 Capitalization

Capital letters are an important signal, either that a new sentence is beginning or that a specific person, place, or brand is being discussed. Capitalize *Carol*, and it's clear that you're referring to a person; write *carol*, and readers will know you're writing about a song sung at Christmas. This chapter offers guidelines to help you know what to capitalize and when.

P-8a Proper Nouns and Common Nouns

Capitalize proper nouns, those naming specific people, places, and things. All other nouns are common nouns and should not be capitalized.

PROPER NOUNS	COMMON NOUNS
Sanjay Gupta	a doctor
Senator Feinstein	a senator
Uncle Daniel	my uncle
France	a republic
the Mississippi River	a river
the West Coast	a coast
Christianity	a religion
Allah	a god
the Torah	a sacred text
Central Intelligence Agency	an agency
U.S. Congress	the U.S. government
Kansas State University	a university
Composition 101	a writing course
World War II	a war
July	summer
the Middle Ages	the fourteenth century
Kleenex	tissues

Adjectives derived from proper nouns, especially the names of people and places, are usually capitalized: *Shakespearean, Swedish, Chicagoan.* There are exceptions to this rule, however, such as *french fries, roman numeral,* and *congressional.* Consult your dictionary if you are unsure whether an adjective should be capitalized.

Many dictionaries capitalize the terms *Internet, Net,* and *World Wide Web,* but you'll see variations such as *Website* and *website.* Whether you capitalize or not, be consistent throughout a paper.

P-8b Titles before a Person's Name

A professional title is capitalized when it appears immediately before a person's name but not when it appears after a proper noun or alone.

Senator (*or* Sen.) Elizabeth Warren   Elizabeth Warren, the senator

P-8c The First Word of a Sentence

Capitalize the first word of a sentence. The first word of a quoted sentence should be capitalized, but not the first word of a quoted phrase.

▶ Speaking about acting, Clint Eastwood notes, "You can show a lot with a look.... It's punctuation."

▶ Sherry Turkle argues that we're living in "techno-enthusiastic times" and that we're inclined "to celebrate our gadgets."

Interrupted quotations

Capitalize the second part of an interrupted quotation only if it begins a new sentence.

▶ "It was just as nice," she sobbed, "as I hoped and dreamed it would be."
—Joan Didion, "Marrying Absurd"

▶ "On the newsstand, the cover is acting as a poster, an ad for what's inside," she said. "The loyal reader is looking for what makes the magazine exceptional."
—Katharine Q. Seelye, "Lurid Numbers on Glossy Pages!"

P-8d Titles and Subtitles

Capitalize the first and last words and all other important words of a title and subtitle. Do not capitalize less important words such as **ARTICLES**, **COORDINATING CONJUNCTIONS**, and **PREPOSITIONS**.

HB-63–65

HB-38

HB-56–57

"Give Peace a Chance"

Pride and Prejudice

The Shallows: What the Internet Is Doing to Our Brains

academic literacies · rhetorical situations · genres · fields · processes · strategies · research MLA / APA · media / design · readings · handbook

Each documentation style has guidelines for formatting titles in notes and bibliographies. You'll find more on titles and subtitles in **MLA STYLE** and **APA STYLE**.

● MLA 548–96
APA 597–636

P-9 Italics

Italic type tells us to read words a certain way. Think of the difference between the office and *The Office*, or between time and *Time*. In each case, the italicized version tells us it's a specific television show or magazine. This chapter provides guidelines on using italics in your writing.

P-9a Titles of Long Works

Titles and subtitles of long works should appear in italics (or underlined). Notable exceptions are sacred writing such as the Qur'an or the Old Testament and historical documents such as the Declaration of Independence.

BOOKS   *War and Peace; The Hobbit; The Brief Wondrous Life of Oscar Wao*

PERIODICALS   *The Atlantic; Teen Vogue; College English*

NEWSPAPERS   *Los Angeles Times*

PLAYS   *Medea; Six Degrees of Separation*

LONG POEMS   *The Odyssey; Paradise Lost*

FILMS AND VIDEOS   *Selma; Inside Out; The Wizard of Oz*

MUSICAL WORKS OR ALBUMS   *The Four Seasons; Rubber Soul*

RADIO AND TV SERIES   *Fresh Air; Modern Family; Game of Thrones*

PAINTINGS, SCULPTURES   the *Mona Lisa*; Michelangelo's *David*

DANCES BY A CHOREOGRAPHER   Mark Morris's *Gloria*

SOFTWARE   *Adobe Acrobat XI Standard*

SHIPS, SPACECRAFT   *Queen Mary; Challenger*

WEBSITES   *Salon; Etsy; IMDb*

A short work, such as a short story, an article, an episode of a series, or a song, takes quotation marks.

P-9b Words Discussed as Words

Italicize a word you are discussing as a word. The same practice applies to numbers, letters, and symbols.

▶ In those 236 words, you will hear the word *dedicate* five times.
—William Safire, "A Spirit Reborn"

▶ Most American dictionaries call for one *t* in the word *benefited*.

▶ All computer codes consist of some combination of *0*s and *1*s.

Some writers use quotation marks rather than italics to signal words discussed as words.

▶ I would learn, when I asked some people who didn't show up the next day, that "definitely attending" on Facebook means "maybe" and "maybe attending" means "likely not."
—Hal Niedzviecki, "Facebook in a Crowd"

P-9c Non-English Words

Use italics for an unfamiliar word or phrase in a language other than English. Do not italicize proper nouns.

▶ *Verstehen*, a concept often associated with Max Weber, is the sociologist's attempt to understand human actions from the actor's point of view.

If the word or phrase has become part of everyday English or has an entry in English-language dictionaries, it does not need italics.

▶ An ad hoc committee should be formed to assess the university's use of fossil fuels and ways to incorporate alternative energy sources.

▶ The plot of *Jane Eyre* follows the conventions of a bildungsroman, or a coming-of-age story.

P-9d For Emphasis

You can use italics occasionally to lend emphasis to a word or phrase, but do not overuse them.

▶ It is, perhaps, as much what Shakespeare did *not* write as what he did that seems to indicate something seriously wrong with his marriage.
— Stephen Greenblatt, "Shakespeare on Marriage"

▶ Despite a physical beauty that had . . . hordes of teenage girls (and a few boys) dreaming of touching his hair *just once*, Depp escaped from the Hollywood star machine.
— Sean Smith, "Johnny Depp: Unlikely Superstar"

P-10 Abbreviations

MTV. USA. OC. DNA. fwiw. DIY. These are some common abbreviations, shortcuts to longer words and phrases. You can use common abbreviations if you are sure your readers will recognize them. If not, spell out the full term with the abbreviation in parentheses the first time it appears. After that, you can use the abbreviation alone.

▶ In a recent press release, officials from the international organization Médecins Sans Frontières (MSF) stressed the need for more effective tuberculosis drugs.

Periods are generally used in abbreviations of personal titles that precede a name and in Latin abbreviations such as *e.g.* or *etc.* They are not needed for state abbreviations such as CA, NY, or TX, or for most abbreviations made up of initials, like AP or YMCA. In some cases, periods are optional (BCE or B.C.E.). Be sure to use them or omit them consistently. If you're not sure about periods for a particular abbreviation, check a dictionary.

P-10a With Names

Most titles are abbreviated when they come before or after a name.

Mr. Ed Stanford   Ed Stanford Jr.

Dr. Ralph Lopez   Ralph Lopez, MD

Prof. Susan Miller   Susan Miller, PhD

Do not abbreviate job titles that are not attached to a name.

▶ The ~~RN~~ ^{nurse} who worked with trauma victims specialized in cardiac care.

P-10b With Numbers

The following abbreviations can be used with numbers.

632 BC ("before Christ")

344 BCE ("before the common era")

AD 800 ("*anno Domini*")

800 CE ("common era")

10:30 AM (*or* a.m.)

7:00 PM (*or* p.m.)

Notice that BC, BCE, and CE follow the date, while AD precedes the date. Remember that the abbreviations in the list cannot be used without a date or time.

▶ By early ~~p.m.,~~ ^{afternoon,} all prospective subjects for the experiment had checked in.

P-10c In Notes and Documentation

With only a few exceptions, the names of months, days of the week, colleges and universities, cities, states, and countries should not be abbrevi-

academic literacies | rhetorical situations | genres | fields | processes | strategies | research MLA / APA | media / design | readings | handbook

ated in the body of a paper. But they often are abbreviated in footnotes and bibliographies; follow the rules of whichever documentation system you are using.

The same applies to Latin abbreviations like *ibid.*, *op. cit.*, and *et al.*: while you may use them in notes and documentation, they're not appropriate in the body of your text. Use equivalent English expressions (such as "and others" for *et al.*) instead.

▶ Being left-handed presents some challenges for writers—e.g., it hurts to write in spiral notebooks, and ink smears across the page and the side of your hand.

[handwritten edit above "e.g.,": for example,*]*

P-11 Numbers

Numbers may be written with numerals (*97*) or words (*ninety-seven*). Spell out numbers and fractions that you can write in one or two words (*thirteen, thirty-seven, thirty thousand, two-thirds*). Use numerals otherwise (*578; 5,788*). Spell out any number that begins a sentence. Be aware, however, that the conventions for writing numbers vary across disciplines.

In the humanities, when the content is not number heavy, **MLA STYLE** recommends spelling out all numbers up to a hundred (*twenty-five*) and using numerals for other numbers (*532*).

● MLA 548–96

▶ In a survey of *two hundred* students, 135 said they spent more than two hours each day writing.

In the social sciences, **APA STYLE** recommends spelling out numbers one through nine and using numerals for all the rest.

● APA 597–636

▶ *Nine* 40-minute interviews of subjects in *three* categories were conducted for this study.

In the sciences, CSE recommends using numerals in almost any situation, but spelling out zero and one to avoid confusion with *l* and *O*.

▶ The physician recommended one dose of 200 mg per day for 8 days.

In most business writing, spell out numbers one through ten and use numerals for all numbers over ten (*ten goals*, 11 *strategies*).

▶ We received *35* applications and identified *five* strong candidates, who we'll interview this week.

For very large numbers that include a fraction or decimal, use a combination of numerals and words.

▶ One retailer sold more than 4.5 million of its basic T-shirts last year.

In addition, numerals are generally used in the following situations.

ADDRESSES   500 Broadway; 107 175th Street

DATES   December 26, 2012; 632 BCE; the 1990s

MONEY IN EXACT AMOUNTS $3.75; $375,000; a deficit of $3.75 trillion

PARTS OF WRITTEN WORKS   volume 2; Chapter 5; page 82; act 3, scene 3

PERCENTAGES   66 percent (*or* 66%)

RATIOS   16:1 (*or* 16 to 1)

STATISTICS   a median age of 32

TIMES OF DAY   6:20 AM (*or* a.m.)

WHOLE NUMBERS WITH DECIMALS OR FRACTIONS   66.7; 66 2/3; 59½

Acknowledgments

IMAGE ACKNOWLEDGMENTS

Page 40: Jacob MacLeod; p. 75: Courtesy of Emily Vallowe; p. 81: Meghan Hickey; p. 84: Ana-Jamileh Kassfy; p. 102: Courtesy of Danielle Allen. © Laura Rose Photography; p. 107: Photo by Kenneth Irby. Courtesy of The Poynter Institute; p. 120: urbanbuzz/Shutterstock.com; p. 121: TOLES © 2007 The Washington Post. Reprinted with permission of ANDREW MCMEEL SYNDICATION. All rights reserved; p. 123: AP Photo/Jeffrey Phelps; p. 124 (both): Courtesy of Ann C. Johns, Ph.D./University of Texas at Austin; p. 131: Michaela Cullington; p. 139: Frankie Schembri; p. 140: Coki10/Shutterstock; p. 143: Courtesy of Jon Marcus, photo by Andrew Kubica; p. 144: Wesley Hitt/Getty Images; p. 157: Joanna MacKay; p. 162: Evan Agostini/Invision/EP Photo; p. 164: Bettmann/Corbis via Getty Images; p. 165: Jafar Fallahi; p. 192: Photo courtesy of www.donlaurencephotography.com; p. 204: Francois Duhamel/© STX Entertainment/Courtesy Everett Collection; p. 211: Keystone Pictures USA/Alamy Stock Photo; p. 212: Matthew M. Miller; p. 224: John Amis/AP; p. 233: Courtesy of Ernie Smith; p. 234: Patryk Michalski/Shutterstock; p. 235: Library of Congress; p. 246: Michael H. Granof; p. 250: Courtesy Dena Betz; p. 256: Courtesy Adam Karsten; p. 257: Courtesy Adalena Kavanagh; p. 258: Courtesy Julia Black; p. 259: Courtesy Darcy Vebber; p. 280: AP Photo/Evan Agostini; p. 377: Jim Mone/AP; p. 407: © Reagan Louie; p. 408: AaronFoster.com; p. 421: All photos © New York Apple Association; p. 428 (left): F. Carter Smith/Bloomberg via Getty Images; p. 428 (right): Richard Carson/REUTERS/Newscom; p. 437: Photo by Swim Ink 2, LLC/CORBIS/Corbis via Getty Images; p. 449: Michigan Economic Development Corporation; p. 460 (all): Patricia Reitz (butteryum.org); p. 492 (all): Nicholas S. Holtzman, Simine Vazire, Matthias R. Mehl. "Sounds Like a Narcissist: Behavioral Manifestations of Narcissism in Everyday Life." *Journal of Research in Personality*; p. 494 (both): Houston Community College; p. 497: Permission to publish courtesy of EBSCO; pp. 500–501: Wright State University Libraries; p. 567: Michael Segal, "The Hit Book That Came from Mars." *Nautilus*. Nautilus Think, 8 January 2015. Web. 10 October 2016; p. 569: Jessamyn Neuhaus, "Marge Simpson, Blue-Haired Housewife Defining Domesticity on The Simpsons." *Journal of Popular Culture* 43.4 (2010); p. 573: Amana Fontanella-Khan, *Pink Sari Revolution: A Tale of Women and Power in India*. New York: Norton, 2013; p. 579: John McIlwain, Molly Simpson, and Sara Hammerschmidt. "Housing in America: Integrating Housing, Health, and Resilience in a Changing Environment." *Urban Land Institute*. Urban Land Institute, 2014. Web. 17 Sept. 2016; p. 591: Bettmann/Getty Images; pp. 613: C. F. Guthrie, (2013). "Smart Technology and the Moral Life." *Ethics & Behavior*, 23, 324–37. https://www.tandfonline.com/doi/full/10.1080

/10508422.2013.787359; p. 615: M. P. Lazette, (2015, February 25). "A Hurricane's Hit to Households." Federal Reserve Bank of Cleveland. Retrieved from www .clevelandfed.org/en/Newsroom%20and%20Events /Publications/Forefront/Katrina.aspx; p. 616: Joseph E. Stiglitz, *The Great Divide: Unequal Societies and What We Can Do about Them.* New York: Norton, 2015; p. 647: Used with the permission of Inter IKEA Systems B.V; p. 655 (left): National Gallery of Art; p. 655 (right): Library of Congress; p. 657 (all): RNGS/ RTR/Newscom; p. 658 (top): NASA Image Collection/ Alamy Stock Photo; p. 658 (center): This map was created by the National Renewable Energy; Laboratory for the U.S. Department of Energy; p. 661: Caricature of an artist painting vigorously, ca. 1885–1886. Francis Davis Millet and Millet family papers, 1858–1984, bulk 1858–1955. Archives of American Art, Smithsonian Institution; p. 666: Courtesy of National Park Service. No protection is claimed in original US government works; p. 667: Smithsonian National Museum of History; p. 668: Courtesy of Ann M. Lawrence, PhD, University of South Florida; p. 671: Courtesy Richard Bullock; p. 673: Library of Congress; p. 674: Courtesy of Judy Davis; p. 688: Photo: Heather Waraksa; p. 693: Courtesy Tanya M. Barrientos; p. 697: Chris Felver/ Getty Images; p. 704: Daniel Hamilton; p. 715: Photo by Jim Harrison/Courtesy of Laurel Thatcher Ulrich; p. 718: John Springer Collection/CORBIS/Corbis via Getty Images; p. 721: Montgomery County Sheriff's Office/AP; p. 726: Courtesy of Diana George; p. 729: Dennis MacDonald/Alamy Stock Photo; p. 738: Isabelle Gill; p. 753: The New York Times/Redux; p. 757: Jason J. Hasler; p. 764: Courtesy Eleanor J. Bader; p. 770: Steven Senne/AP; pp. 771–72 (both): Photographs by Stephen Buel; p. 779: Courtesy of Alina Tugend; p. 780: Monkey Business Images/Shutterstock; p. 789: Colin McPherson/Corbis via Getty Images; p. 790: The Everett Collection; p. 794 (left): Hi-Story/Alamy Stock Photo; p. 794 (right): akg-images/Newscom; p. 797: The

Kheel Center for Labor-Management Documentation and Archives; p. 799: Achinthamb/Shutterstock; p. 804: Eva Derzic; p. 808: Sarah Dzubay; p. 816: Courtesy of danah boyd; p. 823: © 2017 The Atlantic. Photo by: Leah Varjacques; p. 828: Courtesy of Natalie Standiford. Photo by Tobias Everke; p. 832: Ashley Foster; p. 838: Bailey Basinger; p. 851: Röhnert/Ullstein Bild via Getty Images; p. 861: Photo by Fred Viebahn; p. 862: Pictorial Press Ltd/Alamy Stock Photo; p. 879: Walter Oleksy/Alamy Stock Photo; p. 881: Everett Collection Inc/Alamy Stock Photo; p. 883: Yonhap News/YNA/Newscom; p. 891: Courtesy of Kevin Harkins; p. 898: Michele McDonald/The Boston Globe via Getty Images; p. 900: Dave Warren/LNP/REX/ Shutterstock; p. 906: © Heinemann 2011. Photo by Melissa Cooperman; p. 915 (top): Courtesy of James Hamblin; p. 915 (bottom): Sarah Natsumi Moore; p. 916: Sarah Natsumi Moore; pp. 918–20: Courtesy of The Dumpster Project; dumpsterproject.org; p. 923: Courtesy of Ana Pacheco; p. 928 (top): Karen Gordon, Karenscape Photography; p. 928 (bottom): Jason Raish Illustration; p. 929: Claire Middlebrooks/Yeti; p. 933: Geoff Pugh/Shutterstock; pp. 934–35: Jack Naughton/ The New York Times/Redux; p. 940: AP Photo/Seth Wenig; p. 942: Mario Tama/Getty Images; p. 949: Photo by Jonathon Baron; p. 953: Monty Soungpradith/Open Image Studio via M+A Architects; p. 954: Frances Roberts/Alamy Stock Photo; p. 955: Margaret Price; p. 956: Aimi Hamraie; pp. 960-65: Ogden County Schools, Toronto District School Board p. 970: AP Photo/MPI10/MediaPunch/IPX; p. 977: Courtesy of Heather Kresge; p. 983: Vann R. Newkirk II; p. 987: Beth Nguyen; p. 992: Ryan Enn Hughes/The New York Times/Redux; p. 999: Courtesy of Anu Partanen; p. 1000: Jinnnnnnnnnn/Shutterstock; p. 1013: Sneha Saha; p. HB-68: © 20th Century Fox. All rights reserved/Courtesy Everett Collection; p. HB-70: Mike Twohy/The New Yorker Collection/The Cartoon Bank.

TEXT ACKNOWLEDGMENTS

Danielle Allen: From *Our Declaration: A Reading of the Declaration of Independence in Defense of Equality* by Danielle Allen. Copyright © 2014 by Danielle Allen. Used by permission of Liveright Publishing Corporation.

E. J. Bader: "Homeless on Campus" from *The Progressive*, July 2004. Copyright © The Progressive. Reprinted by permission.

Dennis Baron: "Don't Make English Official—Ban It Instead." Reprinted by permission of the author.

Tanya Barrientos: "Se Habla Español," from the August 2004 issue of *Latina*. Reprinted by permission of the author.

Dave Barry: "Introduction: Guys vs. Men" from *Dave Barry's Complete Guide to Guys: A Fairly Short Book* by Dave Barry, copyright © 1995 by Dave Barry. Used by permission of Random House, an imprint and division of Penguin Random House LLC. All rights reserved.

Lynda Barry: "Lost and Found" from "One Hundred Demons," Salon.com, November 17, 2000. This article first appeared in Salon.com, at http://www.Salon.com. An online version remains in the Salon archives. Reprinted with permission.

Bailey Basinger: "Tension, Contradiction, and Ambiguity: Gender Roles in 'A Rose for Emily.'" Copyright © 2018 by W. W. Norton & Company.

Cynthia Bass: Excerpt from "Gettysburg Address: Two Versions," *The San Francisco Examiner*, November 19, 1997. Reprinted by permission of the author.

Michael Benton, Mark Dolan & Rebecca Zisch: "Teen Film$: An Annotated Bibliography" from *Journal of Popular Film and Television*, Vol. 25, No. 2, Summer 1997, pp. 83–88. Reprinted by permission of the publisher Taylor & Francis Ltd, http://www.tandfonline.com

Hannah Berry: "The Fashion Industry: Free to Be an Individual." Copyright © 2012 by Hannah Berry.

Dylan Borchers: "Against the Odds: Harry S. Truman and the Election of 1948." Copyright © 2009 by Dylan Borchers.

danah boyd: "*Wikipedia* as a Site of Knowledge Production" from *It's Complicated: the social lives of networked teens* by danah boyd. Copyright © 2014 by danah boyd. Reprinted by permission of Yale University Press.

Rick Bragg: "All Over But the Shoutin'" from *All Over But the Shoutin'* by Rick Bragg, copyright © 1997 by Rick Bragg. Used by permission of Pantheon Books, an imprint of the Knopf Doubleday Publishing Group, a division of Penguin Random House LLC. All rights reserved.

Rachel Brinkley, Kenneth Ricker, and Kelly Tuomey: From "Esthetic Knowing with a Hospitalized Morbidly Obese Patient," *Journal of Undergraduate Nursing Scholarship*, Vol. 9, No. 1, Fall 2007. Reprinted by permission of The University of Arizona College of Nursing.

Nicholas Carr: "Is *Google* Making Us Stupid?" *The Atlantic*, July/August 2008. Copyright © 2008 The Atlantic Media Co., as first published in The Atlantic Magazine. All rights reserved. Distributed by Tribune Content Agency, LLC. Reprinted with permission.

Cameron Carroll: "Zombie Film Scholarship: A Review of the Literature" from UMW Blogs (htpp://www.umwblogs.org/). Reprinted by permission of the author.

Michael Chabon: "Kids' Stuff" from *Maps and Legends: Reading and Writing along the Borderlands*, published by HarperCollins. Copyright © Michael Chabon. Reprinted by permission of International Creative Management, Inc. All rights reserved.

Nathaniel Cooney: "Self-Assessment." Copyright © 2013 by Nathaniel Cooney.

Glossary / Index

A

a, an, HB-64

abbreviations
  overview, HB-105
  periods with, HB-86
  plural forms, HB-94

abstract, 185–89 A writing GENRE that summarizes a book, an article, or a paper, usually in 100–200 words. Authors in some academic fields must provide, at the top of a report submitted for publication, an abstract of its content. The abstract may then appear in a journal of abstracts, such as *Psychological Abstracts.* An *informative abstract* summarizes a complete report; a briefer *descriptive abstract* provides only a brief overview; a *proposal abstract* (also called a TOPIC PROPOSAL) requests permission to conduct research, write on a topic, or present a report at a scholarly conference. Key Features: SUMMARY of basic information • objective description • brevity
  key features, 187
  reading: "Boredom Proneness," 185–86
  types and examples
    informative, 185–86
    proposal, 186
    science fields, 303
  writing guide, 187–89

abstract and concrete words, HB-45
"Abuse of an Unnamed Wife: Is She Familiar?" (Moore), 845–50
academic fields. *See* fields of study
academic habits of mind, 45–52
Academic Search Complete, 502
Academic Search Premier, 502

academic writing, 3–9 Writing done in an academic or scholarly context, such as for course assignments. Key Features: evidence that you've carefully considered the subject • clear, appropriately qualified THESIS • response to what others have said • good reasons supported by evidence • acknowledgment of multiple perspectives • carefully documented sources • confident, authoritative STANCE • indication of why your topic matters • careful attention to correctness.
  in arts and humanities, 307–9
  in business, 313–14
  in education, 315–16
  in engineering and technology, 316–18
  in health sciences and nursing, 318–20
  rhetorical situation, 305–6
  in science and mathematics, 309–11
  in social sciences, 311–13

accept, except, HB-51
acknowledging other viewpoints. *See* multiple perspectives, incorporating

---

Note: This glossary / index defines key terms and concepts and directs you to pages in the book where you can find specific information on these and other topics. Please note the words set in SMALL CAPITAL LETTERS are themselves defined in the glossary / index.

analogy A STRATEGY for COMPARISON that explains something unfamiliar in terms of something familiar. *See also* figurative language

  comparison and contrast with, 429–30

  false, 414–15

analysis A writing GENRE that methodically examines something by breaking it into its parts and noting how they work in relation to one another. *See* literary analysis; textual analysis

"Analysis of All Terrain Vehicle Crash Mechanisms" (Tanner et al.), 317

"An Ancient Remedy Reexamined" (Hasler), 757–63

and

  avoiding overuse of, HB-38

  comma with, HB-78

  in compound subjects, HB-25–26

  parallelism and, HB-35–36

anecdote A brief NARRATIVE used to illustrate a point.

  beginning with, 153, 379

  endings with, 382

Angelou, Maya, 462–63, 465–66

angle, in profiles, 240, 243

annotated bibliography, 190–98 A writing GENRE that gives an overview of published research and scholarship on a topic. Each entry includes complete publication information and a SUMMARY or an ABSTRACT. A *descriptive annotation* summarizes the content of a source without commenting on its value; an *evaluative annotation* gives an opinion about the source along with a description of it. Key Features: statement of the scope • complete bibliographic information • relevant commentary • consistent presentation • brevity

  key features, 193–94

  types and examples

    descriptive: "Teen Film$," 190–92

    evaluative: "Researching Hunger and Poverty," 192–93

  writing guide, 194–98

annotating

  as reading strategy, 16–19

  textual analyses and, 116

antecedent, 358 The NOUN or PRONOUN to which a pronoun refers. In *Maya* lost *her* wallet, Maya is the antecedent of *her*. *See also* pronoun

any, HB-27

anyone, anything

  pronoun-antecedent agreement, HB-29–30

  subject-verb agreement, HB-27

APA style, 597–636 A system of DOCUMENTATION used in the social sciences. APA stands for the American Psychological Association.

  comparison with MLA style, 545–47

  directory, 597–99

  fields of study

    business, 313

    education, 315

    engineering and technology, 317

    health sciences and nursing, 318

    science and mathematics, 310

    social sciences, 311

application letters, 273–79   Letters written to apply for a job or other position. Key Features: succinct indication of qualifications • reasonable and pleasing tone • conventional, businesslike form. *See also* résumés

arguing, 397–417   A STRATEGY that can be used in any kind of writing to support a claim with REASONS and EVIDENCE.

arguing a position, 157–84   A writing GENRE that uses REASONS and EVIDENCE to support a CLAIM or POSITION and, sometimes, to persuade an AUDIENCE to accept that position. Key Features: clear and arguable position • necessary background • good reasons • convincing support for each reason • appeal to readers' values • trustworthy TONE • careful consideration of other positions

    key features, 170–72

    with other genres, 284

    readings

        "In Defense of Writing Letters," 804–7

        "Is *Google* Making Us Stupid?," 789–803

        "Organ Sales Will Save Lives," 157–62

        "Our Blind Spot about Guns," 162–65

        "An Outbreak of the Irrational," 808–14

        "Should Gamers Be Prosecuted for Virtual Stealing?," 785–88

        "U Can't Talk to Ur Professor Like This," 165–70

    strategies for

        dialogue, 452

        narration, 462

    writing guide

        choosing a topic, 172–74

        considering a rhetorical situation, 174

        design, 182

        drafting, 180–81

        editing and proofreading, 183

        generating ideas and text, 174–78

        organizing, 178–80

        responses and revision, 182–83

        taking stock, 184

        ways of rewriting, 355

article, HB-63–65 The word *a, an,* or *the,* used to indicate that a NOUN is indefinite (*a* writer, *an* author) or definite (*the* author).

    when to use *a* or *an,* HB-64

    when to use no article, HB-65

    when to use *the,* HB-64–65

articles. *See* periodical articles

arts, academic writing for, 307–9

ArtStor, 504

as

    commas with, HB-83

    comparisons with, HB-33

    similes with, 429

    vs.*as if* and *like,* HB-52

as a matter of fact, in fact, HB-49, HB-50

as far as . . . is concerned, HB-59

assessing own writing

    in body of work, 347

    clarity, 346–47

    focus, 344–45

    organization, 345–46

    portfolios and, 365–68

    process and, 347

    rhetorical situation and, 343–44

    support for argument, 345

assigned topics, 149

at, on, in, HB-56–57

At Day's Close: Night in Times Past (Ekirch), 402

atlases, 498

at the time that, HB-59

"At This Academy, the Curriculum Is Garbage" (Schlossberg), 933–38

at this point in time, HB-59

audience, 57–60 Those to whom a text is directed—the people who read, listen to, or view the text. Audience is a key part

e-portfolio, 364 An electronic collection of writing and other evidence selected by a writer to show their work, including a statement assessing the work and explaining what it demonstrates.

essential element, HB-80 A word, PHRASE, or CLAUSE with information that is neces-sary for understanding the meaning of a sentence: *French is the only language that I can speak.*

evaluation, 202–10 A writing GENRE that makes a judgment about something—a source, poem, film, restaurant, whatever—based on certain CRITERIA. Key Features: description of the subject • clearly defined criteria • knowledgeable discussion of the subject • balanced and fair assessment

IMRaD, 303, 311, 318 An acronym representing sections of scientific reports: Introduction (asks a question), methods (tells about experiments), results (states findings), and discussion (tries to make sense of findings in light of what was already known). In some fields, an abstract, literature review, and list of references may also be required.

indefinite pronoun A PRONOUN—such as *all, anyone, anything, everyone, everything, few, many, nobody, nothing, one, some,* and *something*—that does not refer to a specific person or thing.

independent clause A CLAUSE, containing a SUBJECT and a VERB, that can stand alone as a sentence: *She sang. The world-famous soprano sang several popular arias.*

infinitive To plus the base form of the verb: *to come, to go.* An infinitive can function as a NOUN (*He likes <u>to run</u> first thing in the morning*); an ADJECTIVE (*She needs a campaign <u>to run</u>*); or an ADVERB (*He registered <u>to run</u> in the marathon*).

informal writing, HB-42, HB-50–51 Writing not intended to be evaluated, sometimes not even to be read by others. Informal writing is produced primarily to explore ideas or to communicate casually with friends and acquaintances. *See also* formal writing

modal, HB-17–19   A helping VERB—such as *can, could, may, might, must, ought to, should, will,* or *would*—that does not change form for person or number and indicates probability or necessity.

modifier   A word, PHRASE, or CLAUSE that describes or specifies something about another word, phrase, or clause (*a <u>long, informative</u> speech; the actors spoke <u>in unison;</u> the <u>man who would be king</u>*).

mood, HB-20–21   A characteristic of VERBS that indicates a writer's attitude toward the action or condition the verb expresses. The *indicative mood* is used to state fact or opinion: *I'm waiting to buy tickets.* The *imperative mood* is used to give commands or directions: *Sit down, and take off your shoes.* The *subjunctive mood* is used to express wishes, requests, or requirements or to indicate unlikely conditions: *I wish the ticket line were shorter. I suggest that you be ready for a long wait.*

multimedia, 504–5   Using more than one medium of delivery, such as print, speech, or electronic. Often used interchangeably with MULTIMODAL.

multimodal, 504–5   Using more than one mode of expression, such as words, images, sound, links, and so on. Often used interchangeably with MULTIMEDIA.

O

pronoun, HB-4, HB-29–34 A word that takes the place of a NOUN, such as *she, anyone, whoever.*

proofreading, 359–60 The final PROCESS of writing, when a writer checks for correct spelling and punctuation as well as for page order, missing text, and consistent use of FONTS. *See also* editing; revising; rewriting

proposal, 246–55 A GENRE that argues for a solution to a problem or suggests some action. Key Features: well-defined problem • recommended solution • answers to anticipated questions • call to action • appropriate TONE. *See also* topic proposal

response, 348–50 A PROCESS of writing in which a reader gives the writer their thoughts about the writer's title, beginning, THESIS, support and DOCUMENTATION, ORGANIZING, STANCE, treatment of AUDIENCE, achievement of PURPOSE, handling of the GENRE, ending, and other matters.

résumé, 264–73 A GENRE that summarizes someone's academic and employment history, generally written to submit to potential employers. Key Features: organization that suits goals and experience • succinctness • design that highlights key information.

revision, 350–53 The PROCESS of making substantive changes to a draft so that it contains all the necessary content and presents it in an appropriate organization. During revision, writers generally move from whole-text issues to details with the goals of sharpening their focus and strengthening their position.

rewriting, 353–55 A PROCESS of composing a new draft from another perspective—with a different POINT OF VIEW, AUDIENCE, STANCE, GENRE, or MEDIUM, for example.

subordinate clause   A clause that begins with a SUBORDINATING WORD and therefore cannot stand alone as a sentence: *She feels good <u>when she exercises.</u> My roommate, <u>who was a physics major,</u> tutors students in science.*

subordinating word, HB-6–8, HB-11   A word, such as a RELATIVE PRONOUN or a subordinating conjunction, that introduces a SUBORDINATE CLAUSE: *The ice sculpture melted <u>because</u> the ballroom was too hot.* Common subordinating words include *although, as, because, if, since, that, which,* and *why.*

summary, 33–35, 534–35   The use of one's own words and sentence structure to condense someone else's text into a briefer version that gives the main ideas of the original. As with PARAPHRASING and QUOTATION, summarizing requires DOCUMENTATION.

summary and response essay, 33–44   A GENRE of writing that demonstrates one's ability to convey a text's main ideas in condensed form and to engage with those ideas by ARGUING a position, ANALYZING the text, or writing a REFLECTION on its content. Key Features: clearly identified author and title • concise summary of the text • an explicit response • support for that response

synthesizing ideas, 519–25   Bringing together ideas and information from multiple

Submitting Papers for Publication by W. W. Norton & Company

We are interested in receiving writing from college students to consider including in our textbooks as examples of student writing. Please send this form with the work that you would like us to consider to Marilyn Moller, Student Writing, W. W. Norton & Company, 500 Fifth Avenue, New York NY 10110. For questions, or to submit electronically, email us at composition@wwnorton.com.

Text Submission Form

Student's name _____

School _____

Address _____

Department _____

Course _____

Writing assignment the text responds to _____

_____

_____

_____

_____

Instructor's name _____

(continued next page)

Please write a few sentences about what your primary purposes were for writing this text. Also, if you wish, tell us what you think you learned about writing from the experience writing it.

_____

_____

_____

_____

_____

_____

_____

_____

Contact Information

Please provide the information below so that we can contact you if your work is selected for publication.

Name _____

Permanent address _____

Email _____

Phone _____

Revision Symbols

abbr	abbreviation **HB-105**		*ital*	italics **HB-103**
adj	adjective **HB-60**		*jarg*	jargon **HB-43**
adv	adverb **HB-60**		*lc*	lowercase letter **HB-100**
agr	agreement **HB-24, HB-29**		*mm*	misplaced modifier **HB-62**
art	article **HB-63**		*num*	number **HB-106**
awk	awkward		¶	new paragraph
cap	capitalization **HB-100**		//	parallelism **HB-35**
case	pronoun case **HB-32**		*pass*	passive voice **HB-19**
cliché	cliché **HB-44**		*ref*	pronoun reference **HB-31**
◡	close up space		*run-on*	comma splice or fused sentence **HB-10**
cs	comma splice **HB-10**		*sexist*	sexist language **HB-67**
def	define **432–42**		*shift*	confusing shift **HB-39**
⌒	delete		*sl*	slang **HB-42**
dm	dangling modifier **HB-63**		#	insert space
doc	documentation **544–636**		*sp*	spelling
emph	emphasis **HB-105**		*trans*	transition **14**
frag	sentence fragment **HB-7**		‿	transpose
fs	fused sentence **HB-10**		*vb*	verb **HB-12**
hyph	hyphen **HB-98**		*wrdy*	wordy **HB-59**
∧	insert		*ww*	wrong word **HB-51**

A Directory to MLA Style

A Directory to APA Style

A Menu of Readings